# CHILDREN, SPACES AND IDENTITY

Childhood in the Past Monograph Series: Volume 4

# CHILDREN, SPACES AND IDENTITY

*edited by*

Margarita Sánchez Romero, Eva Alarcón García
and Gonzalo Aranda Jiménez

Oxbow Books
*Oxford & Philadelphia*

Published in the United Kingdom in 2015 by
OXBOW BOOKS
10 Hythe Bridge Street, Oxford OX1 2EW

and in the United States by
OXBOW BOOKS
908 Darby Road, Havertown, PA 19083

Paperback Edition: ISBN 978-1-78297-935-7
Digital Edition: ISBN 978-1-78297-936-4
A CIP record for this book is available from the British Library

Printed in the United Kingdom by Hobbs the printers

For a complete list of Oxbow titles, please contact:

UNITED KINGDOM
Oxbow Books
Telephone (01865) 241249, Fax (01865) 794449
Email: oxbow@oxbowbooks.com
www.oxbowbooks.com

UNITED STATES OF AMERICA
Oxbow Books
Telephone (800) 791-9354, Fax (610) 853-9146
Email: queries@casemateacademic.com
www.casemateacademic.com/oxbow

Oxbow Books is part of the Casemate Group

*Front cover: Image from the exhibition "The last Carpetans. The oppidum of El Llano de la Horca (Santoraz, Madrid)" (2012). Museo Regional de Madrid. Author: Arturo Asensio.*

# CONTENTS

List of contributors ......................................................................................... viii
Acknowledgements ............................................................................................ xi

## PART I
### CHILDREN, SPACES AND IDENTITY

1. Children, Childhood and Space: Multidisciplinary Approaches to Identity ........... 2
   *Margarita Sánchez Romero, Eva Alarcón García and Gonzalo Aranda Jiménez*

2. Steps to Children's Living Spaces ................................................................. 10
   *Grete Lillehammer*

## PART II
### PLAYING, LIVING AND LEARNING

3. Complexity, Cooperation and Childhood: An Evolutionary Perspective .............. 26
   *Juan Manuel Jiménez-Arenas*

4. Children as Potters: Apprenticeship Patterns from Bell Beaker Pottery
   of Copper Age Inner Iberia (Spain) (*c.* 2500–2000 cal BC) .............................. 40
   *Rafael Garrido-Pena and Ana Mercedes Herrero-Corral*

5. Social Relations between Adulthood and Childhood in the
   Early Bronze Age Site of Peñalosa (Baños de la Encina, Jaen, Spain) ................ 59
   *Eva Alarcón García*

6. Gender and Childhood in the II Iron Age: The Pottery Centre
   of Las Cogotas (Ávila, Spain) ...................................................................... 75
   *Juan Jesús Padilla Fernández and Linda Chapon*

7. Playing with Mud? An Ethnoarchaeological Approach to Children's
   Learning in Kusasi Ceramic Production ......................................................... 88
   *Manuel Calvo Trias, Jaume García Rosselló, David Javaloyas Molina
   and Daniel Albero Santacreu*

8. Infantile Individuals: The Great Forgotten of Ancient Mining
and Metallurgical Production........................................................................ 105
*Luis Arboledas Martínez and Eva Alarcón García*

9. Learning to Be Adults: Games and Childhood on the Outskirts
of the Big City (San Isidro, Buenos Aires, Argentina) .................................... 122
*Daniel Schavelzon*

10. Disabled Children and Domestic Living Spaces in Britain, 1800–1900 ......... 136
*Mary Clare Martin*

11. La evolución de los espacios de aprendizaje de la infancia a través
de los modelos pedagógicos .......................................................................... 155
*Victoria Carmona Buendía and Elisa Valero Ramos*

12. Montessori y el ambiente preparado: un espacio de aprendizaje para
los niños ....................................................................................................... 168
*Fátima Ortega Castillo*

13. Didactics of Childhood: The Case Study of Prehistory ................................ 179
*Antonia García Luque*

14. *Once upon a time...* Childhood and Archaeology from the Perspective
of Spanish Museums...................................................................................... 193
*Isabel Izquierdo Peraile, Clara López Ruiz and Lourdes Prados Torreira*

15. Home to Mother: The Long Journey to not Lose one's own Identity ............. 208
*Angela Anna Iuliucci*

## PART III
### SPACE, BODY AND MIND: CHILDREN IN FUNERARY CONTEXTS

16. Use of Molecular Genetic Procedures for Sex Determination
in 'Guanches' Children's Remains .................................................................. 218
*Alejandra C. Ordóñez, Matilde Arnay-de-la Rosa, Rosa Fregel,
Guacimara Ramos-Pérez, Emilio González Reimers and José Pestano*

17. Salud y crecimiento en la Edad del Cobre. Un estudio preliminar de los
individuos subadultos de Camino del Molino (Caravaca de la Cruz,
Murcia, España). Un sepulcro colectivo del III milenio cal. BC..................... 230
*Susana Mendiela, Carme Rissech, María Haber, Joaquín Lomba,
Azucena Avilés and Daniel Turbón*

18. Infant Burials during the Copper and Bronze Ages in the Iberian
    Jarama River Valley: A Preliminary Study about Childhood
    in the Funerary Context during III–II millennium BC .................................... 243
    *Raquel Aliaga Almela, Corina Liesau, Patricia Ríos,*
    *Concepción Blasco, and Lorenzo Galindo*

19. Premature Death in the Vaccean Aristocracy at Pintia
    (Padilla de Duero/Peñafiel, Valladolid). Comparative Study of the Funerary
    Rituals of Two Little 'Princesses'....................................................... 262
    *Carlos Sanz Minguez*

20. Dying Young in Archaic Gela (Sicily): From the Analysis of the
    Cemeteries to the Reconstruction of Early Colonial Identity .......................... 282
    *Claudia Lambrugo*

21. Maternidad e inhumaciones perinatales en el *vicus* romanorrepublicano
    de el Camp de les Lloses (Tona, Barcelona): lecturas y significados.............. 294
    *Montserrat Duran i Caixal, Imma Mestres i Santacreu*
    *and M. Dolors Molas Font*

22. Children and Funerary Space. Ritual Behaviours in the Greek Colonies
    of Magna Graecia and Sicily ........................................................... 310
    *Diego Elia and Valeria Meirano*

23. Children and Their Burial Practices in the Early Medieval Cemeteries
    of Castel Trosino and Nocera Umbra (Italy)....................................... 327
    *Valentina De Pasca*

24. La cultura lúdica en los rituales funerarios infantiles: los juegos
    de velorio .............................................................................. 342
    *Jaume Bantulà Janot and Andrés Payà Rico*

25. Compartiendo la experiencia de la muerte. El niño muerto y el niño
    frente a la muerte ..................................................................... 355
    *Virginia de la Cruz Lichet*

# LIST OF CONTRIBUTORS

EVA ALARCÓN GARCÍA
Departamento de Prehistoria y Arqueología,
Universidad de Granada, Spain
eva@ugr.es

DANIEL ALBERO SANTACREU
Departamento de Ciencias Históricas y
Teoría de las Artes, Universidad de las Islas
Baleares, Spain
d.albero@uib.es

RAQUEL ALIAGA
Laboratorio de Arqueología Forense,
Universidad Autónoma de Madrid, Spain
raquel.aliaga@live.com

GONZALO ARANDA JIMÉNEZ
Departamento de Prehistoria y Arqueología,
Universidad de Granada, Spain
garanda@ugr.es

LUIS ARBOLEDAS-MARTÍNEZ
Instituto de Historia, Centro de Ciencias
humanas y Sociales, CSIC
arboledas@ugr.es

MATILDE ARNAY-DE-LA ROSA
Departamento de Geografía e Historia,
Universidad de La Laguna, Spain
matarnay@gmail.com

AZUCENA AVILÉS
Departamento de Prehistoria, Arqueología,
Historia Antigua, Historia Medieval y
Ciencias y Técnicas Historiográficas,
Universidad de Murcia, Spain
azuavi@hotmail.com

JAUME BANTULÀ JANOT
Universitat Ramon Llull, Barcelona, Spain
jaumebj@blanquerna.url.edu

CONCEPCIÓN BLASCO
Departamento de Prehistoria y
Arqueología,Universidad Autónoma de
Madrid, Spain
concepcion.blasco@uam.es

MANUEL CALVO TRIAS
Departamento de Ciencias Históricas y
Teoría de las Artes, Universidad de las Islas
Baleares, Spain
manuel.calvo@uib.es

VICTORIA CARMONA BUENDÍA
Architect
Universidad de Granada, Spain
victoriacb@outlook.com

LINDA CHAPON
Universität Tübingen, Germany
lindachapon2002@hotmail.com

VIRGINIA DE LA CRUZ LICHET
Universidad Francisco de Vitoria, Madrid,
Spain
vcruzlichet@gmail.com

VALENTINA DE PASCA
Dipartimento di Beni Culturali e Ambientali,
Università degli Studi di Milano, Italia
valentina.depasca@gmail.com

MONTSERRAT DURAN I CAIXAL
Centre d'Interpretació del Camp de les
Lloses, Barcelona, Spain
vicustona@e-tona.net

DIEGO ELIA
Dipartimento di Studi Storici, University of
Turin, Italy
diego.elia@unito.it

ROSA FREGEL
Departamento de Genética, Facultad de
Biología Universidad de La Laguna, Spain
Department of Genetics, School of Medicine,
University of Stanford, USA
rfegel@gmail.com

LORENZO GALINDO
Arqueoestudio Coop, Spain
lorenzo.galindo@arqueoestudio.com

ANTONIA GARCÍA LUQUE
Departamento de Didáctica de las Ciencias
Universidad de Jaen, Spain
agalu@ujaen.es

JAUME GARCÍA ROSSELLÓ
Departamento de Ciencias Históricas y
Teoría de las Artes, Universidad de las Islas
Baleares, Spain
jaume.garcia@uib.es

RAFAEL GARRIDO-PENA
Departamento de Prehistoria y Arqueología,
Universidad Autónoma de Madrid, Spain
rafael.garrido@uam.es

EMILIO GONZÁLEZ REIMERS
Departamento de Medicina, Universidad de
La Laguna, Spain
egonrey@ull.es

MARÍA HABER
Universidad de Murcia, Departamento de
Prehistoria, Arqueología, Historia Antigua,
Historia Medieval y Ciencias y Técnicas
Historiográficas, Murcia, España
mariahaber@pi-ma.es

ANA MERCEDES HERRERO-CORRAL
Departamento de Prehistoria, Universidad
Complutense de Madrid, Spain
anaherre@ucm.es

ANGELA ANNA IULIUCCI
Dipartimento di lingue e letterature straniere,
University of Milan, Italy
Angela.Iuliucci@unimi.it

ISABEL IZQUIERDO PERAILE
Dirección General de Bellas Artes y Bienes
Culturales y de Archivos y Bibliotecas,
Secretaría de Estado de Cultura, Spain.
isabel.izquierdo@mecd.es

DAVID JAVALOYAS MOLINA
Departamento de Ciencias Históricas y
Teoría de las Artes, Universidad de las Islas
Baleares, Spain
david.javaloyas@uib.es

JUAN MANUEL JIMÉNEZ-ARENAS
Departamento de Prehistoria y Arqueología,
Universidad de Granada, Spain

Instituto Universitario de la Paz y los
Conflictos, Universidad de Granada, Spain

Anthropological Institute and Museum,
University of Zürich, Switzerland
jumajia@ugr.es

CLAUDIA LAMBRUGO
Università degli Studi di Milano,
Dipartimento di Beni Culturali e Ambientali,
Settore di Archeologia, Milano, Italia
claudia.lambrugo@unimi.it

CORINA LIESAU
Departamento de Prehistoria y Arqueología,
Universidad Autónoma de Madrid, Spain.
corina.liesau@uam.es

GRETE LILLEHAMMER
Museum of Archaeology, University of
Stavanger
grete.lillehammer@uis.no

JOAQUÍN LOMBA
Departamento de Prehistoria, Arqueología,
Historia Antigua, Historia Medieval y
Ciencias y Técnicas Historiográficas,
Universidad de Murcia, Spain
jlomba@um.es

CLARA LÓPEZ RUIZ
Departamento de Prehistoria y Arqueología,
Universidad Autónoma de Madrid, Spain
clara.lopezruiz@uam.es

MARY CLARE MARTIN
Department of Education and Community
Studies, University of Greenwich, United
Kingdom
m.c.h.martin@gre.ac.uk

VALERIA MEIRANO
Dipartimento di Studi Storici,
University of Turin, Italy
valeria.meirano@unito.it

SUSANA MENDIELA
Unitat d'Antropologia, Departament de
Biologia Animal, Universitat de Barcelona,
Spain
susanamendiela@gmail.com

IMMA MESTRES I SANTACREU
Centre d'Interpretació del Camp de les
Lloses, Barcelona, Spain
campdelelloses@e-tona.net

M. DOLORS MOLAS FONT
Facultat de Geografia i Història, Universitat
de Barcelona, Spain
dmolas@ub.edu

ALEJANDRA C. ORDÓÑEZ
Departamento de Geografía e Historia,
Universidad de La Laguna. Departamento
de Prehistoria, Arqueología, Historia
Antigua, Filología Griega y Filología Latina,
Universidad de Alicante, Spain.
alejacalderono@gmail.com

FÁTIMA ORTEGA CASTILLO
Departamento de Teoría e Historia de la
Educación, Facultad de Ciencias de la
Educación, Universidad de Málaga, Spain
fatimaortega@uma.es

JUAN JESÚS PADILLA FERNÁNDEZ
Departamento de Prehistoria,
Universidad Complutense de Madrid, Spain
juanjpad@ucm.es

ANDRÉS PAYÀ RICO
Universitat de València, Valencia, Spain
andres.paya@uv.es

JOSÉ PESTANO
Laboratorio de Genética y Diagnóstico
Molecular, Universidad de Las Palmas de
Gran Canaria, Spain
jpestano@dbbf.ulpgc.es

LOURDES PRADOS TORREIRA
Departamento de Prehistoria y Arqueología,
Universidad Autónoma de Madrid, Spain
lourdes.pradost@gmail.com

GUACIMARA RAMOS-PÉREZ
Departamento de Geografía e Historia,
Universidad de La Laguna. Spain
gmara.ramos@gmail.com

PATRICIA RÍOS
Departamento de Prehistoria y Arqueología,
Universidad Autónoma de Madrid, Spain
patricia.rios@uam.es

CARME RISSECH
Unitat d'Antropologia, Departament Biologia
Animal, Universitat de Barcelona
carmerissech@gmail.com

MARGARITA SÁNCHEZ ROMERO
Departamento de Prehistoria y Arqueología,
Universidad de Granada, Spain
marsanch@ugr.es

CARLOS SANZ MÍNGUEZ
Departamento de Prehistoria, Arqueología,
Antropología Social y Ciencias y Técnicas
Historiográficas and Centro de Estudios
Vacceos 'Federico Wattenberg', Universidad
de Valladolid, Spain
cevfw@uva.es

DANIEL SCHAVELZON
Director del Centro de Arqueología Urbana
de la Universidad de Buenos Aires/
Investigador Principal del Conicet
dschavelzon@fibertel.com.ar

DANIEL TURBÓN
Unitat d'Antropologia, Departament Biologia
Animal, Universitat de Barcelona, Spain
turbon.daniel@gmail.com

ELISA VALERO RAMOS
Architect
Departamento de Expresión Gráfica
Arquitectónica y en la Ingeniería
Universidad de Granada, Spain
evalero@coagranada.org

# Acknowledgements

There are a number of people who helped make this book a success. First and foremost are the individual authors whom we thank for their hard work. It was truly a pleasure working with each of them. We are most grateful to Sally Crawford for her assistance and perseverance in getting the book published. To the Society for the Study of Childhood in the Past (SSCIP) for creating transdisciplinary meeting places for researches with mutual aims and to Oxbow for their support.

The work leading up to this book was carried out as part of the following research projects: "Architecture in Andalusia from a gender perspective: cases, practices and built realities" (HUM-5709) and "Innovation, continuity and hybridization. The Copper and Bronze Ages societies in the southern Iberian Peninsula" (HAR2013-42865) and the support of the research group "GEA. Material Culture and Social Identity in the Recent Prehistory of Southern Iberia" (HUM-065).

Special thanks to the Museo Arqueológico Regional of Madrid and to Enrique Baquedano, Gabriela Martens, Miguel Contreras and Gonzalo Ruiz Zapatero, directors of the fieldworks in El Llano de la Horca (Santorcaz) and Arturo Asensio, illustrator, for the cover image of this volume.

# PART I

## CHILDREN, SPACES AND IDENTITY

# 1

## CHILDREN, CHILDHOOD AND SPACE: MULTIDISCIPLINARY APPROACHES TO IDENTITY

### *Margarita Sánchez Romero, Eva Alarcón García and Gonzalo Aranda Jiménez*

Twenty-five years ago, in 1989, Grete Lillehammer wrote "A Child is Born. The Child's World in an Archaeological Perspective",[1] the first publication in which children were considered not as an object of study, but as active subjects within societies of the past. Lillehammer's article laid the foundations for historic research into children and childhood from then on. The main issue was the invisibility of children in the interpretation of historic processes, which undermined their potential to contribute to social history in general.

Twenty five years later, the study of childhood has undergone a significant change. Work has been focussed primarily on three aspects: the relation of children with the world that surrounds them, their relation with adults and, finally, their relation with other children, defining what is known as the "child's world".[2] Current topics of interest include the definition of the concepts "child" and "childhood", innovation in methodologies used for analysis, and issues surrounding the transmission of knowledge from one generation to the next through learning, play and socialisation.

The aim of this volume is to present a transcultural view of how children construct their social space, living space, space for knowledge acquisition and learning, with a view to offering scholars new possibilities for diachronic analyses of age categories and the study of childhood from different perspectives. In all the texts included in this book, children are presented as the main actors in historic dynamics of social change, from prehistory to the present day.

With regard to the organisation of the volume, we have opted for a classical division into three main thematic sections. The first is an introductory section offering general notions on space, childhood and the construction of both the individual and the group identity of children. There are a further two sections ordered diachronically, the first of which focuses on analysing and identifying the spaces which contribute to the construction of children's identity during their lives: the places they live, learn, socialize and play. The final section deals with these same aspects, but focuses on funerary contexts, in which children may lose their capacity to influence events, as it is adults who establish burial strategies and practices. Such is the structure of the book, for organisational reasons. However, in this introductory chapter, which serves as a reflection on children, space and identity, we will not follow the division outlined above for two basic reasons. Firstly, because the spaces of life and death, and the experiences of life and death do not stand alone, but normally form a continuum, and can only be understood with reference to each other. Secondly, because the reference to experiences which are distant from each other in time and space reinforces the idea of childhood, children and the creation of identity as cultural constructs.

CHILDREN AND MATERIAL CULTURE

The study of childhood in recent decades has focused on three elements: material culture, children's bodies and the spaces they occupy. Studies on material culture have had a decisive influence on research into childhood and have fomented interdisciplinarity in this field. Written texts often limit our view of childhood, either because children are not reflected in them or because texts do not deal with those aspects which are of interest to us. Therefore, studies on the material nature of childhood, in all periods of history, are becoming the basis upon which our knowledge of children is constructed. Interdisciplinarity in the study of childhood is seen through material culture (archaeology, history), the study of bodies (bioarchaeology, medicine), texts (history, literature), representations (pedagogy, museology) or spaces (architecture, anthropology). Such interdisciplinarity, undoubtedly, enriches the discourse we wish to convey and all these disciplines benefit from the advances made individually in each of them.

Significant results and publications have been forthcoming in the study of objects directly related to children and their bodies. However, study of the spaces these children occupy and share is proving more difficult. The study of social space in any human group is, in itself, fraught with limitations, and to these we must add the further limits involved in the study of childhood. Therefore, the aim of this volume is to build a body of theoretical and methodological approaches about how space is articulated and organised around children and how this disposition affects the creation and maintenance of social identities. Such approaches involve different disciplines: architecture, archaeology, pedagogy, literature or anthropology and in the different spaces analysed: ritual, working, learning, funerary, living... In each case authors ask questions such as: how do adults construct spaces for children? How do children manage their own spaces? How do people (adults and children) build (invisible and/ or physical) boundaries and spaces?

CHILDREN AND SPACE

How can we comprehend the space occupied by children? Indeed, it is the chapter contributed by Grete Lillehammer herself which gives us the exact pointers to understand the purpose of this volume. Her re-reading of Edward Soja[3] offers the variables that facilitate our approach. Space always has a threefold nature consisting of physical aspects which can be quantified and explained, mental aspects which imply social significance and a third element involving how individuals occupy spaces. Without the action of these individuals the spaces concerned would hold no meaning for us.

These three variables explain the way in which children perceive space and, in turn, how space helps them to shape their own identity. For children, the spaces in which they live may be hostile, pleasant, uncomfortable, unsuitable, appropriate, comfortable (Martin), but moreover, they are the place where they build and negotiate their identity. This is very clear in the story of the three Australian aboriginal girls who are removed from their home town and sent to a school situated far away, separating them not only from their territory (space) but also from their culture, uprooting them and provoking an identity crisis. Their escape and return home constitutes not only a reunion with their friends and relatives but also a return to the feeling of connection and belonging to a place, and in the final analysis, a return to their identity (Iuliucci).

How do children contribute to the creation and organisation of such spaces? To answer this question, we must explore children's capacity to participate in decision-making or to transform these places once adults have created the space. I am referring here to child agency, as Grete Lillehammer points out: "Children do not write history, they make it".[4] It is obvious that both in life and in death the construction of these spaces will depend on two factors, namely what is understood by "child" and "childhood" in each social group and how children are perceived in such societies. A good example is that of the Kusasi girls (Calvo *et al.*) who enjoy a certain amount of freedom when choosing who will teach them pottery, for example, and which learning method they prefer. Something similar occurs in the case of the girls' "ladies and maids" games in 19th century Buenos Aires (Schavelzon). One may wonder to what extent the adult roles of a highly hierarchical society are reproduced in that mental and social space. Are there spaces in which the girls can subvert the social order? Do they do so? Or do their games only serve to reproduce class awareness? It is necessary to analyse what type of work they do, what kind of learning process takes place, and whether they are separated by sex and age with regard to their responsibilities. From a methodological standpoint, therefore, it is necessary to know the children's biography if we are to better understand the type of life they lived and, as a result of that, the spaces they felt the need or the desire to occupy.

It is also possible to identify those spaces through the study of the objects made or used by children. This allows us to create three different scenarios (Lillehammer), as follows: spaces created by children outside the range of adults, spaces shared by adults and children related to learning and technology, and a third scenario related to spaces for life and death created by adults for children.

At the beginning of this chapter it was stated that one of the main questions regarding the study of children and childhood, which had not been given serious attention by scholars, was the study of the transmission of knowledge. However, there is no doubt that socialisation and learning by the youngest members of a social group is essential to explain the community itself and to explain the link between the adult world and the world of children, whether in early Bronze Age societies (Alarcón) or in the Kusasi populations of Ghana (Calvo *et al.*). Special importance is afforded to the learning of technological processes that cannot be considered exclusively in terms of transmission of technical knowledge, but rather as an integral part of the socialisation process by which ideas are transmitted about the identity of populations, such as gender identity (Calvo *et al.*).

Learning processes vary with regard to their location, starting age, time of the year, knowledge transmission strategies, learning phases, technologies learned, raw materials used and type of final product, amongst other aspects (Garrido and Herrero; Calvo *et al.*). However, the basic element is that all human beings, unlike other animals, undergo much longer learning and socialisation phases. Our species is characterised by being the most complex, fragile and conflictive of all species and culture gives us the tools necessary to interact successfully with the world that surrounds us. It is obvious that learning will play an essential role in the transmission of that cultural knowledge, since neglect in this field will create immediate risks for the community. Our fragility at birth, our dependence on breastmilk, our long period of infancy, mark our passage from the specific care of our mother to the collective care of the group. Socialisation and learning processes take place within the group, which cooperates to ensure the progress of the community's new members (Jiménez-Arenas).

How are these spaces used to coordinate learning processes? Doubtless, the appearance of a certain type of material culture in specific spaces gives us the necessary clues to learn more about such processes. Small, badly manufactured objects, or objects with variations in style or decoration could be considered as learning elements, such as those which appear in Bell Beaker contexts (Garrido and Herrero; Aliaga *et al.*) or in the Iron Age (Padilla and Chapón). However, they could also be considered signs of creativity by children. To what extent does child agency appear in those learning processes? Does the appearance of objects made during the learning process and which form part of these populations' burial rituals mean that they form part of the identity of the person buried? (Garrido and Herrero; Alarcón). On other occasions, material culture shows us how learning processes are much shorter or even non-existent since they transform the children into fully-fledged producers immersed in working processes, such as mining or metal work, for example (Arboledas and Alarcón). These activities, carried out in the same locations as adult labour, reinforce the invisible nature of child labour, since they minimize the influence of child agency, by showing how the participation of children may have involved the capacity to decide, on some occasions, how to do their job most effectively. But that is not all. They also prevent us from seeing how the introduction of new technologies and materials in the daily lives of human groups change those lives, not only at an economic or technological level but also at a social and ideological level, changing their world view and therefore changing the way in which processes of knowledge transmission take place.

Learning spaces can be recognised through the description of contexts. They may appear in specific locations, specially prepared for that purpose, or in places where many other of the population's daily life tasks are carried out. On some occasions these spaces overlap. For example, traditional learning in non-formal education settings such as pottery manufacturing may coexist with formal school-based education. However, when defining those spaces we must also bear in mind the significance of separate spaces for boys and girls, which is related both to the type of technology being learned, as in the case of the Kusasi girls (Calvo *et al.*) and with gender identity. Girls are seen in play rooms and boys playing outside the domestic area, in surrounding areas (Schavelzon).

It is much simpler to recognise and analyse spaces of childhood education and learning in societies where formal education itself analyses these locations. In the western world, specific locations for the education of children did not appear until the 14th century and no interest was shown in this type of construction until well into the 18th century, when Rousseau's new ideas on the concept of childhood changed the previous models (Carmona and Valero). From Friedrich Froebel's open, dynamic and flexible spaces to María Montessori's places conceived for freedom, activity, independence and individuality (Ortega), or Loris Malaguzzi's conception of communal-based, participatory education, all these models are reflected in clearly different and unique architectural structures (Carmona and Valero).

How do these learning processes reflect the populations involved? How is social organisation and personal identity expressed in learning practices? There is no doubt that ethnology and ethnoarchaeology can play an interesting role here. The study of the organisation of pottery production in the contemporary period opens the doors to the interpretation of previous periods, for example the Iron Age, at times when essential changes in communities were taking place, such as the introduction of new technologies, new spaces of production or changes in the forms of social and productive organisation (Padilla and Chapón).

Similarly, nowadays we can learn about contemporary societies through the ways in which they transmit knowledge about history, whether it is in the subject curricula in elementary schools or from exhibitions and representation in museums. With regard to the first of these strategies, we find that the way in which notions of prehistory are learned has changed very little over the last thirty years and new research topics (e.g. gender or age) have not been incorporated into the discourse, although this is more evident in the texts used than in the images, where a gradual change is slowly becoming evident (García Luque). With regard to museums, so much remains to be done, including not only specific content for a young audience but also the coordination of cultural and educational activities (Prados *et al.*). In both cases the invisible nature of children in traditional historic discourse can be seen both in the discourse used in schools and in that used for general dissemination.

What place does the analysis of children occupy in the processes of research and knowledge generation about past societies? One of the most interesting questions when working with children is that their invisibility inevitably leads to new theoretical and methodological proposals for studying them. Such new methodologies help to place our knowledge about children at the service of research about past societies. Much of our current methodology comes from the osteological analysis of infant populations and obliges us to think of children not only in terms of their biological age but also in terms of their cultural age. Our information is derived from the results of bioarchaeology and physical anthropology techniques to analyse the bodies of children who developed to adulthood or those of children who did not survive beyond an early age. One of the most obvious problems we find when attempting to observe children in the spaces they inhabit is our difficulty with sex identification, a crucial element for interpreting their biography, their capacity to act in society and how these societies articulate gender relations and identities. The traditional method for sexing bodies through grave goods in burial sites leads to errors and presuppositions which do not generate valid knowledge.

The availability of molecular genetics permit sex identification through DNA screening but, when working with children, it is more difficult to apply tooth-based techniques, as they are more susceptible to contamination, or long bone techniques, as children's bones are more fragile. The choice of phalanges – much more compact bones – has been of significant use in determining children's sex, (Arnay *et al.*). Determining the sex of children is especially interesting when analysing questions such as health and growth patterns, especially with a view to detecting inequalities between boys and girls. The study of 25 infant bodies from the Camino del Molino Copper Age site in Caravaca de la Cruz, Murcia, Spain, shows us a population with anaemia, acquired when they were no longer protected by the safety of the breastfeeding period, with growth not becoming normal again until the onset of adolescence (Mendiela *et al.*).

## CHILDREN AND IDENTITY

In addition to learning the use of technologies, children must also familiarize themselves with the world they belong to, by acquiring knowledge of rituals and social identities and being aware of the their place in the society they live in. Most of these socialisation practices are influenced by "habitus", the logical practice and sense of order learned subconsciously through norms established in daily life.[5] On some occasions, these socialisation processes leave their mark on the archaeological record. This happens through the "performance" constituted by the burial ritual, which does not only occur in a physical area, i.e. the burial site, but also at a psychological level, with regard to the place that those people (in our case, children) occupied in the social imaginary of the group (ethnicity, hierarchy, gender) and with regard to feelings of loss and affection.

The appearance of children in the funerary record is an element of vital importance with regard to recognition within their social group. When the funeral ritual is used as a form of appropriation of the territory (Copper Age) or as a way to legitimise social status (Bronze Age), the appearance of children in the funerary record, fully involved in the ritual processes of these populations, is a direct indication of their place in society. This occurs for example during the Copper Age in the Jarama River Valley, where the appearance of children over the age of six in collective tombs for the elites of the Bell

Beaker populations has been considered a reflection of social status which is probably hereditary (Aliaga *et al.*). Moreover, the appearance of elements for adornment linked to the bodies of children gives us information about their age, gender or social status and indirectly about the organisation of the society itself (Alarcón).

The wealth of tombs 127 and 153 in Pintia (Valladolid, Spain) belonging to the Vacceai (Iron Age), not only offers information about the place in the social hierarchy occupied by the girls who are buried there, but also their identity as children, their role as transmitters of Vaccean traditions and their connection with the myths about the origins of society. All this converts these tombs into palimpsests of multi-layered information which can be interpreted in numerous ways (Sanz). Similarly, the use of tradition both in rituals and in grave goods in infant tombs, linking the child with the past of those societies, is also evident in the early medieval cemeteries of Castel Trosino and Nocera (De Pasca). Likewise, the infant tombs in Archaic Gela (Sicily) reveal a world of colonial movements in the Mediterranean, new spaces occupied by new populations who, in principle, use burial rituals not only as a way of appropriating the new territory but also in order to reaffirm their original identity. However, gradually, the phenomenon of hybridisation between indigenous populations and the colonisers generates new identities which require ratification in the material world and which are reflected in an additional effort during the burial ritual of children and adolescents (Lambrugo).

An excellent example of hybridisation processes between populations is to be found in the use of indigenous burial rituals in the new forms of Roman Republican settlement in Camp de les Lloses (Barcelona). The local tradition of burying perinatal bodies inside dwellings allows us to state that the female component of this Roman military settlement was made up of indigenous women who give an apotropaic character to these practices. This fact places women and children in spaces normally denied to them, as such spaces are usually exclusively linked to male activities (Molas *et al.*). This invisibility of perinatal tombs contrasts with the use of grave markers in the Greek colonies of *Magna Graecia* and Sicily for children and adolescents (Elia and Meriano).

We have stated that funeral rituals constitute a way to discover the place of children in the social imaginary of the group, but these rituals also constitute an approach to feelings of loss and of how to express affection. We find proof of this in the games played during vigils (Bantulà and Payà) or photographs of dead children (De la Cruz). Playful elements during a "vigil for an angel" are a way of facing up to the pain and loss felt at the death of a child, at both a social and emotional level, through the use of festive elements such as play and dance. Similarly, post mortem depiction of children signifies the need to certify the existence of those children at a specific time and place. Sometimes such images are the only evidence of their brief lives and serve to place them in a virtual space so that they can be contemplated.

NOTES

1  Lillehammer 1989
2  Lillehammer 2000, 2005, 2008, 2010
3  Soja 1996
4  Lillehammer 2010:22
5  Sánchez Romero, 2008a, 2008b

REFERENCES

Lillehammer, G. 2000. The world of children, pp. 17–26 in Sofaer Derevenski, J. (ed.) *Children and Material Culture*. London: Routledge.
Lillehammer, G. 2005. Archaeology and children. *Kvinner I Arkeologi I Norge (K.A.N.)* 24, 18–35.
Lillehammer, G. 2008. Transforming images: Exploring powerful children. *International Journal of Childhood in the Past* 1, 94–105.
Lillehammer, G. 2010. Archaeology of childhood. *Complutum* 21:2, 15–44.
Sánchez Romero, M. 2008a. An approach to learning and socialisation in children during the Spanish Bronze Age, pp. 113–124 in Dommasnes, L. H. and Wrigglesworth, M. (eds) *Children, identity and the past*. Cambridge: Cambridge Scholars Publishing.
Sánchez Romero, M. 2008b. Childhood and the construction of gender identities through material culture. *International Journal of Childhood in the Past* 1, 17–37.
Soja, E. W. 1996. *Thirdspace. Journeys to Los Angeles and Other Real-and-Imagined Places*. Oxford: Blackwell Publishing.

# 2

# STEPS TO CHILDREN'S LIVING SPACES

## *Grete Lillehammer*

## INTRODUCTION

The globalisation of science and the arts has triggered studies of landscape, space and place to form a steadily growing field of interest. To include the cross-cultural perspectives of children's places,[1] the choice of this volume's title and its profile 'Children, spaces and identity' are therefore well-timed. As we may look directly for children in our local backyards, it is important to take steps forward and ask about their living spaces in the past. In relationship to children's worlds, we may define space as equivalent with living place, and refer living places to location, landscape, environment, architecture, building, home, city, region, territory, geography, and so on. Yet to find what children's living spaces are in the multitudes of scenic landscapes and geographies is another matter. Using the academic background from archaeology, art history, and ethnology I would like to share some spaces and experiences from forty years of approaches to children in the past.[2]

According to the geographer Edward Soja, we are inclined to confine spatial thinking in general to two approaches of a dual nature, either as 'firstspace' of concrete material forms to be mapped, analysed and explained; or as 'secondspace' of mental constructs, ideas about and representations of space and its social significance. These two approaches tend, however, to reduce spatiality to a peripheralised background of reflection, container, stage, environment or external constraint upon human behaviour and social action. Soja offers an alternative, and a third approach, one that comprehends both material and mental dimensions of spatiality, and moves beyond them to new and different modes of spatial thinking. This seems to require a strategic re-opening and rethinking of possibilities and induces radical scepticism towards established epistemologies, and a return to the ontological spatiality of existential being and becoming.[3] As ontological similarity and difference exist in the positions between children and adult and their perception and experience as 'human beings' and 'human becomings',[4] I find Soja's approach constructive for thinking 'children' in the broadest sense of human existence. The critique has served to demonstrate the three approaches at work in archaeology and cultural heritage.[5]

To highlight some main points here, we will return to the fundamental questions of what and where children's living spaces are, and who is looking for them. To focus on what in particular are the interests with reference to children's living spaces, child agency would seem a natural approach in general, if this could be understood and explained within activities of reproduction, transformation, and change. Seen from the potentials of children's existential beings and becomings, more perspectives have to be explored than child agency. In this volume, children are presented explicitly to form the leading subject. We may think the childhood perspective is taken for granted, but this is not so. We will have also to extend the queries further. We will have to approach those who overlook children and analyse how they perceive them. In doing a close-up of the variety of childhoods embedded in the material and immaterial worlds of children's living spaces in the past, we allow possibilities and scepticism towards the scientific evidence of children in the academic establishment to be explored in the open.

### THE RUSSIAN DOLL

Studies in sociology have pointed out that there is no single theory of childhood,[6] and studies in social anthropology have shown large variations and difference in childhoods.[7] In social theory, childhood has been defined by several scholars as a social construction of agency that put constraints on what children do.[8] As a social construct it has been defined as the contemporary reflection of society.[9] The concept is found to be ambiguous as an analytical category for the study of children's worlds:[10] the contents defining characteristics and qualifications, both innate and acquired, or given to humans in retrospect, are temporally and passively constructed. Working it is like playing with a Russian doll.

As the familiar logic – there is no childhood without children – goes, a basic fact is that all adults once were children. It is a matter of great concern to stress the variety and complexity of aspects, structures, dimensions, and perspectives linked with the concept 'childhood'. It is of vital importance to reflect on ontological and epistemological universals and divides in being a child in the present, and its potentiality in becoming an adult of a future, and then one whose childhood is left retrospectively to history. It is necessary for the adult researcher who aims at approaching children's living spaces to acknowledge the possibility of competing versions of childhood.[11]

Given the general terms of childhood[12] as 1) the time and age of being a child, and 2) the state and quality of an early period in the life cycle from infancy to puberty, it is necessary to supplement the two attributes with analytical perspectives of relevance for the study of childhood, such as 3) the early biological and cognitive indicators of health, nutrition, and disease of 1 and 2, and 4) the recollections of memory in 1–3. However, to study children's biological and cultural faculties and functions is a multidimensional task. On the structural level, and considering the variety in the material and immaterial evidence of childhood such as the relationships within the macro-cosmos and micro-cosmos of children and adults and in-between these, complexities in the disciplinary divide between biological and cultural studies need appropriate handling. In bridging structural complexities and overcoming relevant obstacles in dealing with a manifold Russian doll of childhood, and without losing a grip on the child-centred discourse, this strategy in the study of children's living spaces is a great challenge. In particular this seems to be evident with regard to children's life cycles, since being a child of time and age and becoming something of state and quality from infancy to puberty, exclude spatiality from the general definition of childhood.

Therefore let us repeat the terminology test and focus on 'the real thing' in its physical and mental entity, the child itself. In English, the concept of 'child' is defined[13] as an unborn, new born, and young human being; someone not far advanced in life, development or existence and not yet old, but immature and inexperienced; one's son or daughter, descendant, follower or product of one; and a childish or innocent person. From this listing we have to acknowledge that the child-being in the world is associated biologically and cognitively with physical and mental development and experience of human offspring, and socially and historically with gender, family, generation, and authority. Yet the concept refers nonetheless also to adult persons. With regard to the potentiality of biological and cognitive abilities, we are dealing with functional and dysfunctional faculties of minors *and* adults. In addition to its fluid character, and similarly to that of childhood, the concept excludes spatiality and reduces children's worlds to social and historical relationships.

In the advancement of knowledge, understanding, and explanation about the past we have come to realise that many children died and not everyone reached adulthood, therefore more children were alive and kicking than adults. If we were to take a group of hunter-gatherers in the Northern European Mesolithic, recent burial studies suggest recognition of a period of childhood[14] and different series of children.[15] If we estimate as much as 50% or more of total deaths occurring,[16] one out of two children grew up to conceive, produce, and bring up children. As half the children reached adulthood, this indicates a population of relatively young individuals and short alternation of generations. On the long term-scale, a hypothesis of life course put forward is the pattern of slowly becoming more skilled at caring for themselves and performing various tasks from an early age, and finally becoming caretakers of their own children.[17] This may indicate a role for older children in taking care of siblings, and for the youngest to adapt easily to the environment and to partake in the subsistence as resource-group from a very early age. In regard to the consequences of the physical contribution and their active role in production as biologically stressful to the young body,[18] this hypothesis of duties and constraints calls for a variety of children's bodies and living spaces to be investigated.

If we were also to take steps to bridge the nature and culture divide further in the scientific discovery of children, we would have to keep on searching for reproductive and transformative spaces and examine continuity and change in the sequences of the life course; to discuss hypotheses of slow or rapid cultural transmission between generations; to continue technological studies of knowledge and experience in the acculturation of material culture. We would have to properly consider children's local biologies,[19] to recognize implications in ageing and modelling of the body, in particular spatial factors which have heavy or low impact on children as resource group. In terms of children's workload, we would have to understand better the expectation and value of their spatial participation compared to adults, and the biological, cognitive, and cultural indicators as to what stages and thresholds constitute idealisations of life's prime. Contrasted with the period, state and quality of old age even the spatial memory of elders may give high cultural significance and value to keeping children's survival kit alive. Regarding the acknowledgement of potentials and barriers in the problematic of standard methods and appropriated materials, this involves the selection of relevant bioarchaeological results best fitted for spatial studies of children.

Life's moulding experience on the materiality of the body,[20] and individuals' intentional modification of the body,[21] which are the dominant factors in hypothetical modelling of the spatiality of children's worlds in relation to chronological and biological age versus social, economic, religious, and political age, show clearly the complexity in strengthening studies of those spaces belonging to children compared to those that do not. But what scholar will volunteer to come forward to ask about children's bodies and living spaces?

'HOLE IN THE WALL'

Viewing the study of childhood and children in the past, I think it appropriate to ask about the present state. During the years of my involvement in the discipline, the topic has passed several stages from non-centred and random recognition of children, to associated and centred recognition of children. Since the 1970s, and thanks to the 2005 inauguration[22] and 2007 establishment[23] of SSCIP, we have accomplished a child-centred advancement of knowledge and understanding about children and childhood in the past.

In order to understand the present state of the subject, regular reference to the general indexes in the academic literature provide an instructive guide.[24] For this approach, and looking particularly at subject indexes of the concepts 'child/children'/'childhood' in the standard literature of archaeology, I searched recent books profiling topics on theory, method, and the study of humans in the past. Four library books containing anthologies published 2009–2012 were picked out randomly: 'Archaeological Theory Today',[25] 'Becoming Human',[26] and 'The Human Past'.[27] Finally, I compared the results to general surveys of archaeological periods. Altogether the books feature authors with a gendered overweight of 2/3 (75 out of 106) males. During many years of experience with these type of tests, I have repeatedly found only Childe with capital letter C, and nothing else but the famous archaeologist Gordon Childe, and so also on this occasion. By contrast, the Oxford Handbook of Anglo-Saxon Archaeology[28] presents a chapter with focus on the human body and life cycle.[29] The concepts in the general index listed 'children' read as follows:[30] 'Burial; Christianity; grave goods; inhumation practices; interpretation of terms; invisibility of agency; Mill Hill burials.'

In the advancement of theory and method on becoming human in the past, it seems relevant on the basis of a random search to point to the status quo as a 'hole in the wall'. To put the case clearly for everyone to see: the subject is visible in academic discourse, but few speak of children's living spaces in general narratives of the human past. Crawford looks at the funerary remains of children and adults to reach for evidence of lived experience before and at death.[31] In the anthologies of Hodder, Renfrew, Morley, and Scarre, the authors look away from the agenda of children as humans. Notwithstanding references to one of the grand old men of British archaeology, the attitudes profile reserve, restriction and withdrawal.[32] The authors seem weighed down by thoughts of the whole humanity, and to deal with an agenda of presenting humans in full bloom developed from nothingness. A dominant perception of humanity still prevailing is the irrelevance of children.

Crawford's model on the adult-artefact pathways into the archaeological record through child agency illustrates that children have been muted and made invisible basically because of adult-centred interests among researchers in the present.[33] According to mute theory, activities of the muted group are seen as less valid or important than those of the dominant group. Consequently, gendered attitudes in the discipline have led to the reproduction and enforcement of adult-centred discourse. The entire process of entry is governed by adults thinking and handling adult worlds.

As the study of children and childhood has not made a great impact in the mainstream archaeology, it is timely that we keep on asking how to deal with dominance of the dominant. From the beginning many efforts were made to illuminate the subject of childhood and children in the past by way of anthologies.[34] But the activities of the majority of those born in the past continue to be an asymmetry in the interests of a minority in the present. Gender identifications separate and discard the material and immaterial evidence of children from academic research interests. Could the images of ancient children possibly be tainted by the representation of a conventional mother and child bondage, the gendered ties of pre-modern paternity prevailing, and being difficult for scholarship to escape?[35] Or is it the materiality in the material evidence that sets restrictions on creating innovations and making successful discoveries?

From the very outset of the study of children and childhood in the past, Anne-Sofie Gräslund has been a pioneering example of the complexity of combining spatial thinking with the use of methods. In order to extend the evidence of funerary remains of non-adults further among the inhumation burials in the Viking cemetery at Birka, Sweden,[36] a direct approach was applied to the 45 children's graves accounted for. Due to scarcity in the remains of skeletal material, the quantitative method was used to measure the internal spatiality of burial shafts and cists and to systematise the equipment associated with undersized interments on the basis of grave plans. In four of the smallest shafts and cists, bronze bells were found. As similar bells were located in six burials categorised as adults, the funerary remains were suggested tentatively to represent children buried together with adults. [37]

At this transitional stage between cultural history archaeology and processual archaeology in Scandinavia,[38] the presence of children's burials in the cemetery was not discussed in relation to ideology and religion, such as the manifold death beliefs of extended life course among the Pagan Norse. Regardless of the problem in a restricted body of archaeological material, in the child-centred analysis the evidence of fragmented sets of data was tentatively associated with children. Considering carefully how to prove beyond reasonable doubt that the funerary equipment was evidence of children's living experience prior to death, she reconsidered the data by the systematic use of comparative methods and analogies.

In her analysis, Gräslund pointed to the occurrence of bells in female burials from the Viking Period in Finland and the Baltic. Based on North-European museum collections of rattles and painted or drawn images of children from the 15th to 19th centuries Anno Domini;[39] it was proposed that the use of bells in the Birka graves represented a ritualized content as well as the part of something 'alive as a child's rattle'; i.e. playthings.[40] Instead of arguing that bells were detached from a concept of child agency, it seems highly relevant to consider the items as both playthings and attachments that adorned children's clothing, and to view the cultural practice as widespread. However far Gräslund reached in order to identify non-adults in the burial evidence of Birka, on a general level of knowledge and understanding much wider inferences were gained than the just use of bells by children. It was demonstrated that sound making instruments were parts of children's living spaces in the representative states of everyday life and celebrations of death.

SMALL SCALE SCENARIOS

In advancing the subject of children and childhood in the past on the academic scene, the direct and indirect evidences of children have been clearly understood to be first and second priorities of study. In the child-centred approach, these are the scientific evidences of children as subjects, and their bodily features or skeletal remains as objects, of investigation. Then what follows next are the evidences of the material and immaterial worlds of children's own creations; i.e. the separate space of children's worlds. Last come the material and immaterial worlds created and developed by adults for children. From the experience of these approaches comes the acknowledgement that one of the main paths to finding steps which lead to children has been turning the priority-model bottom up; i.e. the evidence gained of children's worlds is based on the accumulated knowledge, understanding, and explanation of adult worlds. In order to acknowledge the children we have had first to recognise the parents, guardians, and carers.

Considering the childscape of environmental experience of worlds hidden in the body of humans,[41] and children's preference for park-style visual landscapes to be innate,[42] from a children's perspective at first glance these may seem reductive for examining the spatial potentials of identity, growth, engineering, and bricolage. The study of toys has demonstrated difficulties in drawing demarcated lines between worlds of children and adults.[43] The children manifested in scenes of rock art move around together with the adults,[44] but among themselves also in worlds of their own. As the human body moves objects around and from place to place, material objects could be moved around through various processes of attrition, such as child's play.[45] These worlds may represent a mixture of anomalies, crossbreeds, and alterations, and may be found to exist in the hybrid interrelationships in-between children, adults, and the children themselves.

In 'thirdspace', as existential beings and be comings, to look beyond the constraints of sociality and historicality, the exploration of children's spatiality could mean freedom from the bondage of parents, carers, and family. From the radical perspective of super-modernity, this could involve questioning whether a child asks to be born or to choose its parents or guardians and place in the world, and to ask if ever ancient children were or became less associated with the natural and cultural environment. These implications require inquiries into children's potentialities for remembering, recovering, and restructuring space; to move our perception of children further and beyond the masters of bricolage, and to search for children in the arenas of transformation, otherness, and alteration or something hybrid, liminal, marginal or differently new. Whether humans are bodies first and minds second, and their brains evolve not so much to think as to do,[46] children's sighted abstractions, multidimensional character of experiment, transformation, and unexpected moves in the ordering of objects are specific compared to adults.[47]

In order to investigate the spatiality of worlds, and to study the creation, experience, and development of living spaces, a modified model of children's worlds is suggested:[48]

1. Separate spaces of children and adults.
2. The spaces in-between children and adults.
3. The adult spaces for living and dead children.

Thinking of spatiality as the essential part of children's existential beings and be-comings in the formation of material and immaterial worlds, a return to the human life cycle of childhood seems appropriate. Many pathways may be singled out, but an extended list drawn tentatively here to consider possible sequences shows a variety of spaces associated with children depending on growth, circumstance, and agency (Table 2.1).[49] Not all the spaces refer to living individuals. As shown from the cases of Gräslund and Crawford, it is important to acknowledge the potentials and barriers for drawing lines between life and death in the material and immaterial

*Table 2.1. The distribution of spaces of life and death in the human life cycle corresponding with potential sequences of circumstance, growth, and agency in the worlds of children (cf. Lillehammer 2012, 12, table 1).*

| SPACE OF HUMAN LIFE CYCLE |
|---|
| • Space of conceived |
| • Space of abortion |
| • Space of birth |
| • Space of infanticide |
| • Space of rites of passage |
| • Space of sacrifice |
| • Space of growing up |
| • Space of eating |
| • Space of sleeping |
| • Space of learning |
| • Space of play |
| • Space of work |
| • Space of travel and journey |
| • Space of ritual celebration |
| • Space of worship |
| • Space of defence and war |
| • Space of illness and decease |
| • Space of death |
| • Space of deposal of the body |

evidence of children vs. childhood, and to contrast children's and adults' memories of childhood with adult responses to remembered children. To clarify my points 1–3, a holistic approach is conducted below in order to include both children and adults in the human life cycle. In all research work to discover the potentiality of children and childhood in the past, the following excursions (cf. A–C) will briefly present scenarios in the past and the present in which spatiality moves further than the sociality and historicality of children, and beyond the space of living children.

## A. The First Excursion: Separate Spaces of Children's Own Creations

The scenarios in 'A' refer children's living spaces to separate arenas outside the worlds of adult control, or where adult roles are open for communication.[50] They could be approached in the spatial examination of historical consciousness or found to exist in the personal, secret, and hidden places of subjects and objects of investigation.[51] They are situated far from and close to home and dwelling, or at home outside or inside shelters and buildings (cf. C).

The experience of a separate space came to mind while doing a landscape project which analysed heritage conflicts in the cultural practice of modern farmers in the Norwegian country side.[52] Asking informants to draw mental characteristics of their farm landscape – the Jæren farm – and to plot places of cultural heritage,[53] the sessions were rounded up with questions about favourite childhood play arenas. According to the farmers, the places were located to groves and forests, and along beaches, streams and river beds, on the farmland fringes and situated as far as possible from farmyard and home range because of work obligations.[54] Some farmers had problems in mapping places in the present landscape. The landscape perception of playing fields had survived only in the adult memory of childhood. As a result of intensive modern farming practices, the separate spaces of childhood were extinct and made non-places of the past.[55] One farmer, thinking about the coming generations, regretted that he was not able to pass on his childhood places in real time and space when he shared the history of landscape adventures with his grandchildren.

To counterbalance children's escape and retreat far from home, the evidence drawn from archaeological excavations at the 19th century North American Felton farm house gives another picture of child agency in the past. Children's living spaces are located in places closer to home and mainly in the farmyard near the garden and animal pen.[56] These spaces occur also in the paintings of children's games at a Flemish town square, as compared to the distinctive patterns of play arenas at Late Medieval settlements in the English countryside[57] or in the spread of toys and bricolage from a third millennium BC Harappan settlement, India.[58]

## B. The Second Excursion: Spaces of Relationships in-between Children and Adults

The scenarios in 'B' present children's living spaces especially with regard to technology and learning processes. At an early stage in the study of children and childhood, some archaeological researchers experimented with finding child agency at a modern garbage site,[59] or in the space of a Stone Age site,[60] or comparatively in the measurement of thumbs and flint cores.[61] Later, several studies of serial sequence and technological practice in the spatial pattern of discards, flint assemblages, and working areas[62] have demonstrated processes and end-products of novice knapping, but importantly also the recognition of child-empty spaces.[63]

The scenarios in 'B' bring to mind the oddity and otherness of children further and beyond the manifestation of cultural heritage in the landscape and modern museums, such as in the sideways experience of interactions between places. One of my first recollections of the multidimensional character of child agency was in the link of awareness between heaps of flint on the working table at the museum and playthings at home.[64] At the time a mother of three minors, the daily routine was to clear play arenas at home and in the museum to process flint material from excavated Stone Age sites. The work in the museum always ended up sorting three heaps of flint, one of weapons and tools, one of chips and debris, and one of miscellaneous flint with uncertain classification as to weapons, tools or debris. At the time it dawned on me that oddities in the uncertain heaps of flint might actually relate to ancient children experimenting with materials and learning the tools of flint making, rather than to the inexperienced knowledge and expertise of modern adults in understanding the acculturated practice of stone technology.

## C. The Third Excursion: Spaces of Adult Creation for Living and Dead Children

The scenarios in 'C' refer children's living spaces to integrated spaces of dominant adult worlds, and to environments in which children adapted and socialised during childhood, or where their existential beings were staged, manipulated, and remembered after death. They relate to a variety of habituations and settlements and to funerary places and deposits of children living and dead, in the vicinity or far away from dwellings, within and outside shelters, buildings, cemeteries and graves, or in the liminal and marginal places such as hills and wetlands.

The Late Mesolithic midden occupation inside and outside a cave on the south-western coast of Norway includes features of hybridity and otherness. Alongside the innermost wall a fifteen year old adolescent (possibly male) had been deposited among the debris 7500 years ago. Physically fit, but extremely short, the individual had been born with *scaphocephaly*, a congenital abnormality which makes the skull long and narrowed.[65] This has triggered an enquiry into how and why the corpse was located in the cave.[66]

Children's liminality and transformation could be explored also in the interrelationships between spaces of abandonment, infanticide or sacrifice, and spaces of their transformed bodies into ghosts and spiritual beings. In the Andes children were chosen to be sacrificed messengers to deities.[67] In the tradition of the Norse unwanted new born, children were carried out alive in the landscape, and the practices have survived in the legends of folklore and place-names in the Nordic countries to this day.[68]

CONCLUSION

The search for steps to children's living spaces has opened new and old pathways to the past and the past in the present. Faced with great complexity in the time consuming multi-disciplinary and inter-disciplinary working for a discovery beyond the unique, exclusive, and rare, this has meant challenging the knowledge and understanding of spatiality in the invisibility and fluidity of children's material and immaterial worlds of agency, hybridity, liminality, otherness, alteration, and transformation. In these excursions, exploring theoretical and methodological potentials and barriers, we have looked for children in the most obvious places of reproduction and change, and particularly in the elusive nature of learning, work and play, and widespread deposition of their bodies. We have moved further than their lives and deaths and considered responses to remembered and unwanted children and to those who survived and grew into adulthood and themselves had children. In the pursuit of children's living spaces we have transcended beyond the past to include the recycled, renewed and recuperated space of their cultural heritage in the present.

While looking for the spatial manifestations of children's worlds we have refrained from defining explicitly the concept 'living'. The interested reader may have noticed that it is a lived space and not altogether an empty or a muted space, silenced by academia's attitudes towards the study of children and childhood in the past. Having reached a research state where I want to cross over boundaries set both by others and myself respectively, that always makes me curious and wanting to push forward as researcher. Granted children's living spaces to have been almost anywhere, it would seem there are spaces not assigned to children. For children's living spaces to be examined we have to keep on pushing beyond the present state. One of the main intentions of science and the arts coming together is the creation of a dialogue to air questions and discuss results and to look for answers to challenging calls. In the spatial studies of children and childhood in the past, finding common and complementary grounds where we can join forces and move forward are exciting prospects for future research. Why not touch the future now and initiate international programs and projects on the subject of children and childhood in the past?

NOTES

1  Olwig and Gulløv 2003
2  Lillehammer 2010a
3  Soja 1996, 71–2, 81–2
4  Qvortrup 1994, 4
5  Lillehammer 2012
6  Frønes 1994, 146–8
7  Montgomery 2009
8  James *et al.* 1998; James and James 2004
9  Mejsholm 2009
10  Lillehammer 2010a, 2010b
11  Sofaer Derevenski 2000, 11
12  Elliot *et al.* 2001, 118

13  Elliot *et al.* 2001, 118, 897
14  Fahlander 2012
15  Fahlander 2011
16  Chamberlain 2000, 207–9
17  Welinder 1998, 194–5
18  Halcrow and Tayles 2011, 342–4
19  Gilchrist 2012, 3
20  Sofaer 2006, 77
21  Gowland and Thompson 2013, 173
22  Murphy 2008, 1
23  Crawford and Lewis 2008, 5
24  Lillehammer 2010a, 35, fig. 3
25  Hodder 2012
26  Renfrew and Morley 2009
27  Scarre 2009
28  Hamerow *et al.* 2011
29  Crawford 2011
30  Hamerow *et al.* 2010, 1048–9
31  Crawford 2011 631
32  Whitehead 2002
33  Crawford 2011 628–9, fig. 32.1
34  Alt and Kempes-Grottenthaler 2002; Gilchrist 2000; Moore and Scott 1997; Sofaer Deverenski 2000, 1996; Johnsen and Welinder 1995
35  Lillehammer 2000, 2010a
36  Arbman 1943
37  Gräslund 1973, 164–71, figs 1–2
38  Olsen 1997
39  Lie 1960, 164, fig. 4; Eriksson 1960
40  Gräslund 1973, 168–71, my translation
41  Gamble 2008
42  Chamberlain 2008, 103
43  Rogersdotter 2008, 130
44  Bea 2012
45  Chapman 2008, 195
46  Humpfreys 1997
47  Lönnquist 1992, 80
48  Lillehammer 2010a, 30
49  Lillehammer 2012, 12, table 1
50  Lönnquist *ibid.*
51  Högberg 2007, 38–41
52  Lillehammer 2004
53  Lillehammer 2009
54  Lillehammer 2007, 172
55  Augé 1995
56  Baxter 2005, 76, fig. 7
57  Lewis 2009, 98–104, figs 5–13
58  Rogersdotter 2008
59  Hammond and Hammond 1981
60  Bonnichsen 1973
61  Knutsson 1986

62  Dugstad 2011, 69, fig. 4; Sternke and Sørensen 2009; Högberg 2008; Grimm 2000, 60, fig. 5.6
63  Eigeland 2010, 80
64  Lillehammer 1987
65  Barber 2011, 96–7; Bang-Andersen 1983
66  Lillehammer 2012, 8
67  Ceruti 2010
68  Lillehammer 2011; 2010b, 55–6, fig. 3; 2008, 101–3

REFERENCES

Alt, K. W. and Kemkes-Grottenthaler, A. 2002. *Kinderwelten. Anthropologie – Geschichte -Kulturvergleich*. Köln: Böhlau.

Arbman, H. 1943. *Birka I. Die Gräber*. Uppsala: Kungl Vitterhets Historie och Antikvitets Akademien.

Augé, M. 1995. *Non-places. Introduction to an Anthropology of Supermodernity*. London/New York: Verso.

Bang-Andersen, S. 1983. *Svarthåla på Viste – boplass i 6000 år* (summary in English. The Black Cave – A Stone Age Dwelling-Place). (AmS-Småtrykk 13). Stavanger: Arkeologisk museum i Stavanger.

Barber, J. 2011. *Facial Reconstruction and Exhibition of the Skeletal Find from Viste: A Discussion of problems and Solutions when dealing with Archaeological Material*. Unpublished M.Sc. Thesis, University of Dundee.

Baxter, J. E. 2005. *The Archaeology of Childhood. Children, Gender, and Material Culture*. Walnut Creek: Altamira Press.

Bea, M. 2012. Representaciones infantiles en el arte levantino, pp. 31–55 in Vicente, D. J. (ed.) *Niños en la Antigüedad: Estudios sobre la infancia en Mediterráneo antiguo*. Zaragoza: Prensas de la Universidad de Zaragoza.

Bonnichsen, R. 1973. Millie's camp: An experiment in archaeology. *World Archaeology 4*, 277–91.

Ceruti, C. 2011. The religious role of the children in de Andes – Past and present, pp. 125–133 in Lillehammer, G. (ed.) *Socialisation. Recent Research on Childhood and Children in the Past*. (AmS-Skrifter 23). Stavanger: Museum of Archaeology, University of Stavanger.

Chamberlain, A. 2000. Minor concerns: A demographic perspective on children in past societies, pp. 206–12 in Sofaer Derevenski, J. (ed.) *Children and Material Culture*. London: Routledge.

Chamberlain, A. 2008. Pre-Homo Sapiens life worlds, pp. 102–8 in David, B. and Thomas, J. (eds) *Handbook of Landscape Archaeology*. Walnut Creek: Left Coast Press.

Chapman, J. 2008. Object fragmentation and past landscapes, pp. 187–201 in David, B. and Thomas, J. (eds) *Handbook of Landscape Archaeology*. Walnut Creek: Left Coast Press.

Crawford, S. 2011. Overview: The body and life course, pp. 625–40 in Hamerow, H., Hinton, D. A. and Crawford, S. (eds) *The Oxford Handbook of Anglo-Saxon Archaeology*. Oxford: Oxford University Press.

Crawford, S. and Lewis, C. 2008. Childhood studies and the Society for the Study of Childhood in the Past. *Childhood in the Past* 1, 5–16.

Dugstad, S. A. 2010. Early child caught knapping. A novice Early Mesolithic flintknapper in south-western Noway, pp. 65–75 in Lillehammer, G. (ed.) *Socialisation. Recent Research on Childhood and Children in the Past*. (AmS-Skrifter 23). Stavanger: Museum of Archaeology, University of Stavanger.

Eigeland, L. 2010. Children of the Neolithic Revolution. How a child's perspective can change the way we think about Stone Age, pp. 75–82 in Lillehammer, G. (ed.) *Socialisation. Recent Research on Childhood and Children in the Past*. (AmS-Skrifter 23). Stavanger: Museum of Archaeology, University of Stavanger.

Elliot, J., Knight, A. and Cowley, C. (eds) 2001. *Oxford. Dictionary & Thesaurus*. Oxford: Oxford University Press.

Eriksson, G. 1960. Skallror. *Kulturen 1960*, 72–83.

Fahlander, F. 2011. Subadults or subalterns? Children as serial categories, pp. 14–23 in Lally, M. and Moore, A. (eds) *(Re)Thinking the Little Ancestor*: *New Perspectives on Archaeology of Infancy and Childhood*. (BAR International Series 2271). Oxford: Archaeopress.

Fahlander, F. 2012. Mesolithic childhoods: Changing life-courses of young hunter-fishers in the Stone Age of Southern Scandinavia. *Childhood in the Past* 5, 20–34.

Frönes, I. 1994. Dimensions of childhood, pp. 145–66 in Qvortrup, J., Bardy, M., Sgritta, G. and Wintersberger, H. (eds) *Childhood Matters*: *Social Theory, Practice and Politics*. Aldershot: Avebury Press.

Gamble, C. 2008. Hidden landscapes of the body, pp. 256–262 in David, B. and Thomas, J. (eds) *Handbook of Landscape Archaeology*. Walnut Creek: Left Coast Press.

Gilchrist, R. (ed.) 2000. Human Lifecycles. *World Archaeology* 31. Routledge: London.

Gilchrist, R. 2012. *Medieval Life. Archaeology and the Life Course*. Woodbridge: The Boydell Press.

Gowland, R. and Thompson, T. 2013. *Human Identity and Identification*. Cambridge: Cambridge University Press.

Grimm, L. 2000. Apprentice flintknapping: relating material culture and social practice in the Upper Paleolithic, pp. 53–71 in Sofaer Derevenski, J. (ed.) *Children and Material Culture*. London: Routledge.

Gräslund, A.-S. 1973. Barn i Birka. *Tor 1972–3*, 161–79.

Halcrow, S. E. and Tayles, N. 2011. The bioarchaeological investigation of children and childhood, pp. 333–60 in Agarwal, S. C. and Glencross, B. A. (eds) *Social Bioarchaeology*. Oxford: Wiley-Blackwell.

Hamerow, H., Hinton, D. A. and Crawford, S. (eds). *The Oxford Handbook of Anglo-Saxon Archaeology*. Oxford: Oxford University Press.

Hammond, G. and Hammond, N. 1981. Child's play: A distorting factor in archaeological distribution. *American Antiquity* 46, 634–36.

Hodder, I. (ed.) 2012. *Archaeological Theory Today* (second edition). Cambridge: Polity.

Humphreys, N. 1997. How the mind works out. *New Scientist* 153 (2065), 37.

Högberg, A. 2007. The past is the present – Prehistory and preservation from a children's point of view. *Public Archaeology* 6:1, 28–46.

Högberg, A. 2008. Playing with flint. Tracing a child's imitation of adult work in a lithic assemblage. *Journal of Archaeological Method and Theory* 15, 112–31.

James, A., Jenks, C. and Prout, A. 1998. *Theorizing Childhood*. Cambridge: Polity Press.

James, A. and James, A. L. 2004. *Constructing Childhood*: *Theory, Policy and Practice*. Basingstoke: Palgrave MacMillan.

Johnsen, B. and Welinder, S. (eds) 1995. *Arkeologi om barn*. (Archaeology of Children). (Occasional Papers 10). Uppsala: University of Uppsala.

Knutsson, K. 1986. Några ord om barn, stötkantkärnor och *pieces esquilles*. *Fjölnir 1986*, 1, 29–39.

Lewis, C. 2009. Children's play in the Later Medieval English countryside. *Childhood in the Past* 2, 86–108.

Lie, I. M. 1960. Gullranglen og andre barnerangler. *Kunstindustrimuseet i Oslo Årbok 1950–1958*, 162–81.

Lillehammer, G. 1987. Small scale archaeology, pp. 33–4 in Bertelsen, R., Lillehammer, A. and Næss, J.-R. (eds) *Were They All Male? An Examination of Sex Roles in Prehistoric Society*. (AmS-Varia 17). Stavanger: Arkeologisk museum i Stavanger.

Lillehammer, G. 2000. The world of children, pp. 17–26 in Sofaer Derevenski, J. (ed.) *Children and Material Culture*. London: Routledge.

Lillehammer, G. 2004. *Konflikter i landskapet. Kulturminner og kulturforståelse. Analyse av alvedans og utmark i Hå kommune i Rogaland*. (AmS-Varia 42) Stavanger: Arkeologisk museum i Stavanger. Available at: http://am.uis.no/publikasjoner/ams_nett/article14014-5016.html.

Lillehammer, G. 2007. The past in the present. Landscape perception, archaeological heritage and marginal farmland in Jæren, South-western Norway. *Norwegian Archaeological Review* 40, 2, 159–87.

Lillehammer, G. 2008. Transforming images: Exploring powerful children. *Childhood in the Past* 1, 94–105.

Lillehammer, G. 2009. Making them draw. The use of drawings when researching public attitudes towards the past, pp. 253–69 in Sørensen, M. L. S. and Carman, J. (eds) *Heritage Studies. Methods and Approaches*. London: Routledge.

Lillehammer, G. 2010a. Archaeology of childhood. *Complutum* 21:2, 15–44.

Lillehammer, G. 2010b. Introduction to socialisation. Recent research on childhood and children in the past, pp. 9–19 in Lillehammer, G. (ed.) *Socialisation. Recent Research on Childhood and Children in the Past.* (AmS-Skrifter 23). Stavanger: Museum of Archaeology, University of Stavanger.

Lillehammer, G. 2011. The children in the bog, pp. 47–62 in Lally, M. and Moore, A. (eds) *(Re) Thinking the Little Ancestor: New Perspectives on Archaeology of Infancy and Childhood*. (BAR International Series 2271). Oxford: Archaeopress.

Lillehammer, G. 2012. Travels into thirdspace: The archaeological heritage of children's spaces. A view from beyond. *Childhood in the Past* 5, 7–19.

Lönnquist, B. 1992. *Ting, rum och barn. Historisk-antropologiska studier i kulturella gränser och gränsöverskridande.* (Things, Space and Children). (Kansatieteellinen Arkisto 38). Helsingfors: Suomen Muinaismuistoyhdistys – Finska Fornminnesforeningen.

Mejsholm, L. 2009. *Konstruksjonen av tidig barndom och begravningsritual vid tiden för kristnandet av Skandinavien.* (Borderland. Construction of Early Childhood and Burial Rituals during the Christianisation in Scandinavia). (Occasional papers in Archaeology 44). Uppsala: Uppsala Universitet.

Montgomery, H. 2009. *An Introduction to Childhood. Anthropological Perspectives on Children's Lives.* Oxford: Wiley-Blackwell.

Moore, J. and Scott, E. (eds) 1997. *Invisible People and Processes*. London: Leicester University Press.

Murphy, E. 2008. Editorial. *Childhood in the Past* 1, 1–2.

Olsen, B. 1997. *Fra Ting til Tekst: Teoretiske Perspektiv i Arkeologisk Forskning*. Oslo: Universitetsforlaget.

Olwig, K. F. and Gulløv, E. (eds) 2003. *Children's Places. Cross-cultural Perspectives*. London and New York: Routledge.

Qvortrup, J. 1994. Introduction. pp. 1–23 in Qvortrup, J., Bardy, M., Sgritta, G. and Wintersberger, H. (eds) *Childhood matters. Social Theory, Practice and Politics*. Aldershot: Avebury Press.

Renfrew, C. and Morley, I. 2009. *Becoming Human*. Cambridge: Cambridge University Press.

Rogersdotter, E. 2008. *Socializing Children's Toys. An Archaeological Inquiry into Third Millennium BC Harappan Terracotta Remains from Gujarat, India*. Saarbrücken: VDM Verlag Dr. Müller.

Scarre, C. 2009. *The Human Past* (second edition). London: Thames & Hudson.

Sternke, F. and Sørensen, M. 2009. The identification of children's flint knapping products in Mesolithic Scandinavia, pp. 722–29 in McCartan, S., Schulting, R., Warren, G. and Woodman, P. (eds), *Meolithic Horizons Volume II*. Oxford: Oxbow Books.

Sofaer, J. 2006. *The Body of Material Culture. A Theoretical Ostearchaeology*. Cambridge: Cambridge University Press.

Sofaer Derevenski, J. (ed.) 1996. *Perspectives on Children and Childhood*. (Archaeological Review 13:2). Cambridge: Department of Archaeology.

Sofaer Derevenski, J. 2000. Material Cultural shock: Confronting expectations in the material culture of children, pp. 3–16 in Sofaer Derevenski, J. (ed.) *Children and Material Culture*. London: Routledge.

Soja, E. W. 1996. *Thirdspace. Journeys to Los Angeles and Other Real-and-Imagined Places*. Oxford: Blackwell Publishing.

Welinder, S. 1998. The construction of childhood in Scandinavia 3500 BC–1350 AD. *Current Swedish Archaeology* 6, 185–205.

Whitehead, S. M. 2002. *Men and Masculinities*.Cambridge: Polity Press.

# PART II

## *Playing, Living and Learning*

# 3

# COMPLEXITY, COOPERATION AND CHILDHOOD: AN EVOLUTIONARY PERSPECTIVE

## *Juan Manuel Jiménez-Arenas*

---

INTRODUCTION: WHAT ABOUT HUMANS?

Anatomical modern humans present a set of characteristics with which an important part of humanity feels identified. Some of them, such as bipedalism, are shared by all members of the hominid family. Others, such as lithic tool production, are linked to the genus *Homo* and, last, a big group of them are exclusive to our species *Homo sapiens*.[1] Amongst the latter, we would like to highlight five in this chapter:

1. A big brain. The size of the brain of our species can be four times as large, in absolute terms, as that of one of our closest living relatives, chimpanzees. Thus, their measure is located near 370 cm$^3$ and the members of our species of the Pleistocene reach 1,450 cm$^3$. Furthermore, if we are speaking about its relative size in relation to the corporal mass (Encephalization Quotient),[2] modern humans treble the value of chimpanzees. It is relevant to point out that the absolute and relative sizes of the brain (above all the first) are related to the cognitive abilities of non human primates.[3] In the singular case of the anatomical modern humans it traditionally relates to a special type of intelligence, the symbolic.

2. A difficult birth. First, because the *H. sapiens* neonates present an enlarged brain size (400–450 gr.), which exceeds the average size of adult chimpanzees and represents approximately 30% of the size of human adults. The chimpanzees, on their side, are born with brains of 150 gr., which supposes 40% of the adult's size.[4] Second, because anatomically modern human females (and also Neanderthal ones) present a relatively narrow birth canal, due to the biomechanical impositions related to bipedalism. Such a pelvic feature implies a process of dilation and also need for rotation of the newborn (see the work of Karen Rosenberg for a revision of this fundamental topic in human evolution).[5] These two opposed selective strengths, the sizes of neonate's heads and of the birth canal, have resulted in the expression 'obstetrical dilemma' which supposes an important evolutionary constraint.

3. Very fragile and altricial neonates, insomuch as they are born absolutely dependent, basically of the mothers, on breastfeeding, for much longer than our closest relatives. Once weaning occurs, which happens between three and four years old (three years and two month average in 'archaic societies'),[6] dependency, which continues being important, is no longer exclusive of mothers. Chimpanzees, instead, wean their young later (at five years).[7]

4. On the other hand, and related to the previous point, the chronological length of human development until reaching physical maturity (considered as a fully erupted permanent dentition) is very long in comparison with our closest relatives, chimpanzees. That species has all their teeth by the age of 12.4 years,[8] meanwhile modern humans have them around the 20s.[9]

5. Last, human beings present a rich culture, which has no comparison with other species. This does not mean that other species do not develop extrasomatic modifications acquired and transmitted by means of social learning. Thus, birds, and more specifically corvids, are assisted by certain natural elements to obtain food,[10] although it is our closest relatives who seem to develop something similar to what we call cultural traditions.[11]

Based on the above points, the objective of the present chapter is to establish how complexity, cooperation and childhood are related and how the interactions, produced among the five previously described characteristics, have contributed, and contribute, to the evolutionary success of our linage.

THEORETICAL BACKGROUND: COMPLEXITY AND PEACE RESEARCH

*Complexity*

Our investigations are based on and inscribed in ideas about complexity. Of all the meanings and characteristics which have developed from this concept, we would like to outline three in this chapter. The first one is the existence of different quantitative and qualitative entities and relations (interactions and feedbacks). So the things that are relevant for a system to be considered more or less complex, is not given as much by the number of elements and relations that constitute it, but by the quantity and quality of interactions produced among the elements that make up the system. These relations are conflicting in the sense that they arise from differences in the projects, interests, objectives or perceptions, in the case of human beings, among the different elements that constitute such system. The second one is the existence of nodes and transitions between order and disorder. This takes us to an idea which we think fundamental: the existence of nodes and transitions implies, as they are critical moments, that the interrelations may or may not come to fruition. From there we propose that the more complex a system is, the more fragile it becomes. Now, the fact of being complex also entails that a system has more resources to maintain its conditions of existence (resilience, dynamic balances).

This latter point links with the third characteristic we will outline in relation to complexity: the coexistence of aspects which, apparently, can seem exclusive (for example peace and violence). We do not consider the concept of peace as oppositional to violence. Peace is not only the absence of violence. Peace is based on conflict management where it promotes the development of human capabilities[12] and, given its imperfection (of peace), coexists with violence.[13] Furthermore, peace can also be considered a trans-disciplinary field. Due to its complexity, peace cannot be studied by a single discipline. Therefore, it is fundamental that multiple disciplines converge to create a new theoretical and methodological corpus, which, together with those of each discipline, gives answers to the axiological, methodological, epistemological and ontological elements of peace.

## Peace research

We assume that humans are the most complex, fragile and conflictive species known in nature. This will be one of the main starting points of our investigation. We consider that human beings are, and form part of, non lineal systems. The actions and survival of our linage, since its appearance seven million years ago[14] until the present, depend completely on adaptation to complex and changing contexts in which we are included and relate with the rest of living beings, in nature, on Earth and in the universe. In fact, the resultant complexity of the transformation and evolution of the universe, the planet Earth, of life and culture leaves a legacy of elections for the management of information or for the energy, the organization or forms of life, with which humans cohabit. This heritage facilitates life, achieving a relatively (in)stable and dynamic balance which living beings assume and manage.[15]

One of the methods organisms have to manage complexity is cooperation. Obviously, cooperation is not exclusive of human beings. Thus, for example, following the postulates of the endosymbiotic theory, cooperation serves to explain one of the most crucial episodes in biotic evolution: the emergence of eukaryotic cells.[16] So, cooperation configures a fundamental part of the repertoire that permits us to overcome the fragility human beings are immersed in, especially during the first years of existence. Cooperation is linked to the five previously discussed characteristics, as well as to the conflictivity of our species. Likewise it relates to the satisfaction and development of human capabilities, ergo, to the concepts for constructing peace. And, last, we would like to outline that the cooperative, altruist, and philanthropic behaviours have been constant and have played a fundamental role along the evolution of our lineage.

## The importance of ontological models

If cooperation, altruism and philanthropy have been constants along our (pre)history, why is our way of reconstructing the past not gathering more evidence of it? To a large extent it is due to the anthropological and ontological models we employ and which depend on our practice as professionals of the sciences of the past.

In the case of occidental society, the predominant model is negative; it proposes that humans are violent by nature. Such a proposal has its roots in the Judeo-Christian Hebrew Bible, which is based on the narrative of the expulsion from Paradise and the emergence of original sin. Consideration of the violent nature of humanity reaches one of its apogees with Thomas Hobbes and his affirmation of the primal condition of humanity: 'war of all against all' (*bellum omnium contra omnes*). One of the consequences of this type of affirmation is ontological, provoking very important biases in the design and the access to knowledge, the epistemology. So the balance between authors who had tried to support the violent nature of humanity and those who had tried to sustain the peaceful nature of it, is moving in favour of the first. Thus, there have been many specialists, from multiple disciplines, who tried to argue in favour of the negative nature of humanity.[17]

Alternatively, we find a sensible smaller group of investigators who have endeavored to prove a pacific human 'nature' (or biological condition mediated by culture). One of the reasons for this small number was pointed out by one of the most influential proponents of the positive conception of humanity, Jean-Jacques Rousseau, who describes the difficulties in studying the natural state of humanity. The Genevan philosopher coined the expression 'the myth of the noble savage' to explain that the inequalities in humanity come from private property and civil society. To a certain point, Rousseau's concept builds on 'the ages of humanity' of the Greek poet Hesiod. Human beings are born by nature morally and politically equal: it is the historic (cultural) contexts, created by humans, which provoke the – unjustified – inequalities. The natural state of humanity is – consequently – kind and generous. Another author, partially influenced by Rousseau, who joined the positive concept of humanity, was Piotr Kropotkin. In his most famous work *Mutual Aid*,[18] he tries to answer the Darwinists (not Darwin) over the cruelty of the struggle for subsistence. From his libertarian perspective, the author is 'naturalizing' cooperation and solidarity in order to justify them as forms of making politics. The ideas of Rousseau and Kropotkin had a certain continuation in anthropology. We outline Margaret Mead and Ashley Montagú. The first one because she conducted a study with three different groups from Papua New Guinea and revealed that peaceful and violent behaviours are not related to the gender of individuals.[19] The second one because he articulated a corpus of evidence based on primatology, paleontology and ethnology to dispel the myth of consubstantial badness in humanity.[20]

Both the negative and positive ontological models are based on essentialist approaches. However, for us it is much more important to characterize entities than to be looking for essences. So, we consider human beings as complex and with capacity to make peace as well as be violent. Humans are neither violent nor pacific by nature.[21] Both, violence and peace, are cultural constructions and as such, contingents.

But it is not only about focusing on direct violence. For example, gender archaeology has contributed in a substantial manner to deconstruct ideas about human nature (for example the sexual division of labour) which are at the base of the andocentric idea of inequality between women and men based on a presumed physical superiority which would limit women, for example, in venery activities.[22] Nowadays, we know that for most of human (pre)history, we were scavengers, therefore gatherers, and we cannot sustain naturalizing sexual division of labour.[23] Finally, the visualization of the subjects of history, forgotten by traditional – and predominant – historiography, also forms part of pacifism in the sense that we now contemplate them, as an act of justice. And this is what has happened recently with infants and children.

All the previously discussed theory converges to what we call an 'epistemological and ontological turn' which permits us to centre on aspects that, throughout history, have implemented the peaceful regulation of conflicts, the development of capabilities, all of which we can include as peace practices. As historians, we want to reconstruct the history of peace, and we propose the *Hominid Pax* as idea which can be useful in this sense. *Hominid Pax* serves to recognize the altruistic, cooperative and philanthropic behaviours (today considered peaceful) of our ancestors which, with bipedalism, encephalization, and reduction of canines and postcanine dentitions, have contributed fundamentally to the successive evolutionary successes of our family because they have contributed to the development of human capabilities, of the past and present.[24]

## WHAT DOES CHILDHOOD MEAN?

The vast majority of the mammal species moves from infancy to the adult state without passing intermediate phases. That is, they reach sexual maturity (puberty) and meanwhile the growth rate, the pace of maturation, declines significantly. On the other hand, the most social species, among which we find the primates and some other carnivorous species, tend to pass a juvenile phase, implying a postposition of the arrival of sexual maturity. Only humans display five clearly separated and accepted phases: infancy, childhood, youth, adolescence and adulthood (Fig. 3.1).[25]

Each of these phases is well characterized through a set of features. Thus, infancy is the phase that elapses from birth until weaning which, in 'archaic societies' does not occur until the 38th month. During this period, infants are basically dependent on the mothers (or other women) given that, in normal conditions, the production of milk is exclusive to women. Thus, infancy is the period in which offspring are mainly dependent on mothers (although other females can be included) given lactation. Now, that fact that infants are mainly dependent on females (mothers in most of the cases) does not mean that other members of the groups do not participate in the childcare and socialization. Early childhood is characterized by individuals who are still dependent in terms of alimentation and caretaking but the participation of other group members, joined together the mothers, is considerably bigger. Youth presents independent individuals in terms of alimentation and survival, but they are not yet sexual mature. Adolescence starts with puberty, the moment at which individuals reach sexual maturity which usually happens earlier for females than males and is characterized by rapid physical growth. Also, important neurological centers mature, principally the pre-frontal cortex which is in charge, to a large extent, of the control of behaviour.[26]

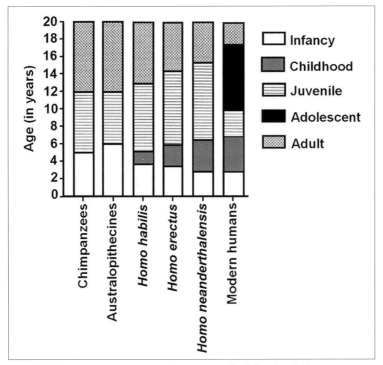

*Figure 3.1. Bar chart where we represent the age reached by the different ontogenic phases in chimpanzees and anatomically modern humans as well as the estimates of different taxa of hominid fossils. Modified from Bogin and Holly-Smith 1996.*

Therefore, unlike our closest relatives, the big apes, anatomically modern humans give birth to an offspring which is dependent during a long period of time, and therefore fragile, at the same time that from three years age onwards, approximately, it is physiologically independent of mothers (or, in some cases, other women).

*Human paradoxes*

As we have already seen, infants, like children, need caretaking during a long period of time: more than any other species of primates close to us. However, not all aspects of human life history follow this trend. For example, human lactation lasts less time than is observed in chimpanzees, which breastfeed their offspring until five years age.[27] This represents a reduction in the energetic cost which the human mother has to generate, and also has the effect of substantially shortening the interbirth interval.[28] Hence the necessity for the existence of a period that permits the development of immature human individuals while they are still dependent – childhood. Moreover, if we compare the age of weaning with the age of eruption of the first molar, we perceive more clearly this paradox in modern human life history, given that *H. sapiens* is the only species where weaning takes place significantly before the eruption of the first molar (Fig. 3.2).

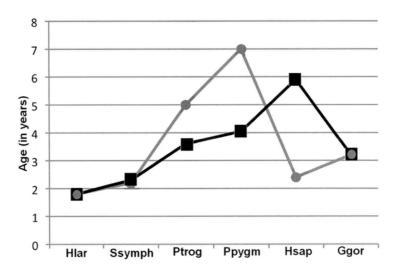

*Figure 3.2. Plot chart representing the weaning age (grey circles) and the eruption of the first molar (black squares) of different anthropomorphic ape species. Legend: Hlar (Hylobates lar); Ssymph (Symphalangus syndactilus); Ptrog (Pan troglodytes); Ppygm (Pongo pygmaeus); Hsap (Homo sapiens); Ggor (Gorilla gorilla). Modified from Humphrey 2010.*

The second paradox is related to the period of learning. So, infancy is the period in which also the chimpanzees learn a good part of their cultural repertoire. It is relevant to point out that one of the activities which most called the attention of investigators is the opening of nuts by the means of rudimentary tools: anvils and hammers. This activity, which might appear simple, requires, however, the acquisition of sufficient abilities and knowledge to find an appropriate primary raw material for the anvils and hammers, as well as the skills to open the nuts effectively. The multiple field observations carried out on groups of chimpanzees point out that the cultural transmission is only passed from mothers to children and that the learning goes on, more or less, the same time as lactation.[29]

On the other hand, human infants-children enjoy a bigger number and degree of interactions given that they are socialized by many members of the group. But not only this. According to this point of view, infancy and childhood necessitate socialization. We propose that the increase of cooperation is more obvious in childhood; that is, the period in which the offspring is still dependent, although not as much from the mothers, and presents, at least partially, a great plasticity linked to development.[30] Obviously, this supposes an increase of complexity and better management of the same type that relates to a cooperative arrangement which is at the base of our peculiar cultural richness. What other consequences have the number of persons (females, males and immature of different ages) implied in the process of learning? Firstly, that learning is richer and therefore more complex. Remember that one of the characteristics which define a system's complexity is the variety of interactions produced between its elements.

So, we can propose that major cooperation just as an increase in the information flows, contributes fundamentally to cultural evolution. Second, and from a perspective which incorporates more clearly biological aspects, the shortening of lactation and the appearance of childhood as differentiated phases in human development, means that women shorten their interbirth interval and that they can, at least theoretically, increase the number of offspring. This is basically due to the existent relation between high levels of prolactine (a hormone related to the maternal milk production) and oligomenorrhea and amenorrhea.[31] This supposes a demographic increase with respect to our closest relatives that could relate to the successive human dispersions which have taken place since the emergence of our lineage.[32]

From a gender perspective, the paradoxes previously exposed also have an influence. By gender we understand those social roles imposed on gendered bodies,[33] which relates to what is expected from each one of them. Cooperation has formed part of the *habitus* of both women and men in such a way that it is expected from the latter to participate actively in the children's learning, socialization and caretaking.

## When, why and how is the link between cooperation and childhood developed?

As announced in the title of this chapter, we give the equation of complexity, cooperation, and childhood an evolutionary perspective. Therefore, the key questions to answer are: when, why and how has the link between these three aspects developed? We can mark a big leap with the appearance of the genus *Homo*. When? It is at least 2.6 million years ago when the first evidences of lithic tools, related to *H. habilis* are registered.[34] On the other hand, the oldest remains of such taxon, associated with the Oldowan techno-complex, are dated to 2.33 million years.[35]

Lithic reduction supposes a substantial cultural difference with respect to the manipulated and transformed objects of distinct raw materials by chimpanzees. So, for the case of our closest relatives and the previously mentioned anvils and hammers to open nuts and the sticks to fish for termites and ants, the relation between the raw material and the final object is very direct. That is, the final result is heavily predetermined by the form/shape of the raw material. Nevertheless, the objects with which they access the interior of nuts and obtain formicids and isopterans present a high degree of standardization, which implies a careful selection of the raw material.[36] In the case of lithic tools, the predetermination is much less evident, which entails much more complex processes of learning. So, from very early (2.34 million years), in the settlement of Lokalalei 2C (Kenya), it is clear that the flintknappers have already interiorized planning notions and prevision for both the procurement of raw material and its manipulation. Beyond the mastery of these basic techniques concerning lithic reduction, *H. habilis* carried out highly controlled processes of reduction following constant technical processes which resulted in a high productivity. Therefore, from the beginnings of lithic tools, these first representatives of the genus *Homo* deployed very complex techno-economical and behavioural patterns.[37]

On the other hand, it does not seem that the obstetrical dilemma affected the *Australopithecus*, who presented significantly smaller brains than those of the first representatives of the genus *Homo* at the same time as they presented very wide birth canals which would confer to the *Australopithecus* female an easier birth. Nevertheless, it is relevant to point out that the birth of *H. habilis* neonates also did not seem to be marked by the posterior difficulties (Neanderthals and anatomically modern humans). In any case, the evidence suggests that the offspring of the first representatives of the genus *Homo* were born more immature then those of *Australopithecus*. This is possible to glimpse because the time of development of the australopithecine infants and children is sensibly shorter than of the second. At least this is inferred from the dental development of the *Australopithecus* and the first representatives of the genus *Homo*.[38] Therefore, the offspring of the first representatives of the genus *Homo* would be born more fragile and, therefore, dependent (qualitatively and quantitatively) and would require more time for learning a richer cultural repertoire which would allow them to unfold with more effectiveness and efficiency in a complex surrounding. Furthermore, this richness also links to a bigger participation of the group members, by increasing cooperation at the time of teaching the infants-children. At the same time, this bigger interdependence could have contributed to the way adults related amongst themselves because dependence is not linked exclusively to the mothers (or other women) through lactation anymore. This would suppose that the children enjoy an increase of highly energetic and easily digestible food intake which permits them to confront the energetic demands of development[39] in which many of the group components should have participated. This fact should have implied the collaboration of males in this type of task.[40] And this, at the same time, could be linked with an increase of the dietary quality, via a bigger participation of animal products in the diet, which is linked to the first representatives of the genus *Homo*.[41]

In this way, we could propose that the appearance of childhood as a distinct phase in human development could contribute notably to an increase of cooperation and, at the same time, would have not been possible without mentioned increase. Could we consider this change, apparent in the genus *Homo*, as the beginning of roles and relations of gender? In our opinion, yes, because the caretaking of children is a sort of 'denaturalized'[42] behaviour and becomes a part of the cultural patrimony of the groups. For this reason, males and females incorporate 'what they are', 'what is expected from them', meaning, they integrate a series of socially recognized roles which relate to the different sexes.

A second step is taken with the appearance of Neanderthals and anatomically modern humans. Both taxa present big brains when born, although Neanderthals present faster growth rates than those of anatomically modern humans.[43] On the other hand, there is evidence that Neanderthal and anatomically modern human females faced similar problems derived from birth, given that to the big size of the neonate's head the relatively small birth canals of both taxa[44] must be added. From the last study, Ponce de León and colleagues could reconstruct the birthing process of Neanderthal females and it seems that it was very similar, in terms of difficulties, to anatomically modern human females. Now, the difference lies in that if the growth of anatomically modern humans was slower than that of Neanderthals, the children and infants of the former would be more fragile and both infancy and childhood would enlarge over time. Therefore, the possibilities of cooperation, of behaviours which can be considered pacific, by the group members of anatomically modern humans would increase.

## FINAL REMARKS

Childhood and cooperation have played a key role in human evolution. Therefore, the appearance and extension of childhood suppose a better adaption to a complex surrounding and help to manage our fragility and to increment the cultural richness of the genus *Homo* through cooperation, which, recursively, made us more complex. This change in our life history, fundamental for our historic evolution, helps to propose that co-responsibility forms a fundamental part of the success of offspring, which poses an important gap regarding our closest living relatives, chimpanzees. These processes of socialization in which infants and children, women and men are immersed, in which cooperation has been a fundamental factor, help to make the pacific behaviours visible which have been relevant during the evolution of our linage and form part of the *Hominid Pax*.

Finally, the approach we present in this contribution, where we interact complexity, peace studies, and evolutionary and human life history, helps us to understand the relations derived from the link between childhood and cooperation, which at the same time permits us to progress in the recognition of pacific behaviours and in the conformation of our pacific identity.

## ACKNOWLEGDEMENTS

I acknowledge the insightful comments and helpful criticism contributed by editors Margarita Sánchez Romero, Eva Alarcón and Gonzalo Aranda. I am grateful to Francisco Muñoz Muñoz for his theoretic support underlining this whole contribution. I also thank María Ruiz Hilillo for her stylistic corrections and Sally Crawford for her suggestions for improving English usage and style in the manuscript. This research has been funded by the Spanish Ministry of Science and Innovation (projects CGL2011-30334 and HAR2011-27718) and supported by the Department of Economy, Innovation and Science, Junta de Andalucía, Spain (Research Group HUM-607). This study has been possible thanks to a Return Contract (University of Granada, Spain).

## NOTES

1   On the basis of the possibility of hybridation between Neanderthals and anatomically modern humans (Green *et al.* 2010) we include in this species both *H. neanderthalensis* and *H. sapiens*
2   Jerison 1973
3   Deaner *et al.* 2007
4   DeSilva and Lesnik 2006

5   Rosenberg 1995
6   Marlowe 2005. The archaic adjective has to be understood in its own etymologic sense. It comes from the Greek αρχή which means 'source', 'beginning' or 'origin'
7   Godfrey *et al.* 2001
8   Zihlman *et al.* 2004
9   Smith *et al.* 1994
10  Hunt 1996
11  Whiten *et al.* 1999, Lycett *et al.* 2007
12  For the issue of capabilities, cf. Max-Neef 2000, Nussbaum 2000, Sen 1985
13  Muñoz Muñoz 2001
14  Lebatard *et al.* 2008
15  Muñoz Muñoz and Molina Rueda 2009
16  Margulis 1970
17  E.g. Ardrey 1976, Bowles 2009, Dart 1959, Dawkins 1976, Eibl-Eibesfeldt 2007, Guilaine and Zammit 2002, Huxley 1888, Lorenz 2002, Wilson 1975
18  Kropotkin 2005
19  Mead 2001
20  E.g. Montagú 1976
21  Martínez Fernández and Jiménez Arenas 2003
22  Cf. Dalhberg 1975, Sanahuja Yll 2002, Sánchez Romero 2005
23  Jiménez Arenas 2011
24  *Ibíd.*
25  Bogin and Holly-Smith 1996
26  Thompson-Schill *et al.* 2009
27  Humprey 2010
28  Gettler 2010; Humphrey 2010
29  *vid.* Boesch 2003 and references contained there
30  Black 1998
31  MacNeilly 1979, Gray *et al.* 1990
32  Given that *Sahelanthropus tchadensis*, the first recognized hominid, was found in Chad (Central Africa) and attributed a chronology of seven million years old, and *Orrorin tugenensis* was discovered in Tanzania with a chronology of six million years old (Senut *et al.* 2001), the most plausible hypothesis is that there was a south-east dispersion with a date previous to six million years
33  Scott 1986
34  Semaw *et al.* 1999, de la Torre, 2011
35  Kimbel *et al.* 1996
36  Haslam *et al.* 2009
37  Delagnes and Roche 2005
38  Smith 1986, Beynon and Wood 1987
39  Gettler 2010, Humprey 2010
40  Gettler 2010
41  Kennedy 2005
42  If we consider natural the scenery presented for the chimpanzees, that is, offspring which are dependent on their mothers until they convert into independent individuals
43  Ramírez Rozzi and Bermúdez de Castro 2004
44  Ponce de León *et al.* 2010

REFERENCES

Ardrey, R. 1976. *The Hunting Hypothesis: A Personal Conclusion Concerning the Evolutionary Nature of Man*. London: MacMillan Publishers.

Beynon, A. D. and Wood, B. A. 1987. Patterns and rates of enamel growth in the molar teeth of early hominids. *Nature* 326, 493–6.

Black, J. E. 1998. How a child builds its brain: Some lessons from animal studies of neural plasticity. *Preventive Medicine* 27, 168–71.

Boesch, C. 2003. Is culture a golden barrier between human and chimpanzee? *Evolutionary Anthropology: Issues, News, and Reviews* 12, 82–91.

Bogin, B. and Holly-Smith, B. L. 1996. Evolution of the human life cycle. *American Journal of Human Biology* 8, 703–16.

Bowles, S. 2009. Did warfare among ancestral hunter- gatherers affect the evolution of human social behaviors? *Science* 324, 1293–8.

Dalhberg, F. 1975. *Woman the Gatherer*. London: Yale University Press.

Dart, R. 1959. *Adventures with the Missing Link*. New York: Harper.

Dawkins, R. 1976. *The Selfish Gene*. Oxford: Oxford University Press.

Deaner, R. O., Isler, D., Burkart, J. and van Schaik, C. 2007. Overall brain size, and note encephalization quotient, best predicts cognitive ability across non-human primates. *Brain, Behaviour and Evolution* 70, 115–24.

Delagnes, A. and Roche, H. 2005. Late Pliocene hominid knapping skills: The case of Lokalalei 2C, West Turkana, Kenya. *Journal of Human Evolution* 48, 435–72.

DeSilva, J. and Lesnik, J. 2006. Chimpanzee neonatal brain size: Implications for brain growth in *Homo erectus*. *Journal of Human Evolution* 51, 207–12.

Eibl-Eibesfeldt, I. 2007. *Human Ethology*. New York: Aldine Transaction.

Freud, S. 2000. *Conflict and Culture: Essays on His Life, Work, and Legacy*. New York: Vintage.

Geetler, L. T. 2010. Direct male care and hominin evolution: Why male-child interaction is more than a nice social idea. *American Anthropologist* 112, 7–21.

Godfrey, L. R., Samonds, K. E., Jungers W. L. and Sutherland, M. R. 2001. Teeth, brains and Primate life histories. *American Journal of Physical Anthropology* 114, 192–14.

Gray, R. H., Campbell, O. M., Apelom R., Eslami, S. S., Zacur, H., Ramos, R. M., Gehret, J. C. and Labbok, M. H. 1990. Risk of ovulation during lactation. *The Lancet* 335, 25–9.

Green, R. E., Krause, J., Briggs, A.W., Maricic, T., Stenzel, U., Kircher, M., Patterson, N., Li, H., Zhai, W., Fritz, M. H., Hansen, N. F., Durand, E. Y., Malaspinas, A. S., Jensen, J. D., Marques-Bonet, T., Alkan, C., Prüfer, K., Meyer, M., Burbano, H. A., Good, J. M., Schultz, R., Aximu-Petri, A., Butthof, A., Höber, B., Höffner, B., Siegemund, M., Weihmann, A., Nusbaum, C., Lander, E.S., Russ, C., Novod, N., Affourtit, J., Egholm, M., Verna, C., Rudan, P., Brajkovic, D., Kucan, Z., Gusic, I., Doronichev, V. B., Golovanova, L.V., Lalueza-Fox, C., de la Rasilla, M., Fortea, J., Rosas, A., Schmitz, R. W., Johnson, P. L., Eichler, E. E., Falush, D., Birney, E., Mullikin, J. C., Slatkin, M., Nielsen, R., Kelso, J., Lachmann, M., Reich, D. and Pääbo, S. 2010. A draft sequence of the Neandertal genome. *Science* 328, 710–22.

Guilaine, J. and Zammit, J. 2004. *The Origin of War: Violence in Prehistory*. New York: Wiley-Blackwell.

Humphrey, L. 2010. Weaning behaviour in humans. Seminars in Cell & Developmental Biology 21, 435–61.

Hunt, G. R. 1996. Manufacture and use of hook-tools by New Caledonia crows. *Nature* 379, 249–51.

Huxley, T. 1888. *The Struggle for Existence in Human Society*. http://aleph0.clarku.edu/huxley/CE9/str.html (3 October 2013).

Jerison, H. J. 1973. *Evolution of the Brain and Intelligence*. New York: Academic Press.

Jiménez Arenas, J. M. 2011. Pax homínida. Una aproximación imperfecta a la evolución humana, pp. 65–93 in Muñoz Muñoz, F. A. and Bolaños Carmona, J. (eds), *Los Habitus de la Paz. Teorías y Prácticas de la Paz Imperfecta*. Granada: Editorial de la Universidad de Granada.

Kennedy, G. E. 2005. From the ape's dilemma to the weanling's dilemma: Early weaning and its evolutionary context. *Journal of Human Evolution* 48, 123–45.

Kimbel, W. H., Walter, R. C., Johanson, D. C., Reed, K. E., Aronson, J. L., Assefa, Z., Marean, C. W., Eck, G. G., Bobe, R., Hovers, E., Rak, Y., Vondra, C., Yemane, T., York, D., Chen, Y., Evensen, N. M. and Smith, P. E. 1996. Late Pliocene *Homo* and Oldowan tools from the Hadar Formation (Kada Hadar Member), Ethiopia. *Journal of Human Evolution* 31: 549–61.

Kropotkin, P. 2005. *Mutual Aid: A Factor of Evolution*. Manchester (NH): Extending Horizons Books.

Lebatard, A.-E., Bourlès, D. L., Duringer, P., Jolivet, M., Braucher, R., Carcaillet, J., Schuster, M., Arnaud, N., Monié, P., Lihoreau, F., Likius, A., Mackaye, H. T., Vignaud, P. and Brunet, M. 2008. Cosmogenic nuclide dating of *Sahelanthropus tchadensis* and *Australopithecus bahrelghazali*: Mio-Pliocene hominids form Chad. *Proceedings of the National Academy of Sciences* 105, 3226–31.

Lorenz, K. 2002. *On Aggression*. London: Routledge.

Lycett, S. J., Collard, M. and McGrew, W. C. 2007. Phylogenetic analyses of behavior support existence of culture among wild chimpanzees. *Proceedings of the National Academy of Sciences* 104, 17588–92.

Margulis, L. 1970. *Origin of Eukariotic Cells*. New Haven: Yale University Press.

Marlowe, F. W. 2005. Hunter-gatherers and human evolution. *Evolutionary Anthropology: Issues, News, and Reviews* 14, 54–67.

Martínez Fernández, G. and Jiménez Arenas, J. M. 2003. Los humanos prehistóricos, ni violentos ni pacíficos por naturaleza, sino todo lo contrario, pp. 59–126 in Muñoz Muñoz, F. A. and Pérez Beltrán, C. (eds) *Experiencias de Paz en el Mediterráneo*. Granada: Editorial de la Universidad de Granada.

Max-Neef, M. 2000. *Desarrollo a Escala Humana*. Barcelona: Icaria.

McNeilly, A. S. 1979. Effects of lactation on fertility. *British Medical Bulletin* 35, 151–4.

Mead, M. 2001. *Sex and Temperament in Three Primitive Societies*. New York: Harper Perennial.

Montagú, A. 1976. *The Nature of Human Aggression*. New York: Oxford University Press.

Muñoz Muñoz, F. A. (ed.). 2001. *La Paz Imperfecta*. Granada: Editorial de la Universidad de Granada.

Muñoz, F. A. and Molina Rueda, B. 2009. Una cultura de paz compleja y conflictiva. La búsqueda de los equilibrios dinámicos. *Revista de Paz y Conflictos* 3, 44–61.

Nussbaum, M. 2000. *Women and Human Development: The Capabilities Approach*. Cambridge: Cambridge University Press.

Rosenberg, K. and Trevathan, W. 1995. Bipedalism and human birth: The obstetrical dilemma revisited. *Evolutionary Anthropology: Issues, News, and Reviews* 4, 161–8.

Ramírez Rozzi, F. V. and Bemúdez de Castro, J. M. 2004. Surprisingly rapid growth in Neanderthals. *Nature* 428, 936–9.

Sanahuja Yll, M. E. 2002. *Cuerpos Sexuados, Objetos y Prehistoria*. Madrid: Cátedra.

Sánchez Romero, M. (ed.). 2005. *Arqueología y Género*. Granada: Editorial de la Universidad de Granada.

Scott, J. W. 1986. Gender: A useful category of historical analysis. *The American Historical Review* 91, 1053–75.

Semaw, S., Renne, P., Harris, J. W. K., Feibel, C. S., Bernor, R. L., Fesseha, N. and Mowbray, K. 1997. 2.5-million-year-old stone tool from Gona, Ethiopia. *Nature* 385, 333–6.

Sen, A. K. 1985. *Commodities and Capabilities*. Oxford: Oxford University Press.

Senut, B., Pickford, M., Gommery, D., Mein, P., Cheboi, K. and Coppens, Y. 2001. First hominid from the Miocene (Lukeino Formation, Kenya). *Comptes Rendus de l'Academie des Sciences Series IIA Earth and Planetary Science* 332, 137–44.

Smith, B. H. 1986. Dental development in *Australopithecus* and early *Homo*. *Nature* 323, 327–30.

Smith, B. H., Crummett, T. L. and Brandt, K. L. 1994. Ages of eruption of primate teeth: a compendium for aging individuals and comparing life histories. *Yearbook of Physical Anthropology* 37, 177–231.

Thompson-Schill, S. L., Ramscar, M. and Chrysikou, E. G. 2009. Cognition without control: When a little frontal lobe goes a long way. *Current Directions in Psychological Science* 18, 259–63.

Whiten, A., Goodall, J., McGrew, W. C., Nishida, T., Reynolds, V., Sugiyama, Y., Tutin, C. E. G., Wrangham, R. W. and Boesch, C. 1999. Cultures in chimpanzees. *Nature* 399, 682–5.

Wilson, E. O. 1975. *Sociobiology: The New Synthesis*. Boston: Harvard University Press.

Zihlman, A., Bolter, D. and Boesch, C. 2004. Wild chimpanzee dentition and its implications for assessing life history in immature hominin fossils. *Proceedings of the National Academy of Science* 101, 10541–3.

# 4

## Children as Potters: Apprenticeship Patterns from Bell Beaker Pottery of Copper Age Inner Iberia (Spain) (c. 2500–2000 cal BC)

### *Rafael Garrido-Pena and Ana Mercedes Herrero-Corral*

Towards an Archaeology of Childhood

As it has been frequently pointed out the study of childhood is one of the most interesting and innovative fields of research during the last two decades in archaeology,[1] although in Iberia it has just begun in the last years.[2] It now seems clear that it is impossible to display a coherent picture of past societies while excluding important parts of the population such as the infant members.[3] Perhaps archaeologists had previously ignored childhood because of the strong influence of the contemporary vision of children in the western world as helpless and dependent creatures.[4]

Nevertheless, if archaeology pretends to obtain information about this group of past populations it is important to ask the appropriate questions to the archaeological record, designing suitable research strategies to properly ask them.[5] Otherwise, those indicators will be lost or ignored during excavation and post-excavation. One of the most traditional ways of approaching childhood in archaeology has been the direct analysis of juvenile burials, and certainly bioanthropological research yields very interesting information on the health, diet or the quality of life of children in the past.[6] But boys and girls do not only die – they also live, play, celebrate and learn.[7] There are other indirect methods to get data about children's lives in the past, such as the collaboration of other disciplines including ethnography, experimental archaeology, history, etc.[8]

Moreover, the presence of children has been frequently identified just through artefacts recovered in the excavations that have been interpreted as toys, in other words artefacts specially designed for children's play that do not have homologues among the adult objects.[9] But children have been rarely considered active agents in the production of material culture.[10] If we want to overcome this bias, one of the most suitable areas for studying children's activities in archaeology is through craft working, and especially pottery.[11] Craft knowledge and traditions are transmitted from one generation to the next from master crafters to apprentices, who are mostly children in pre-industrial societies. Therefore it seems clear that they had a very significant role in the reproduction of culture as active members of the group.

CHILDREN AS POTTERS IN THE ETHNOGRAPHIC RECORD

Craft pottery learning has been one of the best-studied topics in ethnographic literature; however several works have focused on the male crafter with woman and children as passive, subordinate, but necessary assistants (for clay procurement and preparation, or moving the pots during the drying process, for instance).[12] Instead, several reports indicate that ceramics in pre-industrial societies were mainly made by women, at a domestic level, with the transmission of knowledge within the closer kinship group, from mothers, aunts or grandmothers to daughters or granddaughters.[13] Different ethnographic data across the world have shown that children learned crafting pottery at a very early age:[14] amongst the Swahili between two and five years old,[15] and similarly amongst the Asurini do Xingu (Brazil),[16] for instance. In the Dii of Cameroon, apprenticeship starts from around the age of seven and lasts between five to eight years, with an average of four hours of training per day during the dry season and two hours per day during the rest of the year, corresponding to the physical, psychological, and social maturation of the child.[17]

The process of craft learning is always very complex and a variety of teaching methods have been documented in the ethnographic record. Sometimes it was sequential, starting with easier forms then proceeding to more complex, and mainly in unstructured informal contexts apparently viewed as play by children,[18] although sometimes apprentices are treated harshly.[19] A significant Japanese term for traditional craft pottery apprenticeship is 'minari', literally one who learns by observation.[20] Moreover, when a young apprentice asked the master a question he was admonished because he has not paid attention to the potter at work, otherwise the answer would be obvious.[21]

Different studies of North America indigenous groups illustrate diverse learning processes: sometimes the girl takes lessons and practice on vessels previously made by adults where decorative patterns were just roughly sketched (for instance amongst the Shipibo-Conibo), but in other contexts the apprenticeship is much more passive, with observation of potters, eventually accompanied by short verbal instructions.[22] But children did not always mechanically reproduce adult designs, and sometimes they showed their creativity.[23]

The children's tasks can also vary during the process of learning, as Wallaert[24] has shown in a very interesting study of the Dii Potters from Cameroon, West Africa. During the first two years, the young girl helps by fetching clay, water or wood, but there is no formal instruction during this stage, and the girl learns through observation and is allowed to play with pieces of clay only to sense the texture of the raw material. Around age nine, and for approximately a year, the apprentice is discharged from some domestic duties to focus on pottery making (small miniature models with no decoration), where again no questions are welcome and usually the child sits near her mother and watches her work in a kind of observation-imitation process. At the age of ten the girl shapes small cooking pots with minimal decoration (partial designs), following exactly every gesture of the mother, with trial and error method now forbidden. The apprentice experiments under a lot of pressure, since even corporal punishments and verbal humiliations are used to ensure that the rules are respected, mistakes being interpreted as an immoral challenge to the authority of the mother.

Around age fourteen, girls prepare a greater variety of models, and handle the whole process, working form clay and taking care of the pre- and post firing treatments. The apprentice is now capable of describing every stage of the making process, but she still does not handle the firing by herself. Learning, at this stage, continues to be focused on observation and imitation, with very little use of language, and the mother just intervenes to correct major mistakes. Only when the girl is fifteen does she learn to handle firing the pottery on her own, with occasional advice and assistance from other potters in the following years. The apprenticeship ends when the girl is capable of making every type of vessel, and this is marked by a celebration where she receives a set of tools from her mother, and then she is ready to look for a husband as an adult woman.

However, amongst the Ari People (Southern Ethiopia), pottery makers do not learn each making stage step by step, but from the very beginning they do all the making stages to form the whole shape of a pot. Girls move from small size to bigger size by using exactly the same finger movement patterns, although they could not make all kinds of pots. The social role of pottery-makers as daughters, wives, and mothers influences their choice of making techniques, since it is not just a technological matter but has much more to do with their social, cultural, and economic situation.[25]

One of the most widely documented procedures of ceramic apprenticeship is to make the so-called miniatures of the usual standard adult vessels. As Donley-Reid[26] shows, at between three to five years of age, Swahili girls began doing small pots that they also use as toys with which they learn to cook, increasing the size of the pots they make until they grow enough and can finally reproduce the standard size vessels. Miniaturization is also the main didactic resource for young potters amongst the Asurini do Xingu (Brazil),[27] the Atzompa from Oaxaca (Mexico),[28] or the indigenous cultures of the North American southwest.[29] It is very easy to identify the pots made by inexpert apprentices, because they tend to be roughly shaped and finished, with irregular rims and evident mistakes in the decoration.[30]

CHILDREN AS POTTERS IN THE ARCHAEOLOGICAL RECORD

While many aspects of the learning process may not be visible in the archaeological record or in the material culture recovered from sites, certainly there are other ones that can be identified.[31] In fact, while the role of children in stone tool knapping,[32] or in the elaboration of adornment items such as necklace beads,[33] for instance, has been studied, relatively much more work has been done in relation to ceramics.[34]

As Jaya Menon and Supriya Varma,[35] Kathryn Kamp[36] or Patricia Smith,[37] amongst others, have pointed out most archaeologists agree that the products of novices may differ in shape from those usually manufactured, and there are plenty of criteria to identify them, such as the small size and imperfect forms and decorations (pinch pot technique, inadequate sealing of coils, asymmetry in vessel profiles, uneven thickness of vessel walls, rough finish, small drying cracks, asymmetry of designs). Given that novices may not have the necessary knowledge or motor skills for ceramic production, this may result in imperfect products or unusual decorations, typical of an inexpert workmanship. However, Smith[38] argues that those deviations from the norm in decorations need not necessarily imply a lack of conceptual mastery, but may in fact reflect innovation on the part of children, that also influenced each other, as she points out in her study of the juvenile pottery from the Huron prehistoric groups from Ontario (Canada) (AD 1400–1650).

Identifying the gender of beginners may be obviously very difficult in the archaeological record, but it is possible to estimate the age of crafters, which is crucial also to identify the hands of children in archaeological pots. Kamp[39] has shown that the age of crafters can be assessed from the fingerprints accidentally left by them on the ceramics. By the seventh month of natal development the dermatoglyphic patterns for the fingers are complete, and no further modifications occur during maturation. During growth the overall size of hands increases, the fingerprints increase in size but without adding new ridges. Through complex experimental work on individuals of different ages she could estimate the age of the producers of ceramics and terracotta figurines dated between AD 1100–1250 from the Sinagua region of northern Arizona.[40] The experimental data of those studies showed that, even when prints were partial, the high correlation between age and ridge breadth allowed an estimation of the age of the producer enough to discriminate adult prints from those of children.[41] The parameters of small size, crudeness and lumpiness, asymmetrical profiles and lack of proportion, inexpert workmanship in the lack of surface smoothness, previously mentioned, were also used together with the presence of fingerprints and nail marks as indicators of child productions in those analyses.[42]

## BELL BEAKERS: A VERY SPECIAL TYPE OF POTTERY IN THE 3RD MILLENNIUM CAL BC OF WESTERN EUROPE

Bell Beaker pottery appears, together with other accompanying paraphernalia (copper weapons, mainly tanged daggers, bone and ivory adornments, such as V-perforated buttons, and other symbolic items such as the stone wrist-guards) in most of Western Europe during the 3rd millennium cal. BC (*c.* 2600–2000 BC). The interpretation of this intriguing problem has been one of the main concerns of European Prehistory, an authentic intellectual challenge,[43] and therefore the cause of many debates, theories and publications since the beginning of the 20th century.

The first scholars, working fully inside the culture-historian prehistory of that time, considered Bell Beakers as the material remains of a culture/ethnic-racial group, originating in Iberia, which spread across Western Europe. Since the 1970s, with the pioneer work by David Clarke,[44] our vision of this complex phenomenon changed completely. For him, Bell Beakers and accompanying objects were not, in fact, purely domestic items of a given people, but very special ones with a high social value: prestige elements that circulated between the Chalcolithic groups through the exchange systems at a moment where significant economic and social transformations were evolving, with the emergence of social ranking. Incipient political leaders were trying to reinforce their weak position by manipulating those special objects, which accompanied them in their graves, in several social contexts.

Later on, Andrew Sherratt[45] completed Clarke's model, stressing the importance of a supposedly alcoholic beverage consumed in Bell Beaker pots as a means of recruiting supporters in social strategies to legitimate power through social institutions such as hospitality rituals, or the so-called work-party feasts. Recent chemical content analyses of the residues collected inside many Iberian Bell Beaker pots have identified different

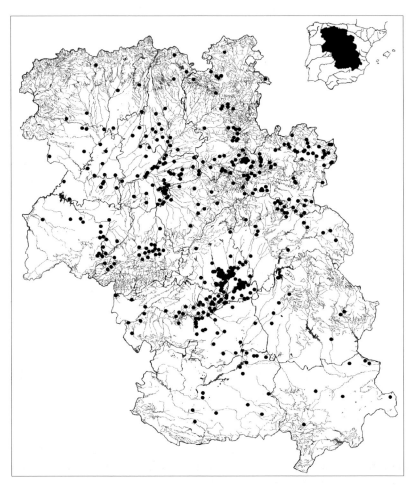

*Figure 4.1. Map of the distribution of Bell Beaker finds in the interior of Iberia (after Garrido-Pena 2000).*

alcoholic drinks, mainly beer.[46] The study of the combination of Bell Beaker ceramic capacities and forms in burial and domestic sets in Central Iberia (Fig. 4.1) has further explored the internal features of the commensality rituals which were celebrated with them inside the settlements, where it represents just 1–4% of the pottery, and in the funerals too (burial symposia).[47]

Perhaps for the emergent leaders and their closer kinship groups in 3rd millennium Western Europe, it was essential to maintain control over the exchange networks, which probably were based more on social than purely economic transactions. In such a social context, marriage exchanges would have been extremely valuable to recruit supporters, to obtain political alliances, and to increase kinship links and therefore the economic bases (land, livestock). And, in fact, strontium isotope analyses on Bell Beaker cemeteries of Central Europe seem to illustrate the movement of certain individuals, especially women.[48] If we assume that women were the potters, marriage exchanges could perhaps explain the diffusion across Western Europe of the peculiar forms and decorative patterns which are characteristic of Bell Beaker pottery.

Therefore, the analysis of learning patterns in Beaker pots must consider, first, that they are special productions, not for everyday domestic or purely culinary tasks. The thin walls (4–5 mm), the careful modelling and finishing, the highly sinuous profiles and the fine and highly standardized decoration, clearly indicate that they were luxury productions for social and ritual use. Beaker pottery in Iberia displays a reduced set of standardized forms (Bell Beakers, bowls, carinated bowls, cups, small carinated bowls), usually found in combined sets of vessels, especially in burials, the most typical of them being the 'Ciempozuelos trio' (Bell Beaker, bowl and carinated bowl) (Fig. 4.2).

These pots were carefully decorated with extremely complex but also regular patterns that have been classified in broad stylistic variants (Maritime, Geometric comb-decorated, Ciempozuelos and other very similar local styles). They use a particular repertoire of designs which repeat and combine (just around three motifs per vessel) in very complex but also highly standardized patterns (only 21 sets of patterns), frequently symmetric. It seems that behind the elaboration of this fine luxury pottery there was a very complex and interesting apprenticeship process, probably transmitted mainly from mothers to daughters to dominate those standardized norms. Perhaps we may infer that such a specialized manufacture will not be elaborated by all the potters but that a certain degree of specialization existed.

CHILDREN AND BELL BEAKER POTTERY IN THE INTERIOR OF THE IBERIAN PENINSULA

The detailed analysis of several examples documented amongst Bell Beaker pottery in the interior of Iberia, our case study area (Fig. 4.1), illustrates several aspects of the apprenticeship process of such a complex and sophisticated craft. However, this is just a preliminary approach, since this interesting line of research is still beginning. We have identified the phenomenon of 'miniatures', those replicas of the Beaker standardized vessels but on a smaller scale, which has been extensively documented

*Figure 4.2. Ciempozuelos style pottery trio from the eponymous site of Ciempozuelos (Madrid) (Photograph Museo Arqueológico Nacional): Bell Beaker to the left, Beaker Carinated bowl in the centre and Beaker Bowl to the right.*

in the ethnographical record from different areas of the world, as a way for children to learn craft pottery, as we have already mentioned. Miniature objects have been often associated with children as toys, but can be used in other ways, such as grave offerings, as ritual and votive artefacts, or as containers for unguents and pigments.[49]

We have documented several examples of 'miniature' Beaker vessels in the interior of Iberia (Table 4.1 and Fig. 4.3). Most of them were recovered in burial contexts, and, in fact, although the rest of the vessels lack a clear archaeological context, they probably also came from destroyed graves as chance finds, given that they are complete pots. Some of these miniature Beakers recovered in tombs are significantly associated with infantile individuals, as for instance, a Ciempozuelos style small Bell Beaker found together with a bigger plain bowl in Aldeagordillo (Ávila)[50] (Fig. 4.3:5 and Fig. 4.4: 1), or a Ciempozuelos style Beaker trio with two miniatures, a Bell Beaker (Valle de las Higueras 1) (Fig. 4.3: 7) and a Beaker bowl (Valle de las Higueras 2) (Fig. 4.3: 15) deposited inside a bigger Beaker bowl with two infantile individuals in the 'nicho 3a' of one of the graves of the Valle de las Higueras (Toledo) cemetery.[51]

*Table 4.1. Examples of "miniature" Bell Beaker pots in the interior of Iberia.*

| Site | Context | Ceramic form | Rim diameter (mm) | Total height (mm) | Average rim diameter in this form (mm) | Average total height in this form (mm) |
|---|---|---|---|---|---|---|
| *Vascos 1* | Unknown | Bell Beaker | 100 | 80 | 120–146 | 110–150 |
| *Vascos 2* | Unknown | Bell Beaker | 115 | 105 | 120–146 | 110–150 |
| *Aldeagordillo* | Infantile burial | Bell Beaker | 110 | 100 | 120–146 | 110–150 |
| *Algete* | Unknown | Bell Beaker | 110 | 110 | 120–146 | 110–150 |
| *Palencia* | Unknown | Bell Beaker | 117 | 110 | 120–146 | 110–150 |
| *Santibáñez de Ayllón* | Unknown | Bell Beaker | 130 | 110 | 120–146 | 110–150 |
| *Valle de las Higueras 1 (nicho 3a)* | infantile burial | Bell Beaker | 100 | 90 | 120–146 | 110–150 |
| *Galisancho* | Burial | Carinated bowl | 119 | 75 | 200–300 | 80–115 |
| *La Maya* | Unknown | Carinated bowl | 130 | 55 | 200–300 | 80–115 |
| *Camino de las Yeseras 1* | Triple adult burial | Carinated bowl | 163 | 82 | 200–300 | 80–115 |
| *Camino de las Yeseras 2* | Single adult burial | Bowl | 111 | 47 | 115–160 | 40–75 |
| *Camino de las Yeseras 3* | Triple adult burial | Bowl | 110 | 51 | 115–160 | 40–75 |
| *Valle de las Higueras 2 (nicho 3a)* | infantile burial | Bowl | 95 | 40 | 115–160 | 40–75 |

However, there are also Beaker miniatures which were found associated with inhumations of adult individuals, as for example in the Camino de las Yeseras (Madrid) cemetery. In the so called 'covacha 2', remains of three inhumations were discovered, the first of them being the worst preserved because it was displaced by the other two. The second inhumation (a young woman) had as grave goods a small and very roughly made Beaker carinated bowl of Ciempozuelos style (Camino de las Yeseras 1) (Fig. 4.3: 12 and Fig. 4.5: 1), together with a plain non-Beaker pot and a possible grinding stone. The third body was an adult man, although the sex identification is very uncertain, which was accompanied by a miniature Beaker bowl (Camino de las Yeseras 3) (Fig. 4.3: 13 and Fig. 4.5: 3), together with another one of bigger dimensions (Fig. 4.5: 4) and a Bell Beaker (Fig. 4.5: 7), both also very rough but standard in its size, all of them of Ciempozuelos style, and a copper awl.[52] These last pots are combined in an atypical trio where the missing carinated bowl characteristic of the Ciempozuelos trio, perhaps was substituted in the ritual by a bigger bowl, as in the already mentioned case of Valle de las Higueras. In another

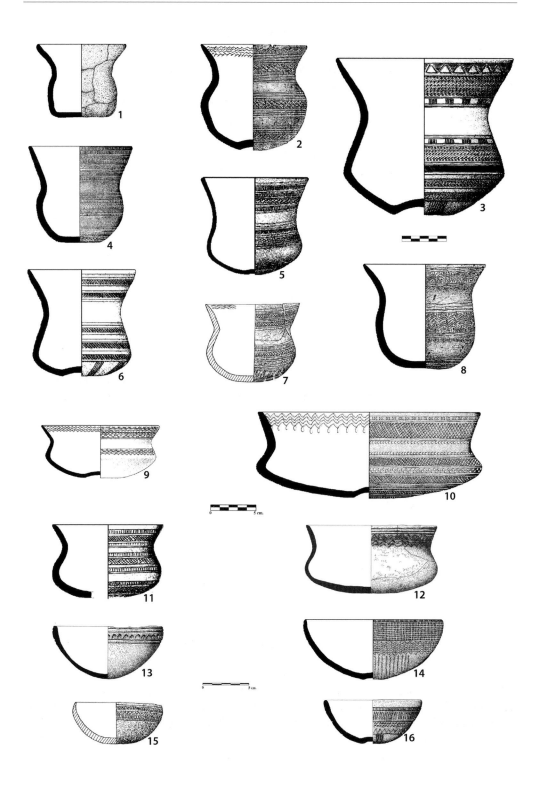

grave of Camino de las Yeseras, the so called 'covacha 1', an individual inhumation of an adult woman was accompanied by a standard size Bell Beaker with fine decoration (Fig. 4.5: 5) and a miniature Beaker bowl very roughly made and ornamented (Camino de las Yeseras 2) (Fig. 4.3: 16 and Fig. 4.5: 6).[53]

All these Beaker vessels are considered 'miniatures' mainly because they are identical replicas of the standard Beaker pots but on a smaller scale (Table 4.1). The miniature Bell Beakers here analysed have rim diameters lower than 12–14 cm and total heights lower than 11–15 cm, where 60% of the Bell Beakers in the interior of Iberia are included.[54] The same occurs with the miniature Beaker carinated bowls studied here, which are far smaller than the standard measures of most of this type of ceramic in the interior of Iberia (60% of them have diameters of 20–30 cm and are 8–15 cm high).[55] Even excluding the big dishes, the measurements of miniature Beaker bowls are also smaller than the usual ones amongst standard Beaker bowls in this area (54% have diameters ranging from 15.5 to 16 cm and total heights of around 4–7.5 cm).[56]

Amongst these Beaker miniatures we can clearly distinguish those vessels that, given the careful shaping and finishing, can be attributed to skilled crafters, from those more probably related to the apprenticeship of children. The first ones are, for example, several of the pieces without a clear context such as the Bell Beakers of Vascos 2, Algete or Palencia, or the carinated bowls from Galisancho or La Maya (Fig. 4.3: 4, 2, 6, 11 and 9). But there also are well manufactured Beaker miniatures recovered from the burials of Aldeagordillo (Fig. 4.3: 5 and Fig. 4.4: 1) and Valle de las Higueras (Fig. 4.2: 7 and 15), significantly associated with children. Thus, it seems that adult expert potters made those Beaker miniatures to be deposited as grave goods inside the grave of certain infantile individuals to represent, perhaps, the social identity of those children, not just within a certain status category but also inside a particular age group. Turek[57] interpreted similar finds of Beaker miniatures in cemeteries of central Europe in the same way, and other researchers have made similar proposals about the so called 'pygmy cups' discovered in Bronze Age child burials.[58]

However, other Beaker miniatures show clear indications that they were created by novices, such as the pinch pot technique, especially in bowls, or the asymmetry in profiles, the rough finish and the asymmetry and mistakes in the designs. These vessels clearly illustrate different aspects of the apprenticeship process necessary to make such fine pottery as Bell Beakers.

*Figure 4.3. (opposite page) Miniature Bell Beaker vessels from different sites of the interior of Iberia, and standard size ones for comparison (3, 10 and 14): 1) Los Vascos (Madrid), 2) Algete (Madrid), 3) Palencia, 4) Los Vascos (Madrid), 5) Aldeagordillo (Ávila), 6) Palencia, 7) Valle de las Higueras (Toledo), 8) Santibáñez de Ayllón (Segovia), 9) La Maya (Salamanca), 10) Ciempozuelos (Madrid), 11) Galisancho (Salamanca), 12–13) Camino de las Yeseras (San Fernando de Henares, Madrid), 14) Ciempozuelos (Madrid), 15) Valle de las Higueras (Toledo), 16) Camino de las Yeseras (San Fernando de Henares, Madrid). Sources: Garrido-Pena 2000, Fabián 1992, Bueno et al. 2005, Municio 1984, Blasco et al. 2005.*

Amongst the Bell Beaker miniatures, the plain Bell Beaker of Los Vascos (Madrid) offers a clear example, being very coarsely made, with an irregular profile and rim and no sign of surface finishing (Fig. 4.3: 1). The other interesting example is the Ciempozuelos style small Bell Beaker from Santibáñez de Ayllón (Segovia)[59] (Fig. 4.3: 8 and Fig. 4.4: 2). It was found inside a cave, and although we do not know the exact context, it was probably a tomb. The sinuous profile shows a clear disequilibrium between the heavy body and a short neck, with a rough modelling and very poor finish of the surface. But what it is even more striking is the decoration where we can find the main basic conventions of a Bell Beaker of Ciempozuelos style (zoned organization, the usual designs, a cruciform schema in the base), but clearly executed by a novice potter. The motifs are too tightly grouped in parts of the friezes, and too separated in others as they were impressed along the perimeter of the vessel. But it is the pattern at the base where these irregularities are more evident: the last frieze is a very coarse hachure with evident discontinuities and the cruciform schema is atypical, not only because it was coarsely made, but also and especially because the asymmetric arms cross at the centre, not avoiding the omphalos, as is the norm for this pattern.[60] Finally, the linear impressed designs are so unskilled that, seen from the bottom of the pot, they are more polygonal than concentric circular lines as is the norm in Bell Beakers.

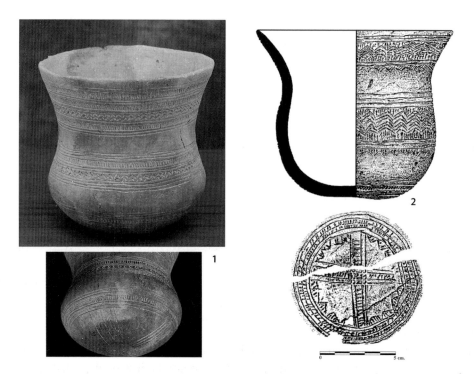

*Figure 4.4. Bell Beaker miniatures from the interior of Iberia: to the left Aldeagordillo (Ávila) (Fabián 1992), to the right Santibáñez de Ayllón (Segovia) (Municio 1984).*

Within the corpus of miniature Beaker carinated bowls we have identified another possible apprenticeship pot. It is the Camino de las Yeseras 1 vessel (Fig. 4.3: 12 and Fig. 4.5: 1), a very atypical example of this form, especially if it is compared with other standard fine productions found at the same site (Fig. 4.5: 2). It was only coarsely ornamented at the neck, with a very irregular design which unsuccessfully tries to reproduce a well-known Beaker motif (10c of Ciempozuelos style),[61] but the body remains undecorated, which is exceptional. Given these irregularities and the rough modelling of this pot together with its small dimensions it is likely to be considered as a possible novice ceramic.

The miniature Beaker bowls also show good examples of apprenticeship pots. Perhaps it was the easiest form to replicate by novices applying the pinch pot technique to model very small vessels, which were also very coarsely decorated. In the 'covacha 2' of Camino de las Yeseras, two bowls were deposited together with a Bell Beaker and a copper awl with an adult man in a triple burial, although the sex identification of this individual remains unclear. One of the bowls is a true miniature by its size (Camino de las Yeseras 2) (Fig. 4.3: 13), but the three vessels exhibit clear irregularities in their shape, finishing and especially in their decoration, where motifs that are perfectly typical of the Ciempozuelos style are very coarsely executed (very sinuous lines irregularly traced) (Fig. 4.5: 1, 3 and 5). But perhaps the strangest thing is the lack of zoned decoration in the Bell Beaker (Fig. 4.5: 7), which is one of the main basic features of this Beaker style, and for that reason this vessel is unique within the central Iberia sample. Given that neither this pot nor the other accompanying bowl were miniatures but look very much like a learning ceramic, could they represent, perhaps, other stages of the apprenticeship process following the first dedicated just to miniatures, as we have previously described in several ethnographic examples? The potter who made this vessel shows his ability to make a standard size Bell Beaker, but it is evident that they still had very much to learn to properly finish the complex and very structured patterns of the decoration.

In the 'covacha 1' single burial of the same site, an adult woman had two Beaker pottery vessels; one is a perfectly standard Bell Beaker, both in its form and decoration (Fig. 4.5: 5), and a miniature Beaker bowl with all the features of novice authorship (Camino de las Yeseras 3) (Fig. 4.5: 6), as is shown by both the shape and the very coarse and irregular decoration, which has undulating instead of straight lines, very irregularly filled friezes, and in particular a very atypical and asymmetrical cruciform pattern, where the very short and coarse arms are so unevenly distributed that one of them almost touches the other.

Finally we will give another very good example of a novice pot which exceptionally reveals very interesting details on the apprenticeship process, as we have suggested.[62] It is a small, but not miniaturized, Beaker shouldered bowl of Geometric comb decorated style that was discovered amongst the Bell beaker grave goods in the La Sima Mound (Soria) (Fig. 4.6). Although it was found in the burial chamber where two adult individuals were deposited with other Beaker grave goods, it was displaced from the bodies. Apparently, this small vessel presents all the basic and canonical features of a

*Figure 4.5. Bell Beaker pottery vessel from Camino de las Yeseras (San Fernando de Henares, Madrid) (Blasco* et al. *2005 and Museo Arqueológico Regional de Madrid).*

*Figure 4.6. Bell Beaker shouldered bowl from the La Sima Mound (Miño de Medinaceli, Soria) (Rojo et al. 2005 and Museo Numantino).*

shouldered bowl of this Beaker style (comb impressed geometric patterns, the usual designs, etc.), but a careful analysis discovers very interesting clues.

First, the shaping is rather irregular, being especially atypical the sinuous rim or the oval instead of circular omphallos at the base, clearly displaced from the geometrical centre. But the most interesting feature is the decoration, where the straight and parallel lines of the body were made with a very tricky and completely atypical technical resource: making a spiral line instead of the canonical equidistant lines progressively descending down the profile, which are much more difficult to maintain, especially in such a tiny pot with such an inclination in the walls. Externally, the resultant effect is the same, but the way of doing things is clearly atypical. Nevertheless it is in the base of this vessel where we find the most curious details, since here a characteristic star-like pattern created by chevrons is very unskilfully executed. A failed first attempt to do it closest to the omphallos remains half done, but interestingly is preserved, as a sort of crossing-out in a written text. Finally the star-like pattern was done slightly outside the other and it is very coarse and asymmetrical. Another curious and atypical feature is the isolated chevron between two of the parallel lines in the lower part of the body of the vessel, just before the base, which perhaps was another failed attempt to begin the star-like design, as a sort of amendment, perhaps as a result of the master's indication. It is tempting to interpret all these details as the result of a novice who was unsuccessfully trying to copy another model of Beaker shouldered bowl under the more or less attentive gaze of another person.

However, there is an apparent paradox with those last vessels, because although they probably were made by children learning how to create Beaker pottery, they were finally deposited in adult graves. Probably we will never know the reason behind that mysterious fact, but we can imagine possible explanations in this context, such as offerings made by young relatives (sons, daughters, etc.), or even that they were the apprenticeship pieces modelled by them when they were children and were learning, and were preserved during their lifetime to accompany them, for some reason, to the other world.

## CONCLUDING REMARKS

It is necessary to consider the importance of the role of infantile individuals in past societies, and so to be able to design adequate strategies to find the clues with which to detect their presence in the archaeological record. In our case study area, the societies of the 3rd millennium in the interior of Iberia, the direct way to do this is through the material culture, and especially the Bell Beaker pottery.

We have shown that it is possible to identify miniatures, which are closely related with juvenile individuals, whether as a part of their apprenticeship in crafting pottery or as grave goods specifically made by adults to accompany them in their tombs. We have also shown that it is possible to identify several vessels that were probably crafted by children, and we could even detect pots possibly belonging to different stages of that learning process and interesting details about it.

To sum up, through a detailed analysis of Bell Beaker pottery which looks for the aspects that we have discussed here, it is possible to discover traces of the activities of children when they were becoming potters capable of crafting those fine and complex high quality productions. It is a promising line of research that is just beginning, but that will yield very interesting results in the future provided that we learn to contemplate those famous and beautiful ceramics through different eyes.

## NOTES

1 Sofaer-Derevenski 2000; Baxter 2008, 2005; Kamp 2001b
2 Rojo, Kunst, Garrido-Pena, García and Morán 2005, 136–7; Vidal and García 2009; Sánchez-Romero 2004, 2010
3 Kamp 2001b
4 Ruttle 2010, 66
5 Sánchez-Romero 2007
6 Schwatzman 2005, 126
7 Lillehammer 2012, 13
8 Lillehammer 1989, 103
9 Politis 2005, 129
10 Menon and Varma 2011, 86
11 *Ibid.*, 87
12 *Ibid.*, 87
13 Silva 2008, 233; Bowser and Patton 2008
14 Smith 2005, 67–8

15 Donley-Reid 1990, 113–14; Kamp 2001a, 427, 2001b, 13
16 Silva 2008, 234
17 Wallaert 2001, 2008, 188
18 Kamp 2001a, 430
19 Wallaert 2001, 2008, 190
20 Singleton 1989, 14
21 *Ibid.*, 26
22 Kamp 2001a, 428–9
23 Smith 2005, 71
24 Wallaert 2008, 188–92
25 Kaneko 2005
26 Donley-Reid 1990, 113–4
27 Silva 2008, 34–5
28 Smith 2005, 67–8
29 Kamp 2010, 113
30 Silva 2008, 234
31 Minar and Crown 2001; Wendrich 2012
32 Finlay 1997; Shea 2006
33 Arnold 2012
34 Crown 2001; Kamp, Timmerman, Lind, Graybill and Natowsky 1999; Kamp 2001a
35 Menon and Varma 2011, 89
36 Kamp 2001a
37 Smith 2005, 67
38 *Ibid.*
39 Kamp 2001a
40 Kamp 2001a, Kamp *et al.* 1999
41 Kamp *et al.* 1999, 309
42 Menon and Varma 2011, 89
43 Garrido-Pena 2005
44 Clarke 1976
45 Sherratt 1987
46 Rojo, Garrido-Pena, García, Juan-Treserras and Matamala 2006
47 Garrido-Pena, Rojo-Guerra, García-Martínez de Lagrán and Tejedor-Rodríguez 2011; Garrido-Pena 2000
48 Price, Grupe and Schröteret 1998; Garrido-Pena 2006
49 Baxter 2005, 47–8; Park 2006; Menon and Varma 2011, 85–6
50 Fabian 1992
51 Bueno, Barroso and Balbín 2005, 76 and fig. 7
52 Blasco, Liesau, Delibes, Baquedano and Rodríguez 2005, 461–2 and figs 9–11; Gómez, Blasco, Trancho, Ríos, Grueso and Martínez 2011, 115
53 Blasco *et al.* 2005, 460 and figs 7–8; Gómez *et al.* 2011, 115
54 Garrido-Pena 2000, 83
55 *Ibid.*, 89
56 *Ibid.*, 94
57 Turek 2000
58 Donnabháin and Brindley 1990
59 Municio 1984
60 Garrido-Pena 2000, 124 and fig. 55
61 *Ibid.*, fig. 46
62 Rojo *et al.* 2005, 136–7

REFERENCES

Arnold, J. E. 2012. Detecting apprentices and innovators in the archaeological record: the shell bead-making industry of the Channel Islands. *Journal of Archaeological Method and Theory* 19, 269–305.

Baxter, J. E. 2008. The archaeology of childhood. *Annual Review of Anthropology* 37, 159–75.

Baxter, J. E. 2005. *The Archaeology of Childhood: Children, Gender, and Material Culture*. CA Alta Mira Press: Walnut Creek.

Blasco, C., Liesau, C., Delibes, G., Baquedano, E. and Rodríguez, M. 2005. Enterramiento campaniforme en ambiente doméstico: el yacimiento de Camino de Las Yeseras (San Fernando de Henares, Madrid), pp. 457–79 in Rojo, M., Garrido-Pena , R. and García, I. (coords), *El Campaniforme en la Península Ibérica y su contexto europeo/Bell Beakers in the Iberian Peninsula and their european context*. Valladolid: Universidad de Valladolid-Junta de Castilla y León.

Bowser, B. J. and Patton, J. Q. 2008. Learning and transmission of pottery style: women's life histories and communities of practice in the Ecuadorian Amazon, pp. 105–29 in Stark, M. T., Bowser, B. J. and Horne, L. (eds), *Cultural Transmission and Material Culture: Breaking Down Boundaries*. Tucson: University of Arizona Press.

Bueno, P., Barroso, R. and Balbín, R. 2005. Ritual campaniforme, ritual colectivo: la necrópolis de cuevas artificiales del Valle de Las Higueras, Huecas, Toledo. *Trabajos de Prehistoria* 62(2), 67–90.

Clarke, D. 1976. The Beaker network-social and economic models, pp. 459–77 in Lanting, J. N. and Van der Waals, J. D. (eds), *Glockenbecher Symposium, Oberried, 1974*. Fibula-van Dishoeck: Bussum/Haarlem.

Crown, P. L. 2001. Learning to make pottery in the Prehispanic American Southwest. *Journal of Anthropological Research* 57, 451–69.

Donley-Reid, L. W. 1990. A structuring of structure: the Swahili house, pp. 114–26 in Kent, S. (ed.) *Domestic Architecture and the Use of Space*. Cambridge: Cambridge University Press.

Donnabháin, B. Ó. and Brindley, A. L. 1989. The status of children in a sample of Bronze Age burials containing Pygmy Cups. *The Journal of Irish Archaeology* 5, 19–24.

Fabián García, J. F. 1992. El enterramiento campaniforme Túmulo 1 de Aldeagordillo (Ávila). *Boletín del Seminario de Estudios de Arte y Arqueología* LVIII, 97–132.

Finlay, N. 1997. Kid knapping: the missing children in lithic analysis, pp. 203–12 in Moore, J. and Scott, E. (eds), *Invisible People and Processes. Writing Gender and Childhood into European Prehistory*. Leicester: Leicester University Press.

Garrido-Pena, R., Rojo-Guerra, M. A., García-Martínez de Lagrán, I. and Tejedor-Rodríguez, C. 2011. Drinking and eating together: the social and symbolic context of commensality rituals in the Bell Beakers of the interior of Iberia (2500–2000 Cal BC), pp.109–29 in Aranda, G., Montón, S. and Sánchez, M. (eds), *Guess Who's Coming to Dinner. Feasting Rituals in the Prehistoric Societies of Europe and the Near East*. Oxford: Oxbow Books.

Garrido-Pena, R. 2006. Transegalitarian societies: an ethnoarchaeological model for the analysis of Copper Age Bell Beakers using groups in Central Iberia, pp. 81–96 in Díaz-del-Río, P. and García Sanjuán, L. (eds), *Social Inequality in Iberian Late Prehistory*, (BAR International Series S1525). Oxford: Archaeopress.

Garrido-Pena, R. 2005. The Beaker Labyrinth: brief history of an intellectual challenge, pp. 45–60 in Rojo, M., Garrido-Pena, R. and García, I. (coords), *El Campaniforme en la Península Ibérica y su contexto europeo/Bell Beakers in the Iberian Peninsula in their European context*. Valladolid: Junta de Castilla y León-Universidad de Valladolid.

Garrido-Pena, R. 2000. *El Campaniforme en la Meseta Central de la Península Ibérica (c. 2500–2000 A.C.)*. (BAR International Series S892). Oxford: Archaeopress.

Gómez, J. L., Blasco, C., Trancho, G., Ríos, P., Grueso, I. and Martínez, M. S. 2011. V.1. Los Protagonistas, pp. 101–32 in Blasco, C., Liesau, C. and Ríos, P. (eds), *Yaciemintos calcolíticos con campaniforme de la región de Madrid: nuevos estudios.* Madrid: Servicio de Publicaciones de la Universidad Autónoma de Madrid.

Kamp, K. A. 2010. Entre el trabajo y el juego: perspectivas sobre la infancia en el suroeste norteamericano. *Complutum* 21(2), 103–20.

Kamp, K. A. 2001a. Prehistoric children working and playing: a southwestern case study in learning ceramics. *Journal of Anthropological Research* 57(4), 427–50.

Kamp, K. A. 2001b. Where have all the children gone?: The archaeology of childhood. *Journal of Archaeological Method and Theory* 8(1), 1–34.

Kamp, K. A., Timmerman, N., Lind, G., Graybill, J. and Natowsky, I. 1999. Discovering Childhood: using fingerprints to find children in the archaeological record. *American Antiquity* 64(2), 309–15.

Kaneko, M. 2005. Learning process of pottery making among Ari People, Southern Ethiopia. *African Study Monographs Suppl.* 29, 73–81.

Lillehammer, G. 2012. Travels into thirdspace: the archaeological heritage of children's spaces. a view from beyond. *Childhood in the past* 5, 7–19.

Lillehammer, G. 1989. A child is born: the child's world in an archaeological perspective. *Norwegian Archaeological Review* 22(2), 89–105.

Menon, J. and Varma, S. 2011. Children playing and learning: crafting ceramics in Ancient Indor Khera. *Asian Perspectives* 49(1), 85–109.

Minar, C. J. and Crown, P. L. 2001. Learning and craft production: an introduction. *Journal of Anthropological Research* 57, 369–80.

Municio González, L. J. 1984. Cerámica campaniforme de Santibáñez de Ayllón (Segovia). *Trabajos de Prehistoria* 41(1), 313–22.

Park, R. W. 2006. Growing up north: exploring the archaeology of childhood in the Thule and Dorset cultures of Arctic Canada, pp. 53–64 in Baxter, J. E. (ed.), *Children in Action: Perspectives on the Archaeology of Childhood*, Archaeological Papers of the American Anthropological Association 15. Berkeley: University of California Press.

Politis, G. 2005. Children's activity in their production of the archaeological record of hunter-gatherers: an ethnoarchaeological approach, pp. 121–43 in Funari, P. P., Sarankin, A. and Stovel, E. (eds), *Global Archaeological Theory: Contextual voices and contemporary thoughts*. New York: Plenum Publishing Corporation.

Price, T. D., Grupe, G. and Schröter, P. 1998. Migration in the Bell Beaker period of central Europe. *Antiquity* 72(276), 405–11.

Rojo, M. A., Garrido-Pena, R., García, I., Juan-Treserras, J. and Matamala, J. C. 2006. Beer and bell beakers: drinking rituals in Copper Age Inner Iberia. *Proceedings of the Prehistoric Society* 72, 243–65.

Rojo, M. A., Kunst, M., Garrido-Pena, R., García, I. and Morán, G. 2005. *Un desafío a la eternidad: tumbas monumentales del Valle de Ambrona*. Soria: Memorias, Arqueología en Castilla y León n° 14.

Ruttle, A. 2010. Neither seen nor heard: looking for children in Northwest Coast archaeology. *Canadian Journal of Archaeology* 34, 60–88.

Sánchez-Romero, M. 2004. Children in south east of Iberian Peninsula during Bronze Age. *Ethnographisch-Archäologische Zeitschrift* 45, 377–87.

Sánchez-Romero, M. 2007. Actividades de mantenimiento en la Edad del Bronce del sur peninsular: El cuidado y la socialización de individuos infantiles. *Complutum* 18, 185–94.

Sánchez-Romero, M. (ed.) 2010. *Infancia y cultura material en arqueología*. Complutum 21(2) número monográfico. Publicaciones Madrid: Universidad Complutense.

Schwartzman, H. B. 2005. Materializing children: challenges for the archaeology of childhood. *Archaeological Papers of the American Anthropological Association* 15/1, 123–31.

Shea, J. J. 2006. Child's play: reflections on the invisibility of children in the Paleolithic record. *Evolutionary Anthropology* 15, 212–16.

Sherratt, A. 1987. Cups that cheered, pp. 81–114 in Waldren, W. H. and Kennard, R. C. (eds) *Bell Beakers of the Western Mediterranean. Definition, Interpretation, Theory and New Site Data.* The Oxford International Conference 1986. (BAR International Series 331). Oxford: Archaeopress.

Silva, F. A. 2008. Ceramic technology of the Asurini do Xingu, Brazil: an ethnoarchaeological study of artifact variability. *Journal of Archaeological Method and Theory* 15(3), 217–65.

Singleton, J. 1989. Japanese folkcraft pottery apprenticeship: cultural patterns of an educational institution, pp. 13–30 in Coy, M. W. (ed.), *Apprenticeship: From Theory to Method and Back Again.* (SUNY Series in the Anthropology of Work). Albany: State University of New York Press.

Smith, P. E. 2005. Children and ceramic innovation: a study in the archaeology of children. *Archeological Papers of the American Anthropological Association* 15, 65–76.

Sofaer-Derevenski, J. (ed.) 2000. *Children and Material Culture.* London: Routledge.

Turek, J. 2000. Being a Beaker child. The position of children in Late Eneolithic society. *Památky archeologické (Supplementum 13 – In memoriam Jan Rulf,* 424–38.

Vidal, A. and García Roselló, J. 2009. Dime cómo lo haces: una visión etnoarqueológica de las estrategias de aprendizaje de la alfarería tradicional. *Arqueoweb (revista sobre arqueología en internet),* 12.

Wallaert, H. 2008. The Way of the Potter's Mother: apprenticeship strategies among Dii Potters from Cameroon, West Africa, pp. 178–98 in Stark, M. T., Bowser, B. J. and Horne, L. (eds), *Cultural Transmission and Material Culture: Breaking Down Boundaries.* Tucson: University of Arizona Press.

Wallaert, H. 2001. Learning how to make the right pots: apprenticeship strategies and material culture, a case study in handmade pottery from Cameroon. *Journal of Anthropological Research* 57, 471–93.

Wendrich, W. 2012. *Archaeology and Apprenticeship: Body Knowledge, Identity, and Communities of Practice.* The University of Arizona Press.

# 5

# SOCIAL RELATIONS BETWEEN ADULTHOOD AND CHILDHOOD IN THE EARLY BRONZE AGE SITE OF PEÑALOSA (BAÑOS DE LA ENCINA, JAEN, SPAIN)[1]

## Eva Alarcón García

## AGE, CHILDHOOD, HOW?

Speaking of age and childhood in recent archaeological investigation is not something exceptional. Many papers[2] and congresses can be referred to when speaking about this topic. Under the investigation of this field we can highlight the congresses of Berlin (2004), Germany (2008), Norway (2006), United Kingdom (2005, 2007, 2011), United States (2009), Greece (2010) or Spain (2012), six of the last seven having been organized through the Society for Study of Childhood in the Past (SSCIP).

It has not always been like this. As with other social categories, age has not formed part of the interests of general investigation and, in particular, the disciplines of history and archaeology did not take it into account when interpreting past societies. Childhood has been invisible to investigation for three reasons. The first is because of the concept that exists of *childhood* in modern occidental societies.[3] Boys and girls have not been considered as active members in the economic and social dynamics of communities. Second, there is an apparent difficulty in recognizing the archaeological evidence related to children,[4] when it is really a *blindness* of the discipline, which, in general, has had almost no interest in articulating different research strategies for a better knowledge of this group. The third reason is related to the fact that the practices of care, socialization, and learning, associated with childhood, have generally been included as part of woman's tasks, with the scarce recognition that these practices have had in explanations of social development. Therefore, for many years, children have been considered passive members of any society, inactive beings in the economic and social processes,[4] biologically and socially incomplete, and thus, lacking the interest of historical explanation, alien to any social or human signification.

This panorama has been changing. With the development of post-procedural positioning in archaeology, new fields of research were opened, some of which postulated paying more attention to people as active agents in societies of the past, as well as in terms of identity, such as gender and age, intimately related to the archaeological study of the body. It is at this moment when an important context started to build, from where many questions would be developed, related to minor social groups, which, until this moment, had never interested researchers, and that began to be included in different research projects. Nevertheless, it was with the development, during the last decades, of feminist theory, when research about women, the relations and identities between genders, and the analysis of maintenance activities and the interest in childhood in the past reached its maximum. These new research settings have inspired the re-reading and reinterpretation of archaeological data, paying more attention to the minorities that until this moment (in the best cases) had been set aside to a secondary stage in the construction of our past, such as woman and children.

Nowadays, we can say that the scientific discipline of archaeology has started to consider this reality as a proper field of investigation in its own right, by considering children as objects of investigation in themselves, and analyzing the relationships they held among a social group. Children must be understood as active agents of biological reproduction and as leading actors of social development in human groups.[6] The following pages continue this statement, putting special interest in the social relations between adults and children, taking as a starting point the fact that they live together and share the same vital reality.

## SOCIAL PROCESSES BETWEEN ADULTS AND CHILDREN

We apprehend that childhood is not a transitional phase towards adulthood,[7] but must be understood as an active process, a social practice, an empiric phenomenon, which, without any doubt, leaves an archaeological trace. Its heterogeneity makes it necessary to understand its specific nature based on the principle that each social-cultural context must not be pre-assumed, but must promote its analysis and study.[8]

This biological and cultural period through which all children of the past, present and future must go, is characterized by common processes by which abilities are acquired, knowledge is developed, education on the use of technologies is undertaken, belief systems are assumed, and social values and aptitudes for behaviour during life are acquired. This long process in the life of any child is done through the mechanisms of socialization and learning, accompanied by biological and social well-being.[9]

The objective of every social group is to transform new born children into social agents capable of interacting with other subjects and their surroundings, finally being incorporated into adulthood. This is only achieved by means of socialization[10] developed through interaction between children and adults, children among themselves, and children and their environment. Boys and girls usually spend many hours in the company of other children, practising games through which they develop a series of capacities and abilities, by imitating behaviours, activities, relations, etc., of the adult world.[11] We suggest that the social relations and inter-relations amongst children, other subjects, and their environment allow them to reach and pass through this vital period.

This socialization process is characterized by the acquisition of knowledge and the development of abilities which play an important role in learning. This is conceived as a formative and educational process which is understood as being long, continuous, progressive and cyclic. Through this process, children (and adults) will acquire the necessary know-how, developing skills that will give the necessary experiences to introduce them into a specific social sphere, knowing and acquiring characteristics that belong to their gender, identity and social status. Through this mechanism children are included in relational systems, forming part of the social and economic structures of the group they belong to, where they turn into social subjects and are determinant to the group, learning different concepts related to their own identity, and reaching their social and biological reproductions.[12]

Different areas of research, such as ethno-archaeology, psychology, didactics, etc., explain learning systems, such as imitation, direct observation, instruction, etc. However, we must take into account that learning is a cultural process and, as such, is defined by the internal rules of each human group. Because of this, we can find social groups that have only one educational system, cases in which different systems are merged together[13] or those that opt for no formal or direct instruction, such as are the case of the North American Inuits. Among these societies, learning is characterized by subtle interactions, which can be verbal, by which they teach different values and social roles, combined with the development of abilities, techniques and practical know-how.[14]

In any case, in any of these systems, games and toys play a fundamental role. Games and toys are one of the means by which children experiment and learn, settling them as main characters of the social structures in their group.[15] With these mechanisms not only do they learn new concepts and techniques, but they also enforce their education and the behaviour that is appropriate at their age, gender or social class, but also, these mechanisms are used by adults, on many occasions, to start delegating different tasks and responsibilities to children. By this means, toys and other game systems act as a tool that transmits cultural messages, and act as a mediator between adults and children.[16] Through this process they learn how to produce and introduce themselves in the economic sphere, promoting their incorporation as members of a community in which the social categories of gender, sex, age, or social class must be reproduced.[17]

Obviously, learning requires observation, imitation and instruction, but the basis of these systems, as also the ones of general education, is that personal and social relations are present. We believe that it is precisely in these relations where the more subtle, progressive and patient education lies, characterized by the internal rules of everyday life, coexistence, interaction, etc., which intervene in the development of children and turn them into co-leading actors of the history of their group, making them participants of a same vital reality. This kind of teaching is due to, one the one hand, the personal relations that transfer the internal characteristics of the social structures, and on the other, to the small and subtle details, expressions, values, etc., that not only define their identity, but also channel and transmit the most intimate characteristics of the group they belong to, acting as authentic memory frames. This learning is determined by the rhythms proper to everyday life, coexistence, and contact among social subjects of different social category, gender and age.

## LIFE AND DEATH IN A SAME SOCIAL SPACE

With this research we move onward to the Southeast of the Iberian Peninsula, more specifically to the province of Jaen (Baños de la Encina, Jaen) where we can find the Early Bronze Age site of Peñalosa. Twenty six years of systematic archaeological research have allowed a deep knowledge of the social structure of the group that lived at this site, spatially and temporally speaking. This site presents the typical settlement patter of the EBA in the Southeast of the Iberian Peninsula (Fig. 5.1): it is found upon a slate spur upon the bank of the river Rumblar, with rectangular houses along the slope of the hill built by artificial terracing of the slope. The different terraces are connected by narrow streets. The settlement is naturally defended by a series of cliffs on its western and northern side, while the rest of the settlement is defended by a wall, reinforced by bastions, to which houses are attached. To date, 14 households and productive spaces have been identified (domestic contexts) in which a total of 32 tombs have been found.[18]

During the EBA of the Southeast of the Iberian Peninsula (also known as the Argar Culture), households or domestic spaces have a great economical and subsistence value, but also hold a high social signification, which is determined by their use and double functionality. Everyday life and rituality coexist in the same space.

*Figure 5.1. View of the location and settlement site of Peñalosa (Baños de la Encina, Jaén, Spain) (Proyecto Peñalosa).*

## THE CONTEXTS: SCENARIOS OF SOCIAL REPRODUCTION

### *Everyday life*

When talking about everyday life we refer to a specific temporal frame, defined by a *daily time*,[19] which is marked by tasks, social practices related to production, and the maintenance of the life of men and woman of different age and categories. In this time scale the human and historical experience, which belong to human life cycles, is concentrated and expressed. This is only achieved by the accumulation of memories, experiences, knowledge, tasks, production and relations that are reflected in the material culture (objects and bodies) of the archaeological evidence,[20] and, thus, a specific spatial frame: domestic contexts. These scenarios amass conducts, decisions and ways of life of a particular society, where the essential routines of daily life are structured and reproduced;[21] they manifest the differences between genders, sex, age, status; and also build and generate a nexus of relationships: relations between generations (children and adults).[22]

The relevance of domestic space lies in its relational nature, as spaces created and lived in by individuals of different sex, age, and status, who by living together have given it a significance and social definition.[23] In the domestic spaces, a large set of personal relations, marked by living together, cooperation, interaction and complementarities, turn theses spaces in to focal points of social relations and into frames of reproduction and manipulation of the social identities of each member that makes up each domestic unit.[24] Thus, the social spaces that make up the settlement of Peñalosa respond to a series of determined structural and spatial criteria.

The fourteen household units that have been identified at this site to date present a structured inner organization, focused on the development of daily life and marked by their social and economical interests. Every household shares a series of fundamental tasks for the social, ideological, economical and political development of what we have defined as maintenance tasks.[25] These activities are as follows (Fig. 5.2):

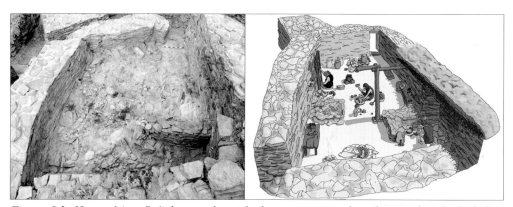

*Figure 5.2. House 14 at Peñalosa and an ideal reconstruction based on archaeological data (Proyecto Peñalosa).*

- Storage Areas. These are located in the more sheltered areas of the houses.
- Processing and milling of cereals. In each building a rough stone structure dedicated to this task has been identified, as well as a great number of grinding stones and mortars which allow this task to be carried out in any other area.
- Preparation and cooking of food. This task is intimately related to the previous two.
- Food consumption and metallurgical production. Usually both activities share the same spaces and structures. Generally, in the central spaces of the household, they appear associated with rough stone benches which circumscribe the interior perimeter of the houses.
- Textile production, textiles and sewing. Unlike the activities that have already been mentioned, in this case this activity has only been documented in four houses of the settlement. Its distribution seems to respond to the social and spatial organization of the settlement. When identifying this activity, in all four cases, this production is found in areas with very good illumination, close to doors or openings into the interior of the households.
- Learning and socialization. We understand that the social space of these activities would encompass the whole settlement. Nevertheless, empirically speaking, we find remains of material culture that indicate phases of the learning process and, therefore, of children's socialization. These objects are usually associated with the benches, in the central areas of the houses, and next to doors or passing lanes of the settlement.

This internal organization diagram has been documented in all the households of Peñalosa. This leads us to confirm that in this EBA settlement, the set of social relations was directly related to only one space: domestic contexts. All these activities form part of daily tasks, even metallurgical production. All of them coexist, are interrelated and share the same spatial and temporal frame. Differentiations of space depending on the activity has not been identified, nor are spatial restrictions influenced by cultural factors, which makes us think that there would not be any distinction depending on gender or age. Logically, if these activities share the same spaces, structures and objects, they also would be shared by the social subjects that carry them out (men, woman, and presumably children), thus understanding that interpersonal and social relations would be assured.

Thus, in Peñalosa we find common spaces, day to day productive spaces where adults and children lived together, related with each other, reunited and shared the same vital and historical experience, obviously determined by the nature of the internal domestic structure. These areas for relating and socializing are indubitable frameworks for learning and socialization. Boys and girls would have a direct, constant, daily and continuous contact, but would also experiment with objects, activities, social agents, spaces and time. This learning process, marked by coexistence of different social subjects, through social relations, would allow the assimilation of small messages, subtle expressions, etc., which will define, identify and characterize them as a part of a specific human group, turning into a vehicle for transmitting knowledge and identity throughout generations as authentic *traces of living memory*.

DAILY LIFE AND DEATH

The double use and functionality of domestic spaces during the EBA in the southeast of the Iberian Peninsula is defined by its standardized funerary ritual. Living and dead coexisted in the same spatial and temporal frame of daily life. Adults and children shared the same vital reality regulated by a series of rules and parameters learned and acquired through social relations. In a social group such as this one, where life and death are entwined in the funerary ritual, it is conceivable that social structures would be expressed through burial organization.[26] Therefore if we study these contextual frames, we can determine different aspects in relation to their social structures.[27]

In addition, the funerary space allows us to analyze the direct relation between objects and bodies;[28] it is a space where proof remains of how identity is created, manipulated and changed through time, and allows us to approach the biographies of these people through the study of their bodies.[29] The analysis of funerary contexts has turned into one of the most important instruments used to understand the construction of the social categories of children, and to establish their own social relations, among themselves and with adults.[30]

The internal structures of the EBA societies of this area evidence that buried individuals (adults and children) are neither the total population, nor do all burials survive. Determining why some individuals were buried and others were not is complicated, and may or may not respond to criteria marked by the social identity of this culture. What we do know is that the decision of the group is not determined by the category of age. Adults and children share the same symbolic act by being buried. This turns them into individuals with full rights from the first years of their life, fully recognized and considered by the rest of the social group.

All the burials (adults and children) are found in the interior of domestic spaces, under the occupational ground or hidden among production structures, benches or other areas of the household. The burials are defined by individual, double, triple or, exceptionally, quadruple interments, accompanied or not by grave goods. There are four types of burials: in cists, pits, wells and urns.

There are a total of 32 burials at Peñalosa divided into individual, double or triple interments, representing a minimum number of 40 individuals, of which 14 are children between the ages of 18 months and 6 years. This supposes a representation of more than 33% of the total sample that has been found to date.

Adults and children, in most cases, share the same funerary structure, cists built of stone slabs. This is the structure chosen for 7 children, including double and triple interments next to adults. In spite of this, unlike adult burials, in children's burials there seems to exist standardization when choosing the type of structure, the most important one, above cists, being the *pithos* or large, straight walled ceramic recipients, such as those chosen by the rest of the community for individual burials (Fig. 4.3).

When referring to the spatial distribution of tombs, in the case of Peñalosa, areas marked by social differences have not been established, and the burials of children, as also those belonging to adults, are present in almost all the households that have been excavated to date.

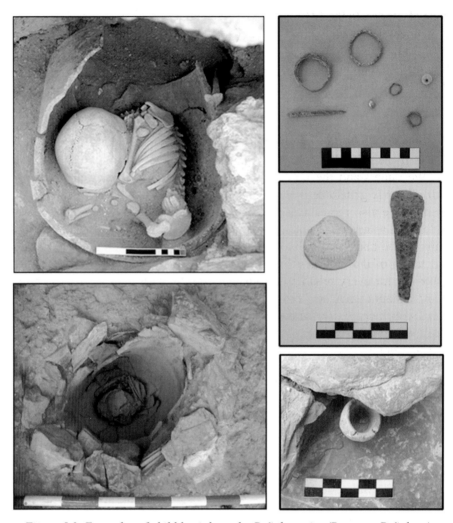

*Figure 5.3. Examples of child burials at the Peñalosa site (Proyecto Peñalosa).*

But, their relations are represented by sharing the same funerary space. In the case of Peñalosa, individual burials make up 73% of the total sample, while 47% belong to sub-adults, again represented equitably, which leads us to think that their determination would be ruled by social categories such as sex or status, but not age. In the cases of shared burials we find equivalence between the association adult-adult and adult-child, but on the other hand we have not located any burial with two children, although this has been observed in other EBA sites.

Another pattern that is shared by adults and children is the position of the body. In the cases that we have been able to document, the interments are flexed, in a right or left supine position.[31] Patterns in position have been identified in adults, marked by the category of gender. In the EBA culture of this area, research has identified that, in most cases, women are usually found in the right supine position, while men are found to the left.[32] In the case of children, we have not been able to identify a distinction in the positioning of the bodies according to gender. Nevertheless, something that draws our attention is that in children of very young age, this kind of pattern in burial position can be identified, but is not influenced by age or social status.

### The bodies: materiality of a reality

Logically, if we talk about materiality, we have to refer to the remains of human beings. We understand the bodies as *instruments through which all the knowledge about societies is* generated and transmitted.[33] Human remains are not only material entities, but are also representations that act as containers of the social construction of gender, and as a vehicle that manifests that identity.[34] In our research we advocate the study of the body as a cultural subject, since it is the receptacle and the material representation of the vital development of a person,[35] and is also in charge of acting as a mediator for every relation established with the world.[36] This new point of view, taken into account when studying human remains, has been defined by the concept of *embodiment* or *corporeity*,[37] materialized in the so called *archaeology of the body*.[38]

When we speak of the archaeology of the body we do not only refer to the of sex and age determination, but we also must study diseases and pathologies, food consumption patterns, the development of different activities or the treatment of the external aspect of the bodies, such as clothes, hairstyles, ornaments, etc., which is a particular manifestation of the way we present ourselves to the rest of the world.[39]

Unfortunately, in the particular case of Peñalosa, bones are poorly preserved, which, combined with the impossibility of determining the gender of juvenile individuals, has affected the conditions of the anthropological analysis. On the other hand, the age of all these individuals has been estimated. All the children are younger than six years of age, and only one case has reached this age. Five of them are about eighteen months old; one lived till approximately two years of age, while another four reached three years of age. Three other individuals were around the ages of four and five.[40]

Based on these ages, we can observe a first large group of children between the ages of eighteen months and three years, leaving a second group represented only by two individuals that are older. In all these cases the probable cause of death was linked to hygiene conditions and poor alimentation, expressed as pathologies which appear as infections, episodes of nutritional stress, or changes in the patterns of food consumption (dentition and weaning), such as hyperplasia of the enamel and *cribra orbitalia*.[41]

The studied pathologies that were present in the bones of adult individuals indicate that both age groups share the same environmental, hygienic-sanitary, and economic and subsistence conditions, due to having experienced the same environment and living conditions.

*The objects: fragments of reality*

The objects that surround us form part of our lives; they are pieces of reality that connect us to daily life. These objects are intimately linked to the social relation derived from members of a community based on the function of their values, symbolism, ideas and even emotions, which can become direct expressions of past experiences, lived histories, events, etc., which create an emotional link between people and society that is hard to break,[42] and act as anchors between the individual, his space, and his time. They are tangible metaphors that connect the experiences and memories of individuals (adults and children) to their contexts.[43]

In the archaeological evidence of Peñalosa we found objects that could form part of children's games (small stone and clay chips, pellets of hardened mud, etc.) made by adult hands,[44] or that possibly formed part of the learning and socialization processes. We think that the second option would better explain the finds of small drinking cups associated with the central areas of the households. These cups, are characterized by using clay that has not been decanted, by being of very small dimensions, being completely asymmetric, by presenting rough and irregular manufacture, unfired and without any surface treatment (Fig. 5.4:1–5 and Fig. 5.4: 7–9). All the identified cases recreate ceramic forms related to the consumption of food in the EBA world of adults, such as semi-spherical vessels and carinated vessels (Fig. 5.1: 5–10). Furthermore, in two houses (9 and 14) we have identified two possible learning phases of this production (Fig. 5.4). A first phase where the lack of technical abilities is clearly seen, being very rough and primary vessels, and a second one where the acquisition of better technical abilities can be observed. Associated with these ceramic objects we have identified small clay *pellets* that seem to respond to the process of ceramic modelling.

Elizabeth Bagwell speaks of *phases* in the children's learning processes of ceramic production. This author concurs that children under the age of four would not be able to create determined ceramic forms and that only from the age of five onward could children start creating recognizable ceramic forms, achieving full ability at the age of nine.[45] If we take into account these studies of the learning process of ceramic production, which are very standardized during the EBA in this area, and the work and time that is needed to develop this skill, we can think that we have identified objects that were probably made by children as part of their learning and socialization process.[46]

Independent of the interpretation of these objects, we consider that objects are temporal guides of our vital development, which help in the construction of our social, individual and collective identities, and that are part of the journey of our life.[47] Furthermore, these objects retain part of the essence of the individuals who made them, used them and deposited them. Therefore, the presence of these ceramic objects as grave goods of infants in the settlement of Peñalosa, as also in other EBA sites in the Southeast, leads us to believe that these objects had a special incidence in the social identity of children,[48] as also its absence in funerary grave goods would have a social explanation. Children and adults share the same funerary rituals that are represented by their active participation in the same social strategies of this social group. These

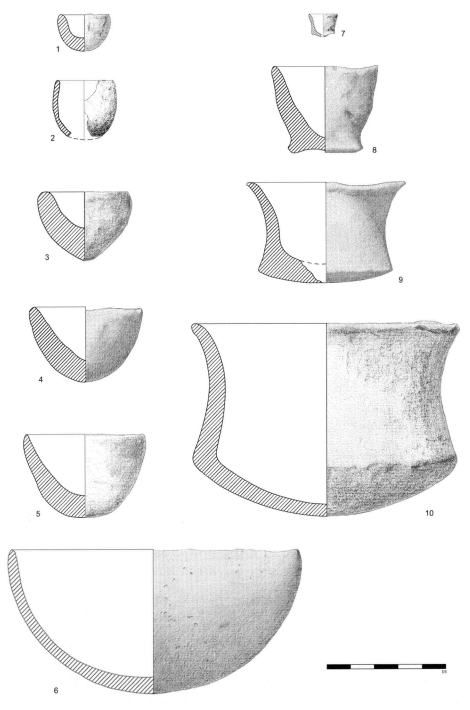

*Figure 5.4. Adult and children pottery production (Proyecto Peñalosa).*

rituals are organized by the same internal rules of the group. Because of this we can find burials with or without grave goods, independent of gender or age. The reasons for the presence or absence can be found in the internal rules of the group,[49] probably determined by the social perception of the deceased person and his/her connection with the social roles and activities carried out by this person during his life. Therefore in juvenile (all these cases correspond to juvenile individuals, which allow us to assure the relationship between object and individual) and in adult burials we find objects that can be identified and defined in the frame of daily life. Nevertheless, a particularity can once again be identified in juvenile burials, where the elements related to personal ornaments are more common, as will be explain below.

An example of this situation is Burial 5, which contained two necklace beads, one made of jasper in a tubular shape, and the other of quartzite, with a copper awl, and two ceramic containers for consumption of medium dimensions. In the double Burial 21, an infant had three silver rings associated with different fingers, two of them being spiral rings and the other a simple ring; furthermore, a silver bracelet was found *in situ* on the left arm. At neck height, two necklace beads were found, both made of rock crystal, and an undetermined element made of gold between the neck and the skull was also found, which could possibly be part of an earring or a pendant (Fig. 5.3). A metallic awl or needle, a semi-spherical bowl and animal remains also formed part of the grave goods of this burial. In Burial 22 the only goods that have been recovered were a meat offering and a semi-spherical bowl, the same as in Burial 23, which also included a ceramic bottle of small dimensions (Fig. 5.3). By contrast, the juvenile individual of tomb 31 had a semi-spherical cup, of very small size, which had not been baked and was very roughly made, a two rivet dagger, also of very small dimensions, and a valve shell of a mollusc (*Glycimeris sp.*) dipped in white. Last of all the individual of tomb 15 was associated with two ceramic bowls of small dimensions and of a similar nature to the ones already described above, a copper dagger and a stone object.[50]

The remainder of the juvenile burials are all multiple burials; therefore we cannot confirm the association between the objects and the individual. Nevertheless, we want to mention the case of a double grave (adult-child) where we found, as part of the grave goods, two small ceramic cups similar to those described above, next to other ceramic objects of large dimensions and a metallic dagger.

## Conclusions

As we have been able to contrast, in the settlement of Peñalosa, there is a special social significance determined by the coexistence, relations and interrelations between children and adults, daily life and rituality. This creates, without any doubts, an unmatchable frame for learning and socialization.

Children and adults of the EBA site of Peñalosa share the same social and symbolic reality, and the same history, which turns them into members with full rights of this cultural and human group of the EBA, and particularly of this site located in the Upper Guadalquivir valley. This reality turns young juvenile individuals into participants of the social strategies, playing a leading role in the social dynamics of this group. This is represented in the standardized funerary pattern (taking into account its internal rules). The materialization, the representation of expressions and the common contacts between adults and children in the funerary world can only be understood if these actions, rules and behaviours are accepted, recognized and assumed by the group. This is only possible if they had occurred and were assumed previously, within the framework of daily life. We believe that a ritual, which is conditioned by symbolism, taboos, rules, etc, and defined as a funerary ritual, can exclusively be determined by the social conditions of these individuals' lives and, most of all, because of the consideration and recognition that the rest of the group held towards these people.

As a final consideration, we must state that the archaeological evidence from this site clearly reveals that children and adults coexisted and shared the same space and time in their daily life, which makes them participants of the same symbolic and social reality.

NOTES

1  This paper was included in the research project I+D+i: *La minería en el Alto Guadalquivir. Formas de construcción histórica en la Antigüedad a partir de la producción, consumo y distribución de los metales (HAR2011-30131-C02-01)*

2  Among others, James and Prout 1990; Golden 1990; James, Jenks and Prout 1998; Moore and Scott 1997; Crawford 1999; Sofaer Derevenski 2000; James and James 2004; Galinadou and Dommasnes 2007; Crawford and Shepherd 2007; Dommasnes and Wrigglesworth 2008; Wileman 2005; Baxter 2005; Gusi and Muriel 2008; Sánchez Romero 2010; Justel Vicente 2012

3  Baxter 2005

4  Lillehammer 1989; Baxter 2005

5  James *et al.* 1998

6  Sánchez Romero and Alarcón García 2012

7  Elliot *et al.* 2001, 118

8  Sánchez Romero 2004

9  Nájera *et al.* 2010

10 Baxter 2005

11 Kamp 2010

12 Prout 1999, 7; Kamp 2010; Nájera *et al.* 2010

13 Rogoff 1990, 129–131

14 Park 2010

15 Smith 2000

16 Sofaer Deverenski 2000, 7; Baxter 2005, 42

17 Lillehammer 1989, 94

18 Alarcón García 2010

19 Picazo 1997

20 González Marcén and Picazo 2005, 148

21 Richards 1990, 113; Hendon 1996, 47

22 Gilchrist 1999, 100

23 Bourdieu 1007; Sørensen 2000

24 Alarcón García 2010

25 Alarcón García 2010

26 Parker Pearson 1999; Rautman and Talalay 2004; Sofaer 2007

27 Aranda *et al.* 2009

28  Sofaer Derevenski 2000, 397
29  Gilchcrist 1999; Sofaer Derevenski 2000
30  Sánchez Romero and Alarcón García 2012
31  Sánchez Romero and Alarcón García 2012
32  Schubart 2004; Sánchez Romero 2009
33  Joyce 2005
34  Prout 1999; Sofaer 2007
35  Sofaer 2007, 60
36  Merleau-Ponty 1945
37  Csordas 1994
38  Joyce 2005
39  Sánchez Romero 2008
40  Alarcón García 2010
41  Sánchez Romero and Alarcón García 2012
42  Hooper-Greenhill 2000
43  Wood 2009
44  Politis 1998, 10
45  Bagwell 2002, 91
46  Kamp 2010; Crown 2002, 108–109
47  Freeman 1993; Cunningham 1995; Wood 2009
48  Sánchez Romero and Alarcón García 2012
49  Wood 2009
50  Alarcón García 2010

REFERENCES

Alarcón García, E. 2010. *Continuidad y cambio social: análisis de las actividades de mantenimiento.* Unpublished PhD. thesis, City University of Granada.
Aranda, G. *et al.* 2009. Death and everyday life: the Argaric societies from South-East Spain. *Journal of Social Archaeology* 9/2, 139–162.
Bagwell, E. 2002. Ceramic form and skill. Attempting to identify child producers at Pecos Pueblo, New Mexico, pp. 90–107 in Kamp, K. A. (ed.), *Children in the Prehistoric Puebloan Southwest.* University of Utah Press: Salt Lake City.
Baxter, J. E. 2005. *The Archaeology of Childhood.* Walnut Creek.
Bourdieu, P. 1977. *Outline of a Theory of Practice.* Cambridge: Cambridge University Press.
Crawford, S. 1999. *Childhood in Anglo-Saxon England.* Stroud: Sutton.
Crawford, S. and Shepherd G. 2007. Children, childhood and society: An introduction, pp. 1–14 in Crawford S., Shepherd, G. (eds), *Children, Childhood and Society. Studies in Archaeology, History, Literature and Art.* (BAR International Series 1696). Oxford: Archaeopress.
Crown, P. L. 2002. Learning and teaching in the Prehispanic American Southeast, pp. 108–124 in Kamp, K. A. (ed.), *Children in the Prehistoric Puebloan Southwest.* University of Utah Press: Salt Lake City.
Csordas, T. J. 1994. Introduction: the body as representation and being-in-the-world, pp. 1–24 in Csordas, T. J. (ed.), *Embodiment and Experience: The Existential Ground of Culture and Self.* Cambridge: Cambridge University Press.
Cunningham, H. 1995. *Children and Childhood in Western Society Since 1500.* London: Pearson Longman.
Dommasnes, L. H. and Wrigglesworth, M. 2008. *Children, Identity and the Past.* Cambridge: Cambridge University Press.
Elliot, J., Knight, A. and Cowley, C. 2001. *Oxford Dictionary & Thesaurus.* Oxford: Oxford University Press.

Freeman, M. 1993. *Rewriting the Self: History, Memory, Narrative*. London: Routledge.

Galinadou, N. and Dommasnes, L. H. 2007. *Telling Children about the Past. An Interdisciplinary Perspective*. International Monographs in Prehistory: Ann Arbor.

Gilchrist, R. 1999. *Gender and Archaeology: Contesting the Past*. London: Routledge.

Golden, M. 1990. *Childhood in Classical Athens*, Baltimore: The Johns Hopkins University Press.

González Marcén, P. and Picazo Gurina, M. 2005. Arqueología de la vida cotidiana, pp. 141–158 in Sánchez Romero, M. (ed.), *Arqueología y Género*. Granada: Universidad de Granada.

Gusi, F. and Muriel, S. 2008. *Nasciturus, Infans, Puerulus. Vobis mater terra*. Castellón: Sèrie de Preistòria i Arqueologia.

Hendon, J. A. 1996. Archaeological approaches to the organization of domestic labor: Household practice and domestic relations. *Annual Review of Anthropology* 25, 45–61

Hooper-Greenhill, E. 2000. *Museums and the Interpretation of Visual Culture*. London: Routledge.

James, A. and Prout, A. (eds) 1990. *Constructing and Reconstructing Childhood*, Basingstoke: Falmer.

James, A., Jenks, C. and Prout, A. 1998. *Theorizing Childhood*. New York: Wiley.

Joyce, R. A. 2005. Archaeology of the body. *Annual Review of Anthropology* 34, 139–158.

Justel, D. 2012. *Niños en la Antigüedad. Estudios sobre la Infancia en el mediterráneo antiguo*. Zaragoza: Prensas Universitarias de Zaragoza.

Kamp, C. 2010. Entre el trabajo y el juego: perspectivas sobre la infancia en el suroeste americano, pp. 103–120 in Sánchez Romero, M. (ed.), *Infancia y cultura material en arqueología*, Complutum, 21/2.

Lillehammer, G. 1989. A child is born. The child's world in an archaeological perspective. *Norwegian Archaeological Review* 22/2, 89–105.

Merleau-Ponty, M. 1975. *Fenomenología de la percepción*. Barcelona (first published as *Fenomenologia de la perception*. Paris: Gallimard, 1945.

Moore, J. and Scott, E. (eds) 1997. *Invisible People and Processes. Writing Gender and Childhood into European Archaeology*. London: Routledge.

Nájera, T. *et al.* 2010. La población infantil de la Motilla del Azuer: Un estudio bioarqueológico, pp. 69–102 in Sánchez Romero, M. (ed.), *Infancia y cultura material en arqueología*, Complutum 21/2.

Park, R. 2010. Finding childhood in the archaeological record of Arctic Canada, pp. 121–134 in Sánchez Romero, M. (ed.), *Infancia y cultura material en arqueología*, Complutum, 21/2.

Parker Pearson, M. 1999. *The Archaeology of Death and Burial*. Stroud: Sutton Publishing Ltd.

Picazo, M. 1997. Hearth and home: the timing of maintenance activities, pp. 59–67 in Moore J. and Scott, E. (eds), *Invisible people and processes. Writing Gender and Childhood into European Archaeology*. London: Leicester University Press.

Politis, G. 1998. Arqueología de la infancia: una perspectiva etnoarqueológica. *Trabajos de Prehistoria* 55, 5–19.

Prout, A. 1999. Childhood bodies: construction, agency and hybridity, pp. 1–18 in Prout, A. (ed.), *Body, Childhood and Society*. London: Palgrave Macmillan.

Rautman, A. E. and Talalay, L. 2000. Introduction: diverse approaches to the study of gender in archaeology, pp. 1–12 in Rautman, A. E. (ed.), *Reading the Body. Representation and Remains in the Archaeological Record*. Philadelphia: University of Pennsylvania Press

Richards, C. 1990. The late Neolithic house in Orkney, pp. 111–124 in Samson, R. (ed.), *The Social Archaeology of Houses*. Edinburgh: Edinburgh University Press.

Rogoff, B. 1990. *Apprenticeship in Thinking: Cognitive Development in Social Context*. New York: Oxford University Press.

Sánchez Romero, M. 2004. Children in south east of Iberian Peninsula during Bronze Age. *Ethnographisch-Archäologische Zeitschrift* 45, 377–387.

Sánchez Romero, M. 2008. Childhood and the construction of gender identities through material culture. *International Journal of Childhood in the Past* 1, 17–37.

Sánchez Romero, M. 2010. *¡Eso no se toca! infancia y cultura material en arqueología*, pp. 9–14 in Sánchez Romero M. (ed.), *Infancia y cultura material en arqueología*, Complutum, 21/2.

Sánchez Romero, M. and Alarcón García, E. 2012. Lo que los niños nos cuentan: individuos infantiles durante la Edad del Bronce en el sur de la Península Ibérica, pp. 57–98 in Justel Vicente, D. (ed.), *Niños en la Antigüedad. Estudios sobre la Infancia en el mediterráneo antiguo*. Zaragoza: Prensas Universitarias de Zaragoza.

Schubart, H. 2004. Das reiche Grab einer jungen Frau aus dem el argar-zeitlichen Fuente Álamo. *Madrider Mitteilungen* 45, 97–107.

Smith, S. 2000. Children at play, pp. 79–98 in Mills, J. and Mills, R. (eds), *Childhood Studies: A Reader in Perspectives of Childhood*. London: Routledge.

Sofaer Derevenski, J. 2000. Material culture shock: confronting expectations in the material culture of children, pp. 3–16 in Sofaer Derevenski, J. (ed.), *Children and Material Culture*. London: Routledge.

Sofaer, J. 2007. Engendering children, engendering archaeology, pp. 87–96 in Insoll, T. (ed.), *The Archaeology of Identities: A Reader*. Abingdon: Routledge.

Sørensen, M. L. S. 2000. *Gender Archaeology*. Cambridge: Polity Press.

Wileman, J. 2005. *Hide and Seek. The Archaeology of Childhood*. Stroud: Tempus.

Wood, E. 2009. Saving childhood in everyday objects. *Childhood in the Past* 2, 151–162.

# 6

# GENDER AND CHILDHOOD IN THE II IRON AGE: THE POTTERY CENTRE OF LAS COGOTAS (ÁVILA, SPAIN)

## *Juan Jesús Padilla Fernández and Linda Chapon*

### INTRODUCTION

Children? Women? The preconceived archaeological inferences used to explain these circumstantial milestones typical of our ancestors, have neglected the important role played by non-adult human collectives, active participants in the quotidian events who constantly produce material culture. The same happens with the female social sector, which has never been taken into account by so called 'traditional archaeology', but which is key in the obtaining of an accurate and complete understanding of human behaviour.

From the unique evidence of the archaeological remains, and the consigning of women and children to oblivion, rather simplistic behavioural interpretations have been elaborated, as well as partial technological models, which are essentially masculine and which reconstruct a biased positivist history. Nevertheless, since the 1980s and '90s, post-processual archaeology has started to contradict the unilineal point of view, characteristic of processualism, with a new interest in understanding other ways of comprehending the world. New perspectives have appeared that consider women and children as objects of study in themselves, analyzing the relationships, biological as well as cultural, which they have with and within the human group to which they belong.[1]

Thanks to the opening of new methodological doors through ethnoarchaeology, the pre-roman pottery centre of Las Cogotas (Cardeñosa, Ávila) permits us to explore the prominence of children and women in order to obtain a satisfactory understanding of the potteries' *chaîne operatoire*. Indeed, they play an important role in the economical and social organization of this production centre, a fact that, in the last instance, allows us to approach their way of conceiving the reality that surrounds them.

### THE POTTERY CENTRE OF LAS COGOTAS: A CENTRE OF 'GREMIAL' CHARACTER

Employing a clear archaeological methodology and using the material culture as a backbone, the pottery centre of Las Cogotas became the epicentre of our study, providing us with valuable information about the relationships that both spheres, the adult and the juvenile, have.

Between 1986 and 1990, the archaeological excavations directed by Dr Gonzalo Ruiz Zapatero[2] discovered, in the territory known as 'Vetton' in the classical sources, a specialized area of pottery production belonging to the second century BC. Within an area greater than 300 m², it is possible to distinguish a perfect compartmentalization of all the rooms, unique in itself (Fig. 6.1).[3]

The conception of archaeological entities, and within them material culture, cannot be understood as isolated elements, but as forms produced by social action, and therefore only understandable if related to the context within which they are included, forcing the study from a technological point of view through the concept of *chaîne operatoire*.[4] Only in this way would we be able to differentiate, on the one hand the technical chain, as the sequence of the phases developed throughout the manual process, since the moment of acquisition of raw materials, to the achievement of the final product, and on the other hand, the cultural, economical, and social factors as also imaginary determinants, which converge and mark all the manufacturing process of the technological chain. As Lemonier said, to examine social control over fixed technical gestures or strategic tasks, allows us to fill the gap between technical phenomenon and others of social nature.[5]

The need to get a complete understanding of the 'how' in order to explain the 'why', and the meaning of the pottery production in the centre of Las Cogotas, turns analogical reasoning into a source of first importance, searching for answers in current human groups, as well as in ethnohistorical and ethnographical data; that is, without falling into the use that has been traditionally given to ethnography in archaeology and which is known as 'direct approximation', or what J. Yellen (1977) named the *buckshot approach*.

The contrast between the archaeological evidence found in the pottery centre and its association with each one of the phases documented ethnologically within the technical chain (Fig. 6.1), are involved in the perception of a complex socio-economical panorama of pyramidal type, where men, women and children interact. The configuration of a new political setting imposed by Rome brings, along with the establishment of new conventions, the alteration of collective rules. A progressive change in individualism generates a structural change in identities, which demands the existence of perfectly definite and autonomous workshops, capable of dealing with the needs required by the new times. The adoption of the pottery wheel as a primary technical resource consigns domestic pottery to a secondary place. The increase of power status and handcrafted specialization induces the members of a specific community to start to make differences between them. This happens as a consequence of the rising, in interpersonal relationships, of a hostile desire above a loving one,[6] understanding the former as a 'type of desire that operates as a distinguishing Me/Not-Me' and the latter as 'a desire to link which connects us with others'.[7]

Technological and material control promotes the appearance of a patriarchal system which organizes work in a gremial or collective way, but centred on the domestic sphere. Connected with the *pater familias*, a solid nucleus is defined involving children, apprentices who continue with the lineage, women – guarantor of the idea of 'us', and the men, who sanctioned the qualified profession.

*Figure 6.1. Top: panoramic view of the pottery centre of Las Cogotas. Below left: plan of the pottery centre complex of Las Cogotas. Below right: sequence of the thrown pottery production process (Padilla Fernández 2013).*

The anthropological study of the Egyptian potter community of Ehnasya el Medina, confirms in a material way the existing relationship between handcraft specialization and the establishment of a system of gremial nature.[8] Furthermore, it allows us to generate behavioural expectations in analogous societies of the past, confirmed subsequently through the search for common agents in the archaeological record.

Nowadays, in Middle Egypt the initiation of a standardized and quasi-industrial productive system entails an exclusive and constant dedication, favouring the establishment of the domestic habitat in the area surrounding the working zone. This obsession for rationalizing space agrees with the finding in Las Cogotas of a household structure annexed to the pottery complex, compartmentalized and of great dimensions. The existence of more than five fireplaces, hundreds of millstones and diverse pottery groups with an absence of firing defects, keeps a strong connection with material culture elements traceable at an ethnological level in Ehnasya el Medina today (Fig. 6.2).

In the same way, and this time alluding to patterns of ethnographical and ethnohistorical nature, the daily familiar coexistence and gremial conception of the pottery handcraft profession was perfectly observable in rural Spain of the first half of the 20th century. Popular centres such as Úbeda or Bailén, both found in the province of Jaén, have been the object of anthropological memories, unique witnesses of the survival of a profession that has remained unchanged over more than 2,000 years (Fig. 6.3).[9]

Are we therefore in front of a Second Iron Age potter's house in Las Cogotas *Oppidum*? It is more than probable. Beside its family group, the potter would have been in charge of the operation of the workshop, transmitting the basics from generation to generation, and the necessary technical patterns for manufacturing wheel-thrown products.

CHILDHOOD AS A SYNONYM OF LEARNING

The post-modern and contemporary world in which we are living conceives children as indifferent agents, largely growing up surrounded by television and new technologies, without receiving education from their parents or guardians. This concept, imposed since the end of the 19th century,[10] has set children aside to suffer oblivion in certain socio-economical aspects of our society, a society that traditionally has omitted the cultural transcendence this group has had throughout the history of humanity.

Leaving aside the preconceived image of invisible individuals, who are also at the same time untouchable, we must be conscious of the change in concept that the communities which are not pervaded by the globalization process have of them. We must not ignore that in those communities, children play an essential role in the economic as well as in social contributions, as they are considered an active part of the system itself.[11] Age, as well as gender or social status, is a culturally constructed category, and thus is subject to the characteristics typical of each social group.[12]

In our case study, a strongly hierarchical society which demands a standardized and specialized thrown pottery production, the juvenile workforce gains an important role. It is an economic strategy, and at the same time, a socializing tool which intends to transmit cultural values as well as technological knowledge. Even though work and learning are difficult to isolate ethnographically, and even more to identify through the archaeological evidence,[13] the pottery centre of Las Cogotas permits us to carry out interesting interpretations of the transmission process of the profession.

*Figure 6.2. Top: archaeological cross section showing the domestic material found in the household structure annexed to the pottery complex culture. Inset: one of the millstones documented. Below: the pottery centre of Ehnasya el Medina where we could appreciate a direct connection between the working and domestic areas (Photographs by the author).*

Accepting that the subjects (individuals) as well as the objects are intimately connected and that they cannot be understood in isolation;[14] the archaeological record of the workshop confirms the establishment of a marked learning pattern. Children, seen as 'heirs', would be considered as students. They would receive, therefore, proper lessons through verbal education, demonstrations and assigned tasks. The finding of

*Figure 6.3. Families of handcraft potters found in the late 1950s in the towns of Úbeda and Bailén (Agudo and Cárdenas 2012).*

pieces of defective workmanship (Fig. 6.4) within the archaeological record could confirm the existence of a formal education in order to acquire complex abilities such as modelling on the potter's wheel. Most of those pieces are characterized by being badly made, with wide and rough walls, lumps, breaks and asymmetry, even though some of them appear very carefully modelled. The evidence of different levels associated with the manufacturing defects would also demonstrate that there is no need for adults as first instructors, and that learning is possible for mixed aged groups, where the care of the younger children falls on the older ones who possess greater knowledge. The discovery of small decorated boxes and toys (rag dolls) of unfired clay (Fig. 6.4), also implies that a great part of this knowledge would be transmitted through games or by imitation. We must then contemplate sequential learning, where teaching begins with the simplest challenges in order to improve progressively towards the more complex ones.

Although the archaeological testimony is only able to express the possible contributions of children in the phases ascribed to the modelling and finishing touches of pottery pieces, it is not absurd to suggest their active participation in other necessary stages of production, such as the extraction of raw materials and their transport, the clay preparation, or the supply of materials needed for the firing process. In fact, the

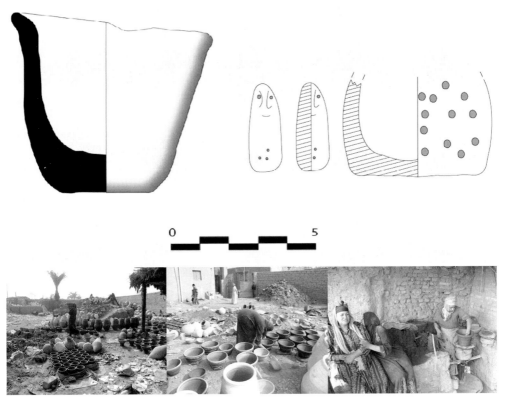

*Figure 6.4. Top left: thrown pottery vessel with manufacturing defects, coming from the pottery centre of Las Cogotas; right: small doll and clay box found within the pottery centre of Las Cogotas (illustration by the author). Below: ethnological sequence that documents the work and role of women in the pottery centre of Ehnasya el Medina (Photographs by the author).*

learning of these practices seems to be much easier than modelling or decoration, thus it is probable that juvenile groups would contribute to pottery manufacturing through these complementary functions.[15] Ethnographical and ethnological evidence observed in the potters' community of Ehnasya El Medina, as well as some ethnohistorical ones found in the Iberian Peninsula,[16] also seem to corroborate this participation.

Dermatoglyphs stamped when the clay was still damp, confirmed the actual involvement of children during the ceramic productive process and the establishment of a familiar gremial pattern type. With the objective of coming to decisive conclusions about the utility of examining the ancient fingerprints seen at an archaeological level, we have been developing a study among 150 individuals between 5 and 60 years old, all of them members of the potters' community which still exists in the town of Bailén in the province of Jaén (Andalusia). Starting from the premise that the fingerprints' shape grow proportionally to the rest of the body and that their variability is due to age,[17] we asked individuals of different age ranges for an approximate execution of those pieces that had been found in the pottery centre of Las Cogotas, which, because of their form characteristics, had been associated with children.

These fingerprints stamped unintentionally on the archaeological pieces as well as on the modern reproductions have been accurately measured in width and length in order to fulfil statistical comparative studies. The results have been encouraging and have allowed the establishment of a direct connection between age and width/length of the fingerprint. The data obtained from widths have been especially taken into account, as this is the most reliable variable because, unlike length, it does not vary depending on the morphology of the mark. The archaeological evidence shows dermatoglyphs width measures, 1.1 cm (60%), 1.2 cm (22%), 1.3 cm (11%) and 1.5 cm (7%) successively as being more common, data which agree precisely with the current marks made in our study by children between 6 and 16 years old. We are able therefore to confirm the effective involvement of children within the technical-operative chain through these specific pieces, such as toys and boxes.

THE WOMEN: TRANSMITTING CODES OF IDENTITY

The influence of Rome and the advance of socio-economical complexity in each one of the communities within the Celtiberian tradition of the *meseta*, marks a definitive break with a general feeling of identity and pertaining to a specific group. Men reinforce, even more if possible, the differences within the group, projecting their hostile desire through the development of positions of power.[18] Nevertheless, as we have mentioned previously, facing this growing individualism the feminine gender assumes the role of promoting the loving link, without which the human being would not be able to survive.[19]

The distribution of work within the pottery centre of de Las Cogotas perfectly responds to this new conception of the world. For reasons merely patriarchal and positivist men would be in charge of giving form to the pieces, while women would employ their ability by carrying out, beside the apprentices, all the peripheral tasks, connected with the transport, drying and decoration of the pottery pieces. Sadly, archaeology does not allow us to see this kind of behaviour directly, but it is possible to visualize it by paying attention to ethnological and ethnohistorical data, as we have highlighted previously (Fig. 6.4).

The growing power-knowledge relationships would motivate a socialization that structures gender roles from childhood, fixing not only future abilities but also a sexual division of work, significantly emphasized in the adult world.[20] Therefore, women became in charge of promoting loving desire and maintaining the collective feeling already reduced to local spheres (settlements) and relatives *gens*. Painted brush decoration, common in archaeological contexts of the western *meseta* at the beginning of the Second Iron Age, is seen as a concrete case of a study that corroborates the interest of expressing on the pottery vessels ideas pertaining to particular realities of identity and ethnicity.[21] The absence of this pottery type in the centre of Las Cogotas demonstrates that they are earlier than the final phase of the big *oppida*. They are set aside for pieces that possess geometrical motifs of Celtiberian tradition, which respond to different socio-cultural contexts and are at the heart of our general study. Preliminary work has begun to offer good indications about the meaning they contain, although it is still too premature to adopt definitive conclusions. Could women be responsible for expressing, through the decoration which 'adorns' the pottery vessels, those bonds and codes of identity? At least for now, it is impossible to know. Nevertheless we could affirm that they are closely related to these codes of identity which show the symbolism typical of parental societies and which have been, up to now, obviated by the scientific community.

The importance of fusing the archaeology with testimonies coming from ethnological, ethnographical and ethnohistorical evidence is that it allows a reconsideration of the problematic concept of ethnicity. The comparison of different wheel-turned pottery centres, all of them relating to the Mediterranean sphere,[22] demonstrates that they are repeating the same canons. Women are provided with a 'marginal' role, linked to activities which do not demand a great technical ability.

CONCLUSIONS

The search for considerations that attempt to explain the role developed by women and children within our history proved that it was necessary to put in practice a more authentic social archaeology. The archaeological record must be understood as a multiplicity of causes[23] in order to be able to find in it the story of the facts where the individuals and their own experiences have the leading role.[24] In addition, the initiation of a whole view which combines the archaeological perspective with those of ethnology, ethnography and ethnohistory, would allow us to explore in an authentic way the identities and the social groups which have traditionally been forgotten from a historiographical point of view.

With the objective of applying this methodological shift, we have set out in the pottery centre of Las Cogotas a socio-economical type study, but also a symbolical one, attempting to give an answer to basic questions such as: who was in charge of utilizing the workshop owing these distinctive features; or how and why a specialized handcraft work is maintained.

The material evidences indicate the adoption of a new system based on the search for prestige and status. The possibility of being able to utilize a pottery production centre such as the one discovered in the *oppidum* of Las Cogotas, generates the establishment of artisanal families that organized the work starting from a pyramidal system, where the base is characterized by children and women, leaving the peak exclusively to the men. It became a parental pattern of patriarchal nature, where masculine individuals searched for difference through the achievement of power, the feminine individuals maintained group links, and the juvenile individuals were educated with the roles that consolidate and justify the necessity of a growing hierarchical organization. The learning process became a fact which determined the future of these societies, giving them a prominent standing within familiar relationships. Carried out progressively and gradually, it gives access to each one of the notions and skills that are necessary in order to develop thrown pottery production. Regardless of whether the instruction is primary or mixed, games and imitation became the main knowledge transmitting channels; knowledge not only reduced to the purely technical sphere, but also of identity and gender organization. Women, kept away since childhood from concepts of individualism and power, are trained in the control of emotions and maintenance of the collective, this being a social function expressed in a subliminal way through the material culture that they produced.

The purpose of this work does not lie in the concept of fixed interpretative categories, but in the creation of a set of instructions or references which may help to explore the material culture typical of a wheel-thrown pottery centre, keeping always in mind the totality of the social agents operating within it. Ultimately, we are asserting the prominence that juvenile activities, as well as gendered activities, had at the close of the Second Iron Age in productive settings like these.

NOTES

1   Sánchez Romero 2010, 9
2   Mariné Isidro and Ruiz Zapatero 1988; Ruiz Zapatero and Álvarez-Sanchís 1995; Mariné Isidro 2005
3   Álvarez-Sanchís 2008; Padilla Fernández, 2011 and 2012
4   Lemonnier 1986, 1990, 1992 and 2012
5   Lemonnier 1992. *Cit. in* González Ruibal 2003, 30
6   Hernando Gonzalo 2007, 171
7   Burín 2003, 51
8   Padilla Fernández 2013
9   Curtis 1962; Guerrero Martín 1988; Sempere 1992; Seseña 1976 and 1997; Cárdenas and Agudo 2012, Padilla Fernández, forthcoming (a)
10  Cunningham 1996
11  Lancy 2008
12  Sofaer Derevensky 2000; Lucy 2005; Sánchez Romero 2004 and 2007; Sánchez Romero and Alarcón García 2012
13  Kamp 2010
14  Sánchez Romero 2008, 18
15  Kamp 2010, 114
16  Padilla Fernández, forthcoming (b)
17  David 1981
18  Hernando Gonzalo 2007, 172
19  Hernando Gonzalo 2005
20  Bradley 1993; Keith 2005
21  Ruiz Zapatero and Álvarez-Sanchís 2002; Álvarez-Sanchís 2010
22  Djordjevic 2005, 2012 and 2013
23  Politis 1998, 16
24  González Ruibal 2006, 236

REFERENCES

Álvarez-Sanchís, J. R. 2008. El descubrimiento de los Vettones. Las Cogotas y la cultura de los Verracos, pp. 14–42 in Álvarez-Sanchís, J. (coord.), *Arqueología Vettona. La Meseta Occidental en la Edad del Hierro* (Zona Arqueológica 12). Alcalá de Henares: Museo Arqueológico Regional.

Álvarez-Sanchís, J. R. 2010. La cerámica con decoración a peine, de 'fósil guía' a indicador de etnicidad, pp. 293–318 in Romero Carnicero, F. and Sanz Mínguez, C. (eds), *De la Región Vaccea a la Arqueología Vaccea*. Valladolid: Vaccea Monografías 4.

Bradley, C. 1993. Women's Power, Children's Labor. *Cross-Cultural Research* 27, 70–96.

Burín, M. 2003. El deseo de poder en la construcción de la subjetividad femenina. El 'techo de cristal', en la carrera laboral de las mujeres, pp. 71–136 in Hernando, A. (Coord.), *¿Desean las mujeres el poder? Cinco reflexiones en torno a un deseo conflictivo*. Madrid: Minerva Ediciones.

Cardenas, A. and Agudo, J. A. 2012. *La Edad del Barro*. Granada: Port-Royal.

Cunningham, H. 1996. The History of Childhood, pp. 27–35 in Hwang, C. P. Lamb, M. E. and Sigel, I. E. (eds), *Images of Childhood*. Mahwah: Lawrence Erlbaum Associates Publishers.

Curtis, F. 1962. The Utility Pottery Industry of Bailén, Southen Spain. *American Antropologist* 64/3, 486–503.

David, T. J. 1981. Distribution, Age and Sex Variation of the Mean Epidermal Ridge Breadth. *Human Heredity* 31, 279–282.

Djorjevic, B. 2005. Some ethnoarchaeological possibilities in the pottery technology investigations, pp. 61–69 in Prudêncio, M. A., Dias, M. A. and Waerenborgh, J. C. (eds), *Understanding people Through their pottery, proceedings of the 7th European Meeting on Ancient Ceramics (EMAC'03)* (Trabalhos de arqueología 42). Lisbon: Portuguese Institute of Archaeology.

Djorjevic, B. 2012. *Intangible Cultural Heritage. An analysis of the Traditional Pottery Production related legislation* (Monograph 15). Belgrade: National Museum of Belgrade.

Djorjevic, B. 2013. Las tecnologías tradicionales de cerámica y sus orígenes europeos como potencial etnoarqueológico, pp. 393–423 in Girón, L., Lazarich, M. and Conceiçâo Lopes, M. (coords) *Actas del I Congreso Internacional sobre Estudios Cerámicos. Homenaje a la doctora Mercedes Vegas, Cádiz 2010*. Cádiz: University of Cádiz.

González Ruibal, A. 2003. *La experiencia del otro, una introducción a la etnoarqueología*. Madrid: Akal.

González Ruibal, A. 2006. Experiencia, Narración, Personas: Elementos para una arqueología comprensible. *Complutum* 17, 235–246.

Guerrero Martín, J. 1988. *Alfares y alfareros de España*. Madrid: Ediciones del Serbal.

Hernando Gonzalo, A. 2005. Mujeres y Prehistoria. En torno a la cuestión del origen del Patriarcado, pp. 73–108 in Sánchez Romero, M. (ed.), *Arqueología y género*. Granada: University of Granada.

Hernando Gonzalo, A. 2007. Sexo, Género y Poder. Breve reflexión sobre algunos conceptos manejados en la Arqueología del Género. *Complutum* 18, 167–174.

Kamp, K. 2010. Entre el trabajo y el juego: perspectivas sobre la infancia en el suroeste americano. *Complutum* 21/2, 103–120.

Keith, K. 2005. Childhood Learning and the Distribution of Knowledge in Foraging Societies, pp. 27–40 in Baxter, J. E. (ed.), *Children in Action: Perspectives on the Archaeology of Childhood*. Washington D.C.: Archaeological Papers of the American Anthropological Society 15.

Lancy, D. F. 2008. *The Anthropology of Childhood: Cherubs, Chattel, Changelings*. Cambridge: Cambridge University Press.

Lemonnier, P. 1986. The study of material culture today: toward an anthropology of technical systems. *Journal of Anthropological Archaeology* 5, 147–186.

Lemonnier, P. 1990. Topsy turvy techniques. Remarks on the social representation of techniques. *Archaeological Review from Cambridge* 9/1, 27–37.

Lemonnier, P. 1992. *Elements for an anthropology of technology*. Ann Arbor. Michigan: University of Michigan Press.

Lemonnier, P. 2012. *Mundane Objects. Materiality and non- verbal communication* (UCL Institute of Archaeology Critical Cultural Heritage Series). California: Left Coast Press.

Lucy, S. 2005. The archaeology of age, pp. 43–66 in Díaz-Andreu, M., Lucy, S., Babic, S. and Edwards, D. N. (eds), *The archaeology of Identity. Approaches to gender, age, status, ethnicity and religion*. London: Routledge.

Mariné Isidro, Mª. (Coord.) 2005. *El descubrimiento de los Vetones: Los materiales del Museo Arqueológico de Madrid*. Ávila: Gran Duque de Alba Institution. Diputación Provincial de Ávila.

Mariné Isidro, Mª. and Ruiz Zapatero, G. 1988. Nuevas Investigaciones en Las Cogotas. Una aplicación del 1% Cultural. *Revista de Arqueología* 84, 46–53.

Padilla Fernández, J. J. 2011. El alfar de Las Cogotas (Cardeñosa, Ávila): Una mirada etnoarqueológica y experimental. *Arqueología y territorio. Departamento de Prehistoria y Arqueología de la Universidad de Granada* 8, 115–128.

Padilla Fernández, J. J. 2012. El proceso de producción cerámica en el alfar de Las Cogotas (Cardeñosa, Ávila): una aproximación etnoarqueológica y experimental, pp. 239–246 in Cascalheira, J. and Gonçalves, C. (eds), *Actas das IV Jornadas de Jovens em Investigação Arqueológica. JIA 2011* (Vol. II). Faro: Universidad de Faro.

Padilla Fernández, J. J. 2013. Redescubriendo el proceso productivo cerámico: La manufactura del fondo umbilicado en el alfar de Las Cogotas (Cardeñosa, Ávila), pp. 505–524 in Girón, L., Lazarich, M. and Conceiçâo Lopes, M. (coords) *Actas del I Congreso Internacional sobre Estudios Cerámicos. Homenaje a la doctora Mercedes Vegas, Cádiz 2010*. Cádiz: University of Cádiz.

Padilla Fernández, J. J. forthcoming (a). Decantation process in Las Cogotas pottery (Cardeñosa, Ávila, Spain): an Ethnoarchaeological approach, in *Minutes of the Congress of Tradicional Pottery Making from the ethnoarchaeological point of view. Scientific Research and Safeguarding of intangible Heritage*. Belgrade: National Museum of Belgrade 2011.

Padilla Fernández, J. J. forthcoming (b). Thousand-year-old knowledge pottery in Andalusia: the popular tradition as a build bridge with the past, in *proceeding of the 6th Italian Conference on Ethnoarchaeology, The intangible elements of culture in the ethnoarchaeological research*, Rome 2012.

Politis, G. 1998. Arqueología de la Infancia: Una perspectiva etnoarqueológica. *Trabajos de Prehistoria* 55/2, 5–19.

Ruiz Zapatero, G. and Álvarez Sanchís, J. R. 1995. Las Cogotas: Oppida and the Roots of Urbanism in the Spanish Meseta, pp. 209–236 in Cunliffe, B. W. and Keay, S. J. (eds), *Social Complexity and the Development of Towns in Iberia: from the copper age to the second century ad* (Proceedings of the British Academy 86). London: Oxford University Press.

Ruiz Zapatero, G. and Álvarez Sanchís, J. R. 2002. Etnicidad y Arqueología: Tras la identidad de Los Vettones. *SPAL* 11, 253–275.

Sánchez Romero, M. 2004. Children in South East of Iberian Peninsula during Bronze Age. *Ethnographisch-Archaologische Zeitschrift* 45, 377–387.

Sánchez Romero, M. 2007. Actividades de mantenimiento en la Edad del Bronce del sur peninsular: el cuidado y la socialización de individuos infantiles. *Complutum* 18,185–194.

Sánchez Romero, M. 2008. Childhood and the construction of gender identities through material culture. *International Journal of Childhood in the Past* 1, 17–37.

Sánchez Romero, M. 2010. ¡Eso no se toca! Infancia y Cultura Material en Arqueología. *Complutum* 21/2, 9–14.

Sánchez Romero, M. and Alarcón García, E. 2012. Lo que los niños nos cuentan: individuos infantiles durante la Edad del Bronce en el sur de la Península Ibérica, pp. 57–98 in Justel Vicente, D. (ed.), *Niños en la Antigüedad. Estudios sobre la infancia en el Mediterráneo antiguo*. Zaragoza: University of Zaragoza Publications.

Sempere, E. 1992. Catalogación de los hornos de España y Portugal, pp. 186–237 in *Tecnología de la cocción cerámica desde la antigüedad a nuestros días*. Alicante: Museum of pottery of Agost.

Seseña, N. 1976. *Barros y Lozas de España*. Madrid: Prensa Española and Magisterio español.

Seseña, N. 1997. *Cacharrería popular. La alfarería de basto en España*. Madrid: Alianza Editorial.

Sofaer Derevensky, J. 2000. Material culture shock: confronting expectations in the material culture of children, pp. 3–16 in Sofaer Derevensky, J. (ed.), *Children and material culture*. London: Routledge.

Yellen, J. E. 1977. *Archaeological approaches to the present: model for reconstructing the past*. New York: Academic Press.

# 7

# PLAYING WITH MUD? AN ETHNOARCHAEOLOGICAL APPROACH TO CHILDREN'S LEARNING IN KUSASI CERAMIC PRODUCTION

## Manuel Calvo Trias, Jaume García Rosselló, David Javaloyas Molina and Daniel Albero Santacreu

### INTRODUCTION

The study of technology, as an essentially social phenomenon, is not just restricted to the analysis of the materials objects are made of or to the sequence of technical actions leading to a specific aim. We understand that technological praxis, reaffirmed in everyday life as defined by Bourdieu's *habitus*,[1] plays an active role in the configuration, maintenance or subversion of social structures. Thus, the social study of the technological event constitutes a good strategy to analyse human communities.

Hence, technological learning during childhood should not be exclusively conceived as the mere transmission of a series of technical knowledge and internalised psychomotor practices, but as a process of social construction for each technological learning system which originates in a global conception of education, deeply rooted in the philosophy and structures of each community.[2] This social practice of technological knowledge transmission constitutes, in turn, a key factor in children's socialisation, as well as the configuration of a specific way of perceiving and understanding the world. In this sense, the very teaching-learning process allows boys and girls to approach the group's traditions and cultural patterns, together with the development of their social life and position. Thus, the knowledge transmission mechanisms, learning contexts and habits acquired in childhood are key factors favouring the establishment of specific norms for doing things or technological traditions, both spatially and temporally located. At the same time, they also imply the assimilation of certain structures which, when preserved in adulthood, tend to position the individual within the social praxis of the group, from which social identity and stability phenomena will eventually emerge.

In this light, the learning process is conceived as a social act rather than an individual event in a master-apprentice relationship as not only the technological *savoir faire* of the master is transmitted but also the technological knowledge of the group and, ultimately, a particular way of seeing, perceiving and being in the world.

From this perspective, this chapter will approach the analysis of children's technological learning through the threefold concept of *representation*:[3]

1. *Representation* understood as the existence of mental operations and psychomotor actions in every technological act, frequently internalised and unconscious. These mental frameworks are in the very basis of the movements, the position of the hands, etc., i.e. in every action made by the agents involved in a technological process. These unconscious mental frameworks, generated from the *technological habitus*, play a fundamental role in the transmission of technological knowledge. Quite often, this transmission is not carried out by a discursive methodology but rather by practice and repetition, where unconscious mental frameworks and their psychomotor derivations are gradually incorporated in daily practice, learning by imitating the master.

2. *Representation* interpreted as the mental models of the sequence and planning of technological action(s), including materials, tools, space for the operation, agent's position, etc. Many of these mental sequence frameworks are not specific to a technological action; they rather depend on elements from other technological processes, outlines of work distribution and organization or other social structures which are active in the learning process.

3. *Representation* regarding contents or information of an ideological, social or symbolic nature which overlap with the technological acts and the formative process originated during childhood. Such information is effective in a web of supratechnological meanings which affect the entirety of meaning and symbolic frameworks and models of the community being studied.

These different interpretations of *representation* are configured from an unconscious and internalised knowledge through the repetition of psychomotor routines and social praxis which takes place in the daily relationship between master and apprentice. It is from this same technological learning that the apprentice assimilates, both consciously and unconsciously, not only technological knowledge but also social structures and practice.

Thus, we analyse from an ethnoarchaeological perspective the learning strategies related to domestic pottery production amongst the Kusasi ethnic group in northeast Ghana. Our intention is to pay special attention, on the one hand, to learning contexts, psychomotor practices to be assimilated by the apprentices and verbal/non-verbal discourses generated in a learning context, as well as the different phases into which it is organised. On the other hand, we focus on the social dynamics regulating and participating in knowledge transmission and habit acquisition. At the same time, we analyse how the traditional learning process has been deeply transformed by the incorporation of new western customs and praxis in the Kusasi social context, particularly the introduction of formal education and schooling for children.

## STUDY CONTEXTS AND STRATEGIES

### *Study Strategy*

The Kusasi group studied in this chapter is geographically located in north-eastern Ghana (Upper East Region), in the area defined by the Upper White Volta basin to the west, the border with Togo to the east, the Gambaga escarpment to the south and the border with Burkina Faso to the north.

This geographical space is mainly inhabited by Kusasi population from the Mole-Dagbane ethnolinguistic group. However, they coexist with other groups such as the Mamprusi, almost exclusively concentrated in some cities, the Bimoba to the west or the Busanga and Mossi to the north. The Kusasi, participating in the socio-political dynamics of other groups, are organized along the territory in chiefdoms which are further divided into households. They are extended patriarchal and polygenic families which may occasionally nucleate in the same household all the landlord's children and grandchildren as well as their respective wives.[4]

The analysis of the learning processes typically deployed by the Kusasi is part of a more comprehensive project aimed at analysing the context of pottery production, exchange, use and perception in the Upper White Volta basin.[5] With this objective in mind, we designed a methodological protocol where the productive units of the pottery production areas and distribution centres particularly associated with markets were analysed, as well as pottery consumption and use patterns.

The analysis of manufacture contexts consisted of: 1) the reconstruction of *chaînes opératoires* associated to ceramic types and people; 2) the recording of the production context and *loci* using the concept of productive strategy[6] which also includes the kind of work organisation, control of production, socialisation and learning processes, the subsistence base of the group, the infrastructure needed for production and, finally, the spatial analysis of the working area, as well as the manufacture systems, and form and function of vessels.

In the present study, special interest is paid to semi-structured interviews with female apprentices and adult potters aimed at documenting the learning process, technical strategies, and related social dynamics. Furthermore, observation and audiovisual documentation strategies (photography and video) are implemented for the study of the *chaînes opératoires* of pottery production, both by adult potters and young apprentices.

Finally, a comparative analysis of the technical gestures of both potters and apprentices is carried out, as well as the study of their production, highlighting aspects such as morphometry, symmetry, final surface treatment and the remaining elements configuring the *chaînes opératoires* of pottery modelling and manufacture.

### *Ceramic Production amongst the Kusasi*

Among other elements, the learning system is highly conditioned by the production strategy adopted by the productive unit.[7] This strategy can be highly variable and contingent, ranging from models where pottery production and use contexts are located in an exclusively domestic sphere to a production mainly aimed at the commercialisation of the vessels, with productive units segregated from the domestic world and inserted into specialised production contexts. In between, there is a wide range of possibilities where the production strategy developed by Kusasi potters may be found, because although their production is carried out in an exclusively domestic context and is largely used for their own consumption, an important number of vessels are market-oriented.

Regarding pottery production, the Kusasi are the only manufacturers in this region and they distribute their vessels far from their original territory, supplying virtually all Mamprusi and Bimoba groups living to the south.[8]

Kusasi pottery is exclusively manufactured by women and characterised by the elaboration of different forms, although three are dominant: open hemispherical vessels (*la*), preferentially used for the individual consumption of food; S-shaped globular pots (*bersbika* or *yure*), mainly reserved for storing grain and other solid foodstuff; and large casks (*dunke*) to keep water and beer (*pitu*).

From a technological point of view, production is characterised by the use of untempered clays, although generally dry and wet clays are mixed to prepare the paste.[9] Broadly speaking, body modelling consists in the application of overlapping coils, making horizontal lines joined by pressing one of the ends and then the lower joining area. For firing Kusasi pottery, three different strategies are followed. The first one is defined by the presence of adobe one-chamber kilns where fuel, combustant and vessels are partially in contact. The second firing strategy takes place in built structures of a flat or semi-excavated surface where fuel, combustant and ceramic objects are in contact. And the third one consists in the reuse of large containers (*dunke*) with the base broken and placed inversely on three stones to be used as a kind of kiln for firing small and medium size vessels. In these cases, the combustant but not the fuel is in contact with the vessel.

## CHILDREN'S LEARNING IN KUSASI'S CERAMIC PRODUCTION

### *The Contextual Framework of Children's Learning*

In this study learning is not merely considered as the absorption and transmission of knowledge related to psychomotor technical practices, but rather, according to Jean Lave and Etienne Wenger, conceptualised as the process by which the apprentice, when getting into contact with a new material culture, adopts a new role in the everyday activities of the domestic group.[10] This new role also implies the establishment of a new relationship with adults, some of them now masters, thus contributing in the reconfiguration of the apprentice's position in the community.[11] In this process, the potter's apprentices, who also start to participate in other domestic chores of the group due to their age, are reconfigured as well, learning to be active and useful members in the domestic context of their community.[12] From this perspective, we can identify a close relationship between learning and the building of people's identity in the social space which the apprentice currently occupies and will occupy in the future.

Thus, pottery production learning cannot be dissociated from the other kinds of learning that the Kusasi girl follows within her own domestic group. Since birth, Kusasi's babies are carried on their mother's back while she performs the domestic chores and takes care of household members, as well as of the activities taking place outdoors such as the movement to agricultural fields or to the markets. In this way, the baby, while acquiring a notion of the surrounding world, also comes into contact with the activities performed by its mother in her daily life, including pottery production. This close mother-child relationship in a daily context continues throughout childhood, especially in the case of girls. Nevertheless, as boys and girls grow up, they gradually enjoy some freedom and, on many occasions, are looked after by their elder sisters. Anyway, infant individuals are kept in the vicinity of all the chores carried out by their mother. In this sense we consider that pottery production is not unknown.

Growing up implies the incorporation of new roles which are frequently manifested in an early participation of children in the domestic activities taking place in the household. Thus, from the age of 5–6, girls begin to take care of their younger siblings, help their mother in some domestic activities and go with her to fetch water or to agricultural fields. As they grow up, the activities in which boys and girls participate start being differentiated. While girls play a more active role assisting their mothers in domestic chores (cleaning, fetching water, helping in food preparation, participating in agricultural collection, etc.), Kusasi boys help their fathers, especially in herding and agricultural activities.

It is in this progressive inclusion of Kusasi girls into the female universe and domestic chores where, in pottery production domestic groups, the girl is gradually introduced to the learning process of this craft, as just another element of the roles she is taking in the female domestic sphere. Thus, unlike other kinds of technical learning such as metallurgy amongst the Moosi of Burkina Faso,[13] pottery production learning in Kusasi groups should not be conceived as the acquisition of a specific knowledge different from the rest of the domestic chores, but rather as the logical and gradual integration of the girl in these domestic activities. So, although pottery-making implies the acquisition of further technical knowledge as well as the establishment of new relationships between the girl and the rest of her community, this learning should be conceived as just another element in the social universe the Kusasi girl is gradually entering in to define her place.

Regarding pottery production, Kusasi girls observe that in the learning process there is a certain degree of freedom, for instance in the teaching methods selected, occasionally in the apprentice's election of master or even in the lack of interest for pottery production shown by other girls. She also understands that, even when women share the same working *loci*, they carry out this activity individually and are self-sufficient in managing the benefits from the sale of their products. Such individuality in the women of the domestic unit is also evident in food preparation or in the use of certain spaces such as bedrooms, kitchens and bathrooms.[14] So, the girl perceives that this individuality will provide her with certain freedom and independence in the future.

In these early moments, the girl also incorporates ideas like the gendered segregation of tasks or the collaboration of men and women in the different productive activities. Thus, on the one hand, children go with their mother to collect clay and, on the other; men are responsible for building the kiln with the assistance of women and to fetch firewood for firing. Similarly, men, helped by boys, build the walls and roofs of the huts which are later coated and decorated by women, who also prepare the surface. Girls also notice that, while their fathers and brothers are engaged in the care and cultivation of crops, they accompany their mothers and the other landlord's wives to collect and store the crop.

Nevertheless, aside from this general context of Kusasi children's learning, when analysing the technological learning process we should not forget that no technique can be limited to the acquisition of certain psychomotor knowledge – i.e. the mere incorporation of a technical gesture – it has to be conceived as an interaction between physical actions and their material consequences, together with the mental frameworks of a way of working learnt through tradition. This transmission of technical knowledge is based on the close interaction between master and apprentice, allowing the transmission of the physical-motor frameworks needed to develop the *savoir faire* involved in pottery modelling. It should be taken into account that this learning step lasts until the manual operations resulting from everyday practice turn almost automatic and result in a precise psychomotor programme acquired and memorized by the apprentice. It allows the identification of different phases and models in the learning process recorded for Kusasi pottery production.

## From the Game to the School: the First Contact with Mud and the Manufacture of Clay Objects

As aforementioned, the Kusasi pottery-making learning process is perfectly integrated within the domestic chores the girls perform. Actually, in the Kusasi vocabulary for pottery production there is no specific term to unambiguously designate the apprentice. It evidences a fluid and multiform concept of pottery learning closely interrelated to the rest of the roles and activities taking place in the domestic sphere in which Kusasi girls participate.

Actually, sometimes the first contact with clay and pottery modelling, except from Kusasi children's experience when they go with their mothers, takes place in a ludic context when the children are about 5–7 years old and their early psychomotor capacities are quite developed. This first playing phase ends at 11–12, when both boys and girls incorporate new roles and obligations in their domestic sphere, among them, the proper learning of pottery production.

In this ludic context, some children play with clay and make objects which reproduce, symbolise and imitate activities carried out by adults. It is therefore an imitative process lacking explicit impositions by adults both in the final result and regarding the technical processes that children automatically generate to make them. It should be highlighted that in this game both boys and girls participate, unlike in pottery production processes, although we noticed that boys and girls tend to manufacture different kinds of objects which clearly refer to activities differentiated by gender-specific roles. In this sense, we observed that in the same potter family unit in the Zuobuluk area, the girls called Fatima, Esta and Geia, aged 10, 13 and 10 respectively, modelled small toys, among others, animals such as cows and sheep but, above all, pots and cooking vessels which imitated the ceramic forms made by their mother (Fig. 7.1). However, their elder brother Isiker, aged 14, still made toys but he neither collaborated with his sisters nor did he model pots or miniatures imitating adults' pottery. In fact, he manufactured toys which reproduced the reality he was interested in, such as cows, sheep, anvils or motorcycles with riders (Fig. 7.2). We observed more cases in other productive units like the children of the Sando family in Takori. Similarly, many of the adult female potters interviewed pointed to the same kind of learning in their early childhood.

*Figure 7.1. Girl's ceramic production in the ludic stage (Pusiga).*

The ludic manufacture of clay objects reproduces some of the technical gestures and strategies implied in the pottery manufacture process children see in their domestic context. Thus, for instance, amongst the apprentices in the Zuobuluk area, some pieces such as miniature pots and bowls are modelled broadly following the *chaînes opératoires* the girls witness in their domestic environment. In some cases, the base is mould-made while in others, pinching is the technique used. Coiling is used for the body and

*Figure 7.2. Boy's ceramic production in the ludic stage (Pusiga).*

the vessels are decorated with the same motives and techniques their mothers use, particularly painting with a lighter-coloured slip. These toys are fired together with the pottery manufactured by their mothers, so the girls attentively observe the firing process. Nevertheless, this is not a phase where corrections are made, but a ludic activity which is not conditioned by the characteristics of the final object. Thus, the girls show much interest in imitating and reproducing real forms, though miniaturised, and in following some of the technical processes they observe in adults. However, they neglect other processes, especially those affecting symmetry, which demand much technical expertise, as well as the processes related to surface homogenisation, both in a primary stage and in the final treatments which result in the definite aspect of the pottery. Regarding figurative objects such as sheep and cows, technical sequences are not imitated as there is no reference to adults manufacturing this kind of artefacts, although both boys and girls use techniques frequent in pottery production such as coiling for the body and legs or fixing of appliqué and handles in the secondary modelling stage.

This first contact with clay and modelling in a ludic, free and not maternally directed or restricted context cannot be strictly considered part of the pottery-making learning process due to the participation of boys, who will not continue in the following phases of the technological learning of pottery production. However, this phase should not be regarded as a mere game either, unrelated to the acquisition of technical models or technological practice. In this sense, the game becomes an activity where children, in an unguided way, are particularly receptive to technical frameworks and gestures through their spontaneous trials and experiments during manufacture, where they follow imitative processes which incorporate not only the observation of adult technological practices but also mental duplication as well as gestural and technical memorisation processes.[15]

In this sense, toy elaboration may be considered a kind of 'proto-learning', as its execution would be impossible without the previous acquisition of certain structured technical knowledge which was previously assimilated, recorded and imitated. Thus, this ludic imitation, though spontaneous and unguided, leads to the acquisition of technical knowledge and, in turn, allows children to experiment with the possibilities of materials and tools. This lets them know how clay can be manipulated and what the options for making and modelling objects are, as well as their potential capacity to express ideas and build a social space. In this sense, the complexity of the mental and physical cognitive processes at play will be consolidated in the following and more specific phases of proper learning.

From this standpoint, the game proves to be effective time before apprentices know how to correctly model clay: it allows the girls a first approach to the sensorial characteristics of the material in its different states, an early contact with potter's tools and some praxis which are typical of adult women in this productive context. Furthermore, they learn the changes in state of clay (wet, dry, fired, etc.) and become familiar with the physical qualities of the materials before learning the other phases of pottery manufacture.

The acquisition of this knowledge at an early age favours the development of *habitus* related to the way of perceiving and conceptualising the raw materials which will accompany people during their adult life, be they potters or not, and in the later phases of learning in the cases where they dedicate themselves to pottery. Furthermore, during the game, mnemonic processes of gesture execution and sequences of technical phases are also unconsciously acquired, i.e., elemental *chaînes opératoires* are incorporated and fixed in children's long-term memory.[16] Simultaneously, the girl becomes familiar with the social spaces for pottery production (clay storage, modelling and drying areas, kiln, etc.) well before starting the proper technological learning process. Through this, she incorporates in her daily praxis and for the rest of her life frameworks of spatial-technological sequencing which will be highly important regardless of her dedication or not to pottery manufacture. In this sense, following B. Martinelli, 'Ces activités ont un portée sémantique qui prépare et conditionnne les acquisitions syntaxiques ou procedurales ulterieures'.[17]

### *Between School and Clay: Children's Learning in Ceramic Production*

When she is about 10 years old, the girl combines the game with a new phase where she participates in some pottery activities independently of whether she dedicates herself to this craft or not. These activities involve helping in clay collection – sometimes covering many kilometres to the source – fetching firewood and going with her mother to sell the production in the market many times a week. Learning these activities make the girl develop a certain concept of the landscape she lives in and of the different elements composing and articulating the space.

Previously to the current intensive children's schooling program in Ghana, the Kusasi girl used to progress in the learning of pottery making, overcoming these early phases until she modelled simple vessels first and later, as her skill improved, more complex containers. Nowadays, with the incorporation of formal education, the girl combines her school time with the rest of her activities in the domestic sphere, including pottery production. It results in a delay in the acquisition of psychomotor frameworks associated with modelling and, occasionally, a final break with pottery production learning, which will only be resumed if she marries a potter's son.

This combination of different educational praxis in children (non-formal learning of pottery production versus formal and western-like learning at school) continues until the girl finishes compulsory basic education at 12. If she remains in the domestic unit, it is at this time that the girl consolidates and fixes the whole of the psychomotor programmes needed and gradually develops potter's technical skills. However, it is also at this time that the girl separates from the pottery production learning process if she continues her senior secondary education, as it implies moving from her domestic unit to an urban centre.

During her basic education, the girl collaborates in non-specialised activities which do not demand background knowledge, such as collecting clay, water and fuel. If she is still in her father's household, towards the end of this phase or when she finishes basic education, she starts to be fully incorporated in domestic productive activities, gradually taking more responsibilities as her social position is modified. Such responsibilities will increase throughout her life and be focused in the domestic space following gender differentiation. It is in this context when she devotes more time to pottery production learning. Nevertheless, not every girl who grows up in a potter's domestic unit learns to manufacture pottery, neither do all potters learn during childhood, as only 59% of the 44 potters interviewed were trained at an early age.

When the learning process takes place during these phases, it lasts from 2 to 6 years, depending on the apprentice's perseverance, skill and receptivity to develop new motor habits and enough technical expertise to manufacture products apt for distribution and commercialisation. Broadly speaking, this phase is considered to start when the girl is about 12, coinciding with the end of her basic education. Three years later she will start to make large vessels and, at 18, she will turn into a full potter.

## FROM THE MOTHER TO THE MOTHER-IN-LAW: ADULT LEARNING AND RELEARNING

An important question related to the formation of Kusasi potters is their learning as adults. In order to contextualise this adult learning, it should be noted that Kusasi familiar groups are patriarchal and polygenic, so the married woman not only moves to her husband's house but she also has to share domestic activities and space with other women, i.e. the landlord's mother and wives.

When a new wife enters a home, she is taken under the care of the women of the household – particularly the landlord's mother, or alternatively, the landlady – and introduced to the ways and customs of the family. If the household's women are potters, the new wife may be incorporated into this craft, as well as in the rest of the domestic activities of the group. In this situation, the master re-teaches or adjusts the previous knowledge of the new wife. At the same time, when a wife knowledgeable in pottery making enters a family unit where pottery is not produced, she usually abandons the activity as it does not match the domestic praxis of the new home.

Adult learning of pottery production is a rather frequent phenomenon, verified in 41% of the potters interviewed (*n*=44). In all the cases where the new wife had previous knowledge in pottery-making, she went through a relearning process to be integrated into the ways of the new productive unit.

However, this process does not imply a radical change; it is basically an adaptation of the use of raw materials, tools, size and proportions of the pieces and decorative patterns. The latter is perhaps the most significant change because potters consider the decorative motifs to have a territorial ascription mainly associated to clans and productive units, so the wife with expertise in pottery, relocated in the new domestic space, adopts the decorative motifs of the new group. In our interviews,[18] most of the potters insisted that they knew other decorative patterns and even motifs which they could reproduce on demand, but they basically repeated the decorative patterns taught by their mothers-in-law.

This adult learning-relearning process creates specific relationships between the landlord's mother and his wife in terms of social structures, which help empower the primacy of the former over the latter. This is evident not only in the organisation of pottery production but also in the rest of the domestic activities the new wife is going to participate in.

## 'WHAT YOU LEARN IS WHAT YOU DO': REFLECTIONS ON THE TRANSMISSION OF KNOWLEDGE MODEL

Regardless of the apprentice's age, position and social status, residence or family of birth, the learning model adopted by Kusasi apprentices and masters is highly regulated. Such a model ultimately generates not only the transmission of technical knowledge, as well as associated social and familiar knowledge, but also a close bond between master and apprentice.

Kusasi learning is mainly oriented to achieve two objectives related to the technical difficulties involved in:

1. The different phases of the *chaînes opératoires*.
2. The ceramic form to be made.

Aside from these conditions which may individually prolong or shorten the learning process, pottery knowledge acquisition is rather uniform between the different productive units and organised in four broad stages:

*Stage 1:Raw material procurement, and feeding and cleaning of the kiln*
Continuing with the activities performed by the girl during her first contact with pottery production, the beginning of the learning process implies the execution of mechanical tasks where the master is helped by the apprentice, reducing the working time and at the same time evaluating the true apprentice's disposition. These activities refer to:

A. Clay extraction and transport, where she acts independently but at the direct service of the master.
B. Cleaning of the kiln and participation during the firing by providing fuel, following the instructions of the master or any other woman supervising the process.

*Stage 2: Modelling of hemispherical and globular vessels*
This stage demands a higher time investment; furthermore, it is the phase the master is more interested in. During this period, which may cover between 1 and 3–4 years, the motor habits needed for modelling are developed, together with the technical expertise crucial for the manufacture of a product in agreement with the community's aesthetic and functional cannons.

Firstly, apprentices just look and listen to the steps made and explained by the master. From this moment on, the apprentice tries to emulate the process by trial and experiment, although during the first weeks the results may not be satisfactory. As the apprentice's production is fired in the kiln, the girl learns the problems inherent to the manufacture and the need to achieve a greater technical expertise in the stages before the firing, as she can evaluate the consequences of her mistakes in the final product.

From these first steps consisting of the apprentice's own experimentation by trial and error as well as the observation and imitation of her master, specific learning based on imitation but at the same time directed and controlled by the master starts (Fig. 7.3). The two most important objectives of this learning phase refer to the materiality under study. The first one considers postural and psychomotor questions associated with the correct development of the technical gesture. The second one is linked to sensorial knowledge concerning sight, hearing and specially touch, as it provides the apprentice with information about fundamental aspects such as ductility, plasticity, humidity, consistence, kind of clay texture, etc., which the future potter has to embrace as part of her basic knowledge.

In this way, as the weeks go by, the apprentice starts to practice how to build a vessel assisted by her master, who scaffolds or corrects the steps to follow. This is a strategy that combines imitation, trial and error, and correction by the master, following a learning process based on practical or applied intelligence rather than in a discursive one,[19] as it is by means of the practical action on the matter that the teacher corrects the apprentice.

As the apprentice becomes more skilful, she gains further freedom while still being tutored by her master. On a technical level, the modelling process follows this outline:

a)  The first thing to be learnt is the modelling of the base. This step is of key importance as the entirety of Kusasi ware-making starts in the same way: modelling hemispherical

*Figure 7.3. Technical skill for burnishing in three generations of potters (Kpatia).*

bases. This process implies making a disc that is placed on an upside-down globular pot which serves as a convex mould (Fig. 7.4). It is during this process that the apprentice learns to prepare and identify the optimal characteristics of the clay. Paste preparation consisting of the mixture of dry and wet clay, the confection of the clay disc and the dusting of clay on the mould are all carried out simultaneously.

b) Secondly, the apprentice learns to manufacture hemispherical vessels (*la*). This is the first form to be made. Once the base of the future vessel is modelled, it only needs the application of a small coil around it. In this way, disregarding the decoration, the final form of the vessel is obtained.

 It should be noted that in the Kusasi learning process the apprentice is expected to make the complete vessel, like a full potter. This is one reason why modelling learning is organised according to the technical difficulty of certain profiles and sizes. It is also a kind of learning where decorative techniques are not particularly important. The effort is focused on building up the form rather than on the decorative process.

 Until the apprentice acquires enough technical skill to prove she can manufacture these bowls without help, she is not promoted to the following level. Moreover, it is only when she acquires a certain technical skill and the results are considered satisfactory by both teacher and consumers that she can start selling her products. For this reason, some apprentices do not continue their learning process and only manufacture small vessels, easier to make as they are the first forms they learn and do not demand so much practice.

 When the apprentice is skilful enough to make bowls with convex moulds, she starts improving the coil confection and application techniques for modelling large globular vessels with open mouths and S-shaped profiles. The apprentice starts to build the vessel body by making horizontal rows of coils which are later applied by inside overlapping and joined by flattening and smoothing the ends with a pod.

c) The last level of this stage is the modelling of the globular vessel's rim (Fig. 7.5). Potters specially highlight this step and differentiate it from the previous one due to three reasons: 1. the coiling technique is different to that used for the body; 2. more technical and practical skill is required, and; 3. this phase will determine the final aspect of the vessel. In other words, a complete command of the S-shaped profile and mouth symmetry is mandatory.

 This operation demands a short execution time and a few but highly complex operations. For instance, in the case of the potters in the Kpatia area, coils are placed with external overlapping over the vessel body which is previously slightly bended. The exterior surface is later smoothed with a pod and at the same time the mouth profile is curved. This operation requires high precision both for the size of the final and single coil which will form the rim as well as for the movements needed to achieve a marked S-shaped profile and a perfectly circular and symmetrical opening. Once again, in this learning system the apprentice occasionally completes this step but does not continue with the whole process.

*Stage 3: Placing the vessels in the kiln*
From her first contact with pottery, the apprentice collaborates with the firing stage in different ways. She first collects fuel, then feeds the kiln during firing and finally removes the ashes from the chamber. She also witnesses the result of her work after firing. In this stage she learns to load and unload the kiln helping her teacher and the other women of the household. The apprentice continues her formative process gradually gaining more freedom and control over her product. At this moment she learns how to position the vessels in the kiln, how to cover it, keep it warm, and avoid the fracture of the pieces or their contact.

*Stage 4: Modelling of large cask-like forms*
The last stage of the learning processes, considered by potters as the one which

*Figure 7.4. Girl learning to model a mould-made base tutored by her master (Kpatia).*

*Figure 7.5. Girl learning to model a vessel neck without assistance whilst boys play and experiment with clay (Kpatia).*

demands more expertise, is the making of large cask-like vessels with open mouths. These vessels present certain variations regarding the making of the body, with large coils spiralling over themselves and applied with internal overlapping. The most difficult part, however, is not the acquisition of new motor habits but the high skill and practice which potters need to prevent the collapse of the vessel during modelling or the cracking of the walls in the firing. In order to achieve this, the piece has to be manufactured by segments at different time intervals with a thorough control of drying conditions and the specific humidity required in each phase. For this reason, potters estimate that between 2 and 3 years are needed to master the complete process.

Summing up, this learning model, focused on the manufacture of almost complete vessels in which each phase is related to a progressively more complex specific kind of pottery, embodies the sequential development in the knowledge of the main modelling techniques. In this sense, the making of hemispherical vessels (*la*) in the first place encourages the acquisition of the technical knowledge implied in two of the basic techniques: mould-use and a first approach to coiling with the making of a single coil used to finish the rim. The following phase, the modelling of S-shaped profile vessels (*bersbika* or *yure*) improves the apprentice's knowledge of coiling. When she becomes expert enough at this technique, she is able to perform more complex variations of coiling like the *bersbika* or *yure* rims or the complete modelling of large containers (*dunke*). Although from the very beginning the learning is focused on the manufacture of finished products, the sequence the apprentice has to follow from one level to the following is directly related to the gradual acquisition of more complex technical knowledge.

## CONCLUSIONS

In this study we shed light on the complexity of the pottery production learning process amongst the Kusasi ethnic group in northeastern Ghana and the multiple interactions it involves, from the acquisition of specific psychomotor strategies which are later internalised to the incorporation of social roles, frameworks and worldviews. Furthermore, we analysed the different learning phases of pottery production as well as their connection to the different life stages of the woman and the diverse kinds of knowledge she acquires.

This perspective uncovers the wide diversity of situations generated by learning processes, a fact which greatly hampers the development of generalisation models. Therefore, the example presented here questions two essentialist associations quite widespread in archaeological and material culture research dealing with technological learning processes.

Firstly, it questions the correlation proposed between the existence of toys and their attribution to apprentices. In the Kusasi groups we study, the game cannot be always considered the first stage of learning; in the case of boys, as well as in some girls, their participation in modelling clay never implies the beginning of proper pottery production learning. This 'proto-learning' phase, however, is important for the girls who will become apprentices in the future, but the two processes should be accordingly differentiated. So, the existence of toys imitating craft products does not necessarily imply the presence of apprentices. Furthermore, many aspects are still unknown, such as the implications of this ludic phase for those individuals who, despite not devoting themselves to pottery making, possess a specific and peculiar perspective of the pottery universe due to their contact with this material during childhood.

Secondly, our study case also proves that learning, for the most part, does not necessarily take part at an early age. Many Kusasi potters learn the craft as adults, when they move to a new pottery production unit after marrying.

From our perspective, what is particularly relevant is that, together with the technical aspects, for both children and adults these learning processes comprise a large baggage of knowledge. This knowledge is part of the daily praxis conforming the ways of living in the world and behaving within socially accepted norms: two essential elements for building up the different social identities at play. In our example, we discussed how pottery-making learning processes are closely related to important social and identity aspects such as gender construction and social organisation in the familiar sphere, independently of the individual's eventual dedication or not to this craft.

Thus, we observed that former apprentices continue resorting to their previous knowledge of pottery production after marrying, not only to adapt to the new technical patterns deployed by the women in their husband's household with whom they start a new life, but also to incorporate specific family and social relationship patterns in their new social nucleus.

Summing up, pottery production learning plays an important role in children's socialisation processes as well as in adult women's adaptation to their married life. We discussed how the learning processes revealed in this study are deeply rooted in family daily practice and are constantly acquired and reconfigured as the woman finds and generates her specific place within the household. For this reason, learning should be conceived as a process under permanent construction through which traditions and family cultural patterns are integrated and which entail a constant readjustment according to the social position of the apprentice during childhood, youth and adulthood. Consequently, the learning of technological processes has to be understood as a key strategy amongst all the social relations guiding the individual integration to the social group as his/her own reality is being transformed and readjusted.

Notes

1   Bourdieu 1991, 1997
2   Martinelli 1996
3   Lemonnier 1992
4   Calvo *et al.* 2013
5   Archaeology in the Upper White Volta basin. Northeast of Ghana. Ministerio de Cultura, Spain SGIPCE/AM/cmm (Archaeology Abroad Projects 2010 and 2011)
6   García Rosselló 2008
7   García Rosselló 2009; Vidal and García Rosselló 2009

8   Calvo *et al.* 2011
9   Occasionally, as in the case of Takori potters, another strategy for preparing the recipe is used: mixing clays from different veins
10   Lave and Wenger 1991
11   Ingold 2000
12   Vidal and García Rosselló 2009
13   Martinelli 1996
14   Calvo *et al.* 2013
15   Martinelli 1996
16   Leroi-Gourhan 1965
17   Martinelli 1996, 28: 'These activities embody a semantic significance which facilitates and conditions subsequent syntactic or procedural acquisitions'
18   The potters interviewed are Akuika Sando, Apam Sando, Agaro Sando, Awinma Dabour, Abanja, Ama Abugri and Sheaitu Asugbila
19   Ingold 1990; Cornu 1991

## REFERENCES

Bourdieu, P. 1991. *El sentido práctico* (reprint of 1980 edition). Madrid: Taurus.
Bourdieu, P. 1997. *Razones prácticas sobre la teoría de la acción.* Barcelona: Anagrama.
Calvo, M., Gavua, K., García Rosselló, J., Javaloyas, D. and Albero, D. 2011. Social approaches in pottery distribution networks: the case of Upper East Ghana. *The Old Potter's Almanack* 16 (2), 13–7.
Calvo, M., Fornés, J., García Rosselló, J., Javaloyas, D. and Sastre, M. 2013. Houses and Society. An Ethnoarchaeological Study of the Mamprusi's Houses (Bende, Northeast Ghana), pp. 31–5 in Lugli Assunta, F., Stoppiello, A. and Biagetti, S. (eds), *Ethnoarchaeology: Current Research and Field Methods* Conference Proceedings, Rome, Italy, 13th–14th May 2010 (BAR International Series 2472). Oxford: Archaeopress.
Cornu, R. 1991. Voire y savoire, pp. 83–100 in Chevallier, D. (ed.) *Savoir et pouvoir transmettre.* Paris: Editions de la Maison des Sciences de l'Homme.
García Rosselló, J. 2008. *Etnoarqueología de la producción cerámica: Identidad y territorio en los valles centrales de Chile.* (Mayurqa 32), Mallorca: Universitat de les Illes Balears.
García Rosselló, J. 2009. Cadena operativa, forma, función y materias primas. Un aporte a través de la producción cerámica Mapuche. *Relaciones de la Sociedad Argentina de Antropología* 29.
Ingold, T. 1990. Society and nature and the concept of technology. *Archaeological Review from Cambridge* 9 (1), 5–17.
Ingold, T. 2000. *The perception of the environment: essays on livelihood, dwelling and skill.* London: Routledge.
Lave, J. and Wenger, E. 1991. *Situated Learning: Legitimate Peripheral Participation.* Cambridge: Cambridge University Press.
Lemonnier, P. 1992. *Elements for an anthropology of technology.* Michigan: University of Michigan, Museum of Anthropology.
Leroi-Gourhan, A. 1965. *La geste et la Parole: La mémoire et les Rythmes.* Paruis: A. Michel.
Martinelli, B. 1996. Sous le regard de l'apreni. Paliers de savoir et d'insertions chez les forgerons Moose du Yatenga (Burkina Faso). *Techniques et culture* 28, 9–47.
Vidal, A. and García Rosselló, J. 2009. 'Díme cómo lo haces': una visión etnoarqueológica de las estrategias de aprendizaje de alfarería tradicional. *Arqueoweb* 12.

# 8

# INFANTILE INDIVIDUALS: THE GREAT FORGOTTEN OF ANCIENT MINING AND METALLURGICAL PRODUCTION[1]

## Luis Arboledas Martínez and Eva Alarcón García

## THE GREAT FORGOTTEN

Oversight, insensibility and indifference are some of the adjectives we could use to define the historiographic treatment of childhood and the implication of children throughout history.[2] If we unite childhood, or in this case, children (both boys and girls) and metallurgical production in antiquity, this ignorance is even greater, being an almost non-existent subject, appearing in very few, short references, remarks or notes found in different reports belonging to mining companies.

The production of metallic objects has been considered as one of the most complex technological activities carried out by humans. Recognized as one of the most important technological activities, metallurgy has had great relevance and influence on the social-economic development of past societies, being directly related to the increase of social complexity, guided by a specific technology and production methods filled with novelties. Like other productive activities of great influence, metallurgy has been considered by most as entirely masculine, leaving out both woman and children.[3]

When studying this subject there is a clear evolution, beginning with works that exclusively described the geological and technological aspects of metallurgy,[4] continuing with those focused on the study of the development of social complexity, based on the control of metallurgical production and trade of copper and bronze,[5] to end up with those works that consider the significance of metallic objects as key expressions of asymmetric relations of gender and age, the basis of the differential exercise of power.[6]

The technical examination that has been the main focus of scientific production relative to mining and metallurgical production has set aside another set of variables that determines its operative chain. We understand that, in the same way as any other social process or cultural phenomenon, the production of metallic objects implies negotiation, ideology and manipulation of human and material resources. Its analysis, without any doubts, will allow us to fill the existing void between technical phenomenon, and the social and cultural implications that were essential for its development.[7]

This change in the paradigm in the archaeological discipline has come hand in hand with new theoretical positions. Post-processualism, linked with the rise of feminist movements and combined with studies of women and relations between gender and age in social and technological contexts, has been able to enhance the analysis of the whole set of factors (*Chaine Operatoire*) that are part of this manufacture (social, cultural, as well as fiscal and technical), while focusing on the social agents as leading actors in the development and changes in a technological process. Thanks to this, we have been able to start understanding material culture as the direct product of social action and interaction among individuals and their contexts.

In spite of these epistemological changes, the analysis of age groups in productive and technological processes has found many other obstacles. Starting in the 19th century, occidental society has suffered obscurantism due to the changes in attitude related to the growing social conscience over the exploitation of child labour. This feeling led to the idea that children must learn and play and not work; idyllic conscience, since this did not occur in mining production, though it did help in forgetting the role played by children in mining since remote times. Due to this, children were disconnected from this kind of labour and the spaces where they had been participating throughout history, nullifying their consideration as an active part of this process and their actual situation.[8]

In this work our objective is to highlight a reality that, for sure, can be tracked back more than 4000 years, the active role that children played in the exploitation of mines and metallurgical production. Among other questions we will try to respond to the following throughout this chapter: what role did children play in mining production? What uses, spaces and social differences existed? What were the costs and sacrifices? To be able to give an answer to these and other questions we will analyze the category of age and childhood through archaeological, ethnographic, and written evidence (texts and epigraphy). We will also refer to modern societies where mining is the day to day lifestyle of thousands of children, being the only social reality that they have access to.

## REAL SCENARIOS

The introduction of metalwork, especially during recent prehistory, not only meant a technological innovation, which obviously influenced the development of daily life in prehistoric societies, but also most probably changed the previous social structures where woman and children were included.[9] Authors such as J. Robb or S. J. Shennan defend that this technological change only benefitted men, while worsening even more the inequality between members of these social groups.[10] Nonetheless, we believe that some woman or children, is it individually or as social groups, benefited from this situation, reaffirming their identity in terms of wealth or social status, proven in the rich metallic grave goods of many burials belonging to children found in the South of Spain.[11] This leads us to believe that the appropriation on behalf of a few members of the productive process or the final product does not affect the rest of the society in terms of gender or age, but in terms of status, power and hierarchy. Due to this we consider that the advance of technology produced by daily experience in creating metallic objects or by using them, cannot be related exclusively to the experience and practice on behalf of part of the population: men;[12] this is especially true since there are no objective, scientific or empiric reasons that specify the exclusion of the social groups of gender or age in this particular technological process of past societies, which is nowadays an obvious reality.

## Archaeological Sources

All the actions that take place during the process of metallurgical technology in the past have left evidence in the archaeological record. Tracking this evidence is not easy; nevertheless, archaeology has four basic analytical principles that allow us to come closer to the structures and internal experiences of the mining-metallurgical technological process: time, space, objects and bodies.

The analysis of these four variables gives us hints that allow is to believe that since the beginning, children participated in the operative chain for the creation of metal. To argue this idea we will centre on the Bronze Age metallurgical settlement of Peñalosa (Baños de la Encina, Jaén, Spain). In this site, the metallurgical process is integrated in the domestic units made up of human groups with blood ties or affinities, be it family cores or not, but whose ties are established and reinforced through daily life.[13] This perfect interrelation is an important fact that allows us to analyze how it is articulated, how it develops, how it is negotiated and how work is distributed among different members of the community, reaching the conclusion that, on the contrary to the preceding period (Copper Age), during the Bronze Age, metallurgy had turned in to a common daily task, immersed in the set of social relations, and directly related to the learning and socialization processes of children.[14]

We find similarities, taking into account the spatial and temporal differences, in a Nigerian society at the end of the 19th century where iron mining was the core of the social structure, supported by a daily subsistent agriculture. In this case, as could have occurred in the daily life of Peñalosa, all the members of the group, men, woman and children, played active roles in different phases of this technological process (from smelting to the forging of iron). This makes them all participants of the same spatial concepts and social strategies. Children are introduced as active workers at the age of five or six, carrying out the same tasks as adults, sharing spaces and instruments initially thought for adults.[15] In this particular case study we observe how the learning and socialization processes of children are entwined in a cohesive social strategy: work, encouraged from the adult world.

Logically, we cannot, and should not extrapolate ethnographic evidence to the past; nevertheless, it does allow us to take in to account possible correlations of activity patterns and social behaviours. In our study of the children's role in recent prehistoric metallurgy and mining we have found many obstacles due to the nature of the archaeological record: the conservation of juvenile bones and the determination of the activity patterns of members of young age. In spite of the biased information we do count with findings (objects and bodies) that allow us to argue for the active participation of children in both the extraction of mineral (inner mining) and its processing (exterior mining). To understand this we can refer to the Neolithic mining of black flint in Strepy (Belgium) where the remains of a child ranging in age from four to five next to an adult, and accompanied by a dog and a pick made from a deer antler were found. These cases, and another finding of the remains of an adult individual in anatomic position with a pick in his right hand found at the Belgian flint mine of Orenburg, are the only surviving examples for this period of European recent prehistory, and have been interpreted as fatal accidents occurring inside the mine. The most probable cause of this accident, as happens throughout the history of mining, is due to unfortunate collapses inside the mines.[16] The remaining human remains found at different European mines, such as the variscite mines of Can Tintorer in Gavà[17] or the copper mines in the Sierra del Áramo,[18] have been related to burials or primary graves in extraction areas that have already been totally exploited.[19]

If we advance in history, reaching Roman times, and concentrate on a gallery located in the Northern Vein at the mines of Riotinto (Huelva, Spain), different human remains (skulls) belonging to two possible young individuals, of approximately age ten, have been found. In close proximity, in a small gallery different mining instruments used for opening galleries and the extraction of minerals were found (Fig. 8.1). These instruments

*Figure 8.1 Tools and juvenile skull fragments found in a gallery at Filón Norte de Riotinto (Museo Minero de Riotinto, photographer: Aquilino Delgado Domínguez).*

were a double pick, a pick and a pick-axe. The pick-axe has some interesting particular characteristics. Its size and weight are considerably less than the other two picks, and it does not reach 400 grams in weight and 16 centimetres in length. If we connect both findings we can think that at least this singular instrument was used by one of the juvenile individuals, who worked side by side with adults in the interior galleries at the Northern Vein, and therefore, directly building and influencing the immediate natural and physical space of these individuals. Furthermore, the implications in the development of specific interior mining tasks could be even greater. We believe that due to the physical characteristics of these spaces (galleries) and the size of ten year olds, in many instances children would be in charge of opening new galleries. These tasks have been recorded in mining reports later in history in mines in the South of Spain (reports from 1873 of the mining company of Riotinto), in the United Kingdom (Victorian period) or in Australia (the mining site at Dolly's Creek to the West of Melbourne).[20]

Other mining objects/instruments that could belong to children from ancient times have reached us thanks to the environmental circumstances of mines that have allowed good conditions of preservation. We refer to the baskets made of organic materials destined to carry and transport minerals and water in and out of the mine, and would most possibly be carried by children or teenagers. In Spain we count some examples that, due to their size (volume and dimensions), adjust to the size of children of young age (approximately around ten). The dimensions of these objects vary from around 23–29 cm in height by 23–27 cm in diameter,[21] perfectly adjusting to the size of children. The use of these objects has been evidenced at the mine of La Fortuna (Mazarrón, Spain) where a basket filled with mineral was found ready to be transported outside the mine. What is interesting about this find is that very close to the basket two wooden tablets with inscription were located with the names *M. MINVF* (') and *L. MINVTI,* that probably, as suggested by G. Gossé, belong to father and son. These inscriptions have been interpreted as identifiers of the names of two miners (father and son) that were tied to the baskets used for transporting mineral. The objective of this system would be that once the worker exited the mine with the minerals, their cargo could be identified thus receiving the corresponding salary.[22]

The analysis of both the spaces, objects and bodies is very important for the study of social and labour relations not only in mining and metallurgical production, but also for studying any other technology in prehistory. In our case, the existence of small galleries and reduced spaces, very frequent in ancient mines, has been taken into account as a revealing and indicative piece of evidence for child labour, since the size of children makes them the only ones that can freely move around and work in these spaces. This fact has been pointed out in many occasions by 19th and 20th century mine engineers when they discovered ancient galleries while mining during the industrial era. As an example, the mining engineer C. Caride when describing an ancient gallery found at the mine of La Loba, Cartagena, indicated that '… through them no one but children could be able to move around with baskets filled with mineral, they would move upward, out of the mine, inclined and with their hands on the sides of the galleries, which seem polished mirrors due to the continuous contact'.[23] This text illustrates the dimensions of these galleries and the exploitation of labour and contemporary conditions. Examples of ancient subterranean labour have been documented in most mining areas of the Iberian Peninsula such as the Northern Vein at Rio Tinto[24] or the mines of El Centenillo or Cartagena.[25]

Obviously the dimensions of the galleries are not irrefutable proof or definitive evidence of the work and the spaces occupied by children in ancient mining. Nevertheless, there are reasons to suspect that due to the technical conditions of ancient subterranean mining, with reduced and tortuous spaces, next to the physical conditions and stature, young children would surely participate in mining activities. In many instances they would be in charge of initially opening new galleries, as well as the exploitation and transport of minerals in small, reduced areas.

Nevertheless, we must be careful when we create and accept the connection between child labour and the conditions of the extractive techniques in mines (small spaces). But, this relation is possible if we consider that children have been used in mining in other historical periods for transporting mineral, due to their skills and abilities, independently of the size of the galleries. Their involvement in this task, as well as in other side-tasks would be determined by the need for a cheaper labour force, thus concentrating adults in, presumably, more burdensome tasks. We also have take into account the socioeconomic factors of family life, which we will consider further in this chapter.

The association between adult and children's bodies, and the possible link to specific objects/instruments and mining spaces indicates the implications and the development of child labour in these tough and dangerous activities in ancient times. Children not only shared the same existence as adults, but they also were leading actors in many of the tasks that had to be carried out during the mining process, having been recognized both by mining companies and the rest of the workers, a fact proved by their direct inclusion in old mining records.

## WRITTEN SOURCES

The archaeological data is completed and corroborated by other evidence and precise information that mainly comes from written sources, classic authors and epigraphy. Normally, most authors refer to slaves, free workers (*mercenarii*) and *damnati ad metalla* and almost never make any distinction between gender and age. Texts sources are very scarce in mining and metallurgical references, and are even scarcer when trying to locate information about the age group we are trying to study. Nonetheless, a text survives belonging to the Greek historian and geographer Agatharchides de Cnido, who carried out his studies and investigations in Alexandria under the reigns of Ptolomy VI and Ptolomy VIII. In Book V (24–29) he carefully describes how the gold mines of the Nubian Desert were exploited and what kind of workers were used. This description was recorded afterwards, during the, 1st century AD by Diodorus Siculus in his *Bibliotheca Historica*.[26]

Agatharchides of Cnidus narrates:

> Young boys, who go down through the galleries to the areas of rock that have been excavated, laboriously pick up the rock that is being dug out bit by bit and carry it outside to a place near the entrance. Men over thirty years of age, take it from them, and pound a fixed amount of the quarried rock on stone mortars with iron pestles until they reduce it to the size of a vetch seed. The women and older men receive from them the seed sized rock and cast it into stone mills, several of which stand in a line; and standing beside them, two or three to a handle, they grind it until they reduce the portion given them to a flour-like state. Since there is general neglect of their bodies and they have no garment to cover their shame, it is impossible for an observer to not pity the wretches because of the extremity of their suffering. For they meet with no respite at all, not the sick, the injured, the aged, not a woman by reason of her weakness, but all are compelled by blows to strive at their tasks until, exhausted by the abuse they have suffered, they die in their miseries. For this reason the poor wretches think that the future always will be more fearful than the present because of the extreme severity of their punishment, and they consider death more desirable than life.[27]

While Diodorus Siculus states:

> The boys there who have not yet come to maturity, entering through the tunnels into the galleries formed by the removal of the rock, laboriously gather up the rock as it is cast down piece by piece and carry it out into the open to the place outside the entrance. Then those who are above thirty years of age take this quarried stone from them and with iron pestles pound a specified amount of it in stone mortars, until they have worked it down to the size of a vetch. There upon the women and older men receive from them the rock of this size and cast it into mills of which a number stand there in a row, and taking their places in groups of two or three at the spoke or handle of each mill the grind it until they have worked down the amount given them to the consistency of the finest flour. And since no opportunity is afforded any of them to care for his body and they have no garment to cover their shame, no man can look upon the unfortunate wretches without feeling pity for them because of the exceeding hardships they suffer. For no leniency or respite of any kind is given to any man who is sick, or maimed or aged, or in the case of a woman for her weakness, but all without exception are compelled by blows to persevere in their labours, until through ill-treatment they die in the midst of their tortures. Consequently the poor unfortunates believe, because their punishment is so excessively severe, that the future will always be more terrible than the present and therefore look forward to death as more to be desired than life.[28]

Both what Agatharchides and Diodorus described about the people who worked at these royal mines (during the reign of Ptolomy VIII) represents an exception in classic historiography. This is mainly because of the desire to explain reality, which at some moments is very harsh, posing the different daily tasks of the different groups of gender and age who worked at the Nubian gold mines. Agatharchides and Diodorus indicate the difference between workers is based on age and sex, though Agatharchides description is more detailed. In his case he does not follow a hierarchical description of labour, but rather follows the criteria of age, children being his first category.[29]

In their descriptions, both authors also explain the differences between specialized and non-specialized workers who carried out different tasks.[30] They refer to the existence of specialized workers, or foremen, who would be in charge of organizing the mining process, and soldiers/guards, possibly mercenaries, because they speak a different language, which would be in charge of controlling and overseeing how the slaves worked in these areas far from political centres. They also refer to young and energetic workers who opened new galleries and extracted minerals, under the watch of the soldiers, minerals that would subsequently be transported out of the mine by children, to finally be processed and ground by women and older people.

Both authors also briefly describe the operative chain with the specific functions for each age and gender group. First of all, children would be in charge of picking up the extracted mineral and then transporting it through the galleries out of the mine (Fig. 8.2). These children, who had not reached puberty, would be children of the condemned (slaves), whose families had to accompany them by royal mandate. The use of children in tasks according to their age is a reality in mining history, from antiquity to modern times, a fact that is also corroborated by archaeology (as we have already mentioned), epigraphy and modern information. Children, like older or sick people, carried out different tasks according to their strength, as did women, referred to by Diodorus.

Though both texts confirm the presence of children and women in ancient mining and metallurgy, these categories of age and sex must have been significantly smaller (physically) than men in perfect conditions, but would be very representative and meaningful.

*Figure 8.2. Reconstruction of a child working inside a gallery in the Museo Minero de Riotinto (Museo Minero de Riotinto, photographer: Aquilino Delgado Domínguez).*

## Epigraphic Sources

The epigraphic testimonies follow the same characteristics and present the same problems as archaeological evidence and textual sources.[31] In the Lex *Metalli Vipascensis*, two bronze plaques found in Aljustrel (Portugal), the third chapter of the first plaque legislates and regulates the use of the baths in this mining-metallurgical centre,[32] exempting children, soldiers, free people, and imperial slaves from having to pay for entrance. The presence of children in this legislation proves the existence of this age group in mining and metallurgical centers, being accepted and recognized as a group who, accompanied or not by their families, would share the same public and private spaces as adults. In the same sense, the wax boards of *Alburnus Maior*, Dacia (Rosa Montanta, Rumania),[33] proves the presence of children in the silver and gold mines in this area. The text indicates the cost of workers where a slave girl of age six costs around 205 denarius, while a slave teenager would cost around 600.[34] This proves the interest of workers based on the categories of sex and age due to the costs, rather than social or economical status of children.

The funerary stela dating from the early empire found near the mine of Polígono (Baños de la Encina, Jaén, España) is even more difficult to interpret. This stelae represents a four year old slave or freed boy named *Q(v)artvlvs* or *Q(vintvs) Artvlvs*, depending on different authors,[35] dressed with a short *sagum* above the knees, barefoot and carrying a pick-hammer and a basket (Fig. 8.3). The interpretation varies depending on the authors - for some,[36] this is a representation of the son of a miner. For others,[37] the objects that he is carrying are not necessarily related to this profession, on the other hand they could be symbols with a special signification, or that represent a community, like the eleven decorated children's tombstones found in

*Figure 8.3. Funerary stelae of Q(v)artvlvs o Q(vintvs) Artvlvs, Baños de la Encina, Jaén, España.*

the Upper Guadalquivir. This would mean that it would not be related to the mining world or its meaning.[38]

Recently, A. Giardina has proposed a new epigraphic interpretation, based on the size, the age of the child and the strange abbreviation of *annoru(m) (an[n]orv[m] IIII)*, which does not have any parallels in the Iberian Peninsula. This author argues that the person who made this figure made a mistake in the interpunctuation between *annorum* and the numeral, and should be read as: *Q(v)artvlvs an[n]or[um] VIIII si[t]/[tibi terr]a le[vis]* (Quartulo age nine). This interpretation would correct the discordance between the inscription and the figure, being more coherent and closer to the age of children related to mining in roman Hispania and in modern times in the rest of Europe at the end of the 19th century.[39] If we accept this theory we would have a representation of a nine year old (and not four) miner recognized as a professional, and directly or indirectly related to the mines of the eastern area of Sierra Morena.

Among the 57 miners related to the mining census of C. Domergue for Roman Hispania,[40] we only know the age of death of 22 workers. Among these 22 individuals only three were children, one slave and two free: *Tonginus* who died at the age of 10 (Andiñuela, León), and *Modestianus* (Aljustrel, Portugal) and *T. Boutius* (Três Minas, Portugal) who died at the age of 10 and 11. Though, based on these numbers, we are lead to believe that the presence of children in mines would be scarce, though if globally observed, we can also say that their presence is completely normalized, assumed and accepted, as in modern Europe (in the North of England, France, the South of the Iberian Peninsula, the Linares-Baeza district, etc.). Their presence is so normalized that during the 19th and 20th centuries specific laws regulating children working in mines were passed in different countries. As an example, the Spanish 'Benot law' (July 24th 1873) established that children could work in mines and auxiliary factories at the age of 10.[41]

## High Costs for Small Individuals

Based on the information that we have analyzed we can reach a first, irrefutable, conclusion. Children played an important role in interior and exterior mining, carrying out different tasks that were initially believed to be for adults, and also shared the same social spheres and working places, and, above all, they were socially recognized and economically rewarded for their work.

The second observation that we can make is that there is a specific age range for working in mines that goes from Roman times to modern times or at least is a bridge between childhood and adulthood. This age range would be between eight and eleven. Nevertheless it is true that the use of illegal child labour was a normal practice during the 19th and 20th centuries. An example can be found during the Victorian era in the United Kingdom or in actual reports belonging to the International Labour Organization explicitly accusing the use of child labour of boys and girls of very young ages (from four years of age onward) in mines in Ghana, Nigeria, Peru, and the United Republic of Tanzania.[42] This situation of non protection and child labour is due to lack of control and the difficulty in determining the age of the exploited children.[43]

But, why were – and are – children implicated so quickly in the mining process? Have they lost their childhood? Or is it a socialization mechanism (socialization or exploitation?). To be able to respond to these questions we must understand the implication of children in mining and metallurgical tasks both in ancient times and in recent societies and the factors that determine their inclusion in mines and metal production (social and economical factors).

From the 19th century onward, in industrialized counties, children entered the mining labour market due to the economic necessities of their families (Fig. 8.4). On occasion, as happened in the southeast of the Iberian Peninsula (Murcia and Alicante) at the end of the 19th century, the premature death of fathers, leaving widows with many children, obliged these children to work in hard and dangerous conditions, putting at risk their health and physical development. On other occasions, low family incomes made children want to start working in mines to help their families.[44]

Without wanting to extrapolate this situation to preindustrial societies of the past, family needs have also been observed in Roman times, during the 2nd century AD., even though it was a slave society. This can be observed in the reference belonging to the 10th tablet of the *Alburnius Maior*, where the salary belonging to an adult miner actually is the sum of both his and of his sons' salaries.[45] In prehistoric times, for example during the Bronze Age in the Iberian Peninsula, the presence of children in the mining an metallurgical process is also assured, and, as in other moments of history,

*Figure 8.4. La Culebrina mine, late 19th century (El Centenillo, Jaén, España), print of family groups at the mine. Colectivo Arrayanes.*

it would serve as a way of learning and acquiring the skills necessary for mining and metallurgy, therefore, continuing this technology.

Among other causes we can put forward the mining companies' need of a cheap labour force to carry out minor and auxiliary tasks, especially in places where adults could not enter. Child labour, as signalled by classic sources and modern mining reports, was mainly linked to picking up and transporting the ore, carrying it to the foundry or doing other tasks depending on their physical condition (such as ore classification, grinding, etc.).[46] The working conditions in both areas are obviously very different from different points of view: when referring to health and physical effort, and when referring to labour efficiency.

Nevertheless, how did their early involvement in mining affect their lives? The first, direct, consequence was the loss of their childhood, understanding childhood as the vital period characterized by the acquisition of knowledge and the development of skills, united to the assuming of a system of beliefs that will forge the personality and identity of each individual. To be able to determine the characteristics that define childhood, and therefore the category of age, in the past is very difficult, as also occurs with gender, since both depend on the culture and the internal structures of each society. In this chapter we have been able to observe how there are no sources that evidence the learning phases and games that should correspond to childhood. In our case we believe their full categorization as working social subjects completely immersed in the work of metal.

Throughout this chapter we have been able to compare how different sources establish an age, at around ten, as an inflexion point in the life of children, becoming active members of mining and metallurgical activities. A great example is the testimony of an eight year old Victorian child, James Sanderson, who stated: 'I work in the new pit (Messrs Houldsworth's). I am a trapper [opens and shuts doors for coal wagons to pass], I like it very well. I sit in the dark all day, or I run to the bottom of the pit and come back. I am used well; I take my dinner with me, and have my dinner when I like. I don't know how long I have been in the pit. I go to Sunday-school every Sunday. (He could make out some letters, but could not read and scarcely knew anything)'.[47]

The worst consequence was his physical wellbeing. For most children who are growing and physiologically developing, their inclusion in extractive mining activities, and all the consequences it entails, provokes illness such as rickets or infections. This health deterioration entailed the growth of child mortality due to mining accidents, insalubrious conditions and a poor diet.

There is no doubt that the life and labour conditions of miners throughout history have been very arduous and difficult. Text sources,[48] epigraphy and archaeology prove that mining would be characterized by long working shifts, poor diet, humidity, insalubrities, high physical decay and would be extremely dangerous, which all together create a short lifespan and high mortality. In Roman Hispania, of the 22 funerary gravestones belonging to mining areas in C. Domergue's census gives us an average age of death at 30, where 40 was the average in Northern Europe during this same period.[49] But, we must take in to account that we cannot assume that all the people that appear in the inscriptions were miners and that only the richest ones could afford to make a gravestone. Therefore, this average would actually indicate the average age of people who lived in mining areas, but were not necessarily miners.[50]

What is a reality is that both exterior and interior mining exposed miners to extreme conditions of insalubrity, favouring dangerous illnesses, a fact that seems more marginal and contemporary, but has existed since the beginning of mining and metallurgy, environmental contamination being a direct or indirect consequence of the health conditions of these human groups.[51] For example, poor illumination was capable of producing an incapacitating illness such as *nystagmus* (vulgarly 'deer's eye') that produces partial or total blindness. Another common illness is lung infection or saturnism, very extended among lead miners. People who are affected by saturnism have gastrointestinal problems (already referred to by Plinio and Hippocrates), anemia, renal disorders, polyneuritis, and problems in the nervous system, muscular injuries, etc.[52] Beside these illnesses, bone fractures and muscular injuries were very common. Because of this, the study of the remains found in the galleries of ancient mines and necropolis close to mining areas, such as Riotinto or Cartagena, can provide interesting results in respect of illnesses, diets, etc.

The study of health and environment nowadays is one of the main focuses of the International Labour Organization, which warns that in many mining areas boys and girls are exposing themselves to dangerous terrain, earth and rock collapses, mercury contamination, and sharp rock shards on which children frequently walk barefooted.[53]

FINAL THOUGHTS

The different sources demonstrate that children were leading actors and active agents, recognized transversally through time and space in the mining and metallurgical sphere. Some even prove that their role and social value overstepped the adult sphere. Children would work both in extracting and transporting ore in areas inaccessible to adults, as well as in secondary industries that depend on mining (such as carpentry, blacksmithing, coal production, etc.). They would frequently supplement adult work, but often they would be the only actors and directly responsible for their work.

There is no context where the relations between work and socialization are easily distinguished since both the categories of age and gender are culturally influenced.[54] Nevertheless, in our investigation we have observed how children are directly introduced into adulthood through work, living and sharing the same reality. This reaches a point where in many cases we can observe how children are recognized as active working adults, being parted from their age category and all it supposes. In this way, part of their life is taken from them, incorporated directly to adulthood without going through the intermediate stages defined as part of childhood. This is why one of our objectives is to prove the economic contribution that children had in their social sphere and the high costs they suffered.

In metal production the relations between child labour and socialization processes are so interconnected that it is almost impossible to distinguish one from the other since the significance of the work oversteps the sphere of socialization.

NOTES

1    This work is included in the framework of the Research Project: *La minería romana en Sierra Morena oriental: formas de estructuración de un territorio a partir de la producción, consumo y distribución de metales*. (2012–2017). Junta de Andalucía
2    Baxter 2005; Sánchez Romero 2010; Kamp 2010
3    Alarcón García and Sánchez Romero 2010
4    Childe 1944
5    Kristiansen 1984; Shennan 1986; Tylecote 1987; Mohen 1989
6    Gilman 1981; Sofaer Derevenski 1999, 389
7    González Ruibal 2003
8    Cunningham 1995; Baxter 2005, 65; Wileman 2005, 55; Lancy 2008; Nájera *et al.* 2010
9    Sánchez Romero and Moreno 2005
10    Robb 1994; Shennan 1993
11    Sánchez Romero and Alarcón García 2012
12    Sánchez Romero and Moreno 2005
13    Sanahuja 2007, 48
14    Alarcón García 2010; Kamp 2010
15    Bellamy 1904, 101–102
16    Shepherd 1980, 103
17    Villalba 2000
18    Blas Cortina, 1996; 1998
19    Shepherd 1980, 103; Villalba 2000, 70
20    Lawrence 1998
21    Domergue 1990, 442
22    Gossé 1942, 53
23    Caride 1978, 32
24    Pérez *et al.* 1996
25    Caride 1978
26    Diodorus B. H. III, 12–14; Sánchez León 2000
27    Agatárquides De Cnido V, 26 Trans. and ed. Stanley M. Burstein, 1989
28    Diodorus, D. S., III, 13, trad. Oldfather, 1953: 115–121
29    Diodorus, D. S., III, 13; Aga. V. 26; Sánchez León 2000, 180–181
30    Diodorus, D. S., III, 13; Aga. V. 26
31    Diodorus, D. S., III, 12–13; Aga. V. 24–29
32    Domergue 1983; Mangas y Orejas 1999, 316
33    CIL, III, I–XXV
34    Mangas y Orejas 1999, 289
35    CIL, II, 3.258; CIL, III, 214: 238
36    Pastor *et al.*, 1981; Arboledas 2009
37    González and Mangas 1991, 238
38    Mangas 1994, 376–378
39    Giardina 2000, 416
40    Domergue 1990, 339–340
41    C.L.M., II, 80–81
42    Alarcón García and Sánchez Romero 2010
43    Pérez de Perceval and Sánchez Picón 2005
44    Martínez Carrión 2005, 201–202
45    CIL. III, X; Mzorek 1989, 169
46    Pérez de Perceval 1989, 89–90; Arboledas 2009, 974–976
47    https://www.nationalarchives.gov.uk

48 Diodorus, D. S., III, 12; 13, 3; *V*, 38, 1
49 Domergue 1990, 358
50 Domergue 1990, 358
51 Fernández Jurado 1988–89, 207–210; Healy 1993, 133
52 García Romero 2002, 439
53 Alarcón García and Sánchez Romero 2010
54 Lillehammer 2010

REFERENCES

Agatárquides De Cnido 1989. *On the Erythraean sea/Agatharchides*; translated and edited by Stanley M. Burstein. London: The Hakluyt Society.

Alarcón García, E. 2010. *Continuidad y cambio social: análisis de las actividades de mantenimiento.* Unpublished PhD. thesis, University of Granada.

Alarcón García, E. and Sánchez Romero, M. 2010. Relaciones de género y organización del trabajo de la Edad del Bronce del sureste peninsular, pp. 207–18 in *Actas del V Simposio Internacional sobre Minería y Metalurgia Históricas en el Suroeste Europeo. Homenaje a Claude Domergue (León, 19–21 de Junio de 2008).*

Arboledas, L. 2009. La epigrafía minera romana del distrito de Linares-La Carolina, *Anales de Arqueología Cordobesa* 20, 269–90.

Baxter, J. E. 2005. *The archaeology of childhood.* Walnut Creek.

Bellamy, C.V. 1904. *A West African smelting house.* London: Journal of the Iron and Steel Institute.

Blas Cortina, M. A. 1996. La minería prehistórica y el caso particular de las explotaciones cupríferas de la Sierra del Aramo. *Gallaecia* 14–15, 167–95.

Blas Cortina, M. A. 1998. Producción e intercambio de metal: la singularidad de las minas de cobre prehistóricas del Aramo y El Milagro, pp. 71–103 in Delibes, G. (coord.), *Minerales y metales en la Prehistoria reciente. Algunos testimonios de su explotación y laboreo en la Península Ibérica.* Valladolid: Studia Archaeologica 88.

Caride Lorente, C. 1978. *Historia de las minas del Centenillo.* Madrid: Colegio Oficial de Ingenieros de minas de Levante.

Childe, G. 1944. *Archaeological ages as technological stages.* Indianapolis: Bobbs-Merrill

C.I.L. *Corpus Inscriptionum Latinarum* (Berlín).

C.L.M.: *Colección Legislativa de Minas.* Formada por la Junta Superior Facultativa de Minas, tomos I–XXXI, 1889–1935

Cunningham, H. 1995. *Children and Childhood in Western Society Since 1500.* London: Pearson Longman.

Diodorus D. S./B. H.: Diodoro De Siculo 1953. *The Loeb classical library/Diodorus of Sicily; with an English translation by C. H. Oldfather*, vol. II, Cambridge (Mass.) London (England): Harvard University Press)

Domergue, C. 1983. *La mina antique d'Aljustrel (Portugal) et les Tables de de Bronze de Vipasca.* Paris.

Domergue, C. 1990. *Les mines de la Peninsule Ibérique dans l'antiquité romaine*, CEFR 127, Rome.

Fernández Jurado, J. 1988–89. Aspectos de la minería y metalurgia en la protohistoria de Huelva. *Huelva Arqueológica X–XI,* 178–214.

García Romero, J. 2002. *Minería y Metalurgia en la Córdoba romana.* Córdoba: Universidad de Córdoba.

Giardina, A. 2000. Bambini in minera: Quartulus e gli altri. *Miscellanea epigráfica, in onore di Lidio Gasperini* vol. 1, 407–16.

Gilman, A. 1981. The development of social stratification in Bronze Age Europe, *Current Anthropology* 22 (1), 1–23.

González, C. and Mangas, J. 1991. *Corpus De Inscripciones Latinas de Andalucía. Volumen III. Jaén.* Sevilla: Junta de Andalucía.

González Ruibal, A. 2006. Experiencia, Narración, Personas: elementos para una arqueología comprensible, *Complutum* 17, 235–46.

Gosse, G. 1942. Las minas y el arte minero de España en la antigüedad. *Revista Ampurias* 4, 43–68.

Healy, J. F. 1993. *Miniere e metallurgia nel mondo greco e romano*, L'Erma di Bretschneider, Roma.

Kamp, C. 2010. Entre el trabajo y el juego: perspectivas sobre la infancia en el suroeste americano, pp. 103–20 in Sánchez Romero M. (ed.), *¡Eso no se toca! infancia y cultura material en arqueología, Infancia y cultura material en arqueología*, Complutum, 21/2

Kristiansen, K. 1984. Ideology and Material Culture: An Archaeological Perspective, pp. 72–100, in Spriggs, M. (ed.), *Marxist Perspectives in Archaeology*. Cambridge: Cambridge University Press.

Lancy, D. F. 2008. *The Anthropology of Childhood: Cherubs, Chattel, Changelings*. Cambridge: Cambridge University Press.

Lawrence, S. 1998. Gender and community structure in Australian colonial goldfields, pp. 39–58, in Knapp, A. B., Pigott, V. C. and Herbert, E. W. (eds), *Social Approaches to an Industrial Past: The Archaeology and Anthropology of Mining*. London: Routledge.

Lillehammer, G. 2010. Archaeology of children, pp. 15–46, in Sánchez Romero, M. (ed.), *Infancia y cultura material en arqueología*, Complutum 21/2.

Mangas, J. 1994. Niños esclavos en la Hispania Altoimperial: Bética y alto Guadalquivir, pp. 365–80 in González, C. (ed.), *La sociedad de la Bética. Contribuciones para su estudio*. Granada: Universidad de Granada

Mangas, J. and Orejas, A. 1999: El trabajo en las minas en la Hispania Romana, pp. 207–335, in Rodríguez Neila and González Román, C. (eds), *El trabajo en la Hispania Romana*. Madrid.

Mangas, J. 1994. Niños esclavos en la Hispania Altoimperial: Bética y Alto Guadalquivir, pp. 365–80 in González Román C. (ed.), *La Sociedad de la Bética. Contribuciones para su estudio*. Granada: Universidad de Granada.

Martínez Carrión, J. M. 2005. Estatura, salud y nivel de vida en la minería del sureste español, 1830–1936. *Revista de Demografía histórica* 23 vol. 1, 177–210.

Mohen, J. P. 1989. Les relations Bronze atlantique, Bronze continental à l'âge du Bronze Moyen, Dynamique du Bronze Moyen en Europe occidentals, pp. 39–46 in *Actes du 113 Congrés national des Socétés savantes*, París.

Mzorek, S. 1989. Le travail des homes libre dans les mines romaines, pp. 157–169 in Domergue C. (eds), *Minería y metalurgia en las Antiguas Civilizaciones Mediterráneas y Europeas, tomo I*. Madrid: Ministerio de Cultura.

Nájera, T., Molina, F., Jiménez-Brobeil, S., Sánchez, M., Al-Oumaoui; I., Aranda, G. and Delgado, A. 2010. La población infantil de la Motilla del Azuer: Un estudio bioarqueológico, pp. 69–102 in Sánchez Romero M. (ed.), *Infancia y cultura material en arqueología*, Complutum 21/2.

Pastor, M., López, M., Soria, M. and Carrasco, J. 1981. Aproximación al estudio de la minería hispano-romana de Jaén y su provincia. *Grupo de Estudios Prehistóricos. Memorias de actividades II*, 59–80.

Pérez de Perceval, M. 1989. *La minería almeriense en el periodo contemporáneo*. Murcia: Universidad de Murcia.

Pérez de Perceval, M. A. and Sánchez Picón, A. 2005. El trabajo infantil en la minería española 1850–1940, *VIII Congreso de la Asociación Española de Historia Económica* http://www.um.es/hisminas/wpcontent/uploads/2012/06/a1_perez_perceval_sanchez_picon.pdf.

Pérez, J. A., Gómez, F., Flores, E. and Álvarez, G. 1996. Minería antigua en la Faja Piritifera Ibérica. El Filón Norte de minas de Riotinto (Huelva). *Vipasca* 5, 11–27.

Robb, J. 1994. Gender contradictions, moral coalitions and inequality in Prehistoric Italy, *Journal of European Archaeology* 2/1, 20–49.

Sanahuja, M. E. 2007. *La cotidianidad en la prehistoria: la vida y su sostenimiento*. Barcelona: Icaria.

Sánchez León, Mª. L. 2000. Grupos de edad y relaciones de dependencia en la antigüedad. El mundo minero, pp. 175–89 in Myro, Mª. Del Mar, Casillas, J. M., Alvar J. and Plácido, D. (eds). *Las edades de la dependencia durante la Antigüedad*. Ediciones Clásicas.

Sánchez Romero, M. and Moreno Onorato, A. 2005. Mujeres y producción metalurgia en la prehistoria: el caso de Peñalosa (Baños de la Encina, Jaén), pp. 261–82 in Sánchez Romero, M. (ed.) *Arqueología y género*. Granada: Universidad de Granada.

Sánchez Romero, M. 2010. *¡Eso no se toca! infancia y cultura material en arqueología*, pp. 9–14 in Sánchez Romero M. (ed.), *Infancia y cultura material en arqueología*, Complutum 21/2.

Sánchez Romero, M. and Alarcón García, E. 2012. Lo que los niños nos cuenta: Individuos infantiles durante la Edad del Bronce en el sur de la Península Ibérica, Justel, D. *Niños en la Antigüedad. Estudios sobre la Infancia en el mediterráneo antiguo*. Zaragoza: Prensas Universitarias de Zaragoza

Shenna, S. J. 1986. Interaction and change in third millennium B.C. western and central Europe, pp. 137–148 in Renfrew, C. and Cherry (eds), *Peer polity interaction and socio-political change*. Cambridge: Cambridge University Press.

Shenna, S. J. 1993. Commodities, transactions and growth in the central-European Early Bronze Age, *Journal of European Archaeology* 2/1, 59–72.

Shepherd, R. 1980. *Prehistoric Mining and Allied Industries*. London: Academic Press. Inc.

Sofaer Deverenski, J. 1999. Rings of life: the role of early metalwork in mediating the gendered life course, *World Archaeology* 31(3), 389–406.

Tylecote, R. F. 1987. *The Early History of Metallurgy in Europe*. London: Longman.

Villalba, Mª. J. 2000. Minería neolítica en Europa occidental: el sílex y la calaita. *I Simposio sobre la Minería y la Metalurgia Antigua en el SW Europeo, Serós* 2000, 1.3, 61–76

Wileman, J. 2005. *Hide and Seek. The Archaeology of Childhood*. London: Stroud.

# 9

# LEARNING TO BE ADULTS: GAMES AND CHILDHOOD ON THE OUTSKIRTS OF THE BIG CITY (SAN ISIDRO, BUENOS AIRES, ARGENTINA)

## Daniel Schavelzon

## INTRODUCTION

Johan Huizinga was the first to open our minds to the need to study play in archaeology, to define its central role in the construction of civilization. He began bluntly by saying: 'Play is older than culture, (…) and animals did not have to wait for man in order to learn to play'.[1] But the controversy that was triggered by the methodical study of childhood in the west, namely the books of Philippe Ariès[2] and Lloyd deMause[3] (1982) with their erudite footnotes and dozens of bibliographical references each, brought a realisation that archaeology still had much distance to cover in this respect. It was not easy to probe into this area in the early days of historical archaeology in Latin America, not just because of the sheer dimensions involved, but also because there were great controversies among authors, which made it difficult to take sides. In order to achieve what Europe was doing in Nordic archaeology – where the question of the archaeology of childhood came forward in the 1970s – we lacked experience and excavations in an activity that was only just beginning here.[4]

Knowledge of the archaeology of childhood eventually grew in the region. The controversy surrounding Processualism and gender archaeology[5] led to penetration into uncommon fields, the latter in particular looking into minorities and the unrepresented, moving away from the mainstream and towards marginal or subjugated individuals and groups.[6] By the 1990s the issue had taken root, and by 2000 papers and congresses had appeared all over the world. By the time the Society for the Study of Childhood in the Past and its corresponding journal had been created, the issue had grown and was recognised by historical archaeology.[7]

Changes in the way childhood was viewed advanced from the recognition of the most obvious objects (marbles, dolls and other toys) to finding play spaces and the social role that this represented. One example shows us this process: in 1764, Johann J. Winckelmann, wrote in what is now considered a foundational text for archaeology,

*Geschichte der Kunst des Altertums*: 'among these (Greek ceramic) vessels are to be found every kind and shape, from the smallest, which must have served as playthings for children…'.[8] Winckelmann made various assumptions: that those ceramics had been for children and were not models for other artisans – or some other thing beyond our knowledge – as scale models were, and that they were also toys, for children to play with. Our understanding, and surely that of the 18th century too, is that to play is to have fun, and according to the *Diccionario de la Real Academia de la Lengua Española*, the first definition of the word '*jugar*' (to play) is 'to do something with joy and for the sole purpose of entertaining oneself or having fun'.[9] We might also add that it is also part of psychological mechanisms for constructing fantasies. From a modern viewpoint it may not seem that those vessels had had such a purpose; in playing, a child does many other things, basically reproducing the universe she is part of, and logically what Winckelmann believed was for entertainment was no more than what adults gave to children so that their world continued without change, to be reproduced over and over again. That is, if we accept that they were toys and had no other function.

Any attempt to explore the archaeology of children is no easy task, and this can be seen in the slow progress of the bibliography on the subject, beginning with the issue of gender in the 1970s, to then move on to the recognition of the absence of children and childhood. There are still questions of childhood that have not been studied and we will try here to explore one of these. Without leaving aside the toys whose significance is now recognised in archaeology, it is important to understand which children played and how and where they played. For this we will see the material evidence of play in objects, not all of which are toys.[10] We will see it reflected in indicators that show actions over the material culture by children but which judging by their simplicity and low cost cannot necessarily be explained by differences in social class, but by the type of activity performed and the physical place in which it took place. It may be that parts of a broken porcelain doll were replaced with carved wood, the interpretation being that the doll was passed down to servants or slaves, but it may also be the solution of someone who was simply poor. But the intact doll may have belonged to a girl from the family but used for playing with a slave girl. We shall also see that this was the local custom. Imagine a society when children can interact with the children of slaves or servants until puberty (by the age of 12 such play came to a complete stop) and this custom is sustained until the 20th century (Fig. 9.1).

Have children always played? This is a question to which the initial answer appears to be yes, from our point of view influenced by modern psychology. We can assume that play has indeed been a constant presence in the history of childhood, which in turn brings up the need to define what we understand as *play* in each time. Hence this is not a question that can be answered with any certainty. Neither documentary history nor archaeology appears to be able to confirm it, at least in our understanding of the word. We do however believe that entertainment has always existed, that there must always have been fantasy; children played with whatever they had to hand, whether adults' objects or objects made especially for them. They fought, ran and got up to what we would now call mischief,

*Figure 9.1. The Alfaro family reconstructed in their social roles: father and daughter play-fighting with the black servant in the courtyard of their house (San Isidro Museum, Library and Historical Archive).*

transgressing adult codes, and since Roman times this has been documented in art. They may have been punished as sinners for this, or such transgressions may have been part of teaching about freedoms, but it still happened. And we know that adults' reactions were violent to the point of verging on sadistic, and so biographies, letters and memoirs of childhood throughout the world rarely describe happy situations prior to the 19th century. Such situations are anecdotal, remembered affectionately, memories that water down the conflictive elements, but they are still loveless. We have 19th century paintings and prints of street scenes in which poorly-clothed children play-fight, rolling on the ground or intruding into the adult leisure activities, as Ariès argued, while the well-dressed show off their clothes, clean and upstanding. Parents' tyrannical obsession leading to infanticide was not a 19th century construction;[11] restrictions on freedom and child labour have always existed and are not inventions of the modern family.

In local art the social differences can be clearly seen from the 1820s on, although of course one has to see it behind the facades of model families in their functioning, as seen in the Alfaro family described here. It is that society that gave us artists such as the French-educated Carlos Pellegrini, who in the early 19th century painted children, games and social roles as part of everyday reality. While children began to appear in the iconography at the start of that century, children's stories would have longer to wait, at least until 1860, as did children's hospitals and memoirs of childhood. It is interesting that such memoirs were not written to be read by children but by adults. For children, reading meant manuals of etiquette. Noé Jitrik writes that in this regard, that attitude of remembering childhood was part of:

> ...a feeling of pride at belonging to a preordained class and the most brilliant group (...) which makes its members constantly return to themselves. There is a reclaiming of the family and of childhood (...) to establish a family line, to somehow explain this preordination, the mission to be fulfilled.[12]

Is it a problem that there is a lack of toys or certain objects because they did not survive? It is hard to say. It is true that mass use of toys occurred in the 19th century, and locally around the middle of the 19th century toy numbers increased greatly with large-scale imports from 1852 with the re-opening of the port to British imports.[13] But we can ask a simple question regarding toy soldiers, known from the 16th century, which were common in training the child for an undoubtedly violent future. Hans Christian Anderson published one of his most widely-known stories, *Den Stanhaftige Tinsoldat* (*The Steadfast Tin Soldier*) and from that time and until my generation tin soldiers were used and every child had as many of them as were affordable. There were surely hundreds of thousands of them buried under the city, and yet not one has ever been found. There is a no doubt a complex explanation for this, but what we have learned is that although many non-perishable objects existed en masse, this does not indicate that they will be frequently found.

The role of children in a male adult society, where they were considered *potential adults*, even beings who if not involved or straightened out in their infancy would become deformed adults, appears to have been far more common than the outrage that this causes in us today appears to indicate. It is interesting that it is thought to have been a custom that came to an end with the Enlightenment, an end inspired by Rousseau,[14] and which only occasionally continued into the 19th century. My own generation saw that in various Latin American countries up until the 1970s, our children's friends were constrained for years (Fig. 9.2).

The questions of love versus authority, the difference between boys' and girls' clothes, and the possibility of outdoor activities applying only to boys developed differently

*Figure 9.2. Image of infant Jesus in swaddling clothes c. 1910 (Museum of Sacred Art, La Rioja).*

according to the country and continent. It was thus understood that the passing of child education and orphanages to the state was part of the modern concept of progress. Consequently, the bourgeois revolution exhorted mothers and the industrial production system in society to forge closer ties between parents and children, producing toys that influenced these relationships and constructed new adult responsibilities towards childcare and achieving family happiness. This again is Ariès' hypothesis regarding the great change that occurred in the late 18th century, but it is also true that this did not guarantee that it would be done.[15] It is true that the bourgeois revolution produced the social construct of childhood, but it was not the only cause, and the words of deMause are still true when he paraphrases St. Augustine many centuries before Freud: 'Give me other mothers and I will give you another world'.[16]

Perhaps because of this it is so common that in ancient places in the world where playthings have been found, they are associated with the entertainment of adults. The link between chance and entertainment and divination is one commonly made: knucklebones, chips, dice, dominoes, chess, backgammon or coins tossed in the air, all activities that do not appear to have been related to children like today. We still use the words game and play for adult competition, such as in sport and the Olympic Games. Play, as we know thanks to Johan Huizinga and his 1955 book on the world of play (2000), was associated with the amusement of baroque courtiers, soldiers with their colourful uniforms and flags, and the leisure of wealthy social classes. Even in the lower classes in colonial times, the sadistic entertainment of cockfighting was out of bounds for children. Dolls and miniatures in Egyptian tombs, or Pharaohs' games, including the Royal Game of Ur at the British Museum, were always for adults; no child could have touched the magnificent miniatures of domestic life found in the great Egyptian tombs. And in the shorter term material evidence continues to provide scant information for before the late 18th century.

In each period and place the relationship between children and adults has been varied, complex, invariably one of suffering, if not cruelty. Not all children played or were happy or had a universe of fantasy like the 19th century imagined and psychology encouraged in the late Victorian period. At least in general terms parents did not feel affection for their children, did not prevent unfortunate situations, exploited their children and even drove them to their deaths without feeling guilt. The renowned Argentine children's writer Eduarda Mansilla tells us how during her joyful and wealthy childhood her father, for whom she felt great affection, would at Christmas give her and her siblings exquisitely-wrapped gifts which were sometimes found to contain potatoes and carrots, so that when they excitedly unwrapped them they would learn to 'prepare for disappointments and heartache'. And that in the mid-19th century, among upper-class European-educated people.[17] It is not surprising, then, that all of Mansilla's stories end in tragedy (Fig. 9.3).

Generally childhood has been a time of suffering for the vast majority of children, to the extent that the concepts of family happiness are considered ideas developed in modern times – understood as after the Ancien Régime – at least in terms of an ideal to be sought by all of society. If our sense of childhood was invented in the 19th century or in the Enlightenment, or even if it already existed, it remains controversial in history. Ultimately it is not a problem different to that of the material presence of other non-dominant social groups, such as women, old people, the disabled and the sick, sexual diversities or servants of all kinds.[18] Slavery, gender and indigenous groups have been able to gain visibility in recent archaeology and today occupy a place, which children presently occupy, while the rest still await their turn.[19]

## LOCAL PRECEDENTS

Historic archaeology studies into childhood in Argentina began in the 1980s with urban archaeology. The issue came to light when a primary school was excavated in the town of Quilmes in 1995 and no other objects were found that were not school objects.[20] But in many others excavations

*Figure 9.3. Details from the painting Fiestas Mayas (25th May Celebrations) by Carlos E. Pellegrini in 1841: boys and girls in various stances, both formal and informal, according to their social status and clothing (Collection of the Urban Archaeology Centre, Universidad de Buenos Aires).*

that had been carried out at houses and rubbish pits in Buenos Aires before that, child objects had indeed appeared that could be attributed to that social group, such as clothing and toys, but the condition of these finds did not allow any further analysis besides mere recognition.[21] So before the end of the 20th century we already had a list of what a white middle to upper-class girl or kid usually wore. It was in 2000 that we managed to find, in a house built in the late 18th century, what we consider to be a 'children's room'.[22] There the objects were related to study, sewing practice, female child beauty and play. This was, then, the place where children learned their future role as adults, boys and girls separately, through a private home education still in the colonial tradition, where they took lessons in reading and writing (boys) and sewing and how to dress (girls). And they also played. The evidence was quite clear: while the number of marbles in two square metres was 26, in all the rest of the house – an excavation of 30 square metres – there were only three. While writing implements numbered 21 per square metre, in the rest of the house there were four in total. The dating of the place was determined by coins from 1854 to 1886, which coincides with the establishment of free State education in Argentina. And it is highly possible that the high number of coins was also due to children's games too. Later, in 2004, we found under the wooden floor of a brewery which then became a school, there was a school context from *c.* 1970 in which toys were mixed with learning elements.

When a rubbish pit was excavated at a suburban residence in San Isidro in 2003, in a place that today is a residential neighbourhood for people with high purchasing power, it was possible to identify the difference between games and toys. The pit contained family waste from between 1833 and *c.* 1900.[23] There we found two types of evidence: traditional toys and objects that had clearly been used for playing. We are interested in analysing objects from domestic life that children used for play as the mark from this activity is left on them. In addition to this there were photographs of the children and their family and various written documents.

The questions that arise are: are handmade toys prior to the period of great development of commercial toys or from the same time? Were they the toys used by slaves' and house servants' children who could not afford others? Or was it the boys who played outside the house with objects that were impossible to use inside? Did they invent those games and toys because the import market did not offer enough variety, i.e. are they the fruit of their own creativity?

## THE CULTURAL MATERIAL OF TOYS

In the case of Buenos Aires, the material evidence shows that the presence of children and childhood is visible in material remains, whether as objects created for children's play or as evidence that indicates it, but until now only from the early 19th century on. It is evident that many of those artefacts were mechanisms that, judging by their form and the way they were used, not only reflected the cultural standards of their time but also taught children to reproduce them, but there were also many other objects that were simply for fun. One object is a white, luxuriously-dressed doll in a house where tea was taken from miniature tea sets; another is marbles which were played with on the dirt floor: boys and girls were separated by their physical relationship with play which indicated the future of each gender.[24]

The reality of the children who constructed their world shows that it is true that 'children do not write history, they make it'[25] and that not all toys and games are evidence of children training for adult life, but fortunately more than that.[26] But play was part of the indoctrination of future generations in their social roles, in what they should and should not be, do and appear to be or do. We want to maintain that although there is little evidence, children created and recreated from their own fantasy, that all was not mechanical, cause and effect, and that childhood also had a place for freedom and creativity, to varying degrees. To deny this is to think that the human being has no capacity to respond to the cultural imposition, including being a child; not all games are bought.[27] There are infinite ways of escaping reality, the imagination has no limits, and children might swim in the river, roll down hills and run through surrounding farmland, where they would eat what grew there, even though they would be punished for it. Children broke taboos and then hid this, and this was why there was such a strict prohibition on so much as setting foot in the 'third courtyard', that of the servants, after the age of 12.

## THE ALFARO FAMILY HOME

In 1833 a wealthy businessman, the scion of a Spanish family, bought a house in a new settlement on the outskirts of Buenos Aires on his return to the city after years living in the city of Carmen de Patagones, on the southern frontier of the territory Argentina had taken from the indigenous. His name was Don Emilio Alfaro.[28] Within a few years he would once again have an important role, becoming the town's first Mayor and founding a family with great local power. He was murdered for his participation, albeit minor, in the political events of the time. Fortunately for the archaeologists, the house remained physically unchanged for over a century and rubbish was thrown into a pit in the garden during the same period, between 1833 and the late 19th century. The discovery of this enormous pit, with a surface area of two squared metres and nearly eight metres deep, was one of the most interesting finds in Argentine archaeology, especially since the enormous amount of animal fats in the pit (beef invariably tended to go to waste), meant that most of the content was airtight and completely preserved.

Among the objects recovered were some which could be attributed to the children of the family, who we know from documents and photographs of the second owner of the house, son of Don Fernando, Fernando Máximo Ireneo del Corazón de Jesús Alfaro. He was an amateur photographer who photographed his children, including when they were playing. What is most striking is that the children did not only use toys that we imagine were traditional among the wealthy classes of the 19th century, such as marbles, dolls, or writing on blackboards, but also invented different games and

made their own fun with objects reused or adapted through their own inventiveness. We wonder who invented these games and non-commercial toys, whether it was the householder's children or the slaves', and I think we can show evidence that it was both (Fig. 9.4).

Taking advantage of the institutional irregularity stemming from the beginning of the independence movement, San Isidro was founded without legal authorization around 1810 by a parish priest who used church land to obtain money.[29] The site is on the south bank of the River Plate, on the road from Buenos Aires that goes north along the riverbank, with a slight incline towards the water. As the area produced a great deal of fruit, wood and cattle, and the nearest town had constant floods, San Isidro grew rapidly. And the children's games have close ties to the geographical location of the place and its ecology. In tune with the ownership of the house, the evidence of the games

*Fig. 9.4. Mistress and servant playing (posing?) in the courtyard of the Alfaro family with the former's dolls, around 1890 (Museum, Library and History Archive of San Isidro).*

corresponds mostly to a white, European-influenced society, but not all the games are standardised or determined by the market. As for the servants' children's games – African servants were still enslaved at the start of this family's history, and would later be freed – not only do we not know anything about them, but also the photographs of the family show us that they played games with the children of the house; we do not know if they had other games. And we believe that the supposition that anything handmade necessarily belonged to the children of the servants is not a valid option. This could be due to poverty, or because it was not possible to replace toys due to restricted access to imported goods, and other personal decisions. There is no doubt that slaves' and servants' children had different toys, but the attribution of one to the other is not necessarily a question of costs, it may be merely a generational transfer.

In this respect, dolls are an important cultural marker. Although play itself goes back to antiquity and no one knows how far back the idea of using scale human figures goes, what is interesting is how much this transformed into a mechanism for reproducing social roles: dolls as a female game, in which girls learn and repeat over again until they have incorporated ways of dressing, behaving, using the house, and understanding their physical and social limits. Observing dolls' houses is an excellent way to see the dos-and-don'ts of the social class they belonged to; of course, the girl who had a house and dolls to play with was one who could afford them, and in play saw all the levels of the fixed social scale, especially hers and those of the servants, and understood where each object went.[30] What is interesting about the case of the Alfaro family, reproducing the local custom of having slaves at home,[31] is that children could play together up until puberty. The photographs show this situation: the poorly-dressed African child poses with a doll that she would never have been able to afford and dressed in clothes that she would never be able to wear. Perhaps for the young girl of the Alfaro family, even for her parents, this would have been an act of sharing, a very Christian sentiment. Psychologically for the other girl it would have reinforced daily her situation of inferiority and lack of future, knowing that when she reached the age of twelve that world would come to an end. Participating with the toys of the mistress, actively or passively in the patriarchal domination, reproduced the system of domination and hierarchies. It may be no coincidence that there are no photographs of boys playing, only of girls, because the photographs were taken inside the house. Boys ran, got dirty, and rolled on the ground with their marbles and other games. There was always this element of outside-inside, male-female, movement or rigidity.

### Fishing with a Wine Bottle

From some unknown time and up until the 20th century, children used bottles to fish for small fish called *mojarritas* on the coast of rivers, lakes or ponds. The system involved taking a wine bottle, usually with a push-up, and perforating it with gentle taps until a hole was made in the bottom and the top of the bottle was corked. When the bottle was floated horizontally on the water with breadcrumbs inside, the little fish would swim into the bottle to eat the breadcrumbs but would not be able to get out because of its tendency to swim along the side of the bottle. It was taken out of the water using a string tied to the side to the bottom of the bottle so that the bottle would come out with the top down and the water would not spill out. It was simple, effective, cost nothing and was no doubt fun. Bottles of this type were found which had been broken intentionally and would otherwise be inexplicable. Furthermore, in other contexts their significance would be quite different.[32]

## Bottle Races

In a few places in Buenos Aires and its surrounding area where the land was uneven, such as the hill leading to the river as just from the Alfaro house, so-called bottle races were common. This involved placing bottles horizontally on the ground, filled with dirt or water to give them weight and speed when they turned, then send them rolling down the hill. The winning bottle was the one that arrived first and in one piece, avoiding obstacles, stones or other hurdles placed by the players. This was seen in bottles with innumerable blows, wear and rolling marks on the exterior surface (Fig. 9.5).

## Cutting the Bottle

This is a simple and entertaining game: cutting a bottle in half in seconds. There are two ways: one is to place a string around an upright bottle on the part which is to be cut, whether horizontally or obliquely. The string is dipped first in a flammable product, such as alcohol, kerosene or oil, and knotted. This is then set alight until the burnt string comes off and in that instant the bottle is placed in water and quickly breaks in half, cleanly and effectively, because of the difference in temperature. It naturally leaves sharp edges, but the fun was in making complex oblique or partial cuts. In one case the 'shoulder' of the wine bottle was cut off, leaving an oval-shaped window or hole. The other way is to scratch the bottle with a sharp object and then strike it, cleaning

*Fig. 9.5. Bottle with irregular rolling marks on the surface, a possible result of games on the hill down to the river (photograph Patricia Frazzi).*

cutting at least one of the halves, although the other half may break. We have found four bottles with the incision made prior to being cut.

## The Catapult or Slingshot

A universal toy, the elastic slingshot was common in the 19th century and was constantly used by children for entertainment, as being a weapon, albeit a rather tame one, it could be used to hunt birds, an activity described by Henry William Hudson in the south of Buenos Aires in the early 19th century,[33] and for fights, and among the boys of the house and their friends or enemies.

We have no evidence of the slingshot itself, as wood and elastic do not leave visible remains, but we do have the ammunition. In the region, because of the high humidity of the land, it is common to find a palm tree (*Jubaea Chilensis* or Chilean Wine Palm) of low proportions whose round fruit is known locally as 'coquito', a little over two centimetres in diameter, with a small hole that is left when detached. When it falls from the tree and dries it becomes a perfect projectile, spherical, cost-free and effective when thrown at high speed. Its presence in the rubbish pit may indicate its use in these domestic wars – it is not edible – or that it was thrown out in the cleaning. But one has been found filled with small lead balls of two-three millimetres. This must have given the projectile a rare force and speed which may have been lethal, which may explain how it ended up in the rubbish pit.

## Board Game Pieces

Traditional pieces, that is, pieces rounded by friction and taken from broken ceramic objects, have been common finds in all historic archaeology in Argentina since the 17th century.[34] Those measuring 3–5cm in diameter are considered to be part of board games but used for other purposes. The most common game in which these pieces were used was backgammon and draughts, for which we believe the board, was chalked out on the floor and the game played there. The pieces are made with quality materials, ivory in this case and bronze at other sites in the city. We cannot verify whether this, in addition to use outside the house, implies ethnicity or poverty. One uncommon piece has been found, made with a fragment of decorated white pottery with gold painted relief in which it is evident that the motif was chosen intentionally. Another piece is square.

## Games inside the House

Various objects have been found that indicate games that were possibly made at home and for which traditional toys produced by the market were used: European porcelain dolls, tea sets for doll's houses, ceramic, earthenware or glass marbles, a pane of glass in which the family surname has been written, and a dog that must have been the upper part of an English earthenware tureen. In this case it is interesting that the object was salvaged after a possible breakage in order to play with it. And while they are not games but objects for children's use, there are various blackboards, one of which features sums carved with an inexpert hand, possibly as part of a school exercise.

## The Knucklebone[35]

Lastly there is a game which in all probability belonged to the adults, although one so simple that children must have played it too, or at least participated in the activity with the grown-ups: knucklebones. The bone had on its two flat sides a bronze or iron surface and generally a lead interior to give it the right balance; depending on the way it fell one would win or lose. In the case of this bone the metals were removed before it was thrown away, no doubt to be reused. We know of its use as a gambling game since 1646, as a custom brought over from Spain.

ACKNOWLEDGEMENTS

Thanks to Patricia Frazzi for her photographs and historical information about San Isidro, and to The Museum, Library and History Archive of San Isidro for allowing us to use their photographs of the Alfaro family.

## NOTES

1   Huizinga 1955, 1
2   Ariès 1960
3   deMause1974
4   Lillehammer 1989; 2011
5   Gilchrist 1999; Scott 1999; Díaz-Andreu 2005; Baxter 2005a
6   Sofaer Derevenski 2000; Wilke 2000; Wileman 2005
7   Baxter 2005a; 2005b; Leilly and Moore 2011; Sofaer Derevenski 2000; Crawford and Lewis 2008
8   Winckelmann 2011, 64
9   R. A. E. L. 2001
10  Sánchez Romero 2010; Andrade Lima 2012
11  Cowen 2001
12  Jitrik 1982, 35
13  Hamlin 2007; Sofaer 2000
14  Robertson 1982
15  Sánchez Romero 2010
16  deMause 1982,16
17  Molina 2010, 14
18  Lucy 2005
19  Schavelzon 2000, 129
20  Quatrín and Perussich 1996
21  Schavelzon 1997; 1991; 2000; 2004
22  Schavelzon 2001; 2012, 186
23  Schavelzon and Silveira 2001
24  Chudakoff 2007
25  Lillehammer 2011, 22
26  Bossard 1948; Wileman 2005
27  Hamlin 2007; Formanek-Brunell 1993
28  Lozier Almazan 1987
29  *Ibid.*
30  Formanek-Brunell 1998
31  Schavelzon 2003

32  Deetz 1996
33  Hudson 1918
34  Schavelzon 1997
35  Zapata Gollán 1972

REFERENCES

Andrade Lima, T. 2012. The dark side of toys: in nineteenth Century Rio de Janeiro, *Historical Archaeology* 46-(3), 63–78.
Ariès, P. 1960. *El niño y la vida familiar en el Antiguo Régimen*. Madrid: Taurus.
Baxter, J. E. (ed.) 2005a. *The Archaeology of Childhood: Children, Gender and Material Culture*. Walnut Creek: Altamira Press.
Baxter, J. E. 2005b. Children's in action: perspectives on the archaeology of childhood. *Archaeological Papers of the American Anthropological Association*. 15 (1).
Bossard, J. H. S. 1948. *The Sociology of Child Development*. New York: Harper & Brothers.
Chudacoff, H. 2007. *Children at Play: an American History*. New York: New York University Press.
Cowen, M. P. 2001. Un niño no es una cosa. Niños, padres y conflicto en Buenos Aires (1788–1829). *Anuario del Instituto de Historia Argentina* 2, 119–144.
Crawford, S. and Lewis, C. 2008. Childhood studies and the Society for the study of childhood in the past. *Childhood in the Past* 1, 5–16
deMause, L. (ed.) 1974. *Historia de la infancia*. Barcelona: Akal.
Deetz, J. 1996. *In Small Things Forgotten: an Archaeology of Early American Life*. New York: Anchor Books.
Díaz-Andreu, M. 2005. *The Archaeology of Identity: Approaches to Gender, Age, Status and Religion*. London: Routledge.
Formanek-Brunell, M. 1998. *Made to Play Home: Dolls and the Commercialization of American Girlhood 1830–90*. New Haven: Yale University Press.
Gilchrist, R. 1999. *Gender and Archaeology: Contesting the Past*. London: Routledge.
Hamlin, D. D. 2007. Work and play: the production and consumption of toys in XIXth Century Germany. *Journal of Social History* 36-(4), 857–869.
Hudson, W. H. 1918. *Far Away and Long Ago, a History of my Early Life*. London: J. M. Dent & Sons.
Huizinga, J. 1955 *Homo Ludens, a Study of the Play Element in Culture*. Boston: Beacon Press.
Jitrik, N. 1982. El mundo del ochenta, *Capítulo* 5, Buenos Aires: Centro Editor de América Latina.
Leilly, M. and Moore, A. (eds), 2011. *Thinking the little ancestors: new perspectives on the archaeology of infancy and childhood*. Archaeopress. Oxford: BAR International Series.
Lillehammer, G. 1989. A child is born; the child's world in an archaeological perspective. *Norwegian Archaeology Review* 22-(2), 89–105.
Lillehammer, G. 2011. Archaeology of children, *Complutum* 21-(2), 15–45.
Lozier Almazán, B.1987. *Reseña histórica del partido de San Isidro*. San Isidro: Edición del autor.
Quatrín, Z. and Perussich, X. 1996. *Informe de excavaciones 1995–1996*. Quilmes: Municipalidad de Quilmes.
Real Academia Española de la Lengua 2001. *Diccionario de la lengua Española*, 22a. edición, Madrid: RAE.
Robertson, P. 1982. El hogar como nido: la infancia de la clase media en la Europa del siglo XIX, pp. 444–471, in deMause, L. (ed.), *Historia de la infancia*, Barcelona: Akal.
Sánchez Romero, M. 2010. ¡Eso no se toca! Infancia y cultura material en arqueología, *Complutum* 21(2), 9–13.
Schavelzon, D. 1991. *Arqueología histórica de Buenos Aires (I), la cultura material porteña de los siglos XVIII y XIX*. Buenos Aires: Editorial Corregidor.

Schavelzon, D. 1997 Las fichas de juego en la arqueología histórica argentina, Buenos Aires. www.danielschavelzon.com.ar/?p=2927

Schavelzon, D. 2000 *The Historical Archaeology of Buenos Aires: a City at the End of the World*. New York: Kluwer/Academic-Plenum Press.

Schavelzon, D. 2001. *La 'Casa más antigua de Buenos Aires': buscando el espacio de los niños*. Paper presented at the XIV Congreso Nacional de Arqueología Argentina. Rosario www.iaa.fadu.uba.ar/cau/?p=2055

Schavelzon, D. 2003. *Buenos Aires Negra, arqueología histórica de una ciudad silenciada*. Buenos Aires: Editorial Emecé.

Schavelzon, D. 2004. La cerveza en el piso: arqueología de rescate en una cervecería en Mercedes, Mendoza: *XVI Congreso Nacional de Arqueología Argentina* III, 1077–1080.

Schavelzon, D. 2012. *La Casa del Naranjo: arqueología de la arquitectura en el contexto municipal de Buenos Aires*. Buenos Aires: Aspha Editor e Instituto de Arte Americano.

Schavelzon, D. and Silveira, M. 2001. *Excavaciones arqueológicas en San Isidro*. San Isidro: Municipalidad de San Isidro.

Scott, E. 1999. *The Archaeology of Infancy and Infant Death*. Oxford: Archaeopress.

Sofaer Derevenski, J. (ed.) 2000. *Children and material culture*. London: Routledge & Co.

Wileman, J. 2005. *Hide and Seek: the Archaeology of Childhood*. Stroud: Tempus.

Wilkie, L. 2000. Not merely child's play: creating a historical archaeology of children's and childhood, pp. 100–113, in Sofaer Derevenski, J. (ed.) *Children and Material Culture*, London: Routledge & Co.

Winckelmann, J. J. 2011. *Historia del arte en la antigüedad*. Barcelona: Akal.

Zapata Gollán, A. 1972. Juegos y diversiones públicas. Santa Fe: *Boletín del Departamento de Estudios Etnográficos y Coloniales* 8.

# 10

## DISABLED CHILDREN AND DOMESTIC LIVING SPACES IN BRITAIN, 1800–1900[1]

### *Mary Clare Martin*

INTRODUCTION

While children's living spaces have recently received more attention from historians,[2] there has been little focus on disabled children and the domestic interior. This is surprising, given the incidence of disability in the nineteenth century.[3] Given the limitations of their conditions, homes could be even more important to disabled children than to their able-bodied counterparts. Thus, from the 1870s, workers at the Passmore Edwards settlement in London found that disabled children might be locked in all day while their parents were at work.[4] Anne Borsay and Pamela Dale argued that, between 1850 and 1970, the home was a site of 'contested caring' between parents and different agencies.[5] While the home and domestic ideology in the period 1780–1850 have been a focus of fierce controversy within women's history,[6] there has been little debate on children's use of living space. Current studies concur on the spatial separation of children from adults in the middle class home from the mid-nineteenth century.[7] Indeed, John Gillis argued that such children were 'islanded' within their homes.[8] More recently, however, Leonore Davidoff emphasised that many middle class homes were quite crowded and that spatial separation occurred mainly in the late nineteenth century.[9]

Disability theory has been shaped by present-centred and sociological approaches, mainly developed in the 1970s and 1980s, rather than by a primary focus on childhood in the past. According to these paradigms, in the nineteenth century, disability was regarded in terms of a 'medical model' of impairment and disabled people as a burden. The 'social model' in which disability is viewed as the failure of society to accommodate the needs of disabled people, was only identified from the 1970s and 1980s.[10] Borsay and Dale have recently critiqued the social model as it applies to children, on the grounds that its emphasis on independence is not appropriate for children, by definition dependent beings.[11] Quite different models can be derived from other contemporary nineteenth-century texts. Thus the 'School of Pain' presented the disabled person as an exemplar of fortitude and the sickroom as the centre of the house. While this model, sometimes characterised as 'heroic', could be perceived as making unfair demands on the disabled person, it nevertheless conferred a superior status to that of the able-bodied.[12]

This chapter will consider the relevance of these models to disabled children's experiences of domestic spatial arrangements, and to factors of class and gender, in the nineteenth century. While historians have argued that childhood was structured by gender in this period,[13] it is an open question as to whether boys' masculinity was problematized by disability. Marianne Farningham argued that 'A sick daughter is as an angel in the house',[14] and Lois Keith represented disability as coded feminine.[15] However, mid-century literature for adults contained sympathetic images of disabled boys of different social classes, notably Charles Dickens' Tiny Tim in *A Christmas Carol* (1843) and Paul in *Dombey and Son* (1848),[16] while Claudia Nelson argued that boyhood was feminised over the nineteenth century.[17] Class difference is also significant. Iain Hutchison argued that 'the professional classes found it harder to accept people who did not conform to their idea of normality'.[18] Seth Koven cited the Queen's Nurse, Margaret Loane, who stated in 1917 that 'the rich closeted their crippled children out of shame' as in Frances Hodgson Burnett's *The Secret Garden* (1911). Conversely, Loane argued, the poor were more accepting, and might even exhibit disabled children.[19] This contrasts with Humphries' findings that many working-class families tried to conceal their disabled children.[20] Moreover, as Hutchison argued, the wealthy indubitably had more resources with which to ameliorate their children's conditions.[21]

## Sources: discourse and experience

Borsay and Dale have shown the difficulty of recovering the voices of disabled children, which are often obscured in official documents constructed for other purposes.[22] While life-story writing or oral history has been used effectively for the twentieth century,[23] there have been few studies from the nineteenth century. Iain Hutchison, one of the few authors in this field, has argued that 'the most important published narratives of the experience of disability should be found in works produced by people with disabilities. Yet authorship of this nature is relatively sparse and gives a skewed overview'.[24] Despite the methodological difficulties of recovering the 'voice of the child',[25] Jane Hamlett and others have argued that autobiographies can be used to recover children's experiences.[26] This chapter will draw on surviving autobiographies and biographies, some by family members, to consider the relevance of models of disability to children's lives over the nineteenth century. Given the paucity of sources available, I undertook a keyword search on 'disability' in the *Oxford Dictionary of National Biography* (2004) and examined any accounts which referred to the authors' childhoods. The narratives range from abuse, to affection, heroism, stoicism, a belief that all were 'in the hand of God', to a more secular view that disability provided improved opportunities. While such sources could be regarded as unrepresentative, in that my subjects became famous, or were at least memorialized in print, these examples represent images of disabled people as active rather than as victims. Of course, such sources have limitations, one being that the narrative was shaped by the preoccupations of the time in which they were written (from the 1870s to the 1960s). 'Domestic biography' written by family members, might intentionally conceal information from the public domain.[27] However, another perspective is that some autobiographers exaggerated their hardships, or were unduly harsh about family members.[28]

Different types of text, such as fiction, poetry, drama, and biography may reflect the same themes at any one period of time, and that of the 'School of Pain' can be found in children's literature such as *What Katy Did* (1872) or *Pollyanna* (1899).[29] Fanny Bickersteth's biographers referred to the 'School of Patience', in both 1860 and 1892.[30] Advice books, such as *Little Scholars in the School of Pain,* were still being published in the 1900s.[31] While the autobiography, published in 1938, of Agnes Hunt, the future nurse and pioneer of clinics and open-air schools for children, was ironical and self-deprecating in tone, she also used the language of the 'apprenticeship to crippledom' and 'the great education of pain'.[32]

## BACKGROUND

The subjects explored here came from a range of class and occupational backgrounds, from the aristocratic Campbells of Scotland, the family of the Duke of Argyll, to lesser gentry and professionals, manufacturers, businessmen, artisans and labourers. Some lived in country houses with large grounds, others rectories, small houses, and town houses. While the upper and the middle classes are better represented, the wide spread of occupations also facilitates examination of different kinds of homes, both urban and rural. It also shows the instability of class position. The father of Joseph Barker (1806–75) was a small cloth merchant who fell into 'absolute want', like many others in the post-Napoleonic period.[33] The business of Florence White's father was affected by the agricultural depression of the 1870s.[34] After an examination of types of disability, this chapter will consider home as a place of danger, including accidents and abuse, as well as a site of medical treatment. More specific attention to exclusion and inclusion will be gained through examination of the uses of different rooms, and experiences of the outdoors. The implications of disability for relationships with household members will be considered, as well as education both inside and outside the family home. Throughout, I will consider disabled adults' reflections on their life-stories, and whether they felt they were disadvantaged by their condition and its treatment.

The nature of the household and of family structure over the period affected children's experiences. Joseph Barker was the fourth of eleven children.[35] By the late nineteenth century, average completed family size in the middle and upper classes was six, a decline from the 'large sprawling families of mid-century.[36] Whereas upper and middle class children lived in households which would include a number of servants, the lower middle class would be more likely to have just one, and the poor, none at all.[37] While Anna Davin has highlighted how home could be peripatetic for poor working class children,[38] many of the upper classes moved between several residences. The aristocratic Campbells had two homes in Scotland, including Rosneath Castle, from 1803, as well as Argyll Lodge in London, though Frances Balfour (née Campbell, 1858–1931) claimed that her parents would have been just as happy in an encampment.[39]Augustus Hare (1834–1903) and his mother, related to country clergy, moved to Stoke Rectory for five months every winter from Lime, near Hurstmonceaux in Kent.[40] Over the life-cycle, rooms might be used very differently. Florence White's family moved three times, and each time the configuration of the rooms changed, according to whether there were young children, and they could afford or have room for live-in servants.[41] Households also varied in size. Augustus Hare lived alone with his adoptive mother and a servant Mary Ann Lea for twenty-five years.[42] Families with substantial resources, such as the Campbells, might adapt their lifestyles to help produce a cure for the ill or disabled person, visiting the sea or watering-places all together.[43] Relatives' and friends' homes were also important as places to convalesce, and could be preferred to those of parents.[44]

## TYPES OF DISABILITY

Disability is not a fixed state: indeed, Altenbaugh and Verstraete noted how many disability theorists characterize the majority as 'temporarily non-disabled'.[45] Nor were all my subjects disabled throughout their entire childhood. In the nineteenth century, the major threats to life and health were measles, scarlet fever, diphtheria, smallpox, typhus, typhoid, whooping-cough, phthisis, pneumonia, bronchitis,and convulsions.[46] Despite medical developments such as the smallpox vaccine, and the decrease in virulence of the killers scarlet fever and measles by 1900, the 'white plague' tuberculosis was still a threat to health, and could cause lasting bone malformations.[47] Four of my subjects suffered from partial blindness,[48] two deafness,[49] while Dudley Ryder (1798–1888), the second Earl of Harrowby, had a speech impediment.[50] Many suffered lameness or paralysis, often as a result of illness.[51] Frances Balfour, future suffragist, had disease of the hip joint, which was later named tuberculosis.[52] These conditions were not entirely disabling, for many of these subjects lived active lives and became well known. By contrast, Fanny Bickersteth (1830–1854), who suffered from irritation of the nervous system and pulmonary disease, died young in 1854.[53] Some had learning disabilities. 'Little Charles Waring' Darwin (1856–8) 'was so clearly backward...he made strange grimaces' and was described as 'lacking in the full measure of intelligence' now categorised as Down's syndrome. His sister Bessy (1847–1926) had some similar symptoms.[54] Cecil Tyndale-Biscoe (1863–1949), later schoolteacher in Kashmir, had meningitis in infancy which he considered left him 'a weakling' and unable to learn by heart.[55]

## HOME AS A PLACE OF DANGER: ACCIDENTS, OVERWORK, ABUSE

While 'separate spheres' ideology delineated home as a haven, and John Tosh has argued that both Evangelicals and Romantics thought children should be protected within the home,[56] it could also be a site of danger from birth onwards, caused by accidents or ill-treatment. These were often attributed to servants, which marks a well-known theme of 'the enemy within'.[57] Dudley Ryder's father reputedly saved his life when he interrupted a servant who was giving Dudley, aged four, the 'hot treatment', after he had been vaccinated for smallpox.[58] The family of the future politician, Herbert Morrison (1886–1965), son of a policeman, blamed the midwife for his partial blindness.[59] Accidents occurred when children were alone, with siblings, or even with adults. Fanny Bickersteth fell on her head when she was eighteen months. She initially suffered from pulmonary disease and her 'whole system became disorganised' as she grew older and eventually died.[60] The blindness of the poet Philip Marston was attributed to an accidental blow received playing with other children, aged four.[61] Cuthbert Heath (1859–1939), a pioneer in insurance broking, had an accident aged twelve while playing with his siblings which seemed to exacerbate his latent deafness.[62] The father of Florence White, the future cook, brought home a chameleon top with a spring when she was eight. The wire jumped out and hit her in the eye, leading to partial blindness.[63] The future scientist Alfred Newton (1829–1907) was playing riotous games with his brothers in the family home at Elveden in Suffolk, when he fell and hurt one of his knees, causing permanent lameness. 'Little was made of it, but serious injury had been done, and his right leg never grew equally with the other, causing permanent harm'.[64] In similar vein, Agnes Hunt (1867–1948), nurse and pioneer of treatment for the disabled, indicated how the culture of stoicism prevented discovery of her condition. She had two abscesses when she was nine which led to blood-poisoning, but thought they were due to growing pains: 'Children in Victorian days were not encouraged to complain'.[65] Lady Frances Balfour was taught that tears were inappropriate, and did not speak about her paralysed leg, as she was afraid it would be cut off.[66]

Others made more direct claims of abuse. Augustus Hare claimed his disabilities were the result of neglect at home: 'I was constantly sick, so thin almost a skeleton-which I really believe now to have been entirely caused by the way in which the miseries of my home life preyed upon my excessively nervous disposition. I was talked to about death and hell and urged to meditate upon them'.[67] Hare had been adopted by an aunt who was over-conscientious about not indulging him and was subject to 'severe discipline' from a young age, which he felt weakened his constitution.[68] Joseph Barker and Louise Jermy (1877–1952) both argued that overwork led to deformity or illness. Barker's story was an indictment of the poverty in which the town of Bramley was thrown after 1815, rather than of his family. In order to pay off the family debts, he worked long hours in the family shop or on the cotton frame, sometimes from three or four in the morning in summer to eight to nine o'clock at night.[69] Louise Jermy, née Withers, whose mother died when she was three, recovered from erypiselas, aged eight. However, she developed a tubercular hip, aged thirteen, turning a mangle all day, taking in washing to help pay off the family loan on the house. 'My health and strength were bartered for that house'.[70] Florence White had to work as general servant and nursery governess after her father's business failed, though her complaint was not the work but the constant criticism from her stepmother.[71] Although Jermy and White were treated as burdens, which would seem commensurate with the medical model, they nevertheless made significant contributions to the maintenance of the household.[72]

DOMESTIC SPACE

While an increased amount of institutional care was targeted at poor children over the nineteenth century, for many, care at home was the only option.[73] In the absence of medical cure, good nursing could alleviate the condition. John Buchan (1875–1940), the future writer, and Constance Smedley (1876–1941), campaigner and founder of the Lyceum clubs, had to lie on their backs for long periods.[74] Randall Davidson (1848–1930), future Archbishop of Canterbury, later considered how it was odd that the only treatment for being shot was staying in bed and care by an old, untrained nurse, even though Lister had begun his studies of antiseptic surgery.[75] The bedroom might be represented and experienced as the centre of the house, as in the mid-nineteenth century imagery of the 'School of Pain', as in the novel *What Katy Did* (1872).[76] This theme also emerges in biography. Fanny Bickersteth spent six years in her bedroom, after her health declined. Her sister Charlotte later noted that 'Fan's bedroom was the brightest place in all the house...She had learnt the difficult lesson of living almost entirely beyond her own little world of disease and pain and opening her heart wide to receive all the sympathies and interests'. She made handicrafts for the London City Mission from 1848 to 1852 and village girls were invited in to be taught ornamental work.[77] In similar vein, Frances Balfour commended the exemplary behaviour of her sister Victoria (1854–1910) in doing her tedious exercises, and described Victoria's couch as 'Bethel'.[78] While this term has religious connotations, Frances also recalled Victoria's bedroom in the autumn of 1868 as 'the centre of the fun and mischief that was going on in the family circle'.[79] Frances herself played games in her own bedroom, 'Counterpane Land', including a pretend duel with her brother, about 1860, and was given a miniature minstrel Blondin who wheeled a barrow on a string across her bed.[80] Yet, even for Fanny Bickersteth, described by her nurse as 'patience itself', confinement could be oppressive.[81] Agnes Hunt recalled the frustration of staying in bed with a fever when everyone else went on a planned outing.[82] As Florence White got older, she was 'sent up to spend most of the day in my room', showing how the bedroom could be a place of punishment.[83]

Davidoff has argued that the middle class home could be a crowded place, with segregated children's quarters only becoming common in the late nineteenth century.[84] Focus on disabled children's experiences of different rooms within the house, as well as the garden, in this section will further call in question the claim that children were usually segregated from adults in nineteenth-century middle class homes.[85] Jane Hamlett's argument that certain children might have privileged access to adult space could be particularly apposite to disabled children.[86] When Fanny Bickersteth was confined indoors all winter in 1846 with a weak chest, she took daily walks around her father's study, her companions being Milton and Beethoven's sonatas.[87] In the 1860s, the invalid aristocrat Frances Balfour was allowed to lie on a sofa in the drawing room, 'while elders had their tea', being fed with milk and 'Inverary' biscuit.[88] In the 1870s, Florence White's elder brother Herbert put her in charge of dusting his room while he was studying for the law.[89]

Rather than being excluded, the social model of adaptation to the needs of the disabled person would seem to be more appropriate. Richard Lane claimed that Anna Gurney, who had infantile paralysis (polio) aged ten months, disliked using a wheelchair and propelled herself around on her hands, which became stronger than in most children. Her cousin Catherine wrote in 1810 how 'Anna is on the floor as usual'.[90] The Balfours played billiards, a game in which disabled children could participate.[91] Indeed, many accounts show disabled and other children sharing family living space with adults, thus calling in question the stereotype of separation. Augustus Hare always had his meals with his mother, never in the nursery, and he was pictured with her in the drawing room, in the house that they shared with their servant Mary Lea.[92] The Scot George Matheson (1842–1906) preached sermons to the whole family as a boy.[93] The Darwin children were allowed to 'toboggan' downstairs on a slide – 'a specially constructed board'.[94] The Campbell children used to distribute themselves around the drawing room after their parents' formal dinner parties, and talk to the guests, 'the more elderly in our group insisting that we should not sit "in a pie"'. Their parents' social lives in London included breakfast parties which started at 10 am, and again included the children.[95]

While John Gillis argued that 'the kitchen was one part of the (Victorian) house that remained unincorporated into the home', and children might be banned from the kitchen,[96] Florence White's experiences of the kitchen ranged from inclusion to exclusion. Her biological mother 'had me with her as much as possible, for example, to help with banging out dough' in the 1860s.[97] However, after her mother's death the family moved, the old servant Eliza was replaced with two fashionable servants and Florence was initially not permitted in the kitchen. As she grew older, she was frequently in disgrace with her new stepmother and was 'much better acquainted with the corner of the room than with the middle'.[98] The drawing-room, from which she was excluded, Cinderella-fashion, was occupied by her father, stepmother and new child.[99] White and Jermy's isolation and banishment to the kitchens of large houses contrasts with the experience of Herbert Morrison, son of a policeman, from a more working-class background, who described playing games devised by their mother round the kitchen range.[100] However, it was not necessarily class, but the fact of remarriage and step-parenting which seems to have caused the most unhappy experiences.

OUTDOORS

Outdoor environments provided many opportunities for disabled children to participate alongside others, and again facilitated adaptation to the needs of the disabled person. The sedate walk taken by Fanny Bickersteth and her sister around the grounds of Watton Rectory in 1846 differed from the more rowdy games of the Gurneys, Hunts, Newtons, and Roydens.[101] Anna Gurney insisted she be taken down to the beach at Cromer aged eight, about 1800, where she learned to swim alongside her able-bodied cousins.[102] Alfred Newton, as good a shot as his younger brother, rode well, as well as engaging in birds' nesting and recording migration of birds.[103] Lady Victoria Campbell used to ride strapped to a Spanish saddle on an island pony at Inverary with her siblings.[104]

The Hunt children had so much freedom that their governess threatened to leave because they were allowed to 'kill ourselves in …many different ways' on their family estate.[105]Agnes Hunt later praised her mother's attitude to her disability, recalling that, 'My brothers and sisters were never made to fetch and carry for me, or to consider me in their games. The consequence was that, without exception, they did what they could to enable me to join in their play and generally to enjoy life'.[106] Thus, one Christmas when they all played ice-hockey she was given a sledge and played goalkeeper, despite falling out endlessly.[107] Maude Royden played dangerous games with her siblings such as lying on railway lines to listen for the approaching train. She later thought she was not very aware of her disability as she was the youngest and weakest anyway.[108] While congruent with Humphries' argument that middle class children were more protected than their working-class counterparts, in their gardens and large grounds,[109] these examples call in question Seth Koven's argument that upper or middle class children were 'hidden away' by their families.[110]

RELATIONSHIPS WITHIN THE HOUSEHOLD

Research on 'the Victorian family' is most likely to note its patriarchal aspect. However, there were multiple forms of family, some female-headed, some single-parent (whether through death, adoption or abandonment), and many with live-in servants, or with relatives.[111] Thus, when Cuthbert Heath had the injury which exacerbated his deafness, he and his siblings were in the care of an aunt, as their parents were in India.[112] Many autobiographies describe warm relationships within the household. Although Steedman has argued that, from the employees' perspective, a good place was one without children,[113] some recalled their childhood attachment to their servants.[114] The Darwins' butler Parslow was a favourite of the baby Charles Waring.[115] Indeed, servants might be kinder than relatives. Hare was devoted to their servant Mary Lea.[116] Florence White recalled how the kindness of female servants contrasted with her stepmother's harshness. She loved her daily governess, who was also a family friend.[117] Elizabeth Knowles, who became Lady Victoria's servant in 1866, was her lifelong and often only companion for thirty-nine years.[118]

Disability could either result in increased intimacy between parents and children, or be a cause of friction. Fanny's sister recorded that, although Mrs Bickersteth's deafness and Fanny's quiet voice made communication between mother and daughter difficult, she developed a close relationship with her father.[119] Frances Balfour's mother cared a great deal when she was suffering pain, but was allegedly unaware of her 'mental agony' during her illness.[120] Given an appropriate environment, children with learning disability could flourish. Thus, Henrietta Darwin believed that 'Emma's sensitive and loving treatment of Bessy had brought out the best in a child who might otherwise have been difficult'.[121]

In several families, however, the discourse of the medical model of disability as a burden is apparent. Harriet Martineau (1802–76) argued that her family were first in denial about her deafness, insisting there was nothing wrong, then blaming her, and only grudgingly agreeing to take action. Indeed, she later claimed that she had never seen a deaf child's education well managed, and that her own temper might have been made a good one 'by indulgence'. So much was learnt from 'oral intercourse' that they became awkward in their manners and suffered more from the ostracism that resulted than the disability itself.[122] Parents and siblings might find the subject's disability harder to bear than the afflicted person. Herbert Morrison recalled that his father's anxiety that he might go blind in both eyes became a cause of friction.[123] Harry Platt felt his parents never came to terms with his disability.[124] Augustus Hare's aunt talked in his presence about how his ill-health made him a burden to his mother, again emphasising the 'medical model'.[125] Indeed, while he recalled being very happy with his adoptive mother, he attributed his most unhappy experiences to other relatives, notably 'Uncle Julius', who beat him.[126] However, relatives outside the nuclear family might provide additional care and support. Lady Victoria Campbell's unmarried aunt Emily MacNeill took a great interest in her and looked after her during her treatments.[127] Florence White liked being with her aunts in the country.[128]

Family size and structure had a significant influence on children's relationships. Augustus Hare, adopted by relatives, and with no resident siblings, was unusual in being forced to play with children he hated, such as his cousin Marcus.[129] Large families provided regular social interaction for the disabled person but also allowed him or her to withdraw temporarily. Indeed, many of these families conformed to the 'social model' of adaptation to the needs of the disabled person. Thus, it was understood that Fanny Bickersteth could not participate with her more vigorous siblings.[130] The deaf Cuthbert Heath's sister Ada recalled that, although he was a little withdrawn, he was integrated into their activities.[131] Frances Balfour, partially paralysed since the age of five, claimed that the youngest of ten did not get much attention but she and her sister were both carried about by or with the others when necessary.[132] Her claim, 'I won through in a full nursery' reflected her poor opinion of the medical care available and attributed her partial recovery to the beneficial effect of a large family.[133]

Davidoff's observation, that brothers as well as sisters might take on caring roles,[134] is also apposite. Fanny Bickersteth's brother was considered as good as a trained nurse, and his sister referred to 'the breezy joyousness of his manner'.[135] Florence White's brother Herbert coached her so she could receive a Sunday breakfast for saying her catechism correctly.[136] Brothers could, however, be harsh. Balfour was teased that she was 'lurching like a ship at sea' when she tried to walk after her recovery.[137] Cuthbert Heath felt his brothers thought him a 'poor fool' because unlike them, he had to go into the City, not the Navy, due to his poor hearing.[138] Conversely, Alfred Newton's biographer claimed that, as he was not able to join in the more boisterous activities of his elder brothers, he became closer to his younger brother Edward as a result of his disability. They both developed a passion for botany which formed the foundation for Newton's future career as a professor. Edward allegedly wished he too was lame, to make up for his brother's disability.[139] Others might be separated from their siblings for long periods, for education or treatment. Dudley Ryder attended a number of different schools, to help with his speech defect.[140] Lady Victoria Campbell was often away from home for long periods, due to her treatment, though all the family went to Brighton in 1864 and Cannes in 1868.[141] Other children might feel very isolated: indeed, Hare, Jermy and Martineau recalled wishing to commit suicide.[142] Florence White 'wished I might go to my mother in heaven'.[143] Indeed, Jermy said she liked hospital better than home as she was treated in a kindly way there.[144]

## EDUCATION

While middle class girls' education in the nineteenth century has been considered as inferior to that of boys, high standards could be reached, whether at school or at home.[145] Indeed, opportunities for 'familiar conversation' and to use their fathers' libraries might provide girls with a more satisfying intellectual experience than boys' diet of enforced Latin grammar.[146] As many girls were educated at home, their disability might be less disruptive of their education than it was for boys. However, some mothers were committed to girls' education and their careers.[147] It has been suggested that, as disabled girls were perceived as less marriageable, their education was even more important.[148]

Many memoirs suggest my subjects were successful in continuing their education, despite or even because of disability. Indeed, the sisters of Fanny Bickersteth and Victoria Campbell commended their dedication to study and methodical approach to organising their time as an example to other invalids.[149] While Victoria's sister Frances Balfour considered that, although their governess had an enthusiasm for knowledge, 'a parish teacher might have been better at imparting it',[150] a cultured atmosphere benefited her, as well as family friends: 'Dr Story made me read Carlyle'.[151] Davidoff noted how some sisters learnt Latin and Greek to share their brothers' 'arcane knowledge', and Harriet Martineau and her sister were taught Latin by her brother.[152] Sisters might also teach their brothers subjects such as Greek.[153] George Matheson's younger sisters learnt Latin, Greek and Hebrew so they could help him study, as he was nearly blind, while his elder sister wrote down his sermons until he became a minister and had a secretary.[154] The blind poet Philip Marston could not read, but others wrote down his poems at his dictation, and his mother aided him to prepare them for press.[155] Such examples might seem to confirm established gender norms of females acting as amanuenses to males, who would then obtain the credit.[156] However, their acknowledgement in the subject's biography did provide some public recognition.

Many middle class boys were taught at home, either, routinely, by governesses when very young, or as a result of illness. Home tuition might have mixed results. Cecil Tyndale-Biscoe recalled that his governess repeatedly boxed his ears for slowness, so he had to endure more punishment than other boys as well as damaged ears. Although this could be interpreted as abuse, retrospectively, he felt this was beneficial, in enabling him to understand other 'dull scholars'.[157] Augustus Hare, who was removed from Harrow School for health reasons and had a private tutor for two and a half years, later wrote about his depression about the 'utter waste of life'. Indeed, his friend Arthur Stanley was shocked by the restriction of educational opportunities available to him.[158] However, he did go to Oxford University, while Harry Platt took medical degrees after home tutoring, mainly in classics and languages.[159] Florence White trained her memory during the six months she was bedridden with bandages over her eyes.[160] She was fortunate in having the same governess, Carrie Loveridge, a family friend, until she was well enough to go to school aged eight. When taken away, aged fourteen and a half, by her stepmother, she took exams from the College of Preceptors to three levels.[161] For Constance Smedley, who had to leave school and lie on her back for some time, Birmingham Art School, where she was taught by May Morris, provided a new opportunity during her recovery.[162] Many claimed they had developed solitary interests as the result of their disability, which might form the basis of their future careers: drawing,[163] music, reading, or writing.[164] Alexander Muirhead, the future electrical engineer, conducted solitary experiments.[165]

Disability might constitute a reason for education away from home rather than maintenance inside it. Indeed, some disabled 'children' claimed they had a better education as a result. To help with his speech impediment, Dudley Ryder was sent away to numerous educational establishments: Mrs Braidwood's school, about 1803, a clergyman's home, and then John Thelwall's school.[166] Joseph Barker was sent to James Sigston's school in Leeds, aged sixteen, because his disability made him unable to work, and his parents' circumstances had improved.[167] Harriet Martineau claimed she was sent to a boarding school in Bristol, aged sixteen as her deafness caused so much tension at home.[168] Although Martineau's case was commensurate with the medical model of disability as a burden, in most families, sending a child away was conceived to be in the child's interests.

## Conclusion

This chapter has analysed the ways models of disability were woven into the accounts of childhoods generated by disabled children in the nineteenth century. Some life-stories, notably those of Fanny Bickersteth and Lady Victoria Campbell, were constructed as exemplary by their sisters and are congruent with the 'School of Pain' theme. Agnes Hunt's autobiography, published in 1930, made more ironical references to this model. Another narrative, that of abuse, mirrors the medical model, since the disabled person was represented as a burden to relatives and family members. However, the same memoirs which link abuse to remarriage or adoption, indicate that these subjects had significant value for their own families. While Augustus Hare, from the professional middle classes, described himself and his mother as 'companions', the memoirs of Joseph Barker, Florence White and Louise Jermy, from the lower middle and upper working classes, indicate that they made a significant economic contribution. Indeed, while Barker and Jermy attributed their disabilities to the hard work they had to do, their labour would seem to have been essential to their family's survival.

Disabled children might be treated as exemplars, and given privileged access to adult living space, while their own bedrooms could be described in ways congruent with the 'School of Pain'. Furthermore, disabled children might be integrated into home life in ways that resembled the 'social model' rather than regarded as burdens. Outdoor space would seem to have had a levelling tendency, allowing children with disabilities to play with others. Clearly upper and upper middle class families such as the Balfours, the Hunts, Newtons, and Gurneys had more resources than the poor to facilitate this, but such adaptations challenge the notion of the rich as wishing to conceal their disabled offspring. Since there is little evidence in these sources of home settings being rigidly differentiated on gender lines, it would be problematic to claim that disability made a great difference to boys' status.

This chapter calls in question the notion that in the nineteenth century, the medical model of disability as a burden or individual tragedy dominated. While some children recalled being abused and being told they were burdens, this was often linked to family circumstances, notably remarriage. The social model of adaptation, assisted particularly by access to the outdoors, was often assisted by large families. Indeed, a frequent theme in life-stories was the beneficial effect of disability. Many subjects retrospectively claimed with the benefit of hindsight that disability provided new educational opportunities, or took them in new directions. While some had little choice about the change of course (Matheson might have gone in for the law, Heath was intended for the Navy),[169] it is plausible that many of their pioneering activities in women's opportunities as well as the professions, the arts and social service, resulted from experiences of solitude, difference and adaptation.

## NOTES

1   Previous versions of this paper were presented at the SSCIP annual conference at the University of Miami in 2009, to the 'Children at Home' conference at the Jeffrye Museum, London, in March 2011, and to the British Society for the History of Paediatrics and Child Health in Liverpool, September 2010. I am grateful to the organisers and participants for their comments and questions, and to Margarita Sanchez Romero for her patience

2   Hamlett 2010, 111–143: Sloane 2008, 42–60. See also recent conferences on this topic: SSCIP in Granada, October 2012, and the Society for the History of Childhood and Youth Biennial Conference, Children and Space, University of Nottingham, June 2013

3   Starkey 2012, 15–28: Ross 1993, 180–181: Dale 2012, 120–1

4   Hollis 1987, 129

5   Borsay and Dale 2012, 1

6   Davidoff and Hall 2002, 74–5, 114–118, 319–20, 364–9, 450–4: Vickery 1993, 388–9: Vickery 1998, 1–12, 285–294: Tosh 1999, 11–26, 43–78, 79–101

7   Hamlett 2010, 111–143

8   Gillis 2008, 316–320

9   Davidoff 2012, 87–8

10   Oliver 2009, 41–57

11   Borsay and Dale 2012, 3

12   Keith 2001, 84–94

13   Fletcher 2008, 3–11, 351–68: Davidoff 2012, 121–124

14   Nelson 1994, 5, 23

15   Keith 2001, 1–14 and *passim*

16   Lerner 1997, 92–3

17   Nelson 1994, 25

18 Hutchison 2007, 168
19 Koven 1994, 1177
20 Humphries and Gordon 1992, 36
21 Hutchison 2007, 105
22 Borsay and Dale 2012, 6
23 Humphries and Gordon 1992: Atkinson, Jackson and Walmsley 1997: Atkinson and Williams 1990: Potts and Fido 1991: Atkinson *et al.* 2000: Wade and Moore 1993
24 Hutchison 2007, 129
25 Hendrick 2002, 51–6: Viner and Golden 2000, 577–579: Newton 2012, 16–27
26 Hamlett 2010, 16–17: Hamlett 2009, 113–114: Dekker 2000, 12–20
27 Tolley 1997, 146–161
28 Martineau 1877, 6: Hunt, 1949, preface by Miss Tizie Kenyon
29 Martin 2014, 36
30 Bickersteth, 1860, 1892, 9–10
31 Bourdillon 1907, 13–15
32 Hunt 1949, 7
33 Barker 1880, 28–36
34 White 1938, 56
35 Barker 1880, 28
36 Sanders 2001, 3: Davidoff 2012, 102–107
37 Steedman 2009, 36–41: Hamlett 2010, 51–9
38 Davin 1996, 31
39 Balfour 1930, 12, 21
40 Hare 1896, I, 69
41 White 1938, 32, 38–9, 50
42 Hare 1896, I, 60
43 Balfour 1911, 8, 33,
44 White 1938, 48,
45 Altenbaugh 2004, 140: Verstraete 2012, 41–44
46 Hardy 1993, 9, 28–9, 56, 80–81, 151, 191, 210: Smith 1979, 142, 154, 171
47 Borsay, 2007, 94–8: Smith 1979, 175
48 Macmillan 1907, 9: Osborne 1926, 3: Morrison, 1960, 12: White 1938, 34–5
49 Brown 1980, 32: Martineau 1877, 72–78
50 Ryder 1891, 3–4
51 Louise Jermy, Harry Platt, Randall Davidson, Alfred Newton, Augustus Hare, Victoria Campbell, Frances Balfour, Maude Royden
52 Balfour 1930, 9
53 Bickersteth 1860, 3, 192–5
54 Healey 2001, 233–8
55 Tyndale-Biscoe 1951, 22
56 Davidoff and Hall 2002, 74–5, 114–118, 319–20, 364–9, 450–4: Tosh 1999, 11–26, 32, 43–78, 79–101
57 Steedman 2009, 228–238
58 Ryder 1891, 3
59 Morrison 1960, 12
60 Bickersteth 1860, 1–4, 78–80, 193–5
61 Osborne 1926, 3
62 Brown 1980, 32
63 White 1938, 34–5
64 Wollaston 1924, 4

65  Hunt 1949, 5
66  Balfour 1930, 9
67  Hare 1896, I, 240–241
68  Hare 1896, 240–41
69  Barker 1880, 36–7
70  Jermy 1934, 19, 22, 29–30
71  White 1938, 42, 44–5, 92
72  Jermy 1934, 85: White 1938, 63–71
73  Levene et al 2012, 15–17, 30: Levene 2013, 327–8:Viner and Golden 2000, 577–79
74  Smith 1965, 14: Smedley 1929, 15
75  Bell 1935, I, 18–19
76  Keith 2001, 84–94
77  Bickersteth 1860, 34, 79–81
78  Balfour 1911, 10
79  Balfour 1911, 33
80  Balfour 1930, 10
81  Bickersteth 1860, 20
82  Hunt 1949, 201–4
83  White 1938, 45
84  Davidoff 2012, 87–8
85  Hamlett 2010, 111–143
86  Hamlett 2009, 120
87  Bickersteth 1860, 2
88  Balfour 1930, 11–12
89  White 1938, 50
90  Lane 2001, 3
91  Balfour 1930, 139
92  Hare 1896, I, 101
93  Macmillan 1907, 20
94  Healey 2001, 197
95  Balfour 1930, 58, 61
96  Gillis 1996, 121
97  White 1938, 25
98  White 1938, 45
99  White 1938, 45
100  Morrison 1960, 37
101  Bickersteth 1860, 1
102  Lane 2001, 3
103  Wollaston 1921, 5–6
104  Balfour 1911, 10
105  Hunt 1949, 4–5
106  Hunt 1949, 4–5
107  Hunt 1949, 7–8
108  Fletcher 1989, 8
109  Humphries and Gordon 1992, 39–40
110  Koven 1994, 1177, citing Loane 1907
111  Davidoff 2012, 78–107
112  Brown 1980, 32. For other examples, see Buettner 2004, 118–20
113  Steedman 2009, 228–238
114  Hamlett 2010, 118–9

115  Healey 2001, 239
116  Hare 1896, I, 60
117  White 1938, 41
118  Balfour 1911, 79–82, 89
119  Bickersteth 1860, 4, 52
120  Balfour 1938, 9–10
121  Healey 2001, 285: Burkhardt and Smith 1991, 142, n. 2
122  Martineau 1877, 73–74
123  Morrison 1960, 27
124  Smith 1986, 864
125  Hare 1896, I, 256
126  Hare 1896, I, 60
127  Balfour 1911, 49
128  White 1938, 75–77
129  Hare 1896, I, 86–88
130  Bickersteth 1860, 3
131  Brown 1980, 32
132  Balfour 1911, 10
133  Balfour 1930, 10
134  Davidoff 2012, 125
135  Bickersteth 1860, 64
136  White 1938, 43
137  Balfour 1930,10
138  Brown 1980, 62
139  Wollaston 1921, 5
140  Ryder 1891, 3–11
141  Balfour 1911, 58–9, 88–9
142  Hare 1896, I, 256: Martineau 1877, 45: Jermy 1934, 30
143  White,1938, 19
144  Jermy 1934, 47
145  Petersen 1989, 68, 72, 160–191: Bellaigue 2007, 10–23, 49–52
146  Cohen 2009, 99–116
147  Hunt 1930, 81–2: Balfour 1930,149
148  Fletcher 1989, 8
149  Bickersteth 1860, 3, 79–81: Bickersteth 1892, 3, 79: Balfour 1911, 9
150  Balfour 1911, 35
151  Balfour 1930, 117
152  Martineau 1877, 53–4
153  Davidoff 2012, 125: Taylor 1969, 75
154  Macmillan 1907, 20–21
155  Osborne 1926, 3–4
156  Gleadle 2009, 109–122, 226
157  Tyndale-Biscoe 1951, 22
158  Hare 1896, I, 261–4, 287
159  Smith 1986, 864
160  White 1938, 161
161  White 1938, 40–2
162  Smedley 1929, 15
163  Hare 1896, I, 82 , 288
164  Morrison 1960, 19–21, 27

165  Birse 2011
166  Ryder 1891, 4
167  Barker 1880, 79, 102
168  Martineau 1877, 83, 91, 93–6
169  Macmillan 1907, 12: Brown 1980, 40, 60

## REFERENCES

Altenbaugh, R. 2004. Polio, disability and American public schooling: a historiographical exploration pp. 137–156 in Whitehead, C. and. O'Neill, M (eds), *Education Research and Perspectives, Essays in Honour of Professor Emeritus Richard Aldrich.* Crawley: University of Western Australia.

Atkinson, D. and Williams, F. (eds) 1990.'*Know Me As I am*'. London: Hodder & Stoughton.

Atkinson, D., McCarthy, M. and Walmsley, J. *et al.* (eds) 2000. *Good Times, Bad Times: Women with Learning Difficulties Telling Their Stories.* Kidderminster: BILD.

Atkinson, D., Jackson, M. and Walmsley, J. (eds) 1997. *Forgotten Lives: Exploring the History of Learning Disability.* Kidderminster: BILD.

Balfour, F. 1911. *Lady Victoria Campbell: a memoir* (2nd edition). London: Hodder and Stoughton.

Balfour, F. 1930. *Ne Obliviscaris: Dinna Forget.* London: Hodder and Stoughton.

Barker, J. 1880. *The Life of Joseph Barker: Written by himself, edited by his nephew John Thomas Barker.* [S.I.] Hodder and Stoughton.

Bell, G. K. 1935. *Randall Davidson, Archbishop of Canterbury.* London: Oxford University Press.

Bellaigue, C. de. 2007. *Educating Women: Schooling and Identity in England and France 1800–1867.* Oxford: Oxford University Press.

Bickersteth, C. 1860. *Doing and Suffering*: memorials of Elizabeth and Frances, daughters of the late Rev. E. Bickersteth. By their sister [Charlotte Bickersteth, afterwards Ward]. London: Seeley, Jackson & Halliday.

Bickersteth, C. 1892. *Doing and Suffering*: memorials of Elizabeth and Frances, daughters of the late Rev. E. Bickersteth. By their sister [Charlotte Bickersteth, afterwards Ward]. London: Sampson Low & Co.

Birse, R. M. 2011. Muirhead, Alexander (1848–1920), rev. Patricia E. Knowlden. *Oxford Dictionary of National Biography*. Oxford University Press, 2004; online edn. http://www.oxforddnb.com/view/article/37794, accessed 13 Aug 2014]

Borsay, A. 2007. Deaf children and charitable education in Britain, 1790–1944, pp. 71–90 in Borsay, A. and Shapeley, P (eds), *Medicine, Charity and Mutual Aid: the Consumption of Health and Welfare in Britain, c. 1850–1950.* Aldershot: Ashgate.

Borsay, A. and Dale, P. (eds) 2012. Introduction: disabled children – contested caring, pp. 1–14, in Borsay, A. and. Dale, P. (eds), *Disabled Children: Contested Caring, 1850–1979*, London: Pickering and Chatto.

Bourdillon, R. 1907. *Little Scholars in the School of Pain.* London: Elliot Stock.

Brown, A. 1980. *Cuthbert Heath: maker of the modern Lloyd's of London.* Newton Abbott: David and Charles.

Buettner, E. 2004. *Empire Families: British Children in India, 1850–1950.* Oxford: Oxford University Press.

Burkhardt, F. and Smith, S. (eds) 1991. *The Correspondence of Charles Darwin, Vol. 7, 1856–8.* Cambridge: Cambridge University Press.

Cohen, M. 2009. 'Familiar Conversation': the Role of the 'Familiar Format' in *Education in Eighteenth- and Nineteenth-Century England*, pp. 99–116 in Hilton, M. and Shefrin, J. (eds), Educating the Child in Enlightenment Britain: Beliefs, Texts, Practices. Aldershot: Ashgate.

Dale, P. 2012. Health visiting and disability issues in Britain before 1948, pp. 117–129 in Borsay, A. and Dale, P. (eds), *Disabled Children: Contested Caring, 1850–1979.* London: Pickering and Chatto.

Davidoff, L. and Hall, C. 2002. *Family Fortunes: Men and Women of the English Middle Class* (2nd edition, 1st edition 1987). London: Hutchinson.

Davidoff, L. 2012. *Thicker than Water: Siblings and Their Relations, 1780–1920*. Oxford: Oxford University Press.

Davin, A. 1996. *Growing Up Poor: home, school and street, 1870–1914*. London: Rivers Oram.

Dekker, R. 2000. *Childhood, Memory and Autobiography in Holland: From the Golden Age to Romanticism*. Basingstoke: Palgrave Macmillan.

Fletcher, S. 1989. *Maude Royden: a Life*. Oxford: Basil Blackwell.

Fletcher, A. 2008. *Growing Up in England: the experience of childhood, 1680–1914*. New Haven, Conn/London: Yale University Press.

Gillis, J. 1996. *A World of Their Own Making: Myth, Ritual and the Quest for Family Values*. New York: Basic Books.

Gillis, J. 2008. Epilogue: the islanding of children: reshaping the mythical landscapes of childhood, pp. 316–30, in Gutman, M. and de Coninck-Smith, N. (eds), *Designing Modern Childhoods: history, space and the material culture of children*. New Brunswick, N. J./London: Rutgers University Press.

Gleadle, K. 2009. *Borderline Citizens: Women, Gender and Political Culture in Britain, 1815–1867*. Oxford: Oxford University Press for the British Academy.

Hamlett, J. 2009. 'Tiresome trips downstairs': middle-class domestic space and family relationships in England, 1850–1910, pp. 118–124 in Delap, L. Griffin, B. and Wills, A. (eds), *The Politics of Domestic Authority in Britain, 1850–1950*. Basingstoke: Palgrave Macmillan.

Hamlett, J. 2010. *Material Relations: Domestic Interiors and Middle Class Families in Britain, 1850–1950*. Manchester: Manchester University Press.

Hardy, A. 1993. *The Epidemic Streets: Infectious Disease and the Rise of Preventive Medicine*. Oxford: Clarendon Press.

Hare, A. 1896. *The Story of My Life. I.* London: George Allen.

Healey, E. 2001. *Emma Darwin, the Inspirational Wife of a Genius*. London: Headline.

Hendrick, H. 2002. The child as social actor in history, pp. 51–70 in Christensen, P. and. James, A (eds), *Research with Children* (reprint of 2000 edition). London: Open University Press.

Hollis, P. 1987. *Ladies Elect: Women in English Local Government 1865–1914*. Oxford: Clarendon Press.

Humphries, S. and Gordon, P. 1992. *Out of Sight: The Experience of Disability 1900–1950*. London: Northcote House.

Hunt, A. 1949. *This is My Life* (reprint of 1938 edition). London, Glasgow: Blackie & Son.

Hutchison, I. 2007. *A History of Disability in Nineteenth-Century Scotland*. Lewiston: Lampeter: Edwin Mellen Press.

Jermy, L. 1934. *The Memoirs of a Working Woman, etc.* Norwich: Goose & Son.

Keith, L. 2001. *Take Up Thy Bed and Walk*. London: The Women's Press.

Koven, S. 1994. Remembering and dismemberment: crippled children, wounded soldiers and the Great War in Great Britain. *American Historical Review* 99, 1167–1202.

Lane. R. 2001. *Anna Gurney, 1795–1857*. Guist Bottom: Larks.

Lerner, L. 1997. *Angels and Absences: Child Deaths in the Nineteenth Century*. Vanderbilt University Press.

Levene, A., Reinarz, J. and Williams, A. 2012. Child Patients, Hospitals and the Home in Eighteenth-Century England, *Family and Community History* 15, 1, 15–33.

Levene, A. 2013. Childhood and adolescence, pp. 321–337 in M. Jackson (ed.), *The Oxford Handbook of the History of Medicine*, paperback edn. Oxford: Oxford University Press.

Loane, M. *The Next Street But One* (1907). London.

Martin, M. 2014. In market, mansion or mountain: representations of disability in reading for the young, 1850–1950, *Childhood in the Past: an International Journal*, 7, 1, 35–48.

Macmillan, D. 1907. *The Life of George Matheson*. London: Hodder and Stoughton.

Martineau, H. 1877. *The Autobiography and Memorials of Miss Harriet Martineau, edited by Edward Russell*. London: Smith, Elder & Co.

Morrison, H. 1960. *Herbert Morrison: an autobiography by Lord Morrison of Lambeth*. London: P. Odhams.

Nelson, C. 1994. *Boys Will be Girls: The Feminine Ethic and British Children's Fiction, 1857–1917*. London: Rutgers University Press.

Newton, H. 2012. *The Sick Child in Early Modern England*. Oxford: Oxford University Press.

Oliver, M. 2009. *Understanding Disability: From Theory to Practice*. Basingstoke: Palgrave Macmillan.

Osborne, C. C. 1926. *Philip Bourke Marston*. London: The Times Book Club.

Peterson, J. 1989. *Family, Love and Work in the Lives of Victorian Gentlewomen*. Indiana University Press, Bloomington

Potts, M. and Fido, R. 1991. *A Fit Person to be Removed: Personal Accounts of Life in a Mental Deficiency Institution*. Plymouth: Northcote House.

Ross, E. 1993. *Love and Toil: Motherhood in Outcast London, 1870–1918*. Oxford: Oxford University Press.

Ryder, D. 1st Earl of Harrowby. 1891. *Autobiography, etc.* London. Privately printed, part of the 'Ryder Family Papers'.

Sanders, V. 2001. *The Brother-Sister Culture in Victorian Fiction: From Austen to Woolf*. Basingstoke: Palgrave.

Sloane, D. 2008. Sick children and the thresholds of domesticity: the Dawson-Harrington families at home, pp. 42–60 in Gutman, M. and de Coninck-Smith, N. *Designing Modern Childhoods: History, Space and the Material Culture of Childhood*. New Brunswick, N.J./London: Rutgers University Press.

Smedley, C. A. (afterwards Armfield). 1929. *Crusaders. The Reminiscences of Constance Smedley.* London: Duckworth.

Smith, F. B. 1979. *The People's Health 1830 to 1910*. London: Croom Helm.

Smith, J. A. B. 1965. *John Buchan: A Biography*. London: Rupert Hart-Davis.

Smith, R. 1986. Sir Henry Platt: 100 not out, *British Medical Journal* 293, 864.

Starkey, P. 2012. Club-feet and charity: children at the House of Charity, Soho, 1848–1914. pp. 15–28 in Borsay, A. and. Dale, P (eds), *Disabled Children: Contested Caring, 1850–1979*. London: Pickering and Chatto.

Steedman, C. 2009. *Labours Lost: Domestic Service and the Making of Modern Britain*. Cambridge: Cambridge University Press.

Taylor, F. M. 1969. Memoirs, Book 1, 1894–1927, unpublished, author's possession.

Tolley, C. 2007. *Domestic Biography: the Legacy of Evangelicalism in Four Nineteenth-Century Families*. Cambridge: Cambridge University Press.

Tosh, J. 1999. *A Man's Place: Masculinity and the Middle-Class Home, 1830–1914*. London and New Haven: Yale University Press.

Tyndale-Biscoe, C. E. 1951. *Tyndale-Biscoe of Kashmir: An Autobiography*. London: Seeley, Service & Co, Ltd.

Vickery, A. 1993. Golden age to separate spheres? A review of the categories and chronologies of English women's history, *Historical Journal*, 36, 2, 398–99.

Vickery, A. 1998. *The Gentleman's Daughter: Women's Lives in Georgian England*. London and New Haven: Yale University Press.

Verstraete, P. 2012. *In the Shadow of Disability: Reconnecting History, Identity and Politics*. Opladen, Berlin, Toronto: Barbara Budrich Publishers.

Viner, R. and Golden, J. 2000. Children's Experiences of Illness, pp. 575–587 in Cooter, R. and Pickstone, J. (eds), *Companion to Medicine in the Twentieth Century*. Amsterdam: Harwood Academic Publishers.

Wade, B. and Moore, M. 1993. *Experiencing Special Education: What Young People With Special Educational Needs Can Tell Us.* Buckingham: Open University Press.

White, F. 1938. *A Fire in the Kitchen: the autobiography of a cook.* London: J. M. Dent and Sons, Ltd.

Wollaston, A. F. R. 1921. *Life of Alfred Newton: Professor of Comparative Anatomy at the University of Cambridge.* London: John Murray.

# 11

# La evolución de los espacios de aprendizaje de la infancia a través de los modelos pedagógicos

## Victoria Carmona Buendía and Elisa Valero Ramos

*The importance of space where childhood education is developed takes value from the first pedagogical models dated in the middle of the seventeenth century. Based in a changing society and in a concept of the child who has passed from being a little man to be understood like a person with his own personal identity, dignity and freedom, the different pedagogical models have evolved, not only from the didactic point of view, but also proposing reforms to those spaces that will accommodate the child.*

*The analysis of different methodologies, such as proposed by F. Froebel, M. Montessori and L. Malaguzzi, reveals how architecture may contribute to the consolidation of innovative educational processes. This contribution will be reflected in the architectural solutions that architects have proposed to the design of schools where they have conducted these methodologies. Distributions that promote the role of the teacher as observer, common spaces that contribute to the socialization of children, furniture adapted to the user or large windows that show the school as a cultural environment for the city, are some of the means through which architecture contributes to learning.*

*The study of the different ways that pedagogy, through history, has designed the space will help us to find the spatial characteristics that must have these architectural works aimed to the children, combining proposals from different disciplines we'll get a firm base where we could lean on to build learning spaces that contribute to the proper physical, mental and social development of children.*

## Introducción

A pesar de que la educación ha estado presente durante toda la historia, los edificios diseñados especialmente para tal fin no surgirían en Occidente hasta el siglo XIV. Hasta ese momento la educación se impartía en espacios que estaban destinados fundamentalmente a otros usos y que en determinados espacios de tiempo eran usados como improvisadas escuelas. A partir del siglo XVII existe un aumento del valor social y del interés por la infancia, lo que se manifiesta en un cambio de actitud de la sociedad hacia los niños. El interés por las construcciones escolares surge a finales del siglo XVIII y XIX, de la mano de la importancia que adquiere la educación y el derecho a saber leer y escribir.[1]

No podemos concebir los espacios escolares como algo estático o definitivo, los ambientes se constituyen en la interacción con los niños y en las relaciones que se establecen entre los grupos de sujetos y el medio. El ambiente va modificándose en el transcurso de estas relaciones promoviendo la construcción de ciertas habilidades en los niños. Estas nuevas habilidades modifican de nuevo el ambiente y el modo en que el niño interacciona con él, generando así la transformación del espacio y el enriquecimiento del sujeto. La base para pensar en el entorno escolar de los niños debe ser el conocimiento de sus necesidades, su manera de progresar, crecer y aprender. Los procesos evolutivos de los niños serán fundamentales a la hora de proyectar los entornos destinados a ellos.

En los modelos pedagógicos tradicionales el papel del alumno en el aprendizaje era totalmente pasivo, el maestro tenía como única función la transmisión de conocimiento mediante la impartición de clases magistrales. Las actividades del niño se basan en la repetición de ejercicios y su evaluación se realizará midiendo hasta que punto habían sido asimilados los conocimientos trasmitidos por el profesor. Estos modelos, al entender el aprendizaje del alumno como una adquisición de saberes, no consideran fundamental el espacio en el que se desarrolla el aprendizaje. Existen datos de cómo estos modelos concebían el espacio escuela, por ejemplo Comenius, en su obra *Didáctica Magna* publicada en 1630 explicaba como las escuelas debían de ser talleres de humanidad. Planteaba unas escuelas con patios y jardines llenos de arboles y de flores para despertar el interés del niño por la escuela. Para Pestalozzi en sus *Cartas para Educación Infantil* de 1819 explicaba como las escuelas deberían de ser talleres, donde los alumnos, en número de cincuenta, cultivaban la tierra, hacían trabajos agrícolas, recolectaban los frutos e iban a venderlos al mercado próximo. Pestalozzi consideraba que en el proceso de estas actividades, lograban aprendizajes importantes en el área del pensamiento abstracto: números, clasificaciones, diferenciaciones.

Dentro de los modelos pedagógicos tradicionales tendríamos que hablar de Rousseau que en 1762 publica su Programa para la Educación General del Niño. Rousseau no propone una tipología propia de espacio escuela pero sus aportaciones al concepto de infancia, con la idea de que el niño es un ser independiente y no un adulto en miniatura, propicia espacios para el desarrollo espontáneo y natural. Sus aportaciones fueron fundamentales para los avances pedagógicos que se producirían en el siglo XVIII.

Una serie de cambios de orden histórico, científico y psicológico hicieron que se produjera una reforma en la concepción de los enfoques pedagógicos que había hasta el momento y de esta forma surge la Escuela Nueva.[2] La Escuela Nueva toma del darwinismo la reivindicación de la acción, al considerar esta como un elemento central en todo proceso de selección natural. Es influenciada por la teoría de la Gestalt, de la que derivan las primeras ideas del carácter global del aprendizaje, que será el marco psicológico que resalta la importancia de la niñez para el futuro del hombre. La Escuela Nueva utiliza los principios filosóficos y las críticas a la educación noble y autoritaria, vigente en la Revolución francesa. De esta tomará el concepto de "hombre" y convertirá al niño en sujeto activo, y no en objeto, de la práctica educativa. Frente el mecanicismo, el autoritarismo y la falta de actividad de la escuela tradicional surge la pedagogía de la acción en la cual el niño tiene la capacidad de educarse a si mismo mediante la experimentación, la actividad espontánea y con una figura del maestro como un mediador en el proceso educativo. En la Escuela Nueva será fundamental la socialización y felicidad del niño y busca preparar al individuo para la vida.

## MODELO PEDAGÓGICO DE FROEBEL

Uno de los representantes más destacados de la Escuela Nueva es F. Froebel (1787–1852). Constituye el primer modelo formalizado de educación preescolar que afecta no sólo a los fundamentos teóricos de la pedagogía infantil, sino también a los repertorios técnicos y materiales de la práctica escolar e incluso aportó un tipo bien definido de arquitectura para la educación

La teoría pedagógica desarrollada por Froebel en su libro *La Educación del Hombre* de 1826, denota la existencia de una base religioso-filosófica, y en ella destacan una serie de principios, tales como:

a) Importancia de la familia en el proceso educativo: Considera la escuela como una extensión del hogar. Froebel recalca el valor de la familia, colaborando así con la visión de familia como núcleo social.

b) Individualidad: Cada educando es singular, y por tanto corresponde a la educación generar formas de atención que tengan en cuenta las diferencias individuales.

c) Libertad: El ambiente educativo que se estructure ha de respetar y preservar la libertad del niño, por lo que se deben ofrecer diferentes opciones de aprendizaje.

d) Autoactividad: La acción es un proceder innato en el hombre, lo cual debe favorecerse desde temprana edad. Se destaca la relación que hay entre la acción motora y otras habilidades y capacidades del niño. Hoy se sigue considerando fundamental que el niño experimente, interactúe con sus iguales y con todos los agentes educativos, porque solo así se favorece su desarrollo y se darán respuestas a sus inquietudes e intereses.

e) Relación: Llamado también de cooperación social, socialización o apertura. Se plantea que en el niño hay una tendencia natural a relacionarse con los demás. Es en el mundo de relaciones en que él vive, el mejor medio para estimularlo y favorecer la producción y creación.

f) La madre como figura fundamental: el papel de la madre era de gran importancia para la educación temprana aunque Froebel consideraba necesario completar el instinto maternal con una formación adecuada para la educación de sus hijos.

El modelo froebeliano centra su atención en el juego como forma de aprendizaje, creando materiales específicos, a los que denomina 'dones' o regalos, y que están constituidos por una serie de juguetes y actividades. Desde este punto de vista concibe la educación como la posibilidad de promover la actividad creadora, espontánea y libre del niño.

## El espacio-escuela de Froebel

El modelo froebeliano configura un nuevo espacio escolar abierto, dinámico y flexible, en el que puedan darse todas las formas posibles de desarrollo, percepciones, expresiones y relaciones del niño, en un medio educativo organizado.

Su modelo escolar, el Kindergarten o Jardín de la Infancia, se contrapone a modelos anteriores mucho más rígidos, como el propuesto por P. Montesino[3] de aulas masificadas, con tarima y gradería. La escuela de Froebel, como señala García Purón,[4] es un 'lugar' para el desenvolvimiento de la vida, la belleza y el conocimiento, donde ha desaparecido 'el fastidio, el cansancio, la pesadez, la rutina... '. Un espacio escolar con predominio de los espacios abiertos, donde el aire, el agua, las plantas y la educación física formaban parte esencial de este patrón pedagógico.

Esta nueva pedagogía de educación integral, armónica y progresiva necesitará para su buena implantación una arquitectura de las mismas características, con espacios cerrados, abiertos y de transición. Se construyeron escuelas específicas que seguían las pautas del modelo froebeliano y que según LaHoz,[5] eran las siguientes:

– El Jardín es el espacio de más extensión en todo el conjunto escolar y elemento fundamental para diferentes funciones. Se compone de varios espacios. El mayor lo ocupan las parcelas individuales, trozos de tierra de un metro cuadrado en forma rectangular para el trabajo individual. Cada niño cultivará a su gusto y manera su parcela correspondiente. El segundo grupo de espacios está dedicado al trabajo colectivo y será cultivado por todos a la vez. Deben estar divididos en partes iguales para grupos de veinticinco niños. Estarán situados rodeando a los jardines individuales. El Jardín ha de tener también espacios cerrados para guardar los instrumentos de la labor y algunos estanques con peces y jaulas para aves y otros animales que los niños puedan observar y estudiar.

– Debe haber dos patios, uno cubierto para los días de lluvia y otro descubierto con porches alrededor. El patio descubierto tendrá plantaciones de árboles, que serán de varias especies, y un círculo central con una fuente o una glorieta con plantas, alrededor de la cual formarán los niños círculos para los ejercicios gimnásticos. Ambos patios estarán enarenados y servirán para los ejercicios de gimnasia y canto, para los juegos libres y para realizar las actividades de labores y trabajos, cuando el tiempo lo permita. Un tercer espacio o patio cerrado es el refectorio, en cuyo centro habrá una fuente-lavabo de forma circular y a su alrededor unas mesas donde los niños se sentarán a tomar la merienda.

– La escuela estará compuesta por un tercer grupo de espacios cerrados que configuran el edificio propiamente dicho. En primer lugar están las salas de trabajo, que serán generalmente dos o cuatro, de forma rectangular o cuadrada, lo suficientemente amplias para trabajar con holgura y bien iluminadas, si es posible con luz bilateral. Cada aula no debe reunir más de 25 niños, y estará conectada directamente con el patio abierto para poder sacar las mesas, bancos y materiales y trabajar al aire libre los días primaverales (Tabla 11.1).

*Tabla 11.1. Propuestas pedagógicas de Froebel y su materialización arquitectónica en su modelo de espacio escuela. Fuente: Elaboración propia.*

| Principio pedagógico | Explicación | Respuesta arquitectónica |
|---|---|---|
| La escuela como extensión del hogar | Recalca el valor de la familia. Colaborando así con la visión de familia como núcleo social y la importancia de esta en el proceso educativo | Carácter familiar del edificio, pequeñas dimensiones y arquitectura sencilla, de aspecto casi doméstico, cuyo estilo puede ser tanto popular como funcional, adecuándose lo más posible a su entorno natural y sociocultural |
| Pedagogía intuitiva, e integral | Se puedan dar todas las formas posibles de percepciones, expresiones y relaciones del niño | Arquitectura abierta, dinámica y flexible |
| Educación armónica y progresiva | Que atienda a los distintos pasos que necesite el desarrollo del niño | Transición desde el edificio cerrado al jardín, pasando por los patios cubiertos y semicubiertos |
| Fondo filosófico naturalista | Instinto infantil a hurgar y manipular la tierra | Comunicación de las aulas con el entorno natural<br>Prevalencia de los espacios abiertos frente a los cerrados |
| Individualidad | Cada educando es singular, y por tanto corresponde a la educación generar formas de atención que consideren esas peculiaridades | Jardín dividido en parcelas individuales de un metro cuadrado para que cada niño cultive a su gusto y manera su parcela |
| Cooperación social | Tendencia natural del niño a relacionarse con los demás | Jardín con espacios dedicados al trabajo colectivo y que serán cultivados por todos a la vez |
| Promover la actividad creadora, espontánea y libre del niño | Utilización del juego como procedimiento metodológico | Mobiliario adaptado y movible. Las mesas han de tener el tablero sin inclinación y dibujada sobre él una cuadrícula para que encajen los "dones" |
| Autoactividad | La acción es un proceder innato que debe favorecerse desde temprana edad | Frente a los modelos rígidos anteriores propone aulas amplias para trabajar con holgura |
| Clara intención educativo-conceptual de las formas geométricas puras | Sirven de refuerzo a los aprendizajes realizados con el resto de los materiales y su metodología | El análisis de la planta nos muestra una disposición con gran simetría, con divisiones en medidas *áureas* y gran repetición de las formas rectangulares, cuadradas y circulares, sin faltar los cubos y cilindros, que añade en forma de cabañas para animales y jaulas para las aves |

Para entender la importancia de la educación en el desarrollo creativo y la influencia del modelo froebeliano y de sus estímulos didácticos en todo el proceso educativo del niño[6] podemos leer la cita del arquitecto Frank Lloyd Wright,[7] uno de los representantes más significativos de la arquitectura moderna, que fue un usuario de estos Kindergarten.

> Fui llevado hacia él a los tres años de edad, y por varios años me senté frente a la pequeña mesa de Kindergarten que tenía líneas trazadas a cuatro pulgadas de distancia en ambas direcciones y que formaban cuadrados de cuatro pulgadas de lado; y junto con otras cosas, jugaba yo sobre esas 'unidades lineales' con el cuadrado (cubo), con el círculo (esfera), y con el triángulo (tetraedro o trípode); todos eran bloques lisos de arce. Luego llegué a formar diseños usando otros elementos. Pero los bloques de arte liso y los triángulos de cartón eran los más importantes. Todavía los siento en la punta de los dedos.
>   La virtud de todo eso era despertar en la mente del niño la idea de la estructura rítmica de la naturaleza, dando el sentido intrínseco de causa y efecto, que de otra manera estaría fuera de su alcance. Pronto fui atraído por esas construcciones, modificando todo lo que veía. Aprendí a 'ver' en esta forma, y cuando veía ya no me conformaba con las apariencias de la naturaleza; quería proyectar.

## El modelo de María Montessori (1870–1952)

El modelo Montessori[8] parte de una fuerte base biologista y psicológica, que no solo se queda en el plano teórico, sino que se concreta en la práctica. Entre sus principios educativos se destacan: el de la libertad, el de actividad, el de independencia y el de la individualidad. Los componentes básicos de este modelo son la estructura y el orden, la realidad y la naturaleza, la belleza, la atmósfera y el desarrollo de la vida en comunidad.

La filosofía Montessori, que tuvo como soporte fundamental la publicación de *El Método Montessori* en 1912, considera la religión como algo esencial al hombre, que nace con él y por lo tanto no puede estar ausente de una educación integral, así como tampoco 'la preparación espiritual del maestro'. Montessori crea materiales especialmente diseñados para posibilitar el proceso de apropiación del conocimiento. Estos materiales no pretenden enseñar habilidades, sino ayudar a la autoconstrucción y el desarrollo psíquico mediante la ejercitación.

Los niños pueden mover sus mesas, agruparlas o separarlas según la actividad, todo el mobiliario es adecuado al tamaño del niño, siendo las manos las mejores herramientas de exploración, descubrimiento y construcción de dichos aprendizajes. Un ambiente que se ha organizado cuidadosamente para el niño, para ayudarle a aprender y a crecer. Este ambiente está formado por dos factores: (a) el entorno y (b) el material. El entorno preparado de tal manera que los niños puedan desarrollar los aspectos sociales, emocionales, intelectuales y morales de un niño. Es importante que también satisfaga las necesidades de orden y seguridad, todo tiene su lugar apropiado y pensado para ello. Montessori comprobó que preparando el medio ambiente del niño con los materiales necesarios para su formación en todas las áreas y dejándole escoger el material de trabajo, abriría el camino para un desarrollo completo. Sería la 'Libertad de elección en un medio ambiente preparado'.

Con el método Montessori se cambia completamente la idea de aula de transmisión frontal. Las aulas fomentaran la interacción con el ambiente y el uso de los materiales

Montessori. Los ambientes están diseñados para estimular el deseo de conocer y la independencia en los niños.

## Las escuelas de Montessori

El arquitecto Herman Hertzberger construyo en Delft una escuela Montessori donde pudo llevar a cabo un modelo de espacio escuela que sintetizará todos los planteamientos de este modelo pedagógico. Los factores que definen el diseño de esta escuela son:[9]

- El usuario del edificio es el principal factor para la toma de decisiones arquitectónicas.
- Cada proyecto es específico en función del contexto urbano y la disposición geométrica de los espacios no está basada en jerarquías formales ni espaciales.
- El proyecto se configura por la agregación de distintas unidades habitacionales, en forma de 'L', autónomas, que el arquitecto concebía como pequeños hogares. Cada unidad tiene su propio baño, una pequeña biblioteca, vestidor, aula (con diferentes zonas de trabajo) y una vitrina para mostrar, hacia el espacio común, las actividades desarrolladas en el aula.
- Los elementos y los espacios tienen múltiples funciones; se adaptan de acuerdo con la necesidad y la imaginación de cada niño o grupo de niños.
- Las formas predominan en la composición arquitectónica, permitiendo la versatilidad espacial y potenciando la creatividad.
- El espacio común se conforma por la disposición de las aulas, como si fuera una calle o plaza de la ciudad. El espacio se puede utilizar con distintos niveles de privacidad, en grupo o de forma individual siempre de una manera informal. Además Hertzberger diseño plataformas elevadas o deprimidas, formadas por bloques, que invitaban al niño a construir su propio espacio.

Con respecto a la utilización del espacio, los niños que están concentrados en tareas individuales o en pequeños grupos de trabajo, se ubican en la parte más baja del salón y cuentan con un mueble con diferentes gavetas, con todo lo que necesitan para que no se tengan que desplazar hasta la otra sección del salón. El trabajo grupal, las exposiciones y las conferencias sobre lo que se ha hecho en el día se realizan en la parte más grande y, a la vez, la más elevada de la 'L' y allí también existen muebles con todas las herramientas necesarias. Se trata por tanto de un espacio multifuncional que permite al niño realizar todas esas acciones tan propias de la pedagogía Montessori como son reunir, encontrar, imaginar, recorrer, permanecer, descubrir, compartir, comunicarse, aprender, observar, mirar, buscar, cuidar, será el lugar para lo imprevisto, para la aventura y el juego.

Los espacios exteriores son considerados como el lugar que permite el contacto del mundo natural y social. Se organizan con una serie de muros bajos que estructuran áreas de juego a modo de areneros-jardines. Se conforman espacios de distintos tamaños que permiten que los niños se apropien de ellos de manera individualizada o en grupo. Los materiales con los que está construida la escuela son madera y hormigón de forma que se cree un ambiente neutro que permite que sea la imaginación de los niños la que les guie en todos sus descubrimientos (Tabla 11.2).

*Tabla 11.2. Relación entre los principios pedagógicos y la respuesta arquitectónica. Fuente: Adaptado de Jiménez Avilés (2009).*

| Pedagogía | | Explicación | Arquitectura |
|---|---|---|---|
| Ambiente preparado | Proporcionado | Acorde a las dimensiones y fuerzas del niño | Cada aula se conforma como un pequeño hogar |
| | Limitado | El mismo ambiente sea el que dirija al niño hacia el conocimiento y lo ayude a ordenar sus ideas y aclare su mente | Cada unidad es reconocible por sus actividades a través de las hallazgos y propuestas de los niños que se muestran al espacio central a través de vitrinas |
| | Sencillo | En la calidad de las cosas y en la línea de las formas | Materiales utilizados: Madera y hormigón, se crea un ambiente neutral que permite que sea la imaginación la que guie a los niños |
| | Lavable | Para que el niño pueda mantener limpio y cuidado el ambiente | Materiales lavables y de fácil mantenimiento |
| Libertad: el niño escoge lo que quiere aprender | | No hay clases magistrales ni colectivas | Aulas que permiten abordar, de forma simultánea, actividades de la vida práctica, habilidades sensoriales y áreas académicas y artísticas |
| Uso del material Montessori como medio de desarrollar habilidades | | El niño aprende mediante la manipulación del material Montessori. Se desarrollan en el niño destrezas específicas según la edad | Zona especial para el uso de este material. Espacio donde el niño pueda estar solo, concentrado, o en comunidad ayudando a otros |
| Silencio, actividad, libertad, autonomía y movilidad. Uso del mobiliario adecuado | | Aprendizaje personal a través del ensayo y el error, que se hace evidente en grandes superficies claras y en silencio | Pocas barreras arquitectónicas verticales. Los estantes para el material Montessori pueden ser las divisiones verticales, pero deben permitir la continuidad visual del espacio |
| Educación sensorial | | Colores, cambios de nivel e interacción directa con la naturaleza | La textura del piso y los cambios de nivel son importantes; son elementos que favorecen el desarrollo de la sensibilidad en el educando |
| Mundo adecuado a la escala del niño | | Diseños que se adaptan a la talla del infante | Muros bajos, ventanas, mobiliario acorde a la talla del niño |
| Maestro como observador | | El maestro no imparte la clase, solo es un guía | Lugar especial para que el maestro pueda observar el intervenir cuando lo considere necesario |

## LOS MODELOS PEDAGÓGICOS ACTUALES

Resulta imposible aunar en un único modelo pedagógico el conjunto de propuestas surgidas de los avances en la psicología y en las teorías del aprendizaje durante el siglo XX. Los cambios en una sociedad mucho más globalizada y la revolución en las telecomunicaciones plantean nuevas demandas educativas. Los modelos pedagógicos anteriores no pueden dar respuesta a los requerimientos que la sociedad contemporánea plantea a la educación.

El desarrollo acelerado de la sociedad moderna implica la elaboración de un currículum activo que desarrolle capacidades y que prepare a los niños para enfrentarse al enorme volumen de información que actualmente se genera. No obstante, en los primeros años, los niños han de adquirir las bases necesarias que les permitan asimilar los conocimientos para el tránsito escolar, creando habilidades generales que sean el cimiento de todo ese andamiaje intelectual necesario para la formación futura.

## El modelo de Loris Malaguzzi (Sistema Reggio Emilia)

Este sistema pedagógico fue iniciado para las madres de familia en 1946, y apoyado por su fundador Loris Malaguzzi (1920–1994), educador italiano, tuvo su fuente de inspiración en las ideas de numerosos autores como Dewey, Wallon, Claparede, Decroly, Makarenko y Vigotsky, así como posteriormente Freinet, Dalton y J. Piaget. El sistema de Reggio Emilia[10] considerado educación progresiva, concibe al niño como un ser intelectual, emocional, social y moral, cuyas potencialidades son guiadas y cultivadas cuidadosamente.

Este modelo se plantea lograr una educación de calidad en la que se enriquezcan intelectualmente no solo los niños sino todos los alumnos que participan en ella. La educación del niño se enfoca de una manera comunitaria y se describe la cultura de forma participativa y conjunta de adulto–niño. El trabajo educativo se organiza en forma de proyectos. Es una continua investigación de temas seleccionados por los niños. El proyecto se diseña para ayudar a los niños a darse cuenta de los distintos fenómenos que ocurren en el ambiente, y de esta forma experimentarlos; los niños son motivados a tomar sus propias decisiones y elecciones en compañía de sus coetáneos.

Los niños no son obligados a cambiar de actividad, sino que se respeta su ritmo y se motivan para repetir experiencias, observando y volviendo a observar, representando, desarrollando sus capacidades a través de la expresión simbólica. Se le estimula a explorar su medio ambiente y a utilizar mil lenguajes: palabras, movimientos, dibujo, pintura, construcción, escultura, teatro de sombras, collage, drama y música. Para ello parten de los siguientes principios:[11]

– Todos los niños están potencialmente preparados, tienen curiosidad e interés para construir su aprendizaje, utilizando todo lo que el ambiente les tiende en su interacción social. Los maestros son conscientes de esta potencialidad y construyen con los niños un programa que los apoye en su desarrollo.
– La educación tiene que potenciar a cada niño, no verlo aislado, sino en relación con los demás niños y con los adultos.
– El bienestar emocional del niño es indispensable para que aprenda, y está relacionado con el bienestar de los padres y educadores.
– La interacción con la familia es variada y parte activa en la experiencia de los niños en el centro infantil.
– La utilización del espacio, la ambientación y el material deben favorecer la comunicación y la relación entre los niños, así como también actividades que

promuevan diferentes opciones y la solución de problemas en el proceso de aprendizaje.
– Al planificar y llevar a cabo las actividades y proyectos, se ha de tener en cuenta el sentido del tiempo y el ritmo de los niños. El educador permanece durante tres años con los niños, lo que le permite conocer el ritmo de aprendizaje y le facilita, por lo tanto, la planificación.

El rol del adulto consiste en escuchar, observar y entender las estrategias que los niños usan para su aprendizaje, en las diferentes situaciones. El maestro se considera como un recurso, un proveedor de ocasiones a quien pueden acudir cuando necesitan un gesto, una palabra y no un sancionador de las actividades que realizan.

## El modelo de espacio-escuela de Reggio Emilia

El método de Malaguzzi es tan vivencial que no podría aprenderse por medio de libros. Una parte fundamental de este proyecto pedagógico es el ambiente, por tanto existe una fuerte relación entre el discurso pedagógico y el arquitectónico (Tabla 11.3). Malaguzzi[12] quería que los edificios tuvieran una estructura unitaria, familiar y acogedora que permita a los niños recorrer todos sus espacios manteniéndose orientado y facilitándole una percepción global del conjunto. Las dimensiones globales del centro han de permitir que todos se conozcan, evitar la necesidad de normas que restrinjan la espontaneidad como ocurre en los grandes centros. En Reggio Emilia ningún centro supera los 70 u 80 niños, según sea primer o segundo ciclo. Las escuelas pequeñas favorecen las relaciones informales, facilitan la flexibilidad del funcionamiento, impiden el anonimato e invitan a la participación de toda la comunidad educativa.

Se utiliza la ciudad, el campo y la montaña como elementos didácticos y ofrece también la escuela como ámbito cultural para la ciudad. Esto se refleja en un diseño arquitectónico de las escuelas, con grandes ventanales, hasta el suelo, de manera que la ciudad entra en la escuela y los niños puedan ir hacia ella. Malaguzzi hablaba de la necesaria conexión entre el 'L' 'dentro' y el 'fuera' de los espacios, de las aulas y los patios así como la fácil visibilidad de lo que ocurre dentro del centro escolar y de su entorno social y cultural.

En cuanto al ambiente humano, en cada sala puede haber hasta 25 niños y 2 maestros, que trabajan conjuntamente con el atelierista y el pedagogo. El arte se ve como parte inseparable del programa, como una representación simbólica del proceso de aprendizaje del niño.

Su modelo también establece que cada salón debe estar ambientado con diferentes áreas de una manera sumamente atractiva, y que todos los materiales deben estar al alcance de los niños y mantener un orden perfecto. El espacio debe permitir dividirse y subdividirse para que los niños puedan reunirse en pequeños grupos. No existe jerarquización de espacio ni roles de forma que los niños pueden recorrer la escuela con libertad, sin límites, salvo los estrictamente necesarios. Incluso la cocina, con una posición central y transparente, toma valor en las escuelas de Reggio Emilia haciendo

*Tabla 11.3. Relación entre el discurso pedagógico y el arquitectónico de Malaguzzi. Fuente: Elaboración propia.*

| Principios Pedagógicos | Explicación | Arquitectura |
|---|---|---|
| Educación comunitaria | La interacción con la familia es variada y parte activa en la experiencia de los niños en el centro infantil | Los espacios deben ser capaces de potenciar la participación social aportando y mostrando documentación cualificada y clara de qué ocurre y mostrando las huellas de la experiencia de los niños |
| Atención a la dimensión estética | El ambiente es concebido como un proyecto pedagógico. Es un educador más | Cada escuela tiene su propio ambiente y su propia identidad arquitectónica en la ideación y finalización de espacios, formas y funciones |
| Importancia de la socialización de los niños | Se debe favorecer la comunicación y relación entre los niños | Gran 'plaza' central, lugar de encuentros, juegos y actividades |
| La escuela sea un ámbito cultural para la ciudad | La escuela no puede estar aislada del territorio urbano y social | Las escuelas gozan hacia el interior y hacia el exterior de grandes cristaleras que hacen que la luz genere paisajes luminosos |
| Estructura de escuela articulada, unitaria y familiar | Las escuelas infantiles acogen a un máximo de 66 niños de 0–3 y de 78 en el ciclo de 3–6 | Escuelas pequeñas en las que todo el mundo es conocido |
| Todos los niños están potencialmente preparados | Los niños tienen curiosidad e interés para construir su aprendizaje utilizando lo que el ambiente les brinde | Cada aula debe de tener diferentes áreas con todos los materiales al alcance de los niños |
| La educación tiene que potenciar a cada niño, no verlo aislado, sino en relación con los demás niños y adultos | Los niños pueden encontrarse en pequeños grupos o en intimidad si lo desean | El espacio permite dividirse y subdividirse |
| No existen jerarquías ni roles | Los niños pueden recorrer la escuela con libertad, sin límites | En la distribución del espacio se evitan también las jerarquías, situando en algunas escuelas la cocina como elemento central |

participe al niño en el proceso de elaboración de la comida y no solo en el resultado. Malaguzzi ve en cada acción cotidiana una oportunidad para educar.

Las aulas se encuentran unidas por una gran plaza central, lugar de encuentros, juegos, amistades y actividades. Las aulas están subdivididas en dos zonas contiguas. Hay también aula de música y un taller de arte o atelier, que contiene una gran variedad de materiales, herramientas y recursos, usado por todos los niños y maestros para explorar, experimentar, expresar y crear pensamientos. El ambiente de la escuela es un lugar de convivencias y de intercambio relacional entre adultos y niños. Un lugar en el que se piensa, discute y se trabaja tratando de reconciliar lo que se sabe con lo que no se sabe, las dificultades, los errores, las expectativas, los éxitos, las dudas y los problemas de elección. (Tabla 11.3).

Después del análisis de las propuestas de espacio escuela que se plantean a lo largo de la historia por los diferentes modelos pedagógicos, podemos extraer los valores fundamentales y más comunes de estas propuestas. Se pretende dejar constancia de la importancia del espacio en los primeros años. Un espacio adecuado a la medida de las necesidades del niño le ayudará a adquirir, además de conocimientos, autonomía, seguridad y hábitos que tan importantes son para un buen desarrollo integral.

– A su vez estos espacios deben tener flexibilidad espacial de forma que permitan y faciliten la respuesta a sus deseos de exploración, y a sus necesidades de movimientos libres, lo que les proporcionará experiencias ricas y estimulantes.
– Para un desarrollo adecuado del niño es fundamental los estímulos que recibe de su entorno en los primeros años de vida. Un entorno rico y estimulante proporcionará oportunidades de aprendizaje, de desarrollo físico, intelectual y emocional.

     Estos espacios deben favorecer la percepción polisensorial del niño, lo que permitirá el desarrollo sensorial además de fomentar y mejorar sus capacidades perceptivas.
– Los espacios deben de atender a la escala del usuario. Las investigaciones de Dudek[13] ponen de relieve el efecto que ejerce el espacio escolar sobre la actividad de los niños, llegando a la conclusión de que los espacios más amplios favorecen una mayor actividad motriz. También, el espacio, debe de contribuir al trabajo individual o en pequeños grupos, mediante el uso de lugares estructurados. Estos permiten al niño configurar su propio espacio en el que sentirse seguro y desarrollar actividades que requieran más atención.
– Es fundamental que los espacios reunan las condiciones necesarias para fomentar el juego. Estas condiciones posibilitan juegos motores de experimentación, juegos simbólicos o de representación, o juego individuales o colectivos que tan importantes son para el desarrollo infantil. Hay que tener en cuenta que aportando posibilidades de juego estamos contribuyendo a la socializacion y a la adquisición, por parte del niño, de habilidades y destrezas psicológicas y psicomotrices.

Con el juego se plantea nuevas situaciones, soluciones a desafios, metas que fomentan la capacidad de organización, planificación y toma de decisiones, lo que termina siendo un ensayo para la vida futura.

NOTES

1   Ramírez 2009
2   Jiménez 2009
3   Montesino 1850
4   García Purón 1919

5  LaHoz 1991
6  Bordes 2007
7  Wright 1962
8  Montessori 2003
9  Marín, 2009
10 Malaguzzi, 2001
11 Ibidem
12 Ibidem
13 Dudek 2007

## Referencias

Bordes, J. 2007. *La infancia de las vanguardias.* Madrid: Cátedra

Dudek, M. 2007. *Schools and Kindergartens: A design manual.* Basel (Suiza): Birkhäuser.

García Puron, J. 1919. "*Sobre la presente obra", El niño y su naturaleza.* Nueva York: D. Appleton y Compañía.

Jiménez, Á. M. 2009. "La Escuela Nueva y los espacios para educar". *Revista Educación y Pedagogía* 21, 103–125.

Lahoz Abad, P. 1991. "El modelo froebeliano de espacio-escuela. Su introducción en España" *Historia de la Educación* 8, 107–35.

Malaguzzi, L. 2001. *La Educacion Infantil en Reggio Emilia.* Barcelona: Octaedro/Rosa Sensat.

Marín Acosta, F. 2009. "La arquitectura escolar del estructuralismo holandés en la obra de Herman Hertzberger y Aldo Van Eyck". *Revista Educación y pedagogía* 21, 67–79.

Montesino, P. 1850. *Manual para los maestros de escuelas de párvulos.* Madrid: Imprenta del colegio de sordo-mudos y ciegos.

Montessori, M. 2003. *El metodo de la pedagogia científica aplicado a la educación de la infancia.* Madrid: Biblioteca Nueva.

Ramírez Potes, F. 2009. "Arquitectura y pedagogía en el desarrollo de la arquitectura moderna", *Revista Educación y Pedagogía* 21, 29–65.

Wright, F. L. 1962. "*Textos de Frank Lloyd Wright"* seleccionados por Edgar Kaufmann y Ben Raeburn. Buenos Aires: Víctor Lerú.

# 12

## MONTESSORI Y EL AMBIENTE PREPARADO: UN ESPACIO DE APRENDIZAJE PARA LOS NIÑOS

### *Fátima Ortega Castillo*

*In 1907, one of the representatives of the educational reform movement from the early twentieth century, Maria Montessori (1870–1952), she had the opportunity to coordinate a day care center for children of the working class who were too young to attend public school. Centered Approach 'whole child', Dr Montessori developed a very different kind of school the traditional focus on the adult. To emphasize this difference, she called her first school the 'Casa dei Bambini' or 'Children's House'. The Montessori classroom wasn't designed for the domain of the adults in charge, but in a meticulously crafted. Usually referred to as class's atmosphere Montessori prepared. This name reflects the care and attention that is given to create a learning environment that will enhance the independence of children and their intellectual development, and which is fully adapted to its characteristics.*

*Spaces and educational materials are always relevant in education, but we would like to emphasize its importance in early childhood education. It is generally accepted that the student has an active role in changing their environment, but also recognizes that the physical features of an area, even if alone do not determine any conduct, self help or hinder your appearance.*

*Classroom organization is an important tool in the hands of the teacher or the teacher, especially in the early ages. It is therefore necessary to put all the care and attention possible to achieve an environment, both enjoyable and practical, enhancing the life and learning of children.*

*Thus, historians have recently shown a growing interest in space. Historians of education have also turned their attention to the spaces for children, classrooms being one of the most representatives. In a progressive manner, from the 50s, has been increasing interest in understanding the relationship between the built environment and human behavior, and adapt the design of the buildings to the characteristics and needs of its users.*

*This chapter is intended to give an overview of how Montessori, from the early twentieth century, found that preparing the child's environment with the materials necessary for their development in all areas possible and letting you choose your work material, open the way for a full development of his being. How developed his scientific pedagogy, how he started his 'children's house', which gave recommendations in his works, in short, how to make their classrooms and how they affect the chances of children. The relevance of the prepared environment (space, materials and their layout) is a cornerstone in her methodology.*

Introducción

Desde mitad del siglo XX y de forma progresiva, ha ido aumentando el interés por conocer las relaciones existentes entre el ambiente construido y la conducta humana, así como por adecuar el diseño de los edificios a las características y necesidades de sus usuarios.[1] En términos generales, los historiadores han mostrado recientemente un interés creciente en el espacio y particularmente los historiadores de la educación también han dirigido su atención a los espacios destinados a los niños, siendo las aulas uno de los espacios más representativos. En general, se admite que el alumno posee un papel activo en la modificación de su medio.[2] Pero también se reconoce que los rasgos físicos de un espacio, aun cuando por sí solos no determinan ninguna conducta, sí facilitan o dificultan su aparición.

En el presente trabajo se pretende dar una visión general de cómo se crean las aulas y cómo influyen en las posibilidades de los niños desde la visión de María Montessori. Esta autora comprobó que preparando el medio ambiente del niño con los materiales necesarios para su desarrollo y dejándole escoger su material de trabajo, abriría el camino para el desarrollo completo del niño. Cabe señalar que la bibliografía actual tiene varias deficiencias que en su mayoría resultan de la falta de investigación interdisciplinaria.

María Montessori y la pedagogía científica

María Montessori (1870–1952) obtiene el doctorado en Medicina hacia 1896. Desde un primer momento destaca su visión pedagógica y comienza a ocuparse de los niños con deficiencias psíquicas, inspirándose en metodologías de los médicos y educadores franceses Jean Itard (1775–1838) y Edouard Sèguin (1812–1880). Sus primeras convicciones e intereses cultivados ya en los últimos años del siglo XIX se reflejan en sus palabras 'a diferencia de mis colegas, tuve la intuición de que la cuestión de los deficientes era preferentemente pedagógica, más que preferentemente médica'.[3]

María Montessori se convierte en una de las representantes del movimiento de renovación pedagógica a partir de principios del siglo XX, el denominado 'siglo del niño'. La educación de Montessori es conocida en la actualidad por muchas características y aspectos, incluyendo un enfoque en la creación de un espacio para niños, con tamaño infantil, elementos y materiales accesibles y juguetes. La importancia del ambiente preparado (espacio, materiales y su diseño) es una parte importante en su metodología.

Montessori desarrolla lo que llama *pedagogía científica*, metodología basada en la organización, el trabajo y la libertad. Ella establece como uno de los principios fundamentales de la pedagogía científica el que la escuela permita las libres manifestaciones de los alumnos, libertad que permita el desarrollo de las manifestaciones espontáneas del niño.[4] El método nace de la idea de ayudar al niño a obtener un desarrollo completo, para lograr al máximo sus capacidades, trabajando sobre bases científicas en relación con su propio desarrollo físico y psíquico. Debemos recordar que en época de Montessori el concepto de infancia, el reconocimiento del niño no estaba establecido ni social ni culturalmente. Por ello el reconocimiento de las diferencias individuales, el respeto por el ritmo de aprendizaje junto con la idea de permitir y favorecer la libre actividad, la espontaneidad y la expresión de los niños está en la base del método Montessori.[5]

Una vez afirmada la concepción del niño como ser, ser activo y reafirmado el principio de que los adultos no deben sustituir al niño (cambio sustancial del papel del docente en el aula), Montessori añade que estas potencialidades tienen que ser *estimuladas por el ambiente*. El objetivo es que el niño desarrolle al máximo sus posibilidades, sus potencialidades, dentro de un ambiente estructurado siendo, a la vez, atractivo y motivador. En este sentido, en la Casa de los Niños[6] se cuidan al máximo los detalles en mobiliario y equipamiento, disposición en el aula, de forma que se pueda vivir y trabajar cómodamente y se favorezca la disciplina autoeducadora.

Tal como cita Lillard,[7] al contrario de muchos filósofos educadores, la doctora Montessori desarrolla su método pedagógico para poner en práctica su filosofía. Partiendo de que las innovaciones en el aula junto con su enfoque educativo entero estaba animado por una experimentación constante basada en la observación del niño. A esto le añade dos componentes básicos de su método: el medio ambiente, incluyendo los materiales y los ejercicios pedagógicos, y las maestras que preparan ese medio ambiente (Montessori siempre piensa en una mujer para realizar la función de maestra, guía, directora, lo que hoy sería independiente de género).[8]

Basa su método en el trabajo del niño y en la colaboración entre el adulto y el niño. Así, la escuela no es un lugar donde la maestra transmite conocimientos a través del método básicamente oral, predominante en la educación tradicional en aquella época, sino un lugar donde la inteligencia y la parte psíquica del niño se desarrolla a través del trabajo libre con material didáctico especializado.

Los principios de la filosofía Montessori se fundamentan de forma directa con los preceptos de la vida. El niño posee dentro de sí, desde antes de nacer, principios para desarrollarse psíquicamente, de forma autónoma. Los adultos somos simples colaboradores en esta construcción que hace de sí mismo. El niño necesita del amor y cuidado de sus padres, pero necesita también que el adulto le facilite un medio ambiente preparado en donde sea posible la acción y la selección, autoconstrucción, siendo el maestro el que transformará la educación y la escuela en ambientes que permitan las libres manifestaciones del niño, exigencia explícita dentro del pensamiento montessoriano.

Para ello, el docente debe ser guía, encargado de mostrar el camino. Debe conocer y manejar e indicar correctamente y de modo claro el uso y los objetivos de cada material, así como ser capaz de guiar al niño hacia el material o actividad que se requiera para lograr un desarrollo armónico y adecuado a su edad dentro de ese *medio ambiente preparado*.

## Educación mediante la libertad en un medio preparado

Ella describe el medio ambiente como un lugar fructífero para el niño, diseñado para satisfacer sus necesidades de autoconstrucción, y para revelarnos su personalidad y sus modelos de crecimiento. Lillard[9] al respecto destaca tres puntos a tener en cuenta:

en primer lugar, Montessori considera al medio ambiente secundario a la propia vida: 'puede modificar en el sentido de que ayuda u obstaculiza, pero no puede crear nunca... Los orígenes del desarrollo, tanto en la especie como en el individuo, yacen adentro'.[10] Desde esta concepción el niño 'crece porque la vida potencial dentro de él se desarrolla, haciéndose visible'.[11] En segundo lugar, el medio ambiente debe ser preparado cuidadosamente para el niño, por un adulto inteligente y sensible. En tercer lugar, el adulto debe participar en la vida y el crecimiento del niño dentro del mismo.

> 'Simplemente, el medio ambiente debe estar lleno de vida, dirigido por una inteligencia más elevada, y arreglado por un adulto que esté preparado para cumplir su misión. Es en esto que nuestro concepto difiere tanto de aquel del mundo en el que el adulto hace todo para el niño, como del medio ambiente pasivo en el que el adulto abandona al niño a sí mismo... Esto significa que no es suficiente colocar al niño entre objetos que estén en proporción con su tamaño y fuerza; el adulto que quiera ayudarlo debe haber aprendido cómo hacerlo'.[12]

Un ambiente que se ha organizado y preparado de forma minuciosa para el niño, para ayudarle a aprender y a crecer. Este ambiente está formado tanto por el entorno como por el material disponible en él, preparado de tal manera que derive en un desarrollo social, emocional, intelectual, pero también que satisfaga las necesidades de orden y seguridad, ya que todo tiene su lugar apropiado. Montessori pretende ordenar la vida del niño para que su esencia investigadora tenga libertad en el aula y de esta forma se exprese a sí mismo sin coacción alguna (Fig. 12.1).[13]

*Figura 12.1: Niños y niñas en el aula. (Montessori, 1912: 349).*

La Dra. Montessori comprobó que preparando el medio ambiente del niño con los materiales necesarios para su periodo de desarrollo (pertinencia al ritmo de aprendizaje del niño) en todas las áreas posibles y dejándole escoger su material de trabajo, abriría el camino para un desarrollo completo de su ser: *libertad de elección en un medio ambiente preparado*.

> 'Comencemos por proveer a las necesidades del niño disponiendo de un ambiente adaptado a su personalidad. Ello es una obra de servicio social, porque aquél no puede desenvolver una vida en el ambiente complicado de nuestra sociedad y menos aún en el de los refugios y prisiones que llamamos escuela... En el lugar de esto, debemos prepararle un ambiente donde la vigilancia del adulto y sus enseñanzas se reduzcan al mínimo posible; cuanto más se reduzca la acción del adulto, tanto más perfecto será el ambiente. Éste es un problema fundamental de la educación... Es preciso preparar con solicitud el ambiente, es decir, crear un nuevo mundo, el mundo del niño'.[14]

De esta manera, no se trata de preparar sólo al docente, hay que adaptar la escuela, con todo lo que esto implica a las nuevas ideas en que se apoya el método: 'para que nazca la pedagogía científica es preciso que la escuela permita las libres manifestaciones naturales del niño; ésta es la reforma esencial'.[15]

La creación de un ambiente adaptado, elaborado, a la vez que apropiado para el desarrollo de la atención, la voluntad, la inteligencia, la imaginación creativa, y la educación moral, es otra de sus grandes aportaciones. 'La clave es organizar el espacio de forma que los niños sean los protagonistas de su aprendizaje y que sepan usar el material sin depender constantemente de sus educadores. La totalidad del ambiente debe mantenerse, además, escrupulosamente ordenado, ya que el orden externo refuerza el orden de la mente del niño'.[16]

La principal singularidad de este material es su carácter autocorrector que permite que el niño se eduque a sí mismo, comprobando su actividad realizada. Esta idea de la autoeducación es central en el método montessoriano, relacionado con la autonomía y la libertad del infante. Siendo otras características del material: el realismo, la accesibilidad, la estética y su estructuración, organización.

De esta manera, la maestra/o, en este ambiente autoeducativo, debe respetar el ritmo interno del niño, y su decisión de qué hacer en cada momento en un entorno agradable, diseñado y equipado en especial para satisfacer sus necesidades.

Para Montessori la escuela, el ambiente de la clase tiene que ser extremadamente favorable a la educación:

> 'Comencé por crear un ambiente y una decoración escolares que fuesen proporcionales a la infancia y respondiese a la necesidad de actuar de manera inteligente...hice construir unas mesitas sólidas, pero ligerísimas, que dos niños pequeños de cuatro años las pudiesen transportar fácilmente, también sillitas, algunas de boga y otras de madera, y a poder ser elegantes y proporcionadas a la forma del cuerpo infantil'.[17]

## MONTESSORI Y EL MOBILIARIO ESCOLAR

Fue a finales del siglo XIX cuando se empezaron a tener en cuenta las necesidades físicas de los niños en el mobiliario escolar. En algunas publicaciones resalta la conveniencia de sujetar a los niños a los pupitres para, de este modo, evitar molestias físicas como las desviaciones de columna. Montessori se mostrará totalmente contraria a tales planteamientos.

'Es el principio de la esclavitud el que inspira toda la pedagogía y reina en la escuela. Una prueba de lo que afirmamos, la que más salta a la vista es el banco.

El banco escolar constituye una prueba luminosa de los errores de la primitiva pedagogía científica materialista, la cual pretendía reconstruir el viejo edificio escolar con unas cuantas piedras dispersas. Existía en otro tiempo el banco sucio sobre el cual se amontonaban los alumnos. Viene la ciencia, perfecciona el banco y para esta tarea pone a contribución la antropología y tiene en cuenta: la edad del alumno y la longitud de las piernas para hallar la altura exacta que ha de tener el asiento. No contenta con esto, calcula minuciosamente la distancia entre el asiento y la mesa para que la columna vertebral no sufra la escoliosis. Por último, (¡oh intuición profunda!) separa los asientos, los mide en el sentido de la anchura con el fin de que el niño que esté sentado no pueda moverse hacia los lados y quede bien independiente de su vecino. El banco está construido de modo que el niño esté lo más a la vista posible en su inmovilidad y pueda ser vigilado para prevenir los actos de perversión sexual en plena clase. ¿Qué pensaremos de este exceso de prudencia en una sociedad donde sería escandaloso enunciar principios de moral sexual por temor de contaminar la inocencia? Pero he aquí que la ciencia se presta a esta hipocresía perfeccionando los bancos de modo que la inmovilidad del niño sea la más completa posible'.[18]

El principio de libertad en el medio preparado del niño no encaja en los planteamientos del banco rígido basado en una idea de origen preventivo en el aula. Según Montessori, para combatir posibles dolencias físicas de los niños es mejor, en primer lugar, cambiar la forma de su trabajo de tal modo que no se vean obligados a permanecer durante muchas horas del día en una posición defectuosa. Aspecto muy ligado a la libertad y a la libre manifestación de la espontaneidad.

El método de la observación se establece sobre una sola base fundamental: la libertad de los niños en sus manifestaciones espontáneas. De este modo el mobiliario y el ambiente han de adaptarse a este principio.

La principal modificación del ambiente tradicional es la supresión de bancos, que los niños puedan entrar y salir libremente del aula. Las mesas, sillas y sillones son ligeros y fáciles de llevar, permite que el niño escoja la posición que más le conviene, lo cual constituye un signo de libertad y un medio educativo. Todo está hecho a la medida de las necesidades y posibilidades de los niños.

'Sentar a los niños en filas, como en las escuelas comunes, y asignarle a cada pequeño un lugar, y proponer que así se queden sentados en observación del orden de la clase como en una asamblea, esto puede obtenerse más tarde, al comienzo de la educación colectiva. Porque también en la vida sucede a veces que debemos quedarnos sentados y quietos, cuando, por ejemplo, asistimos a un concierto o a una disertación. Y sabemos bien que incluso para nosotros, como adultos, esto no se hace sin sacrificio. Si podemos – cuando hemos establecido la disciplina individual – enviar a cada uno a su propio sitio, en orden, tratando de hacerles entender que es una buena cosa estar ubicados así; que hay entonces un orden agradable en el cuarto, este ajuste ordenado y tranquilo de su parte, quedándose en sus sitios quietos y silenciosos, será el resultado de una especie de lección, no de una imposición'[19] (Fig. 12.2).

*Figura 12.2. Aula Montessori. Álbum "Historic Photos of Montessori around the World". Disponible en http://www.montessoricentenary.org.*

Los armarios han de ser bajos para que el niño alcance un objeto encima del mismo, a la vez que largos para que pueda tener muchos cajoncitos, cada uno de un alumno el cual podrá abrir y cerrar a voluntad para poder guardar dentro objetos de su propiedad.

Dentro del mobiliario también se destaca el espíritu estético que se ha de configurar tanto en el orden general como en cada uno de los objetos que los escolares pueden utilizar.

'Encima de las pizarras cuelgan cuadros que representan niños, escenas de familia, escenas campestres, animales domésticos, en forma simple y graciosa. Entre estos cuadros figura siempre en Roma el cuadro de la familia real de Italia. Un gran cuadro, reproducción en color de la "Virgen de la Silla", de Rafael, preside a todos los demás. Lo hemos escogido como símbolo de la Casa dei Bambini, porque éste no representa tan sólo un progreso social, sino un progreso del sentimiento humanitario'.[20]

## MATERIALES SENSORIALES

El niño en sus primeros años, según Montessori, tiene una fuerza interior que se manifiesta hacia los objetos del mundo exterior. Forma sus primeras ideas abstractas a través de sus sentidos, con ayuda de la educación. De este modo, el mundo de la materia constituye el principal medio de formación del espíritu y de construcción de la inteligencia. Aprenderá, en primer lugar, la relación entre el objeto y el nombre del mismo, para continuar por la existente entre un nombre y la idea que representa.[21]

Montessori desarrolla una propuesta para el aprendizaje en la que considera esenciales la práctica, la imitación, la repetición y la ordenación y clasificación. A través de la práctica y la experimentación el niño se apropiará de unas habilidades de tipo lógico y clasificatorio esenciales para el posterior desarrollo de operaciones mentales de mayor complejidad. Esta pedagoga crea para ello una serie de materiales y ejercicios didácticos, cuyo objetivo es el desarrollo de la educación intelectual, motriz y sensorial. De esta manera el método de Montessori pretende seguir la naturaleza funcional y psíquica del niño.

Desde un primer momento, establece el material que ella crea con cualidades destinadas a los niños y en ningún caso como una ayuda para el maestro, sino para que el niño trabaje de forma autónoma e independiente. Dentro de sus materiales y actividades para el desarrollo motriz, desarrollo centrado en la *vida práctica*, propone una serie de ejercicios individuales y colectivos tanto gimnásticos y psicomotrices como relacionados con la vida práctica y con el ambiente, en los que los alumnos, a la vez que progresan en la adquisición de dominio psicomotriz, están desarrollando tareas útiles para resultar seres cada vez más autónomos y prepararse para la vida en sociedad. Se considera importante la ayuda al niño para desarrollar la coordinación, concentración, independencia, orden y disciplina. Abarca ejercicios para la relación social, la tolerancia y la cortesía, el control perfecto y refinamiento del movimiento. Entre las diferentes actividades, los alumnos se abrochan las batas, se peinan, ponen la mesa, limpian el aula y objetos, anudan diferentes tipos de cierres en los bastidores creados para ello, entre otras (Fig. 12.3).

El desarrollo sensorial, se refiere tanto al progreso como al refinamiento de los cinco sentidos: vista, sonido, tacto, olor y gusto. El propósito de los ejercicios es educar los sentidos, así el niño puede aprender sobre el ambiente, y ser capaz de discriminar sus aspectos más sutiles. Montessori elabora una serie de materiales que provocan la libre manipulación por

*Figura 12.3. Niñas con bastidores (Montessori, 1912: 145).*

parte de los niños y el aprendizaje individualizado, prestando gran atención a la estética.

Estos materiales tienen como objetivo primordial ayudar al niño a desarrollar su inteligencia a través de la práctica, del desarrollo de diferentes acciones, organizando y clasificando sus percepciones sensoriales siguiendo siempre un orden lógico. Pretende, del mismo modo, ordenar la infinidad de impresiones que el niño percibe, considerando este desarrollo práctico como preparatorio interno para su vida intelectual. Montessori de esta manera crea un material específico para el desarrollo de cada sentido.

Algunos de estos materiales, de forma resumida:[22] tres colecciones de ajustes de sólidos denominados *Encajes sólidos* (cilindros ajustados dentro de sus moldes en tres piezas de madera); tres colecciones de sólidos en tamaños graduados desde cubos (color rosa, incluye su *Pink Tower*), prismas (color castaño oscuro) y listones de madera de color verde o coloreados alternativamente de rojo y azul; varios sólidos geométricos prisma, pirámide, esfera, cono, etc.; tablitas rectangulares con superficies lisas y ásperas llamadas *Tablas del tacto*; una colección de varias telas; pequeñas tablitas de madera de diferentes pesos; dos cajas, con 64 tablitas con colores; una caja de cajoncitos, conteniendo ajustes de figuras planas conocidos como *Encajes planos*; tres series de tarjetas con dibujos de formas geométricas de papel; una colección de cajas cilíndricas cerradas (para los sonidos); una doble serie de campanitas musicales cada una con un sonido diferente que corresponden a la escala musical, entre otros.

Finalmente, en cuanto a los materiales para el desarrollo del lenguaje y para el desarrollo matemático, hemos de afirmar que una vez más la introducción a los números y a las letras es de forma sensorial.

En primer lugar, en el desarrollo aritmético, el niño aprende a asociar los números a las cantidades, trasladándose gradualmente a formas más abstractas de representación. La educación temprana de este sentido, ayuda al niño a poner la base para la lectura y el aprendizaje de las matemáticas. Las actividades desarrolladas con los materiales sensoriales hacen que el niño pase de lo concreto a lo abstracto y le ayude a discriminar tamaños, colores, formas, peso, etc. Del mismo modo, el primer paso hacia la lectura y la escritura, también, es sensorial.

Los niños utilizan su dedo índice para conocer sensorialmente cada letra a través del uso de letras contorneadas con papel de lija. Esto les ayuda a reconocer las formas geométricas, al mismo tiempo que desarrolla su destreza y aprende las letras fonéticamente. Más adelante, se sustituye el dedo por un lápiz para a continuación, escribir. De esta manera, el aprendizaje de la lectura y la escritura se logra en el niño de forma natural.

Dentro del material didáctico desarrollado para la preparación a la escritura y a la aritmética,[23] podemos destacar, entre otros: pupitres sueltos con varios ajustes de metal; series de tarjetas con letras de papel de lija; dos alfabetos de letras de cartulina recortadas de diferentes tamaños; series de tarjetas con números de papel de lija; una serie de grandes cartones conteniendo las mismas figuras en papel liso para la numeración desde diez en adelante; dos cajas con pequeños palillos en forma de huso para contar, etc. (Fig. 12.4).

*Figura 12.4. Material didáctico de escritura y aritmética (Montessori, 1912: 187).*

## Discusión

Montessori no descuida que la sociedad se organiza para satisfacer, de manera casi exclusiva, las necesidades de los adultos. Pone como comparación de esta idea la concepción del interior de las casas: todo se prevé para y en función de las demandas del adulto. Pero, sobre todo, los adultos se refieren generalmente a sus propias necesidades sin tener en cuenta la vida psíquica y física del niño.[24] Por este motivo, esta pedagoga desde un primer momento reitera la vital necesidad de adaptar el ambiente, el clima educativo, los materiales a las necesidades de la infancia.

María Montessori entiende la tarea del docente como preparador del ambiente en el que se ha de desarrollar el niño, éste lo concibe como el sujeto del experimento, y a la escuela como terreno o medio de cultivo.

Del mismo modo, introduce en el aula infantil prácticas, materiales, actividades que hoy en día podemos considerar habituales, pero en su época fueron innovadoras.

En la práctica rompe con las tradicionales conceptos escolares, por ello desaparecen los pupitres y la cátedra, que entorpece el libre movimiento del niño, tanto las sillas, mesas, cuadros, adornos como diferentes objetos de manipulación, todos son hechos a la medida del niño. También introduje los materiales sensoriales para la educación intelectual y de cada uno de los sentidos.

NOTES

1   Suárez Pazos 1987
2   Cooper 1980
3   Montessori 1909, 28
4   Montessori 1937
5   Pla Molins, Cano García y Lorenzo Ramírez 2002, 78
6   En 1907 abre, en el barrio de San Lorenzo de Roma, la primera *Casa dei Bambini* para niños de tres a siete años
7   Lillard 1984
8   Montessori 2003, 41
9   Lillard 1984, 80
10  Montessori 1964
11  *Ibidem*
12  Montessori 1963, 224
13  Montessori 1937
14  *Ibidem*
15  Montessori 2003, 47
16  *Ibidem*
17  Montessori 1937
18  Montessori 2003, 99,100
19  Montessori 1994
20  Montessori 2003, 144
21  Yaglis 2004
22  Montesssori 1994
23  *Ibidem*
24  Yaglis 2004

REFERENCIAS

Cooper, I. 1980. La conducta de nens i professors i el disseny dels edificis escolars: l'experiència britànica en educació primaria, en Pol, E. y Morales, M. (eds): *L'entorn escolar: problemática psicológica, educativa i de disseny*. Barcelona: Universitat de Barcelona.

Lillard, P. P. 1984. *Un enfoque moderno al método Montessori*. México, D.F.: Diana.

Montessori, M. 1909. *Il Metodo della pedagogia scientifica aplicato all'educazione infantile delle case dei bambini*. Città di Castello: Lapi.

Montessori, M. 1912. The Montessori Method. Nueva York: Frederick A. Stokes Company.

Montessori, M. 1937. *El Método de la Pedagogía Científica*. Barcelona: Araluce.

Montessori, M. 1963. *The Secret of Childhood*. Calcutta: Orient Longmans.

Montessori, M. 1964. *The Montessori Method*. Nueva York: Schocken Books.

Montessori, M. 1994. *Ideas generales sobre el método. Manual práctico*. Madrid: CEPE.

Montessori, M. 2003. *El método de la Pedagogía científica aplicado a la educación de la infantil*. Ed. y estudio introductorio de Carmen Sanchidrián. Madrid: Biblioteca Nueva.

Pla Molins, M., Cano García, E., y Lorenzo Ramírez, N. 2002. María Montessori: el Método de la Pedagogía Científica, pp. 69–94 en Trilla, J. (coord.). *El legado pedagógico del siglo XX para la escuela del siglo XXI*. Barcelona: Grao.

Suárez Pazos, M. 1987. Diseño espacial del aula y conductas escolares. *Enseñanza & Teaching*, Vol. 5, 307–319.

Yaglis, D. 2004. *Montessori. La educación natural y el medio*. México D.F.: Editorial Trillas.

# 13

## DIDACTICS OF CHILDHOOD:
## THE CASE STUDY OF PREHISTORY

### *Antonia García Luque*

CHILDHOOD IN RESEARCH, THE GREAT FORGOTTEN…

The study of childhood in different social sciences (anthropology, ethnography, archaeology, history…) is as new as it is necessary. The investigation of childhood in archaeology has always attracted very little attention, becoming more important due to the rise of gender studies in archaeology, driven by post-processual trends.[1] Only when women started to be considered as part of archaeological research, as historical individuals and social agents, did interest in the study of childhood arise, due to its undeniable link with the female sphere. We cannot forget the fact that woman/maternity are two concepts traditionally linked together from the beginning of gender studies. Thus, we can claim that Gender Archaeology has lead to the appearance of what now is known as Childhood Archaeology, whose objective is to study children through the analysis of their relationships within the social group, considering them as active social agents, and not as dependent or unproductive individuals.[2]

The history of childhood has a longer tradition than it does in archaeology, as is demonstrated by the large amount of monographs that exist, which have studied different child rearing practices, and have studied the different concepts and ideas of childhood throughout a diverse number of historical moments and geographic spaces.[3] Its importance in Spain can be seen by its incorporation in different undergraduate programs in pedagogy or other graduate degrees in Spanish universities, as is, for example, in the Nation University of Long Distance Studies (UNED Universidad Nacional de Educación a Distancia), which has a course in the History of Childhood whose objectives are to offer the student a deeper understanding of the significance of childhood throughout the historical process;[4] to approach the history of childhood from the point of view of childhood being a dynamic process that sees children not only as receptors of educational processes throughout history, but as subjects, authors and actors that build history, be it from an individual or a collective point of view, to include it in the historiography that develops the evolution of the learning fields of childhood; and to analyze the educative agents that act upon children during each period in its historic coordinates.

With this kind of teaching of the history of childhood we find ourselves faced with a series of difficulties that are hard to overcome, since what is taught about the lives of children in different historic periods usually only goes back to the Greco-Roman period, so that very little or nothing at all is taught about childhood in prehistory and protohistory, for which we must turn to childhood archaeology, recently incorporated into Spanish research, and rarely seen at a university educational level.

As with Gender Archaeology in Spain, Childhood Archaeology has arrived late if we compare it to the rest of Europe, but there is no doubt that it has implanted itself very strongly and with great celerity in the discipline of archaeology. To see its first steps we must go back the monographic publication in the journal *Cuadernos de Prehistoria y Arqueología Casellonenses,* 14 (1989), which studied children's burials in the Mediterranean area of Spain between the 7th century BC and the 2nd AD. Almost twenty years later a new monograph was published, edited by Francesc Gusi, Susanna Muriel and and Carmen Rosa Oláría, *Nasciturus, infants, puerulus, vobis mater terra* (2008), with the intention of reconsidering childhood death with renewed interest, and on a larger temporal and spatial scale, studying its different rituals and its social significance throughout prehistory and history.[5] Additionally, in 2010 the journal *Complutum* dedicated the second volume of number 21 to a monograph on childhood and material culture in archaeology.

Based on these first reflections, we are going to analyze how the scientific knowledge of childhood is transferred in the classrooms of basic general education in Spain, and more accurately in Elementary school, with the final objective of considering how some specific categories of analysis, such as gender and age, are taught when transmitting historic knowledge. With this study we want to demonstrate how far apart investigation is from the teaching and transmission of historical knowledge at a basic educational level.

## THE CURRICULUM IN ELEMENTARY SCHOOL: A HANDICAP TO PREHISTORIC KNOWLEDGE

The absence of childhood as a part of archaeological research can be one of the causes of its invisibility in the educational process and learning of prehistory in obligatory basic education. In Spain, the education system's own curriculum (Fig. 13.1) is a barrier for knowledge of this period, as we will now discuss.

The Spanish education system[6] is organized in stages, cycles, school years, courses, and education levels to assure the transition between and among each other. The education offered by the system is as follows:

a) Kindergarten
b) Elementary School
c) Obligatory Secondary Education
d) High School

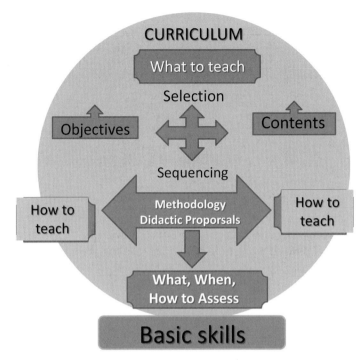

*Figure 13.1. Spanish curriculum structure.*

e) Professional Education
f) Language Education
g) Art Education
h) Sports Education
i) Adult Education
j) University Education

Elementary School and Obligatory Secondary education constitute what we consider basic education. In this chapter we are going to centre on Elementary School,[7] made up of three cycles of two years each, which are usually run between the ages of six and twelve. It is organized in areas with a global and compound nature, which are: Natural, Social and Cultural Science; Artistic Education, Physical Education, Spanish Language and Literature, and, in locations with a co-official language, again another group of Language and Literature; Foreign Language; and Math. Historical contents are included in the curricular areas of Natural, Social and Cultural Science, which is structured in seven areas: 1, *The environment and its conservation*; 2, *The diversity of living beings*; 3, *Health and personal development*; 4. *People, cultures and social organization*; 5, *Changes throughout time*; 6, *Material and energy*; and 7, *Objects, machines and technologies.*

Each block is composed of its own contents structured in cycles. In our case we are going to focus on block 5, *Changes throughout time,* which 'is the beginning of the learning of History, that includes contents on how time is measured, and approaches the concept of historic time, by means of the study of the nature and roll of societies in different historic periods, historical facts, and relevant people for the History of Spain'.[8] Table 13.1 shows how contents are relate to the teaching of Prehistory and Protohistory in this block, where we can observe that the first approach to historic time, and further on that of chronological time,[9] takes place from the third cycle onwards, the moment at which students, because of their age, have already acquired a cognitive development that allows them to do exercises in the abstraction of knowledge, based on the theories of evaluative psychology posed by Jean Piaget.[10]

However, when we analyze the didactic resources used in classrooms to teach this historic period, basically text books, we observe an obvious limitation to the transmission of contents, mostly favoured by the maintenance of traditional concepts, and the absence and failure of being able to incorporate and transfer new investigations in prehistory to the didactics of social sciences. Therefore we must not be surprised

*Table 13.1. Relation of the contents that are entwined to the teaching of prehistory and protohistory existent in block 5 of the Royal Decree 1513/2006.*

| Elementary Education. Area: Knowledge of the Natural, Social and Cultural Block 6. Changes over time Royal Decree 1513/2006 | | |
|---|---|---|
| *First cycle* <br> *6–7 years* | *Second cycle* <br> *8–9 years* | *Third cycle* <br> *10–11 years* |
| Using the basics of time | – Using temporary measure units (decade, century) and introduction to the concepts of management succession planning and concurrency <br> – Recognition and assessment of the meaning of some ancient footprints in the environment <br> - Using written and visual documents for historical information and develop different jobs <br> – Identification of the role of men and women in history | – Conventions dating and periodization (b. C., a.C. age) <br> – Using techniques to locate in time and space past events, to perceive the duration, simultaneity and the relationship between events <br> – Factors explaining human actions, historical events and social changes <br> – Characterization of some societies in historical eras: prehistoric, classical, medieval, discoveries, industrial development and the world in the twentieth century, through the study of lifestyles <br> – Knowledge, appreciation and respect of significant manifestations of historical and cultural heritage <br> – Using different sources of history, geography, art, etc. for reporting and other works of historical content <br> – Evaluation of the role of men and women as subjects of history |

that in the texts used in educational and learning processes, with or without the same methodology, traditional knowledge linked to the classic periods of this historical moment are perpetuated (Paleolithic, Neolithic, Iron Age). Thus, if we compare a text book used thirty years ago, to one used today, we could observe that no considerable change in the ideas that are transmitted has taken place, therefore, we can affirm that the results of the recent lines of research, such as gender and age, have not been incorporated to the didactics of prehistory, or have, but on a minor scale.

A different situation can be observed when we concentrate on the illustrations in text books, in which we can see a prominent change, having incorporated woman in the images carrying out maintenance activities proper to this collective, and, at a minor scale, an age group that corresponds to childhood, normally performing some recreational activity or one of the aforementioned activities. However, this advance in the images is not accompanied by the necessary change in the conceptual contents that are transmitted.

With all this, we must consider, from a critical point of view, why women and children are absent in the texts, the studies, the lectures…, and how patriarchal ideology was, and still is, transmitted in the classrooms in the area of Natural, Social and Cultural Science.

The first question, already stated by other researchers is, is this omission due to the sex of woman? Or in other words, does gender lead to invisibility? If not, then why?

Woman have carried out, since prehistoric times, what are known as maintenance activities, which are analytical categories created by a group of catalan feminist archaeologists[11] which designate those chores that provide the support and wellbeing of the social group during its life cycle, from birth to death, which include pregnancy, child care, weaving, food processing, work related to health, care, wellbeing, healing and hygiene, management of death, and basically, every activity that traditionally has been considered as domestic, and that creates, as Paloma Gonzalez Marcén and Marina Picazo state, 'the temporal fabric and the relation with the cycle of everyday life that constitute the forms of city and which create and conserves the social structures of society'.[12] These activities, usually carried out by woman, taking place in different spaces and at routine times, generate important social networks, in which different agents interact, such as gender, age, ethnic group, time and space, in a way that articulates and transforms the social practices of a group and its historic development, and therefore, it configures the social space of the domestic group.

It is possible that in the ideological association between woman and maintenance, and between men and change, we can find one of the causes for the marginality of maintenance activities in history. Change is linked to development, innovation, power, and positive perception, while maintenance is the contrary, in other words, linked with what is static, what is non innovational, and what is negative.[13] Both concepts, change and maintenance, are at the same time related to different paces and timing, the first related to a faster and more dynamic temporal scale (change-development-technology), whose effects can be perceived more immediately, while maintenance is associated with routine, to what is daily, unchanging, whose effects, therefore, can barely be perceived because they are immutable or change very little throughout the centuries.

Therefore, the question is whether it is not women that have been ignored by history, but their activities,[14] and hence, the omission of these activities in the educational processes of history is another strategy to exclude and hide this collective, since what is not known does not exist, and what is not taught or transmitted is not known or assimilated.

There are many studies that demonstrate the current sexism in text books and other didactic resources.[15] On the other hand, when the problem has been detected, the next stage is to find a solution, proposing different alternatives that incorporate gender and age into the transmission of knowledge:

1. To add maintenance activities in the processes of teaching/learning history, as important activities that constituted our past, which are necessary to understand the social construction throughout time and different cultures, omitting in lectures the undervaluation to which it has been submitted. When we incorporate these activities to the teaching/learning process we are also incorporating the teaching of the spaces and timing of these activities, what constitutes daily routine, so that it makes it easy for elementary students to understand and assimilate, which also expands the kind of time that is taught in this educational phase.
2. The best strategy for obtaining change comes from education in the equality of genders among the university graduate students of Elementary School education, who will be the future teachers educating future citizens.

Therefore change begins in university classrooms, from where it will be transferred, as a network, to the classrooms of kindergarten, elementary, secondary education, etc.

It would be convenient to indicate that university students should study the didactics of social sciences, and that what has been taught to them is not a historic reality and is but an historic knowledge, built, till a very few decades ago, almost exclusively by white men of high social status, who were the ones who had access to such knowledge and therefore held public power. Thus, what we know about our past is a distortion of reality manipulated by multiple variables, ideology and gender being fundamental for its understanding. This way, we teach students that we do not write history, we do not reconstruct the reality of our past; we just simply build a partial historical knowledge, since, until a few decades ago, research and investigation in social sciences has been marked by unquestionably biased information (androcentrism etc.).

The incorporation of these other perspectives will not break the subjective partiality of historical education, but it will oblige us to take into account other points of view, and therefore we can reconstruct history with more accuracy and integrity, than if we took into account only one point of view.

Therefore, we want to point out that new content is being created. As an example we must stress the R+D project *Los trabajos de las mujeres y el lenguaje de los objetos: renovación de lasreconstruccioneshistóricas y recuperación de la cultura material femenina como herramienta de transformación de valores* ('Woman's work and the language of objects: renovation of historic reconstructions and the recovery of the female material culture as a tool for the transformation of values'), coordinated by professor Paloma Gonzalez Marcén (UAB). The objective of this project is to visualize woman in prehistory and protohistory through the creation of new images of the social realities of these periods. The final objective was to create databases of graphic data, accessible to any professional form of historic dissemination (education, museography, press), and that are better adjusted to the reality of different periods and cultures.

The process of the construction of the graphic material begins with an earlier creation of an index card for each of the taught periods of prehistory and protohistory, including the archaeological register, the materials and the techniques used for each activity, and the daily tasks carried out by woman. Based on the collected information we can create new images in which woman and men of all ages are represented, next to texts that accompany them.[16]

SOME TEACHING PROBLEMS...

As we have already noted, the curricular contents of Elementary education take very little consideration of prehistory, reducing it, in the best cases, to one didactic unit in the third cycle. This absence can be due to different reasons:

*Absence of an epistemological consideration on behalf of the faculty members*

When teachers do not meditate on this, they are exposed to carrying out a practical activity (teaching) without a scientific foundation, which heads toward the mandates and conceptions of the dominant ideology, thus carrying out an aligned action.[17] This creates what Pilar Maestro defined as an educative action with no sense, costly and with no benefit, stiff, and sometimes incomprehensible, depending only on the capacity of communication of the recipe.[18]

Nobody doubts that a deep knowledge in the subject that is going to be taught is a necessary condition for any teacher, nevertheless, it is not enough, since knowledge must reach the epistemological level, this is the theoretic, ideological and philosophical basis of knowledge in its different dimensions: conceptual, methodological and the value of these. In this respect, Antonio Luis Garcia Ruiz and José Antonio Jimenez López indicate the educational system demands a new model of a reflexive teacher, independent and critic, with enough knowledge of the discipline, as well as a didactic knowledge that will allow the teacher to teach better.[19] For this to happen, knowledge of the subject should not be limited to the general contents of the course, but should be deeper, allowing the teacher to reach a theoretic, ideological and philosophical basis on which the mentioned contents are inspired, in other words, the historical paradigms and currents. Definitely, teaching practice should be well founded: what does he/she do? Why does he/she do it? What does he/she do it for?

The curriculum, the selection of the general objectives and final purposes of education, depend greatly on the theoretical perspective in which we are situated, because each way of understanding the world prioritizes some ideas and concepts susceptible of being applied to education, and establishes its priorities and values. Therefore, the contents of prehistory found in the official curriculum of Elementary education must be submitted to this mitigation, since this will be the only way that will ultimately allow us to change the educational system. This way, taking in to account the didactics of prehistory, an immersion in the theoretical and ideological field could respond to questions such as: why do we study prehistory, or what should we teach in prehistory? This all depends on the scientific option chosen by teachers, whom we consider have the responsibility of achieving a balance between their own ideology and the dominant ideology from critical and autocratic positions, for which it is absolutely necessary to carry out this paradigmatic consideration.

Therefore, an epistemological consideration will help understand the relativity of knowledge, the existence of different positions, different explanatory models and interpretations of social reality. To understand this is fundamental when we decide what do we teach? Why do we teach it? What is obtained when it is taught?

Without this worry, teachers would never be conscious of the need to introduce in the teaching of prehistory what we know about those collectives that have been ignored by the traditional interpretations and explanations of history, such as woman and children, and therefore this kind of education would stay immutable, static and alien to new investigations.

As a conclusion, we understand that contributing conceptual and methodological systems to the content, from the point of view of different paradigmatic positioning, is a fundamental requisite for the construction of knowledge, as it is for one's training in that knowledge. Thus, the addition of new perspectives in the teaching of prehistory and history, such as gender and childhood, is not only a scientific option, but a need.

## *Complexity of the conceptualization of social and historic time*

The problem associated with the process of the conceptualization of historic time can also find ways of being resolved by epistemological consideration.

Historic time can be understood, taking in to account the historic epistemology existent at the beginning of the 21st century, as the simultaneity of durations, movements and diverse changes that have taken place in a human group throughout a determined period. Usually we tend to confuse or compare chronologic time with historic time so that history has been interpreted from a positivist point of view as uniquely linear, leading to the conception that facts or events must be accurately fixed by chronology, and thus they are generally reduced to the intentions, decisions and actions of famous people in power, excluding woman or children.

As a consequence of this temporal conception, the learning of history in schools is fundamentally constituted by the memorization of political facts or events, embodied by certain people and linked to accurate dates. Historical periods are established the same way, as hermetic drawers, limited by chronological dates chosen based on the dominant criteria (patriarchal), in which the presence of woman and children passes unaware.

The most recurrent argument to justify the maintenance of this kind of historic education is related to the complexity of the concept of time, comprehensible only from a wide and trans-disciplinary point of view. To be able to assimilate this, elementary schoolchildren, because of their age, are not ready to understand it, since they understand history as more of a personal and anecdotic sequence, finding difficulty in understanding more abstract ideas such as social, political or economic aspects.

*Intercession of different disciplines in the construction of historic knowledge*

Interdisciplinarity is enriching for any research or investigation, but in the case of prehistory, it may be more important due to the large amount of disciplines that intercede to be able to reconstruct historic knowledge (carpology, antracology, archeometry, forensic anthropology, ethnography, etc). This handicaps the teaching of prehistory to elementary school students, because of the difficulty in explaining, based on their cognitive development, that the same object can be studied by different disciplines and that their interaction creates an integrated knowledge of reality. It is very likely that these kinds of students are not able, due to their lack of abstraction, to understand interdisciplinary studies, but are able, on the other hand, to understand multidisciplinary studies, but, depending on the teaching methodology employed, this problem can or cannot be solved, as we will see in the next section.

TOWARDS A NEW LEARNING OF PREHISTORY

To be able to change how we learn history we must necessarily begin by changing the methodological basis. We can define methodology as the series of pre-planned activities taking place inside classrooms, based on a series of principles of which we can highlight:

–   Starting from the previous knowledge of the students, this is known as significant learning, and allows us to connect new knowledge to previous learning, thus creating learning networks and hierarchies.
–   Promote the role played by students in the learning process by developing skills that will allow them to build their own knowledge, and which will help them learn how to construct their own knowledge independently.
–   Teachers must adopt the role of a mediator and act as a guide towards knowledge.
–   Help the students develop the critical abilities.
–   Promote active learning by enhancing the student's participation.
–   Base the educational action on a process of communication and interaction between teachers and students as equals.
–   One must adapt oneself to the diversity of students by creating an effective and trustworthy atmosphere.
–   Promote the students' creativity by developing activities that enhance consideration, thought, inquiry, decision making, etc.

In order to fulfill these values we must introduce an educative methodological strategy that is able to bypass direct traditional teaching, and produces the change that is needed when teaching prehistory. The heuristic method responds to this need if we situate ourselves at the level where learning is part of how one resolves the problem, and obliges the student to participate in learning in an active way. In our case the problem is the omission of a particular group of individuals when teaching prehistory and history. To be able to carry out this kind of education, several stages must be followed (Fig. 13.2).

With this methodology we focus on the procedural contents. The contents taught are composed of a series of cultural, social, political, economic scientific and technological ideas that conform to the different disciplinary areas, and are considered essential for how an individual learns.[20] This is the basis on which we must build the program of teaching-learning activities with the ultimate goal of achieving what has been expressed in the objectives.

In our educative system, contents are structured in three categories: conceptual, attitudinal and procedural. We have observed, when we study the actual didactics of prehistory in elementary school, a clear unbalanced relationship between all three, conceptual contents being the most used to the detriment of the other two.

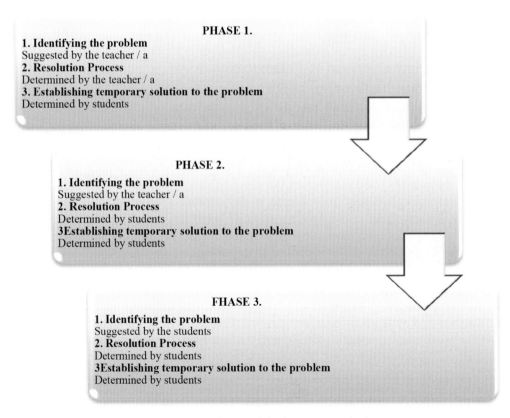

*Figure 13.2. Phases of the heuristic method.*

We consider procedures, which are the set of organized actions directed towards reaching a target, necessary for the didactics of prehistory. In other words, procedures are made up of a series of strategies, methods, skills, and abilities, which a student must learn to be able to 'know how'.[21]

A procedure is nothing else but the skill which we want to help the student to build; it is the object of educative planning and interaction, which can be learned by employing different methods. Procedural contents design a series of actions and ways of acting to be able to solve tasks. It is knowledge that allows us to know how to do things.

This makes us want to develop these procedures by employing different strategies:

a) Learning by discovery, following the traditional scientific method (Table 13.2)

b) Learning by inquiry, which does not follow a predetermined process or pattern, the emphasis is situated in the process of how we investigate a problem, more than using the scientific method to solve it. This way students can use different strategies to obtain more information about the same problem (Table 13.3).

c) With all the information that has been recovered we can do an exercise of experimental archaeology applied to elementary school classrooms that will produce an important change in how students learn prehistory, this is, by direct practice: for example, by carrying out simulations of different activities done by children in prehistory; pottery workshops, lithic workshops, etc.

*Table 13.2. The traditional scientific method.*

| General Scientific Research Model |
|---|
| *1. Identify the problem* <br> ○ To raise awareness of the problem <br> ○ State the problem |
| *2. Develop possible solutions* <br> ○ Propose testable hypotheses |
| *3. Collection of information* <br> ○ Gather evidence <br> ○ Conduct experiment/s <br> ○ Study of a sample |
| *4. Analysis and interpretation of data* <br> ○ Perform data supported claims <br> ○ Testing hypotheses <br> ○ Establish relationships and patterns <br> ○ Make generalizations |
| *5. Conclusions* <br> ○ New data <br> ○ Check conclusions |

*Table 13.3. The inquiry process.*

| Inquiry process |
|---|
| *1. Identify the problem* <br> ○ To raise awareness of the problem <br> ○ State the problem |
| *2. Working on finding solutions* <br> ○ More important to find a solution to the solution itself. <br> ○ Does not use the scientific method of Table X. <br> ○ The students thought their own strategies |
| *3. Develop solutions* <br> ○ Success does not depend on the achievement of a particular outcome. <br> ○ Personal experience for each subject involved. |

CONCLUSIONS

The conceptualization of time and space under particular historical postulates that have directed social sciences research has been one of the responsible factors for the omission of women and children collectives in history teaching and learning procedures in Spain. The diagnosis of this situation was carried out by experts in this matter, and therefore it is time to reconsider the methods and the strategies used in the teaching-learning process, which we must incorporate into the actual educative system, thus eradicating the sexism that still remains in the transmission of historical knowledge and also in contents related to woman and children.

To be able to achieve this objective, a transformation must take place, not only of the idea of how we teach, which poses a limit to the learning capacities at a determined moment in the stages of cognitive development of students, but also by changing the inner circle of the actual legislation of our educational system, which has turned into a wall for the teaching of prehistory, thus creating an education without any biases at the first stages of primary education.

NOTES

1   Chapa 2003,117
2   Sánchez Romero 2010
3   DeMause 1974; Delgado 1998; Bajo,1998; Rodríguez and Mannrelli 2007
4   http://portal.uned.es/portal/page?_pageid=93,25467331&_dad=portal&_schema=PORTAL&idAsi
    gnatura=01489234&idPrograma=-1&idContenido=1
5   Gusi *et al.* 2008
6   Ley Orgánica 2/2006, de 3 de mayo de Educación (B.O.E. núm. 106 de jueves 4 de mayo de
    2006)
7   Real Decreto 1513/2006, de 7 de diciembre, por el que se es Tablecen las enseñanzas mínimas
    de la Educación Primaria. (B.O.E. núm. 293 de 8 de diciembre de 2006)
8   R. D. 1513/2006
9   Pagés 1997, 1999; Santisteban and Pagés 2011
10  Piaget 1979; Flavell 1982; Aebli 1984
11  Bardavio and González Marcén 1996; Colomer 1996, 2005; Sanahuja 1997a, 1997b; Picazo,
    1997; Colomer, González Marcén and Montón 1998; González Marcén 2000; González Marcén
    and Picazo 2005; Montón 2005
12  Gonzalez Marcén and Picazo 2005, 143
13  Hernando 2006; Dommasnes 1987, 2006
14  Hernando 2006
15  Subirats 1993; Hernández García and Fernández Alonso 1994; Ruiz Oliveras and Vallejo Martín
    1999; García Luque and Peinado Rodríguez 2012
16  www.pastwomen.org
17  Mainer 2008
18  Maestro 1993, 313
19  García Ruiz and Jimenez López 2010
20  Odreman 1996
21  Michel, Osnaya and Mora 2009

REFERENCES

Aebli, H. 1984. *Una didáctica fundada en la psicología de Jean Piaget.* Publicación Buenos Aires: Kapelusz (first edition).

Agudelo, A. M. and Flores de Lovera H. 1996. *El proyecto pedagógico de aula y la Unidad de clase. La planificación didáctica en el contexto de la reforma educativa del nivel de Educación Básica.* Panapo, Venezuela.

Bajo, F. 1998. *Breve historia de la infancia.* Madrid: Temas de Hoy.

Bardavio, A. and González Marcén, P. 1996. La vida cuotidiana a la prehistoria: l´estudi de les activitats de manteniment, *Balma* 6, 7–17.

Chapa, T. 2003. La percepción de la infancia en el mundo ibérico, *Trabajos de Prehistoria* 60 1, 115–138.

Colomer, L. 1996. Contenidors cerámics i processament d´aliments a la prehistoria, *Cota Zero* 12, 47–60.

Colomer, L. 2005. Cerámica prehistórica y trabajo femenino en el Argar: una aproximación desde el estudio de la tecnología cerámica, pp. 177–219 in Sánchez Romero, M. (ed.), *Arqueología y Género,* Biblioteca de Humanidades/Arte y Arqueología, Universidad de Granada.

Colomer, L., González, P. and Montón, S. 1998. Maintenance activities, technological knowledge and consumption patterns: a view of Northeast Iberia (2000–500 Cal BC), *Journal of Mediterranean Archaeology* 11, 53–80.

Delgado, B. 1998. *Historia de la infancia.* Ariel. Barcelona.

DeMause, LL. 1974. *Historia de la infancia.* Madrid: Alianza.

Dommasnes, L. H. 2006. Su corazón se modeló sobre una rueda: las mujeres entre la ideología y la vida en el pasado nórdico, pp. 73–91 in González Marcén, P., Montón, S. and Picazo, M. (eds), *Dones i activitats de manteniment en temps de canvi,* Treballs D´Arqueologia, 11.

Flavell, J. H. 1982. *La psicología evolutiva de Jean Piaget.* Edt. Paidós, Barcelona.

García Luque, A. and Peinado, M. 2012. Género y ciudadanía en la educación obligatoria: de la intencionalidad a la realidad, pp. 291–300 in Martín Clavijo, M. (ed.) Actas *Congreso Internacional De La Asociación Universitaria De Estudios De Las Mujeres. Más igualdad. Redes para la igualdad,* AUDEM.

García Ruiz, A. L. and Jiménez López, J. A. 2010. *El valor formativo y la enseñanza de la Historia,* Universidad de Granada.

González Marcén, P. (ed.) 2000. *Espacios de Género en la Arqueología,* Arqueología Espacial, *22.* Teruel.

González Marcén, P. and Picazo, M. 2005. Arqueología de la vida cotidiana, pp. 141–159 in Sánchez Romero, M. (ed.), *Arqueología y Género.* Biblioteca de Humanidades/Arte y Arqueología, Universidad de Granada.

Gusi, F., Muriel, S. and Olària, C. (eds) 2008. *Nasciturus, infans, puerulus vobis mater terra: la muerte en la infacia,* Diputació de Castelló, Servei d'Investigacions Arqueològiques i Prehistòriques.

Gutiérrez, A. and Pernil, P. 2004. *Historia de la infancia, itinerarios educativos.* UNED. Madrid.

Hernández, J. and Fernández, R. 1994. El sexismo en los libros de texto. *Educadores,* 169, 29–59.

Hernando, A. 2006 "¿Por qué la Historia no ha valorado las actividades de mantenimiento?, pp. 91–115 in González Marcén, P., Montón, S. and Picazo, M. (eds), *Dones i activitats de manteniment en temps de canvi,* TreballsD´Arqueologia, 11.

Maestro, P. 1993. Epistemología histórica y enseñanza, *Ayer (Asociación de Historia Contemporáneas),* 12, 135–181.

Mainer, J. 2008. *Pensar críticamente la educación escolar: perspectivas y controversias historiográficas,* Prensas Universitarias de Zaragoza.

Mestres, J. 1994. *Cómo construir el proyecto curricular de centro.* Vicens Vives Primaria, Barcelona.

Michel, P., Osnaya, G. and Mora, R. 2009. El aprendizaje y la enseñanza de los procedimientos, in *http://www.slideshare.net/Gabrielos/contenidos-procedimentales*

Odreman, N. 1996. *La reforma curricular venezolana*. Educación Básica.

Pagés, J. 1997. El tiempo histórico, pp. 189–208 in Benejam, P. and Pagés, J. (eds) *Enseñar y aprender ciencias sociales, geografía e historia en la Educación Secundaria*: Horsori: Universitat de Barcelona, Instituto de Ciencias de la Educación.

Pagés, J. 1999. El tiempo histórico: ¿Qué sabemos sobre su enseñanza y su aprendizaje? Análisis y valoración de los resultados de algunas investigaciones, pp. 241–278 in Pagés, J. (ed.), *Aspectos didácticos de las ciencias sociales, 13*, Universidad de Zaragoza, Instituto de Ciencias de la Educación.

Piaget, J. 1979. *Epistemología de las Ciencias Humanas*. Paidós. Buenos Aires.

Picazo, M. 1997. Estudios clásicos y feminismo en los noventa, pp. 25–35 in Segura Graiño, C. (ed.), *La Historia de las Mujeres en el Nuevo paradigma de la Historia*, Asociación Cultural AL-MUDAYNA.

Rodríguez, P. and Mannarelli, M. E. 2007. *Historia de la Infancia en la América Latina*, Universidad Externado de Colombia.

Ruiz, L. and Vallejo, C. 1999. ¿Qué queda de sexismo en los libros de texto? *Revista Complutense de Educación, Vól. 10, núm. 2*, 125–145.

Sanahuja, E. 1997a. Marxismo y feminismo, *Boletín de Antropología Americana, 31*, 7–14.

Sanahuja, E. 1997b. Sexuar el pasado. Una propuesta arqueológica, pp. 15–24, in Segura, C. (ed.), *La Historia de las Mujeres en el Nuevo paradigma de la Historia*, Asociación Cultural AL-MUDAYNA.

Sánchez Romero, M. 2010. ¡Eso no se toca! Infancia y cultura material en arqueología. *Complutum 21, vol. 2*, 9–13.

Santisteban, A. and Pagés, J. 2011. Enseñar y aprender el tiempo histórico, pp. 229–247 in Santisteban, A. y Pagés, J. (eds), *Didáctica del Conocimiento del Medio Social y Cultural en la Educación Primaria: ciencias sociales para aprender, pensar y actuar*, Síntesis.

Subirats, M. (ed.) 1993. *El sexismo en los libros de texto: análisis y propuesta de un sistema de indicadores*. Madrid: Instituto de la Mujer.

# 14

## Once upon a Time…
## Childhood and Archaeology from the
## Perspective of Spanish Museums[1]

### Isabel Izquierdo Peraile, Clara López Ruiz
### and Lourdes Prados Torreira

---

### Museums and Children

Museums are cultural institutions which, despite their origins as temples of knowledge reserved for a privileged few, have undergone numerous changes. Nowadays, museums try to open their doors to all areas of a society; a society that is increasingly complex, cosmopolitan and diverse. Their new social dimension has given rise to regeneration along with a new educational focus. This process has always been and always will be a slow one. With the birth of this *New Museology*, new concepts of the museum as an entity are established in the community: the ecomuseums in Europe and Canada, regional museums in the United States and community museums in Latin America. Based on the latter, and by applying the principles of the 'comprehensive museum', the educational museum is born, as first conceived by Larrauri.[2]

At present, it is the diffusion of knowledge that links the museum directly to society, connecting its content and its visitors, transmitting the message, aims and values of the institution itself.[3] The museum materializes as an educational centre and a place where culture and heritage is promoted; an entity capable of transmitting a series of universal values to its visitors and to children in particular. In this way, in its more social dimension, the museum could become a tool for educating children in equality and respect for heritage. It must be noted here that there is no one kind of visitor to museums: visitors belong to various age groups, have had different types of education, have various interests and expectations, etc. In this study, we will focus on children between the ages of 4 and 12 years, a group that makes up a portion of any museum's visitors.

The first attempts to involve child visitors were made by North American museums, pioneers in this field, due to their educational projection. Particularly deserving of mention are the Brooklyn Children's Museum (New York, 1899) and the Boston

Children's Museum (1913). Nordic museums (Scandinavian ones in particular) also joined this cutting-edge educational movement with the creation of open-air museums designed to reach out to popular culture. However, it is science museums that are essentially educational and have traditionally tried to aim their collections at children. Through experimenting and handling objects, these institutions have managed to bring science closer to the youngest of children. In Spain, various initiatives stand out in particular, including those of the Fundación Cosmocaixa, the Museo Nacional de Ciencias Naturales (National Natural Science Museum) or the Parque de las Ciencias de Granada (Granada Science Park). We also have a wide range of institutions that maintain a strong relationship with children, including toy museums (also of North American origin), dinosaur museums and railway museums, which allow a direct link with their youngest visitors, becoming an educational, recreational and tourism destination for families and school groups.

## ARCHAEOLOGY MUSEUMS AND CHILDREN

Material culture, an essential tool for human understanding, is an exceptional means of communication. Objects 'fossilize' the past, as J. Ballart Hernández notes in his reflections on the construction of the meanings of museum objects.[4] If we refer to archaeological or historical museums in particular (but also anthropological or ethnographical museums), whose collections are based on material culture, these objects that are so charged with meaning can also be used to promote a series of social values. Aside from the curiosity, romanticism, magic or mystery surrounding the knowledge of the past that these objects inspire, in the words of G. Clark,[5] archaeology allows us to see things from a wide perspective and promotes human solidarity, since it covers everything from the 'great works' to the remains of rubbish through direct and immediate sources. It provides us with evidence on identities and basic human concerns, allowing us to connect with other interests and topics, encouraging respect towards the collective value of heritage, and awakening social conscience towards racism, xenophobia and social inequality. Material fragments from the past represent unique raw material to be used as a vehicle of knowledge and communication. Added to this is the growing presence of archaeology in society, in the mass media, as a recent phenomenon that manifests itself in various forms and through various mediums[6] including films.[7]

Given this concept of material culture and society's growing interest in archaeology, we should take time to reflect on how evidence from the past is selected, prepared and presented in the museum, taking centre stage in the exhibition, ultimately reflecting a vision of the world and of society, a vision that empowers it as a cultural entity, a space for interpretation and renovation.[8] The selection of the display pieces and the vision of the exhibition are therefore key in our understanding of the story or stories are being told, what values are being transmitted, how the events transpired and who is who in the story or who is the leading character and who has been left out of the picture. From this point of view, archaeological museums, as historical places and centres of social communication, are a means of promoting values, of expressing ideas and of visualizing areas of society that are traditionally invisible. The permanent collection provides many possibilities for increasing the awareness of visitors and the interaction of the public. In this area, there are great opportunities to organize stories and talks for visitors that can and should be heard by different social and ethnic groups, as well as both genders and people of different ages.

With regards to who the traditional leading characters of the story are and who is usually left out of the picture, in another recent article[9] we have focused our attention on the need to include women in the stories of the past that are told in museums. In the article, our main aims are to dismiss the traditional messages that link men to the main tasks and attribute a passive approach to women. Our aim is to explain that the division of work, in its sexual or gender-based specialization, indicates difference and not pre-eminence or hierarchy in the tasks of each group, as has been traditionally assumed by archaeology and reflected in traditional museology. To summarize, we hope to distance ourselves from the traditional approach towards the invisibility, inferiority, minimal social function or importance of women.[10]

In this work, we have centred our attention on children in three ways, as we shall now explain: first, from an assessment of visitors, with recent statistics from the *Laboratorio Permanente de Público de Museos del Ministerio de Cultura* (the Ministry of Culture's Permanent Laboratory of Museum Visitors).[11] Secondly, we have looked at the necessary projection and visibility of child visitors in the exhibition itself from a museological perspective and, above all, based on recent considerations within the field of archaeology that are giving rise to new possibilities. Thirdly, we will examine some interesting examples of the museographical application of these ideas on different areas of the exhibition in some of the latest archaeological museums and temporary exhibitions in Spain.

With regards to the relationship between museums and children under the age of 12 (pre-school and primary school), there is still much work to be done in museums in general, and in archaeological museums in particular. The general visitor profile for the Spanish state museums studied shows that 70.5% of adults and young people visited individually and that only 8.2% of adults and children came to museums on school trips. 5.7% of adults and children visit museums on other kinds of organized trip, with 10.5 of child visitors on family visits and 5.1% on school trips. The general figure for visiting children is 15.6% in Spanish state museums. In some archaeological museums, this number increases significantly, for example when it comes to the Museo de Altamira (Altamira Museum) (22.5%), whilst other museums have slightly less visiting children (14% at the Museo Arqueológico Nacional (National Archaeology Museum) before it was closed for refurbishment). It is interesting to note that, at least until the age of 12, children tend to visit museums individually or on family trips rather than with their schools.

It is important to highlight the value of the concept that visiting museums is a social activity. Social interaction is an integral part of family visits because children ask questions and adults answer them. For this reason, it is essential that the exhibition itself facilitates the task of bringing cultural artefacts closer to children, providing precise answers to their questions. Their visit to the museum should not be a missed opportunity to learn or, even worse, give children a sense of failure. Observing, questioning, comparing, commenting are all just some of the actions that, when shared with other members of the group, make the visit a gratifying experience that is capable of capturing their attention.[12]

School trips to state museums make up 13.4% of the total number, with 38.4% of these at primary school level (under the age of 12). From this average, there are vastly differing figures amongst archaeological museums: the Museo de Altamira (Altamira Museum), for example, is 15% above this average, whilst the Museo Arqueológico Nacional (National Archaeology Museum) is 7.1% below. A look at the visitor statistics can also tell us a great deal. With regards to other studies carried out on the same state museums in the last ten years,[13] it has been proved that these museums have not gained young visitors to compensate for the evident aging amongst its usual visitors. A series of recommendations that are worthy of note are suggested to compensate for the low numbers of child visitors to museums and are designed to increase the appeal of museums for families. These suggestions include increasing the services on offer to ensure that their visit is a comfortable one, considering the child's point of view when designing the exhibitions and activities, and promoting and encouraging the idea that visiting museums should be something to do culturally as a family. It is also proposed that the number of activities on offer for children and families be increased so that visiting becomes a habit for the future, meaning a gradual generational replacement in the museum's visitors.[14]

## MUSEOLOGY, ARCHAEOLOGY AND CHILDHOOD

It should be no surprise to us that children from different geographical and historical cultures are barely included in the exhibitions of archaeological museums, since they are almost completely invisible in archaeological research itself.[15] Although we know that they are present in almost all everyday situations (at home, within the community, etc.), it is noteworthy that their existence is hardly covered in archaeological studies. This means a double loss since involving them more in museums through the relicts of their material culture could partly alleviate their absence from historical texts.[16] The lack of clearly identified traces of children in archaeology is the result not only of a methodological problem but also of a conceptual one, making it a similar case to that of the apparent invisibility of women. In fact, in many instances, the interest shown towards childhood in archaeological studies is directly related to the development of archaeology and gender studies. The post-processual tendencies of past two decades have stressed the importance of the individual as a social agent, whilst at the same time granting importance to considerations surrounding gender, age, etc.

It is possible that the remains of children may have not survived at many archaeological sites as easily perishable materials or fragile skeletal remains. It is also possible that their remains are not recorded by archaeologists in the excavations because they fail to identify them as such, or due to the momentary and general nature of children's activities.[17] The Norwegian researcher Grete Lillehammer highlights the three main areas of interest of the so-called archaeology of infancy and childhood;[18] how boys and girls see their world; what the relationships between children and adults are like; and, finally, how adults understand the world of children. Generally speaking, we can highlight a series of general topics on childhood that have a leading role in archaeological research.

## *Funerals: Death and Burials*

Until very recently, societies have had to deal with a high percentage of infant deaths, both during pregnancy and in birth, and the first few months of age. Often, the mother dies along with the baby at the puerperal stage. A number of studies have been carried out in this area[19] with regards to peninsular prehistory and proto-history. Infant burials can include skeletal remains and grave goods or stores of objects, gathered together in the tomb for ritual or eschatological reasons. Generally speaking, the greatest contributions towards our knowledge of childhood in archaeology tend to come from this area of study. When it comes to anthropological remains, alongside the problems arising from rituals such as cremation, we also have to deal with the fragility of skeletal remains themselves and difficulties in determining gender. Other physical factors have also led to these remains going unnoticed in excavations that are not as rigorous as others.[20] On many occasions, children occupy different funerary areas to the rest of the population: underneath houses, for example. They may also follow different rituals such as interment as opposed to cremation, and their different treatment provides important information about the social structure and ideology of groups from the past. With regards to the grave goods, these may include small decorative objects such as jewels, pieces of pottery and sometimes even toys and amulets. Often objects linked to the adult world are also found, such as weapons or remains from the funeral banquets, since the funeral rites are carried out by adults who transmit the idea that they wish to convey of the child in question in his/her tomb.

## *Living Space: Subsistence and Maintenance*

Beyond the more traditional area of study relating to death and burials, and within the topics most covered by contemporary archaeology, we must highlight here those studies carried out on the arrangement of objects and the definition of areas of activity, fields in which children have played a crucial role in the societies of the past (albeit one that is not well known). Amongst the most important areas, we include those activities associated with the maintenance of the community as such, for example the transformation and preparation of food, the provision of care for members of the community, the production of certain crafts such as pottery,[21] basket making, weaving, etc. The same goes for any other decisive activity for the community that required a learning process such as hunting, making stone tools, etc. In the prehistoric world, hunting, for example, must have been a group task involving men, women, children and the elderly. Each of these groups would possibly have had a specific task, from keeping watch and locating the animal, the hunting of the animal itself, quartering it and treating and moving the meat, etc.

*Child Material Culture: Games, Miniatures...*

The material culture traditionally associated with children poses an interesting area of study in archaeology, with preconceptions and research difficulties coming together. This area seems to be limited to toys, pieces from the adult world that are made into miniatures, and objects that are clearly linked with the care of unweaned babies or young children, food, clothes and child adornment. From this group, which is often masked or lost due to its organic nature, toys have without a doubt stood out in particular. In the words of Sharon Brookshaw, toys are adults' favourite way of representing child material culture.[22] These objects could have been made by adults or by children. In fact, toys provide us with an insight into their role as mediators between children and adults.[23] They also allow us to trace their use, as a means of learning, not only of skills but also of roles and ways of behaving, how to understand the community, the territory, beliefs, etc. We are often not sure of the meaning of miniatures: could they be toys made by or for children as part of a learning process, such as tools as work instruments, or small pieces of pottery made by children themselves? Would each case depend on the context in which it is found? In shrines, for example, a miniature may substitute the real-size object and have a symbolic meaning. Material culture therefore opens up new areas of consideration on the function and meaning of pieces in their own context.

*Images of Children themselves: Codes of Representation*

Despite their scarcity, iconographic representations of children on funerary monuments, votive offerings in shrines, pieces of pottery or small objects, etc. provide us with a great deal of information.[24] Through these representations, we have access to codes of identification that are reflected in the clothes, hairstyles, head-dresses, adornment, tattoos, etc. that are difficult to value in archaeological findings, and can be used as rites of passage between one age and another to define age categories as cultural constructions. The female appearance in Iberian imagery is codified within the characteristics of their dresses, hairstyles and adornment. Although rare, images of the family as a whole, with their scales of representation, provide us with information of equal importance. Together with the male, the female is represented on a greater scale than children or young people, as part of the phenomenon of the visualization of social relationships of citizen structures, present in Iberian shrines from the 3rd century BC.[25]

To summarize, we can assert that from death to habitat; from the material culture of childhood or the representations of children themselves on different mediums, there is great deal to be explored and researched. The role of archaeological museums may be crucial in this sense. It is important that we consider the need to revise the collections of museums that keep a wide range of objects that could be analyzed from this point of view; objects that may be related to childhood and have been ignored until now due to a lack of awareness or the fact that they are not of interest for certain fields of research. By revising their collections, museums can enrich their displays and represent this part of society that is usually forgotten in exhibitions, this 'universal minority in all societies' as it is aptly defined by Sharon Brookshaw 2010,[26] thus underlining the critical role of museum collections and the possibilities that this represents for exhibitions.

## MUSEOGRAPHIC RESOURCES AND CHILDHOOD

The language of the exhibition includes, together with the artefacts themselves, a wide range of resources for communication, essential in all exhibitions nowadays to support the transmission of information.[27] These resources take the form of texts of various styles and formats, as well as explanatory illustrations, both documentary and evocative. They may also include photographs, animations, diagrams, maps, plans, chronologies and other kinds of graphs, sculptures, models, scale models and other 3D resources, as well as new technologies that are interactive to various degrees and multimedia. All of the exhibition resources, as part of its architecture and museography (accesses, visitor circulation patterns, room shape, flooring, walls and ceilings, textures, colours, lighting and general atmosphere), provide a particular experience for the visitor. From a child's point of view, we would highlight the importance of scale (the height of the displays, texts, font size, height and the accessibility of the interactive and manipulative elements), and sensory stimulation (ranges of colour in the exhibition architecture, inside display cabinets and graphical elements, as well as adequate lighting). We also believe in the importance of putting on interesting talks, powerful acoustics, and meaningful sounds, complementary resources to stimulate the sense of smell and touch, as well as other factors that all affect the enjoyment and comfort of visitors and their understanding of the exhibition.

### *Images in Two Dimensions: Illustrations, Animations, etc...*

The graphic art displayed at exhibitions present possibilities for the representation of children. However, there is still a long way to go: although landscapes, houses, pottery, etc. are illustrated with precision and detail, they often provide little information on the men and women they depict. We know little of their age, what they are doing, what their attitudes and gestures are, whether they should take centre stage or a have a secondary role in the scenes, etc. These elements are of extreme importance since they leave an impression on visitors to museums and transmit ideas on values, roles or functions, as well as social relationships, especially in children, who make up the main foundations of society of the future. By means of an example, we should draw attention here to the illustrations at the recently-opened permanent exhibition (2011) (Fig. 14.1) at the Museo Arqueológico de Asturias (Asturias Archaeological Museum) in Oviedo, with children depicted in daily life scenes. These large illustrations stand out for their communicative efficiency and the elegance of their technique and presentation. The children are depicted within the family nucleus and are involved in the activities and daily life of the cave.

Temporary archaeology exhibitions are beginning to incorporate these themes into their content and museographical form. The recent exhibition at the Museo Arqueológico Regional de Madrid (Madrid Region Archaeological Museum), *Los últimos carpetanos. El oppidum de El Llano de la Horca (Santorcaz, Madrid) (The last Carpetans. The*

*Figure 14.1. Scene of family daily life, part of the prehistory series of the Museo Arqueológico de Asturias (Asturias Archaeology Museum) in Oviedo (2011). © Ministry of Culture.*

*oppidum of El Llano de la Horca [Santorcaz, Madrid]*) (2012), for example, recalls important aspects of life in the Second Iron Age in the centre of the Peninsula, based on the El Llano de la Horca site (Fig. 14.2). Within the same museum, we should also mention the exhibition opened in December 2012 entitled *Arte sin artistas: Una mirada al Paleolítico* (*Art without artists. A look at the Paleolithic*). The symbolic image used to advertise this exhibition and on the cover of the guide depicts a woman with a baby painting in the cave whilst another child watches them.

*Sculptures, Scenes and other 3D Resources*

3D images of children from long ago are increasingly common in museums as an educational tool. The representation of the four-year-old Neanderthal based on a mould of the cranium found at Roc-de-Marsal (Périgord) (40.000 B.P.) on display at the National Museum of Prehistory in Les Eyzies-de-Tayac, Dordogne (2008), and sculpted by Elisabeth Daynès, is a true work of art that is full of compassion. The same sculptor did another extraordinary 'reconstruction' for the Museo de la Evolución Humana (Museum of Human Evolution) in Burgos (2010), this time of the *homo ergaster*. The impressive sculpture is known as the *niño de Turkana* or Child of Turkana, even though the piece is really of a young person.

The Museo de Almería (Almería Museum) (2006) offers a spectacular large-scale scene named *el círculo de la vida* (*The circle of life*). Made up of a set of modern metal-based sculptures, a woman takes centre stage in a birthing scene (Fig. 14.3). On the

Figure 14.2. Scene of daily life in the oppidum El Llano de la Horca, from the exhibition Los últimos carpetanos. El oppidum de El Llano de la Horca (Santorcaz, Madrid) (2012) (The last Carpetans. The oppidum of El Llano de la Horca). © Museo Arqueológico Regional de Madrid (Madrid Region Archaeological Museum).

Figure 14.3. El círculo de la vida (The circle of life). Birth scene from the permanent exhibition at the Museo de Almería (Almería Museum) (2006).© Ministry of Culture.

*Figure 14.4. 3D display at the temporary exhibition Play Evolución. Atapuerca y el MEH en paisaje Playmobil (Play Evolution. Atapuerca and the Museum of Human Evolution in Playmobil Landscape) (2012). © Museo de la Evolución Humana, Burgos (Museum of Human Evolution, Burgos).*

other hand, models, peep-hole scenes and scale models, of a more traditional format, can also include children in the scenes they depict. A recent contribution to this field was made by the Museum of Human Evolution in Burgos, whose permanent collection includes peep-hole scenes and scale models with children. The same museum has also recently opened an attractive temporary exhibition on the world of Atapuerca named *PlayEvolución. Atapuerca y el MEH en paisaje playmobil* (*Play Evolution. Atapuerca and the Museum of Human Evolution in Playmobil Landscape*) (2012) (Fig. 14.4).

### Audiovisual and/or Interactive Productions or Multimedia

Audiovisual productions are a real plus to exhibitions, presenting moving images, acoustic effects, speech and settings that all enrich the visitors' experience. Other interactive resources and multimedia, with greater or lesser technological components, that are adapted for the youngest of visitors, offer many possibilities for communication and allow children to connect with the past easily. Of these interactive resources, the audiovisual resources at the Museo Monográfico Puig des Molins (Puig des Molins Monographic Museum) in Ibiza deserve a mention. Recently opened (2012), the resources display the grave goods found at the Phoenician-Punic necropolis of Puig des Molins. Young girls take us on a journey from the Phoenician era to the present, connecting with the exhibitions' visitors effectively and even managing to play down somewhat the drama of death.

Another interesting and widely-accessible interactive resource that stimulates the senses is to be found at the Museo Arqueológico de Asturias (Asturias Archaeological Museum) (2011), under the name of 'i-punto'. The resources include easily-manipulated replicas, scale models and controllable elements related to smell and sounds, as well as interactive games. Interactivity, as well as functionality (or virtuality in some cases) and sustainability is thus added to education, experimentation and recreation on offer.

## EDUCATION AND CULTURAL ACTION: TEACHING ACTIVITIES

Programmes that have been adapted for children in museums offer an important source of recreation for families nowadays. A large number of museums are aware that they should adapt and personalize the resources they have on offer for child visitors in order to facilitate their educational duties. Museums are gradually being included in the diaries of families and schools as cultural and leisure centres to be visited. Although children tend to visit museums with their schools, their mothers and fathers are gradually joining them and are actively taking part in the activities offered by these centres. The creation of educational departments in the nineties has slowly started to yield its benefits.

Nursery schools demand material from the world of publishing in order to work in close proximity with these cultural institutions. In order to complement the information given in exhibitions and its museography, therefore, teaching activities and strategies should be suggested to replace the more traditional ones. These could take the form of various teaching materials that are increasingly available in the digital world. In this sense, the previous ideas worked on by the school are crucial, and the revision of texts and school materials is an important task. We would like to insist here on the publications offered to child visitors by museums, since, as Gonzalo Ruiz Zapatero states, institutions and researchers need to work together more.[28] Much work needs to be done on educational manuals for children since they are essential for their education and are, therefore, also essential for museums.

Education in museums could become a means of social transformation and revising the content of exhibitions could make real and marked contribution to this gradual social change. Cultural, teaching and educational activities also play a huge part in working towards this aim. To give an example of educational activities for children, we should mention the tours, workshops and various activities arranged every month or every three months in museums. A quick glance at the schedules of state museums proves that, despite current austerity, there are still a number of workshops and themed child visits, family workshops, games and other recreational activities of interest on offer.[29]

The activities of the Museo de Altamira (Altamira Museum) stand out in particular, since here it is possible to prepare a 'tailor-made' visit adapted to the needs of each visitor (individual adults, families with children, teachers, tourism professionals, media professionals, researchers, etc.) In addition to its permanent exhibition, 'Los tiempos de Altamira' ('The eras of Altamira'), the *Museoteca* is also exclusively open to families with children interested in learning more, playing, reading, creating things together. At ARQUA (Museo Nacional de Arqueología Subacuática de Cartagena – the

National Underwater Archaeology Museum in Cartagena), workshops are offered for each educational level (nursery, primary, secondary, sixth-form, as well as workshops for families). Another example is that of the Museo de América (Museum of America) which has a programme in place for children with storytelling, children's films, a summer school, workshops and specific activities.

Other examples of continual educational activity that is also accessible via internet can be found in the material and initiatives of the Museo de Prehistoria de Valencia (the Valencia Prehistory Museum), whose content can be viewed on its webpage.[30] The Museo Romano de Oiasso (Oiasso Roman Museum) also has resources on hand for teachers, with educational programmes and material available via internet.[31] The Museo de Arqueología de Cataluña (Catalonia Archaeology Museum), Barcelona,[32] also offers workshops for children and families aimed at experiencing and discovering. Together with Arqueoxarxa, the museum network, and archaeological sites in Cataluña, this museum organized a series of interesting activities around the animation film *Las Aventuras de Tadeo Jones*, to promote the understanding and enjoyment of archaeology amongst children.

## Final Considerations

In this chapter, our aim has been to highlight how archaeological museums may have a key role as educational centres in the spreading of cultural heritage aimed at children, since they are centres for transmitting the memories of a community and, as such, of the construction of culture, essential to the education of children. At the same time, they are also an essential tool for teaching equality.

Childhood has, for various reasons, generally been masked or limited in its representation in museums. It should come as no surprise to us that the world of children is scarcely represented in the exhibition content of archaeological museums. The lack of clearly identified traces of children in archaeology is the result not only of a methodological problem but also of theoretical foundations, making it similar to the apparent invisibility of women in archaeological remains. In this way, archaeological museums could have an important role in revising historical content through research, with new approaches towards their collections, and not only those traditionally related to children such as toys, but also cultural material linked to different biological stages, their daily lives, their games and learning, their beliefs and the rituals related to their death. This would therefore suppose a means of discovering the key elements to the social and ideological organization of any human group from the past.

Although educational programmes have been increasing the resources they have on offer for children, a much greater effort it needed for archaeological museums to become an attractive prospect for this portion of the population. Proof of this can be found in the statistics which show that the number of children visiting museums has not risen in the last ten years. It still surprises us that children visit museums more with their families than as part of school trips. This leads us to question, on the one hand, the need for compulsory interaction between museums and educational centres and, on the other hand, the need to provide teaching materials designed specifically for these family visits.

In terms of the exhibition itself, the permanent museum display should allow children to build up their own understanding by interacting with the pieces on display with the help of adults.[33] Active learning therefore needs to be promoted within the museum. The museum should have a layout that allows visitors to look at collections comfortably, read texts without difficulty and it provide educational tools for different ages, without forgetting that the preparation given before the tour is essential. At the same time, the organization of temporary exhibitions with themes of interest to children is an ongoing challenge and, in this sense, archaeological museums could be truly inspirational.

Simultaneously, activities aimed at children should promote learning though playing and discovery. In this context of diffusion, we cannot forget the use of new technologies, which have a great potential for the development of applications for the tablets and smart phones that children use intuitively with ease and skill ('a la carte' exhibition, themed visits of the exhibition, a plan of the museum adapted for each age group, games for the mobile phone, etc.). Aside from the collection, however, we should not forget that suitable infrastructure and services in the museum will provide families and children with a better experience and higher levels of satisfaction. With regards to visiting children, a welcome area should also be available where their visit can be planned, with lockers at the same height as the smallest children, and equipment such as fountains, benches, rest areas, adapted toilets and childcare areas. Rooms to carry out workshops, presentations and other activities and to store material for teaching activities are also a good idea. At the same time the museum can also connect with child visitors through their public services, whether this is by offering a children's menu in the cafeteria, by taking care of the image it projects to the outside world, or by offering specialized material in its bookshop: informative books for children, teaching guides, stories, costumes, games, etc.

## NOTES

1   The research for this chapter was carried out as part of research project "I+D *La discriminación de la mujer: los orígenes del problema. La función social y educativa de los museos arqueológicos en la lucha contra la violencia de género* (2013–2015), funded by Instituto de la Mujer (Ministerio de Sanidad, Servicios Sociales e Igualdad)
2   Decarli 2003, 9
3   Valdés Sagüés 2004, 68
4   Ballart Hernández 2012
5   Ruiz Zapatero 2010
6   Ruiz Zapatero 2012
7   A popular recent example of production by 'made in Spain' (2012): One of the most successful children's animation films in Spain is *Las aventuras de Tadeo Jones*, whose main character is a young workman who dreams of becoming an archaeologist-explorer. Although the film is packed with stereotypical assumptions about those working in archaeology and evident gender biases, it serves as proof of the recognition of archaeology in the media, its popularity and its social attractiveness, as well as its success amongst children, and those above the age of 4 in particular

8    Grau 2012
9    Izquierdo, López and Prados 2012
10   Sada Castillo 2010
11   http://www.mcu.es/museos/MC/Laboratorio/index.html
12   AAVV 2011, 72
13   *Ibid.* 2011, 82
14   *Ibid.* 2011, 250
15   Brookshaw 2010
16   McKerr 2008
17   Wileman 2005, 8
18   Lillehammer 2010
19   Sánchez Romero 2008
20   Chapa Brunet 2003, 117
21   Králik *et al.* 2008
22   Brookshaw 2010
23   Sánchez Romero 2010
24   Prados 2013
25   Izquierdo 2013
26   Brookshaw 2010
27   Hernández Hernández 2010, 216–21
28   Ruiz Zapatero 2012
29   http://www.mcu.es/museos/docs/agenda_octubre12.pdf
30   http://www.museuprehistoriavalencia.es/didactica_museo.html
31   http://www.irun.org/oiasso/home.aspx?tabid=89
32   http://www.mac.cat/Educacio
33   Pastor 2004

References

AA.VV. 2011. *Conociendo a nuestros visitantes. Estudio de Público en museos del Ministerio de Cultura*, Laboratorio Permanente de Público de Museos, Ministerio de Cultura, Madrid.
Ballart Hernández, J. 2012. De objeto a objeto de museo: la construcción de significados, pp. 99–114 in Ferrer, C. and Vives-Ferrándiz, J. (eds), *Construcciones y usos del pasado. Patrimonio Arqueológico, Territorio y Museo. Jornadas de debate del Museo de Prehistoria de Valencia*, Museo de Prehistoria de Valencia.
Brookshaw, S. 2010. The Archaeology of Childhood: A Museum perspective. *Complutum*, Vol. 21 (2): 215–232.
Chapa Brunet, T. 2003. La percepción de la infancia en el mundo ibérico. *Trabajos de Prehistoria*, 60, 1: 115–138.
Decarli, G. 2003. Vigencia de la Nueva Museología en América Latina: conceptos y modelos, pp. 1–22, *Revista ABRA de la Facultad de Ciencias Sociales de la Universidad Nacional*, EUNA, Costa Rica, June–December 2003.
Grau, L. 2012. Territorio de cambios: algunas conjeturas sobre museos y otras ilusiones, pp. 75–98 in Ferrer, C. and Vives-Ferrándiz, J. (eds), *Construcciones y usos del pasado. Patrimonio Arqueológico, Territorio y Museo. Jornadas de debate del Museo de Prehistoria de Valencia*, Museo de Prehistoria de Valencia.
Hernández Hernández, F. 2010. *Los museos arqueológicos y su museografía*, Trea, Gijón.
Izquierdo, I. 2013. Aristócratas, ciudadanas y madres: imágenes de mujeres en la sociedad ibérica, pp. 103–128, in Domínguez Arranz, A. (ed.), *Política y Género en la Propaganda en la Antigüedad, Antecedentes y Legado*, Trea, Piedras Angulares.

Izquierdo, I., López, C. and Prados, L. 2014. Infancia, museología y arqueología. Reflexiones en torno a los museos arqueológicos y el público infantil, *Archivo de Prehistoria Levantina*, Vol. XXXI, 401–418. Valencia.

Izquierdo, I., López, C. and Prados, L. 2012. Exposición y género: El ejemplo de los museos de arqueología, pp. 271–286, in Asensio, Pol, Asenjo and Castro (eds), *SIAM. Series Iberoamericanas de Museología. Vol. 4*, Universidad Autónoma de Madrid.

Králik, M., Urbanová, P. and Hlozêk, M. 2008. Finger, Hand and Foot Imprints: The Evidence of Children on Archaeological Artefacts, pp. 1–14 in Dommasnes, L. H. and Wrigglesworth, M. (eds), *Children, Identity and the Past*, Cambridge.

Lillehammer, G. 2010. Archaeology of children. *Complutum*, Vol. 21 (2): 15–46.

McKerr, L. 2008. Towards an archaeology of childhood: children and material culture in historic Ireland, pp. 36–50 in Dommasnesand, L. H. and Wrigglesworth M. (eds), *Children, Identity and the Past*, Cambridge.

Pastor Homs, I. 2004. *Pedagogía museística. Nuevas perspectivas y tendencias actuales*, Ariel Patrimonio.

Prados Torreira, L. 2013. ¿Por qué se ofrecían los exvotos de recién nacidos? Una aproximación a la presencia de "bebés enfajados" en el santuario ibérico de Collado de Los Jardines (Sta Elena, Jaén, España), pp. 325–340, in Rísquez, C. and Rueda, C. (eds), *Santuarios Iberos: Territorio, ritualidad y Memoria*, Jaén.

Ruiz Zapatero, G. 2010. Los valores educativos de la Prehistoria en la Enseñanza Obligatoria. *Marq, arqueología y museos*, 4: 161–179.

Ruiz Zapatero, G. 2012. Presencia social de la arqueología y percepción pública del pasado, pp. 31–74, in Ferrer, C. y Vives-Ferrándiz, J. (eds), *Construcciones y usos del pasado. Patrimonio Arqueológico, Territorio y Museo. Jornadas de debate del Museo de Prehistoria de Valencia*, Museo de Prehistoria de Valencia.

Sada Castillo, P. 2010. ¿Mujeres invisibles? La presencia de la mujer en los discursos expositivos de la Historia, pp. 229–247 in Domínguez Arranz, A. (ed.), *Mujeres en la Antigüedad Clásica. Género, poder y conflicto*. Madrid: Sílex.

Sánchez Romero, M. 2008. Childhood and the construction of gender identities through material culture. *International Journal of Childhood in the Past*, 1: 17–37.

Sánchez Romero, M. 2010. *¡Eso no se toca! infancia y cultura material en arqueología. Complutum*, Vol. 21 (2): 9–14.

Valdés Sagüés, M. C. 2004. La difusión, una función del museo. *Museos.es*, 4: 64–75.

Wileman, J. 2005. *Hide and Seek: The Archaeology of Childhood*. Stroud: Tempus.

# Home to Mother: The Long Journey to not Lose one's own Identity

## *Angela Anna Iuliucci*

The connection between space and identity has always been an attractive but difficult literary topic. The complexity of this issue is due to the fact that to define the concept of identity in a distinct and precise way is often a problematical task. As noticed by Ashild Lappergard Hauge, in fact, identity is 'a complex term, especially in interdisciplinary fields. Each discipline has its own definitions, and uses the term differently according to its own traditions. Even within the same discipline, "identity" may be seen as a term with indistinct borders'.[1] Hauge also observes that 'many factors – genetic, social, and cultural as well as the built environment – combine to shape identity'.[2] Among all these elements, space is beyond question particularly relevant and it plays an important role in framing identity. However, also defining space is rather difficult. In the essay 'Body, self and landscape: A geographical inquiry into the place-world', Casey makes an interesting distinction between space and place. He defines space as 'the encompassing reality that allows for things to be located within it'[3] and place as 'the immediate ambiance of my lived body and its history, including the whole sedimented history of cultural and social influences and personal interests that compose my life-history'.[4] This is the same concept expressed by Setha M. Low and Denise Lawrence-Zúñiga when they speak about the embodied space: 'Embodied space is the location where human experience and consciousness take on material and spatial form'.[5] It is 'the space occupied by the body, and the perception and experience of that space contracts and expands in relationship to a person's emotions, and state of mind, sense of self, social relations, and cultural predispositions'.[6] Putting aside the different definitions and approaches, what is certain is that place/space and identity influence each other mutually in a very intense way: 'People affect places, and places (and the way places are affected) influence how people see themselves'.[7]

As already pointed out, many elements work together to shape identity, and therefore they also affect the search for the self. According to John Hodgson, 'everyone exists in the specific society into which they are born and the effects of that society, both negative and positive, influence the nature, quality and the outcome of the search for self'.[8] As a result, the search for the self entails a sort of negotiation with all the elements that can influence it, including space. It is interesting to notice that when the person dealing with the space is a child, the bond between space and identity becomes more complex because 'physically smaller, often less knowledgeable, and frequently barred from full inclusion in society, children must adapt to their landscapes [...] from an inherently marginal position, even when they belong to dominant groups'.[9] It is during childhood that we start to look for an identity and children's literature can be very helpful to make children aware of this search. As stated by Margaret Meek, in fact, 'If we agree that literature offers and encourages a continuing scrutiny of 'who we think we are', we have to emphasize the part that children's literature plays in the development of children's understanding of both belonging (being one of us) and differentiation (being other)'.[10]

On the basis of all these remarks, I have decided to examine the relationship between children and their living spaces through the analysis of *Home to Mother*, a children's book published in 2006 illustrated by Janice Lyndon and written by Doris Pilkington Garimara.[11] Actually, *Home to Mother* is the younger reader's version of Pilkington's bestseller *Follow the Rabbit-Proof Fence*, first published in 1996. The novel takes place in Australia in 1931 and tells the true story of Molly (the author's mother), Gracie and Daisy, three young Aboriginal girls who are taken away from the community of Jigalong, where they live with their families, to be led to the Moore River Native Settlement.

I have chosen to take into consideration this book because the story allows us to stress the importance of the connection between space and identity and because, being a children's book, it enables us to examine 'the ways in which children's literature addresses the processes of coming both to know oneself as situated in space and how the spaces one inhabits shape one's self'.[12] Moreover, as underlined in the Introduction to *Space and Place in Children's Literature*,

> [...] no work of literature can capture in words or images the fullness of being in a place, any specific lived-in social place. Children's literature nevertheless introduces young readers to new places and ways of understanding them, whether through imaginary otherworlds that reflects upon reality or explications of spaces in our own world that cast them in a particular light. These spaces and places of children's literature demonstrate the ways in which setting can influence identity, and also lie open to interpretation and appropriation by readers who may wish to transform them for their own purposes.[13]

One of the crucial passages in *Home to Mother* is the one describing Molly, Gracie and Daisy's forced removal from the community of Jigalong:

> Addressing no one in particular the man uttered those fateful words, 'I've come to take Molly, Gracie and Daisy, the three half-caste girls, with me to send them to school south.'
>
> The man's name was Constable Riggs. He was a Protection Officer and also a policeman with orders to search for children of Aboriginal mothers and white fathers. The Department of Native Affairs called these children 'the half-castes' and was rounding them up from all over Western Australia's East Pilbara region.
>
> The girls had no choice but to obey and go with him – it was the law. With tears streaming down their faces, Molly and Gracie climbed up on the constable's big bay horse.

'Where is Daisy?' the Constable asked.

'She's with her mother at Murra Munda.'

'Well then, we'd better go there and find her,' said Constable Riggs and they rode away in the direction of Murra Munda Station.

Behind them the mothers' high pitched wails filled the air, followed by the cries and sobbing of the families. Molly and Gracie looked back just once before the camp disappeared through the river gums.

It wasn't long before Daisy was caught and joined her cousins on their long and terrifying journey south.[14]

Scenes like this were common in 19th and 20th century Australia, where to be taken away from one's own family and put in the care of the whites was the destiny of all Aboriginal children. As Peter Read states in *The Stolen Generations: The removal of Aboriginal children in New South Wales 1883 to 1969*:

> White people have never been able to leave Aborigines alone. Children particularly have suffered. Missionaries, teachers, government officials have believed that the best way to make black people behave like white people was to get hold of the children who had not yet learned Aboriginal lifeways. They thought that children's minds were like a kind of blackboard on which the European secrets could be written.[15]

Even if 'indigenous children have been forcibly separated from their families and communities since the very first days of the European occupation of Australia',[16] it was the Aborigines Protection Act of 1909 that gave official power over children to the Aborigines Protection Board.[17] Children could be removed without their parents' consent, they could be taken at any age and they were completely cut off from the outside world and from their roots, because the Board's aim was to absorb them into white society, to erase their Aboriginal identity in order to develop a white identity.

In *Children's Literature and National Identity*, Margaret Meek states 'At some point in childhood, children discover the name of the location, country, city, town or village where they are 'at home'. The recorded address becomes an extension of themselves in a world of people they know.'[18] She also underlines the tight connection between identity and space, language and culture, culture that she defines as '[...] what we live for. Affection, relationship, memory, kinship, place, community, emotional fulfilment, intellectual enjoyment, a sense of ultimate meaning; [...]'.[19] The link between identity and space, language and culture is also stressed by Rosemary Ross Johnston who affirms that in children's literature home represents personal significance and care and that the concept of home is inseparable from the concept of nation, where nation is 'not just a geographical space but a history, language, codes of behaviour and dress, codes of relationships between generations, and codes of past and future'.[20]

As a consequence, being taken away did not only mean to lose their parents for the Aboriginal children, but it also entailed the loss of their identity, their space, their language and their culture. The loss of place implies the loss of self because, as underlined by Casey, 'there is *no place without self; and no self without place.*'[21] 'Shhh,' Martha hissed. 'Not allowed to speak 'blackfella talk'. We gotta speak English all the time',[22] says Martha to Molly, Gracie and Daisy during their first day at the

Moore River Native Settlement. But to not speak their own language was not the only prohibition. Every aspect of Aboriginality was not positively affirmed. In an interview given to George Negus, Doris Pilkington Garimara herself, who was taken to the Moore River Native Settlement when she was four and a half, remembers that in the mission the children were told that they were there because their parents did not love and did not want them. 'We were continually told, you know, that Aboriginal culture was evil', she says.[23] The effects of this brainwashing were devastating. When, at the age of eighteen, the children were legally free, they found themselves homeless and they did not know who they were. Like any other children of diasporas, they had a complicated relationship to place and they had to negotiate cultural differences.

If we read the evidences included in *Bringing Them Home: Report of the National Inquiry into the Separation of Aboriginal and Torres Strait Islander Children from Their Families*, we can easily notice that grief and loss are the predominant themes, grief for the forced separation, for the abuses suffered, grief for the loss of years that can never be fully recovered, grief for the loss of an identity. Many witnesses, in fact, speak of 'their strong sense of not belonging either in the Indigenous community or in the non-Indigenous community':[24]

> Our life pattern was created by the government policies and are forever with me, as though an invisible anchor around my neck. The moments that should be shared and rejoiced by a family unit, for [my brother] and mum and I are forever lost. The stolen years that are worth more than any treasure are irrecoverable.
> *Confidential submission 338, Victoria.*[25]

> I went through an identity crisis. And our identity is where we come from and who we are. And, I think, instead of compensation being in the form of large sums of money, I personally would like to see it go into some form of land acquisition for the people who were taken away, if they so wish, to have a place that they can call their own and that they can give to their children. My wife and I are trying to break this cycle, trying our hardest to break this cycle of shattered families. We're going to make sure that we stick together and bring our children up so they know who they are, what they are and where they came from.
> *Confidential evidence 696, New South Wales: man happily adopted into a non-Indigenous family at 13 months in the 1960s.*[26]

> When we left Port Augusta, when they took us away, we could only talk Aboriginal. We only knew one language and when we went down there, well, we had to communicate somehow. Anyway, when I come back I couldn't even speak my own language. And that really buggered my identity up. It took me 40 odd years before I became a man in my own people's eyes, through Aboriginal law. Whereas I should've went through that when I was about 12 years of age.
> *Confidential evidence 179, South Australia: man removed as an 'experiment' in assimilation to a Church of England boys' home in the 1950s.*[27]

> I had to relearn lots of things. I had to relearn humour, ways of sitting, ways of being which was another way totally to what I was actually brought up with. It was like having to re-do me, I suppose. The thing that people were denied in being removed from family was that they were denied being read as Aboriginal people, they were denied being educated in an Aboriginal way.
> *Confidential evidence 71, New South Wales: woman who lived from 5 months to 16 years in Cootamundra Girl's Home in the 1950s and 1960s.*[28]

> Most of us girls were thinking white in the head but were feeling black inside. We weren't black or white. We were a very lonely, lost and sad displaced group of people. We were taught to think and act like a white person, but we didn't know how to think and act like an Aboriginal. We didn't know anything about our culture. We were completely brainwashed to think only like a white person. When they went to mix in white society, they found they were not accepted [because] they were Aboriginal. When they went and mixed with Aborigines, some found they couldn't identify with them either, because they had too much white ways in them. So, that they were either black or white. They were simply a lost generation of children. I know. I was one of them.
> *Confidential submission 617, New South Wales: woman removed at 8 years with her 3 sisters in the 1940s; placed in Cootamundra Girls' Home.*[29]

The morning after her first night at the Moore River Native Settlement, Molly wakes up and looks around the dormitory.

> It was crowded with beds without sheets and for a toilet there was a bucket. In the early light she could see metal bars across the windows. Outside, the jangling noise of keys and the scrape of a padlock left no question. Molly, Gracie and Daisy were no longer free and happy. They were in a gaol. '*I'm not staying here*,' Molly promised herself[30]

In this moment Molly chooses to change a destiny that seems to be already written, the destiny that the whites want to impose on her. Molly is the eldest of the three and so, according to the tradition, she is entrusted with the safety of Gracie and Daisy, and she decides that they will escape to come back home. Molly, Gracie and Daisy's journey will be very long because 1,600 kilometres separate them from home. Without maps or compasses, their only reference point will be the rabbit-proof fence.[31] For the first time since they were born, the three girls are alone and far from home and they have to travel through a land completely unknown to them, a land in which they do not feel safe. Anyway, they succeed in surviving because they rely on what they have learned at home, on the Elders' teachings. This is particularly evident in two passages of the book. In the first one, the three girls have to cross a river. While Daisy and Gracie think that they will not able to do that, Molly is more confident. 'The day before, she had watched the Settlement girls using a long stick to test the depth of the river and she was certain that she could do the same thing'.[32] In the other passage, Molly tries to comfort a tired and hungry Gracie: 'Don't worry, we will find something to eat, you'll see.' Molly put her arm around Gracie. 'This country is different from ours so we gotta learn to find their bush tucker, that's all'.[33] These passages also demonstrate what was stated by Casey when he speaks about *outgoing* and *incoming* body. According to Casey, the body is the link between the self and the lived place. 'Neither body nor place is a wholly determinate entity; each continually evolves, and precisely in relation to the other'.[34] When 'the lived body *goes out to meet the place-world*',[35] we can speak about *outgoing* body. 'But the body not only goes out to reach places; it also bears the traces of the places it has known'[36] and all these places combine to shape the body. This is the *incoming* body.

Molly, Gracie and Daisy's journey does not only show that space influences people, but also that 'people negotiate the social, historical, and physical connotations of space and place to claim their own identities'[37] It proves that landscape is '*the background and foreground*[38] in which humans are embodied (or outlined against), in which they are embedded (given shape and fitted into place); it is a liminal and subliminal presence which, whether it is described or not, commits identity and some sort of social and by extension national attachment'.[39] Molly, Daisy and Gracie escape from the Moore River Native Settlement and face a hard journey full of dangers and troubles to claim the right to be themselves, to not lose their identity.

> As they neared the creek, the girls pulled up suddenly. They could hear the voices from the camp speaking Mardu wangku. They were suddenly overcome with emotions. They had come home to their mothers, their family, their homeland – the warm, red earth, the spinifex grass and wintamarra trees.

> Around the camp fire that night the girls sat with their families and talked about tomorrow's plans. They will be moved to a camp where they would be safe. But for now, this is what Molly and Daisy wanted, sleeping beside their mothers near a big warm fire. Now they knew they were at home at last.[40]

In this passage, it is impossible to not notice a deep sense of connection and belonging, and the idea of land perceived as the place where one belongs to 'can never be owned, nor possessed; it is as innately communal as personal: it is land not only as landscape, not only as a mindscape, but as a soulscape'.[41]

NOTES

1  Hauge 2007
2  *Ibid.*
3  Casey 2001, 404
4  *Ibid.*
5  Low and Lawrence-Zúñiga 2003, 2
6  *Ibid.*
7  Hauge 2007
8  Hodgson 1993, 145
9  Cecire *et al.* 2015, 14
10  Meek 2001, x
11  Doris Pilkington's Aboriginal name is Nugi Garimara. She was born in 1937 on Balfour Downs Station, in the East Pilbara. As a toddler she was taken from her mother to be raised at the Moore River Mission. At 18, Doris left the mission system as the first of its members to qualify for the Royal Perth Hospital's nursing aide training program. Following marriage and a family, she studied journalism and worked in film/video production. Her first book *Caprice: A Stockman's Daughter* won the 1990 David Unaipon National Award. *Follow the Rabbit-Proof Fence* was first published in 1996, and was released internationally in 2002 as the film '*Rabbit-Proof Fence*'. The novel has now been translated into 11 languages worldwide. In 2002, Doris was appointed co-patron of the state and federal Sorry Day committees' Journey of Healing. Her third novel *Under the Wintamarra Tree* was also published in the same year. In 2006, Doris published *Home to Mother,* a children's version of her own mother's courageous 1600-km journey on foot from the Moore River Native Settlement to Jigalong. In the same year, she was awarded an Order of Australia for service to the arts in Indigenous literature. Doris Pilkington Garimara AM is the recipient of the 2008 Australia Council Red Ochre Award. The award pays tribute to an Aboriginal or Torres Strait Islander artist for their outstanding, life-long contribution to Aboriginal and Torres Strait

Islander arts at home and abroad. http://www.australiacouncil.gov.au/news/items/pre-2010/pot_of_gold_at_the_end_of_the_rabbitproof_fence_for_doris_pilkington_garimara_am/doris_pilkington_garimara_am?a=29977

12 Doughty and Thompson 2011, 1
13 Cecire *et al.* 2015, 17–18
14 Garimara 2006, 5–7
15 Read 1981, 3
16 Lavarch 1997
17 '"Aboriginal protection" was constantly debated, as the moving frontier created new groups of dispossessed Aborigines. Could they be "civilised" through contact with whites, or did they need to be protected by being separated from the worst aspects of colonial society? Humanitarians increasingly believed that Aborigines should be moved onto Aboriginal reserves, which would function as asylums caring for "a dying race" or as reformatories where paternal superintendents could "raise" able-bodies Aborigines, particularly the young, by inculcating the virtues of hard work, thrift and sobriety. […] Between the late nineteenth century and the 1930s, many Aborigines were "protected" by special acts of parliament.' This meant that 'governments assumed legal responsibility for Aborigines and established special bureaucracies (generally called "Protection Boards"). These were empowered to control Aborigines' affairs by prescribing their place of residence, determining conditions of employment, and assuming the care and the custody of children.' Davison, Hirst, Macintyre 1998, 10
18 Meek 2001, viii
19 *Ibid.*
20 Johnston 2004, 966
21 Casey 2001, 406
22 Garimara 2006, 11
23 Doris Pilkington Garimara Interview 2003
24 Lavarch 1997
25 *Ibid.*
26 *Ibid.*
27 *Ibid.*
28 *Ibid.*
29 *Ibid.*
30 Garimara 2006, 9–10
31 The rabbit-proof fence is a fence which crosses Western Australia. It was constructed between 1901 and 1907 to keep rabbits and other agricultural pests coming from the East out of Western Australian pastoral areas. Garimara 2002
32 Garimara 2006, 16
33 *Ibid.*, 32
34 Casey 2001, 414
35 *Ibid.*
36 *Ibid.*
37 Cecire *et al.* 2015, 6
38 The terms background and foreground are used by Hirsch and O'Hanlon in their definition of landscape. According to them, in fact, 'landscape entails a relationship between the "foreground" and "background" of social life'. They define as foreground 'the concrete actuality of everyday social life ("the way we now are")', and as background 'the perceived potentiality thrown into relief by our foregrounded existence ("the way we might be")'. Hirsch and O'Hanlon 1995, 3
39 Johnston 2004, 964
40 Garimara 2006, 96–97
41 Johnston 2004, 981

REFERENCES

Casey, E. S. 2001. Body, self and landscape: A geographical inquiry into the place-world, pp. 403–425, in Adams, P. C., Hoelscher, S. and Tills, K. E. (eds), *Textures of Place*. Minneapolis: University of Minnesota Press.

Cecire, M. S., Field, H., Finn, K. M. and Malini, R. (eds) 2015. *Space and Place in Children's Literature, 1789 to the present*. Burlington: Ashgate.

Davison, G., Hirst, J. and Macintyre, S. (eds) 1998. *The Oxford Companion to Australian History*. Melbourne: Oxford University Press.

Doris Pilkington Garimara Interview at *George Negus Tonight*, 25th June 2003. Transcript available at http://www.abc.net.au (Australian Broadcast Corporation). Last accessed October 2012.

Doughty, T. and Thompson, D. (eds) 2006. *Knowing Their Place? Identity and Space in Children's Literature*. Newcastle Upon Tyne: Cambridge Scholars Publishing.

Garimara, D. P. 2002. *Follow the Rabbit-Proof Fence*. St Lucia (Queensland): University of Queensland Press.

Garimara, D. P. 2006. *Home to Mother*. St Lucia (Queensland): University of Queensland Press.

Hauge, A. L. 2007. Identity and place: a critical comparison of three identity theories. *Architectural Science Review*, 50, 1, 44–51. Online version downloadable at http://faculty.arch.utah.edu/benham/ group 3/Place-Identity.pdf. Last accessed March 2013.

Hirsch, E. and O'Hanlon, M. (eds) 1995. *The Anthropology of Landscape: Perspectives on Space and Place*. New York: Oxford University Press.

Hodgson, John 1993. *The Search for the Self: Childhood in Autobiography and Fiction since 1940*. Sheffield: Sheffield Academic Press.

Lavarch, M. 1997. *Bringing Them Home: Report of the National Inquiry into the Separation of Aboriginal and Torres Strait Islander Children from Their Families*. Online version downloadable at http://humanrights.gov.au/ (Australian Human Rights Commission). Last accessed October 2012.

Low, S. M. and Lawrence-Zúñiga, D. (eds) 2003. *The Anthropology of Space and Place: Locating Culture*. Oxford: Blackwell Publishing.

Meek, M. (ed.) 2001. *Children's Literature and National Identity*. Stoke on Trent: Trentham Books.

Read, P. 1981. *The Stolen Generations: The Removal of Aboriginal Children in New South Wales 1883 to 1969*. Online version downloadable at http://www.daa.nsw.gov.au (NSW Government Department of Education and Communities – Office of Communities Aboriginal Affairs). Last accessed October 2012.

Ross Johnston, R. 2004. Australia, pp. 960–983 in Hunt, P. (ed.), *International Companion Encyclopedia of Children's Literature* (second edition). London: Routledge.

# PART III
## SPACE, BODY AND MIND:
## CHILDREN IN FUNERARY CONTEXTS

# 16

## Use of Molecular Genetic Procedures for Sex Determination in 'Guanches' Children's Remains

*Alejandra C. Ordóñez, Matilde Arnay-de-la Rosa,*
*Rosa Fregel, Guacimara Ramos-Pérez,*
*Emilio González Reimers and José Pestano*

### Introduction

The study of childhood is very important from the point of view of the social organisation inside different populations. Children, as well as adults, play outstanding economical and social roles. They should be considered as active social agents by themselves, not just as a reflex of the adult's world.

The categories of childhood, adolescence and youth are clearly cultural concepts. Different societies understand these categories in many different ways, as shown by various transcultural studies of present day societies. For this reason, when we face the study of childhood in the past, we have to make a clear distinction between biological and non-biological age. The first one is related to the physiological maturity of the skeleton. It has more or less standard patterns where growth rhythms are used to determine the age of an individual. On the other hand, non-biological age uses different social and cultural aspects to determine a person's maturity and his or her integration in different life stages. Modern western societies tend to emphasise the chronological age, using rigid categories to establish it. On the contrary, other societies use skills or the involvement in different social activities as a criterion to determine individual maturity.

Once the differences between these two concepts are established and a diachronical analysis of different societies is made, we can assert that our concept of childhood differs from that of past societies. Since the 1960s, the idealist approach in history has been questioned. It assumed that children were ahistorical figures whose attributes and behaviours were part of universal human nature.

When studying past societies, historical references help us to demonstrate that children were part of different social groups from a very young age. This can be also seen in archaeological contexts with the aid of osteoarchaeology. Children's involvement in different group activities many times required a high physical effort, which would leave an imprint in the skeleton.[1] As for the girls, in particular, their entrance into adulthood would come with the menarche, which usually meant being ready to get married.[2] This would normally imply motherhood from a young age, something that would also leave an imprint in the anthropological record.

There are various problems regarding the interpretation of the archaeological record associated with childhood, especially because there is a lack of specific research strategies for this particular group.[3] It becomes necessary to analyse the evidence that will allow us to come closer to the representation of childhood inside the archaeological record, to their place in burial spaces and in different settlements or in contexts were they have been usually concealed for the researchers. We must establish their relationships with the rest of the community, as well as determine the type of grave goods or funerary treatment they receive in different societies. All this can help us to go in depth into the concept of childhood within the societies we study.

Nevertheless, to be able to make any considerations about the concept of childhood, it is necessary to know the sex of the individuals. To know if there are any differences in the way subadults are treated according to their sex, in a specific community, is one of the main keys to understand their behaviour.

## Sex Diagnosis in Children's Remains

Sex identification of non-adult skeletal remains is a very complex task that requires a specific methodology that takes into account the levels of sexual dimorphism between different populations. Methodological proposals introduced for sexual diagnosis of children's remains are diverse, although they are usually focused in morphological and metric criteria.[4] All of them have been used with an acceptable range of effectiveness.

Currently, molecular genetic procedures are being used for this task; the possibility of an unquestionable sex assignation from children's bone is still being researched.

Genetic sex determination is performed by the study of the amelogenin gene.[5] This gene codifies one of the fundamental proteins for teeth development and it shows a length dimorphism between the X and the Y-chromosomes. The great advantage of the amelogenin is that because of its presence on both sexual chromosomes, it acts as an internal positive control. The application of new techniques, such as the Real Time PCR, also known as the quantitative polymerase chain reaction (qPCR), has increased the sensitivity as well as the reliability of amelogenin studies in degraded samples.[6]

Several other studies of sexual determination in non-adult individuals have been made using this technique, some trying to define the sex of victims of infanticide,[7] others looking for characterisation of family groups[8] and others, searching for differences in funerary practices.[9] For these studies genetic sex determination has been performed using different children's bones, such as ribs and long bones.

Sexing of children's remains through molecular genetics – using the amelogenin gene – also presents some problems, most of them derived from the intrinsic characteristics of children's bones and teeth, as they tend to be more fragile and prone to contamination with modern DNA.

In the Canarian adult skeletal remains studied so far, genetic analyses have been made using well-preserved teeth, obtaining satisfactory results in the recovery of ancient DNA (aDNA). These studies have been performed in populations following the Castilian conquest[10] as well as in populations from the aboriginal period from different islands of the archipelago.[11] Recently, cortical bone dyaphysis samples of very well preserved long bones have been analysed, obtaining very good results (unpublished results) (Fig. 16.1). The use of teeth and long bones from children is more difficult. Subadult teeth are more prone to contamination with modern DNA, mainly because of the presence of open roots among other features, and long bones may require a different methodological approach, due to their size and fragility (Fig. 16.2).

Phalanges are very compact bones, even from a young age. Although depending on the soil conditions, phalanges are usually better preserved than other long bones, increasing the possibility of obtaining endogenous DNA. They also tend to be less handled during traditional anthropological study, which decreases the possibilities of exogenous DNA contamination.

In these studies we test the applicability of well-preserved children's phalanges as a source of endogenous DNA that can be used for sex determination.

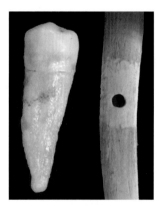

*Fig. 16.1. Samples from adult teeth and cortical bone from diaphysis for the obtaining of aDNA.*

*Fig. 16.2. Selected children phalanx for this research.*

## MATERIAL AND METHODS

A second mandibular left incisive and a medial right phalanx of a seven year old child were selected. This child was buried in an individual cave burial located on the low northwestern border of the Cascajo Mountain, in the municipality of Santiago del Teide, inside a lava flow, at 1700 meters of altitude. In this area the eruption suffered a collapse, forming a great depression. The area is surrounded by steep walls that protected an aboriginal settlement, composed, in addition to the burial, by some caves used as dwellings, one of them with evidence of an important settlement. In the northern wall of the depression there was a longitudinal breach with two different spaces in its interior. The smaller one, closed with a dry stone wall, contained the remains of a child placed on the rocky ground. It showed signs of having been subjected to artificial conservation practices (mummification). The upper part of the body had a goat skin wrapping and it maintained the anatomical connection preserving the majority of the body tissue. The arms were folded over the thorax. The burial site was embedded in the settlement space, being an example of the relationship and proximity between the funerary and the domestic areas, especially when regarding children's remains (Fig. 16.3). Radiocarbon dating yielded and antiquity of 510 ± 40 BP.

## ARCHAEOLOGICAL MATERIAL CLEANING

The manipulation of the archaeological samples was always done using gloves and under strict sterile conditions, to avoid contamination with modern DNA.[12] An extraction of the superficial DNA was performed to the tooth.[13] The possible DNA remains from previous handling will be recovered with the use of a swab soaked in a solution of Guanidinium thiocyanate. Furthermore, the sample was washed with 15% HCl, rinsed with distilled water and radiated with a UV lamp for ten minutes.

## DNA EXTRACTION

The phalanx was reduced to powder with the help of two metallic sheets and the dentine of the tooth was extracted with a dentist's drill. The resulting powder was used to obtain DNA using the PrepFiler Express BTA™ Forensic DNA Extraction Kit (Applied Biosystems). To avoid contamination due to human handling, the samples were automatically extracted using the AutoMate Express™ Forensic DNA Extraction System (Applied Biosystems).

*Fig. 16.3. Child analysed in this study as it was found in an individual cave burial, in Santiago del Teide.*

## Mitochondrial DNA Quantification by qPCR

It is known that the DNA recovered from ancient samples is mostly composed by small size molecules, with a greater abundance of multi-copy loci, like mitochondrial DNA (mtDNA) in comparison with the nuclear DNA.[14] Therefore, before performing the molecular sexing, the number of mtDNA copies was estimated by qPCR, using a Taqman mitochondrial-specific probe.[15] For this purpose, the TaqMan Universal PCR Master Mix (Applied Biosystems) kit was used in the real time thermal cycler 7500 Real-Time PCR System (Applied Biosystems).

As an authenticity criterion, only those individuals where mtDNA was amplified were subject to the analysis of the amelogenin gene. On the other hand, those from which mtDNA amplification was not possible, were discarded from the assay, as the absence of a multi-copy locus such as the mtDNA, also implies the absence of nuclear DNA in the sample.

## Molecular Sexing through the Analysis of the Amelogenin Gene by qPCR

The samples were sexed throughout the amplification of a fragment of the amelogenin gene. This gene is present in the X chromosome as well as in the Y chromosome, but it presents differences that allow sex determination of ancient remains through the PCR. The amelogenin gene amplification was done using primers that amplify a region of the first intron from both sexual chromosomes.[16] This region includes a six pb deletion for the X chromosome.

For a more sensitive detection of the different fragments, the amplification of the amelogenin gene was made through qPCR, using two Taqman probes that are specifically attached to the X and Y chromosomes,[17] as well as an internal control to detect the presence of inhibition.[18] As it was done for the mtDNA, the TaqMan Universal PCR Master Mix (Applied Biosystems) kit was used in the real time thermal cycler 7500 Real-Time PCR System (Applied Biosystems).

This sexing methodology has several advantages. The small length of the fragments (71bp) favours the quantification of severely degraded DNA, whereas the use of two distinct primer sets for the X and Y chromosome amplification helps to reduce allelic dropout.

## Authenticity Criteria

With the aim of avoiding contamination and to assure the authenticity of our results, the standards of prevention and control for the work with ancient material were followed. To achieve this, we followed Pääbo *et al.* recommendations that included those established by Cooper and Poinar.[19]

- Analyses were performed in three independent aDNA-dedicated laboratories. In the first, the excavated material was decontaminated and processed to obtain powdered samples. In the second, DNA extraction and pre-PCR procedures were carried out.

PCR amplifications were performed in a third area. Finally, post-PCR analyses were done in another physically isolated laboratory.

- In each aDNA dedicated area, all personnel were required to wear lab-coats, face-shields, hats and multiple pairs of gloves.
- The equipment and work areas were constantly irradiated with UV lamps and frequently cleaned with bleach. All sample manipulations were performed with dedicated pipettes and sterile filter tips.
- Solutions were commercially acquired whenever possible; otherwise, they were autoclaved and UV-treated.
- All metallic material was sterilised in an oven at 200°C for at least four hours.
- All the amplifications included a negative extraction control and three PCR negatives controls per reaction.
- Whenever possible, the extractions were repeated to confirm the obtained results.

The initial number of amplifiable DNA was determined by the qPCR. To ensure the obtaining of endogenous DNA, in the amelogenin gene studies primers were designed to amplify fragments of less than a 100 pb.

## RESULTS

The quantification values of the mitochondrial DNA showed that the endogenous DNA of the individual is well preserved. We can also observe that the quantity of DNA recovered from the phalanx (3,67E+04 copies/µl) is more than the one recovered from the incisive (1,75E+0,3 copies/µl). We obtained a male profile from the tooth as well as from the phalange, having once again more DNA in the phalange sample (Table 16.1).

*Table 16.1. Table of quantification values of nuclear DNA (nDNA).*

| Sample | mtDNA concentration (num. copies/µl) | Detector | Ct | nDNA concentration(ng/µl) | Sex |
|--------|--------------------------------------|----------|------|---------------------------|------|
| CAS-D | 1.75E+03 | AMGX | 34.7 | 8.71E-03 | Male |
| | | | 35.3 | 3.82E-03 | |
| | | AMGY | 35.4 | 7.65E-03 | |
| | | | 35.5 | 7.45E-03 | |
| | | IPC-qPCR | 23.8 | | |
| | | | 22.6 | | |
| CAS-F | 3.67E+04 | AMGX | 28.9 | 4.25E-01 | Male |
| | | | 27.0 | 1.20E+00 | |
| | | AMGY | 29.3 | 5.76E-01 | |
| | | | 27.0 | 2.86E+00 | |
| | | IPC-qPCR | Undetermined | | |
| | | | Undetermined | | |

DISCUSSION

Even though there had been a great deal of investigation since the 19th century of the Canarian aboriginal populations, the children's remains have usually remained invisible until the 1980s. Since then, the finding of burial sites with children's remains has increased and, throughout the years, with the use of a more demanding field methodology, the perinatal bone remains are starting to be well known in their archaeological contexts.[20] This is the reason why the introduction of series of children's remains in the Canarian anthropological studies is very recent,[21] as well as the researches where their presence, sub-representation or marginality in some burial contexts is taken into account.[22]

The current interest in the study of the children's archaeological and anthropological record has prompted us to begin this research line. Methodological issues constitute the first step. A very important matter, due to the role it can play in the correct explanation of certain social behaviours, is the sex determination of children's remains, using appropriate criteria.

Until now very different approaches have been used. The most popular ones are those based on the study of metric and morphological characteristics. The search of effective methods, based on morphological observations to determine the sex of sub-adult remains started with Von Fehling and Thompson.[23] They saw morphological differences between the pelvic bones of foetus over four months. Reynolds also found differences in the pelvic bone of children up to nine years of age.[24] After these groundbreaking works, an important part of the research has been focused in sex determination based on the anatomical traits that are used for adult sex assignment. Some have used the hipbone[25] or the mandible.[26] A statistically significant dimorphism has been also described for the permanent teeth, specially the canine.[27] The works based on the comparison between the maturity of the postcranial skeleton and the calcification stage of the teeth also deserve mention.[28]

All these procedures have been used with an acceptable range of accuracy, although they always present degrees of uncertainty. Nowadays we can solve the problem of correct sexing with the use of molecular genetic procedures.

The use of molecular biology for sex determination in archaeological human remains constitutes an important step in the analysis of children and adults whose skeletons are incomplete.[29]

For the molecular determination of sex, the use of the amelogenin gene has been generalised.[30] In the last few years, methodology has improved, although the theoretical basis remains the same.[31]

There are several reports dealing with this approach. Faerman *et al.* analysed Roman children from Ashkelon,[32] where skeletal remains of some 100 neonates were discovered in a sewer, beneath a roman bathhouse, which might have also served as a brothel. Due to the characteristics of the burial, infanticide was proposed as a probable hypothesis. Amplification was possible in 19 out of the 43 studied specimens, finding 14 males and 5 females. The authors propose that the prostitutes of Ashkelon would have selectively kept some of their children, preferably girls that would continue with their profession, discarding boys. A similar study was performed in the United Kingdom.[33] Their original hypothesis was once again the presence of female infanticide during the Roman period. Results were obtained only in 13 of the 31 analysed individuals. The difference among sexes was not significantly different from that of natural deaths, probably due to the small size of the sample, which made the results inconclusive. Also of great interest is the work of de De la Cruz *et al.* on the sacrificed children of Tlatelolco.[34] DNA was obtained for 32 of the 37 sub-adults and for six adults. The first results showed they were all males, but only the results of 26 individuals were replicated. The most plausible explanation is that the individuals sacrificed were seen as personifications of the god they were being offered to. Taking into account that Ehecatl-Quetzalcoatl, god of the studied temple, was a male god, male victims would be better personifications of this god.

Faerman also studied 10 children from the Israeli settlement o Tell Teo.[35] The infants were found in jars or under the houses. Genetic sex was determined in 5 of the 9 children studied, being all boys. Authors hypothesise about the possible differentiation in the burial treatment according to gender. The amelogenin gene has also been used for sex determination of adult bone remains in the Canary Islands, with positive results.[36] Until now it has not been applied effectively in children's remains.

With regard to this work where we analysed the remains of a 7-year-old male child that had been subjected to artificial conservation practices (usually referred to as mummification in the Canary Islands), we have some preliminary thoughts. The artificial conservation practice has been considered as an expression of social status, inside the hierarchical Guanche society. Assuming this hypothesis, and taking into account that only a fraction of the children's remains have been subjected to these practices, we can consider the social status as an hereditary condition. This would agree with the information from the written sources of the 16th and 17th centuries. We have diagnosed the sex of mummified infantile remains with reliable methods for the first time. This allows us to open an encouraging research line that can offer some clues for the understanding of this significant Guanche death ritual.

## Conclusions

The specific conditions of the sub-adult teeth and bones led us to consider the phalanx bones as adequate samples for the obtaining of endogenous DNA. The results obtained in this study confirm that the tooth sample and the phalanx are appropriate for the obtaining of endogenous DNA. They are suitable for the analysis of maternal and paternal lineages (mtDNA, Y-chromosome) and also for autosomal STRs. This proves the usefulness of phalanges as a source of genetic material for the analysis of aDNA and for sex determination through the study of the amelogenin gene. It was also shown that the quantity of DNA recovered from the phalanx was higher than the one recovered from the tooth.

ACKNOWLEDGEMENTS

This study is included in a research project funded by Ministerio de Medio Ambiente y Medio Rural y Marino. Organismo Autónomo de Parques Nacionales. Reference 328/2011.

NOTES

1   Chapa 2003; 2008
2   De Miguel Ibáñez 2010
3   Sánchez Romero 2007, 186
4   Rissech 2003
5   Salido *et al.* 1992
6   Fregel *et al.* 2011
7   Mays and Faerman 2001
8   Dudar *et al.* 2003; Simón, M. *et al.* 2011
9   Faerman *et al.* 1998; Faerman and Smith 2008; Di Bernardo *et al.* 2009
10  Maca-Meyer *et al.* 2005
11  Maca-Meyer *et al.* 2004; Arnay *et al.* 2007; 2009; Fregel *et al.* 2009
12  Cooper and Poinar 2000; Pääbo *et al.* 2004
13  Fregel *et al.* 2009
14  Higuchi *et al.* 1984, Pääbo, 1985
15  Almeida *et al.* 2011
16  Sullivan *et al.* 1993
17  Fregel *et al.* 2011
18  Hudlow *et al.* 2008
19  Pääbo *et al.* 2004; Cooper and Poinar 2000
20  Velasco *et al.* 2005
21  Velasco *et al.* 1998; 2003
22  Velasco 2009
23  Villadóniga 2005
24  Villadóniga 2005
25  Ferembach *et al.* 1979; Weaver 1980; Mitler and Sheridan 1992; Schutkowski 1993; Molleson y Cruse 1998; Loth y Heneberg 2001
26  Coqueugniot 2002
27  Goose 1963; Perzigian, 1976; Harris and Nweeia 1980
28  Ferembach *et al.* 1979; Rissech 2003
29  Schmidt *et al.* 2003
30  Nakahori *et al.* 1991a; 1991b; Maca Meyer 2002
31  Codina 2009; Gibbon *et al.* 2009
32  Faerman *et al.* 1998
33  Mays and Faerman, 2001
34  De la Cruz *et al.* 2008
35  Faerman 2008
36  Arnay *et al.* 2007; 2009

## ABBREVIATIONS

aDNA:    ancient DNA.
mtDNA:   mitochondrial DNA.
nDNA:    nuclear DNA
qPCR:    Quantitive Polymerase Chain Reaction.

## REFERENCES

Almeida, M., Betancor, E., Fregel, R., Suárez, N. M. and Pestano, J. 2011. Efficient DNA extraction from hair shafts. *Forensic Science International: Genetics Supplement Series* 3(1): e319-e320.

Arnay de la Rosa, M., González Reimers, E., Fregel, R., Velasco Vázquez, J., Delgado Darias, T., González, A. M. and Larruga, J. M. 2007. Canary Islands aborigen sex determination based on mandible parameters contrasted by amelogenin analysis. *Journal of Archaeological Science* 34, 1515–1522.

Arnay de la Rosa, M., Gámez Mendoza, A., Navarro Mederos, J. F., Hernández Marrero, J. C., Fregel, R., Yanes, Y., Galindo Martín, L., Romanek, C. S. and González Reimers, E. 2009. Dietary patterns during the early prehispanic settlement in La Gomera (Canary Islands). *Journal of Archaeological Science* 36, 1972–1981.

Chapa Brunet, T. 2003. La percepción de la infancia en el mundo ibérico. *Trabajos de Prehistoria* 60, 115–138.

Chapa Brunet, T. 2008. Presencia infantil y ritual funerario. Nasciturus, Infans, Puerulus vovis mater terra, pp. 619–641 in Gusi., F. Muriel, S. and Olaria, C. (eds), *SIAP-Diputació de Castelló*, Castelló.

Codina, A. E., Niederstatter, H. and Parson, W. 2009. 'GenderPlex' a PCR multiplex for reliable gender determination of degraded human DNA samples and complex gender constellations. *International Journal of Legal Medicine* 123 (6), 459–464.

Cooper, A. and Poinar, H. N. 2000. Ancient DNA: Do it right or not at ALL. *Science* 289 (5482), 1139–1139.

Coqueugniot, H., Giacobini, G. and Malerba, G. 2002. L'utilisation de caractères morphologiques dans la diagnose sexuelle des mandibules d'enfants: application à la collection ostéologique de Turin (Italie). *Bull. et Mém. de la Société d'Anthropologie de Paris* 14, 1–2, 131–139.

De La Cruz, I., Gonzalez-Oliver, A., Kemp, B. M., Roman, J. A., Smith, D. G. and Torre-Blanco, A. 2008. Sex identification of children sacrificed to the ancient Aztec rain gods in Tlatelolco. *Current Anthropology* 49 (3), 519–526.

De Miguel Ibañez, M. P. 2012. Una visión de la infancia desde la osteoarqueología: de la Prehistoria reciente a la Edad Media. *Complutum* 21, 135–155.

Di Bernardo, G., Del Gaudio, S., Galderisi, U., Cascino, A. and Cipollaro, M. 2009. Ancient DNA and Family Relationships in a Pompeian House. *Annals of Human Genetics* 73, 429–437.

Dudar, J. C., Waye, J. S. and Saunders, S. R. 2003. Determination of a kinship system using ancient DNA, mortuary practice, and historic records in an Upper Canadian pioneer cemetery. *International Journal of Osteoarchaeology* 13 (4), 232–246.

Faerman, M., Bar-Gal, G. K., Filon, D., Greenblatt, C. L., Stager, L., Oppenheim, A. and Smith, P. 1998. Determining the sex of infanticide victims from the late Roman era through ancient DNA analysis. *Journal of Archaeological Scien*ce 25 (9), 861–865.

Faerman, M. and Smith, P. 2008. Has society changed its attitude to infants and children? Evidence from archeological sites in the southern Levant, pp. 211–299, in Gusi, F. M. and Olaria, S. (eds) *Nasciturus, Infans, Puerulus vovis mater terra*. Castelló: SIAP-Diputació de Castelló.

Ferembach, D., Schwidetzky, I. and Stloukal, M. 1979. Recommandations pour determiner l'age et le sexe sur le squelette. *Bulletins et Mémoires de la Société d'Anthropologie de Paris* série 13 6, 7–4.

Fregel, R., Pestano, J., Arnay, M., Cabrera, V. M., Larruga, J. M. and Gonzalez, A. M. 2009. The maternal aborigine colonization of La Palma (Canary Islands). *European Journal of Human Genetics* 17 (10), 1314–1324.

Fregel, R., Almeida, M., Betancor, E., Suárez, N. M. and Pestano, J. 2011. Reliable nuclear and mitochondrial DNA quantification for low copy number and degraded forensic samples. *Forensic Science International: Genetics Supplement Series* 3 (1), e303-e304.

Gibbon, V., Paximadis, M., Strkalj, G., Ruff, P. and Penny, C. 2009. Novel methods of molecular sex identification from skeletal tissue using the amelogenin gene. *Forensic Science International-Genetics* 3 (2), 74–79.

Goose, D. H. 1963. Dental measurement: an assessment of its value in anthropological studies, pp. 125–148, in Brothwell, D. R. (ed.), *Dental anthropology*. New York: Pergamon.

Harris, E. F. and Nweeia, M. T. 1980. Dental asymmetry as a measure of environmental stress in the Ticuna Indians of Colombia. *American Journal of Physical Anthropology* 53(1), 133–42.

Higuchi, R., Bowman, B., Freiberger, M., Ryder, O. A. and Wilson, A. C. 1984. DNA- Sequences from the Quagga, an Extinct Member of the Horse Family. *Nature* 312 (5991), 282–284.

Hudlow, W. R., Date Chong, M., Swango, K. L., Timken, M. D. and Buoncristiani, M. R. 2008. A quadruplex real-time qPCR assay for the simultaneous assessment of total human DNA, human male DNA, DNA degradation and the presence of PCR inhibitors in forensic samples: a diagnostic tool for STR typing. *Forensic science international Genetics* 2 (2), 108–125.

Loth, S. R. and Henneberg, M. 2001. Sexually dimorphic mandibular morphology in the first few years of life. *American Journal of Physical Anthropology* 115, 179–186.

Maca-Meyer, N. 2002. *Composición genética de poblaciones históricas y prehistóricas humanas de las Islas Canarias*, Unpublished Ph.D. thesis, Departamento de Parasitología, Ecología y Genética, Universidad de La Laguna, La Laguna.

Maca-Meyer, N., Arnay, M., Rando, J. C., Flores, C., Gonzalez, A. M., Cabrera, V. M. and Larruga, J. M. 2004. Ancient mtDNA analysis and the origin of the Guanches. *European Journal of Human Genetics* 12 (2), 155–162.

Maca-Meyer, N., Arnay de la Rosa, M., Flores, C., Fregel, R., González, A. M. and Larruga, J. M. 2005. Mithocondrial DNA Diversity in 17th–18th Century remains from Tenerife (Canary Islands). *American Journal of Physical Anthropology* 127, 418–24.

Mays, S. and Faerman, M. 2001. Sex identification in some putative infanticide victims from Roman Britain using ancient DNA. *Journal of Archaeological Science* 28 (5), 555–559.

Mittler, D. M. and Sheridan, S. G. 1992. Sex determination in subadults using auricular surface morphology: a forensic science perspective. *Journal of Forensic Sciences* 37(4), 1068–1075.

Molleson, T., Cruse, K. and Mays, S. 1998. Some sexually dimorphic features of the human juvenile skull and their value in sex determination in immature skeletal remains. *Journal of Archaeological Science* 25, 719–728.

Nakahori, Y., Hamano, K., Iwaya, M. and Nakagome, Y. 1991a. Sex identification by polymerase chain-reaction using X-Y homologous primer. *American Journal of Medical Genetics* 39 (4), 472–473.

Nakahori, Y., Takenaka,O. and Nakagome, Y. 1991b. A human X-Y homologous region encodes amelogenin. *Genomics* 9 (2), 264–269.

Pääbo, S. 1985. Molecular-cloning of Ancient Egyptian mummy DNA. *Nature* 314 (6012), 644–645.

Pääbo, S., Poinar, H., Serre, D., Jaenicke-Despres, V., Hebler, J., Rohland, N., Kuch, M., Krause, J., Vigilant, L. and Hofreiter M. 2004. Genetic analyses from ancient DNA. *Annual Review of Genetics* 38, 645–679.

Perzigian A. J. 1976. The dentition of the Indian Knoll skeletal population: odontometrics and cusp number. *American Journal of Physical Anthropology* 44, 113–22.

Rissech Badallo, C. 2003. La determinación de la edad en restos esqueléticos infantiles y adolescentes, pp. 47–56, in Isidro, A. and Malgosa, A. (eds), *Paleopatología. La enfermedad no escrita*. Barcelona: Masson.

Sánchez Romero, M. 2007. Actividades de mantenimiento en la Edad del Bronce del sur peninsular: el cuidado y la socialización de los individuos infantiles. *Complutum* 18.

Salido, E. C., Yen, P. H., Koprivinikar, K., Yu, L. C. and Shapiro, L. J. 1992. The human enamel protein gene amelogenin is expressed from both the X and the Y chromosomes. *American Journal of Human Genetics* 50, 303–316.

Schmidt, D., Hummel, S. and Herrmann, B. 2003. Brief communication: Multiplex X/Y-PCR improves sex identification in aDNA analysis. *American Journal of Physical Anthropology*. 121 (4), 337–341.

Schutkowski, H. 1993. Sex determination of infant and juveniles skeleton, I- morphognostic features. *American Journal of Physical Anthropology* 90, 199–205.

Simón, M., Jordana, X., Armentano, N., Santos, C., Díaz, N., Solorzano, E., López, J. B., González-Ruiz, M. and Malgosa, A. 2011. The presence of nuclear families in prehistoric collective burials revisited: The bronze age burial of montanissell cave (Spain) in the light of aDNA. *American Journal of Physical Anthropology* 146(3), 406–13.

Sullivan, K. M., Mannucci, A., Kimpton, C. P. and Gill, P. 1993. A rapid and quantitative DNA sex test – fluorescence-based PCR analysis of X-Y homologous gene amelogenin. *Biotechniques* 15(4), 636–8.

Velasco Vázquez, J., Ruíz González, T. and Sánchez Perera, S., 2005. *El lugar de los antepasados. La necrópolis bimbape de Montaña La Lajura.* Cabildo de El Hierro. Santa Cruz de Tenerife.

Velasco, J., Alberto, V., Hernández, C., Barro, A., Eugenio, C. and Galván, B., 1998. Restos humanos en ámbitos domésticos prehistóricos: el caso de Arenas-3 (Buenavista del Norte, Tenerife). *El Museo Canario*, 53, 85–109.

Velasco Vázquez, J., Delgado Darias, T., Arnay De La Rosa, M. and González Reimers, E. 2003. Unos modos de vida arraigados. La salud oral de la población prehispánica de Gran Canaria en edad no adulta. *Tabona*, 12, 45–67.

Velasco Vázquez, J., 2009. Nacer para morir. Algunas consideraciones sobre las estrategias de reproducción de los antiguos canarios, pp. 215–260, en Suárez Grimón, V., Trujillo Yánez, G. A. y Domínguez Talavera, O. (eds), *Nacimiento, matrimonio y muerte en Canarias. VI Jornadas de Patrimonio Cultural de Teror.* Las Palmas de Gran Canaria: Ed. Anroart.

Villadóniga García, M. 2005. *El conocimiento de las poblaciones del pasado a través de los restos óseos: Determinación del sexo en individuos infantiles a partir de los caracteres morfológicos de la mandóbula.* Universidad Autónoma de Madrid.

Weaver, D, 1980. Sex differences in the ilia of a known sex and age sample of fetal and infant skeletons. *American Journal of Physical Anthropology* 52, 191–195.

# 17

## Salud y crecimiento en la Edad del Cobre. Un estudio preliminar de los individuos subadultos de Camino del Molino (Caravaca de la Cruz, Murcia, España). Un sepulcro colectivo del III milenio cal. BC

*Susana Mendiela, Carme Rissech, María Haber, Joaquín Lomba, Azucena Avilés and Daniel Turbón*

*The present study examines twenty-five infant and juvenile individuals from the archaeological Copper Age site, Camino del Molino (Caravaca de la Cruz, Murcia). The site consists of a collective burial of the III Millennium BC. Growth patterns and pathological conditions of these individuals were examined in order to identify the health conditions of the whole population. A visual comparison of growth curves between Camino del Molino and three documented Iberian samples, two of them dating from the late nineteenth century and early twentieth, and the third from the current living population, revealed that our sample exhibits faltering growth compared with the current population until the growth spurt, in which the growth rate increased greatly. Concerning pathological conditions, a high percentage of porotic lesions was recorded; cribra orbitalia (77.77%), cribra femoralis (80.95%) and porotic hyperostosis of the skull (33.33%) and ischium (33.33%). These lesions were associated with osteopenia, lacelike trabeculae pattern and H-shaped vertebral bodies, in the thoracic spine. The high frequency of porotic lesions together with the lesions observed in the spine could suggest some type of thalassemia endemic in the Mediterranean area.*

## Introducción

En las últimas décadas se ha asistido al aumento de estudios relativos a la infancia tanto desde el punto de vista cultural – prestando atención al rol que desempeñan los individuos infantiles en el grupo y la percepción de los adultos hacia éstos – como desde un punto de vista biológico dado que representan la porción del conjunto más sensible,[1] con una mortalidad más elevada, que puede llegar a representar el 30–40% del total.[2] Si bien es cierto que muchos investigadores han desarrollado nuevas técnicas para diagnosticar las condiciones patológicas que afectan a los subadultos, son menos los que se han basado en los patrones de crecimiento para evaluar, no sólo el estado de salud de la población infantil y juvenil, sino de todo el conjunto de la población.[3] Los niños son especialmente sensibles a periodos de estrés – nutrición deficiente, cambios climáticos, ven retardado su proceso de maduración y alterado su patrón de crecimiento.[4] Sin embargo, los pocos estudios que se han realizado al respecto, se basan en poblaciones medievales o posteriores[5] quedando las poblaciones prehistóricas al margen.

Por este motivo y debido a la importancia del Calcolítico en la prehistoria de la Península Ibérica, por los cambios culturales y el amplio registro antropológico, el objetivo del presente trabajo es evaluar el patrón de crecimiento y el estado de salud de los individuos infantiles y juveniles de una muestra de los individuos inmaduros del sepulcro colectivo Camino del Molino (Caravaca de la Cruz, Murcia, España). Además del estudio del crecimiento se focalizará en las patologías debidas a los estados carenciales y procesos infecciosos.

## Camino del Molino (Caravaca de la Cruz, Murcia, España). Una cueva sepulcral del III milenio cal. BC

Camino del Molino es un yacimiento calcolítico de tipo funerario localizado en la periferia del municipio murciano de Caravaca de la Cruz (Fig. 17.1). Este yacimiento fue excavado mediante una actuación preventiva a lo largo del 2008, a raíz de una promoción inmobiliaria en el perímetro suroriental de Caravaca de la Cruz. La excavación fue coordinada y dirigida por Joaquín Lomba Maurandi, profesor titular de la Universidad de Murcia y por Mariano López Martínez y Francisco Ramos Martínez, ambos de Arqueoweb S. L. Se trata de un enterramiento múltiple y sucesivo en cavidad natural (Fig. 17.1) que según el registro arqueológico y las dataciones radiocarbónicas

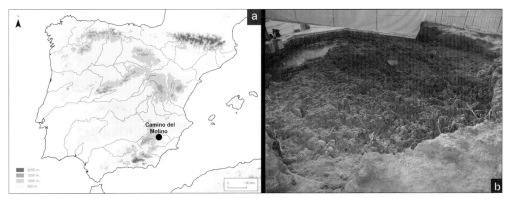

*Figura 17.1. a) Localización del yacimiento Camino del Molino (TM. Caravaca de la Cruz, Murcia, España.) b) Vista del sepulcro en los inicios de los trabajos arqueológicos.*

fue utilizado como necrópolis ininterrumpidamente unos 300–350 años durante el III Milenio BC.[6] Camino del Molino es una cavidad natural de unos siete metros de diámetro por dos metros de profundidad (Fig. 17.1), en su interior, sin embargo, presenta marcas antrópicas de remodelación de las paredes para su uso funerario. Las primeras deposiciones de cadáveres se realizaron en torno al 4,260 ± 40 BP (Beta- 244973), continuando ininterrumpidamente hasta el 3,850 ± 40 BP (Beta-244974).[7]

La primera acumulación de individuos se hizo en torno a las paredes de la cavidad, dejando libre todo el espacio central. Conforme se fue colapsando el perímetro se producían remociones hacia el centro para dejar espacio y seguir acumulando cerca de las paredes. De esta manera, el número de individuos con mayor índice de conexiones anatómicas y en posición primaria se encontró pegado a las paredes de la cavidad, mientras que en el centro, el índice de posición secundaria, astillamiento y fragmentación era muy superior al resto.[8] Es probable que cuando estas remociones se efectuaron, muchos de los individuos aún conservaban tejido orgánico o algún tipo de mortaja, ya que en la zona central, en principio más caótica que los laterales, también se encuentran individuos parcialmente articulados. Llama la atención la escasez de elementos de ajuar, encontrados en número muy inferior al esperado para un enterramiento de las características de Camino del Molino. Por el material documentado, la mayoría de inhumados carecía de ajuar funerario, ya que para un número mínimo de individuos tan elevado (1300 NMI), sólo se documentaron: treinta puntas de flecha, otras tantas láminas, un puñal y diversas tabletas en sílex; en torno a treinta punzones y varillas planas de hueso; 5 hachas pulimentadas; diversas cuentas de collar pertenecientes a unos pocos collares; y en metal, diecisiete punzones de sección cuadrada (uno de ellos aún enmangado en una tibia de perro), una punta y un puñal de lengüeta de treinta y dos centímetros de longitud.[9]

## Material y métodos

El material analizado en este estudio corresponde a una muestra de individuos subadultos del sepulcro colectivo calcolítico Camino del Molino. Al término de la excavación, a finales del 2008, el número de individuos exhumados ascendió a 1300 (NMI). Del total, 182 individuos se catalogaron como 'sujetos' y corresponden a los que se encontraban en posición primaria. Hasta la fecha, de esos 182 se ha realizado el estudio antropológico preliminar de noventa y un individuos en el Laboratorio de Arqueología de la Universidad de Murcia, por la Dra. María Haber Uriarte y Azucena Avilés Fernández.[10] De esos noventa y un individuos estudiados, veinticinco son inmaduros y representan la muestra seleccionada para realizar este trabajo.

El estado de conservación de la muestra se analizó según el Índice de Preservación.[11] Se determinó el sexo mediante la morfología del ilion y la mandíbula siguiendo el método de Schutkowsky.[12] La estimación de la edad se realizó mediante los criterios de erupción de las piezas dentales y su grado de maduración siguiendo el método de Crétot.[13] También se tuvo en cuenta la fusión de las epífisis[14] y el desarrollo óseo.[15]

El análisis de crecimiento se realizó a través de un estudio transversal de los datos de la diáfisis del fémur y la edad, en relación a otras poblaciones de las cuales se tuviera la máxima información posible. Para ello se utilizaron los datos (longitud de la diáfisis del fémur y la edad cronológica) de las colecciones de referencia portuguesas de Lisboa y Coimbra, pertenecientes al siglo XIX y XX,[16] y de una muestra de la población actual viva de Barcelona. Las dos colecciones portuguesas fueron escogidas como un buen elemento de comparación poblacional de la muestra analizada debido a que son colecciones documentadas y contextualizadas de la Península Ibérica, y además son las únicas que contienen individuos subadultos suficientes para poder realizar dicha comparación. De ellas hay documentada mucha información tanto social como biológica, se conoce el sexo, la edad cronológica, el origen biológico, las patologías sufridas, el trabajo de los padres, las relaciones familiares y el contexto social y económico en que vivieron los individuos.[17] Los estudios realizados sobre ambas colecciones indican que los individuos pertenecen a una clase social media-baja, cuyas condiciones no eran muy favorables para el crecimiento infantil y juvenil.[18] Los datos de la población actual viva de Barcelona fueron escogidos de la colección de telemetrías en formato DICOM (Digital Imaging and Communication in Medicine) de la UB formada por 779 individuos (354♂, 425♀) menores de veintiún años, correspondientes a la mitad inferior del cuerpo. Las telemetrías proceden del Hospital Sant Joan de Déu de Barcelona, institución que colabora con el grupo de investigación liderado por el Dr. Turbón. Los datos fueron anonimizados conforme a la Ley Orgánica de Protección de Datos.[19] De este material se seleccionaron dieciséis niños y dieciséis niñas de cero a dieciséis años.

El elemento esquelético para realizar este estudio fue el fémur, por ser uno de los elementos esqueléticos más sensibles al medio, además de no presentar diferencias sexuales hasta después del brote puberal,[20] lo que permite considerar la muestra como una sola serie sexual hasta aproximadamente los dieciséis años de edad. Para evaluar los patrones de crecimiento de la población calcolítica en relación a la contemporánea y la actual, se generaron graficas de dispersión y curvas de crecimiento mediante el método Lowess, observándose las distancias entre ellas.[21] El método Lowess es un método de iteración que se basa en el cálculo de mínimos cuadrados ponderados, sin explicar de forma concreta *a priori* la curva que se podría ajustar al número de puntos de la nube de dispersión.

Los patrones de crecimiento también se analizaron mediante el crecimiento relativo del fémur, para ello se consideró el porcentaje de la longitud total del fémur adulto conseguido a una edad determinada [(longitud de la diáfisis del fémur de cada individuo x longitud femoral adulta estimada)/100]. En cada serie se utilizaron como longitudes adultas la longitud femoral media de los fémures con ambas epífisis fusionadas y esto sucede a partir de los diecinueve años en los niños y los dieciséis años en las niñas.[22]

El estudio paleopatológico se llevó a cabo a través de la observación macroscópica de los restos óseos, siguiendo las indicaciones de Ortner y Lewis.[23] Se observaron las lesiones poróticas, como la *cribra orbitalia* y fueron clasificadas según las recomendaciones de Stuart-Macadam.[24] El resto de lesiones poróticas, con una alta frecuencia en la muestra del presente trabajo, como la *cribra femoralis*, hiperostosis porótica en el parietal y en el isquion (zona acetabular), se diagnosticaron y clasificaron según los trabajos de Lewis, Djuric *et al.* y Walker *et al.*[25]

Así mismo, cuando fue necesario para el diagnóstico, se hicieron radiografías en el Hospital Clínic de Barcelona. El estudio radiológico convencional se realizó digitalmente. Se tomaron dos proyecciones ortogonales, anteroposterior y mediolateral con un equipo médico de radiodiagnóstico Philips Diagnost® a cincuenta kilovolts (kV) y quince miliamperios por segundo con una distancia focal de 120 centímetros. Para ajustar el brillo y el contraste de las imágenes radiográficas hasta su máxima cualidad se utilizó un equipo AGFA MultiSync LCD 18805X®.

RESULTADOS

El conjunto de subadultos estudiados, pertenecientes al yacimiento calcolítico Camino del Molino, consta de veinticinco individuos (siete probables femeninos, cinco femeninos, un probable masculino, tres masculinos, ocho indeterminados y un alofiso) con unos valores medios de IP[1] del 69%, IP[2] del 61.46% y de IP[3] de 57.63%, lo que evidencia una mejor conservación de los huesos largos, especialmente del miembro superior. El rango de edad de la muestra oscila entre uno y dieciocho años (Tabla 17.1).

Se observa que el grupo más numeroso es el de niños de cinco a nueve años y el menos numeroso, de cero a cuatro años. En las poblaciones preindustriales las etapas que albergan un mayor porcentaje de individuos suelen ser los primeros años de vida y se suele atribuir al momento de destete, el cual implica un período complicado para la supervivencia del individuo.[26] Contrariamente, en la muestra analizada se observa un bajo número muestral en los primeros años de vida, muy probablemente debido a la fragilidad del esqueleto de estos individuos, lo que ha provocado una conservación más deficiente. Aunque también podría ser debido a un enterramiento diferencial de los individuos inmaduros.

*Crecimiento*

El gráfico de dispersión (Fig. 17.2a) muestra los valores de la diáfisis del fémur en relación a la edad para los individuos subadultos de Camino del Molino y las dos colecciones de referencia portuguesas de Lisboa y Coimbra. Los resultados indican que los valores de la diáfisis del fémur de Camino del Molino quedan bien integrados dentro de los valores de las demás series documentadas, además de ser muy cortas las distancias de las curvas generadas por el método Lowess, lo que indica un crecimiento similar entre las series. Las similitudes de crecimiento entre los individuos de Camino del Molino y las colecciones portuguesas asociadas a unas condiciones duras para el crecimiento de los individuos infantiles y juveniles indican que existe coincidencia en cuanto al tipo de vida.

Si se compara el crecimiento de la diáfisis del fémur de estas tres series esqueléticas con el crecimiento de la diáfisis del fémur de la población actual viva de Barcelona (Fig. 17.2b), se observa una menor tasa de crecimiento por parte de las series históricas

*Tabla 17.1. Resultados.*

| Cuadro | Código del individuo | Edad | Sexo | Grupo de edad | IP$^1$% | IP$^2$% | IP$^3$ % |
|---|---|---|---|---|---|---|---|
| 1192 | 127 | 1–2 años | Indeterminado | Infantil I (1–5 años) | 58.33 | 47.36 | 45.45 |
| 1323 | 142 | 6 años | Prob. Femenino | Infantil II (6–12 años) | 50 | 31.57 | 27.27 |
| 440, 442 | 29 | 6'5 años | Prob. Femenino | Infantil II | 66.66 | 42.1 | 45.45 |
| 1685 | 172 | 7 años | Indeterminado | Infantil II | 83.33 | 84.21 | 86.36 |
| 1031, 1036 | 101 | 7–8 años | Prob. masculino | Infantil II | 75 | 78.94 | 81.81 |
| 209 | 180 | 7–8 años | Masculino | Infantil II | 0 | 0 | 13.63 |
| 1475, 1484 | 155 | 8 años | Indeterminado | Infantil II | 16.66 | 21.05 | 18.18 |
| 1217, 1228 | 128 | 8–9 años | Prob. Femenino | Infantil II | 91.66 | 73.68 | 63.63 |
| 1237, 1241 | 130 | 9 años | Indeterminado | Infantil II | 100 | 89.47 | 77.27 |
| 1406 | 149 | 9 años | Indeterminado | Infantil II | 75 | 78.94 | 68.18 |
| 1184, 1247 | 126 | 9–10 años | Prob. Femenino | Infantil II | 100 | 94.73 | 90.9 |
| 1667 | 168 | 9–10 años | Prob. Femenino | Infantil II | 100 | 100 | 86.36 |
| 1266, 1274, 1276 | 176 | 10 años | Prob. Femenino | Infantil II | 50 | 47.36 | 40.9 |
| 1437, 1440, 1444 | 153 | 12–13 años | Femenino | Juvenil (13–20 años) | 100 | 84.21 | 72.72 |
| 1696 | 173 | 12–13 años | Alofiso | Juvenil | 83.33 | 68.42 | 68.18 |
| 1614 | 166 | 12–13 años | Femenino | Juvenil | 58.33 | 57.89 | 59.09 |
| 1128 | 121 | 12–14 años | Prob. Femenino | Juvenil | 50 | 57.89 | 59.09 |
| 1663 | 183 | 12–14 años | Indeterminado | Juvenil | 41.66 | 26.31 | 22.72 |
| 1070 | 181 | 13–14 años | Femenino | Juvenil | 58.33 | 57.89 | 50 |
| 1430 | 152 | 14–15 años | Femenino | Juvenil | 100 | 78.94 | 81.81 |
| 1345 | 144 | 16 años | Masculino | Juvenil | 100 | 84.21 | 72.72 |
| 1266, 1274, 1276 | 135 | 16–17 años | Indeterminado | Juvenil | 75 | 52.63 | 45.45 |
| 213 | 10 | 16–18 años | Indeterminado | Juvenil | 50 | 52.63 | 45.45 |
| 1282 | 138 | 17–18 años | Femenino | Juvenil | 75 | 57.89 | 59.09 |
| 1258, 1263 | 134 | 17–18 años | Masculino | Juvenil | 66.66 | 68.42 | 59.09 |

y prehistóricas en relación a la serie actual viva, observándose las mayores distancias entre las curvas de crecimiento entre los cinco y diez años. A partir de los diez años el crecimiento se reactiva en las series esqueléticas, llegando al final de crecimiento, al límite inferior del rango de valores de la curva de crecimiento del fémur de la población actual viva.

La Figura 17.2c muestra los resultados obtenidos durante el estudio del crecimiento relativo del fémur. Aunque los datos son pocos, y por tanto la interpretación ha de ser cautelosa, se observa que los valores de Camino del Molino quedan por debajo de la curva de crecimiento relativo de la población actual viva, evidenciando un ralentizamiento del crecimiento en los subadultos de Camino del Molino; éstos a los quince años sólo han alcanzado un ochenta por ciento de la longitud total del fémur adulto, en cambio los individuos de la población actual a los quince años están cerca del 100%.

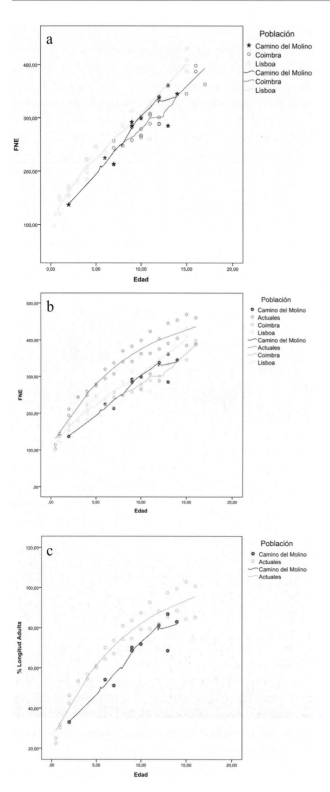

*Figura 17.2. a) Regresión lineal (Lowess) que muestra el patrón de crecimiento de Camino del Molino en relación a las colecciones de Coimbra y Lisboa, teniendo en cuenta la longitud de la diáfisis del fémur (FNE) y la edad de cada individuo. b) Regresión lineal que muestra las tres series anteriores más la población actual viva. c) En esta regresión lineal se muestra el porcentaje de longitud del fémur adulto alcanzado por cada subadulto, comparando los resultados de Camino del Molino con los de la población actual viva.*

## Patologías

El análisis paleopatológico reveló una alta frecuencia de lesiones poróticas. Se observó *cribra orbitalia,* en un 77.77% de los casos (n= 7/9), *cribra femoralis*, en un 80.95% (n= 17/21) siendo la lesión más frecuente, hiperostosis porótica del parietal en un 33.33% (n=3/9) e hiperostosis porótica del isquion en un 33.33% (n=5/15). La edad en que tienen mayor prevalencia en la muestra estudiada es en el intervalo de cinco a nueve años con 62.5%. Por otro lado, el 65% (n=13/20) de los individuos presentaba en la región anterior del cuerpo de las vértebras dorsales (Fig. 17.3), una lesión con patrón trabecular en forma de 'bordado' o 'encaje', estando las cervicales y lumbares libres de ella. Su radiografía revela el cuerpo vertebral en forma de 'H'. Esta lesión en encaje incide especialmente en la franja de edad de 10–14 años con un 87.5% (n=7/8).

No se observa en ella un proceso inflamatorio crónico, que sería la reacción natural a un proceso infeccioso. Al tratarse de un elemento esquelético se observaría un proceso granulomatoso del hueso y/o del periostio que se traduciría en una formación o destrucción de hueso, descartando así la posibilidad de que sea una enfermedad

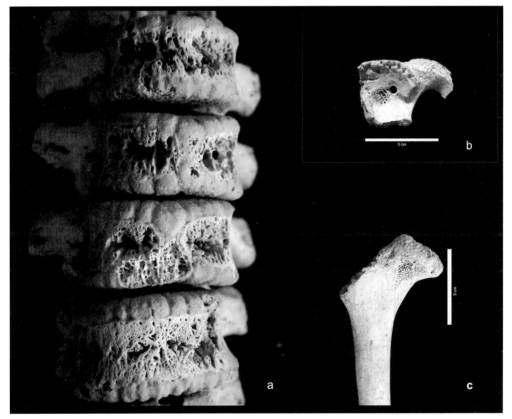

*Figura 17.3. a) Vista macro de la región dorsal del individuo 130 (9 años). b) Isquión izquierdo del inviduo 130 (9 años). c) Fémur derecho del individuo 153 (12–13 años).*

infecciosa. Contrariamente, parece más probable que se trate de una hiperplasia de la medula ósea, tratándose posiblemente de una enfermedad metabólica o hematológica. Dentro de estas últimas, está descrita en las betatalasemias la existencia de un patrón trabecular vertebral en forma de 'bordado' o 'encaje'[27] que coincide con las lesiones observadas. La talasemia es un tipo de anemia genética que suele encontrarse en regiones donde la malaria es endémica y la región mediterránea (centro y este del Mediterráneo) es una de ellas.[28] Tradicionalmente se ha relacionado las lesiones poróticas con deficiencia de hierro y/o con cierto de tipo de infecciones, sin embargo, se ha visto que este tipo de lesión parece estar más relacionada con la anemia genética o con la deficiencia de vitamina B12.[29]

## Discusión

En este estudio se ha realizado un análisis transversal del patrón de crecimiento y el estado de salud de una muestra de veinticinco individuos subadultos del yacimiento calcolítico de Camino del Molino. A pesar del bajo número muestral, que impone extremar prudencia, los resultados indican que estos individuos tenían un crecimiento retardado en relación a la población actual viva española, pero parecido al crecimiento experimentado por las series esqueléticas documentadas de la Península Ibérica, las cuales vivían en condiciones no muy favorables para el desarrollo. Aunque la muestra es pequeña, parece insinuarse que el crecimiento de los individuos de Camino del Molino tiene una disminución de la tasa del crecimiento desde los cinco años hasta la edad del brote puberal. A partir de esta edad, la tasa de crecimiento se reactiva, experimentando una fuerte aceleración hasta que la longitud del fémur alcanza el límite inferior del rango de valores obtenidos en la edad adulta de los individuos vivos actuales. Estos resultados confirman la sospecha de la presencia de un crecimiento retardado en los niños prehistóricos del Mediterráneo.[30] El patrón de crecimiento que parece mostrar los individuos de Camino del Molino, y la variación de la tasa de crecimiento a lo largo de la edad, es similar a la observada en otras poblaciones preindustriales como los grupos ancestrales de los indios Pueblo de Norte América[31] y los Medievales portugueses.[32]

El estudio paleopatológico de la muestra subadulta de Camino del Molino señala una alta frecuencia de *cribra orbitalia* (77.77%), *cribra femoralis* (80.95%), hiperostosis porótica del parietal (33.33%), y del isquion (33.33%), así como la presencia de una lesión en forma de encaje en la región anterior de los cuerpos vertebrales de las vértebras dorsales (65%), pero no en lumbares y cervicales. Destaca también la forma de 'H' de las vértebras. Los resultados del test de la $X^2$ indicaron que no hay diferencias en el porcentaje de presencia y ausencia de los diferentes tipos de lesiones($X2=5,069$ y $p=0,280$), señalando su posible relación. La presencia de lesiones poróticas como *cribra orbitalia* o *hiperostosis porótica* es frecuente en las poblaciones arqueológicas, sobre todo en las etapas más tempranas de vida del individuo.[33] Tradicionalmente se han relacionado estas lesiones con la falta de hierro, anemia genética o adquirida por alimentación deficiente, aunque también pueden ser consecuencia de la acción anemizante de algunas infecciones crónicas como por ejemplo las gastrointestinales,[34] que son una de las causas más importantes de mortalidad en los individuos subadultos de las sociedades del pasado.[35] Durante la infancia, los individuos inmaduros aún no tienen el sistema inmunológico totalmente formado, con lo cual son más propensos a contraer enfermedades,[36] y en especial después del destete. No obstante, se considera que los casos más severos (mayor frecuencia) de lesiones poróticas son los causados por las anemias genéticas o por deficiencia de vitamina $B_{12}$.[37] Así pues, si tenemos en cuenta las altas frecuencias de las lesiones poróticas observadas en los individuos de Camino del Molino, parece posible descartar que éstas sean debidas a algún tipo de infección crónica.

Aunque puede haber periodos de hambruna, se considera que en las poblaciones postmesolíticas, incluido el Calcolítico, habría una ingesta suficiente de vitamina $B_{12}$ para prevenir la anemia megaloblástica y por extensión, una alta frecuencia de lesiones poróticas como hiperostosis porótica y *cribra orbitalia*, por estar su dieta basada en carne y productos lácteos.[38] Además, en este tipo de anemias, las adquiridas, nunca se encuentran descritas lesiones en encaje en los cuerpos vertebrales, ni vértebras en forma de 'H'. Así pues, se puede descartar este tipo de patología.

Si tenemos en cuenta el origen geográfico de la muestra, el alto porcentaje de lesiones poróticas, la lesión en encaje en la cara anterior de los cuerpos torácicos y la imagen radiográfica de estos, que muestra una forma del cuerpo en 'H', se puede afirmar que estos datos coinciden mucho con las descripciones hechas para la ß-talasemia,[39] haciendo pensar que podría tratarse de algún tipo de talasemia, siendo la causante del crecimiento retardado en la muestra. No obstante, sería necesario un estudio más profundo, para realizar cualquier afirmación.

## Conclusión

En conclusión, los resultados de este estudio sobre el crecimiento en una muestra de individuos subadultos del yacimiento calcolítico Camino del Molino, muestra un retardo en el crecimiento (en relación a la población viva actual) acompañado de un alto porcentaje de *cribra orbitalia*, *cribra femoralis*, osteoporosis hiperostósica del parietal y el isquion, junto con una lesión en forma de encaje en la región anterior del cuerpo vertebral de las vértebras torácicas, la cual parece estar íntimamente relacionada con las demás lesiones poróticas. Estas lesiones porosas se consideran indicadores de anemia genética o adquirida debido a estrés nutricional y/o infecciones crónicas. El alto porcentaje en la presencia de lesiones poróticas, la lesión en forma de encaje, la forma de "H" de las vértebras y la relación que parecen tener las lesiones poróticas y la de forma de encaje parece indicar que se trate de algún tipo de talasemia, aunque sería necesario profundizar más en el análisis para poder afirmar cualquier cosa.

## Agradecimientos

Los autores de este trabajo agradecen: al Sr Aniol Pujol Bayona los datos sobre la longitud del fémur de la muestra radiográfica de la población actual viva de Barcelona; al

Dr Xavier Tomàs Batlle, radiólogo del Hospital Clínic de Barcelona, por el radiografiado del material esquelético; y al Dr Manuel Campo por sus comentarios como especialista en la columna vertebral. Y al GRQ – Grup d'Estudis d'Evolució d'Homínids i altres Primats. Generelitat de Catalunya Ref: 2009FaSGR884.

NOTES

1　Roth 1992; Lewis 2002
2　Brothwell 1987; González 1999
3　Cardoso 2006; Lewis 2002
4　Martorell *et al.* 1979; Alvear *et al.* 1986
5　Hoppa 1992; González 1999; Cardoso and García 2009
6　Lomba *et al.* 2009, 144
7　Lomba *et al.* 2009, 155
8　Lomba *et al.* 2009, 151; Haber *et al.* 2012
9　Lomba *et al.* 2009, 153
10　Haber *et al.* 2012
11　Alesán 1990
12　Schutkowsky 1993
13　Crétot 1978
14　Brothwell 1987; Ferembach *et al.* 1980; Krogman y Iscan 1986; Scheuer y Black 2000; Rissech *et al.* 2001
15　Weaver 1979; Scheuer y Black, 2000
16　Rissech *et al.* 2008
17　Rocha 1995; Cardoso 2006
18　Cardoso y García　2009
19　García *et al.* 2010
20　Rissech *et al.* 2008
21　Schillaci *et al.* 2011
22　Scheuer and Black 2000
23　Ortner 2003; Lewis 2007
24　Stuart-Macadam 1985, 1992
25　Lewis 2007; Djuric *et al.* 2008; Walker *et al.* 2009
26　Corruccini *et al.* 1985; Krenz-Niedbala 2001
27　Taylor and Resnik 2000
28　Lewis 2012, 685
29　Walker *et al.* 2009
30　Nájera *et al.* 2010, 86
31　Schillaci *et al.* 2011
32　Cardoso y García, 2009
33　Ortner 2003; Lewis 2007; Walker *et al.* 2009
34　Walker *et al.* 2009, 113
35　Djuric *et al.* 2008, 467
36　Shultz 2007; Djuric 2008
37　Walker *et al.* 2009
38　Walker *et al.* 2009; McClure *et al.* 2011
39　Ángel 1978; Taylor and Resnik 2000; Lagia *et al.* 2011

## REFERENCIAS

Alesan, A. 1990. *Estudi d'una població subadulta de l'Edat del Ferro: demografia, antropometria i creixement.* Tesis de Master en Biología Humana. Inédita. Universitat Autònoma de Barcelona.

Alvear, J., Artaza, C., Vial, M., Guerrero, S. and Muzzo, S. 1986. Physical growth and bone age of survivors of protein energy malnutrition. *Archaeology of Diseases of Children* 61, 257–62.

Angel, J. L. 1978. Porotic hyperostosis in the Eastern Mediterranean. *Medical College of Virginia Quarterly.* 14, 10–16.

Brothwell, D. R. 1987. *Desenterrando huesos* (Traducido en 1987 por Carmen González). Fondo de cultura económica. México.

Cardoso, H. 2006. Brief communication: The collection of identified human skeletons housed at the Bocage Museum (National Museum of Natural History), Lisbon, Portugal. *American Journal of Physical Anthropology.* 129, 173–176.

Cardoso, H., and García, S. 2009. The not-so-dark ages: ecology from Human growth in Medieval and Early twentieth century Portugal as inferred from skeletal growth profiles. *American Journal of Physical Anthropology.* 138, 136–147.

Corrucini, R., Handler, J. and Jacobi, K. 1985. Chronological distribution of enamel hypoplasia and weaningin the Caribbean slave population. *Human Biology.* 57, 699–711.

Crétot, M. 1978. *L'arcade dentaire humaine (Morphologie).* Julien Prélat, Paris.

Djuric, M., Milovanovic, P., Janovic, A., Draskovic, M., Djukic, K. and Milenkovic P. 2008. Porotic Lesions in Immature Skeletons from Stara Torina, Late Medieval Serbia. *International Journal of Osteoarchaeology*, 18, 458–475.

Ferembach, D., Schwidetzky, I. and Stloukal, M. 1980. Recommendations for Age and Sex Diagnoses of Skeletons. *Journal of Human Evolution.* 9, 517–549.

García, F. J., Lucendo, J., Sevilla, J. M., Alemán, I., Rissech, C., Botella, M. and Turbón, D. 2010. Nuevas tecnologías de imagen radiológica y su uso en antropología, pp. 475–479, in Galera V., Gutiérrez-Redomero E. and Sánchez-Andrés A. (eds). *Diversidad Humana y Antropología Aplicada.* Gráficas Algorán, Madrid.

González, A. 1999. *Infancia y adolescencia en la Murcia musulmana. Estudio de restos óseos.* Tesis Doctoral inédita. Universidad Autónoma de Madrid.

Haber, U. M., Avilés, F. A. and Lomba, M. J. 2012. Estudio antropológico preliminar de los restos humanos calcolíticos del enterramiento múltiple de Camino del Molino (Caravaca de la Cruz, Murcia), pp. 236–242, in Trubón, D., Fañanás, L., Rissech, C. and Rosas, A. (eds) *Biodiversidad Humana y Evolución.*

Hoppa, R. D. 1992. Evaluating human skeletal growth: an Anglo-Saxon example. *International Journal of Osteoarchaeology* 2, 275–288.

Krenz-Niedbala. 2001. Biological and cultural consequences of the transition to agriculture in human populations on Polish territories. *Variability and Evolution* 9, 89–99.

Krogman, W. M. and Iscan, Y. M. 1986. *The Human Skeleton in Forensic Medicine,* pp. 1–551. Ch. C. Thomas Ed. Springfield, Illinois.

Lagia, A., Eliopoulos, C. and Manolis, S. 2007. Thalassemia: Macroscopic and Radiological Study of a Case. *International Journal of Osteoarchaeology* 17, 269–285.

Lewis, M. E. 2002. Impact of Industrialization: Comparative Study of Child Health in Four Sites From Medieval and Postmedieval England (A.D. 850–1859). *American Journal of Physical Anthropology,* 119, 211–223.

Lewis, M. E. 2007. *The Bioarchaeology of children. Perspectives from biological and forensic anthropology.* Cambridge.

Lewis, M. E. 2012. Thalassaemia: its Diagnosis and Interpretation in Past Skeletal Populations. *International Journal of Osteoarchaeology* 6, 685–693.

Lomba, J., López, M., Ramos, F. and Avilés, A. 2009. El enterramiento múltiple, calcolítico, de Camino del Molino (Caravaca de la Cruz, Murcia): Metodología y primeros resultados de un yacimiento excepcional. *Trabajos de Prehistoria* 66, 143–160.

Martorell, R., Yarbrough, C., Klein, R. E. and Lechtig, A. 1979. Malnutrition, body size and skeletal maturation: interrelation ships and implications for catch-up growth. *Human Biology* 51, 371–389.

McClure, S. B., Roca de Togores, C., Culleton, B. J. and Kennett D. J. 2011. Osteological and paleodietary investigation of burials from Cova de la Pastora, Alicante, Spain. *Journal of Archaeological Science* 38, 420–428.

Nájera, T., Molina, F., Jiménez-Brobeil, S., Sánchez, M., Al Oumaoui, I., Aranda, G., Delgado-Huertas, A. and Laffranchi, Z. 2010. La población infantil de la Motilla del Azuer: Un estudio bioarqueológico. *Complutum* 21, 69–102.

Ortner, D. 2003. *Identification of Pathological Conditions in Human Skeletal Remains*. New York: Academy Press.

Rissech, C., Sanudo, J. R. and Malgosa, A. 2001. The acetabular point: a morphological and ontogenic study. *Journal of Anatomy* 198, 743–8.

Rissech, C., Schaefer, M. and Malgosa, A. 2008. Development of the femur – Implications for age and sex determination. *Forensic Science International* 180, 1–9.

Rocha, M. A. 1995. Les collections ostéologiques humaines identifiées du Musseé Anthropologique de l'Université de Coimbra. *Antropologia Portuguesa* 13, 17–38.

Roth, E. A. 1992. Applications of demography models to paleodemography, pp. 175–188, in Saunders, S. R. and Katzenberg, M. A. (eds), *Skeletal biology of past peoples: research methods*. New York.

Scheuer, L. and Black, S. 2000. *Developmental juvenile osteology*. London: Academic.

Schillaci, M. A., Nikitovic, D., Akins, N. J., Tripp, L. and Palkovich, A. M. 2011. Infant and Juvenile Growth in Ancestral Pueblo Indians. *American Journal of Physical Anthropology* 145, 318–26.

Schultz, M., Timme, U. and Schmidt-Schultz, T. H. 2007. Infancy and Childhood in the Pre-Columbian Noth American Southwest-First Results of the Paleopathological Investigation of the Skeletons from the Grasshopper Pueblo, Arizona. *International Journal of Osteoarchaeology* 17, 369–79

Schutkowski, H. 1993. Sex determination of infant and juvenile skeletons. I. Morphognostic features. *American Journal of Physical Anthropology* 90, 199–05.

Stuart-Macadam, P. L. 1985. Porotic Hyperostosis: Representative of a Childhood Condition. *American Journal of Physical Anthropology* 66, 391–98.

Stuart-Macadam, P. L. 1992. Porotic Hyperostosis: a new perspective. *American Journal of Physical Anthropology* 87, 39–47.

Taylor, J. A. M. and Resnick, D. L. 2000. *Skeletal imaging. Atlas of the spine and extremities*. Saunders; Table 1–14 (p. 35) and 4–19 (p. 312).

Walker, P. L., Bathurst, R. R., Richman, R., Gjerdrum, T. and Andrushko, V. A. 2009. The causes of Porotic Hyperostosis and Cribra Orbitalia: A Reappraisal of Iron-Deficiency-Anemia Hypothesis. *American Journal of Physical Anthropology* 139, 109–25.

Weaver, D. S. 1979. Application of the likelihood ratio test to age estimation using the infant and child temporal bone. *American Journal of Physical Anthropology* 50, 263–70.

# 18

# INFANT BURIALS DURING THE COPPER AND BRONZE AGES IN THE IBERIAN JARAMA RIVER VALLEY: A PRELIMINARY STUDY ABOUT CHILDHOOD IN THE FUNERARY CONTEXT DURING III–II MILLENNIUM BC[1]

*Raquel Aliaga Almela, Corina Liesau, Patricia Ríos, Concepción Blasco and Lorenzo Galindo*

## INTRODUCTION

This work provides an overview about children's funerary rituals[2] in Copper and Bronze Age in Jarama-Henares Valleys, located at the centre of Iberian Peninsula. Diachronic transformations that occur at children burials over the 3rd and 2nd millennium BC in this area seem to indicate changes in the role and concept of childhood. In this way, it is exposed how funerary spaces, treatments and rituals were not the same for children as for adults, neither in the Copper Age nor in the Bronze Age. In addition, differences in child burial treatment between the Copper and Bronze Ages are indicated and explained as a result of social and cultural changes.

## GEOGRAPHIC AND CHRONOLOGICAL CONTEXT

As far as geographical context is concerned, the study area is located at the centre of the Iberian Peninsula, in the contact zone between the North and South plateaus, being a natural path between them. Because of this fact, many archaeological similarities and influences can be found between this and the surrounding areas (Tajo Valley, Duero Valley, etc.).

Owing to its richness in resources, Jarama river valley would have been densely inhabited from early prehistory onwards.

This study spans more than 1500 years, from the beginning of the 3rd millennium, *c.* 3000 BC, to the middle of the 2nd millennium, *c.* 1400 BC. Throughout this time, farmer livelihoods were developed in stable sites with certain differences in settlement, but, despite the improvement of knowledge in recent years, it is difficult to determine changes and temporal limits, especially in the Bronze Age.[3]

Regarding funerary remains, there are identifiable changes between the two main periods, although radiocarbon dates show some coexistence between different burial customs which also complicate the establishment of clear phases. However, it is possible to establish three burial practices: a first one for the early moments of the 3rd millennium BC (*c.* 2900–2500 BC), with a probable Neolithic tradition; a second one between *c.* 2600–1800 BC, belonging to the Copper Age too and a third one, during the Bronze Age (1900–1400 BC).

## Children and Funerary Spaces during Copper Age in Jarama's Valley

The Copper Age in the Jarama valley can be divided into two phases owing to changes in children's presence in the funerary context, and the break point seems to coincide with the start of the Bell Beaker horizon.

Sixty-seven graves and more than 160 bodies are known for the entire period. On the whole, anthropological data shows the inequality of child and adult burials, the presence of adults being higher (122 adults, but only 40 children). In fact, the rate of child mortality is only 26%, being far from the normal child mortality rate for pre-industrial societies, which is expected to be around 30–50%.[4] In other words, it seems that only part of the child population was buried in this period.

### *Children and the most ancient chalcolithic burials documented (c. 3000–2500 BC)*

The most ancient chalcolithic burials known in the Jarama valley were collective burials in natural caves and a newly-discovered grave type, the burial mound or barrow. Both types are dated to the first half of the 3rd millennium as evidence by two available radiocarbon dates:[5] 2891–2662 cal BC from *Jarama II* cave[6] and 2858–2490 cal BC from *Soto del Henares* barrow.

Burials in natural caves seem to have been the most frequent type of tomb in this period and this geographic area; indeed, we have recovered more than twenty cases with funerary remains.[7]

In relation to the case of these caves, chronology is a difficult question to resolve owing to the strong strata distortion caused by different taphonomic agents, such as animal intrusions and erosive processes, and because of the similarities between archaeological materials throughout this period. However, as has been said, Jarama II cave has given one radiocarbon date, dating this type of tomb in 4185±50 BP (2891–2662 cal BC).[8]

For some of these caves, the existence of nearby or immediate habitats has been proposed, but there is not enough archaeological evidence to establish this relationship. Furthermore, most of the well documented settlements in the region are located in the lower terraces of the main rivers and far away from these caves. This fact makes it difficult to relate what portion of the population is buried in these tombs at this moment and if these caves could include individuals or families from different communities (or different settlements).

The second type of burial was interments under artificial barrows made by rocks and mud.

In the Jarama basin, only two examples of this type of tomb have been found for the moment, one at the site of *Vegas de Samburiel*[9] and another at *Soto del Henares*[10] (Table 18.1). The last one has been dated by radiocarbon AMS method and has given 4074±35 BP (2891–2662 cal BC) as a result.

As far as funerary depositions are concerned, the skeletons in caves are always displaced, sometimes because of natural post-depositional processes, sometimes due to anthropic displacements to create free space for new burials. Therefore, osteological remains are often badly preserved and the information that can be extracted is poor. However, despite this fact, children are well documented in caves (Table 18.1).

In the case of barrows, only *Soto del Henares* has offered osteological and anthropological information owing to its well preserved conditions. Also in this case, as in caves, the study confirms the absence of children younger than one year and the presence of adults up to their fifties, both men and women (Table 18.1).

What happens with the babies in societies which used barrows and caves as tombs is still an unresolved question. They could have been buried in another place which remains unknown, or they could have received another funerary treatment which did not leave any traces.

In spite of sometimes the worst preservation of baby bones, which has been argued as the cause for their absence in archaeological sites,[11] burying babies in a different way to the rest of the population has been common in the past and not rare in prehistory.[12] A reason for this exclusion could be the fact that these children were not members in their own right for the social community, as happened in Ancient Rome or Iberian pre-roman populations.[13] That means that babies would have a different funerary space, being separated from the rest of people from their community.

On the contrary, children older than one year were buried with adults in the same spaces. For this reason, it should be thought that individuals from this age had probably the same right to be interred in these tombs like the rest of population.

Mortality rates of children in their first years of life must have been very high, and this fact could be an important factor to exclude the youngest from the rest of the community. Access to society could be accompanied of some sort of rite of passage which would take place after the first year of life, perhaps accompanied by weaning.[14]

Being buried in the same tomb of the rest of community should have been an important social aspect in the Early Copper Age due to the features of funerary ritual in this time and its ideological meaning. Barrows and caves housed collective burials, which were formed by consecutive deposits made through the life-time of the tomb. This kind of ritual, which keeps the community together after death, was a very successful formula in order to hold on ties between the group and its land. It demonstrated exploitation rights over territory showing the large occupation of the place by the cult of ancestors.[15] Some of these tombs, besides, would have worked as territorial markers in the landscape.[16]

*Table 18.1. The natural caves and barrows with child burials inside (\*Oxcal 4.1 calibrated dates; \*\* Minimal Individual Number).*

| Archaeological Site | Tomb | Date BP | Date BC* | Min** | Age |
|---|---|---|---|---|---|
| SOTO DEL HENARES | MOUND | 4074 ± 35 | 2858–2491 | 10 | ADULT |
| | | | | | **10 years±30 months** |
| | | | | | 1>12 years |
| | | | | | 12-18 years |
| | | | | | **1>12 years** |
| | | | | | **1>12 years** |
| | | | | | ADULT |
| | | | | | 18-24 years |
| | | | | | 40>65 years |
| | | | | | 24 years |
| CANTERA DE LOS ESQUELETOS | CAVE | | | 7 | ADULT |
| | | | | | ADULT |
| | | | | | ADULT |
| | | | | | ADULT |
| | | | | | **7-8 years** |
| | CAVE | | | 4 | **1>12 years** |
| | | | | | ADULT |
| | | | | | **1>6 years** |
| | | | | | ADULT |
| CUEVA DEL DESTETE | CAVE | | | 13 | ADULT |
| | | | | | ADULT |
| | | | | | **1>12 years** |
| JARAMA II | CAVE | 4185 ± 50 | 2891–2622 | 10 | **1>12 years** |
| | | | | | 12>20 years |
| | | | | | 12>20 years |
| | | | | | 12>20 years |
| | | | | | ADULT |
| | | | | | ADULT |
| | | | | | ADULT |
| | | | | | ADULT |
| | | | | | ADULT |
| | | | | | ADULT |
| JUAN BARBERO | CAVE | | | 11 | **5-6 years** |
| | | | | | ADULT |
| | | | | | 12>20 years |
| | | | | | **2 years** |
| | | | | | ADULT |
| | | | | | 20>40 years |
| | | | | | 20>40 years |
| | | | | | ADULT |
| | | | | | 12>20 years |
| | | | | | **6-8 years** |
| | | | | | **6 years** |

\* Oxcal 4.1 calibrated dates

\*\* Minimal Individuals Number

According to this claim, children older than one year would have become 'ancestors' in the same way as adult people in these tombs, being participants in the construction of an ideological and ritual sacred space.

## *Recent child chalcolithic burials* c. *2600–1800 BC*

During the second half of the 3rd millennium there were two different funerary rituals: those which included Bell Beaker pottery as grave goods and those which did not.

As radiocarbon dates of *Camino de las Yeseras* and *Humanejos* have shown, both types were in use in the same period and in the same settlements.[17] In addition, on occasions both kinds of burials are spatially close.

### CHILDREN IN NON-BELL BEAKER TOMBS

From the architectural point of view, non-Bell Beaker tombs are always simple grave-type. All known examples are pits,[18] very similar to the rest of structures of these settlements.

Individual burials seem to be the standard for this type of tomb, occurring in eleven of the nineteen cases. However, not a single child seems to be buried in this way, and they appear only in multiple burials, that is to say, in graves which contain simultaneous depositions of several bodies, between four and ten. These tombs, perhaps older than the others because they seem to not go beyond 2200 BC, would correspond to exceptional circumstances of mortality (epidemics, accidents, war episodes, etc.) in which deceased would be buried at the same time or within few days.[19]

For the Jarama valley, it is difficult to know the reasons which motivated this type of burial, since there is neither osteological damage nor pathological traces in the bones. Only in one case from *Camino de las Yeseras*, which housed the bodies of one teenager, two adults and four children with an age between one and twelve years, might there be some evidence. In this grave, seven arrow points were found, and some of them have impact traces, although none of them appeared stuck into bones. This case could be considered as burial of people who died violently, as has been argued for other similar peninsular cases.[20]

Children appear with high frequency in multiple tombs and sometimes make up 90% of bodies buried inside (Table 18.2). The higher sensitivity of children to epidemics, hunger episodes, etc. could explain this fact, but the question which should be made is – where are the children who died in normal circumstances buried? At this moment, we do not know certainly any single child burial for this period. Only three examples have been documented, but there are no chronological data available.

Leaving these uncertain cases aside, it seems that children only were buried in multiple graves and had no right to be buried in single burials as some adults did. Why, then, were children buried with adults – frequently women – in multiple graves? Perhaps because the unexpected death of many members from the group caused a trauma, making the community choose burying all of them together. As Catherine Rigeade says,[21] the abnormality of the circumstances of these deaths made people adapt their rites and funerary procedures, modifying the norm.

*Table 18.2. Child chalcolithic burials* c. *2600–1800 BC (\*Oxcal 4.1 calibrated dates; Bell Beaker burials in italic).*

| Site | Tomb | Burial Type | Min | Age | Sex | Date BP | Date BC* |
|---|---|---|---|---|---|---|---|
| LA SALMEDINA | *HYPOGEUM* | *COLLECTIVE* | *2* | *40>65 years* | *WOMAN* | | |
| | | | | *6month> 12years* | | | |
| CAMINO DE LAS YESERAS | SIMPLE GRAVE | MÚLTIPLE | 7 | **1–3 years** | | | |
| | | | | **4–5 years** | | | |
| | | | | **8–9 years** | | | |
| | | | | **12 years** | | | |
| | | | | 14–17 years | ? | | |
| | | | | 25–35 years | ? | | |
| | | | | ADULT | ? | | |
| | SIMPLE GRAVE | MÚLTIPLE | 4 | **6 months** | | 4021 ± 30 | 2620–2470 |
| | | | | **2.5 years** | | | |
| | | | | 26–31 years | WOMAN | | |
| | | | | 18–20 years | WOMAN | | |
| | SIMPLE GRAVE | MÚLTIPLE | 10 | **4 years±12 months** | | 3903 ± 35 | 2480–2280 |
| | | | | **12 years** | WOMAN | 3981 ± 30 | 2580–2450 |
| | | | | **6 years±24 months** | | | |
| | | | | **6 years±24 months** | | | |
| | | | | 12–14 years | | | |
| | | | | **4–5 years** | | | |
| | | | | 12 years | | | |
| | | | | 12 years | | | |
| | | | | 18–20 years | WOMAN | | |
| | | | | **6-12 months** | | | |
| | *NICHE-TYPE GRAVE* | *MULTIPLE* | *4* | **5 years±16 months** | | *4004 ± 30* | *2580–2460* |
| | | | | *ADULT* | *?* | *3752 ± 30* | *2290–2110* |
| | | | | *ADULT* | *?* | | |
| | | | | *ADULT* | *?* | | |
| | *HYPOGEUM* | *COLLECTIVE* | *3* | *20-30 years* | *?* | | |
| | | | | *40>65 years* | *MAN?* | | |
| | | | | *6month> 12years* | | | |
| | *ARTIFICAL CAVE* | *MÚLTIPLE* | *2* | *20–30 years* | *WOMAN* | *3525 ± 40* | *1960–1740* |
| | | | | *1-5 years* | | | |
| HUMANEJOS | SIMPLE GRAVE | MÚLTIPLE | 4 | **7 years±24 months** | | 3959 ± 35 | 2580–2340 |
| | | | | **16 years ± 6 months** | ? | | |
| | | | | **4 years** | | | |
| | | | | 18–20 years | WOMAN | | |
| | SIMPLE GRAVE | MÚLTIPLE | 7 | **10–12 years** | | 4009 ± 56 | 2700–2300 |
| | | | | 13–15 years | WOMAN | | |
| | | | | **9–12 years** | | | |
| | | | | 26–27 years | WOMAN | | |
| | | | | **10–12 years** | | | |
| | | | | 27–30 years | MAN | | |
| | | | | 18–20 years | | | |
| | *FALSE HYPOGEUM* | *MÚLTIPLE* | *3* | *20–25 years* | *MAN* | *3825 ± 37* | *2460–2190* |
| | | | | *12 years* | | | |
| | | | | *17–21 years* | *?* | | |

Italics: Bell Beaker tombs

\* Oxcal 4.1 calibrated dates

In spite of the fact that it could be thought that Rigeade is right, this funerary adaptation seems not to be complete at this time. Children found in multiple graves are always older than six months (Table 18.2), so the youngest babies did not receive this treatment, although it seems difficult to think that this part of the population was not affected by mortality crises. On the contrary, they must have been the most affected according to the normal mortality rate for pre-industrial populations.[22]

Maybe, for cultural or ideological reasons, these babies received another funerary treatment, such as exposure or another ritual, and maybe this unknown burial treatment was the norm for children. It would be always applied to babies younger than six months, despite dying in abnormal circumstances.

## CHILDREN IN BELL BEAKER TOMBS

Bell Beaker tombs were different from non-Bell Beaker ones as far as the child population is concerned, in spite of the absence of babies younger than six months.

There were several types of tombs associated to Bell Beaker pottery, and children were buried in all of them, even in the most monumental types, but in all the cases they were accompanied by adults (Table 18.2).[23] As a matter of fact, neither individual burials nor collective nor multiple burials exclusively with children are documented.

According to the archaeological evidence, children shared funerary spaces with adults and also had Bell Beaker pottery in their grave goods. However, the proportion of child individuals is lower than adult, and only a few children were buried in this way. In fact, the majority of Bell Beaker tombs belong to adult men.

Taking into account that Bell Beaker tombs and non-Bell Beaker tombs are contemporaneous,[24] there are several signs which indicate a higher social rank for individuals who were buried in Beaker burials which are added to the special value of the pottery by itself.[25] Firstly, the architecture of tombs, more complex and laborious in most cases; secondly, the presence of gold jewellery and metal weapons as grave goods; and third, the use of cinnabar pigments for body treatment[26] and the presence of ivory ornaments as grave goods,[27] both infrequent and exotic raw materials because of their long distance origin or their special treatment as exclusive materials.[28]

There are also other indications which would support this claim. On one hand, paleodiet analysis from some individuals at the sites of Camino de las Yeseras[29] and also of Aldeagordillo (Ávila)[30] indicate that people from Bell Beaker tombs had a richer diet in meat and dairy products. On the other hand, anthropological data suggest that individuals without Bell Beaker pottery bore more reiterative physical efforts and also seem to indicate that life expectancy was higher for Bell Beaker individuals.[31]

If we consider Bell Beaker tombs and Bell Beaker grave goods as symbols of high social status,[32] the fact that children older than six years were buried with it appears to indicate the possible existence of hereditary status.[33] However, this social status or rank was not for the children by themselves, on the contrary, it seems to be always to have been shared with the adults buried with them in collective tombs.

Collective burials associated to Bell Beaker pottery are common in the Jarama valley. Indeed, around 22% of Beaker tombs – 8 of the 32 Beaker graves at least – housed burials of this type. In other words, 21 of the 57 persons who were buried with Bell Beaker pottery were interred in collective graves.

In these tombs, individuals who were buried together seem to make up family or kinship groups owing to their demographic profile. As matter of fact, association affects only a few individuals, groups of two or four bodies being the most common, and when we know the sex and the age of them, they appear to be members of a family or have kinship relationships despite of the fact that DNA analysis would be necessary to confirm it.

There are several examples in which children are involved, like the burial of one mature woman and one child from the hypogeum of *Salmedina*, or the simultaneous burial of one young woman and one little child from an artificial cave of *Camino de las Yeseras*.

The latter case is one of the burials made inside the second funerary area of the site,[34] in which the child was buried with a little Bell Beaker bowl, a miniature version of their mother's vessel.[35] In this funerary area, two adult burials were also recovered. One of them, possibly male, was buried in a monumental hypogeum with the richest grave goods of the site.[36]

This whole funerary space, like the two others documented in this site, forms a kind of pantheon for a probably high-social-rank kinship group. The presence of one child inside indicates that children were part of these groups and shared special funerary privileges and rites with the rest of its members. However, despite of the fact that some children were buried in Bell Beaker tombs, we must not forget that, regarding the available data, children younger than six months were not buried in these tombs. Actually, according to the archaeological record, baby burials are unknown, as happened with the younger children from the non-Bell Beaker mortuary population.

Although the reasons for this fact would have been the same for both groups of people – buried with Bell Beaker and buried without it – it is difficult to say if the funerary ritual applied to babies was similar or not.

## CHILDREN AND FUNERARY SPACES DURING THE BRONZE AGE IN THE JARAMA VALLEY

From the point of view of funerary practices, the Early and Middle Bronze Ages[37] are rather alike. The change takes place around 1300 cal BC, when burials completely disappear. Before this, interments in simple graves are the norm for the Early and Middle Bronze Ages, despite the exception of a few of them which have a little niche for the body.[38]

We have recorded a total of 107 tombs and 127 skeletons, of which we know the sex and the age in only 95% of the cases.

The most ancient grave at this time is dated to 1880–1660 cal BC, and the most recent to 1490–1290 cal BC. Throughout this period, multiple and single burials have been documented, as well a sort of collective grave made by the association of individual and separated interments inside the same grave. In all these types of tombs children are documented (Table 18.3).

In contrast to what happened in the Copper Age, children were buried in the same way as adult people from their first week of life to twelve years old. Actually, the infantile mortality rate is 45 per cent,[39] which fits in with what is expected in pre-industrial times. In conclusion, it seems that, unlike previous practice, there was no child exclusion from burial treatments.

## *Children and grave goods: elite or natural social status?*

The Bronze Age grave goods in the Jarama valley were formed by complete animals or partial skeletons (50%), pottery (25%), personal ornaments (14%) and copper awls (12%). All these kinds of artefacts were associated with both children and adults (Table 18.4).

The variety of grave goods makes it difficult to recognize their social value,[40] but it would make sense that those formed by offerings of cattle bones and metal awls were the most valued, taking into account the energy cost[41] and the proportional representation of these goods on the whole.[42] Besides, bovines would have possibly been a high value offering, considering that cattle were the most important meat provider according to the studies of faunal remains from habitats.[43]

All in all, and taking into account that only 30% of the buried population had grave goods,[44] the presence of these offerings inside child tombs suggests the social importance of children in these societies. Furthermore, it has to be emphasized that 40% of children were buried with grave goods, but only 23% of adults include them.[45]

If the presence of grave goods is in itself a status sign, owing to the few people who were buried with them, the fact that almost the half of children had grave goods could be explained in two ways. On the one hand, it could be thought that grave goods are the sign of a high social rank, and in this case children buried with goods would be considered as the progeny of higher social rank groups.

On other hand, and we think this is more probable, the higher proportion of children buried with grave goods would lead us to think of the concept of *status by definition,*[46] which refers to a special social consideration obtained by natural causes, and not in *status by property*[47] or *status by achievement.*[48] That is to say, children would have been valued for their age, for the fact that they were not adults yet, and not for their feats, power or richness; or rather the feats, power or richness of their relatives.

According to this thesis, the emotional factor could have been an important reason to explain why children were one of the population sectors which received more attention in death.

Whatever the reasons for it, there was a special burial treatment for children. As a matter of fact, the most interesting and singular burials from this period are those in which children were buried with dogs. One of these cases is the burial of two children (five and nine years old) who were buried face to face with a partial dog skeleton

*Table 18.3. Child burials during the Bronze Age (*Oxcal 4.1 calibrated dates).*

| Archaeological Site | Grave Type | Min* | Age | Sex | Date BP | Date BC* |
|---|---|---|---|---|---|---|
| CALLE PRÍNCIPE 11 | SIMPLE | 1 | 6–7 years | | | |
| CASERÍO DE PERALES | SIMPLE | 2 | 9 years | | | |
| | | | 5 years | | | |
| SOTO DEL HENARES | SIMPLE | 3 | 12 years±36 months | | | |
| | | | 10 years±30 months | | | |
| | | | 1–6 months | | | |
| | NICHE-TYPE | 2 | ADULT | MAN | | |
| | | | 9 years±24 months | | | |
| | SIMPLE | 2 | 16–17 years | MAN | | |
| | | | 11–14 years | | | |
| | SIMPLE | 1 | 1>12 years | | | |
| | NICHE-TYPE | 2 | 3 years±12 months | | | |
| | | | 2–4 years | | | |
| PISTA DE MOTOS | SIMPLE | 3 | 6>12 years | | 3269 ± 21 | 1613–1497 |
| | | | ADULT | MAN | | |
| | | | ADULT | WOMAN | | |
| | SIMPLE | 2 | 17–18 years | ? | | |
| | | | 10 years±30 months | | | |
| LA DEHESA | SIMPLE | 1 | 10 years. | | | |
| | SIMPLE | 1 | 1>6 years | | | |
| LA LOMA DEL LOMO | SIMPLE | 4 | 15–16 years | WOMAN | | |
| | | | 2–3 years | | | |
| | | | 4–5 years | | | |
| | | | 2–3 years | | | |
| | SIMPLE | 1 | 2–3 years | | | |
| | SIMPLE | 1 | 5–6 years | | | |
| | NICHE-TYPE | 1 | 2–4 years | | | |
| | SIMPLE | 1 | 0–3 months | | | |
| | SIMPLE | 1 | 3–4 years | | | |
| | SIMPLE | 3 | 3–4 years | | | |
| | | | 2–3 years | | | |
| | | | 3–4 years | | | |
| | SIMPLE | 1 | 6–7 years | | | |
| | SIMPLE | 1 | 5–6 months | | | |
| | SIMPLE | 1 | 2 years | | | |
| | NICHE-TYPE | 1 | 2 years | | | |
| LOS BERROCALES | SIMPLE | 3 | 20>40 years | MAN | 3540 ± 50 | 1982–1746 |
| | | | 12>20 years | ALOFISO | | |
| | | | 1>6 years | | | |
| | SIMPLE | 3 | 25–35 years | WOMAN | | |
| | | | 2–3 years | | | |
| | | | 1–6 months | | | |
| | SIMPLE | 1 | 3–4 years | | | |
| | SIMPLE | 1 | 3–4 years | | | |
| | SIMPLE | 1 | 2–4 years | | | |
| | SIMPLE | 2 | 20>40 | WOMAN | | |
| | | | 6–8 years | | | |
| | SIMPLE | 2 | 17–25 years | WOMAN | | |
| | | | 6>12 years | | | |
| | SIMPLE | 1 | 5–7 years | | | |
| CAMINO DE LAS YESERAS | SIMPLE | 1 | 2 years±8 months | | | 1460–1290 |
| AMPLIACIÓN DE AGUAS VIVAS | SIMPLE | 1 | 1>6 years | | | |
| | SIMPLE | 2 | 15–17 years | WOMAN | | |
| | | | 7 years±24 months | | | |
| GÓZQUEZ | SIMPLE | 1 | 1>6 years | | | |

Table 18.4. Grave Goods from Bronze Age burials.

| Site | Grave | Age Group | Sex | Type | Pottery | Ornaments | Tools | Fauna |
|---|---|---|---|---|---|---|---|---|
| CASERÍO DE PERALES | SIMPLE | INFANTILE II | | SINGLE | carenated-bowl | stone beads | | |
| | NICHE-TYPE | YOUNG ADULT | WOMAN | SINGLE | | | | |
| | SIMPLE | INFANTILE II | | SHARED | | | | partial dog |
| | | INFANTILE I | | | | | | |
| | NICHE-TYPE | INFANTILE I | | SHARED | carenated-bowl | | | |
| SOTO DEL HENARES | | INFANTILE I | | | | | | |
| | SIMPLE | INFANTILE II | | SHARED | | | mill stone | |
| | | PERINATAL | | | | | | |
| | SIMPLE | JUVENILE | MAN | SINGLE | bowl | | metal awl | 1 leg and 1 complet eskeleton |
| PISTA DE MOTOS | SIMPLE | INFANTILE II | | SHARED | 3 pots | | mill stones | |
| | | ADULT | MAN | | | | | |
| | | ADULT | WOMAN | | | | | |
| | SIMPLE | ADULT | ¿? | SINGLE | | | metal awl | |
| LA DEHESA | SIMPLE | INFANTILE | | SINGLE | | | flint stone chip | |
| | SIMPLE | ADULT | ¿? | SHARED | 1 pot | | mill stone | |
| | | ADULT | ¿? | | | | | |
| VALDOCARROS | SIMPLE | ADULT | MAN? | SINGLE | | | | |
| | SIMPLE | JUVENILE | MAN | SINGLE | | | metal awl | |
| | SIMPLE | ADULT | WOMAN | SINGLE | | | | cattle head |
| LOS BERROCALES | SIMPLE | YOUNG ADULT | WOMAN | SINGLE | | 1 snail necklace | | |
| | SIMPLE | INFANTILE I | | SINGLE | | | thread roll | |
| | SIMPLE | YOUNG ADULT | MAN | SINGLE | | | | dog |
| | SIMPLE | YOUNG ADULT | MAN | SINGLE | | | | ovicaprine |
| CAMINO DE LAS YESERAS | SIMPLE | INFANTILE I | | SINGLE | | | | raven and dog |
| | SIMPLE | JUVENILE | WOMAN | SINGLE | carenated-bowl | | | pigle |
| | SIMPLE | INFANTILE I | | SINGLE | | | | pigle |
| | SIMPLE | INFANTILE I | | SINGLE | | | | pigle |
| | SIMPLE | INFANTILE I | | SINGLE | | drilled seashel | | pigle |
| | SIMPLE | SENIL | MAN | SINGLE | | | | pigle |
| | SIMPLE | SENIL | MAN | SINGLE | bowl | | | cow |
| LA LOMA DEL LOMO | SIMPLE | INFANTILE I | | SINGLE | | | metal awl | pigle |
| | SIMPLE | INFANTILE I | | SINGLE | | drilled seashel | | 2 pigles and 1 dog's cranium |
| | SIMPLE | SENIL | WOMAN | SINGLE | | | | cattle head |
| | NICHE-TYPE | INFANTILE I | | SINGLE | | | bone awl | |
| | SIMPLE | INFANTILE I | | SINGLE | | | | cattle front leg |
| | SIMPLE | INFANTILE I | | SINGLE | | | | lamb |
| | SIMPLE | INFANTILE I | | SINGLE | | | | goat |
| | SIMPLE | INFANTILE I | | SINGLE | | | | bovine horn |
| | SIMPLE | MATURE | MAN | SINGLE | | bovine molar pendants | | |
| LAS MATILLAS | NICHE-TYPE | MATURE | MAN | SINGLE | | | | pigle |

near their feet in the *Caserío de Perales* site.[49] This grave is ascribed to the Middle Bronze Age, within the *Protocogotas* horizon, just like another case from *Camino de las Yeseras* – dated to 3450±40 BP (1460–1290 cal BC) – the singular interment of one two year old child buried with a dog and a raven.[50]

A probable interpretation to these dog-deposits is that they could have accompanied children as guardians, play-mates, pets, etc., although the absence of the hind legs of the dog from *Caserío de Perales* reveals a more complex depositional act than initially might have been supposed, possibly related to a symbolic or a consumption intention.[51]

## *Multiple and collective burials within children: the possible reflection of kinship bonds*

In general, single interment in simple graves was the most common kind of burial in the Jarama valley. Actually, more than 80% of tombs were for a single body. However, the proportion of individuals buried alone changes between adult and child population. Indeed, only 20% of adults were interred in collective or multiple burials, but 40% of children were buried in this way.[52]

Single burials for children were not different from those for adults. Besides, the age range suggests that there was no discrimination by age, considering that the youngest child interred in a single burial was a perinatal and the oldest was 10–12 years old.

As far as collective burials are concerned, all the documented cases were made up by single interments which were disposed inside the same grave, being careful to separate and individuate each burial. Stones and soil were used for this purpose, sealing each one of them clearly.

Although children were the more frequent population sector in collective tombs, they were usually associated with adults. A good example of this association is the burial of three children between two and five years old who were interred in a deep grave one over the other in *La loma del Lomo*.[53] The tomb was closed by rocks and a mud surface, but at some time it was opened again to include a new burial inside, the fourth, which was a sixteen year old woman. Each one of the children from this grave had a piglet as grave good.

Burying several corpses closely in the same funerary space reflects an evident intention of keeping together these individuals after their death. Owing to this fact, these graves would have been a sort of pantheon like Bell Beaker funerary areas, in which several graves were associated, and the reasons for their existence might have been the kinship bonds between the buried. Supporting this claim is the fact that there are two specific cases in the Jarama valley counting on clear parallels in the *Meseta* area which have results of DNA analysis proving these family bonds.

One of these cases is one of the tombs from *Los Berrocales* site, a simple pit grave which housed two consecutive burials. The first one has been dated to 3540±50 BP (1982–1746 cal BC) and it included a young man, a possible female juvenile individual and a child younger than six years old, all of them buried at the same time. The second one was a little later – it has been dated to 3515±40 BP (1952–1739 cal BC) – and was a single burial of a young man. This second burial was on the top of the first one, and there was a clear space filled with sediment and rocks between both of them.

The parallel to this case is the burial of *La Horra* (Burgos, Spain), with the same association between single and multiple interments in the same grave. In this tomb, the DNA analyses showed that the secondary male burial was the brother of one of the men buried in the first interment.[54]

Another case is the multiple burial of *Pista de Motos*, in which were buried a man, a women and a child. This tomb has been dated in 3269±31 BP (1613–1497 cal BC) and its parallel is in *San Román de la Hornija* (Valladolid, Spain), where a very similar burial was found years ago. Recent paleogenetic studies have shown that the woman was the mother of the child,[55] therefore, it could be suggested that the man was the father.

In spite of not having more DNA analyses, the age and sex of the buried population in the rest of the collective or multiple burials which have been found in the Jarama Valley suggest that family or kinship bonds were the reason for these associations.

There are many examples in which adults and children were buried as a nuclear family. In this way, we can mention the triple burial of a 25–35 year old woman with a perinatal and a 2–3 year old child, other of a young man buried with a possible female juvenile and a child younger than six years old, and another burial of a young woman and a 6–8 year old child, all of them from *Los Berrocales*.

In a few cases, those buried together were only children, and because of their age it could be thought that they were siblings. That happens in the mentioned case of *Caserío de Perales*, and in *Soto del Henares*, where there are two more examples: the first one, a three months old baby and a 2–3 year old child buried in the same tomb; and the second one, the triple burial of a neonate, a ten year old child and a twelve years old juvenile.

## Conclusions

Age seems to be a determining factor in funerary practices during the Copper and Bronze Ages in the Jarama Valley.

If it is considered that burial rituals are the result of regulated belief systems and ritual norms directly connected with historical processes,[56] changes observed in the funerary role and space of children should be explained as the result of deep transformations in social structure throughout the 3rd and 2nd millennia BC.

During the first half of the Copper Age, communities started to settle in the Jarama valley in a regular way.[57] In this historical context, legitimizing resource exploitation and land property would have been one of the most important matters for these groups,[58] and the main way would have been establishing bonds between territory and community.

For this purpose, time could have become an argument and the dead became a proof of territorial establishment.[59] Natural caves and funerary barrows, as collective tombs for the community, would be part of funerary practices called 'ritual of ancestors',[60] by means of which death would be used to create sacred ancestral spaces in order to legitimize the community presence and its right over land resources.[61]

However, as has been shown, children younger than one year did not take part in these rituals. It seems that they were not considered part of this ancestral community before this age, probably because they were not full members of society.

In the recent Copper Age, social stratification signs and individualism are clear in funerary remains. Prestige Bell Beaker items, long-distance exchange, specialized craftwork, farming surplus and possibly communal ceremonies are signs of a social change in favour of hierarchy[62] which can be found in the Jarama valley at this time.

Among Bell Beaker groups, collective burials were reserved for a few members of the elite, who were buried with high social value grave goods and in architecturally complex tombs, making up pantheon structures.

Taking into account child Bell Beaker burials, social status was probably hereditary, at least as far as higher social rank was concerned. Children from elites were part of privileged kinship groups and because of this fact they shared funerary spaces with their members.

On other hand, lower status children were not buried like their adult relatives – in single burials into simple graves – and they can only be found in multiple tombs. There must have been another funerary treatment for children which has not been identified and this fact shows the unimportant role which these children played in social stratification. However, this fact does not mean that these children were not important for society and their families.

Only Bell Beaker elites were buried collectively because in these groups familiar bonds mattered in order to inherit privileges and because of that their children were part of these rituals.[63]

In the Bronze Age, however, things totally changed. Collective burials seem to have been used for nuclear families, emphasizing bonds between parents and progeny and siblings.[64] At the same time, children were the object of more funerary attention than before owing to being children and not only because of their lineage, even the younger babies.

It seems that the structural social bases of these communities changed from the broad kinship groups of beginning of the 3rd millennium to the nuclear families of the Bronze Age, throughout the limited kinship group of elite in Bell Beaker horizon.[65] And in all this process, the social role and importance of childhood changed too.

NOTES

1   Study financed by Project HAR2011-28731, *Las sociedades calcolíticas y su marco temporal en la región de Madrid.* Ministerio de Economía y Competitividad. Gobierno de España
2   The study is focus on burials of individuals between zero and twelve years old, according to Ubelaker, 2007, 88
3   Ríos, Blasco and Aliaga 2012
4   Weiss 1973
5   All of the dates mentioned in the text are 2 sigma calibrated results.
6   Jordá and Mestres 1999

7  Aliaga 2014
8  *Ibid.*
9  Jiménez Guijarro, 2008
10 Galindo and Sánchez-Sánchez 2010
11 Guy, Masset and Baud 1997
12 Rihuete 2000, 165
13 Chapa 2003; Fernández Crespo 2008, 200–4; Torija, Baquedano, Cruz 2010
14 Something similar has been documented of Inca culture, which is called *rutuchikuy* ritual. These rites accompanied weaning and consisted, essentially, in cutting the hair of the baby and giving it a new name, establishing kinship with the other members of family and community (González Carré, 2003, chapter II)
15 Barret 1996; Godelier 1990, 168; Zammit 1991; Tilley 1996, 241–3
16 Renfrew 1976 and 1984; Chapman 1981; Criado 1989; Cámara 2000; Márquez 2002
17 Aliaga 2008 and 2014; Blasco, Liesau, Ríos, Blanco, Aliaga, Moreno and Daza, 2009; Ríos 2011; Ríos *et al.* 2012
18 There are nineteen tombs, of which twelve are dated
19 Macarro 2002, 101; Aliaga 2011, 72–5
20 One similar example is the burial of *Cerro de la Cabeza*, in Ávila (Spain), in which some of the buried individuals had arrow points stuck into their bones and others did not. This grave housed the same number of bodies as arrow points, and due to this fact it is said that all of the individuals died by the arrows' impact (Fabián 2006, 311)
21 Rigeade 2007, 9–10
22 Weiss 1973
23 Except in one possible case, but it was too altered and destroyed to know if it really is a Bell Beaker child single burial
24 Aliaga 2008; Blasco *et al.* 2009; Gómez, Blasco, Trancho, Grueso, Ríos and Martínez-Ávila 2011
25 Shenan 1982, 156; Thomas 1991, 34–5; Garrido 2000, 62 and 66; etc.
26 Ríos and Liesau 2011, 367–8
27 Liesau and Moreno 2012
28 Regarding cinnabar, all known Spanish deposits are far away from the Jarama valley (Ríos and Liesau 2011, 367–8). As far as ivory is concerned, FTIR and TC analysis have confirmed that, at least, one bead from an individual grave of Camino de las Yeseras' was made of African savannah elephant. The rest of the pieces of this type were made of extinct forest elephant (Liesau, Banerjee and Schwartz 2011; Liesau and Moreno 2012)
29 Trancho and Robledo 2011
30 Trancho, Robledo, López-Bueis and Fabián, 1996
31 Aliaga 2012, 332–3
32 Shennan, 1982, 156; Thomas, 1991, 34–5; Garrido, 2000, 62 and 66; etc.
33 Andrés 2003, 25
34 Blasco *et al.*, 2009, 55–64
35 Small size imitations of adult's vessels as grave goods for children are documented too in others periods and regions in central Iberian, like in a Bronze Age's child burial from *Motilla del Azuer* (Ciudad Real) (Nájera, Molina, Sánchez and Aranda, 2006, 154)
36 Blasco *et al.* 2009, 59
37 *Protogocotas* and *Cogotas I* horizons at this area
38 From the total of 107 tombs documented for the Bronze Age in this region, only sixteen are of niche-type (15%)
39 Aliaga, 2012, 283
40 Lull, Micó, Risch and Rihuete, 2004. It is the social meaning of a funerary object, taking into account the energy expended on its production (economic value) and its social appreciation

(symbolic value), which comes from factors like the scarcity of its raw material or its exclusivity. This concept must be understood including economic, moral, politic and social aspects. For this reason, Krueger (2008, 9–10) defines it as the object's ability to awaken admiration

41  Tainter, 1973. He defined 'energy cost' as the economic, human and material resources expended in a funeral ritual and said that the higher the cost, the higher would be the status of the deceased

42  There are many systems to recognize the social value of grave good elements, but one of the most employed is estimating the proportional representation of them. Scarcity is considered a sign of more value: Tainter 1975; Brown 1987; Lull and Estévez 1986

43  Molero and Íñigo 2001; García y Liesau 2007; Aliaga y Campos 2011

44  From the total of 134 individuals catalogued, only 39 were buried with grave goods (Aliaga 2012, 345)

45  *Ibid.*

46  Hayawaka, 1969, 110

47  *Ibidem*

48  *Ibidem*

49  Blasco Capilla Calle, Robles, González and González, 1991, 59 and 60.

50  Liesau, Blasco, Ríos, Vega., Menduiña, Blanco, Baena. Herrera, Petri and Gómez, 2008, 108

51  Liesau 2012, 242–3

52  Aliaga 2012, 339–42

53  Valiente 1992, 115–20

54  Esparza Velasco and Delibes 2012, 280

55  Esparza *et al.* 2012, 307

56  Smith 1989, 153

57  Díaz-del Río 2001, 310–11; Ríos, 2011, 318–19 and 587–88

58  Díaz-del Río 2001, 312

59  Hernando 1993, 92

60  Barrett 1996

61  Renfrew 1976; Chapman 1981; Criado 1989

62  Andrés 2005, 137–38

63  Aliaga 2012, 335 and 351

64  Aliaga 2012, 357

65  Aliaga 2012, 406 and 407

REFERENCES

Aliaga, R. 2008. El mundo funerario calcolítico en la región de Madrid. *Cuadernos de Prehistoria y Arqueología de la Universidad Autónoma de Madrid* 34, 23–39.

Aliaga, R. 2011. Los enterramientos múltiples del Calcolítico Peninsular, pp. 23–39, in Aliaga, R. and Parra. J. (eds), *Actas de las IV Jornadas de investigación del dep. de Prehistoria y Arqueología de la UAM (3–5 marzo de 2009)*, Madrid: UAM Ediciones.

Aliaga, R. 2014. *Sociedad y mundo funerario en el III y II milenio a. C. en la región del Jarama* (Bar International Series 2630). Oxford: Archaeopress.

Aliaga, R. and Campos, N. 2011. Los restos faunísticos, pp. 147–164 in Aliaga, R. and Megías, M. (eds), *Los Berrocales (Madrid): un yacimiento de la Edad del Bronce en la confluencia Manzanares-Jarama* (Patrimonio Arqueológico de Madrid 8). Madrid: Universidad Autónoma de Madrid.

Andrés, M. T. 2003. El concepto de la muerte y el ritual funerario en la Prehistoria. *Cuadernos de Arqueología de la Universidad de Navarra* 11, 13–36.

Barret, J. C. 1996. The Living, the Dead and the Ancestors: Neolithic and Early Bronze Age Mortuary Practices, pp. 394–412 in Preucel, R. and Hodder, I. (eds), *Contemporary Archaeology in Theory*. Oxford: Blackwell Publishers Ltd.

Blasco, C., Liesau, C., Ríos, P., Blanco, P., Aliaga, R., Moreno, E. and Daza, A. 2009. Kupferzeitliche Siedlungsbestattungen mit Glockenbeche und Prestigebeigaben aus dem Grabenwerk von El Camino de las Yeseras (San Fernando de Henares, Prov. Madrid). Untersuchungen zur Typologie des Grabritus und zu dessen sozialer Symbolik. *Maddrider Mitteilungen* 50, 40–70.

Blasco, C., Capilla, M. I., Calle, J., Robles, F., González, V. M. and González, A. 1991. Enterramientos del horizonte Protocogotas en el valle del Manzanares. *Cuadernos de Prehistoria y Arqueología de la Universidad Autónoma de Madrid* 18, 55–112.

Brown, J. A. 1987. Quantitative Burial Analyses as Interassemblage Comparison, pp. 294–308 in Aldenderfer, S. (ed.), *Quantitative Research in Archaeology: Progress and Prospects*. Newbury Park: Sage Periodical Press.

Cámara, J. A. 2000. Bases teóricas para el studio del ritual funerario utilizado durante la Prehistoria Reciente en el Sur de la Península Ibérica. *SAGVNTVM* 32, 97–114.

Chapa, T. 2003. La percepción de la infancia en el mundo ibérico. *Trabajos de Prehistoria* 60 (1), 115–138.

Chapman, R. 1981. The emergence of formal disposal areas and the 'problem' of megalithic tombs in prehistoric Europe, pp. 71–89 in Chapman, R., Kinnes, I. and Randsborg, K. (eds), *The archaeology of death*. London: Cambridge University Press.

Criado, F. 1989. Megalitos, espacio y pensamiento. *Trabajos de Prehistoria* 46, 75–98.

Díaz-del Río, P. 2001. *La formación del paisaje agrario: Madrid en el III y II milenio BC* (Arqueología, Paleontología y Etnografía de la Comunidad de Madrid 9). Madrid: Comunidad de Madrid.

Esparza, A., Velasco, J. and Delibes, G. 2012. HUM 2005–00139. Planteamiento y primeros resultados en un proyecto de investigación sobre la muerte en Cogotas I, pp. 259–320 in Rodríguez, J. A. and Fernández, J. (eds), *Cogotas I. una cultura de la Edad del Bronce en la Península Ibérica* (Serie Arte y Arqueología 30). Valladolid: Universidad de Valladolid.

Fabián, J. F. 2006. *El IV y el III milenio AC en el Valle del Amblés (Ávila)* (Monografía de Arqueología de la Junta de Castilla y León 5). Castilla y León: Consejería de Cultura y Turismo.

Fernández Crespo, T. 2008. Los enterramientos infantiles en contextos domésticos en la Cuenca Alta/Media del Ebro: a propósito de la inhumación del despoblado altomedieval de Aistra (Álava). *Munibe* 59, 199–217.

Galindo, L. and Sánchez Sánchez, V. 2010. *Memoria final de los trabajos de excavación arqueológica en el yacimiento "Soto del Henares" (Torrejón de Ardoz)*. Unpublished Archaeological Report.

García, J. and Liesau, C. 2007. Los restos faunísticos, pp. 251–278 in Blasco, C., Blanco, F., Liesau, C., Carrión. H., Baena, J., Quero, S. and Rodríguez, M. J. (eds), *El Bronce Medio y Final en la región de Madrid. El poblado de la Fábrica de Ladrillos (Getafe, Madrid)* (Estudios de Prehistoria y Arqueología Madrileñas 14–15). Madrid: Ayuntamiento de Madrid.

Garrido, R. 2000. *El Campaniforme en la Meseta Central de la Península Ibérica (c. 2500–2000 AC)*. (BAR International Series 892). Oxford: Archaeopress.

Godelier, M. 1990. *Lo ideal y lo material*. Madrid: Taurus Humanidades.

Gómez, J. L., Blasco, C., Trancho, G., Grueso, I., Ríos, P. and Martínez-Ávila, M. 2011. Los protagonistas, pp. 101–132 in Blasco, C., Liesau, C. and Ríos, P. (eds), *Yacimientos calcolíticos con campaniformes de la región de Madrid: nuevos estudios* (Patrimonio Arqueológico de Madrid 6). Madrid: Universidad Autónoma de Madrid.

González Carré, E. 2003. *Ritos de tránsito en el Perú de los Incas* (Colección Biblioteca Andina de Bolsillo 18). Lima: Lluvia Editores.

Guy, H., Masset, C. and Baud, C. A. 1997. Infant taphonomy. *International Journal of Osteoarchaeology* 7, 221–229.

Hayawaka, S. L. 1969. *Símbolo, estatus y personalidad*. Barcelona: Sagitario.

Hernando, A. 1993. Campesinos y ritos funerarios: el desarrollo de la complejidad en el Mediterráneo Oriental (IV–II milenio a. C.). *Trabalhos de Antropologia y Etnologia* 33, 391–398.

Jiménez Guijarro, J. 2008. El concepto no-neolítico del fenómeno megalítico madrileño, pp. 55–66 in Hernández, M; Soler, J. A. and López, J. A. (eds), *IV Congreso del Neolítico Peninsular. 27–30 de noviembre de 2006*. Alicante: Diputación de Alicante.

Jordá, J. F. and Mestres, J. S. 1999. El enterramiento calcolítico precampaniforme de Jarama II: una nueva fecha radiocarbónica para la Prehistoria Reciente de Guadalajara y su integración en la cronología de la región. *Zephyrus* 52, 175–190.

Krueger, M. 2008. Valor, prestigio e intercambio. Los métodos ante la teoría. *Herakleion* 1, 7–19.

Liesau, C. 2012. Depósitos con ofrendas de animales en yacimientos Cogotas I: antecedentes y características, pp. 219–257 in Rodríguez, J. A. and Fernández, J. (eds), *Cogotas I. Una cultura de la Edad del Bronce en la Península Ibérica*. Valladolid: Universidad de Valladolid.

Liesau, C., Banerjee, A. and Schawrz, J. O. 2011. Camino de las Yeseras Ivory Collection: advances in analysis technology used in identifying raw material, pp. 387–396, in Blasco, C., Liesau, C. and Ríos, P. (eds), *Yacimientos calcolíticos con campaniformes de la región de Madrid: nuevos estudios* (Patrimonio Arqueológico de Madrid 6). Madrid: Universidad Autónoma de Madrid.

Liesau, C., Blasco, C., Ríos, P., Vega, J., Menduiña, R., Blanco, F., Baena, J., Herrera, T., Petri, A. and Gómez, J. L. 2008. Un espacio compartido por vivos y muertos: el poblado calcolítico de fosos de Camino de las Yeseras. *Complutum* 19 (1), 97–120.

Liesau, C. and Moreno, E. 2012. Marfiles campaniformes de El Camino de las yeseras (San Fernando de Henares, Madrid), pp. 87–97 in Banerjee, A., Schumacher, Th. X., Marzoli, D. and López, J. A. (eds), *Marfil y elefantes en la Península Ibérica y el Mediterráneo. Coloquio internacional 26–27 Marzo 2008*. Barcelona: Iberia Arqueológica 16(1).

Lull, V. and Estévez, J. 1986. Propuesta metodológica para el studio de las necrópolis argáricas, pp. 441–452, in *Homenaje a Luis Siret (1934–1984)*. Sevilla: Junta de Andalucía, Consejería de Cultura.

Lull, V., Micó, M., Risch, R. and Rihuete, C. 2004. Las relaciones de propiedad en la sociedad argárica. Una aproximación a través del análisis de las tumbas de individuos infantiles. *Mainake* XXVI, 233–272.

Macarro, J. A. 2000. *La Alcalá prehistórica. El poblado de la Edad del Bronce de "La Dehesa"*. Alcalá de Henares: Fundación Colegio del Rey.

Márquez, J. E. 2002. Megalitismo, agricultura y complejidad social: algunas consideraciones. *Baetica. Estudios de Arte, Geografía e Historia* 24, 193–222.

Molero, G. and Íñigo, C. 2001. Estudio de los restos óseos hallados en la zona A/Norte de la Loma del Lomo (Cogolludo, Guadalajara). Campañas de 1984–1994, pp. 281–294 in Valiente, J., *La Loma del Lomo III. Cogolludo, Guadalajara*. Toledo: Junta de Comunidades de Castilla-La Mancha.

Nájera, T., Molina, A., Sánchez, M. and Aranda, G. 2006. Un enterramiento infantil singular en el yacimiento de la Edad del Bronce de la Motilla del Azuer (Daimiel, Ciudad Real). *Trabajos de Prehistoria* 63 (1), 149–156.

Renfrew, C. 1976. Megaliths, territories and populations, pp. 198–220 in De Leet, J. (ed.) *Acculturation and continuity in Atlantic Europe*. London: Gape.

Renfrew, C. 1984. Arqueología social de los monumentos megalíticos. *Investigación y ciencia* 88, 70–79.

Rigeade, C. 2007. *Les sépultures de catastrophe. Aproche anthropologique des sites d'inhumations en relations avec des épidémies de peste, des masacres, de population et des charies militaires* (BAR International Series 1695). Oxford: Archaeopress.

Rihuete, C. 2000. *Dimensiones bioarqueológicas de los contextos funerarios. Estudio de los restos humanos de la necrópolis prehistórica de la Cova des Cârrix (Ciutadella, Menorca), ca. 1450–800 cal ANE* (BAR International Series 1161). Oxford: Archaeopress.

Ríos, P. 2011. *Territorio y Sociedad en la región de Madrid durante el III milenio AC. El referente del yacimiento de Camino de las Yeseras* (Patrimonio Arqueológico de Madrid 7). Madrid: Universidad Autónoma de Madrid.

Ríos, P. and Liesau, C. 2011. Elementos de adorno simbólicos y colorantes en contextos funerarios y singulares, pp. 357–370 in Blasco, C., Liesau, C. and Ríos, P. (eds), *Yacimientos calcolíticos con campaniformes de la región de Madrid: nuevos estudios* (Patrimonio Arqueológico de Madrid 6). Madrid: Universidad Autónoma de Madrid.

Ríos, P., Blasco, C. and Aliaga, R. 2012. Entre el Calcolítico y la Edad del Bronce. Algunas consideraciones sobre la cronología campaniforme. *Cuadernos de Prehistoria y Arqueología de la Universidad Autónoma de Madrid* 37–38, 195–208.

Shennan, S. J. 1982. Ideology, change and the European Early Bronze Age, pp. 155–161, in Hodder, I. (ed.), *Symbolic and Structural Archaeology*. London: Cambridge University Press.

Smith, P. 1989. Aspectos de la organización de los ritos, pp. 147–179 in Izard, M. and Smith, P., *La función simbólica*. Barcelona: Júcar Universidad.

Tainter, J. A. 1973. The social correlates of mortuary pattering at Kaloko, North Kona, Hawaii. *Archaeology and Physical Anthropology in Oceania* 8, 1–11.

Tainter, J. A. 1975. Social Inference and Mortuary Practices: an Experiment in Numerical Classification. *World Archaeology* 7, 1–15.

Thomas, J. S. 1991. Reading the body. Beaker burials practices in Britain, pp. 33–42 in Garwood, P. (ed.), *Sacred and Profane: Archaeological Method and Theory* (Oxford University Committee for Archaeology Monograph 32). Oxford: Oxford University Press.

Torija, A., Baquedano, I. and De la Cruz, C. 2010. Inhumaciones infantiles en el centro peninsular durante la Protohistoria. Algunas novedades en el yacimiento de Cerrocuquillo, pp. 434–444 in Burillo, F. (ed.), *Ritos y Mitos. VI Simposio sobre Celtíberos*. Segeda: Centro de Estudios Celtibéricos.

Trancho, G. J. and Robledo, B. 2011. Reconstrucción paleonutricional de la población del Camino de las Yeseras, pp. 133–153 in Blasco, C., Liesau, C. and Ríos, P. (eds), *Yacimientos calcolíticos con campaniformes de la región de Madrid: nuevos estudios* (Patrimonio Arqueológico de Madrid 6). Madrid: Universidad Autónoma de Madrid.

Trancho, G. J., Robledo, B., López-Bueis, I. and Fabián F. J. 1996. Reconstrucción del patron alimenticio de dos poblaciones prehistóricas de la Meseta Norte. *Complutum* 7, 73–90.

Ubelaker, H. D. 2007. *Enterramientos Humanos; excavación, análisis, interpretación*. Donostia: Sociedad de Ciencias Aranzadi Zient-zi Elkaretea.

Valiente, J. 1992. *La Loma del Lomo II, Cogolludo, Guadalajara*. Toledo: Junta de Comunidades de Castilla-La Mancha.

Weiss, J. 1973. Demographic models for Anthropology. *American Antiquity* 38 (2) Mem 27.

Zammit, J. 1991. L'émergence des sépultures collectives du Néolithique français: Réflexions et Hypothèses. *L'Anthropologie* 95 (1), 237–256.

# 19

# PREMATURE DEATH IN THE VACCEAN ARISTOCRACY AT PINTIA (PADILLA DE DUERO/PEÑAFIEL, VALLADOLID): COMPARATIVE STUDY OF THE FUNERARY RITUALS OF TWO LITTLE 'PRINCESSES'[1]

## Carlos Sanz Mínguez

## INTRODUCTION

The study of the Iron Age in the middle Douro Valley reveals a significant backwardness with respect to its bordering territories. The lack of historiographic tradition, the premature death of F. Wattenberg – pioneer in the research of the Vaccaei[2] – and, mostly, the lack of awareness of the Vaccean necropolises,[3] recently uncovered, may be among the reasons for the non-definition of the Vaccean identity and its dissolution in the illusion of a *Celtic-Iberization,* an intended process of cultural homogenization during the second Iron Age.[4]

As a consequence, until the late 20th century, the Vaccaei have been best known due to the study and discussion of the brief references provided by classical sources – especially to their well-known agricultural collectivization – rather than by their archaeology.[5] However, this scenario is progressively changing in recent times, partly due to research initiatives carried out in the last 30 years in an important city located on the West boundary of the ancient Vaccean territory: *Pintia*, in Padilla de Duero/ Peñafiel (Valladolid). Nevertheless, the lack of research projects within this territory still handicaps the scope of discoveries, and prevents researchers from extending the data obtained in this enclave to the complete territory.

Bearing this in mind, speaking about infancy in the Vaccean society is almost providential. But the Vaccean-Roman necropolis of *Las Ruedas* at *Pintia*, uncovered in the Sixties in the 20th century, makes it possible today. Its study emerges from the excavation works carried out from 1985 to 1987.[6] Excavations in this area of the archaeological site started again in the year 2000. By the end of the 2012 campaign, a total of 260 cremation tombs, dating back from the 4th century BC to the 2nd century AD, were uncovered. This, although a significant figure, is far from the total number of burials there could have been in this cemetery – several thousand – if we consider that the cemetery is estimated to occupy an extension of six hectares, that the city could count on a population of thousands of inhabitants, and that this burial site remained in use for 600 years. These data provide an overview of the wealth of this burial enclave that, together with the rest of the archaeological site, was declared a National Cultural Asset in 1993.

The child tombs identified, either as individual graves or those linked to adult graves (graves 5, 8, 11, 12, 13, 14, 21, 53, 90, 98, 114, 127b, 153 and 247) are under-represented – only 8% of the total sample – as traditional pre-industrial societies are known to have higher infant mortality rates.[7]

An anthropological[8] study was carried out for the identification of child individuals. Data obtained refer to age thresholds, but do not provide information on gender, due to the difficulties encountered to differentiate them at tender ages and after cremation processes. Thus, deductive criteria were adopted according to the configuration of grave goods, awarding certain artifacts a prevailing role for their symbolic significance to their future adult profiles. We will now focus on these pieces.

## GENDER STEREOTYPES REPRESENTED IN THE TOMBS OF *LAS RUEDAS* NECROPOLIS

Before focusing on some intended aspects, it is to necessary to remark on certain age and gender stereotypes represented in tombs. These, in combination with other symbolic elements, set the grounds for the identification of men, women and children. Assuming that grave goods represent people – age, gender, social position, etc.– bonds and affection, and that certain gestures and rites would be replicated according to these profiles, one of the aims of the archaeological analysis with respect to the burial site should try to isolate behavioural standards derived from the artifacts of the deceased.

We will briefly comment on male stereotypes. It seems evident that, besides the criticism deductive models may raise, weapons have traditionally been considered the most representative male burial symbol. However, the study of 80% of the male tombs including warrior grave goods that were uncovered during the preliminary excavation works in *Las Ruedas* necropolis[9] does not reveal the existence of a military class dedicated to the art of war. Besides, we know the economic model was based on an extensive, surplus grain-producing agricultural model, namely, peasantry.[10] Considering that the reading of grave goods is marked by an ideological filter, much different to the readings of daily life living spaces, the Vaccean society – infused by the agonistic ethics where heroic deeds are achieved through weapons on an individual basis, and where there is a *nice death* that deserves a specific rite, such as exposure to vultures[11] – would present males to the afterlife accompanied by certain symbolic artifacts, prevailing weaponry over tools. Graves 148a and 151, unearthed during the excavation campaigns in 2008, placed together real weaponry and miniature tools. This would synthesize the individual's essential condition from a moral or ethical perspective – represented by the use of weapons – not ignoring the basis of their living: agriculture and farming implements.

To sum up, according to these data, the Vaccei would be a peasant society that, for the symbolic representation of male identity for the afterlife, would observe a warrior component, even though, except for aristocracy, individuals would only seldom, if requested, handle weapons.[12] Nevertheless, it should be noted that, in all cases, the use of weapons was probably an essential part of the world view of these peoples and their rites of passage from infancy to adult life, and to their death.

With respect to the tombs of adult women, the characteristic grave goods included, in general, more ceramic artifacts than metal artifacts. Traditionally, the presence of metal, mainly bronze, refers to tombs of a high social status, with the incorporation of artifacts essentially decorative – probably with a high symbolic value, as well as an apotropaic or protective value – such as pendants, necklaces, fibulae, clasps, etc., but also of artifacts with a functional nature – such as sewing needles – that, together with ceramic spindle whorls, perfectly represent the textile function – spinning, weaving, sewing, embroidering – attached to women in the Circum-Mediterranean Ancient World.

## TOMBS OF LITTLE 'PRINCESSES' IN *LAS RUEDAS* NECROPOLISES

Thus, of all the child burials recorded up to date in this cemetery, we will focus on the child tombs 127b and 153, of an earlier chronology, that date back to the 2nd century BC or early 1st century AD (Fig. 19.1). According to the ample variety of rites that accompanied them, together with the grave goods and offerings included in both sites, both burials could belong to two potential Vaccean 'princesses'. The study of both sites, that according to analysis contained artifacts belonging to two pubescent girls of similar ages, allows us to compare the stereotypes existing for the social status of girls close to becoming adult women,[13] who were daughters to local aristocratic families. The expectations put on them, in terms of starting or preserving exogamic relationships with other territorial communities rich in strategic resources, and a dramatic feeling of loss, after the most critical stages of infancy, give evidence of gestures and emotions, accompanied by symbolism, that refer to different semantic levels – funerary feast, protection, ascribed status, the textile function related to women, immortality or regeneration, etc. Let us focus on these aspects.

## GRAVE 127B

The child tomb 127b, uncovered during the campaign of 2007,[14] is tightly related to grave 127a, which corresponds to an adult woman aged 30–40. Together with grave 128 – another adult woman – the three burial sites form a contemporaneous triad. Their layout in the cemetery was accompanied by exclusive funerary rites, as it was found

*Figure 19.1. (opposite page) A. Map of the Vaccean territory and location of Pintia (Padilla de Duero/Peñafiel, Valladolid). B. Pintia in the Douro Valley, with location of its necropolis (rectangle). C. Partial mapping of the cemetery of Las Ruedas (main grid of 40 m side, divided into ten units of 4 × 4 m), indicating excavated areas (in white), infant burials registered (black dots) and tombs 127b and 153 object of study (circles). D. Tombs 127 a and 127b in situ.*

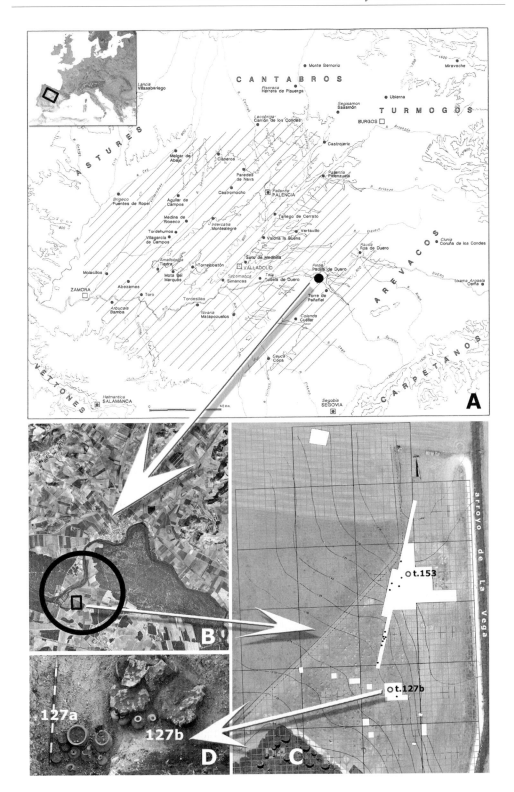

in 2011, when their cremation *bustum* and their commemorative *silicernium*[15] were unearthed when excavation works were expanded to the surrounding area.

Another exceptional element of analysis comes from its location in an ancient area of the cemetery that dates back to the 4th century BC, within the horizontal stratrigraphy defined[16] for it. Such a disposal contrasts with the traditional location adopted for most of the individuals buried in this area.

The burial site, a meter in diameter and displayed in a tangent position with respect to the smaller grave 127a, was 70–140 cm deep, dug in a hole in a sterile terrace of gravel and sands, and protected by five stone slabs of a medium size (35–45 cm long, 20–35 cm wide, and 10 cm thick). Grave 128 was arranged only two meters away to the South-East.

Sixty-nine artifacts (Fig. 19.2) were extracted: 13 painted thrown ceramics (a cup, a goblet, two beaked jugs, three bowls, five flared bottles and a big hollow pot with horizontal handles), two roughly thrown pots (one of them is a funerary urn), four hand-made ceramics (two oval-shaped darkish dishes, comb-decorated; and a pair of small pieces of orange-coloured painted pottery, a conic-frustrum earthenware bowl and a cylindrical bowl with a precise iconic mark);[17] a small animal-shaped box, a rattle and 19 ceramic marbles (14 of them decorated). Amid the stone-made artifacts there were four limestone marbles and an amber bead; the latter was accompanied by three ellipsoid faience beads and six bronze pendants, conforming a sort of necklace. These metal ornaments were found together with six (five bronze and one iron) fibulae – it is shaped like a wolf's head with faience inserted into the eyes – and a small bronze bracelet. A sewing needle and two hemispherical-shaped staples complete the series of bronze artifacts. A tiny grill and tongs were also included, as a symbol of the funerary feast, together with a big-size (probably goose) egg painted in red-coloured tones.

Among the meat offerings, five groups of bones were extracted. After analysis, remains were identified as part of an immature bovid-capra, and an adult leporid.

## GRAVE 153

This tomb, uncovered during the 2008 campaign, yielded the biggest grave good collection found up to date, with 112 artifacts (Figs 19.3 and 19.4). Its location dates back to the late 2nd–1st century BC, so that it may be contemporary to grave 127b. Co-existing with contemporaneous ensembles of notorious richness, it is nevertheless located in a Northern area of the cemetery, in one of its Eastern boundaries, limited by the course of La Vega stream. Its paleochannel – some 40 m away from the current one – has only recently been unearthed.[18]

The grave was found in a round hole 90 cm in diameter, 1–1.40 m deep, in deposits of superimposed levels of a thick appearance.

The burial goods comprised 58 ceramics – 16 hand-made and 42 thrown vessels (amid the latter, there are 22 small unguent bottles). Furthermore, the tomb yielded a variety of unique ceramics: six small animal-shaped boxes, an excise plate with rings, a big marble-rattle, a spindle whorl, 25 marbles (one granite, two clay, and 22 ceramic marbles), eight ceramic pendants and an Hispanic annular fibula (an exceptional copy

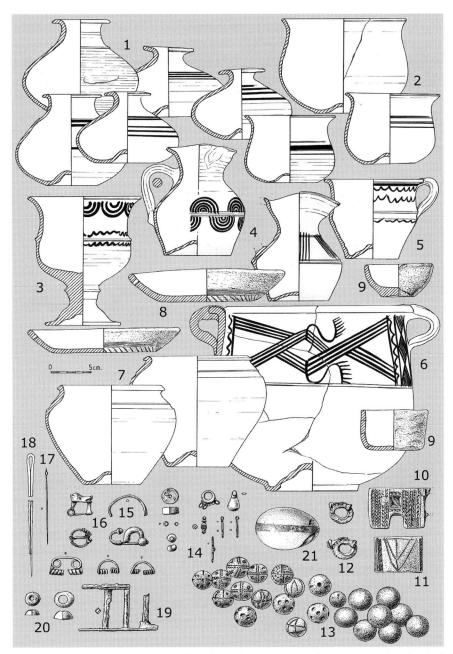

*Figure 19.2. Grave goods and offerings of tomb 127b: 1. Unguent alabastrons; 2. Bowls; 3. Goblet; 4. Beaked jugs; 5. Cup; 6. Large capacity cup; 7. Roughly thrown pot; 8. Hand-made darkish dishes, comb-decorated; 9. Little conic-frustrum and cylindrical hand-made orange-coloured cups; 10. Small animal-shaped box; 11. Rattle; 12. Tendrils for hair; 13. Marbles; 14. Bronze, faience and amber pendants; 15. Little wristband; 16. Fibulae; 17. Sewing needle; 18. Tongs; 19. Grill; 20. Hemispherical-shaped staples; 21. Painted egg.*

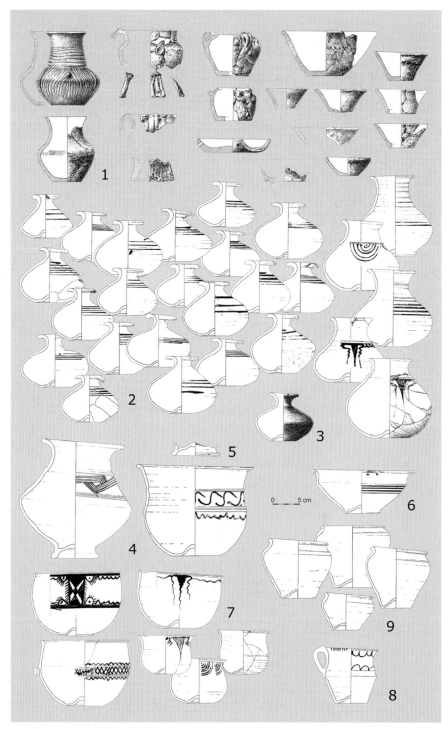

*Figure 19.3. Ceramic containers from tomb 153: 1. Hand-made ceramics; 2. Unguent alabastrons; 3. Polished black-coloured unguent alabastron; 4. Large capacity cups; 5. Trimmed bottom of a ceramic; 6. Darkish dish; 7. Bowls; 8. Cup; 9. Roughly thrown pot.*

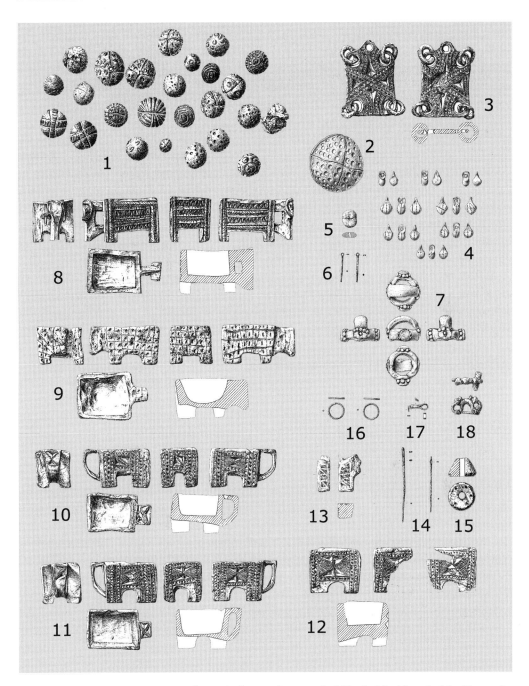

*Figure 19.4. Unique ceramic and metal objects from tomb 153: 1. Marbles; 2. Marble-rattle; 3. Excise plate with rings; 4. Clay pendants; 5. Amber bead; 6. Bronze needle-like pendants; 7. Ceramic Hispanic annular fibula; 8-13. Small animal-shaped boxes; 14. Sewing needles; 15. Spindle whorl; 16. Bronze rings; 17. Iron handle; 18. La Tène symmetrical fibulae.*

of a metal model). Goods also included personal ornaments, like a bead from an amber necklace, and two pins; two bronze needle-like pendants and a symmetric fibula; and an iron handle, maybe from a chest or tiny wooden drawer; as well as two bronze sewing needles. Finally, to emphasise the relevance of this tomb, up to seven groups of meat offerings were also found inside some cups, together with an eggshell.

## COMPARATIVE STUDY

The two girls buried in graves 127b and 153 lived in a period of upheaval, namely between the Celtiberian and Sertorian Wars, during the Roman Conquest of inner *Iberia*, a period that would extend until the turn of the Era, and the subjugation of the Cantabri and the Astures to Augustus. In this dramatic context, both aristocratic Pintian families would have faced the personal tragedy of seeing the expectations to perpetuate their lineage cut short, together with the possibilities of building strategic alliances with other territories through exogamy, as it was traditionally done. [19]

It has been archaeologically demonstrated that, the older the children are before their death, the more prolix and varied their funerary gestures are, as a result of their more developed personality and of tighter affectional bonds.[20] This, together with the privileged position of the families of both girls, makes the semantics of the funerary gestures adopted be of significant dimensions, not common in other child tombs uncovered up to date in *Las Ruedas* cemetery.

The categorization and comparison of the offerings and grave goods of both burials unveil, with certain quantitative variations, the existence of common categories of artifacts that would represent messages of specific intentionality we will analyze in the following paragraphs.

As a result of our finding, diverse categories could be differentiated according to gender, social status, age, ornaments and ostentation, protection, regeneration in the afterlife, etc.

## ASSEMBLAGES UNVEIL THE ARISTOCRATIC SOCIAL STATUS

According to evidence, the assemblages analyzed seem to be among the most outstanding representations documented at *Las Ruedas*, and the tender age of the individuals buried in these graves did not limit the deployment of gestures and offerings traditionally associated with real life achievements, thus proving that social status among the Vaccei would not be acquired, but ascribed.

Graves 127b and 153 yielded 69 and 112 artifacts respectively. After their categorization – joining their parts – the total number is reduced to 56 and 73 artifacts,[21] making them one of the richest discoveries in the cemetery. Before a further count provides a more detailed analysis, and only based on the study of the number of items, the presence of metal artifacts has proven to be a relevant criterion for delimiting the relevance of this necropolis, based on the concept that the presence of metal artifacts in this tomb, in a Vaccean region with limited resources, would add value to the discoveries.[22] In this sense, fibulae, pendants, grills, tongs, sewing needles, bracelets or rings, constitute an expressive record of the richness of these sites, mainly if we consider the usual tradition among the Vaccei to include scarce metal artifacts in female tombs.[23]

Besides, we think that certain ceramic imitations of jewelry – hair-rings in grave 127b (Fig. 19.2: 12) and an Hispanic ceramic annular fibula (Fig. 19.4, 7) and ceramic beads in 153 (Fig. 19.4: 4) – can only be considered indicators of the social status, with a marked symbolism: the replacement of the original gold artifacts used in the world of the living that their rightful heirs would have used in life if death had not taken them away at such an early age.[24]

Summing up, as pointed out in previous lines, there was a direct synchronous link between the girl buried in grave 127b, and graves 127a and 128 belonging to adult women. Her tomb is marked by a splendid sacrificial deployment that included the intake of bovid, suid, bovid-capra, leporid and, even dog. The latter, an unusual example in the cemetery, has an important symbolic meaning.[25]

ARTIFACTS THAT REPRESENT THE FEMALE/INFANT CONDITION

The analysis should first start with those artifacts that would symbolize the female condition of these individuals. Bronze sewing needles and ceramic spindle whorls or spindle counterweights,[26] are some of the explicit references to the textile activity related to women in the Ancient World.[27] Both graves included bronze needles: one in grave 127b (Fig. 19.2: 17) and two in grave 153 (Fig. 19.4: 14). This grave also yielded a tiny ceramic spindle whorl, in a truncated-cone shape and decorated with imprints (Fig. 19.4: 15). In *Las Ruedas* cemetery, grave 12 also yielded a sewing needle associated with a child's tomb, but note that the needle found in grave 24 belonged, according to an anatomical study, to a male individual.[28]

The extraordinary presence of these artifacts in Iberian male tombs does not take importance away from their symbolic value.[29] Nevertheless, these textile materials could also provide a less symbolic and more practical interpretation. This would refer to the fabric as a product with economic, political and social dimensions,[30] well-known through Classical literature, which referred to the renowned Vaccean wool capes – *saga* – as for example, in the campaign of L. Licinius Lucullus in 151 BC,[31] when he demanded them as a war tribute after he besieged *Cauca*.

In this sense, the child characteristics of both assemblages is specially marked by the two ceramic hair-rings (Fig. 19.2: 12) and a pair of bronze rings with rope mouldings (Fig. 19.4: 16) found in graves 127b and 153. Even though there are other ornament artifacts we will also refer to, the present ones are, in our opinion, especially expressive.

The iconic richness displayed by the Iberian world through the large-format stone sculptures in their necropolis, their votive offerings in sanctuaries, their quality ceramics, etc., unveil some of the distinctive attributes of women, and, specially, of their hairdos and dresses in relation to their age. Thus, even though braids were also found in teenage male individuals, they were mainly used by women, and they are adopted as a symbolic-formal characteristic of youth.[32] Probably the little 'ladies' from the necropolis of *Corral de Saus de Moixent* (Valencia) may be the sculptures that best represent the aesthetics of Iberian young women of a high social status. In contrast to the characteristic clothes of Iberian women – with tunics, veils and a thick shawl, dressed and brushed with thick ornaments over their heads and elaborate necklaces or earrings – these ladies are dressed in loose tunics hugged by a belt, with a hairband, pendant earrings, necklace, spiral bracelets, but, most interestingly of all, brushed with long thick braids dressed by hair rings.[33]

According to these data, it seems probable that our Vaccean girls were dressed with similar braids that made reference to their young age, and that all these artifacts – ceramic gold imitation hair-rings or bronze earrings – were used as ornaments. Grave 127b is suspected to have also included a belt to hug her waist, decorated with bronze hemispherical rivets (Fig. 19.2: 20).

We will briefly refer to the presence of beads or marbles: 23 in grave 127b (Fig. 19.2: 13) – four stone and 19 ceramic marbles, six plain and the rest of them decorated, from 20–30 mm in diameter – and 25 in grave 153 (Fig. 19.4: 1) – one granite, two clay and 22 ceramic marbles, from 17 and 40 mm in diameter, all of them showing a specially original and detailed decoration. The presence of spheroids in burials is referenced in the Neolithic, throughout the Bronze Age and up to the Iron Age, but no other context shows such a prevailing use as in the case of Vaccean tombs, associated with child burials, as well as to the tombs of male and female adults.[34] These circumstances obscure our interpretation of these artifacts in some Iberian child burials, following Attic models, as in grave 51 in *Turó dels Dos Pins*, which included one of these ceramic decorated marbles used as symbols of child and female in a single state, that were offered to Persephone short before the wedding as a symbol of the infancy that is left behind.[35]

ARTIFACTS THAT REPRESENT SOURCE TRADITIONS: WHEEL-THROWN CERAMICS AND RELICS

The display of the diverse ceramic well-fired wheel-thrown vessels, or poorly-fired hand-made vessels, must be related to the correspondent food or viaticum offerings to the great beyond, both for the deceased or for gods. The analysis of the remains found in different ceramic containers of *Las Ruedas*, has provided evidence of the presence of animal fats, arropes, oils, dairy products and beverages such as beer, mead or wine.[36] Nevertheless, no specific data have yet been drawn from the vessels collected from graves 153 and 127b.

Amid the pottery artifacts, hand-made vessels really attract attention. In this sense grave 153 (Fig. 19.3: 1) provides a better display than grave 127b (Fig. 19.2: 8). During the late 2nd century or the early 1st century BC, these would be considered *traditional pottery*, as they would no longer be present in domestic uses, and would only be symbolically adopted in the funerary world. As a consequence, in most cases, pottery is not fired, so that its characteristic dark colour comes from a low-temperature combustion process.[37] This grave good collection is formed by heavily burnished bottles and three-legged cups with coming-in rims, that share a taste for a decoration with mamelons and handles; a comb-decorated plate that recalls those earlier peculiar productions nowadays missing;[38] tiny conic-frustrum earthenware bowls, plain[39] or with some eel-shaped imprints, as well as a small dish. In the case of grave 127b, this sort of pottery is only represented by two comb-decorated oval-shaped dishes. These containers might have been used for diverse food offerings.

In short, these artifacts with a limited functionality – or useless – beyond funerary rituals, witness earlier times and ancestral rituals that survive in a context resistant to change.

In archaeology, the concept of 'relic' is used for objects with a chronology that differs significantly from a considerable later context. For instance, the extraordinary scabbard of a *Monte Bernorio* dagger, related to a warrior aristocracy, was found in a Pintian house from the 1st century AD; its production chronology, however, dates from the 4th century BC and refers to its transfer among 20 generations.[40] As a consequence, the Hispanic annular fibula (Fig. 19.2: 16) and the tiny bracelet of the girl buried in grave 127b (Fig. 19.2: 15), both of them made in bronze, could also be identified as 'relics': the fibula is an ancient model that dates from the 4th century BC, whereas the sort of tiny bracelet found in *Las Ruedas* corresponds to models uncovered in ancient layers of the horizontal stratigraphy.[41]

The co-existence, in one context and the other, of artifacts from the 4th century BC is not surprising, as the idiosyncrasy of the Vaccean world develops in this historical moment and, as a result, the myth of origin or the cosmological concept that provided an answer to the Vaccean universe could have come true in the form of certain uses, habits and material artifacts.

## WHEEL-THROWN HEART-SHAPED CERAMICS AND OTHER *VIATICUM* ARTIFACTS RELATED TO THE FUNERARY FEAST

Wheel-thrown ceramics predominate in this area of the cemetery, and unveil certain standardization in ritual gestures, as could be derived from the duplicated forms in both burial sites. It seems evident they might have been associated with specific products.

Thus, first of all, it is worth noting, in the most representative assemblages in the cemetery, the presence of big crater-shaped vessels, outstanding for their size and capacity: grave 153 yielded two (totalling 6,800 ml) (Fig. 19.3: 4 and 5), and grave 127b one (Fig. 19.2: 6) ceramic cooking-pot with two handles (7,500 ml). Studies carried out with similar vessels from *Las Ruedas* unveil the presence of alcoholic beverages such as wine, beer or mead.[42] Small cups – a cylindrical cup (150 ml) and a conic-frustrum cup (75 ml) found in grave 127b (Fig. 19.2: 9), wheel-thrown and fired in an oxidizing ambient that provides the traditional orange colour – are usually related to these big containers and make them be considered unrefined *cyathus* or ladles,[43] used to serve liquids out of the big containers, according to a given measure (50 measures of the cylindrical cup would equal the capacity of the cooking-pot found in grave 127b). No equivalent artifact was found in grave 153, except for a broken base of a wheel-thrown vessel (Fig. 19.3: 5) that could have had the same use (40 ml).

The presence of alcoholic beverages in grave goods found in child tombs[44] may be surprising. Nevertheless, it seems that the aristocratic condition prevailed, as other ceramic sets associated with beverages and the funerary feast are also found: two beak-jugs[45] and a cup in grave 127b (Fig. 19.2: 3 and 4), together with other artifacts traditionally used in food processing, such as a miniature grill and tongs (Fig. 19.2: 18 and 19),[46] and a small spice-box/saltcellar (Fig. 19.2: 10).

Vessels are well represented in both assemblages (Fig. 19.2: 2; Fig. 19.3: 7) – six (6,500 ml) in 153 and three in 127b (2,490 ml) – and, if results from the analysis of graves 20 and 29 in *Las Ruedas*[47] are made extensive, they could have contained dairy products, fresh fruits preserved in honey, and cereals. Curiously enough, both collections include a cup (Fig. 19.2: 5; Fig. 19.3: 8) of similar shape and capacity (530 ml and 430 ml), that would suggest that the same potter manufactured both pieces.

The unrefined pots (Fig. 19.2: 7; Fig. 19.3: 9) were used in both cases as funerary urns, but they were also used as containers for meat offerings (young bovid-capra). It should also be noted the presence of remains of lagomorphs and bovid-capra in both tombs, as well as of suid in grave 153, that bear witness of the funeral feast.

## Unguent bottles and personal hygiene

Grave 153 yielded 22 ceramic flared unguent alabastrons[48] that (Fig. 19.3: 2) shine in their own right. Among all these small orange-coloured containers decorated with simple spiral designs in manganese dioxide, attention focuses on a polished and poorly-fired one with an intense black colour.[49] Together with this tiny bottle, five other similar bottles of a bigger capacity that might have also contained unguents were also found. The capacities of all these containers total some 13 litres of oils, making this amount really extraordinary among the burial sites uncovered up to date in *Las Ruedas*.

Even though under-represented, this ceramic group was also found in grave 127b, with five artifacts (three small and two bigger ones) (Fig. 19.2: 1).

It seems then evident that part of these offerings was devoted to personal hygiene, through the application of oils to the skin, although culinary uses or even uses related to religious ceremonies could not be disregarded.

Could the presence of a small iron handle (Fig. 19.4: 17) – possibly part of a tiny wooden drawer – be related to a woman's dressing table?

## Ornament and protection

To end up with, we will focus on a heterogeneous group of artifacts that might have been granted protective purpose.

From their birth, children are provided special attentions with the aim of ensuring their future development, their family and community integration, and to ward off the curse of evil eye and other bad influences by using simple charms in the form of rings, bracelets or earrings.[50] This protective function would explain why both girls wore necklaces made up of beads of a diverse nature and typology. Grave 127b yielded ten artifacts (Fig. 19.2: 14): three faience ellipsoid beads, a dish-shaped amber bead[51] and six bronze pendants – needle-shaped, acorn-shaped or crescent moon-shaped with pending rings.[52] The girl buried in grave 153 was accompanied by eleven pendants: two bronze needle-like pendants (Fig. 19.4: 6), an amber pendant (Fig. 19.4: 5) and eight clay beads (Fig. 19.4: 4) that probably imitated pieces made in precious metals.

We must now focus on fibulae (Fig. 19.2: 16). Apart from their use to fasten clothing, their protective nature seems evident. Grave 127b included a bronze wolf's head with faience inserted into the eyes. Once fastened on the clothing, this would provide a similar perspective to the overhead view of the four-legged zoomorph also found in different Vaccean and Arevacian foundations, and characterized by its marked protective character.[53] The bronze relic found in this tomb, a Hispanic annular fibula, would serve to call on a genealogical benefactor, an ancestor.

The protective function is also represented by rattles – a circular stamped one in grave 153 (Fig. 19.4: 2) and a cylindrical incised one in grave 127b (Fig. 19.2: 11) – or a mysterious ceramic plate pierced with rings, in a bull skin shape (Fig. 19.4: 3), in grave 153. The universal value of tinkling to chase away evil spirits would be reinforced by the exclusive excise decoration of these original Vaccean productions.[54] Therefore, we think that the six animal-shaped small boxes of grave 153 (Fig. 19.4: 9–13) – together with the one found in grave 127b (Fig. 19.2: 10) – and specially one of them with a mutton's head-shaped handle, may have had some protective role extended in funerary rituals. The over 150 vessels of this type uncovered so far in the cemetery of *Las Ruedas*, explain how their symbolic/eschatological value[55] was extended and accepted. Besides, considering they might have been used, mainly, as saltcellars/spice-boxes, it is to remark the symbolism of the so called 'white gold' in the Ancient World as an element representing wealth and protection.

Finally, the presence in both tombs of ochre and eggs, one of them – grave 153 – painted in wine colours and with its surface divided in three areas, should be considered with respect to their protective/regenerative sense.

We have analyzed the composition of two really extraordinary child burials in the Vaccean cemetery of *Las Ruedas*, and we have found common configuration patterns, with artifacts that, in most cases, refer to material fields similar to the ones found in adult burials. The absence of toys – except for marbles and rattles, which are also present in some adult burials – indicates how, at least for this aristocratic class, prepubescent and pubescent girls could have had a role in the world of adults. In contrast to this situation, differences can also be found in graves 12[56] and 90[57] in *Las Ruedas*. Although these burial sites are not the most representative examples, they indicate certain social status and, according to their anthropological analysis, they belong to individuals of tender age; that is, infants or prepubescent children. Both ensembles include multiple miniature ceramic artifacts, real toys, which seem to unveil a different ritual for more tender ages.

To conclude, the number of child burials in *Las Ruedas* cemetery is surprisingly small, and we consider it is under-represented according to the infant mortality rates traditionally known for pre-industrial societies. The presence of modest burials – such as grave 53 – with a single metal ring as part of the grave goods,[58] or other burials that only contained cremated bones – such as grave 14[59] – rejects the idea that only individuals of a certain social status were buried in this cemetery. There might be specific areas in the cemetery reserved for *mors prematura,* but no evidence has yet been found in this sense. Hopefully, future research campaigns and the preservation of the endangered Pintian cemetery of *Las Ruedas,*[60] will shed light on this, and on the study of infancy in pre-Roman Vaccean societies.

## Notes

1   This work is part of the research project (2011–2013) *Cosmovisión y simbología vacceas. Nuevas perspectivas de análisis* (HAR2010-21745-C03-01) ('World view and Vaccean symbology. New approaches for the analysis'), funded by the Directorate-General for Innovation of the Ministry of Economy and Competitiveness
2   Wattenberg 1959
3   Sanz 2010a
4   Sanz 1997a: 505–512
5   For a detailed synthesis on the historiography of the Vaccei from their sources to the archaeology, and on the lack of dialogue among disciplines, refer to Sánchez-Moreno, 2010
6   Sanz 1990; 1997a
7   Sanz 1997a: 495
8   The analysis of the bone remains found in grave 127b was carried out by Prof. Javier Velasco Vazquez, who estimates an approximate age of 7–8 years due to the lack of eruption of molars. The remains of grave 153 have been studied by Professors Félix de Paz, Mercedes Barbosa and José Francisco Pastor, from the Department of Anatomy and Radiology, of the Faculty of Medicine, University of Valladolid. Their analysis drew similar results: 7 to 12 years old
9   Sanz 1997a
10  For general information on the Vaccei, see Sanz and Martín 2001
11  Eliano (*De Nat. An.* 10,22); Sopeña, 2004
12  Sanz 2008; 2010b
13  The age of both girls would be among *infantia* and *adolescentia*: *puertitia*. This is the moment when the first permanent teeth come out and the age of reason starts. It is to remark the symbolism of number 7 in the Ancient World and throughout the Middle Ages. (Buchet and Séguy 2008, 31; Chapa Brunet 2008, 619–621)
14  Sanz and Romero Carnicero 2008
15  Sanz 2012a; 2012b
16  Sanz 1997a, 467–476
17  De Bernardo, Romero Carnicero and Sanz 2012, 178
18  Sanz and Carrascal 2013
19  Graves 27 and 31 in *Las Ruedas*, include *Bureba* booches, associated to aristocratic burials of warriors 28 and 32, as suggested for the Turmodigi and Vaccei (Romero and Sanz 2009, 82–84; Sanz and Romero 2010, 415–416)
20  In the village *Las Eretas* (Berbinzana, Navarra) of the total number of child burials unearthed, only graves 2 and 5, older than the average (full-term foetus and children within the first three months of life) included grave goods consisting of a small ceramic cup and a stone marble in grave 2, and a small ceramic cup, a necklace bead and a bronze ring in grave 5. (Armendáriz and De Miguel 2006, 38–39)
21  Grave 127b: 42 ceramic artifacts, a rattle, a tiny box, two ceramic hair-rings, a set of 23 marbles, six fibulae, a sewing needle, a grill and tongs, a necklace with ten beads and a painted goose-egg. Grave 153: 58 ceramics, a ceramic Hispanic annular fibula, a rattle, six tiny boxes, an excise

plate with pendant rings, a set of 25 marbles, a textile set with two sewing needles and a spindle whorl, a pair of bronze hair-rings, a necklace with eleven beads, a symmetric bronze fibula and a tiny wooden drawer with its iron handle missing

22 Sanz 1997a, 483

23 Sanz 1997a, 501

24 Sanz and Romero Carnicero 2009; Romero Carnicero and Sanz 2010

25 Sanz 2012a, 11–13

26 Examples of decontextualized ceramic rolls are found in the cemetery of *Las Ruedas*. In *Pintia*, the *pondera* or loom counterweights are almost exclusively present up to date, in domestic settings

27 If we consider textile activity as a productive activity and observe its operative structure, male involvement is referred in Mesopotamia, Egypt and the Aegean during the second millennium BC, mainly related to obtaining, dying and finishing raw material (García, 2005, 137). In the greek ideology, women and textile activity were tightly associated. This bond was used to represent *philergia* as one of the essential virtues of women (Mirón Pérez, 2007, 273). Prados Torreira (2008, 236) recalls Ephor's reference to the Iberian Peninsula: he stresses the importance of fabric among women as indicated by the yearly public exhibition of the fabrics weaved and the election, by a group of men, of the best works

28 Sanz 1997a, 408. Even though the assemblage was much altered and its associations are barely representative

29 In general terms, spinning and knitting have been considered two examples of the female condition in the Iberian world, with explicit iconic representations in potteries, as in *San Miguel de Liria* (Izquierdo 2008). The presence of spindle whorls in some Iberian male tombs does not add a contradictory approach. In any case, as indicated by Binford and Saxe, rituals and burials will frequently be conditioned by the size and volume of the individuals buried, as by the social bonds or the lineage of the deceased. Thus, the presence of spindle whorls in some burials together with weaponry could well be interpreted as offerings, not as grave goods, or belongings. The symbolism of spindle whorls in rites of passage, mainly marriage and death, could also be the answer to their presence in male tombs (Rísquez and García 2007, 156)

30 Rafel Fontanals, 2007, 135. This perspective is considerably marked in the princely female grave goods of grave 200 in *El Cigarralejo*. The grave goods found seem to indicate that the textile activity represents economic control rather than the textile activity associated to the female condition (Rísquez and García 2007, 155–163)

31 Apiano *Iberia*, 50–55

32 Izquierdo 2008, 124–125; Rueda Galán 2008, 67–68

33 Izquierdo 1999; also present in votive offerings associated to rites of passage found in Iberian sanctuaries (Rueda, 2008)

34 Sanz 1997a. Over a thousand of them have been found up to date

35 Chapa Brunet 2003, 128–129. In the Vaccean context, the presence of a small bottle in grave 11 of *Las Erijuelas* necropolis in Cuéllar (Barrio Martin 1988, 134) that used one of these small beads as a top, and another three formed a triangle to stabilize the unguent-bottle, could indicate both functional and symbolic values. In any case, the biggest number of beads found up to date in the necropolis *Las Ruedas* corresponds to graves 127b and 153. In the case of grave 153, the number coincides approximately with an unusual deployment of unguent-bottles. Could they have been used as tops, even though they were not touching their correspondent bottles?

36 Sanz *et al.* 2003

37 These circumstances create important preservation problems. Clay doughs that can barely be isolated, or have been diluted, are frequently found during excavation works

38 First present during the 1st Iron Age, comb-decorated pottery evolved during the 2nd Iron Age, giving rise to more excessive comb-decoration and to specific groups, such as the comb imprints of the Vaccean world (Sanz 1999)

39  Artifacts in other Pintian burials contained remains of animal fats (Sanz *et al.* 2003, 156, group I). Their symbolic value may be associated to cultural structures from the 1st Iron Age, as unveiled in *La Corona-El Pesadero*, where three of these vessels and a *sympulum* were related to grave 24 (Romero Carnicero, Sanz and Górriz 2009, 232–233)

40  Sanz 2008

41  Sanz 1997a, 401–402

42  Group IV of containers includes a *kernoi* (Sanz *et al.* 2003, 155–157)

43  One of these small containers found in grave 84 in Las Ruedas, in *Pintia*, provided remains of tartrates associated to wine consumption, together with a big-size crater-shaped vessel (Sanz, Romero Carnicero and Górriz, 2010:601). Both are atavistic containers in a liturgy timidly adapted to modern times, as represented in their oxidizing firing processes, in contrast to the traditional dark pottery that strongly recall cultural settings of the 1st Iron Age (*see.* footnote 39)

44  The *silicernium* found in grave 20 in *Los Villares* contained three small mugs or greek *coes*, with child decoration. These were offered to three and four-year-old boys during the Dyonisian festival of Anthesteria. This is a surprising finding in an Iberian context, as these artifacts were not normally exported. Nevertheless, their presence is not by chance. Regardless potential similarities, they may have been acquired for child addressees of the family unit (Chapa Brunet, 2008: 631–632). As for the Vaccean world, we have pointed out that the funerary feast expanded not only to aristocratic warriors, but also to their spouses and offspring (Sanz *et al.* 2009; Sanz, Romero and Górriz 2010)

45  410 and 500 ml- jugs, significantly smaller than the traditional jugs (2000 ml) found in other burial sites, may be conditioned by the child profile of the offering. It is also remarkable the ochre coating of one of the jugs. Would it reinforce the wine concept, or the genesis forces?

46  Symbolic artifacts also present in adult burials and that, as a consequence, should not be considered toys

47  II Group of containers (Sanz *et al.* 2003, 155).

48  The interpretation as unguent-bottles is due to the identification in similar containers found in some graves in *Las Ruedas*, of fatty acids (mainly oleic acid) and pollens of *Rosaceae*, *Rosmarinus*, *Pinus*, *Ulmus* and *Salix* that refer to the presence of scented vegetal oils (probably olive). (Sanz *et al.* 2003, 155, group V; Juan Treserras, J. and Carles Matamala 2003, 314 and 315)

49  Romero *et al.*, 2012: 625. Form XI. With a finishing touch surprisingly similar to the one of 'black wheel-thrown pottery', it would be interesting to determine the substance it contained

50  Dasen 2003

51  Together with the one found in grave 153, these are the only beads documented in the cemetery. The analysis of these pieces has not yet been carried out, as the beads present a much damaged surface. Fractures in one of them reveal a red-color core. Nevertheless, it is not yet possible to determine the origin of its raw material: either native from the Iberian Peninsula (diverse locations, generally from the Cretaceous, reddish and more brittle) or of a Baltic origin (more yellowish and of simpler sculpture) (Cerdeño *et al.* 2012)

52  This pendant with rings is identical to the one preserved in the *Lazaro Galdiano* Museum in Madrid, unknown, but probably from *Monte Bernorio*. Curiously, this artifact is accompanied by other elements with a common aesthetics of mobile rings, as in the case of a horse-shaped fibula or more schematic models with up to 29 small rings (Sanz 1997b, 251, fig. 4, 23). For the protective value of tinkling, read *infra*

53  This may be a deity, as suggested by expression of the *Monte Bernorio* dagger handle uncovered in grave 32 in *Las Ruedas* necrópolis – tripled and following the universal conventionalism of representation: centered and bigger in size than the rest of elements – (Sanz 1997a, 439–448; a detailed study in Romero Carnicero and Sanz 1992; and an update in Romero 2010)

54  Small boxes, rattles, bases, small boats, plates, animal shapes, *sympulum* and other containers with a marked liturgical function, share this knife-beveled technique in number 45. This should intrinsically provide protective effects (Sanz 1997a, 169–176, 314–349)

55  Sanz, Carrascal and Rodríguez, 2014
56  Sanz 1997a, 60
57  Sanz and Diezhandino 2007, 99–102
58  Sanz 1997a, 124
59  Sanz 1997a, 61–62
60  We think it is a citizen's duty to use all the possible scenarios to condemn that an area of the cemetery is still being ploughed and dismantled. Efforts at preserving the site are explained in Sanz *et al.* 2013

REFERENCES

Armendáriz Martija, J. and De Miguel Ibáñez, M. P. 2006. Los enterramientos infantiles del poblado de Las Eretas (Berbinzana). Estudio paleoantropológico, *Trabajos de Arqueología Navarra*, 19, 5–43.
Barrio Martín, J. 1988. *Las cerámicas de la necrópolis de Las Erijuelas, Cuéllar (Segovia). Estudios de sus producciones cerámicas en el marco de la II Edad del Hierro en la Meseta norte*, Diputación Provincial de Segovia, Segovia.
Buchet, L. and Séguy, I. 2008. L'âge au décès des enfants: âge civil, âge biologique, âge social?, en F. Gusi, S. Muriel and C. Olària, *Nasciturus, infans, puerulus, vobis mater terra*, SIAP – Diputació de Castelló, Castelló: 25–39.
Cerdeño, M. L., Martínez, J. A., Agua, F., Sagardoy, T. and Monasterio, M. 2012. Ámbar en la Meseta Oriental durante el Bronce Final: yacimientos locales e importaciones bálticas, *Trabajos de Prehistoria*, 69, nº 2, 375–384.
Chapa Brunet, T. 2003. La percepción de la infancia en el mundo ibérico, *Trabajos de Prehistoria*, 60, nº 1, 115–138.
Chapa Brunet, T. 2008, Presencia infantil y ritual funerario en el mundo ibérico, en F. Gusi, S. Muriel and C. Olària, *Nasciturus, infans, puerulus, vobis mater terra*, SIAP – Diputació de Castelló, Castelló: 619–641.
Dasen, V. 2003. Les amulettes d'enfants dans le monde gréco-romain, *Latomus*, 62, fasc. 2, Société d'Etudes Latines de Bruselas, 275–289.
De Bernardo, P., Romero Carnicero, F. and Sanz Mínguez, C. 2012. Grafitos con signario celtibérico en cerámicas de *Pintia* (Padilla de Duero-Peñafiel, Valladolid), *Palaeohispanica* 12, 157–194.
García, A. 2005. Producción textil y división sexual del trabajo en la Antigüedad. Mesopotamia, Egipto y el Egeo en el segundo milenio a.n.e., *Historiae*, 2, 115–142.
Izquierdo, M. I. 1999. Las 'damitas' de Moixent en el contexto de la plástica y la sociedad ibérica, *Lucentum*, XVII–XVIII, 1998–1999, 131–147.
Izquierdo, M. I. 2008, Arqueología, iconografía y género: códigos en femenino del imaginario ibérico, *Verdolay*, 11, Murcia, 121–142.
Juan Treserras, J. and Carles Matamala, J. 2003. Análisis de adobe, pigmentos, contenidos de recipientes, instrumental textil, material lítico de molienda y cálculo dental humano procedentes del yacimiento de *Pintia*, en C. Sanz Mínguez and J. Velasco Vázquez (eds), *Pintia. Un oppidum en los confines orientales de la región vaccea. Investigaciones arqueológicas Vacceas, Romanas y Visigodas (1999–2003)*, Valladolid: Universidad de Valladolid, 311–322.
Mirón Pérez, M. D. 2007. Los trabajos de las mujeres y la economía de las unidades domésticas en la Grecia Clásica, *Complutum* vol. 18, 271–280.
Prados Torreira, L. 2008. Y la mujer se hace visible: estudios de género en la arqueología ibérica, en L. Prados Torreira and C. Ruiz López (coords.), *Arqueología del Género, 1er encuentro internacional de la UAM*, Universidad Autónoma de Madrid, Madrid, 225–250.
Rafel Fontanals, N. 2007. El textil como indicador de género en el registro funerario ibérico, *Interpreting household practices*, Barcelona, 21–24 November 2007. *Treballs d'Arqueologia* 13, 115–146.

Rísquez, C. and García Luque, A. 2007. ¿Actividades de mantenimiento en el registro funerario? El caso de las necrópolis ibéricas, *Interpreting household practices*, Barcelona, 21–24 november 2007. *Treballs d'Arqueologia* 13, 145–173.

Romero Carnicero, F. 2010. Las representaciones zoomorfas en perspectiva cenital. Un estado de la cuestión, en F. Romero Carnicero and C. Sanz Mínguez (eds), *De la Región Vaccea a la Arqueología Vaccea*, Vaccea Monografías, 4, Valladolid: Universidad de Valladolid, Centro de Estudios Vacceos 'Federico Wattenberg', 467–545.

Romero Carnicero, F. and Sanz Mínguez, C. 1992. Representaciones zoomorfas prerromanas en perspectiva cenital. Iconografía, cronología y dispersión geográfica, *II Simposio de Arqueología Soriana,* Soria, 1989, Soria, 453–471.

Romero Carnicero, F. and Sanz Mínguez, C. 2009. Tiempo y género a partir de la Arqueología. Las necrópolis de *Pintia* (Padilla de Duero/Peñafiel, Valladolid), en M.I. del Val, C. de la Rosa, M. J. Dueñas and M. Santo Tomás (coords.), *Protagonistas del pasado. Las mujeres desde la Prehistoria al siglo XX*, Ed. Castilla, 59–103.

Romero Carnicero, F. and Sanz Mínguez, C. 2010. Réplicas en barro de la orfebrería vaccea, en F. Romero Carnicero and C. Sanz Mínguez (eds.), *De la Región Vaccea a la Arqueología Vaccea*, Vaccea Monografías, 4, Valladolid: Universidad de Valladolid, Centro de Estudios Vacceos 'Federico Wattenberg', 437–465.

Romero Carnicero, F., Sanz Mínguez, C. and Górriz Gañán, C. 2009. El vino entre las élites vacceas. De los más antiguos testimonios a la consolidación de su consumo, en C. Sanz Mínguez and F. Romero Carnicero, El Vino y el banquete en la Europa prerromana, Vaccea Monografías, 2, Valladolid: Universidad de Valladolid, Centro de Estudios Vacceos 'Federico Wattenberg', 225–251.

Romero Carnicero, F., Sanz Mínguez, C., Górriz Gañán, C. and De Pablo Martínez, R. 2012. Cerámicas negras bruñidas del oriente vacceo, *Cerámicas hispanorromanas II. Producciones regionales. Monografías Historia y Arte*, Universidad de Cádiz, Cádiz, 619–638.

Rueda Galán, C. 2008. Las imágenes de los santuarios de Cástulo: los exvotos ibéricos en bronce de Collado de Los Jardines (Santa Elena) y los Altos del Sotillo (Castellar), *Palaeohispanica*, 8, 55–87.

Sánchez-Moreno, E. 2010. Los vacceos a través de las fuentes: una perspectiva actual, en F. Romero Carnicero and C. Sanz Mínguez (eds.), *De la Región Vaccea a la Arqueología Vaccea*, Vaccea Monografías, 4, Valladolid: Universidad de Valladolid, Centro de Estudios Vacceos 'Federico Wattenberg', 65–103.

Sanz Mínguez, C. 1990. Rituales funerarios en la necrópolis celtibérica de Las Ruedas, Padilla de Duero (Valladolid), *II Simposio sobre los Celtíberos: Necrópolis Celtibéricas, Daroca*, 1988, Zaragoza, 159–170.

Sanz Mínguez, C. 1997a. *Los vacceos: Cultura y ritos funerarios de un pueblo prerromano del valle medio del Duero. La necrópolis de Las Ruedas, Padilla de Duero (Valladolid)*, Memorias, Arqueología en Castilla y León, 6. Salamanca.

Sanz Mínguez, C. 1997b. Bronces prerromanos de la Meseta Norte en el Museo Lázaro Galdiano, *Goya*, 256, 1997, 241–252.

Sanz Mínguez, C. 2008. Un puñal reliquia vacceo hallado en *Pintia* (Padilla de Duero, Valladolid)", *GLADIUS, Estudios sobre armas antiguas, arte militar y vida cultural en oriente y occidente*, XXVIII, CSIC, Madrid, 177–194.

Sanz Mínguez, C. 1999. La cerámica a peine. Nuevos datos para la definición de un estilo impreso en el grupo vacceo, *II Congreso de Arqueología Peninsular, t. III*, Zamora, 1996, Madrid, 249–273.

Sanz Mínguez, C. 2010a. Un vacío vacceo historiográfico: sus necrópolis, en F. Romero Carnicero and C. Sanz Mínguez (eds), *De la Región Vaccea a la Arqueología Vaccea*, Vaccea Monografías, 4, Valladolid: Universidad de Valladolid, Centro de Estudios Vacceos 'Federico Wattenberg', 193–230.

Sanz Mínguez, C. 2010b. El armamento vacceo, en F. Romero Carnicero and C. Sanz Mínguez (eds), *De la Región Vaccea a la Arqueología Vaccea*, Vaccea Monografías, 4, Valladolid: Universidad de Valladolid, Centro de Estudios Vacceos "Federico Wattenberg", 319–361.

Sanz Mínguez, C. 2012a. Campaña XXII–2011 de excavaciones arqueológicas en *Pintia* (Padilla de Duero/Peñafiel), *Vaccea Anuario, 2011*, 5, Valladolid: Universidad de Valladolid, Centro de Estudios Vacceos 'Federico Wattenberg', 6–14.

Sanz Mínguez, C. 2012b. Aristocracia vaccea en femenino. Las tumbas 127a, 127b y 128 de la necrópolis de Las Ruedas (*Pintia*, Padilla de Duero/Peñafiel, Valladolid), *Gaceta Cultural Ateneo de Valladolid*. Abril–mayo–junio 2012, nº 62, 4–7.

Sanz Mínguez, C. and Carrascal Arranz, J. M. 2013. Campaña XXIII-2012 de excavaciones arqueológicas en *Pintia* (Padilla de Duero/Peñafiel), *Vaccea Anuario, 2012*, 6, Valladolid: Universidad de Valladolid, Centro de Estudios Vacceos 'Federico Wattenberg', 6–12.

Sanz Mínguez, C., Carrascal Arranz, J. M. and Rodríguez Gutiérrez, E. 2014, Saleros-especieros zoomorfos, en técnica excisa, de barro y cerámica, del territorio vacceo (ss. IV-I a.C.), en R. Morais, A. Fernández and M. J. Sousa (eds), As produçoes cerámicas de imitaçao na Hispania, Monografías Ex Officina Hispana II, tomo II, Porto, 199–212.

Sanz Mínguez, C. and Diezhandino Couceiro, E. 2007. en C. Sanz Mínguez and F. Romero Carnicero (eds), En los extremos de la Región Vaccea, León, 99–102.

Sanz Mínguez, C. and Martín Valls, R., Los Vacceos, 2001, en M. Almagro Gorbea (Com.), *Catálogo de la exposición Celtas y Vettones*, Ávila, 314–325.

Sanz Minguez, C. and Romero Carnicero, F. 2008. "Campaña XVIII (2007) de excavaciones arqueológicas en Pintia (Padilla de Duero/Peñafiel)", en C. Sanz Mínguez and F. Romero Carnicero (dirs.), Vaccea Anuario 2007, Centro de Estudios Vacceos 'Federico Wattenberg' de la Universidad de Valladolid, Valladolid, 6–12.

Sanz Mínguez, C. and Romero Carnicero, F. 2009. Joyas de barro vacceas, en C. Sanz Mínguez and F. Romero Carnicero (dirs.), *Vaccea Anuario 2008*, Valladolid: Universidad de Valladolid, Centro de Estudios Vacceos 'Federico Wattenberg', 55–59.

Sanz Mínguez, C. and Romero Carnicero, F. 2010. Mujeres, rango social y herencia en la necrópolis vaccea de Las Ruedas, *Pintia* (Padilla de Duero/Peñafiel, Valladolid), en F. Burillo Mozota (coord.), *Ritos y mitos, VI Simposio sobre Celtíberos, Daroca*, 27–29 de noviembre de 2008, Zaragoza: Centro de Estudios Celtibéricos de Segeda, 403–420.

Sanz Mínguez, C., Romero Carnicero, F. and Górriz Gañán, C. 2010. El vino en *Pintia*: nuevos datos y lecturas, en F. Burillo Mozota (coord.), *Ritos y mitos, VI Simposio sobre Celtíberos, Daroca*, 27–29 de noviembre de 2008, Zaragoza: Centro de Estudios Celtibéricos de Segeda, 595–612.

Sanz Mínguez, C., Romero Carnicero, F., Górriz Gañán, C. and De Pablo Martínez, R. 2009. *El vino y el banquete en la Ribera del Duero durante la Protohistoria*. Valladolid: Universidad de Valladolid, Centro de Estudios Vacceos 'Federico Wattenberg'.

Sanz Mínguez, C., Romero Carnicero, F., Górriz Gañán, C. and De Pablo Martínez, R. 2013. La necrópolis vacceo-romana de Las Ruedas de *Pintia*, Padilla de Duero/Peñafiel (Valladolid). Un paisaje funerario recuperado para la memoria. *VI Congreso Internacional de Musealización de Yacimientos y Patrimonio. Arqueología, Patrimonio y Paisajes Históricos para el siglo XXI.* Toledo, 22 a 25 de noviembre 2010, Consorcio de la Ciudad de Toledo, Toledo, 221–231.

Sanz Mínguez, C., Velasco Vázquez, J., Centeno Cea, I., Juan i Tresserras, J. and Carles Matamala, J. 2003. Escatología vaccea: nuevos datos para su comprensión a través de la analítica de residuos, en C. Sanz Mínguez and J. Velasco Vázquez (eds), *Pintia. Un oppidum en los confines orientales de la región vaccea. Investigaciones arqueológicas Vacceas, Romanas y Visigodas (1999–2003)*. Valladolid: Universidad de Valladolid, 145–171.

Sopeña Genzor, G. 2004. El mundo funerario celtibérico como expresión de un ethos agonístico. *Historiae*, 1, 56–107.

Wattenberg Sanpere, F. 1959. *La región vaccea. Celtiberismo y romanización en el cuenca media del Duero*. Madrid: Consejo Superior de Investigaciones Científicas y Diputación Provincial de Valladolid. Bibliotheca Praehistoria Hispana, IV.

# Dying Young in Archaic Gela (Sicily): From the Analysis of the Cemeteries to the Reconstruction of Early Colonial Identity[1]

## Claudia Lambrugo

### Introduction

My paper will examine the children funerary space in Archaic Gela, the well-known Rhodian and Cretan colony in Sicily, founded in 689 BC on a low hill by the sea on the southern Sicilian coast (Fig. 20.1). The paper has drawn inspiration from other recent works and researches on sub-adult death in Classical antiquity, referring especially to Gillian Shepherd's work on burial and religion in Sicilian colonies,[2] and to the proceedings of the International Round Tables organized between 2008 and 2011 by EMA (*L'Enfant et la mort dans l'Antiquité*) with special sections concerning Magna Graecia and Sicily.[3]

I shall focus on the results of a major new examination of the Archaic cemeteries of Gela, containing mainly 7th and 6th Century burials. I began this work ten years ago as PhD research at the University of Pavia, and then I continued it during postdoctoral research at the University of Milan. The final results of the work have just appeared in a book entitled *Profumi di argilla. Tombe con unguentari corinzi nella necropoli arcaica di Gela.*[4]

### Excavating and re-excavating the Geloan Archaic cemeteries

Gela (whose name was changed in *Terranova di Sicilia* in Medieval times) makes its appearance on the world's archaeological scene at the beginning of the 19th century, when the agricultural development of the hill (where the Rhodian and Cretan colony once stood) led to the discovery of countless exceptionally painted vases. These unexpected treasures, in addition to making a big fortune for local landowners and ancient history buffs, attracted to this obscure village a disparate cohort of wealthy foreigners, who often left with more than a few crates of artefacts for their home museums and collections (among these also Arthur Evans).[5]

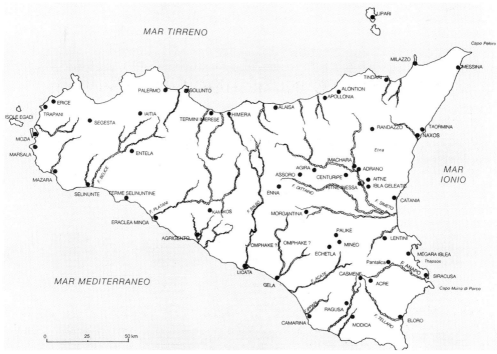

Figure 20.1. Map of ancient Greek Sicily.

Despite the Kingdom of the Two Sicilies having some of the most advanced heritage protection laws of the time, illegal spoliations went on until the turn of the 20th century; in fact it was then (autumn 1897) that the *Direzione degli Scavi di Siracusa* extended its mandate to the Caltanissetta province (which Gela still nowadays belongs to) and its curator, Paolo Orsi, undertook the task of putting the Gela excavations in order.

Orsi's first intervention in Gela concerned the investigation of the well-known ancient city's Archaic *necropolis* (well-known after numerous foreign and private semi-illegal diggings); it was located west of the Greek settlement, in the quarter named *Borgo*, on the west bank of a deep valley (*Vallone Pasqualello*), which represented in antiquity the natural border between the *polis* and its *necropolis*. Orsi was given the opportunity to carry out this investigation by a massive road regeneration project of the quarter owned by the *Comune di Terranova*. Following difficult authorization procedures, finally an agreement was reached with the Municipality regarding archaeological diggings to be carried out before the sewer pipes and road were laid. On March 30th 1900 Orsi managed to start the excavation, which lasted three months, sometimes under unfavorable conditions such as having crowds of shouting and curious sightseers constantly standing on the trench edge, and given the risk of illegal diggers, poor funding, bad hygienic conditions of the roads, typhus or other infections (Fig. 20.2). The main outcome of the excavation was the discovery of almost 570 graves in

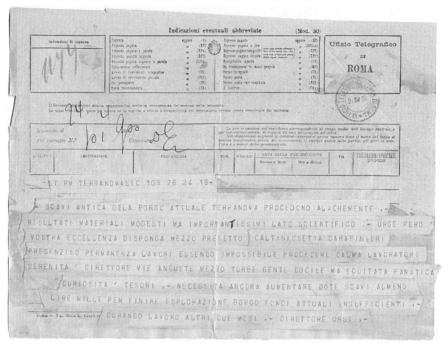

*Figure 20.2. (top) An unpublished letter sent by Orsi from Terranova di Sicilia to Rome (24th April 1900), with some details about the archaeological excavation in the Borgo area (Roma, Archivio Centrale dello Stato; Min. P.I., Dir. Gen. AA.BB.AA., III vers. II serie, busta 19, "Terranova. Scoperte di antichità 1898–1907", fasc. 46/5; autorizzazione 785/09). (bottom) Orsi and his workers in Gela (Archivio Fotografico del Museo Civico di Rovereto, inv. n. 7094/13).*

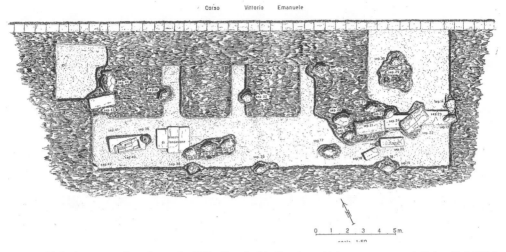

*Figure 20.3. A group of tombs in the Villa Garibaldi Gardens (Adamesteanu and Orlandini 1956, fig. 15).*

the Borgo and Predio La Paglia areas, the latter along the southwest slope of a sunny terrace in the Villa Garibaldi Gardens, just south of the Borgo area.[6]

During the 1950s, seventy other graves were discovered in the Villa Garibaldi Gardens (Fig. 20.3) and in some other little areas of the ancient city by Dinu Adamesteanu and Piero Orlandini, two great figures of Gela archaeology.[7] In total 636 burials were unearthed. Apart from preliminary news, no further information has been delivered with regards to the more recent discoveries made in Gela during hydraulic works in summer 2009.[8]

Even though the available archaeological finds are expected to be partial, as they are limited to a few areas of the Geloan Archaic *necropolis*, nevertheless their reliability and significance are such as to allow a successful analysis.[9] Before addressing children's funerary space in Gela (and in order to better evaluate it) however, some preliminary data are in order.

## CHRONOLOGICAL DATA

No graves of the first generation of *apoikoi* were found in Gela. The same phenomenon was also observed in other *necropoleis* in Sicily and Magna Graecia such as *Pithekoussai*, Taranto, Lentini, *Kamarina* and so forth.[10] This happened either because the graves are to be found elsewhere, for instance (in Gela) along the slopes of the Molino a Vento hill (later the *akropolis*) as suggested by Orlandini,[11] or because they were destroyed by the construction of graves in later periods or, again, they must be identified as the graves without burial goods. In fact, we can argue that the early *apoikoi* were quite poor; therefore, their burials had little funerary visibility.[12]

The chronological distribution of the graves (or at least of those which can be dated), mainly based on Corinthian pottery (which is the most numerous) shows a

significant shift: a gradual increase in the number of graves dated between MPC II and
LPC (26 burials) corresponding to the second and third generation of settlers, then an
exponential increase during the following forty years from TR, throughout EC, to the
very beginning of MC (109 burials), finally a rapid decrease between MC and LC I
(65 burials) starting from 585/580 BC and developing in a widespread '*crisis*' in the
middle of the 6th century BC.[13]

BURIAL RITES AND ARRANGEMENT OF THE GRAVE GOODS

Focusing on the Geloan burial variability requires great attention and caution:[14] in
Archaic Gela the funerary scenario is characterized by a relative lack of burial rites
and grave goods, a well-known tendency observed in almost all Sicilian cemeteries
(also highlighted in recent studies by G. Shepherd)[15] which in Gela resembles a
singular *mesotes*,[16] rigorously curbing the ostentation of wealth. A limited number of
cremations (105 in total), both direct and indirect, can be observed; given the high
costs and symbolic connections with the heroic funerary custom, these cremations
are likely related to wealthy, upper-class adult males. Moreover, in addition to the
above mentioned cremations, the following burial rites were found: little more than
200 children *enchytrismòi* in *amphorae, dolii, pithoi,* basins, clay tubes, *louterion*
bases, and at least 214 inhumations in monolithic *sarcophagi*, stone or clay coffins,
*cappuccine di tegole, fossae* dug into the rock or directly in the soil. Very few cases
of *rannicchiamenti* (contracted burials) and *acefalie* (acephalous burials) are testified.[17]

   The fact that 268 graves out of 636 (little more than 42%) totally lack grave goods
further certifies the funerary variability of Gela in terms of horizontal and vertical
discontinuity. Basically, if present, the grave goods consist of two sets of objects: the
predominant one includes perfume and oil vases of different kinds (mainly Corinthian
but also East Greek, Laconian and Attic), certainly used to perform specific corpse
treatment related to the adoption of elegant and refined customs and to the attempt to
make the dead immortal.[18] The other set includes different kinds of pots for pouring
(*olpai, oinochoai* etc.) and drinking (*kotylai, skyphoi* and *kotyliskoi*), mainly of local
production and connected to a crucial funerary rite, namely libation and the ritual
handling of the liquids (wine, honey, water and *melikraton)* offered to the dead and to
the chthonic deities. Objects used for funeral aristocratic *deipna* such as kraters, *deinoi*
and *stamnoi*, as well as plates, *lekanides* and *kalathiskoi* for the offerings, and *viatica*
for the journey to the underworld, are quite rare.

   A shortage of precious and exotic objects or metal ornaments can be generally
observed, especially if we compare Geloan data to those from other cemeteries (such
as *Megara Hyblaea*, Syracuse etc.).[19]

FUNERARY 'REPRESENTATION' OF FEMININE/MASCULINE GENDERS AND ETHNIC
DIFFERENCES

A third element to be highlighted is the substantial indifference of the Geloan people
in regards to the funerary 'representation' of feminine and masculine genders. This

specificity is once again shared with other Greek Archaic communities of Sicily. Indicators of gender, like tools for spinning and weaving activities, traditionally connected to the feminine sphere, are very rare (not more than 20 artefacts from a total of 636 graves). On the other hand, the grave of the adult man in Gela is even less 'visible'. It is impossible to observe anything that might be connected to the expression of values associated with athleticism or war, so well represented in other areas; extremely modest is also the presence of weapons and working tools.[20]

The analysis of the so called *indicatori etnici* (ethnic signs), both Greek (some specific Cretan or Rhodian ceramics or the problematic Cretan acephalous burials) and indigenous (Sikel funerary rites like contracted burials or the presence of indigenous artefacts, such as *fibulae*, pendants, charms, large containers for food etc.), underlines another crucial point. Even though there have been often recent suggestions that an indigenous element in ancient Greek settlements in Sicily (such as in Magna Graecia) can be detected through funerary customs, and in the light of some important recent revisions (by Mercuri, Shepherd and Albanese Procelli) of the *indicatori etnici* concept itself,[21] the analysis shows that the funerary record cannot be used as a reliable identifier of such groups. The general impression given by Sicilian Greek cemeteries is rather an overall subscription to coherent burial systems, which may be seen as part of an attempt to form a unified and independent cultural new identity, different from the motherland's one. In our case also, it is clear that the Geloan community in the Archaic period, although certainly dominated between the 7th and the 6th century BC by biological and cultural hybridism and characterized by a broad phenomena of people and goods mobility in both directions (Greek and indigenous), does not seem to be particularly interested in discriminating groups of different ethnicity, at least not through funerary rites.[22]

## CONSTRUCTING A NEW CULTURAL IDENTITY, PROMOTING YOUNG GENERATIONS

On the contrary, the biggest effort in 'displaying' a new cultural identity is expressed by the desire to appear as a society in construction or in development. This is achieved with an emphasis on family groups, through the principle of spatial aggregation of adult, adolescent, child and newborn graves of the same household in the same place and for a long time (family plots), and through the adoption (very common since the third generation of colonists onwards) of multiple burials, which integrate adults and sub-adults or only sub-adults, sometimes even of different ages, in the same grave. Some scholars have interpreted this practice as an ethnical indicator, deriving from the collective burial in little caves (very common among the indigenous populations of Sicily), but it may also be viewed as an emphasis on the connection within a family and, consequently, as an urgency to show the crystallization of the young colonial community in social groups and to assert the belonging to specific *oikiai*.[23]

In other words the young *apoikia* chooses to 'represent' itself as a community in formation, emphasizing the family role, in particular that of the aristocratic family, destined to take up central roles in the community, rather than highlighting different ethnic or cultural components that occurred in their society. For this reason, the reunion after death of parents and sons/daughters together, buried close to each other or even in the same receptacle occurs very often, underlying the *anchisteiai*.

Within this framework the young Geloan community of the Archaic period, so reluctant between the middle of the 7th and the middle of the 6th Century BC to organize expensive funerals (limited number of cremations, no bronze cinerary containers), to display luxury goods (little enthusiasm for the deposition of metals and objects of intrinsic prestige) and to build monumental graves (only two hypogean cells, so common on the contrary in *Megara Hyblaea*), shows a careful and constant solidarity in the formalization of infant death. In fact, the anthropometric data carefully reported by the excavators, who unfortunately did not preserve the bone remains as carefully,[24] certify that more than 43% of the graves (276 tombs) belong to sub-adults.

The Geloans not only choose to confer each newborn, child or adolescent a funerary visibility through a formal burial (with *enchytrismòi* and different kinds of inhumations), but they also reserve for a selected group of young or very young people, united by similar high census parameters, special funeral rituals. This implies an economical and cultural effort superior to that employed for the burial of adults, in particular males. In this regard, it is possible to notice how in the graves of sub-adults and particularly in those of adolescents and young girls occur with special and significant frequency (Fig. 20.4):

1. the monolithic sarcophagus, an expensive choice, because of the lack of good cutting stones in the area of Gela;
2. the deposition of exotic or precious artefacts, such as alabaster and *faïence* perfume vases, East Greek plastic vases, gold *stephanai*, earrings, little silver rings, or other metallic ornaments, so rare in adult tombs;
3. a selection of tools/objects that either belonged to children or were dear to them (baby-feeders, statuettes and sea shells probably used as ornaments as well as toys); amongst these, particularly interesting are the fortune charms for travel to the underworld (*coroplastica*, especially female enthroned figurines, amulets etc.);
4. the choice of expensive import vessels (above all Corinthian *alabastra* and *aryballoi*), often iterated in redundant grave goods.

The Geloan choice to promote so carefully the funerary visibility of a *jeunesse dorée* is not an isolated ritual behaviour, but is also shared by other Sicilian colonies between the 7th and the first half of the 6th Century BC, as it has been correctly underlined by Shepherd in her recent works.[25] Even Orsi, at the end of 19th Century, could already notice similar customs in the western *necropolis* of *Megara Hyblaea*:

> La distribuzione quantitativa di essi (oggetti di corredo) pare regolata con questo criterio, che il maggior numero fosse posto attorno ai cadaveri di bambini benestanti, poi attorno a quelli di donne, la minor quantità intorno agli adulti; anzi i cadaveri di fanciulli di agiata condizione scompaiono di solito sotto il cumulo di oggetti, soprattutto dei vasettini (piccoli skyphoi ed oinochoai); in più di un sepolcro il numero di questi (fra interi e rotti) toccò la ottantina.[26]

Something similar may be highlighted also in the *necropoleis* of Syracuse (Fusco), Selinus (Buffa/Gaggera) and Agrigento.[27]

*Figure 20.4. Four children's tombs with their grave goods: (upper left) Gela, Borgo necropolis, Quartiere Ospedale, T. 476, an enchytrismòs containing 'tracce di scheletrino', 650–630 BC, Siracusa, Museo Archeologico Regionale; (upper right) Gela, Villa Garibaldi necropolis, T. 20, burial in monolithic sarcophagus, belonging to 'una fanciulla di 10–12 anni', 630/620 BC, Gela, Museo Archeologico Regionale; (bottom left) Gela, Borgo necropolis, Quartiere Ospedale, T. 419, a multiple enchytrismòs belonging to 'due scheletri dai sette agli otto anni', 630/620 BC, Siracusa, Museo Archeologico Regionale; (bottom right) Gela, Borgo necropolis, Via Pecorai, T. 49, burial in monolithic sarcophagus belonging to a young girl; c. 570 BC, Siracusa, Museo Archeologico Regionale. (Author's photographs).*

This marked visibility conferred after death to an *elite* group of children and adolescents, even if certainly due to emotive factors, can also be interpreted as a 'compensatory' and 'representative' reaction to the strong social investment in the offspring by the household, which aspired to cover *elite* roles within a society in formation. It is exactly through numerous and vigorous offspring, an indispensable resource for the future that the aristocratic *ghene* of Archaic Gela could hope to survive and establish themselves in the territory. It is through sumptuous funerals for premature deaths that the families could reassert their ties and exorcise the danger of dynastic extinction. The closer the young man or the future beautiful bride was to the adult age, the more severe were the pain and the representative effort after death, because they were proportional to the investment of energy, resources and emotion tied to their growth.

## From the Archaeological Data to the Historical Events

Finally it is possible to give an overview of what has emerged from the interpretation of the archaeological data in the light of historical events.

During the period between the middle of the 7th and the first decades of the 6th Century BC, the Geloan *necropolis* revealed a community characterized by a progressive population growth and a social and family structuring, as it is showed by the peak in the number of graves between 630 and 585/580 BC (109 tombs). It is exactly in the same period that the oldest and principal sanctuaries of the colony, the ones in Bitalemi and in Predio Sola, are founded and intensively used. It is interesting that the ritual functions of these sanctuaries are connected to the biological path and to the social development of the aristocratic *nymphai*, as well as brides and mothers, as recently underlined by Ismaelli.[28]

This is also the period in which Gela undertakes significant territorial expansion in southern Sicily.[29] The well-known penetration inland, certainly facilitated by the two big rivers, the Gela and the Salso-Imera, is obviously tied to the agricultural activities of the colony, whose demand for agriculture is displayed by the violent looting of *Omphake* by Antifemo (Pausania, VIII, 46, 2). This is the moment in which, progressively, the big properties are forming, probably organized around farms or rural settlements, but belonging to only a few *ghene*. This was followed by a top-down social restructuring of the young Geloan community, which within a few generations moves from an initial condition of equality, to an unequal concentration of the best farm land in the hands of a few people.

The population growth, the progressive structure of the cemetery layout in large families, some of which were from the very beginning tied to specific funeral areas in full public view (for example the sector on top of the hill and the terrace of the Villa Garibaldi Gardens), and the general well-being observable in the grave-goods, can be interpreted in the light of the above expansion.

This expansion certainly created new dynamics, but probably aroused at the same time an increasing competition among aristocratic families, who were ambitious and eager to secure a growing range of powers.The famous secession of *Maktorion* in Herodotus, VII, 153, 2–4, a tale deriving from an ancient Geloan tragedy, whose date has been indicated in the decades between 620 and 580 BC,[30] can be read as evidence of a social discontent winding through the town in these years. The episode, on which the inexhaustible attention of scholars has been focused, has recently been the object of a new reading, which interprets it as a rampant clash between *ghene*, some of whom were evidently unsatisfied or frustrated in their expectations; hence an internal secession within the oligarchic factions, which may have been complicated by ethnic problems,[31]

Probably the 'golden' children cited above were sons and daughters of these important families; they were rich children and adolescents who died before they could fully assume their place in society or perpetuate an aristocratic bloodline. Their premature deaths were used by the adults to signal certain social conditions and to exorcise the fear of loss or disruption of bloodlines and inheritance.

## ABBREVIATIONS

| | |
|---|---|
| EC | Early Corinthian |
| LC | Late Corinthian |
| LPC | Late Protocorinthian |
| MC | Middle Corinthian |
| MPC II | Middle Protocorinthian II |
| TR | Transitional |

## NOTES

1 Many thanks to the colleagues Cecilia Nobili and Andrea Capra for helping me with English text
2 Shepherd 1995, 1999, 2000, 2005, 2006, 2007, 2011
3 Guimier-Sorbets and Morizot 2010; Nenna 2012; Hermary 2012
4 Lambrugo 2013; on the same argument, but related to some specific details, see also Lambrugo 2005, 2012 and forthcoming
5 Lambrugo 2013, 19–26 with references; see also Vickers 1996 and 2003; Lambrugo 2009
6 For fuller discussion of this issue see Lambrugo 2013, 26–34, with inedit documents published in Appendix 1. See also Ciurcina 2003
7 Lambrugo 2013, 35–8
8 News on some local newspapers, like *La Sicilia* (26th August 2009)
9 The reliability and significance of the material sample have been ascertained through some evaluations; see Lambrugo 2013, 60–3
10 Lambrugo 2013, 381–2 with references
11 Orlandini 1963, 56
12 Lambrugo 2013, 381 and nt. 12
13 For a fuller discussion of the chronological data, see Lambrugo 2013, 381–85, 413
14 For a fuller discussion and references about this issue, see Lambrugo 2013, 61–3, 385–94.
15 Shepherd 2006, 314–315
16 Torelli (2003, 100 and 103) uses the same term of *mesotes*, also dealing with the Classical Geloan burials, comparing them to those of Agrigento and elsewhere in Greek Sicily
17 For the discussion of the contracted and acephalous burials in Gela see Lambrugo 2013, 390–1
18 For a larger analysis of 'perfumed' funerary practices in close relation to a western *habrosyne*, see for Gela Lambrugo 2008; Lambrugo 2013, 324–36 with references
19 With more details in Lambrugo 2013, 360–5
20 For a fuller discussion about this issue with references, see Lambrugo 2013, 394–6
21 Mercuri 2001; Shepherd 2005; Albanese Procelli 2010
22 Lambrugo 2013, 396–8 with more details and references
23 For a fuller discussion on the multiple burial in Sicily, see Lambrugo 2013, 389–90 with references.
24 The same problem occurs also for other numerous Sicilian *necropoleis* excavated during the 19th Century: Elia, Meirano 2012, 429
25 Shepherd 2006, 2007
26 Cavallari and Orsi 1890, 776
27 Lambrugo 2013, 411 with references
28 Ismaelli 2011, 229

29  Lo Presti 2000; La Torre 2011, 76 with references; see also Bergemann 2011, 72 ss
30  Raccuia 2003, 459–63
31  Anello 2003, 397–8; Petruzzella 2003; Raccuia 2003; Sammartano 2011, 228, nt. 39

REFERENCES

Albanese Procelli, R. M. 2010. Presenze indigene in contesti coloniali: sul problema degli indicatori archeologici, pp. 501–8 in Tréziny, H. (ed.), *Grecs et Indigènes de la Catalogne à la mer Noire, Actes des recontres du programme européen Ramses* (2006–2008). Paris: Centre Camille Jullian, Éditions Errance.

Anello, P. 2003. La storia di Gela antica, pp. 385–408 in *Per servire alla storia di Gela, Atti del colloquio* (Gela 1998). *Kokalos*, 45 (1999). Roma: Giorgio Bretschneider Editore.

Bergemann, J. 2011. Il Gela-Survey: 3000 anni di insediamenti e storia nella Sicilia centro-meridionale. *Sicilia Antiqua* 8, 63–100.

Cavallari, F. S. and Orsi, P. 1890. *Megara Hyblaea*. Storia, topografia, necropoli e *anathemata*. *Monumenti Antichi dei Lincei* 1, Part I, 689–950.

Ciurcina, C. 2003. Paolo Orsi e l'avvio di scavi regolari a Gela, pp. 145–47 in Panvini, R. and Giudice, F. (eds), *TA ATTIKA. Veder greco a Gela. Ceramiche attiche figurate dall'antica colonia*. Roma: L''Erma' di Bretschneider.

Elia, D. and Meirano, V. 2012. La typologie des tombes d'enfants dans le colonies grecques d'Italie du Sud, pp. 429–57 in Nenna, D.-M. 2012 (ed.), *L'Enfant et la mort dans l'Antiquité*. II. *Types de tombes et traitements du corps des enfants*, *Actes de la table ronde* (Alexandrie, Centre d'Études Alexandrines 2009). Alexandrie: Centre d'Études Alexandrines.

Guimier-Sorbets, A.-M. and Morizot, Y. 2010 (eds), *L'Enfant et la mort dans l'Antiquité*. I. *Nouvelles recherches dans les nécropoles grecques. Le signalement des tombes d'enfants*, *Actes de la table ronde* (Athénes, École Française d'Athènes 2008). Paris: De Boccard.

Hermary, A. 2012 (ed.). *L'Enfant et la mort dans l'Antiquité*. III. *Le matériel associé aux tombes d'enfant*, *Actes de la table ronde* (Aix-en-Provence, Maison Méditerranéenne des Sciences de l'Homme 2011). Paris/Aix-en-Provence: Centre Camille Jullian, Éditions Errance.

Ismaelli, T. 2011. *Archeologia del culto a Gela. Il santuario di Predio Sola*. Bari: Edipuglia.

Lambrugo, C. 2005. Per la storia di un mondo 'minore'. *Alabastra* e *aryballoi* corinzi nella necropoli arcaica di Gela: esegesi di un indicatore infantile. *Orizzonti* 6, 81–93.

Lambrugo, C. 2008. Les vases à parfum corinthiens en Sicile et en Grande-Grèce, pp. 187–95 in Bodiou, L. and Frère, D. and Mehl, V. (eds), *Parfums et odeurs dans l'Antiquité*. Rennes: Presses Universitaires de Rennes.

Lambrugo, C. 2009. Antichità e scavi aTerranova di Sicilia (Gela) nella seconda metà dell'Ottocento. Documenti inediti dagli archivi comunali, pp. 23–60 in Zanetto, G. and Ornaghi, M. (eds), *Argumenta Antiquitatis* (Quaderni di Acme 109). Milano: Cisalpino, Istituto Editoriale Universitario, Monduzzi Editore.

Lambrugo, C. 2012. La pantera, il cacciatore e il profumo. Riflessioni intorno a due *aryballoi* del *Chimaera Group* a Gela, pp. 257–66 in Frère, D. and Hugot, L. (eds), *Les Huiles parfumées en Méditerranée occidentale et en Gaule (VIIIe s. av.-VIIe s. apr. J.-C.), Atti del convegno internazionale (Roma 2009)*. Rennes: Presses Universitaires de Rennes, centre Jean Bérard.

Lambrugo, C. 2013: *Profumi di argilla. Tombe con unguentari corinzi nella necropoli arcaica di Gela*. Roma: L''Erma' di Bretschneider.

Lambrugo, C. forthcoming. Corinto 'profumata': Afrodite e la via dell'iris in Caruso, F., Gigli, R. and Grasso, L. (eds), *Hierà Sikelikà. Approcci multidisciplinari del sacro nella Sicilia greca, Atti del Convegno* (Catania, IBAM 2010).

La Torre, G. F. 2011. *Sicilia e Magna Grecia. Archeologia della colonizzazione greca in Occidente*. Roma-Bari: EditoriLaterza.

Lo Presti, L. G. 2000. Gela e l'entroterra tra il VII e VI secolo a.C. *Kokalos* 46, 365–80.

Mercuri, L. 2001. Tête sans corps, corps sans tête. De certaines pratiques funéraires en Italie méridionale et en Sicile (VIIIe–Ve siècle avant J.-C.). *Mélanges de L'École française de Rome* 113, 1, 7–31.

Nenna, D.-M. 2012 (ed.). *L'Enfant et la mort dans l'Antiquité.* II. *Types de tombes et traitements du corps des enfants, Actes de la table ronde* (Alexandrie, Centre d'Études Alexandrines 2009). Alexandrie: Centre d'Études Alexandrines.

Orlandini, P. 1963. La più antica ceramica greca di Gela e il problema di Lindioi. *Cronache di Archeologia* 2, 50–6.

Petruzzella, M. 2003. La *stasis* a Gela in età arcaica e la figura dello ierofante *Telines*, pp. 501–7 in *Per servire alla storia di Gela, Atti del colloquio* (Gela 1998). *Kokalos*, 45 (1999). Roma: Giorgio Bretschneider Editore.

Raccuia, C. 2003. La secessione in *Maktorion*, pp. 457–69 in *Per servire alla storia di Gela, Atti del colloquio* (Gela 1998). *Kokalos*, 45 (1999). Roma: Giorgio Bretschneider Editore.

Sammartano, R. 2011. I Cretesi in Sicilia: la proiezione culturale, pp. 223–53 in Rizza G. (ed.), *Identità culturale, etnicità, processi di trasformazione a Creta tra* Dark Ages *e Arcaismo. Atti del Convegno per i 100 anni dello scavo di Priniàs 1906–2006* (Studi e materiali di archeologia greca 10). Palermo: Consiglio Nazionale delle Ricerche, I.B.A.M. Sede di Catania, Università di Catania, Centro di Archeologia Cretese.

Shepherd, G. 1995.The Pride of Most Colonials: Burial and Religion in the Sicilian Colonies, pp. 51–82 in Fischer-Hansen, T. (ed.), *Ancient Sicily.* Copenhagen.

Shepherd, G. 1999. Fibulae and Females: Intermarriage in the western Greek colonies and the Evidence from the Cemeteries, pp. 267–300 in Tsetskhladze, G. R. (ed.), *Ancient Greeks West and East.* Leiden-Boston-Köln: Brill.

Shepherd, G. 2000. Greeks bearing Gifts: religious Relationships between Sicily and Greece in the Archaic Period, pp. 55–70 in Smith, C. J. and Serrati, J. (eds), *Sicily from Aeneas to Augustus. New Approaches in Archaeology and History.* Edinburgh: Edinburgh University Press.

Shepherd, G. 2005. Dead Men tell no Tales: ethnic Diversity in Sicilian Colonies and the Evidence of the Cemeteries. *Oxford Journal of Archaeology* 24, 2, 115–36.

Shepherd, G. 2006. Dead but not buried? Child Disposal in the Greek West, pp. 311–25 in Herring, E. and Lemos, I. and Lo Schiavo, F. *et al.* (eds), *Across Frontiers. Etruscans, Greeks, Phoenicians and Cypriots. Studies in honour of David Ridgway and Francesca Romana Serra Ridgway* (Accordia Specialist Studies on the Mediterranean 6). London: Accordia Research Institute, University of London.

Shepherd, G. 2007. Poor little rich Kids? Status and Selection in Archaic Western Greece, pp. 93–106 in Shepherd, G. and Crawford, S. (eds), *Children, Childhood and Society* (BAR International Series 1696). Oxford: Archaeopress.

Shepherd, G. 2011. Hybridity and Hierarchy: Cultural Identity and Social Mobility in Archaic Sicily, pp. 113–29 in Gleba, M. and Horsnaes, H. W. (eds), *Communicating Identity in the Italic Iron Age.* Oxford: Oxbow Books.

Torelli, M. 2003. Le ceramiche a figure rosse di Gela. Contributo alla costruzione del profilo culturale di una città, pp. 99–144 in Panvini, R. and Giudice, F. (eds), *TA ATTIKA. Veder greco a Gela. Ceramiche attiche figurate dall'antica colonia.* Roma: L''Erma' di Bretschneider.

Vickers, M. 1996. The Greek Pottery Vases from Gela in Oxford: their Place in History and in the History of Art, pp. 181–89 in *I Vasi attici e altre ceramiche coeve in Sicilia. Atti del convegno internazionale* (Catania, Camarina, Gela, Vittoria 1990).*Cronache di Archeologia* 29–30, 1990–1991.

Vickers, V. 2003. '….at Terranova One gets more for One's Money than at Rome': Arthur and Margaret Evans in Gela, 1887–1896, pp. 239–42 in Panvini, R. and Giudice, F. (eds), *TA ATTIKA. Veder greco a Gela. Ceramiche attiche figurate dall'antica colonia.* Roma: L''Erma' di Bretschneider.

# 21

## MATERNIDAD E INHUMACIONES PERINATALES EN EL *VICUS* ROMANORREPUBLICANO DE EL CAMP DE LES LLOSES (TONA, BARCELONA): LECTURAS Y SIGNIFICADOS[1]

*Montserrat Duran i Caixal, Imma Mestres i Santacreu and M. Dolors Molas Font*

*The burial in houses of babies who had died perinatally is a documented practice since the Bronce Age, especially among protohistorical communities located at the southern Gaul and the Northeastern and Eastern Iberic peninsula. The period of greatest diffusion of this type of burials spans from mid-fifth century b.C. to the early second century b.C, and then remains constant during the Roman-Republican period until the Medieval Ages.*

*The present work discloses the finding of nine perinatal burials in the Roman-Republican settlement at El Camp de les Lloses (Tona, Barcelona, Catalonia). It is a small vicus related to the construction of the road network that joins the central Catalan coast with inland territory, and where there have been documented several productive activities possibly related to military logistics. The chronology of the settlement is restricted to a single moment of occupation from 125 BC to 75 BC. The absence of a long occupation, together with the homogeneity of the settlement as a whole, makes this place a reference for knowledge on funeral rituals that, in our view, would be carried out by indigenous women that would share their lives with the men, most of them Italic legionaries and auxiliary troops. The non-deposition of perinatal children in the necropolis could be due to the fact that they were not recognized as social beings, so they lacked social identity. It a rises the possibility that buried perinatal children in houses were those children whose mothers survived their birth, for if both child and mother died at birth, they would have been buried together in the cemetery. The work introduces this and others interpretations related to the presence – or absence – of perinatal burials in the vicus for discussion.*

Introducción

La inhumación de individuos perinatales en los asentamientos es una práctica documentada en Europa desde el Neolítico[2] y, en especial, desde la Edad del Bronce entre las comunidades protohistóricas del sur de la Galia y del noreste y levante de la península ibérica. En esta área, el período de mayor difusión de ese tipo de enterramientos abarca desde mediados del siglo V a.C. hasta inicios del II a.C. y perduró durante la etapa romana y la Edad Media.[3] Se documenta incluso en épocas moderna y contemporánea.[4]

El objetivo del presente trabajo es dar a conocer el hallazgo de sepulturas perinatales en el yacimiento romanorrepublicano de El Camp de les Lloses (Tona, Barcelona, Cataluña). Se trata de un pequeño *vicus*, o *canaba,* relacionado con la construcción de una red viaria que unía la costa central catalana con el interior del país, en el que se llevaron a cabo actividades productivas que cabría relacionar con la logística militar. La cronología del *vicus* corresponde a un único momento de ocupación que se sitúa entre el 125 y el 75 a.C.

La inexistencia de una secuencia larga de ocupación, unida a la homogeneidad del conjunto, convierte al yacimiento en un lugar de referencia para el conocimiento de los rituales funerarios en estudio que, en nuestra opinión, llevarían a cabo mujeres indígenas que compartirían su vida con hombres, ya fueran civiles o militares que vivían o frecuentaban el lugar. El trabajo presenta a discusión esta y otras interpretaciones sobre la presencia – y en su caso ausencia – de enterramientos perinatales en el *vicus.*

Ubicación del Yacimiento

El Camp de les Lloses se ubica a los pies de un cerro (El Turó del Castell) en el municipio de Tona (Barcelona), en la zona intermedia de las cuencas hidrográficas de los ríos Ter y Congost, al sur de la Plana de Vic, zona que se caracteriza por su gran potencial agrícola. Desde la prehistoria reciente, la riqueza agrícola del llano fue determinante para la implantación poblacional en el territorio. El asentamiento está situado en una zona que presenta un relieve de cárcavas que configuran pequeños valles de sección en 'V', formando un modelado generado por la acción erosiva de las aguas torrenciales. Los análisis granulométricos de diversos cortes estratigráficos del yacimiento parecen confirmar que la destrucción de algunas estructuras del asentamiento estaría relacionada con la existencia de un torrente natural que favoreció el arrastre violento de materiales que afectaría notablemente a dichas construcciones (Fig. 21.1).

La Estratigrafía del Yacimiento

*Las Fases Prerromanas*

Los niveles de ocupación más antiguos se remontan al Bronce Final y al periodo preibérico – siglos VIII–VII a.C. – y están documentados por cerámicas modeladas a mano con superficies alisadas y decoraciones de cordones aplicados.[5] Durante las últimas intervenciones arqueológicas, llevadas a cabo entre los años 2008 y 2012, se han exhumado estructuras arqueológicas del periodo ibérico, datadas entre los siglos

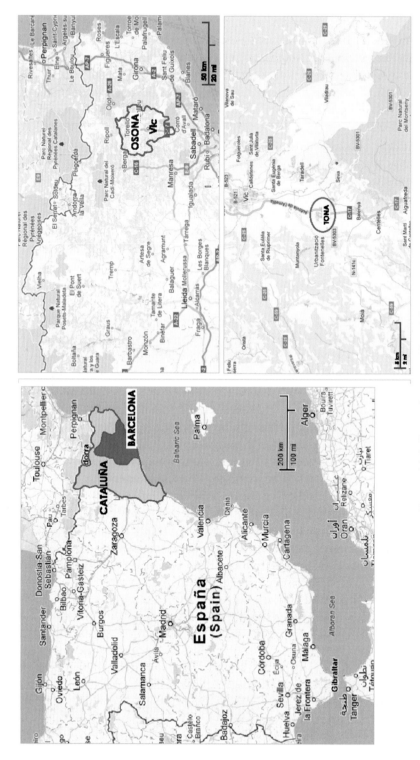

*Figure 21.1. Situación geográfica del yacimiento.*

III y II a.C., junto a restos de pavimentos líticos y algunos hogares. A este mismo período corresponde el hallazgo de silos globulares. En el último cuarto de siglo II a.C., todos estos elementos, enmarcables en el período ibérico, se amortizaron durante la fase constructiva de las nuevas casas romanorrepublicanas.[6]

## La ocupación tardorrepublicana

La fundación estratégica del *vicus* se sitúa entre el 125 y el 75 a.C. y se relaciona con la construcción de una infraestructura viaria secundaria. De ella hay constancia a partir del hallazgo en un lugar cercano al yacimiento de un miliario con el nombre del procónsul *Manius Sergius* (*c*. 110 a.C.). El camino conectaba el interior de la comarca de Osona – territorio del antiguo pueblo íbero de los ausetanos – con un tramo de la antigua Vía Heráclea, que discurría de sur a norte, por las áreas costeras. El trazado interior de esa vía se conoce a través de otros miliarios del citado procónsul descubiertos en las comarcas de Osona y el Vallès Occidental (Barcelona).[7]

El período de actividad del asentamiento se sitúa entre un momento posterior a la toma de Numancia (*c*. 133 a.C.) y el inicio del siglo I a.C. En consecuencia, la ocupación fue relativamente breve y abarcaría unos 50 años. A partir del registro arqueológico se puede afirmar que su abandono no fue repentino, pero si suficientemente rápido, que favoreció la formación de unos conjuntos de amortización muy completos. El material cerámico es sobre todo de origen local: cerámicas ibéricas oxidadas, lisas y pintadas, cerámica gris ampuritana, cerámicas comunes de imitación de modelos itálicos, y algunas cerámicas modeladas a mano. En cuanto a las importaciones, son mayoritariamente de origen itálico: vajilla de barniz negro Campaniense A tardía y de Cales, variante media, algunos vasos cubiletes de paredes finas, tapaderas y *patinae* de cerámica de cocina itálica, así como ánfora itálica del tipo Dr. 1A y brindisiana; también se documenta ánfora púnico-ebusitana, norteafricana tripolitana y, en menor cantidad, del área del estrecho de Gibraltar.[8]

Hasta el momento, se han excavado diez edificios que han sido objeto de musealización en el parque arqueológico. Estas construcciones se articulan urbanísticamente alrededor de un espacio público, presumiblemente una calle pavimentada de piedra. Las casas, adosadas según un eje norte-sur, presentan un diseño inspirado en el patrón de casa itálica tradicional de planta rectangular con diversas estancias dispuestas en torno a un atrio central.[9] Se trata de construcciones de adobe con zócalo o base de mampostería cubiertas por una techumbre de cañizo y cal que sustentaba un envigado de roble.

Se han identificado quince talleres metalúrgicos situados en el interior de las casas o bien en espacios exteriores, ya sean patios o calles, que operaron de forma simultánea. La gran cantidad de *oficcinae* permite formular la hipótesis de que el asentamiento pudiera corresponder a una *canaba* al servicio de un campamento militar, posiblemente situado próximo al lugar. Los militares del *castrum* serían los responsables de la construcción de la infraestructura viaria proconsular.[10]

Otra interpretación es que el asentamiento fuese un puesto de avance militar, directamente relacionado con la logística de los ejércitos romanos que operaban tanto en la *Hispania Citerior* como fuera del territorio provincial. En estos espacios logísticos, pequeñas guarniciones se encargaban de la seguridad y de las provisiones para las tropas en tránsito y, a su vez, de la organización del reclutamiento de auxiliares locales. Estas gestionaban también las *fabricae* que producían o reparaban utillaje y armas, e incluso acuñaban moneda.[11] El resultado de las excavaciones del 2012 señala la posible relación del edificio I, de características singulares, con la presencia de una guarnición militar.

Los hallazgos numismáticos son notables y variados (plata y bronce ibéricos, romanos, de origen masaliota,...). Predominan los bronces ibéricos, que sobrepasan el 90% de las piezas computadas, con escaso grado de desgaste en su mayoría, siendo las cecas mejor representadas las que corresponden al territorio ausetano (*Ausesken, Eusti* y *Ore*). Igualmente hay que destacar el reciente hallazgo de una ocultación de 41 bronces ibéricos en la que, a diferencia de lo visto hasta ahora, prevalecen las monedas de las cecas layetanas e ilergetas. Esta ocultación corresponde al momento de abandono del asentamiento republicano.

## Fase Final y Abandono

La ocupación de El Camp de les Lloses no acaba con el abandono precipitado de los edificios republicanos. El edificio C, asociable a las infraestructuras de una *villa*, se data entre el 40 a.C. y el 60 d.C., y probablemente responde a nuevas formas de implantación en el territorio características de la romanización.

## EL MUNDO CULTURAL Y FUNERARIO: LAS SEPULTURAS PERINATALES Y OTROS HALLAZGOS

La mayoría de las casas romanorrepublicanas presentan el mismo patrón en relación a las inhumaciones perinatales excavadas en el suelo de las mismas, de las que se han exhumado un total de nueve en habitaciones cubiertas. Dada su ubicación y contexto estratigráfico, algunas investigaciones relacionan los enterramientos perinatales con la fundación de la casa o la remodelación de los espacios de habitación, y también con el inicio o fin de actividades productivas en los talleres metalúrgicos.[12] Asimismo, el culto y la ritualidad de los depósitos perinatales han sido interpretados con finalidad profiláctica y propiciatoria, de protección de la casa y del grupo familiar y en relación al culto agrario de fertilidad de la tierra.[13]

Si bien no son objeto de estudio en este trabajo, destaca la presencia en el asentamiento de depósitos rituales de animales de carácter cultual en el interior de las casas y en los espacios de circulación y patios (ovicápridos, suidos, équidos y cánidos). Cabe señalar el depósito de dos neonatos de *Sus domesticus* en el edificio A: uno en el ámbito 2, interpretado como un espacio de *culina* y *triclinium,* y otro en el taller metalúrgico del ámbito 21.[14]

Otro ejemplo descubierto de práctica ritual en el ámbito 12 del edificio B, es la ocultación de una vasija de cerámica emporitana que contenía restos de microfauna, un astrágalo y una moneda de bronce, interpretada con un carácter fundacional por su contexto estratigráfico.

El depósito más singular es el hallado en el pavimento de circulación de una calle que apareció señalizado por una gran losa y diversos adobes. Estaba formado por un vaso plástico que reproduce una cabeza infantil – que tal vez corresponda a un pseudopebetero de origen itálico – escorias de hierro, fragmentos cerámicos y restos de un équido. Se le atribuye un carácter propiciatorio en relación con la metalurgia, una de las actividades más importantes de la comunidad.

Es interesante señalar el descubrimiento casual, en el año 1915, a unos 100 m al este del yacimiento actual, de una estela figurativa ibérica que representa una lucha de guerreros y un lobo. La presencia de esta estela y el hallazgo de inhumaciones fueron relacionados con la posible existencia de una necrópolis o santuario en el asentamiento.[15] Sin embargo esta idea no ha podido ser contrastada arqueológicamente. El estudio iconográfico de la estela permite vincularla a los tipos bajoaragoneses datados a finales del siglo II a.C.[16]

## RITUALIDAD DE LOS CUERPOS INHUMADOS

Las sepulturas de El Camp de les Lloses corresponden a inhumaciones perinatales localizadas fuera del espacio funerario de la necrópolis. Todas las criaturas están enterradas en el interior de las casas, en espacios cubiertos y cerca de las esquinas, si bien la inhumación dos se sitúa en el umbral de la habitación 8 del edificio A. Seis de las inhumaciones (1, 3, 5, 6, 8 y 9) se practicaron en espacios de producción de mantenimiento, y tres (2, 4 y 7) en talleres metalúrgicos, es decir de producción de bienes de intercambio.

La casi totalidad de las criaturas fueron depositadas de forma individual en las habitaciones (1, 2, 3, 4, 5, 7 y 9) y solo dos comparten estancia (inhumaciones 6 y 8); su proximidad induce a pensar que podría tratarse de un parto múltiple, sin descartar que sean enterramientos diacrónicos. En todo caso los análisis de ADN podrán confirmar el supuesto parentesco. Dada su excepcionalidad, los partos múltiples se consideraban de contenido mágico y benefactor.[17]

Las inhumaciones documentadas son primarias, o sea, están depositadas en el suelo en pequeñas fosas en las que se encaja la criatura; algunas posturas forzadas sugieren el uso de mortaja. La conexión anatómica que muchas partes de los esqueletos presentan, indica que la corrupción de los cuerpos se produjo en un espacio colmatado, en el mismo momento del enterramiento o durante la descomposición de los mismos.

Los esqueletos, enterrados en posición fetal, muestran posiciones diversas, decúbito lateral izquierdo o derecho, o bien decúbito supino con piernas más o menos flexionadas. Circunstancias acontecidas después de la deposición de los cuerpos afectaron algunas sepulturas (inhumaciones 1, 4, 6 y 8) y causaron movimientos, post mórtem, acaecidos en el proceso de descomposición o bien provocados por fenómenos externos. Señalar que predominan las sepulturas con una orientación sur, si bien varían en grado (inhumaciones 1, 3, 4, 5, 7, y 9). Asimismo se documentan algunas sepulturas orientadas al norte (inhumaciones 6 y 8) (Fig. 21.2).

El estudio del conjunto de las sepulturas evidencia una cierta diversidad en los detalles de las tumbas. La inhumación 4, practicada en el ámbito 17 del edificio

*Figure 21.2. Detalle de la inhumación 7 documentada en el edificio F, Ámbito 43.*

C, se deposita en un lecho de arenas ocres relacionadas con el trabajo metalúrgico, cuya composición afectó la conservación del esqueleto de la criatura. La inhumación 2, llevada a cabo en el taller metalúrgico del ámbito 8 del edificio A, reaprovecha como tumba un pequeño horno construido con adobes. La reutilización de estructuras artesanales como espacio de sepultura está documentada en la Península y, aunque es poco habitual, se conocen algunos ejemplos.[18] Las tumbas 1, 3, 4 y 7 estaban delimitadas por elementos líticos muy simples y se desconoce si servían para señalizarlas o solo eran visibles en el momento de practicar la inhumación, sin descartar la función protectora de muros, esquinas, bancos y escaleras.[19]

En general las sepulturas no contienen ajuar de forma evidente, a excepción de la inhumación 1, exhumada en el ámbito 13 del edifico B, formado por objetos muy singulares de hierro, un *dolabrum*, una hebilla y diversas piezas hemisféricas.[20] Al valor económico y de prestigio social del ajuar se podría añadir el valor profiláctico del metal. La sepultura se encuentra en la casa más romanizada y es exponente del elevado estatus social de sus habitantes, indicado por: elementos de ornamentación personal, un tesoro monetario y la presencia de un lararió que albergaba una *arula* anepígrafa doméstica del tipo 1[21] y ofrendas formadas por un plato de cerámica Calena f. L.5 y un denario de plata de la ceca de *Bolskan*.

Tres sepulturas (inhumaciones 1, 2, y 4) contenían pequeños fragmentos de cerámica y restos de fauna en los sedimentos de colmatación; en la inhumación 2 se exhumó un incisivo inferior de suido subadulto o adulto, considerado como un elemento de ajuar funerario.[22] En los sedimentos de colmatación de la inhumación 1 había restos de fauna muy fracturada, correspondientes a piezas dentarias de un ejemplar de *Bos taurus,* restos de ovidocáprido y *Sus domesticus*, interpretados como una deposición secundaria y no ritual. La inhumación 4 estaba acompañada de un fragmento de tibia de *Bos taurus* de edad adulta.[23] En definitiva, la escasa cantidad de fauna documentada en los sedimentos de colmatación de las sepulturas dificulta relacionar los restos con algún ritual o banquete funerario. De hecho, la mayoría de inhumaciones infantiles documentadas en la Península y en el sur de Francia raramente albergan ajuares funerarios y solo se acompañan de restos de fauna. Los elementos documentados corresponden mayoritariamente a cerámicas y piezas ornamentales relacionadas con el mundo infantil, probablemente de carácter protector.[24]

En El Camp de les Lloses se han identificado dos posibles rituales funerarios. En la tumba 3 de la habitación 17 del edificio C, se documentó un pequeño encaje de morfología oval que comunicaba el nivel de circulación de la habitación con la sepultura. El orificio se ha interpretado como un posible canal para la práctica de ofrendas y libaciones típicas de los banquetes funerarios. Es posible que la reiteración de dichas prácticas afectara la conservación de las extremidades de la criatura. La inhumación 2 conservaba abundantes restos antracológicos en los sedimentos de colmatación de la tumba que quizá se relacionen con rituales de cremación de elementos vegetales durante la sepultura (Fig. 21.3).

### Diagnóstico de edad, sexo e identificación de patologías[25]

Se trata de 9 inhumaciones perinatales correspondientes a fetos a término entre 38–42 semanas de gestación (inhumaciones 1, 2, 3, 5, 6, 8 y 9) y recién nacidos hasta dos meses de vida (inhumaciones 4 y 7)

De las nueve inhumaciones, se atribuye el sexo femenino a seis (inhumaciones 2, 3, 4, 6, 7 y 8), el masculino a dos (inhumaciones 1 y 9) y una es de sexo indeterminado (inhumación 5). Si los análisis de ADN confirmaran esta proporción en más muestras de campo, podría indicar una mayor mortalidad del sexo femenino durante el proceso de alumbramiento y los días posteriores al parto, o bien que existiera una selección positiva del sexo femenino para recibir sepultura en el ámbito familiar. En ningún caso se han detectado patologías ni malformaciones que se puedan relacionar con su muerte.

Concluimos este apartado con la constatación de que las sepulturas perinatales de El Camp de les Lloses comparten rasgos comunes: se ubican en las casas y las criaturas están depositadas en fosas de carácter primario en posición fetal. A su vez, constatamos una cierta heterogeneidad en la muestra en cuanto al sexo de las criaturas, la posición fetal del cadáver y en los espacios donde se practicó la inhumación. Creemos que esta diversidad se debe a que son sepulturas resueltas en el ámbito doméstico familiar y no en el espacio público y normatizado de la necrópolis (Fig. 21.4).

### Interpretaciones y significados

Según se deduce del registro arqueológico, el componente masculino del *vicus,* o bien *canaba*, estaría básicamente constituido por militares (legionarios itálicos o miembros

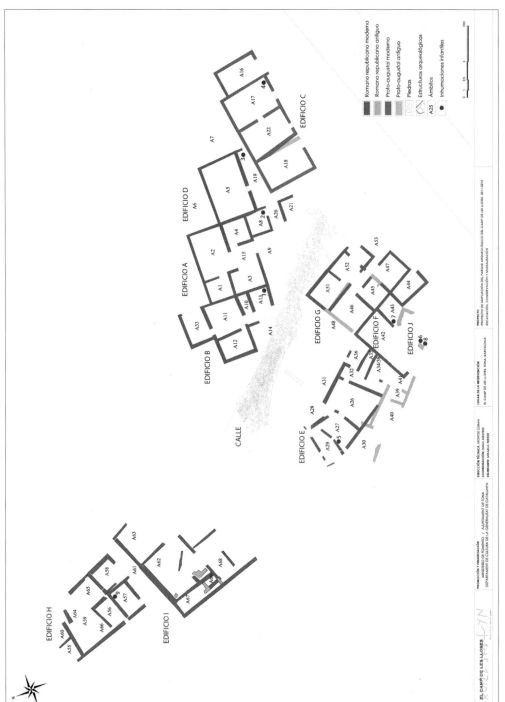

*Figure 21.3. Plano de situación de las inhumaciones.*

| Inhumación | Situación | Edad | Sexo | Talla | Preservación | Tipo de Inhumación | Posición del Esqueleto | Orientación | Carácter del Nivel de Enterramiento |
|---|---|---|---|---|---|---|---|---|---|
| **Inh. 1** CdL.98.143.27 | Edificio B Ámbito 13 | 38–40 sg | Masculino | 49.97 cm | 90.91% | Primaria | Decúbito lateral izquierdo (posición fetal) | 194° S | Producción de mantenimiento |
| **Inh. 2** CdL.98.156.12 | Edificio A Ámbito 8 | 0–1.5 meses post. natales | Femenino | 54.9 cm | 100 % | Primaria | Decúbito supino con piernas flexionadas | 254° S-W | Producción de mantenimiento y producción de intercambio |
| **Inh. 3** CdL.99.227.1 | Edificio D Ámbito 19 | 38–42 sg | Femenino | 53.82 cm | 90.91% | Primaria | Decúbito lateral izquierdo (posición fetal) | 205° S-W | Producción de mantenimiento |
| **Inh. 4** CdL.02.340.1 | Edificio C Ámbito 17 | 0–2 meses post. natales | Femenino | 51.35 cm | 40.91% | Primaria | Decúbito supino | 224° S-W | Producción de mantenimiento y producción de intercambio |
| **Inh. 5** CdL.06.735.1 | Edificio E Ámbito 27 | 40–42 sg | Indeterminado | | 31.82% | Primaria | Posiblemente decúbito lateral derecho | 200° S-E | Producción de mantenimiento |
| **Inh. 6** CdL.09.2232.1 | Edificio J Ámbito 50 | 0–1.5 meses post. natales | Femenino | 54.93 cm | 68.2% | Primaria | Decúbito lateral derecho (posición fetal) | 34° N-E | Producción de mantenimiento |
| **Inh. 7** CdL.09.2091.1 | Edificio F Ámbito 43 | 0–2 meses post. natales | Femenino | 52.15 cm | 95,45% | Primaria | Decúbito supino con piernas flexionadas | 219° S-E | Producción de mantenimiento y producción de intercambio |
| **Inh. 8** CdL.09.2334.1 | Edificio J Ámbito 50 | 0–1 mes post. natal | Femenino | 56.63 cm | 59.09% | Primaria | Decúbito lateral derecho (posición fetal) | 89° N- E | Producción de mantenimiento |
| **Inh. 9** CdL.11.2444.1 | Edificio H Ámbito 57 | 0–2 meses post. natales | Masculino | 52.36 cm | 100% | Primaria | Decúbito lateral derecho (posición fetal) | 190° S | Producción de mantenimiento |

*Figure 21.4. Tabla de las inhumaciones.*

de las tropas auxiliares vecinas) y civiles (indígenas o foráneos), que residían o frecuentaban el lugar. Estos hombres compartirían su vida y se relacionarían con mujeres indígenas que, según nuestra consideración, serían las principales protagonistas de los rituales ofrecidos a los seres perinatales. Después de un siglo de presencia romana en las tierras del noreste peninsular, las poblaciones autóctonas habrían evolucionado, dentro de un proceso de disolución cultural y organizativa, hacia una *koiné* política preeminentemente romana. Sin embargo, la fuerza de la tradición funeraria conservada entre las mujeres daría lugar a que éstas perpetuaran dicha costumbre a pesar de la romanización.

Por lo tanto, el ritual de tradición local de depositar los cuerpos inhumados de perinatales y de bebés en las casas permite, a su vez, establecer que la componente femenina de El Camp de les Lloses estaba integrada, sobre todo, por indígenas, si bien algunas de las criaturas enterradas serían fruto de uniones mixtas con foráneos. Es posible que esa costumbre no fuera extraña para muchos de los hombres de origen itálico, puesto que se documenta en la región del Lacio durante la primera Edad del Hierro.[26] Además, son varias las referencias en textos latinos de épocas diversas sobre la no cremación de las criaturas sin dentición y su deposición en el subsuelo de las áreas de habitación.[27]

Es difícil precisar qué tipo de vínculos unían a las mujeres y a los hombres del *vicus*. No obstante, las características del asentamiento y la diversidad de procedencias y estatus de las personas que vivían en él y de aquellas que lo frecuentaban, originarían situaciones jurídico-estatutarias diferentes y, a menudo, ambiguas, en especial las surgidas de las relaciones entre mujeres y militares. La variedad de marcos jurídico-estatutarios daría lugar a la categorización jerárquica de las criaturas nacidas, pero también de las fallecidas. Este estado de las cosas comportaría que no todos los individuos perinatales fueran suficientemente valorados para ser enterrados en las casas. Ello explicaría que la presencia de este tipo de sepulturas sea relativamente escasa, teniendo en cuenta la más que probable alta mortalidad de las criaturas durante los últimos meses de la gestación, en el parto y también en el posparto. Al parecer, hubo pues una selección entre los individuos fallecidos. Y así, el enterramiento en el subsuelo de las viviendas distinguiría a algunos seres fallecidos en base al estatus o condición social de sus progenitores. Es muy probable que entre los cuerpos estimados como no dignos para recibir sepultura en las viviendas estuvieran los nacidos de prostitutas, de mujeres de condición servil y aquellos que, en un sentido amplio, eran fruto de embarazos no deseados.

Además, planteamos la posibilidad de que los inhumados en el asentamiento fueran las hijas y los hijos de las madres que sobrevivieron al parto y, por consiguiente, que fueran las madres quienes tuvieran el protagonismo en los rituales del enterramiento. Por otro lado, las criaturas y las madres fallecidas durante el alumbramiento – que serían muchísimas, ya que la mortalidad femenina en este proceso había de ser elevadísima – posiblemente serían enterradas juntas en la necrópolis,[28] decisión en la que intervendrían las personas más allegadas. Actualmente se desconoce la ubicación de la necrópolis de El Camp de les Lloses, si bien algunos hallazgos importantes próximos al *vicus,* de marcado carácter funerario, permiten considerar que el santuario o necrópolis se hallaría en las cercanías. Por ello, no sabemos si los perinatales sepultados en el cementerio eran inhumados o bien cremados, como seguramente lo fueron las madres.

La no deposición de perinatales en la necrópolis podría deberse a que no eran reconocidos como seres sociales,[29] es decir carecían de identidad social. A causa de su muerte prematura, estos seres aún no habían llevado a cabo algunos de los rituales de iniciación infantil necesarios para ser aceptados como miembros de la comunidad y tener así el derecho de ser enterrados en el cementerio, el espacio de representación social más importante, aunque fuera en un espacio diferenciado según las subdivisiones de edad infantil. La identidad de una persona como integrante de una colectividad lleva implícita la idea de no pertenencia, es decir de persona extraña a ella. Por esta razón creemos que el término 'identidad social negada' expresa la relación simbólica entre estos seres y la comunidad, manifiesta por la no deposición de ajuar. El ajuar funerario es un elemento identitario de significación social, exponente de cómo las personas que realizan el enterramiento plasman su forma de mostrar en la muerte la identidad de la persona difunta, según su sexo, género, edad, estatus, etnia, condición sexual o creencias religiosas. Y así, su ausencia en las tumbas perinatales reflejaría la no consideración social de estas criaturas y su carencia de individualidad.[30] Además, el uso de la inhumación – dejando a un lado las posibles creencias espirituales asociadas a este ritual – creemos que refuerza esta idea: la inhumación de los cuerpos no requiere del tiempo, ni de la energía, ni de los recursos necesarios aportados para la cremación por un grupo humano que reconoce en este proceso ritual, de tipo colectivo, a uno de los suyos.

Sin embargo, en el conjunto de los nueve hallazgos destaca por su singularidad la inhumación 1 ya que el cuerpo estaba acompañado por un *dolabrum*, una hebilla y elementos hemisféricos de hierro, y la tumba se excavó en una vivienda cuyos residentes se adscribían plenamente a la cultura romana y pertenecían a un estrato social elevado, comparado con el del resto de los habitantes del asentamiento. En este caso, cabría interpretar que las personas que enterraron a la criatura quisieron mostrar, ante todo, su pertenencia a una unidad familiar situada en la parte alta de la jerarquía social del *vicus.* Interpretación que no se contradice con que los objetos ofrendados en la sepultura tuvieran un valor simbólico relacionado con la producción metalúrgica.

No obstante, y ante todo, la sepultura de esas criaturas en las casas – que, como antes hemos indicado, serían solo una parte de las fallecidas en el asentamiento – pone de manifiesto que su muerte era sentida como una pérdida importante para la unidad familiar, ya que frustraba, en cierta medida, su continuidad. Por ello, la deposición de esos cuerpos 'sin malformaciones' en la tierra del ámbito familiar propiciaría, a través de cultos ctónicos, la fertilidad necesaria para la fecundación, procreación y pervivencia del grupo familiar y, en definitiva, de la colectividad. Es importante tener en cuenta que los perinatales fueron enterrados en las casas, donde normalmente se produce el parto,[31] y por esta razón su sepultura en ellas podría ser un símbolo de renacimiento y de deseo materno de guardar memoria de su efímera existencia a través de marcas que indicaran su situación y de periódicas ofrendas florales y vegetales.[32] Y por esta razón, las tumbas se excavaron cerca de los muros, apartadas de las zonas de paso para asegurar su protección.

Los estudios antropológicos no han apreciado patologías como causa de la muerte. El fallecimiento de esos seres se debería a complicaciones endógenas vinculadas a la gestación y al posparto, frecuentes en poblaciones con escasos recursos médicos, deficiente alimentación y escasa higiene, por lo que las enfermedades infecciosas, nutricionales o traumatismos afectarían de forma muy rápida a los recién nacidos provocando una alta mortalidad infantil. Estas causas exógenas difícilmente se detectan en los esqueletos infantiles. Cabe señalar que no hay muestras de violencia en los cuerpos que indiquen muertes traumáticas provocadas. Seguramente su fallecimiento fue un proceso natural.

El análisis de las nueve inhumaciones muestra una gran variedad en los detalles de las sepulturas y los rituales de enterramiento, es decir, hay una cierta individualización en el tratamiento de las muertes perinatales en cada unidad familiar. La diversidad evidencia que este hecho funerario no estaba sujeto a normas establecidas, ya que sería una cuestión que se resolvía en el ámbito doméstico familiar, y no en el público, mediante la implicación, sobre todo, femenina.

En El Camp de les Lloses las inhumaciones perinatales se llevaron a cabo tanto en espacios de producción de mantenimiento, como en espacios de producción de bienes de intercambio. En los estudios sobre este tema se tiende a otorgar significados distintos a los enterramientos según su ubicación sea en un espacio de habitación o bien en un taller artesanal. Nosotras interpretamos que la diferente funcionalidad de los ámbitos que configuran las viviendas del *vicus* no implica, necesariamente, un significado distinto de los enterramientos, ante todo porque los talleres artesanales están integrados en el espacio material donde vivía el grupo familiar. Parecería lógico, y probable, que la fuerza de trabajo utilizada para la producción artesanal estuviera constituida, en buena medida, por personas de la unidad familiar – hombres, mujeres, niños, niñas, ancianos y ancianas – que participarían en las distintas fases productivas según su edad y sus habilidades. Es decir, esos talleres no han de ser clasificados y significados como espacios de masculinidad, alejados del "mundo de las mujeres", sino como espacios compartidos en los que las sepulturas de esos seres queridos podrían, además, propiciar el trabajo productivo del grupo familiar. Esta interpretación se basa en la concepción de las viviendas como un espacio multifuncional, dinámico y de interrelación entre las personas que las habitan y entre estas y aquellas que las frecuentan. La idea estructuralista del espacio – basada en el sistema binario que contrapone el espacio doméstico al público, y el privado al político – impregna, a menudo, la significación de los ámbitos de las casas según sean las tareas en ellos realizadas, asociando de forma estereotipada las funciones y los espacios a uno u otro género, enmascarando así su naturaleza dinámica y su valor como lugar de interrelación social y familiar, y de producción.

## NOTES

1 Este ensayo forma parte del proyecto de investigación 'Claves diacrónicas de la divergencia social entre las construcciones jurídicas y simbólicas de la maternidad', financiado por el anterior Ministerio de Ciencia e Innovación (HAR2009-10035HIST)
2 Stefanovic, 2006
3 Riu, 1982, 32; Mínguez, 1989–1990, 105–22; Lorencio *et al.*, 1998, 309
4 Fernández, 2008, 204–14
5 Clop y Cruells 1991, 51
6 Duran *et al.,* 2013, 48
7 Molas 1982, 66–9; Rodà 2009, 31; Padrós 2010, 253
8 Álvarez *et al.* 2000, 273–5
9 Gros 2001, 30–38 y 82–84
10 Los estudios de territorio y los hallazgos arqueológicos nos permiten plantear la idea de que el campamento estuviera situado en el cerro de El Clascar (Malla, Barcelona), aproximadamente a 3,5 km del yacimiento de El Camp de les Lloses
11 Duran *et al.,* en prensa a
12 Lorrio *et al.* 2010, 253
13 Gusi y Muriel 2008, 297–300; Lorrio *et al.* 2010, 248–50
14 Saña y Valenzuela 2009, 26–45
15 Maluquer 1982, 251–9
16 Quesada 1999–2000, 104
17 Molas 2009; Lorrio *et al.* 2010, 253
18 Lorrio *et al.* 2010, 239; Guérin 2003, 62
19 Lorrio *et al.* 2010, 240
20 Existe un paralelo en el enterramiento perinatal del yacimiento ibérico del Molón (Camporrobles, Valencia) con ajuar funerario formado por escorias de hierro, muy similares a las del perinatal de El Camp de les Lloses, que rodeaban la cabeza y el costado derecho del neonato (Lorrio *et al.* 2010, 251)
21 Montón 1996, 7
22 Saña, y Valenzuela 2009, 37
23 Saña. y Valenzuela 2009, 73–92
24 Gusi y Muriel 2008, 304; Lorrio *et al.* 2010, 245
25 Los estudios antropológicos de las inhumaciones 1, 2, 3 y 4 han sido realizados por A. Alesan, S. Safont y A. Malgosa (Alesan *et al.* 1999, 2001 y 2003) y los de las inhumaciones 5, 6, 7, 8 y 9 por A. Alesan (Alesan, 2009 y 2012). Los criterios diagnósticos para la determinación del sexo se basan en la morfología de la mandíbula e *ilium* siguiendo a Schutkowski (Schutkowski 1993, 199–205) y los criterios diagnósticos para la determinación de la edad se establecen a partir de diversos autores (Alesan 2012,11)
26 Mínguez 1989–90, 115
27 Néraudau 1987, 195–7
28 Chapa-Brunet 2008, 628
29 Chapa-Brunet 2008, 621; Gusi y Muriel 2008, 298; Dedet 2008, 170
30 Dedet 2008, 170
31 Dedet 2008, 170
32 Scott 1999, 107–8

REFERENCIAS

Alesan, A., Safont, S. y Malgosa, A. 1999. *Dues inhumacions infantils del jaciment del Camp de les Lloses (Tona, Osona, 1998). Estudi antropològic.* Informe inédito. Generalitat de Catalunya, Barcelona.

Alesan, A., Safont, S. y Malgosa, A. 2001. *Estudi de la inhumació infantil recuperada al jaciment del Camp de les Lloses (Tona, Osona) durant la campanya de 1999. Estudi del material antropològic.* Informe inédito. Generalitat de Catalunya, Barcelona.

Alesan, A., Safont, S. y Malgosa, A. 2003. *Estudi de la inhumació infantil recuperada al jaciment del Camp de les Lloses (Tona, Osona) durant la campanya de 2002. Estudi del material antropològic.* Informe inédito. Generalitat de Catalunya, Barcelona.

Alesan, A. 2009. *Estudi del material antropològic del jaciment del Camp de les Lloses (Tona). Campanya d'excavacions 2006.* Informe inédito. Generalitat de Catalunya, Barcelona.

Alesan, A. 2012. *Estudi del material antropològic del jaciment del Camp de les Lloses (Tona). Campanya d'excavacions de 2009 i 2011.* Informe inédito. Generalitat de Catalunya, Barcelona.

Álvarez, R., Duran, M., Mestres, I. y Principal, J. 2000. El jaciment del Camp de les Lloses (Tona, Osona ) i el seu taller de metalls, pp. 271–281 en Mata, C. y Pérez Jordà, G. (eds), *IBERS. Agricultors, artesans i comerciants.* Valencia: Universitat de València.

Chapa-Brunet, T. 2008. Presencia infantil y ritual funerario en el mundo ibérico, pp. 619–641 en Gusi, F., Muriel, S. y Olaria, C. (coords.), *Nasciturus, infans, puerulus vobis mater terra. La muerte en la infancia.* Castellón de la Plana: Servei d'Investigacions Arqueològiques i Prehistòriques (SIAP). Servei de Publicacions.

Clop, X. y Cruells, W. 1991. *Memòria de la prospecció d'urgència realitzada en el Camp de les Lloses (Tona).* Memoria de excavación inédita. Generalitat de Catalunya, Barcelona.

Dedet, B. 2008. La mort du nouveau-né et du nourrisson dans le sud de la France protohistorique (Ie-Ier siècles avant J.-C), pp. 143–182 en Gusi, F., Muriel, S. y Olaria, C. (coords.), *Nasciturus, infans, puerulus vobis mater terra. La muerte en la infancia.* Castellón de la Plana: Servei d'Investigacions Arqueològiques i Prehistòriques (SIAP). Servei de Publicacions.

Duran, M., López, F., Mestres, I., Principal, J. y Ñaco, A. (en prensa). Evidencias numismáticas en un espacio logístico tardorrepublicano: El Camp de les Lloses (Tona, Barcelona, Catalunya). *I Workshop Internazionale di Numismatica. Numismatica e Archeologia. Monete, stratigrafie, dati a confronto, Roma, 2011.*

Duran, M., Mestres, I. y Principal, J. 2013. *El Parc Arqueològic del Camp de les Lloses el 2013.* Tona. Llibre de Tona.

Fernández, T. 2008. Los enterramientos infantiles en contextos domésticos en la cuenca Alta/Media del Ebro: a propósito de la inhumación del despoblado altomedieval de Aistra (Álava). *Munibe Antropologia-Arkeologia* 59, 199–217

Gros, P. 2001. *L'architecture romaine du début du IIIe siècle av. J.-C. à la fin du Haut-Empire. 2. Maisons, palais, villas et tombeaux.* Paris: Picard.

Guérin, P. 2003. *El Castellet de Bernabé y el horizonte Ibérico Pleno edetano* (Serie de Trabajos Varios nº 101). Valencia: Servicio de Investigación Prehistórica.

Gusi, F., Muriel, S. y Olaria, C. 2008 (coords.). *Nasciturus, infans, puerulus vobis mater terra. La muerte en la infancia.* Castellón de la Plana: Servei d'Investigacions Arqueològiques i Prehistòriques (SIAP). Servei de Publicacions.

Gusi, F. y Muriel, S. 2008. Panorama actual de la investigación de las inhumaciones infantiles en la Protohistoria del sudoeste mediterráneo europeo, pp. 257– 329 en Gusi, F., Muriel, S. y Olaria, C. (coords.), *Nasciturus, infans, puerulus vobis mater terra. La muerte en la infancia.* Castellón de la Plana: Servei d'Investigacions Arqueològiques i Prehistòriques (SIAP). Servei de Publicacions.

Lorencio, C., Puig, F. y Julià, M. 1998. Enterraments infantils a l'edifici imperial de la Magdalena (Lleida). De les estructures indígenes a l'organització provincial romana de la Hispania Citerior. *Itaca,* Annexos, 299–315.

Lorrio, A. J., Miguel, M. P., Moneo, T. y Sánchez del Prado, M. D. 2010. Enterramientos infantiles en el *oppidum* de El Molón (Camporrobles, Valencia). *Cuadernos de Arqueología Universidad de Navarra* 18, 201–62.

Maluquer, J. 1982. Notes sobre la formació del protagonisme dels Ausetans. *Ausa* X, 251–259.

Mínguez Morales, J. A. 1989–1990. Enterramientos infantiles domésticos en la colonia Lepida/Celsa (Velilla de Ebro, Zaragoza). *Caesaraugusta* 66–67, 105–122.

Molas Font, M. D. 1982. *Els ausetans i la ciutat d'Ausa.* Vic: Patronat d'Estudis Ausonencs.

Molas Font, M. D. 2009. La maternidad negada en las leyendas de los orígenes de Roma, pp. 133–154 en Cid López, R. M. (coord.). *Madres y maternidades. Construcciones culturales en la civilización clásica.* Oviedo: KRK Ediciones.

Montón, F. J. 1996. Las arulas de Tárraco. *Fòrum*, 6.

Néraudau, J.P. 1987. La mort les morts et l'au-delà dans le monde romain. *Actes du Colloque de Caen, 20–22 Novembre 1985*, 195–208.

Padrós, C. 2010. El territorio de la Plana ausetana i el seu entorn des de l'ibèric ple a l'alt imperi. *Cypsela 18,* pp. 247–266.

Quesada, F. 1999–2000. Territorio, etnicidad y cultura material. Estelas "Del Bajo Aragón" en Cataluña Nororiental. *Katathos* 18–19, 95–106.

Riu, M. 1982. Alguns costums funeraris de l'Edat Mitjana a Catalunya, Necròpolis i sepultures medievals de Catalunya. *Acta Mediaevalia.* Annex 1, 29–57.

Rodà, I. 2009. L'arqueologia pre-romana i romana al Montseny. *Monografies del Montseny/*24, 27–40.

Saña, M. y Valenzuela, A. 2009. *Anàlisi arqueozoològica de les restes de fauna recuperades al jaciment del Camp de les Lloses (Tona, Osona).* Laboratori d'Arqueozoologia. Universitat Autònoma de Barcelona. Informe inèdit. Generalitat de Catalunya, Barcelona.

Schutkowski, H. 1993. Sex Determination of Infant and Juvenile Skeletons: I Morphognostic Features. *American Journal of Physical Anthropology* 90, 199–205.

Scott, E. 1999. *The Archaeology of Infancy and Infant Death* (BAR International Series 819). Oxford: Archaeopress.

Stefanovic, S. 2006. The domestication of human birth. *Documenta Praehistorica* XXXIII, 159–164.

Subirà, E. y Molist, N. 2008. Inhumacions perinatals multiples i espais de treball en els assentaments ibers, pp. 365–385 en Gusi, F., Muriel, S. y Olaria, C. (coords.), *Nasciturus, infans, puerulus vobis mater terra. La muerte en la infancia.* Castellón de la Plana: Servei d'Investigacions Arqueològiques i Prehistòriques (SIAP). Servei de Publicacions.

# 22

## Children and Funerary Space. Ritual Behaviours in the Greek Colonies of Magna Graecia and Sicily

### Diego Elia and Valeria Meirano

The International Research Programme recently devoted to children and death in the ancient Mediterranean, intitled *EMA. L'enfant et la mort dans l'antiquité: des pratiques funéraires à l'identité sociale (2008–2011)*, as well as the three related conferences, which took place in Athens, Alexandria and Aix en Provence (Fig. 22.1),[1] represented an important occasion for interdisciplinary exchange between scholars involved in the study of Antiquity. In this frame, a considerable *corpus* of data often neglected in archaeological speculation has been revisited and put in a new perspective, together with the evidence coming from recent investigations. A website (www.mae.u-paris10. fr/ema) was also created to put the results of the programme at scholars' disposal and

*Figure 22.1. The EMA programme: Athens (2008), Alexandria (2009), Aix-en Provence (2011).*

to provide easy access to archaeological data by means of site, necropolis and tomb forms related to pre-adult funerary contexts, from the archaic to the late antique period.

The team of the University of Turin[2] worked on the Greek archaeological contexts of Southern Italy and Sicily, both in a general perspective and focusing on those specific case-studies which offer an abundant and well documented body of material. Moreover, a particular aspect consisted in bringing unpublished evidence concerning the necropoleis of *Locri Epizephyrii* into discussion.

The aim of our paper is to provide a contribution towards the reconstruction of child-related space in funerary contexts, focusing on the Greek colonies of Southern Italy and Sicily. By the way, the investigation on space is not the sole field in which one encounters difficulties in the attempt to draw proper attention to the presence of children in the necropoleis of Western Greece.

*Cherchez l'enfant!* is the beginning of the title of the contribution by Véronique Dasen in the third *EMA* conference[3] and could also efficaciously epitomize the effort which is necessary to detect the traces of children in funerary areas. If pre-adults played a socially-weak role in ancient communities, especially in Greek ones, as marginal and under-tutelage individuals – like women and slaves – nevertheless their *status* was somewhere recognized, for exemple in Athens, in relation to specific official religious festivals and occasions, like the *Choes*, when three year old male children could taste wine for the first time in their life. Moreover, they received attention in the iconography, e.g. on attic figured vases and tomb *stelai*.[4] On the contrary, on the basis of ancient sources and archaeological data, we should infer that in Western Greece children were given very little attention by their communities, in comparison to many regions of Greek Mainland, especially Attica. This attitude – we could say – is reflected by modern research, which has been neglecting the study of children in the Greek societies of Southern Italy and Sicily for a long time; only in the last few years do we notice a new interest in this field.[5]

## CHILDREN AND SPACE IN *MAGNA GRAECIA* AND SICILY THROUGH FUNERARY EVIDENCE

Pre-adult individuals are attested to at the necropoleis of Greek cities of Southern Italy and Sicily, even though their occurrence largely varies according to contexts and chronological periods; moreover, their presence is not related to particular funerary areas, exclusively or mainly reserved to specific age-classes. In the cemeteries where child burials are known, they are rather scattered among adult tombs.

Our approach is based on the analysis of two factors that represent different aspects of the relation existing between children and space in funerary contexts: grave markers and grave containers. The former implies the concept of *visibility* accorded to children by their communities, while the latter concerns the way adults performed the preparation of the space eternally devoted to house the deceased children, so a more *intimate* space. In both cases, we deal with the roles the society attributed to children.

## Grave Markers

Grave markers – *semata* or *epitymbia*, as the Greeks used to say – represented a crucial element of ancient funerary landscapes, used for the indication of tombs on the surface of the necropoleis. They could be monumental and accurate – like architectural structures, *naiskoi* in the form of small temples, earth moulds or *tumuli*, sculpted or inscribed *stelai*, statues, columns, pillars, large marble or ceramic vases – as well as simpler elements – like *cippi*, uncarved *stelae*, pebble heaps, stone circles, etc.

In general, even for adult deceased, the evidence concerning grave markers and indication systems on surface is very poor in *Magna Graecia* and Sicily, notwithstanding the intensive excavation of many necropoleis. The analysis of published data shows the poorness of the archaeological elements recovered and the difficulty in collecting and refering them to precise tombs or tomb groups.[6] This is striking, if we consider the extent of the funerary areas explored and the number of burials discovered at sites like *Poseidonia*, *Metapontum*, Taranto, and, in Sicily, Syracuse, *Megara Hyblaea*, *Kamarina*, Agrigento, *Selinus*, etc. In general, we can assume that the lack of documents is partly due to the circumstances in which excavations took place in past decades, as well as to the destruction and spoliation phenomena occurred in ancient and modern times. The perishable nature of many *semata* – made of wood, mudbricks, earth etc. – could also be among the causes of their disappearance. Nevertheless, all these circumstances cannot contradict the fact that in Western Greece grave markers are seldom attested, especially in comparison with other areas of the Greek world. Moreover, the evidence is very heterogeneous according to chronological periods: during the archaic and the classical age, the examples are absolutely rare and the majority of them come from Sicilian Greek sites.[7]

In the light of this meagre gathering, what is the occurrence of *semata* related to children? If adult tombs were very seldom indicated on the surface, grave markers constitute an absolute exception for infant burials.[8]

At Syracuse (Fig. 22.2), in Sicily, two funerary *stelai* are probably attributable to adolescents,[9] and in the Fusco necropolis a *bathron* made in stone blocks surmounted a communal shaft grave containing an incineration and an inhumation belonging to a child.[10] At Gela (Fig. 22.2), in the necropolis of Capo Soprano, pebbles and a stone heap indicated the tomb of a young individual.[11]

Apart from these few Sicilian exemples, the funerary area of San Montano on the island of *Pithekoussai*, modern Ischia (Fig. 22.2), constitues probably the unique context in which one can recognise, between the 8th and the beginning of the 6th century, a precise relation between the graves and the indication system on surface, in which child tombs played a role.

At *Pithekoussai*, the funerary ritual varies according to the *status* and the age of the deceased. Incineration concerns almost exclusively adult individuals of both sexes.[12] The ashes were disposed in pits, surrounded by stone circles and surmounted by *tumuli*. On the contrary, children and adolescents were usually buried in wooden coffins (perhaps surmounted by little *tumuli*) and newborn individuals were put in

*Figure 22.2. Magna Graecia and Sicily: main sites cited in the paper.*

amphoras or in cooking pots. In every case, the location of the graves was indicated on surface by stone heaps.

The grave-marker system played a major role at San Montano: the archaeological data show that the funerary space was accurately planned and divided in family plots, where the *tumuli* pertaining to new tombs progressively incorporated the previous ones.

The analysis of the stratigraphy brought into evidence that the rite implied the respect of previous burials.[13] In family plots, pre-adult graves were integrated in the common system: the renowned example published by Buchner and Ridgway (Fig. 22.3)[14] is emblematic of this phenomenon of progressive agglutination involving also child and newborn tombs, till the beginning of the 6th century.

First, the tomb group is constituted by the inhumation of a newborn baby surmounted by a stone (a) and by the incineration of an adult with its *tumulus* (A). Then, the group is made larger thanks to the progressive *agglutination* we mentioned: the earth mould

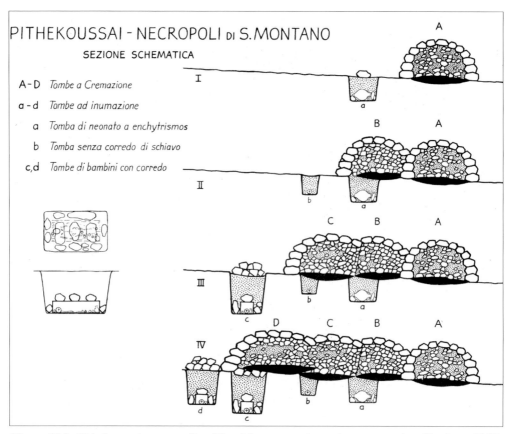

*Figure 22.3. Pithekoussai, necropolis of San Montano: schematic cross-section (Buchner 1975, pl. II).*

is doubled to accomodate the incineration of another adult (B), which covers the infant burial (a). This process is repeated during the following phases of the necropolis: other shaft graves covered by stone heaps (c and d) belonging to pre-adults are added to the initial group as well as adult incinerations (C and D). As the *tumuli* of the adults merge, infant tombs are incorporated and lose their individual identity. It is noteworthy that some tombs belonging to subordinate individuals, consisting in inhumations without any grave good (e.g., b), are involved in the same phenomenon.

The case of *Pithekoussai* represents a rare document in the general picture offered by Greek necropoleis in Southern Italy and Sicily,[15] but we can now add new elements to this frame presenting the data coming from the necropoleis of *Locri Epizephyrii*, a Greek colony on the Ionian coast of Southern Calabria (Fig. 22.2), explored on several occasions during the 20th century. The Parapezza-Lucifero funerary area, counting almost 2000 tombs dated between the 6th and the 3rd century, has been the object of a systematic re-examination and partial re-edition in the last few years.[16]

The analysis of unpublished excavation journals and a new evaluation of several indications have permitted to ascertain the existence of grave markers previously neglected by archaeological literature, like stone bases, ionian capitals, several architectural elements, many stone *cippi*, as well as column fragments, a marble sculpted *hydria*, terracotta *arulae* and a few inscribed stones dated to the 3rd and 2nd century. In addition, at least 5% of the tombs were indicated on surface by means of heaps made of large pebbles.

In the light of the evidence recovered, the funerary landscape we can now reconstruct is extremely varied and constitutes a rare case in *Magna Graecia* between the archaic period and the 3rd century.

At Parapezza-Lucifero, pre-adult burials represent 22.5% of the total (17% belonging to children, 5.5% to adolescent individuals), a percentage that, like in the majority of ancient funerary areas, is largely lower than expected for a preindustrial society, due to the fact that only a small part of pre-adults received what we call "formal burial".[17]

Recent research enables us to detect the traces of the links existing between the surface indication system and some infant burials. In a child cist tomb dated to the first half of the 6th century (n. 1956/B: Fig. 22.4), three terracotta *arulae* – small altars – laid one upon the other and constituted one of the walls of the grave and the grave marker as well.[18] The three specimens derive from the same mould and they all show the same iconography: the hero Heracles fighting against a human-head bull we can identify as Acheloos.[19] We may assume that the image of this labour by Heracles, the hero triumphant over the dangers, was intentionally selected due to its prophylactic value, as a *viaticum* for the journey of the infant deceased to the Underworld.[20]

A later example of marker is attested for tomb n. 773, dated to the 3rd century, which was surmounted by a monumental *epitymbion* made of stone blocks;[21] moreover, many child graves where covered and delimited by pebbles and stone splinters, used to make rudimentary heaps.[22]

Thus, it is ascertained that at least some of the child tombs were provided with individual markers of different shapes at

*Figure 22.4. Reconstruction of the south wall of tomb 1956/B of the Parapezza-Lucifero necropolis at Locri Epizephyrii (Elia 2010, 72, pl. 5).*

Locri: may we assume that child burials could sometimes also be integrated in tomb groups marked on surface by commonal *semata*?

In 1913, a broken column with its lower part still *in situ* was discovered: it clearly acted as a communal grave marker for a group of tombs. Another tomb group excavated in 1914 shows the association between a quadrangular stone *cippus*, probably the socle of the proper communal marker, and a gravel layer, underscoring the unity of the complex.[23] In the two groups (Fig. 22.5), dated between the end of the 6th and the 5th century, where both male and female individuals were buried, the graves mutually respected each other, being parallel or superimposed at different levels. Sometimes, new tombs partly damaged previous graves: in this case, the use of a *privileged* space prevailed over the respect for more ancient burials. In these groups, adolescents (tombs nn. 653 and 661) and children (tombs nn. 1062, 1071 and 1066, containing two little girls aged 4 and 7, and a child aged 9 respectively) are attested, which means that their burials were totally integrated in the spatial organisation we mentioned.

A context excavated in 1956, dated between the second half of the 6th and the first half of the 4th century, shows clear analogies with the two tomb-groups previously described.[24] In this case, it is possibile to trace back the progressive distribution of the graves, making a circle around an area which was left free and marked on surface by a piece of a column and by several pebbles. Among the tombs, two belong to pre-adult individuals we can identify as a foetus (tomb n. 11) and a child (tomb n. 8).

The cases examined confirm the existence of markers of different types, used to show tomb groups on surface; in these groups, the graves are linked by specific spatial relations which imply family ties. Moreover, at Locri this system concerns pre-adults at different age-stages who did participate in the spatial organisation of the burial area, with all the social implications related.

Starting from the 6th century – especially from the second half – we notice a general increase of *semata* in Western Greece, both monumental and small ones, which lead us to imagine the existence of more varied and heterogeneous funerary landscapes, especially in Sicily. New types of markers are characteristic of this period, like the

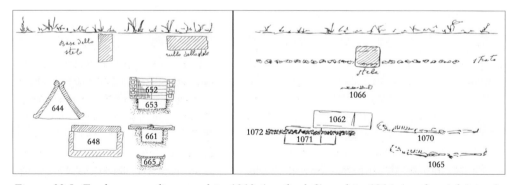

*Figure 22.5. Tomb groups discovered in 1913 (on the left) and in 1914 (on the right) in the necropolis of Parapezza-Lucifero at Locri Epizephyrii (Elia 2010, 337, figs 1 and 2).*

stepped pyramid *epitymbia*; at the same time, *mausolea* and rock-cut tombs with architectural *façades* show a momentous development.[25]

This different scenario enables us to trace the elements of some indication systems where infants were involved in Sicily.[26]A tomb group in the Fusco necropolis at Syracuse was surmounted by a *mnema koinon,* a communal marker: the plot counted a very young individual.[27] Two child burials of Scala Greca, always in Syracuse, were indicated on surface by stone *cippi*.[28]

In the necropolis of Valle San Mauro at *Leontinoi* (Fig. 22.2), four stepped pyramid *epitymbia,* dated between the end of the 4th and the beginning of the 3rd century, show a common orientation and correspond to a distinguished group (tombs nn. 1, 2, 6, 9). Even though all the burials belong to adult individuals, a young deceased was buried in the narrow space between two *epitymbia*.[29] This case clearly shows the deliberate choice of a specific space to accomodate the non-adult. In the same funerary area, the *enchytrismos* of a baby was indicated on surface by a rudimentary marker constituted by a stone circle.[30]

On the other hand, several sites of Southern Italy – like Reggio, Naples, *Herakleia, Metapontum* and especially Taranto – offer a rich and detailed body of documents, but, unfortunately, it is neither possibile to trace the associations of the majority of the markers, nor to ascertain their provenance. Among the cases in which the original contexts are known, no grave marker is attributable to an infant burial.[31]

*Grave containers*

The second aspect concerned by our paper is the *aménagement* of the space directly surrounding the body of deceased children. The degree of scrutiny spent during the excavations, especially in past decades, as well as the heterogeneous level of the documentation make it hard to evaluate the occurrence of tomb types used for children. As it is impossible to provide such a general picture, we choose to examine some case-studies from *Magna Graecia* which prove representative and enable us to highlight some recurrent tendencies.[32]

In the necropolis of San Montano at *Pithekoussai*, between the 8th and the beginning of the 6th century, the majority of child burials are *enchytrismoi*, corresponding to more than 25% of the tombs of the entire burial area.[33] The most common containers are transport amphoras, large jars (*pithoi*), jugs, *ollae,* biconical vases, etc., among which smaller vessels are used for foetuses.[34] The remaining non-adult individuals are buried in shaft graves:[35] among these tombs, some show a more complex structure, with wooden coffins and grave markers  – as we have seen – and are attributed to the middle or high social *milieu* of the community due to their furnishings.[36] On the contrary, other pre-adults are buried, sometimes in flexed position, in simpler shaft tombs without any grave good, and are generally considered to belong to the subordinate class.[37]

This synthetic picture shows the variability of burial customs during the first phases of the settlement: the funerary practice reflects the ideology that determined a specific treatment for every member of the community, appropriated to his/her level of social integration; in this frame, age criteria played a fundamental role.[38]

Between the 6th and the 3rd century, some case-studies show the predominance of common tendencies in the choice of tomb types related the age-classes. An exemple is constituted by the necropoleis of the territory of the colony of *Metapontum* on the Ionian coast (Fig. 22.2), where the quality of the documentation and the osteological analyses provide a systematic *corpus* of data.[39] Only 21.2% of the tombs for which an age determination is possible belong to non-adults.[40] Incineration is by far the minority rite for children,[41] while among the inhumations we notice the use of less rich and accurate containers in comparison with adults, a choice which seems to be the result of a precise strategy. Cist tombs, stone graves and sarcophagi are intended for adults, with a very few exceptions; even among tile graves, accurate vault tombs are used for adults only.[42] Other tomb types are shared by all age classes, like shaft and *a cappuccina* tombs.[43]

On the contrary, the structures made in laconian tiles (laconian *a cappuccina* and cradle burials: Fig. 22.6) belong almost exclusively to pre-adults: they correspond to about half of the deceased of this age group (45%), among which many are newborn. Tiles could also be used to build modest versions of adult cist tombs to accomodate children.[44] Babies aged under six months were also buried in sort of terracotta bathtubs of undetermined function, as well as in amphora *enchytrismoi*.[45]

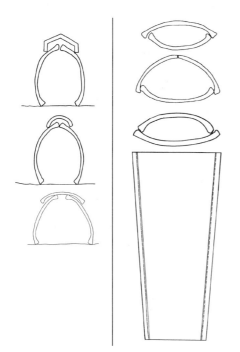

*Figure 22.6. Laconian a cappuccina tombs and cradle burials from the necropolis of Pantanello, Metapontum (Carter 1998a, figs 3.52, 3.55, 3.56).*

Further south on the Ionian coast is the colony of *Kaulonia* (Fig. 22.2). In the necropolis of Vallone Bernardo, dated between the archaic and the hellenistic period,[46] inhumation concerns the majority of the deceased and all the children. Shaft and tile graves (cist and *a cappuccina* types) are used both for adults and non-adults, while about half of the children are buried in *enchytrismoi*, mainly obtained using cooking pots, amphoras or even large bowls. In addition, some terracotta containers exclusively recur in infant graves and are attested by a unique specimen: this is the case of a *cilindro fittile con armille alle estremità*, probably the base of a *louterion* (large basin), and of an *arula* (?).[47]

At Locri, in the Parapezza-Lucifero necropolis, the study conducted on a large sample of tombs shows that the incineration was used for non-adults, even though it is impossibile to ascertain its occurrence.[48] As far as inhumation is concerned, the majority of infant and adult burials was made of terracotta elements.[49] Although some terracotta tomb types were reserved to adults (e.g. the *a mezza botte* and the *a cassa* graves made of bricks and vertically oriented tiles), the majority of adult tombs belong to two types which were commonly used also for children: tile and shaft graves. In these cases, the choice consisted in burying children in adult tomb types of reduced or simplified versions.

At the same time, we notice a tendency in adopting other types, exclusively conceived for non-adults, both in the case of adolescents (8.3% of non-adults inhumations) and, particularly, in that of children (more than 40% of non-adults inhumations). *Enchytrismoi* are not widely attested and concern mainly newborn individuals, buried in transport amphoras and also in black-glaze specimens during the second half of the 6th century.[50] The use of large *pithoi* is documented in two cases, probably pertaining to adolescents.[51]

A rare kind of *enchytrismos* consists in the use of tubular terracotta elements: in tomb n. 842, this was probably a beehive, as it is attested to in Attica and in other western sites.[52] This kind of container shows symbolic implications related to the values of honey, both as an imputrescible substance and as one of the nourishments given to newborn babies.[53]

Among the tombs conceived for children are those made by small terracotta basins: at Parapezza-Lucifero this type is attested between the end of the 5th and the first half of the 4th century for foetuses or very young individuals (Fig. 22.7). Moreover, typically Locrian child graves are those encircled by *arulae*. We've already examined

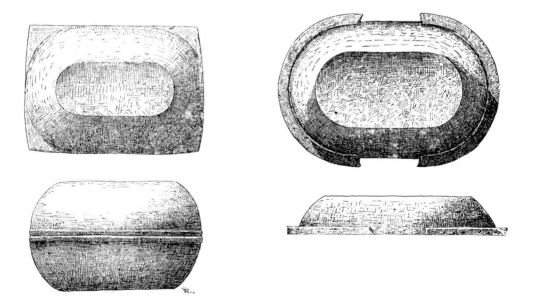

*Figure 22.7. Tombs made with terracotta basins from the necropolis of Parapezza-Lucifero at Locri Epizephyrii (Orsi 1913, figs 5 and 7).*

the tomb showing small altars bearing the iconography of Heracles and Akeloos (n. 1956/B), which recurs on an *arula* in tomb n. 1347 too.[54] In another burial (n. 1224), dated between the second half of the 6th and the beginning of the 5th century, two altars were used, bearing an animal fight scene and the depiction of a four-horse chariot respectively.[55] In tomb n. 1956/13 the south wall was made by two *arulae* without any decoration.[56]

Between the 5th and the 3rd century, new heterogeneous tomb types develop at Parapezza-Lucifero, mostly belonging to newborn or very small children, made of poor, occasional and usually fragmentary materials, like pieces of tiles and *arulae*, stone splinters and pebbles, etc.[57] Notwithstanding the use of building material, it is impossible to identify a precise structure in these graves which sometimes protected only a minor part of the corpses.[58]

The review of the documentation related to Southern Italy colonial centres shows the heterogeneous level of the data at our disposal. For the most ancient phases, the case of *Pithekoussai* is emblematic of the strict link existing between tomb-types and social organisation on the base of age and *status*.[59]

On the other hand, the *corpus* of material provided by *Magna Graecia* between the second half of the 6th and the 3rd century is largely more abundant and varied. In this period, when funerary ritual and customs are standardized and the tendency to emphasize the social role of the deceased by means of grave goods is generally abandoned,[60] the development of tiles and terracotta elements in the making of tomb structures modifies the funerary evidence. In this frame, some sites offer material for a comparative reading: certain grave types (e.g., those made of stone, like *sarcophagi* and cist tombs, as well as particular terracotta types, like the *a mezza botte* and vault tombs attested to at Locri and in the territory of *Metaponum*) are exclusively conceived for adults. Other types are common to different age classes, like the *a cappuccina* and shaft graves (e.g., in the *Metapontum* area, at *Kaulonia* and Locri): they just vary in the dimensions and in the complexity of the structures in comparison with those belonging to adults.

On the contrary, many different solutions are adopted to bury infants and adolescents. *Enchtrismoi* are less common, like in the *Metapontum* territory and at Locri, notwithstanding the major evidence in the necropoleis of *Kaulonia* and *Pithekoussai*, as far as this chronological phase is concerned.[61]

On the majority of the sites, new terracotta containers of cylindrical shape are made with varied elements: curved roof tiles, sometimes associated with ordinary tiles or *kalypteres hegemones*, laconian tiles to make *cradle burials* – like in the *Metapontum* area – bases of *louteria*, etc. Rare solutions are adopted sometimes, like the bathtub tombs in the *Metapontum* area and the bottle-shaped vase used in tomb n. 846 at Locri.[62] The choice is usually determined by the suitability these objects show for the making of children funerary structures; nevertheless, the use of particular containers, like small terracotta basins, as well as the rare beehive from tomb n. 842 at Locri, is not fortuitus, but probably related to specific symbolic values pertaining to the infant sphere. The Locrian tombs showing sculpted *arulae* are the result of an accurate iconographic selection, as well as the hellenistic foot-shaped sarcophagus of Reggio, which constitutes an *unicum* so far.[63]

In conclusion, in the frame provided by the funerary variability of the necropoleis examined, the strict relation existing between tomb types and age-classes is clearly documented; on the contrary, it proves difficult to recognize a systematic relation between the choice of funerary containers and the representation strategy of the social *status* of the deceased. It is noteworthy that on many sites, as at Locri, accurate tombs structures and containers are not necessarily associated to *rich* and articulated grave good assemblages.

NOTES

1    Guimier Sorbets and Morizot 2010; Nenna 2012; Hermary and Dubois 2012
2    Dr. Barbara Carè and Carla Scilabra participated in the programme with the authors
3    Dasen 2012
4    The bibliography concerning children in ancient Attica is particularly abundant: see e.g. Golden 1990; Hamilton 1992; Houby-Nielsen 2000; Neils and Oakley 2003; Beaumont 2012
5    See for exemple: Bouffier 1999; 2012; Carè 2006; 2012 and forthcoming; Elia 2012; Elia and Meirano 2010; 2012; Lambrugo 2005; forthcoming and *supra*, in this volume; Meirano 2012; Scilabra 2012; 2013 and forthcoming; Shepherd 2006; 2007
6    Elia and Meirano 2010
7    All the dates cited in the text are BC, with the exception of those related to archaeological explorations
8    For a general outline, see Elia and Meirano 2010
9    From Contrada Taracati: Orsi 1915, 193, fig. 8 (end of the Vth century); from Tyche: Libertini 1929, 160; Villard and de Miré 1955, 293, fig. 14 (beginning of the IVth century)
10   Orsi 1895, 130 (tomb n. CLXXXV)
11   Orsi 1906, col. 399, fig. 291 (tomb n. 12: Vth century). Concerning the renowned archaic *kourotrophos* found in the necropolis of Megara Hyblaea (Gentili 1954, 99–102, fig. 24, tomb I; Elia and Meirano 2010, 291), the archaeological evidence does not corroborate the hypothesis that the statue was somehow related to the infant tomb found nearby, as stated by V. Dasen (2005, 201)
12   With some rare exceptions concerning adolescents: *cf.* Elia and Meirano 2012, 431, note 7, for discussion and bibliography
13   See Buchner and Ridgway 1993; see also Buchner 1975; 1982; Ridgway 1984, 61–95; Nizzo 2007; Elia and Meirano 2010, 297–98
14   Buchner 1975, pl. II; Ridgway 1984, fig. 6
15   See Buchner 1975. The occurrence of incinerations surmounted by *tumuli* continues between the end of the VIth and the IVth century at San Montano: see Buchner and Ridgway 1993, 49 (tomb n. 21), 52 (tomb n. 27), 82 (tomb n. 61), 109 (tomb n. 86), etc.
16   See Orsi 1913; 1917; Cerchiai 1982; Elia 2003; 2010, with the complete bibliography concerning the necropolis; 2012, *passim*; Elia and Meirano 2010, 304–8; 2012, 439–48; Meirano 2012, *passim*
17   Morris 1987; see also d'Agostino and D'Onofrio 1993
18   Elia 2010, 58, 269–70, 332–35, tomb B; Elia and Meirano 2010, 306, fig. 4; 2012, 446–48, fig. 11.
19   The structure of another Locrian child tomb (n. 1347) was partly built with an *arula* showing the same scene: *cf.* Orsi 1917, 119–20, fig. 24; Elia 2010, 268, 335; Elia and Meirano 2010, 306; 2012, 445–46, fig. 10

20 For further discussion, see Elia and Meirano 2010, 306; 2012, 448. Other specimens and fragments of *arulae*, found sporadic on the surface of the necropolis, could have been part of child tombs or markers (Elia and Meirano 2010, 306, note 168)

21 Orsi 1913, 33; Elia and Meirano 2010, 306–07, fig. 5

22 Elia and Meirano 2012, 445

23 Elia 2010, 336, figs. 1 and 2; Elia and Meirano 2010, 307, fig. 6a–b

24 Elia 2010, 336–39, fig. 3; Elia and Meirano 2010, 307–08, fig. 7

25 Elia and Meirano 2010, 298–301, with further bibliography

26 Elia and Meirano 2010, 301–02

27 Orsi 1897, 480–82, figs 13–16 (tombs nn. DXLV–DXLVIII)

28 Orsi 1897, 494 (tomb n. IX; IVth century); 501 (tomb n. LIII)

29 Rizza 1954, 72; 1955, 305, figs 8 and 20 (tomb n. 10)

30 Rizza 1955, 311–12, fig. 17 (tomb n. 133)

31 See Elia and Meirano 2010, 302–04, for discussion and references

32 See Elia and Meirano 2012, 429–30, for the methodological problems and the criteria followed to select the case-studies presented

33 Nizzo 2007, 13

34 Nizzo 2007, 32; Buchner 1982, 277

35 Buchner 1982, 277; d'Agostino 2000, 106; see also Shepherd 2006, 311

36 Nizzo 2007, 30–1; Elia and Meirano 2012, 431

37 Buchner 1982, 279; see also Ridgway 1984, 61–2, 90; Nizzo 2007, 13, 31; d'Agostino 2000; Elia and Meirano 2012, 431

38 *Cf. supra*, for other aspects of the ritual concerning *status* and age classes

In the following phases of the necropolis, the documents are less abudant; nevertheless, some of the previous tendencies are confirmed: see Elia and Meirano 2012, 433

39 Carter 1998a

40 Carter 1998b, 180, table 6.4; *cf.* also Elia and Meirano 2012, 435, note 31

41 Elia and Meirano 2012, 435–6, note 34

42 Elia and Meirano 2012, 436

43 Carter and Hall 1998, 247, 275; Elia and Meirano 2012, 437

44 Carter 1998b, 97–103; Elia and Meirano 2012, 437, fig. 3

45 *Cf.* Carter 1998b, 103, 108, tomb n. 191; Carter and Hall 1998, 333, 373, tombs nn. 308 and 337; see also Elia and Meirano 2012, 437, fig. 4

46 Orsi 1914; Palomba 2004

47 Orsi 1914, col. 910, tomb n. 7; cols. 923–4, tomb n. 54; *cf.* Elia and Meirano 2012, 439, notes 50 and 51

48 Elia 2010, 15, with further bibliography; Elia and Meirano 2012, 439–40, note 57

49 With a few exceptions: Elia 2010, 50 and note 18; Elia and Meirano 2012, 440

50 Elia and Meirano 2012, 440–2

51 Orsi 1917, 103, 106, tombs nn. 1011 and 1106

52 See also tomb n. 846, showing a bottle-shaped container of indefinte function: Elia and Meirano 2012, 442

53 Elia and Meirano 2012, 442–43, note 73

54 *Supra*, note 19

55 As in tomb n. 1347, the *arulae* show evidence of reuse: Elia and Meirano 2012, 446, note 90, fig. 9.

56 Elia 2010, 51, 58; Elia and Meirano 2012, 446

57 Elia and Meirano 2012, 443–44

58 Elia and Meirano 2012, 445, with discussion

59 Close parallels for the *Pithekoussai* necropolis are provided by Sicilian sites: Elia and Meirano 2012, 449, note 98

60  See Elia 2012 for discussion and the examination of meaningful exceptions
61  *Supra*, note 15
62  *Supra*, note 52
63  See Meirano 2012, 122–123, fig. 6, also for the symbolic value of the foot iconography related to young female individuals and for the different kinds of shoes as *status* indicators

## References

Beaumont, L. A. 2012. *Childhood in ancient Athens. Iconography and social history*, London-New York: Routledge.

Bouffier, S. 1999. Des vases pour les enfants, pp. 91–6 in Villaneuva Puig, M. C., Lissarrague, F. and Rouillard, P. (eds), *Céramique et peinture grecques: modes d'emploi. Actes du Colloque International, École du Louvre, 26–28 avril 1995*. Paris: La documentation française.

Bouffier, S. 2012. Mobilier funéraire et statut social des enfants dans les nécropoles grecques de Sicile, pp. 131–148 in Hermary, A. and Dubois, C. (eds), *L'enfant et la mort dans l'antiquité, III. Le matériel associé aux tombes d'enfants, Actes de la table ronde internationale organisée à la Maison Méditerranéenne des Sciences de l'Homme (MMSH, Aix-en-Provence, 20–22 janvier 2011)*, BiAMA 12. Paris: Éditions Errance.

Buchner, G. 1975. Nuovi aspetti e problemi posti dagli scavi di Pithecusa con particolari considerazioni sulle oreficerie di stile orientalizzante antico, pp. 59–86 in *Contribution à l'étude de la société et de la colonisation eubéennes*, Cahiers du Centre Jean Bérard II. Naples: Centre Jean Bérard.

Buchner, G. 1982. Articolazione sociale, differenze di rituale e composizione dei corredi nella necropoli di Pithecusa, pp. 275–87 in Gnoli, G. and Vernant, J.-P. (eds), *La mort, les morts dans les sociétés anciennes*. Cambridge/Paris: Cambridge University Press.

Buchner, G. and Ridgway, D. 1993. *Pithekoussai I. Le necropoli: tombe 1–723 scavate dal 1952 al 1961*, Monumenti Antichi dei Lincei LV, s. mon. IV. Rome: G. Bretschneider.

Carè, B. 2006. Alcune osservazioni sulle sepolture di defunti in età pre-adulta nelle necropoli greche d'Occidente: la diffusione dell'astragalo, *Orizzonti. Rassegna di Archeologia* VII, 143–52.

Carè, B. 2012. L'astragalo in tomba nel mondo greco: un indicatore infantile? Vecchi problemi e nuove osservazioni a proposito di un aspetto del costume funerario, pp. 403–416 in Hermary, A. and Dubois, C. (eds), *L'enfant et la mort dans l'antiquité, III. Le matériel associé aux tombes d'enfants, Actes de la table ronde internationale organisée à la Maison Méditerranéenne des Sciences de l'Homme (MMSH, Aix-en-Provence, 20–22 janvier 2011)*, BiAMA 12. Paris: Éditions Errance.

Carè, B. forthcoming. "Where are the children?" again. Infants and 'age markers' in the necropoleis of Western Greece, in *Between Life and Death: Interactions Between Burial and Society in the Ancient Mediterranean and Near East, Liverpool, May 11–12 2012*.

Carter, J. C. 1998a (ed.). *The chora of Metaponto: the necropoleis*. Austin: Universiy of Texas Press.

Carter, J. C. 1998b. Burial Rites and Tomb Types, pp. 57–111 in Carter, J. C., *The chora of Metaponto: the necropoleis*. Austin: Universiy of Texas Press.

Carter, J. C. and Hall, J. 1998. Burial Descriptions, pp. 237–447 in Carter, J. C., *The chora of Metaponto: the necropoleis*. Austin: Universiy of Texas Press.

Cerchiai, L. 1982. Sesso e classi d'età nelle necropoli greche di Locri Epizephiri, pp. 289–298 in Gnoli, G. and Vernant, J.-P. (eds), *La mort, les morts dans les sociétés anciennes*. Cambridge/Paris: Cambridge University Press.

d'Agostino, B. 2000. La colonizzazione euboica nel golfo di Napoli, pp. 99–113 in Gras M., Greco E., Guzzo P. G. (eds), *Nel cuore del Mediterraneo antico. Reggio, Messina e le colonie calcidesi dell'area dello Stretto*. Corigliano Calabro: Meridiana Libri.

d'Agostino, B. and D'Onofrio, A. M. 1993. Review of: Morris I., *Burial and Ancient Society. The Rise of the Greek City-state*, Cambridge, 1987, *Gnomon* 65, 41–51.

Dasen, V. 2005. *Jumeaux, jumelles dans l'antiquité grecque et romaine*. Kilchberg: Akanthus.

Dasen, V. 2012. Cherchez l'enfant! La question de l'identité à partir du matériel funéraire, pp. 9–22 in Hermary, A. and Dubois, C. (eds), *L'enfant et la mort dans l'antiquité, III. Le matériel associé aux tombes d'enfants, Actes de la table ronde internationale organisée à la Maison Méditerranéenne des Sciences de l'Homme (MMSH, Aix-en-Provence, 20–22 janvier 2011),* BiAMA 12. Paris: Éditions Errance.

Elia, D. 2003. L'offerta di sostanze alimentari liquide presso la tomba e l'uso rituale del cratere nelle necropoli greche d'Occidente. *Orizzonti. Rassegna di Archeologia* IV, 145–54.

Elia, D. 2010. *Locri Epizefiri VI. Nelle case di Ade. La necropoli in contrada Lucifero. Nuovi documenti.* Alessandria: Dell'Orso.

Elia, D. 2012. Sepolture di pre-adulti nelle necropoli greche dell'Italia meridionale: osservazioni sulle strategie di rappresentazione tra periodo tardo arcaico ed eta classica, pp. 97–110 in Hermary, A. and Dubois, C. (eds), *L'enfant et la mort dans l'antiquité, III. Le matériel associé aux tombes d'enfants, Actes de la table ronde internationale organisée à la Maison Méditerranéenne des Sciences de l'Homme (MMSH, Aix-en-Provence, 20–22 janvier 2011),* BiAMA 12. Paris: Éditions Errance.

Elia, D. and Meirano, V. 2010. Modes de signalisation des sépultures dans les nécropoles grecques d'Italie du Sud et de Sicilie. Remarques générales et le cas des tombes d'enfant, pp. 289–325 in Guimier-Sorbets, A. M. and Morizot, Y. (eds), *L'enfant et la mort dans l'antiquité, I. Nouvelles recherches dans les nécropoles grecques. Le signalement des tombes d'enfants, Actes de la table ronde internationale (Athènes, 28–30 mai 2008),* Travaux de la Maison René Ginouvès 12. Paris: De Boccard.

Elia, D. and Meirano, V. 2012. La typologie des tombes d'enfant dans les colonies grecques d'Italie du Sud: problèmes et cas d'études, pp. 429–57 in Nenna, M. D. (ed.), *L'enfant et la mort dans l'antiquité, II. Types de tombes et traitement du corps des enfants dans l'antiquité gréco-romaine, Actes de la table ronde internationale, (Alexandrie, Centre d'Études Alexandrines, 12–14 novembre 2009),* Études Alexandrines 28. Alexandrie: Centre d'Études Alexandrines.

Gentili, G. V. 1954. Megara Hyblaea (Siracusa). Tombe arcaiche e reperti sporadici nella proprietà della "Rasiom", e tomba arcaica in predio Vinci. *Notizie degli Scavi di Antichità*, 80–113.

Golden, M. 1990. *Children and Childhood in Classical Athens*, Baltimore/London: The Johns Hopkins University Press.

Guimier-Sorbets, A. M. and Morizot, Y. (eds) 2010. *L'enfant et la mort dans l'antiquité, I. Nouvelles recherches dans les nécropoles grecques. Le signalement des tombes d'enfants, Actes de la table ronde internationale (Athènes, 28–30 mai 2008),* Travaux de la Maison René Ginouvès 12. Paris: De Boccard.

Hamilton, R. 1992: *Choes and Anthesteria. Athenian Iconography and Ritual.* Ann Arbor: University of Michigan Press.

Hermary, A. and Dubois, C. (eds) 2012. *L'enfant et la mort dans l'antiquité, III. Le matériel associé aux tombes d'enfants, Actes de la table ronde internationale organisée à la Maison Méditerranéenne des Sciences de l'Homme (MMSH, Aix-en-Provence, 20–22 janvier 2011),* BiAMA 12. Paris: Éditions Errance.

Houby-Nielsen, S. 2000. Child burials in ancient Athens, pp. 151–66 in Sofaer Derevenski, J. (ed.), *Children and Material Culture.* London/New York: Routledge.

Lambrugo, C. 2005. Per una storia di un mondo "minore". *Alabastra* e *aryballoi* corinzi nella necropoli arcaica di Gela: esegesi di un indicatore infantile. *Orizzonti. Rassegna di Arceologia* VI, 81–93.

Lambrugo, C. forthcoming. La visibilità dell'invisibile: lo spazio funerario infantile nella Sicilia arcaica. Il caso di Gela, in Panvini, R. and Sole, L. (eds.), *La Sicilia in età arcaica. Dalle* apoikiai *al 480 a.C., Atti del Convegno Internazionale, Caltanissetta, 27–29 marzo 2008.* Palermo: Centro regionale per l'inventario, la catalogazione e la documentazione.

Libertini, G. 1929. *Il Regio Museo Archeologico di Siracusa.* Rome: La Libreria dello Stato.

Meirano, V. 2012. Les terres cuites dans les sépultures d'individus immatures en Grèce d'Occident, de l'époque archaïque au milieu du IVe s. av. J.-C.: types, contextes, significations, pp. 111–30 in Hermary, A. and Dubois, C. (eds), *L'enfant et la mort dans l'antiquité, III. Le matériel associé aux tombes d'enfants, Actes de la table ronde internationale organisée à la Maison Méditerranéenne des Sciences de l'Homme (MMSH, Aix-en-Provence, 20–22 janvier 2011)*, BiAMA 12. Paris: Éditions Errance.

Morris, I. 1987. *Burial and Ancient Society. The Rise of the Greek City-state*. Cambridge: Cambridge University Press.

Neils, J. and Oakley, J. H. (eds) 2003. *Coming of Age in Ancient Greece. Images of Childhood from the Classical Past*. New Haven: Yale University Press.

Nenna, M. D. (ed.) 2012. *L'enfant et la mort dans l'antiquité, II. Types de tombes et traitement du corps des enfants dans l'antiquité gréco-romaine, Actes de la table ronde internationale (Alexandrie, Centre d'Études Alexandrines, 12–14 novembre 2009)*, Études Alexandrines 28. Alexandrie: Centre d'Études Alexandrines.

Nizzo, V. 2007. *Ritorno ad Ischia. Dalla stratigrafia della necropoli di Pithekoussai alla tipologia dei materiali*. Naples: Centre Jean Bérard.

Orsi, P. 1895. Siracusa. Gli scavi nella necropoli del Fusco a Siracusa nel giugno, novembre e dicembre del 1893. *Notizie degli Scavi di Antichità*, 109–192.

Orsi, P. 1897. Siracusa. Di alcune necropoli secondarie di Siracusa. *Notizie degli Scavi di Antichità*, 472–504.

Orsi, P. 1906. Gela. Scavi del 1900–1905. *Monumenti Antichi dei Lincei* XVII, cols. 5–758.

Orsi, P. 1913. Scavi di Calabria nel 1913 (relazione preliminare). *Notizie degli Scavi di Antichità*. Suppl., 3–54.

Orsi, P. 1914. Caulonia. Campagne archeologiche del 1912, 1913 e 1915, *Monumenti Antichi dei Lincei* XXIII, cols. 685–948.

Orsi, P. 1915. Siracusa. *Notizie degli Scavi di Antichità*, 175–208.

Orsi, P. 1917. Locri Epiz. Campagne di scavo nella necropoli Lucifero negli anni 1914 e 1915. *Notizie degli Scavi di Antichità*, 101–167.

Palomba, D. 2004. La necropoli del Vallone Bernardo a Caulonia, pp. 351–430 in Parra M. C. (ed.), *Kaulonía, Caulonia, Stilida (e oltre). Contributi storici, archeologici e topografici, II, Annali della Scuola Normale Superiore di Pisa, Quaderni* 17–18.

Ridgway, D. 1984. *L'alba della Magna Grecia*. Milan: Longanesi.

Rizza, G. 1954. Scavi e ricerche nella città di Leontini negli anni 1951–1953. *Bollettino d'Arte* XXXIX,1, s. IV, 69–73.

Rizza, G. 1955. Campagne di scavi 1950–1951 e 1951–1952: la necropoli della Valle S. Mauro; le fortificazioni meridionali della città e la porta di Siracusa. *Notizie degli Scavi di Antichità*, 281–376.

Scilabra, C. 2012. *Veneri pupa negata*. Giocattoli in tomba: casi di studio dall'Occidente greco, pp. 387–402 in Hermary, A. and Dubois, C. (eds), *L'enfant et la mort dans l'antiquité, III. Le matériel associé aux tombes d'enfants, Actes de la table ronde internationale organisée à la Maison Méditerranéenne des Sciences de l'Homme (MMSH, Aix-en-Provence, 20–22 janvier 2011)*, BiAMA 12. Paris: Éditions Errance.

Scilabra, C. 2013. *Identità e status dell'individuo preadulto nel mondo greco dal periodo arcaico a quello classico: fonti letterarie, iconografiche e testimonianze materiali*, Dottorato in Storia del patrimonio archeologico e artistico, Università degli Studi di Torino, XXIV ciclo, unpublished PhD thesis.

Scilabra, C. forthcoming. Riflessioni sull'identità sociale dei defunti immaturi in età arcaica e classica. Note in margine ad alcune tendenze nelle necropoli magnogreche e sicelіote. *Orizzonti. Rassegna di Archeologia* XIV.

Shepherd, G. 2006. Dead but not buried? Child disposal in the Greek West, pp. 311–25 in Herring, E. *et al* (eds), *Across frontiers. Etruscans, Greeks, Phoenicians & Cypriots. Studies in honor of*

*David Ridgway and Francesca Romana Serra Ridgway*. London: Accordia Research Institute, University of London.

Shepherd, G. 2007. Poor little rich kids? Status and selection in Archaic Western Greece, pp. 93–106 in Crawford, S. and Shepherd, G. (eds), *Children, Childhood and Society*, BAR International Series 1696. Oxford: Archaeopress.

Villard, F. and de Miré, G. and V. 1955. *Sicile grecque*. Paris: M. Girodias.

# CHILDREN AND THEIR BURIAL PRACTICES IN THE EARLY MEDIEVAL CEMETERIES OF CASTEL TROSINO AND NOCERA UMBRA (ITALY)

## *Valentina De Pasca*

### CASTEL TROSINO AND NOCERA UMBRA: AN INTRODUCTION

The early medieval cemeteries of Castel Trosino and Nocera Umbra[1] share a similar destiny. Both localized in central Italy, they were discovered accidentally during agricultural activities at the end of the nineteenth century and their knowledge is fundamental to the study of the Italian early medieval necropolis. Their importance is also highlighted from the great names of Italian archaeologists and researchers who excavated and recorded the cemeteries: Raniero Mengarelli and Giulio Gabrielli in the case of Castel Trosino; Angiolo Pasqui and Roberto Paribeni in the case of Nocera Umbra.

Being a first attempt to examine child burial practices in these contexts, my purpose is primarily to outline some observations about infant grave goods that I believe are fundamental to future studies. I think we could imagine this paper only as a first step on a longer stairway. It is for this reason that I will start by giving a brief description of these early medieval sites, and then outlining the typologies of burial practices we can identify in infant tombs.

### CASTEL TROSINO

The site of Castel Trosino (Fig. 23.1) is located in the Marche, a central Italian region, not far away from Ascoli Piceno, and its necropolis is dated between the late 6th and the beginning of the 8th century. Marche was inhabited during the early Medieval Age by Italic people, Byzantines and Lombards: the presence of heterogeneous populations influenced and enriched the burial practices of the inhabitants of this site, and their material culture, which is the widest source of information about italic-byzantine handiwork in the early medieval age. In fact, the cemetery is defined as '*una preziosa testimonianza del primo stanziamento longobardo in uno strategico ambito del bacino*

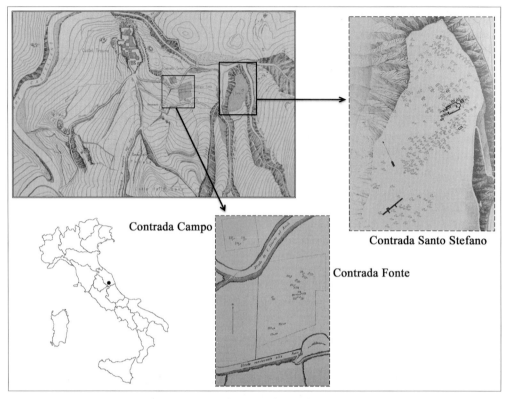

Contrada Campo

Contrada Santo Stefano

Contrada Fonte

*Figure 23.1. The site of Castel Trosino.*

*del Tronto a monte di Ascoli Piceno, e della trasformazione degli usi funerari al crocevia tra influssi ancora tardo romani e bizantini e nuovi apporti germanici'.*[2] The complexity of the archaeological records means that hypotheses about the ethnic groups which inhabited this site are still conflicting, because of the different decorative styles: we find grave goods belonging to germanic animal art next to objects characterised by byzantine-mediterranean style which proves trade with the East, or the existence of skilled employees. However, the hypothesis about the reason for settlement here is unanimous: in Castel Trosino they had an administrative role, which may be confirmed by comparison with Nocera Umbra's cemetery, where grave goods have a strong military and strategic character, highlighted in most cases by horse equipment referring to the military function of deceased men. In fact at Castel Trosino, archaeologists have discovered military grave goods in only a few graves.

Although we can find reference to the presence of *barbarian* remains in documents dated to the fifteenth and sixteenth centuries,[3] the cemetery was excavated for the first time between 1893 and 1896[4] after a rich burial was unearthed accidentally in 1872.[5] Given the richness of its grave goods, the tomb was named 'the knight's grave', but unfortunately after the discovery the grave goods were partly lost and partly scattered worldwide, in particular items merged into the collections of the French Musée des Antiquités Nationales in Saint-Germain-en-Laye, and of The Metropolitan Museum of Modern Art of New York.[6] During excavations archaeologists discovered a necropolis consisting of 289 graves[7] and divided into three main areas:[8] Contrada Santo Stefano (270 burials), Contrada Fonte (16 burials) and Contrada Campo (3 burials). The deceased were oriented east-west with skulls to the west and feet to the east.

An exhaustive study highlights the fact that just a little more than half of Castel Trosino's tombs contains grave goods but only in a few of them we can identify a high status burial defined on the basis of the value and the quantity of the objects accompanying the deceased on their journey into the afterlife. The cemetery area containing the majority of tombs belonging to deceased of high rank is Contrada Santo Stefano, which also has significance because of the church of the same name built at the centre of it. The religious building, in addition to its central position, contained some burials:[9] both these features are a reminder that Santo Stefano's church could have been the funeral chapel of the leading family.[10] This hypothesis is, in my opinion, strengthened not only by the period in which the church was built (the end of the 7th century) and by the aristocratic custom of erecting buildings with a religious function, but also and in particular by the finding, during the most recent excavations, of a gold seal ring[11] in grave 49.[12] I believe it is no coincidence that the only two gold seal rings discovered in Castel Trosino were found in 'the knight's grave'[13] and in the male burial 49 within the church. If we consider the high symbolic meaning attributed to these precious objects[14] we cannot deny that most likely they were markers of high ranking personalities, who undoubtedly had considerable status during the period of use of the cemetery.[15]

The investigations into the necropolis have also highlighted the need to wonder where the inhabited area of Castel Trosino was placed. It is possible to give a first answer to this question, without claiming to be complete, thanks to Mengarelli's description[16] of what was dug up during his excavations: it would appear that an early medieval residential zone was in the area near Contrada Pedata.

Finally, from the beginning of the conservation history of Castel Trosino's archaeological finds, Italian institutions[17] decided they would be preserved in the Museo Nazionale Romano (now Museo dell'Alto Medioevo) in Rome,[18] and a few of them in Ascoli Piceno's Museo dell'Alto Medioevo.

NOCERA UMBRA

The site of Nocera Umbra (Fig. 23.2), located in central Italian region called Umbria, is forty kilometres north-east from Spoleto and it is in a strategic position on the route named the Via Flaminia that connected Ravenna to Rome. The site was occupied by Longobardic people who came from the Adriatic Sea in 571. It is no coincidence that the necropolis is dated between 571 (*terminus post quem*) and the second half of the 7th century, although we can distinguish three chronological phases: the first one post 571, the second one between the late 6th and the 7th century, and the third one identified

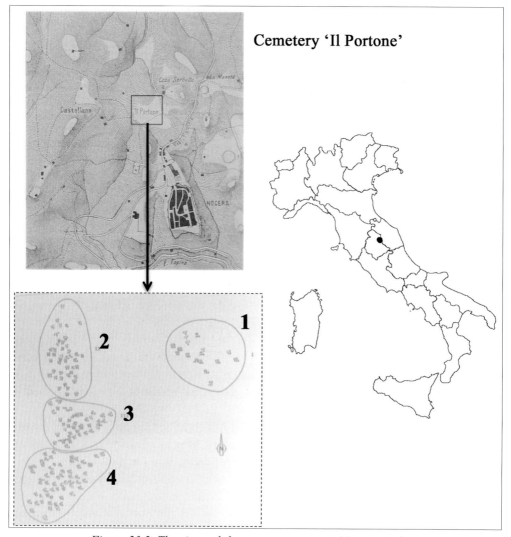

*Figure 23.2. The site and the cemetery areas at Nocera Umbra.*

with the first decades of 7th century.[19] In the cemetery it is possible to recognize four contemporary cemetery, although Cornelia Rupp[20] affirms that in areas one to three, graves of the first two periods outnumber those of the third one, while in the fourth area we find a greater number of tombs belonging to the last period of the necropolis' use. She also highlights that within the four areas of the cemetery it is possible to make a gender distinction: children's tombs are for the most part near women's ones, so it there may also be a discrimination based on age, too.[21]

Also in this case, the first grave of the necropolis was discovered by chance in 1897 when the Blasi – owner of the field – came across the burial while during the planting of grapevines.[22] Regular excavations began a year later and brought to light 165 graves containing 169 inhumations. The deceased were laid supine, with feet pointed eastward and the majority had their hands on their stomachs: they were laid in the grave after being placed in a wooden coffin.[23]

Unlike Castel Trosino, where excavations brought to light proofs demonstrating the ancient inhabited area, at Nocera Umbra it is very difficult to hypothesize the settlement where people buried in the cemetery lived. In this regard Pasqui and Paribeni, the archaeologists who excavated the site, observed that the distance existing between the necropolis and the urban settlement lead them to believe the cemetery was unrelated to the residential area.[24] Still today the most strongly recommended hypothesis identifies Nocera Umbra's necropolis as the cemetery of a military garrison.[25] Although we have no archaeological record attesting the ancient presence of a stronghold,[26] we can not disallow that it was a military unit because '*gli uomini sepolti nel cimitero sono sempre armati di tutto punto e si può anche stabilire che molti di essi erano cavalieri, data la presenza di morsi per cavalli*'.[27] The hypothesis of a military function for people settled in Nocera Umbra during that period is also corroborated by the position of the site: a hundred metres away from the cemetery it is possible to identify an elevated spur from which people had a view that extended widely, especially over the strategic junction of the Via Flaminia.[28] Researchers are inclined to believe people in Nocera Umbra had a military function[29] and Jørgensen highlighted not only that '*Nocera Umbra has over 200% more weapon graves in relation to Castel Trosino*'[30] but also '[…] *men with full weapons set appear more frequently at Nocera Umbra, while Castel Trosino usually produces only part set*'.[31]

Not only the presence of military grave goods, but also jewellery, gold coins, *sellae plicatiles*[32] lead researchers to speak about upper-class graves characterized by an evident display of power. This is the reason for why Felice Bernabei – who thought the grave goods were complementary to Castel Trosino ones – persisted in the conservation of objects brought to light in Nocera Umbra in the Museo Nazionale Romano.[33]

## CHILDREN, FUNERARY SPACES AND BURIAL PRACTICES

It is hard to find studies concerning children in Italian contexts dated to the 6th to 8th century. Until now Italian studies about medieval children have focussed on the Late Medieval era and in particular on the similarities between Christ and the Virgin's infancy,[34] their iconography in paintings and illuminations,[35] and the daily life of contemporary children.[36] In this paper we would like to take a step backward and focus our attention on societies not yet completely converted to Christianity, societies where we still find burial practices bound to paganism. Although the deposition of grave goods cannot be interpreted only as a religious expression,[37] I think in pagan society people had more reasons to practice this custom since their belief in the afterlife was more connected with their daily life. If afterlife for Christians is strictly connected with one's own behaviour in everyday life,[38] on the contrary heathens believed afterlife was a simple continuation of everyday life: it was for this reason they cared that the deceased would be buried with adequate grave goods which could accompany them in their second life.

The significant presence of children's graves in the cemeteries of Castel Trosino and Nocera Umbra together with good documentations of the two sites' excavations let us deepen this theme outlining some observations closely linked to grave goods data. After a quantitative analysis of grave goods and a qualitative one, I will present a first attempt to outline how during early medieval era mortuary practices relating to children were complex because of a kind of cultural and ritual 'melting pot'. Thanks to the evidence from the two cemeteries it is reasonable to identify three groups of children's grave goods: a first one which refers to the classical world; a second one that presupposes the renewal of ancient traditions and finally, a third one, which shows new customs.

## CHILD BURIAL PRACTICES IN CASTEL TROSINO AND NOCERA UMBRA

### Child Burial in Castel Trosino

Children's graves in Castel Trosino amount to sixty-nine: in Contrada S. Stefano we can notice thirty-four infant burials with grave goods and twenty-eight without, in Contrada Fonte seven children's graves are without grave goods, while in Contrada Campo there are no infant tombs. The percentage of graves belonging to infants and young boys and girls is significant: it is approximately 30 per cent throughout the cemetery.

Lars Jørgensen assessed the status of families buried in Castel Trosino in a wide sociological study,[39] and I believe records regarding infant graves reinforce his hypothesis. After a quantitative analysis of grave assemblages in female and male burials, he argued that people buried nearby the church, in the area named Contrada S. Stefano, belonged to the wealthiest families. If we consider that grave goods associated with infant burials only occur in Contrada S. Stefano, the infant graves support this hypothesis.

Compared with Nocera Umbra, Castel Trosino's infant grave good are fewer, probably because of a greater presence of Italic people than German ones and also because of a greater conversion to Christianity which necessarily entailed a gradual change of burial practices.

Observing children's grave goods we can notice that the most frequent markers are, at first, glass beads,[40] secondly jugs[41] and necklaces,[42] then glass bottles, earrings, pins and pierced coins. Obviously there are other kinds of objects but they appear less frequently: glass or pottery vessels like jars and dishes, buckles, combs, rings, little gold crosses, knives, belt adornments, but also a little bell, a pair of stirrups, a little glass sphere and an armilla. We can identify among them objects that reflect markers of the classical world, but in the mean time we should notice the absence of markers which in were strictly connected with infant burials in the classical world, such as shells, terracotta figurines of animal or human shapes, little dolls and astragali.

### Child Burial in Nocera Umbra

The cemetery of Nocera Umbra counts fifty-six child burials, fifty-five furnished with grave goods and only one without.[43] Also in this case, like Castel Trosino, the percentage of graves belonging to children and young boys and girls is meaningful:

it is more than 30%. Except for an infant grave,[44] all the children's graves are located in areas two, three and four, apparently without a defined order with the exception of their proximity to women's graves and the fact they formed a kind of group, albeit interspersed with other burials.

It is not only the high percentage of furnished graves that draw our attention, but also the amount of grave goods contained in Nocera Umbra's burials and their variety. These last features contribute to differentiate clearly this necropolis from that of Castel Trosino where, if we can find a good percentage of tombs containing grave goods, at the same time it is not possible to distinguish funerary goods characterised by the same variety and richness. I believe that the above-mentioned features argue in favour of a greater presence of a barbarian population in Nocera Umbra's settlement than in Castel Trosino, where in my opinion there is a more noticeable integration between local people and German ones.

I think another proof in the direction of a massive presence in Nocera Umbra of German people or people strongly conditioned by German funerary rituals is given by the discovery of weapons in most infant graves: archaeologists found knives, little knives, knife edges, spears, a scramasax, a dagger, a sword and arrow tips, in particular three edged ones.

However, as I have previously indicated, in this site the wide range of grave goods that parents chose to accompany their offspring in after life is also significant: we can distinguish a lot of objects such as, for example, pottery or glass vessels (particularly clay mugs and bowls), brooches (disc brooches and cross ones), coins, jewels (necklaces, rings, bracelets), glass beads, hairpins, scissors, ivory caskets, bone combs, eggshells, seashells, little crystal balls and gold crosses, to cite those of particular interest.

## CATEGORIES OF GRAVE GOODS IDENTIFIED IN THE TWO NECROPOLIS

A careful analysis of grave goods brought to light in the cemeteries of Castel Trosino and Nocera Umbra let us observe that from 6th to the 8th century, italic society settled in those sites make use of mortuary practices typical of the classical world which in part adopted the addition of new symbols. Although this behaviour towards the deceased could be noticed both in adults' graves and in children's ones, our attention in this study is focused on child burial practices which clearly display elements of ancestral tradition blended with elements linked to contexts.

It is possible to identify three main categories of infant grave goods in both necropolis: one composed from objects strictly connected to the past and to the ancient traditions; a second category formed by elements reflecting the past but that show a strong influence of the cultural context in which they are inserted, and finally a third one including objects completely new in terms of ancient customs. To reinforce and give reliability to this observation we will examine some examples of the three categories from both cemeteries.

Let us start with the first group: funerary goods that forcefully call on ancient funerary rituals. Coins and pierced coins,[45] pottery and glass vessels, clay mugs and bowls, eggshells, seashells and chicken bones belong to this category and it is significant that also their position is inherited from the tradition and remains unchanged. Coins and pierced ones were positioned on the chest or in the hand of the dead,[46] whereas pottery or glass vessels rather than clay mugs and bowls were next to the feet of the deceased or by his head.

The presence of elements that reflect ancient practices together with the fact that their position remained unchanged leads me to suppose that also their function and their meaning held steady. In my opinion coins continued to be interpreted as Charon's obol[47] or as something magic and characterised by an apotrophaic function. Given their metal composition and their round shape, they were used also as amulets: if the talismanic properties of metal composition were highlighted in Plinius' *Naturalis Historia*,[48] it was commonly believed evil spirits would not enter into any round object.[49] Vessels, mugs and bowls, which referred to the food offering, had the same unaltered function: the remains of animal bones vouch for that ritual.

Analyzing the second case, we can notice the correspondences between grave goods connected to the past and new ones. An example is the presence of beads in the majority of graves (especially in Castel Trosino) – that at the moment of the burial formed simple necklaces – along with jewellery objects as necklaces, bracelets and rings distinctive of the group identity of the deceased (especially in Nocera Umbra). Elements connected to the adornment sphere also draw comparison to the byzantine tendency to exhibit pride and status by adorning their offspring with jewellery and luxurious garments, a tendency that they perpetuated in mortuary rituals.[50]

As regards Castel Trosino's burials which prove the habit of renewing ancient customs, I believe depositions 128,[51] 164[52] and 169[53] are meaningful. Grave 128 was a double burial containing a woman and a little girl, probably a mother with her daughter. The woman's grave goods consisted of a pair of gold basket earrings, two silver pins and a little pottery jug, while those belonging to the little girl were a necklace made up of twenty-seven glass beads and two ivory beads, and a bronze armilla. The presence of ivory in the necklace enriched its value: if we consider these beads were also carved and grooved and that in Pliny's *Naturalis Historia* ivory is described as a luxurious material,[54] we can assume that the inclusion of that particular material was the result of a specific choice. A similar situation is revealed in graves 164 and 169, where archaeologists founded two necklaces consisting of glass beads and with further amber and crystal beads. Pliny wrote that women wore amber jewels as ornaments or with a therapeutic purpose against fever and sore throat, and children took delight in wearing amber amulets.[55] In the same book, the ancient author describes also curative features linked to crystal: the choice to include particular gemstones was clearly intentional.

Nocera Umbra graves 39, 63, 69 and 102 are significant at this respect, although we might cite other examples (graves 10, 35, 85 and 148). Burial 39[56] belonged to a young girl who wore a necklace composed of precious stones: crystal, amber and opal beads, the latter one was described by Pliny as a stone that combines the qualities of most precious stones.[57] Her grave goods also included a clay mug, four pierced coins, a fragmentary bone comb and a fragmentary knife, a silver tip and a bronze brooch. The girl buried in grave 63[58] was accompanied by a necklace composed of amethyst, and topaz and gold-in-glass beads, a bronze ring and a brooch of the same material, a hairpin and, finally, a seashell. Another rich burial including a precious jewel is burial 69:[59] The young girl had a necklace composed of glass beads interspersed with gold pendants. This grave is also significant for the variety and richness of its grave goods: a little gold cross, an ivory and two bronze bracelets, a bronze ring, a scramasax, a fragmentary ivory casket (containing a coin and a seashell), a hairpin, a crystal ball, a fragmentary bone comb, a bottle base. Finally, grave 102 belonged to a little girl and although there were only three objects amongst the grave goods – a fragmentary amphora, a little buckle and a necklace – this latter is particularly precious being composed of gold studs.

Deposition of jewellery entailed, in my opinion, at least two meanings. If we think of glass beads which formed simple necklaces, the function should have been merely affective because they were cheap stuff, as we could note also in ancient funerary practices. This statement obviously changes if we focus our attention on gold or silver pieces of jewellery: their real value means the necklaces were not merely decorative. Precious jewels had also the function of proving that the individual, children in the above mentioned cases, were related to an influential group and belonged to élite. If we examine carefully, for example, necklaces made from amber beads, we could suppose that given the presence of this precious stone – that Pliny in his *Naturalis Historia* describes also as one of the most luxurious objects – it is a jewel of great value, to which we have to add an apotropaic character for sure, and maybe also an affective one.

Not only jewels belong to this category but also, for example, three fibulae characterized by a horse shape brought to light in three little girls' graves[60] in Castel Trosino. In this case, it is significant that reference to childhood is symbolized by common objects strictly connected to the tradition. The object – the fibula, in this case – undergoes a change, a transformation and acquires a childish feature. This behaviour brings me to suppose that people, parents in particular, had a specific attention towards infant burial practices. They cared about the best way to furnish objects appropriate to the age of the deceased to accompany their children to the after life.

The third category – which includes objects strictly related to new customs – consist of infant burials marked out by little gold crosses that clearly articulate Christian symbols. In Castel Trosino's necropolis, there are two graves containing crosses (graves 37 and 41), compared to Nocera Umbra where we count nine graves (43, 59, 69, 89, 101, 108, 147, 148 and 149) that present this kind of grave good. We could cite Castel Trosino's grave 37[61] where the cross was placed on the right shoulder: it was a gold foil Greek cross decorated with two triangular shapes. Crosses like this were widespread from the arrival of the Lombards in Italy.[62] They are usually found on the face or on the chest of the deceased, probably they were sewed onto the shroud: which is likely because of the presence of small holes on the edges. I believe that also gold crosses reflected an apotropaic meaning strictly connected with the major Christian symbol, therefore crosses would not only have the function of marking Christian burials.

## WHAT SPACES FOR EARLY MEDIEVAL CHILDREN?

Analysing the two central Italian cemeteries, it becomes clearer how in the early medieval period only funerary spaces return us a tangible evidence of children.[63] At other periods it is possible to find other traces of childhood: it seems strange but the only way to investigate children's lives in this period is to begin from the dramatic event of their death.

The care given to the rites of children's burial in the two necropolis above mentioned highlights not only how those people worried about their children, but also what kind of spaces they dedicated to them. I believe we can speak in particular about emotional and economic spaces.

Emotional spaces could be interpreted like something deeply human in a primitive society as well as the early medieval one: we find 'proofs' of them observing apotropaic grave goods and objects that have a talismanic function, which had to protect the deceased. In the matter of this theme, Didier Lett[64] affirms *'[...] les objects et les vêtements trouvés dans leur tombes témoignent d'une réelle volonté parentale ou sociale de rendre hommage au petit mort et traduisent sans doute des gestes d'affection'*. In this way parents saw that their children felt less lonely. They inserted into infant burials objects that created a connection between life and afterlife and proved the strong affection of the family: in fact it was a common practice to bury children with a beloved object which had the function of a security blanket and kept them company during a frightening journey.[65] These observations bring me to affirm that we have to be cautious in claiming that in the medieval era *'the death of a child was generally less dramatized than it is today'*.[66]

The economic sphere is the most complex to understand because we cannot forget that by enriching children's tombs the society lost wealth. Therefore children played a social role, otherwise one could not explain why households lose so much of their precious goods to the grave. In this respect, in my opinion it is relevant to observe burials of young boys and girls because their grave good choice shows a specific purpose: their own features place them in a definite position, they do not belong anymore to infant graves but they are not adult burials yet. They symbolize two rites of passage *par excellence*: the passage from life to death and from childhood to adult age. I think it is for this reason they present the main and symbolic markers of both ages. Their rich and elaborate mortuary equipment seems to refer to the role they would have had after the rite of passage to the adult age. But this is another question.

NOTES

1   The necropolis discovered in Nocera Umbra were three in all: the cemetery *Il Portone* (Pasqui and Paribeni 1918; Rupp 2005), the small necropolis of *Piazza Medaglie d'Oro* (Rupp 2003, Profumo 1995) and finally that of *Pettinara – Casale Lozzi* (von Hessen 1978). Although they have been discovered in neighbouring places, their features are very different. In this paper our attention will be paid to the greater one, the cemetery of *Il Portone*, which will be named *necropolis of Nocera Umbra* from this point forward for the sake of simplicity

2   Profumo and Staffa 2007, 383:'[…] a valuable record of the first Lombard allocation in a strategic area of the Tronto's basin upstream of Ascoli Piceno and of the transformation of the burial practices at the crossroads of continuing Late Roman and Byzantine influences and new Germanic ones'

3   Colucci 1794, 45

4   The cemetery was investigated also in recent years (2001–2003) to judge its conservation and to verify any possible presence of graves yet undiscovered (Profumo and Staffa 2007)

5   Mengarelli 1902

6   Paroli 2004; Paroli 2000; Vallet 1995

7   The most widespread kind of grave was that earth dug, but it was possible to distinguish other types: graves with stone cladding and with mortar, graves with stone plate roofing (*Deckplattgrab*) and with dry stone walls

8   The *knight's grave* was discovered in a different area, Contrada Pedata. Since the beginning of investigations archaeologists assumed it was isolated and this has been confirmed by recent surveys of the site (Profumo and Staffa 2007, 390). The fact that burial was lonely together with the richness of grave goods led researchers to presume its importance in Castel Trosino was without equal (Paroli 2000; Profumo and Staffa 2007, 390–5)

9   Mengarelli 1902, 174

10  Chavarría Arnau 2009

11  Profumo and Staffa 2007, 395–6

12  Paroli and Ricci 2007, 58–9

13  Researchers (Paroli 2000, 91) are inclined to identify it with the gold seal ring conserved at The Metropolitan Museum of Modern Art (accession number 95.15.4)

14  De Marchi 2006; Lusuardi Siena 2006

15  This is not the context to investigate the above-mentioned suggestions, however I think a study in that direction could throw light on adult burial rituals in Castel Trosino and in particular on the symbolism of grave goods and on their connection with the role which the deceased had during their life

16  Mengarelli 1902, 152

17  Gagliardi 1995, 325

18  Arena and Paroli 1993; Paroli 1983; Felletti Maj 1967

19  Rupp 1997, 33

20  *Ibid.*, 31

21  *Ibid.*, 26

22  Pasqui and Paribeni 1918, 141

23  *Ibid.*, 141

24  *Ibid.*, 142

25  Jørgensen 1991, 31

26  Rupp 1997, 39

27  von Hessen 1997, 132: '[…] men buried in the cemetery were well armed and it is possible to determine that many of them were knights, given the presence of bits for horses'

28  Von Hessen 1985,131–4

29  In particular, Jørgensen 1991, 31

30  *Ibid.*, 45

31  *Ibid.*, 45

32 Arena 1994
33 Arena 1997, 15
34 Baragli 2012; Becchi 1996; Giallongo 1990
35 It might be linked to Giotto's Scrovegni Chapel (*c.* 1303–5), in particular scenes such as the Virgin's nativity, or to the illumination of the *Holy Family at Work, Saturday Hours of the Virgin: Sext* within the Hours of Catherine of Cleves, in latin, illuminated by the Master of Catherine of Cleves (*c.* 1440) now conserved in the Morgan Library and Museum (MS M. 917)
36 Although I believe the study of childhood in the Middle Ages only in the Christian perspective is very limiting, we can not hide the fact that the importance given to children in the Gospels certainly entailed a re-evaluation of the figure of the child and all that could concern it. See also Becchi 1996, 61–2
37 James 1989, 26
38 For example, Luke 20:27–38
39 Jørgensen 1991, 34–44
40 Glass beads were found in the following graves: 41, 80, 85, 96, 113, 158, 161, 184. See Paroli and Ricci 2007
41 Jugs were found in the following burials: D, 3, 74, 82, 161. See Paroli and Ricci 2007
42 Necklaces were found in graves 117, 128a, 164, 169, 187. See Paroli and Ricci 2007
43 Rupp 2005, 159–60
44 Grave 4. See Rupp 2005, 6–7
45 In reference to Castel Trosino, coins – all pierced – were found in the following graves: 80, 85, 96, 164 (see Paroli and Ricci 2007, 112–9). On the contrary, only four coins brought to light in grave 39 in Nocera Umbra were pierced. In Nocera Umbra coins were brought to light in burial 4, 11, 56 (gold solidus), 69, 85 (gold solidus) and 107
46 In Nocera Umbra's grave 39 (belonged to a young girl) coins were found in the area of the knee (see Rupp 2005, 57–9): we could acknowledge they were part of a pendant that ran down her side. Something similar coud be noticed in a young girl's grave found in Verona (Calomino 2008) and in another young girl's grave brought to light in Chiusi (Asolati 2012)
47 D'Angela 2006; Cantilena 1995; Peduto 1995; Stevens 1991; Grinsell 1957; Sullivan 1950
48 Pliny, *Naturalis Historia* XXIV–XXXII
49 Pera 1993, 349
50 Pitarakis 2009, 177–8
51 Paroli and Ricci 2007, 88–9
52 *Ibid.*, 96–7
53 *Ibid.*, 98–9
54 Pliny, *Naturalis Historia* XVIII, 4
55 *Nat. Hist.* XXXVII, 40
56 Rupp 2005, 57–9
57 *Nat. Hist.* XXXVII, 80–81
58 Rupp 2005, 79–81
59 Rupp 2005, 87–9
60 Castel Trosino's graves containing fibulae featured with a horse shape are 121, 136 and 171. In Nocera Umbra nothing similar has been discovered
61 Paroli and Ricci 2007, 54–5
62 Giostra 2010
63 See also Lett 1997, 56–7
64 Lett 1997, 59: '[…] objects and garments found in graves are witness of a real familial and social will to honour deceased children and translate gestures of affection'
65 Muggia 2004, 217
66 Papacostantinou 2009, 9

ABBREVIATIONS

*Nat. Hist.* Pliny *Naturalis Historia:* Plinio, G. 2000. *Storia Naturale. Libro XXXVII. Gemme e pietre preziose* (translated by C. Lefons). Livorno: Sillabe.

REFERENCES

Arena, M. S. and Paroli, L. (eds) 1993. *Museo dell'Alto Medioevo Roma*, Roma: Istituto Poligrafico e Zecca dello Stato.

Arena, M. S. 1994, Le sellae plicatiles di Nocera Umbra, pp. 7–10 in Arena, M. S. and Paroli, L. (eds), *Arti del fuoco in età longobarda: il restauro delle necropoli di Nocera Umbra e Castel Trosino*. Roma: Museo dell'Alto Medioevo.

Arena, M. S. 1997. La necropoli longobarda di Nocera Umbra: cento anni di scoperte, pp. 11–22 in Paroli, L. (ed.), *Umbria Longobarda. La necropoli di Nocera Umbra nel centenario della scoperta* (Roma, Museo dell'Altomedioevo, 27 luglio 1996–10 gennaio 1997). Roma: De Luca.

Asolati, M. 2012. Bracciale con monete romane e bizantine da una tomba longobarda da Chiusi, pp. 173–83 in Asolati, M. (ed.), *Praestantia Nummorum. Temi e note di numismatica tardo antica e alto medievale*. Padova: Esedra Editrice.

Baragli, S. 2012. Il Medioevo dei bambini, *Medioevo. Un passato da riscoprire* 2 (181), 71–95.

Becchi, E. 1996. Medioevo, pp. 61–90 in Becchi, E. and Dominique, J. (eds), *Storia dell'infanzia. 1. Dall'antichità al Seicento*. Roma-Bari: Editori Laterza.

Calomino, D. 2008. Una 'collana' di monete bronzee in una tomba longobarda a Verona, pp. 431–443 in *EST ENIM ILLE FLOS ITALIAE. Vita economica e sociale nella Cisalpina romana*, Atti delle Giornate di Studio in onore di Ezio Buchi (Verona, 30 novembre–1 dicembre 2006). Verona: QuiEdit.

Cantilena, R. 1995. Un obolo per Caronte?, *La Parola del Passato* 50, 165–77.

Chavarría Arnau, A. 2009. *Archeologia delle chiese. Dalle origini all'anno Mille*, Roma: Carocci Editore.

Colucci, G. 1794. Narrazione istorica della fondazione, e della situazione di Castel Trosino Stato d'Ascoli, pp. 44–9 in Colucci, G., *Delle antichità picene dell'abate Giuseppe Colucci patrizio camerinese* 21. Fermo: Colucci.

D'Angela, C. 2006. L'Obolo a Caronte. Usi funerari medievali tra paganesimo e cristianesimo, pp. 89–96 in C. D'Angela, *Studi di Antichità Cristiane*. Bari: Edipuglia.

De Marchi, M. 2006. Gli anelli aure sigillari longobardi: un simbolo di potere, fedeltà e memoria, pp. 25–39 in Lusuardi Siena, S. (ed.), *Anulus sui effigii. Identità e rappresentazione negli anelli-sigillo longobardi*. Milano: Vita e Pensiero.

Felletti Maj, B. M. 1967. Il museo dell'alto medioevo in Roma, *Alto medioevo* I, 1–8.

Gagliardi, G. 1995. *La necropoli di Castel Trosino*, Ascoli Piceno: Giannino e Giuseppe Gagliardi Editori.

Giallongo, A. 1990. *Il bambino medievale*, Bari: Edizioni Dedalo.

Giostra, C. 2010. Le croci in lamina d'oro: origine, significato e funzione, pp. 129–40 in Sannazzaro, M. and Giostra, C. (eds), *Petala aurea: lamine di ambito bizantino e longobardo dalla Collezione Rovati*, Catalogo della mostra (Monza,15 dicembre 2010–16 gennaio 2011). Milano: Johan & Levi

Grinsell, L. V. 1957. The Ferryman and His Fee: A Study in Ethnology, Archaeology, and Tradition, *Folklore* 68, I, 257–69.

von Hessen, O. 1978. *Il cimitero altomedievale di Pettinara – Casale Lozzi (Nocera Umbra)*, Quaderni del Centro per il collegamento degli studi medievali e umanistici nell'Università di Perugia, 3, Perugia: Università degli Studi di Perugia.

von Hessen, O. 1985. Il rituale funerario longobardo e i rinvenimenti di Nocera Umbra, pp. 106–125 in *Il territorio nocerino tra protostoria e altomedioevo*, Catalogo della mostra (Nocera Umbra, Pinacoteca S. Francesco, 8 giugno –15 settembre 1985). Firenze: Centro Di.

von Hessen, O. 1997. Testimonianze archeologiche longobarde nel ducato di Spoleto, pp. 131–4 in Paroli, L. (ed.) *Umbria Longobarda. La necropoli di Nocera Umbra nel centenario della scoperta* (Roma, Museo dell'Altomedioevo, 19 aprile –26 ottobre 1997). Roma: De Luca.

James, E. 1989. Burial and Status in the Early Medieval West, *Transactions of the Royal Historical Society* 39, 23–40.

Jørgensen, L. 1991. Castel Trosino and Nocera Umbra. A Chronological and Social Analysis of Family Burial Practices in Lombard Italy (6th–8th Cent. A.D.), *Acta Archaeologica* 62, 1–58.

Lett, D. 1997. L'enfant dans la chrétienté ($V^e$–$XIII^e$ siècles), pp. 17–125 in Alexandre-Bidon, D. and Lett, D. (eds), *Les Enfants au Moyen Age $V^e$–$XV^e$ siècles*. Paris: Hachette.

Lusuardi Siena, S. 2006. Esibizione di 'status', senso di appartenenza e identità nei sigilli aurei, pp. VII–XI in Lusuardi Siena, S. (ed.), *Anulus sui effigii. Identità e rappresentazione negli anelli-sigillo longobardi*. Milano: Vita e Pensiero.

Mengarelli, R. 1902. La necropoli barbarica di Castel Trosino presso Ascoli Piceno. *Monumenti Antichi* 12, 145–379.

Muggia, A. 2004. *Impronte nella sabbia: tombe infantili e di adolescenti nelle necropoli di Valle Trebbia a Spina*. Firenze: All'Insegna del Giglio.

Papacostantinou, A. 2009, Introduction: Homo Byzantinus in the Making, pp. 1–14, in Papacostantinou, A. and Talbot, A.-M. (eds) 2009, *Becoming Byzantine. Children and Childhood in Byzantium*. Washington: Dumbarton Oaks Research Library and Collection.

Paroli, L. 1983. Prospettive per un museo archeologico medievale di Roma, *Archeologia Medievale* 10, 19–42.

Paroli, L. 2000. Tomba di cavaliere longobardo da Castel Trosino. Località Pedata, pp. 88–92 in Bertelli, C. and Brogiolo, G. P. (eds), *Il futuro dei Longobardi. L'Italia e la costruzione dell'Europa di Carlo Magno*, Catalogo della mostra (Brescia, Monastero di Santa Giulia, 18 giugno–19 novembre 2000). Milano: Skira Editore.

Paroli, L. 2004. La tomba del fondatore dello stanziamento rinvenuta in loc. Pedata nel 1872, pp. 24–5 in *Il ritorno dei Longobardi. I nuovi scavi di Castel Trosino (2001–2004) ed il Museo dell'Altomedioevo ascolano*, Guida alla mostra (Ascoli Piceno, Palazzo dell'Arengo, 28 febbraio – 31 agosto 2004). Ascoli Piceno: Comune di Ascoli Piceno.

Paroli, L. and Ricci, M. 2007. *La necropoli altomedievale di Castel Trosino*. Firenze: Edizioni All'Insegna del Giglio.

Pasqui, A. and Paribeni, R. 1918. Necropoli barbarica di Nocera Umbra, *Monumenti Antichi* 25, 137–352.

Peduto, P. 1995. La moneta in tomba. Osservazioni sul rito in epoca medievale, *La Parola del Passato* 50, 311–318.

Pera, R. 1993. La moneta antica come talismano, *Rivista Italiana di Numismatica* 95, 347–361.

Pitarakis, B. 2009. The Material Culture of Childhood in Byzantium, pp. 167–182 in Papacostantinou, A. and Talbot, A.-M. (eds), *Becoming Byzantine. Children and Childhood in Byzantium*. Washington: Dumbarton Oaks Research Library and Collection.

Profumo, M. C. 1995. La necropoli di Nocera Umbra (Piazza Medaglie d'Oro), pp. 329–35 in Paroli, L. (ed.), *La necropoli altomedievale di Castel Trosino: bizantini e longobardi nelle Marche*, Catalogo della mostra (Ascoli Piceno, Museo Archeologico Statale, 1 luglio–31 ottobre 1995). Milano: Silvana Editoriale.

Profumo, M .C. and Staffa, A. 2007. Le necropoli altomedievali ed il sito fortificato di Castel Trosino, pp. 379–425 in Catani, E. and Paci, G. (eds), *La Salaria in età tardoantica e altomedievale*, Atti del Convegno di Studi (Rieti, Cascia, Norcia, Ascoli Piceno, 28–30 settembre 2001). Roma: L'Erma di Bretschneider.

Rupp, C. 1997. La necropoli longobarda di Nocera Umbra (loc. Il Portone): l'analisi archeologica, pp. 23–40 in Paroli, L. (ed.), *Umbria Longobarda. La necropoli di Nocera Umbra nel centenario della scoperta* (Roma, Museo dell'Altomedioevo, 27 luglio 1996–10 gennaio 1997). Roma: De Luca.

Rupp, C. 2003. Langobardische und Romanische Grabfunde in Umbrien, pp. 677–9, in *I Longobardi dei Ducati di Spoleto e di Benevento*, Atti del XVI Congresso internazionale di studi sull'alto medioevo (Spoleto, 20–23 ottobre 2002; Benevento, 24–27 ottobre 2002). Spoleto: Fondazione CISAM.

Rupp, C. 2005. *Das Langobardische Gräberfeld von Nocera Umbra. 1. Katalog und Tafeln*. Firenze: Edizioni All'Insegna del Giglio.

Sigismondi, G. 1979. *Nuceria in Umbria. Contributi per la storia dalle origini all'età feudale*. Foligno: Ediclio.

Stevens, S. T. 1991. Charon's Obol and Other Coins in Ancient Funerary Practice, *Phoenix* 45, III, 215–229.

Sullivan, F. A. 1950. Charon, the Ferryman of the Dead, *The Classical Journal* 46, I, 11–17.

Vallet, F. 1995. Une tombe de riche cavalier lombard découverte à Castel Trosino. *Mémoires – Association française d'archéologie mérovingienne* 9, 335–49.

# 24

## LA CULTURA LÚDICA EN LOS RITUALES FUNERARIOS INFANTILES: LOS JUEGOS DE VELORIO

### Jaume Bantulà Janot and Andrés Payà Rico

*There have always been many rituals related to the treatment of the deceased: banquets, funerary feasts, propitiatory sacrifices, funerary chants, processions accompanied by music and dances, etc. This paper approaches one of the various funerary ceremonies, the vigil celebrated when the deceased is a child. Even though the sadness and sorrow for the loss of an infant, it also takes place a festive and lively aspect, in which the play, dance and joy are also part of the celebration. The presence of the ludic element has aroused the interest for a better knowledge of the play activity accompanying the infant vigil. This ritual is known in Latin America as velorio de angelito (vigil for an angel).*

*As this is a common practice among the black population in various Latin American countries it is considered to have its origin in the African slaves. Nevertheless, this ritual also takes place in Central and South America countries in which indigenous population is more common that the black one. Researchers have seen it as an evidence of its precolonial origins. This kind of vigil does also exist in Spain in different places, thus it could be said that its entrance in the new continent came with the conquerors. But a checking of the vigil for deceased infants in America will reveal that it is not only the transfer of a funerary tradition from a continent to the other, but a confluence of different rituals from various cultural identities.*

## INTRODUCCIÓN

En todos los tiempos han existido una variedad de rituales en torno al tratamiento del muerto, banquetes y fiestas funerarias en honor del difunto, sacrificios propiciatorios, cantos funerarios, procesiones acompañadas de música y danzas, etc. El objetivo central de este trabajo, no es otro que el de abordar una de las posibles ceremonias fúnebres, nos referimos al velatorio. Con la intención de ilustrar la importancia que se atribuía al velatorio de difuntos en otros tiempos, hemos querido estudiar de más cerca una tipología concreta de velatorio, aquella que se realiza cuando el muerto es un niño. Nos hemos interesado básicamente por esta ceremonia por el hecho de que pese a la situación de tristeza y abatimiento que se produce por la pérdida de un niño, durante el ritual también se pone de manifiesto una vertiente festiva y alegre durante la cual el juego, la danza, el baile y la algazara también forman parte de la celebración.

Este ritual se conoce en América Latina como 'velorio de angelito'. El hecho de que esta ceremonia acontezca una práctica habitual entre la población negra de varios países latinoamericanos ha sido interpretado, como una señal que indica que su origen proviene del África negra y que fue introducido por los esclavos africanos. No obstante, este ritual también tiene cabida en países de Centro América y América del Sur en los cuales la población indígena es muy importante, a la vez que la presencia de población negra es más bien escasa. En estos casos los investigadores lo han interpretado como un signo inequívoco de su origen precolonial. Ahora bien, este tipo de velatorio, ha sido localizado al mismo tiempo en diferentes lugares de España, sobre todo por Valencia, Murcia, Extremadura y las Islas Canarias. Por esta razón, se podría argumentar que esta tipología de ritual tiene su entrada en el nuevo continente de la mano de los conquistadores. Pero una revisión de cómo se desarrolla el velatorio de niños en territorio americano nos mostrará que no se trata simplemente del traspaso de una costumbre funeraria de un continente a otro y que en este tipo de velatorio confluyen otros rituales propios de otras identidades culturales.

Además de profundizar en cada una de estas hipótesis, aquello que más llama la atención es que el velatorio está impregnado de un espíritu festivo donde tienen cabida cantos, danzas y bailes, y varias manifestaciones lúdicas. Ha sido esta presencia del elemento lúdico la que nos ha despertado el interés por conocer de más cerca cuáles acostumbran a ser los juegos de velatorio que acompañan, no sólo el velatorio de los niños, sino también el de los adultos. De todo esto se desprenden algunas cuestiones: ¿se juega por entretener al difunto?, ¿se juega el muerto su destino o bien su eternidad?, ¿el juego será de utilidad para cohesionar y consolidar la comunidad de los vivos?

### LOS RITUALES FUNERARIOS, UNA MANIFESTACIÓN HUMANA DE CULTO A LOS MUERTOS

Como nos recuerda el refrán 'la muerte no perdona a nadie', todavía hoy en día, en nuestra sociedad, cada vez más la muerte se esconde y es un tema tabú que preferimos silenciar y vivir de espaldas. Sin embargo, no es éste el espacio indicado para desarrollar una reflexión entorno al fenómeno de la muerte y la multiplicidad de creencias y rituales que la acompañan desde antaño. Aunque la naturaleza de los rituales funerarios y de luto son definidos socialmente y reflejan el contexto sociocultural donde suceden, el sentido de estos rituales podría asociarse a varias cuestiones que están presentes en varias culturas: certificar la muerte del otro; facilitar el camino, el retorno y la llegada del muerto a su lugar de destino; asustar a los malos espíritus; ofrecer un buen trato al difunto por su papel de mediador entre el más allá y los seres vivos; facilitar la adaptación a la realidad de la muerte y obtener el apoyo de la comunidad.

Si el juego está presente a lo largo de la vida del hombre, no debe resultar extraño que en el momento de la muerte, las manifestaciones lúdicas también nos acompañen. De hecho, es conocido el origen funerario de los juegos olímpicos. En el mundo griego, era habitual la realización de varios juegos de carácter competitivo como rituales que se celebraban en honor de los personajes importantes.[1] En tiempos de los romanos, a los nueve días del sepelio tenía lugar el banquete fúnebre conocido como 'novendalia'. Tanto en la antigua Grecia como en la Roma imperial era costumbre jugar dentro de los cementerios, testigo de lo cual son los hallazgos de tabas, dados y cubiletes en los mismos. Antiguamente 'el día de Todos Santos', se celebraban auténticas bacanales en recuerdo y honor de los difuntos. La Iglesia combatió estos abusos, como por ejemplo, en el concilio de Braga (572) en donde se recordaba la prohibición de celebrar banquetes en los cementerios o depositar ofrendas en honor a los muertos. En cambio, pese a las constantes prohibiciones a lo largo de la época medieval, en el s. XVI todavía era frecuente en España celebrar el día de los difuntos ofreciendo alimentos a los muertos. Se trataba, por lo tanto, de prácticas arraigadas en las costumbres populares, no sólo propias de la cultura greco-latina, sino también presentes en la cultura china y entre los egipcios, y más tarde heredadas también por los árabes.

En este trabajo nos ocuparemos de una de las posibles ceremonias fúnebres, el velatorio. De las diversas acepciones del término, el velatorio significa pasar la noche al cuidado de una persona que ha muerto recientemente. Una palabra derivada de velar, que aparece en el siglo XIII proveniente del latino *vĭgĭlare*, que significa 'estar despierto; 'vigilar', derivado de *vigēre* 'tener vida, vigor; estar desvelado'. Con la intención de ilustrar la importancia que se atribuía al velatorio de difuntos en otros tiempos, hemos querido estudiar la vela de niños. A la hora de interpretar este ritual hará falta tener en cuenta diversas consideraciones. De entrada nos parece oportuno detenernos en dos de ellas. En primer lugar, remarcar que desde el siglo II hay referencias en el cristianismo que expresan la creencia de que los niños que morían no debían ser despedidos con pena pues todavía no había tenido tiempo de pecar. En segundo lugar, debemos tener presente que la muerte hasta entrado el siglo XX era algo familiar y natural, no se escondía y no era revestida de gran dramatismo. Incluso era costumbre no dar nombre a los niños al nacer, y esperar un tiempo prudencial para saber si sobrevivirían o no. La mortalidad infantil era bastante elevada y cotidiana y los padres mantenían cierta actitud de resignación ante la muerte de los hijos.

EL VELATORIO INFANTIL EN ESPAÑA Y SU INCIDENCIA EN VALENCIA

El velatorio infantil y el carácter lúdico a él ligado que describiremos a continuación, era una práctica arraigada antaño en diversos puntos del territorio español. Así, se tiene constancia de estos juegos en Valencia, Murcia, Extremadura, Islas Canarias, así como en algunos lugares del centro y sur peninsular. A propósito de esta costumbre en el archipiélago canario, gracias a la historia oral, José Luis Concepción recoge el testimonio de un 'velorio de los angelitos' en 1896 en Herquito (La Gomera):

> Cuando un niño moría, hasta los siete años inclusive, lo amortajaban y el primero en bailar al niño muerto era el padrino, a ritmo de tambor y chácaras, que tocaban los acompañantes del velorio. El padrino daba una vuelta al local y la madrina repetía lo mismo; después ponían el niño en la mesa, vestido de blanco y sin caja, sólo lo metían en la caja cuando lo llevaban a enterrar. Sólo bailaban al niño estas dos vueltas; luego, los acompañantes del velorio se pasaban la noche bailando y cantando al niño[2]

Otra de las escasas referencias existentes, nos la brinda el historiador Manuel Hernández al recordarnos el carácter festivo del velorio, en el cual *'jóvenes y adultos de ambos sexos burlaban embriagados por el alcohol y el baile sus traumas y preocupaciones y, en definitiva, la muerte que a cada paso les golpea'*,[3] al mismo tiempo que practican el 'juego del difunto', recogido por Bethencourt en Candelaria (Tenerife):

> Encaminado a burlar a los mozos inexpertos, consiste en tenderse un individuo en el suelo a manera de cadáver, rodeado por los doloridos que llevan en la mano un zapato a guisa de cirio, mientras que otros desfilan aproximándose al fingido cadáver para abrazarlo y besarlo, dando ayes y suspiros, llorando a la vez que dicen las cosas más picarescas y ocurrentes alusivas a la vida del finado. Y así continúan la zumba hasta que toca el turno al cándido a quien preparan la velada y tan pronto se acercan al cadáver lo abrazan y lo retienen mientras los doloridos descargan un diluvio de zapatazos sobre el incauto.[4]

Pero donde más presencia e incidencia tuvo este tipo de velatorio y los juegos que lo acompañan, fue en el Levante español, concretamente en Valencia, especialmente en tierras alicantinas. Por esta razón nos centraremos en estudiar con mayor detenimiento el caso valenciano, más documentado y en donde este tipo de ritual recibe el nombre de *vetlatori de l'albaet*. En Valencia era costumbre cuando un niño menor de siete u ocho años moría, la celebración de un rito funerario que se convertía en motivo de fiesta alegre durante la cual se comía, bebía y bailaba. El motivo de permanecer alegres era porque prevalecía la creencia de que los niños a estas edades tan tempranas no habían tenido tiempo de pecar, por lo cual se convertían en ángeles que, desde el cielo, podían interceder por todos los parientes y amigos.

A lo largo del día se hacían los preparativos. En la cocina, encima de una mesa se ponía al niño muerto, denominado 'albaet' porque había muerto apenas encontrándose en el alba de la vida. La mesa se guarnía con sábanas o telas blancas para acoger al niño vestido también de blanco, con los pies desnudos, los labios y las mejillas pintadas de carmín y coronado con flores blancas de tela o de papel. Este uso intensivo del color blanco podría guardar relación con el hecho de que ya desde la época medieval se creía que este color era repulsivo del alma y así se facilitaba su separación del cuerpo.

A este respeto, Duque corrobora que el motivo por el que se empleaba el blanco era para que el alma huyera de este color, no debiendo tampoco de faltar la luz en la habitación del difunto para guiar así el alma y que encontrara el camino al cielo,[5] si bien hay quien opina que las velas también se encendían para purificar el ambiente y alejar los malos espíritus.

En otra mesa de la cocina se preparaba la comida con la que se invitaba a la noche a los asistentes. Llegada la noche, 'l'albaet' era velado *alegremente durante toda la noche con el ritmo marcado por castañuelas, guitarras, bandurrias y acordeones*.[6] Una pareja de bailadores empezaba la 'dansa del vetlatori', entrando y saliendo las parejas a bailar hasta la madrugada. Al acabar todas las parejas juntas bailaban formando cuadras y un círculo. Se trataba de un baile ceremonial de movimientos lentos y suaves. Al final, cinco estrofas invitaban al baile a la vez que se consolaba a los padres y se hacía referencia a 'l'albaet', tal y como sucede en la 'dansa del vetlatori' de Xàtiva (Valencia).

Este ceremonial del 'velatori de l'albaet' se realizó con fuerza en Valencia, siendo más propio de la zona costera del levante mediterráneo, aquella que va de Castellón a Murcia, si bien también también se localiza su práctica en Extremadura, Islas Canarias, así como en varios lugares del centro y sur de España. Entre las fuentes documentales que dan cuenta del uso de este ritual destaca la petición del obispo de Orihuela (Alicante) para que actúe prohibiendo las fiestas de los 'mortichuelos' o 'mortixolets' que es como denominaban la fiesta de l'albaet:

> se ha introducido la barbara costumbre de los Bayles nocturnos con motivos de los Niños que se mueren llamados vulgarmente Mortichuelos (...)suelen juntarse hombres, y mujeres, la mayor parte Mozos, y Doncellas en las casas de los Padres de los difuntos, y contra las leyes de la humanidad, se gastan chanzas, invectivas, y bufonadas, contrarias á la modestia, y consideraciones christianas que presentan la muerte de un hijo, y despues se bayla hasta las dos, ó tres de la mañana, en que se retiran alborotando las calles con griteria, relinchos, y carcajadas, y muchas veces no dexando fruta en los campos, con no pocas quexas y sentimientos de sus Dueños.[7]

Pese a que se evidencia en este real acuerdo de la Audiencia de Valencia la disconformidad por parte de la Iglesia a la celebración de este rito funerario, su práctica se mantendrá en el tiempo de manera inalterable. Así es cómo lo describe, en el año 1862, el barón Ch. Davillier mientras realiza un viaje por España, cuando de manera fortuita se encuentra con la celebración de un velatorio de infantes en Jijona (Alicante):

> Nous fûmes un jour témoins à Jijona d'une cérémonie funèbre dans laquelle, à notre gran étonnement, les assistants dansaient la Jota. Nous passions dans une rue deserte, quand nous entendimes un fronfon de guitarre accompagné du chant aigu de la bandurria et d'un cliquetis de castagnettes. Nous poussâmes la porte entre'ouverte d'une maison de cultivateurs, croyant tomber au milieu d'une noce: c'était un enterrement. Dans le fond de la pièce nous aperçûmes, étendue sur une table couverte d'un tapis, une petite fille de cinq à six ans, habillée comme pour un jour de fête (…) un jeune homme et une jeune fille, portant le costume de fête des labradores valenciens, dansaient une Jota en s'accompagnant de leurs castagnettes[8]

La literatura valenciana de finales del siglo XIX y principios del XX, contiene varias referencias a estos ritos funerarios con descripciones llenas de sentimiento y tradición popular valenciana. Éste es el caso, por ejemplo del poema 'A [l]'albat' de Constantí Llombart (1888), premiado en el certamen literario de los Juegos Florales de la ciudad de Valencia. Una década después, en 1898, Vicente Blasco Ibañez, publicaría su famosa novela *La Barraca*. En el octavo capítulo de su obra –que nos abstenemos de reproducir aqui por su longitud – describe ampliamente el velatorio de un albaet. Otras referencias las podemos encontrar también en el cuento 'L'albaet' de Vicent Plá Mompó (1924) o los versos d'Eduardo Buil (1927) titulados 'L'albaet. A la blanca memoria del nene Paquito'.[9]

Con los ejemplos mencionados se pretende poner de manifiesto la vigencia de este ritual, sobre todo en el levante mediterráneo. Ahora bien, este ritual no fue una costumbre arraigada sólo en la península ibérica y las islas Canarias. Por todas partes de Iberoamérica también es una práctica ritual muy extendida territorialmente, destacando aquellos lugares poseedores de una elevada población afroamericana o indígena, como veremos a continuación.

## EL VELATORIO DE INFANTES EN IBEROAMÉRICA

La realización del ceremonial anteriormente descrito en una basta y dispersa extensión territorial dio pie a indagar sobre cuál podría ser su origen y su difusión. El hecho de que la ceremonia tuviese lugar entre la población afroamericana de Colombia, Ecuador, Venezuela, Puerto Rico y otros países iberoamericanos, permitió especular que se trataba de un ceremonial importado de América por los esclavos. No obstante, la constatación del ritual funerario entre indígenas de Bolivia, Ecuador, Perú, Guatemala, México, etc..., sugería a los investigadores que la ceremonia tenía un origen precolonial. Pero, su presencia en Valencia, donde hay documentación que avala la realización del velatorio de infantes y de la danza del *albaet* desde el siglo XVI hasta el inicio de la guerra civil española, así como su localización en otros lugares, obligan a pensar que fueron los conquistadores españoles quienes extendieron el ceremonial en el nuevo mundo:

> [esta costumbre] es hispana, y a España la llevaron los árabes. [En España, el velatorio del Angelito se ha encontrado principalmente en el sur de ese país, en las províncias del Mediterráneo, Extremadura y las Islas Canarias. En Valencia, Alicante y Murcia, esta práctica se conoce con el nombre de aurora. En una aurora el cuerpecito del niño se envolvía en un velo de gasa o chifón]. Lo demás es sencillo: con la cruz y la espada trasplantáronse al Nuevo Mundo junto con el cancionero que siguió las huellas del conquistador o se superpuso a ellas, una y otra costumbre peninsular, que un aislamiento geográfico protegió favoreciendo su conservación hasta nuestros días.[10]

Del mismo modo, Pelegrín señala que *'el primitivo origen de este funeral de párvuls, está relacionado con la presencia de los árabes en territorio español, desde los inicios de la conquista a partir del siglo VIII'*.[11] Así pues, para aclarar este origen es necesario hacer una revisión de cómo se desarrolla el velatorio de niños en territorio americano, en la cual podremos ver cómo confluyen otros rituales mágico-religiosos.

En Argentina hay bastantes fuentes documentales que indican la existencia de una fuerte presencia de la celebración del velatorio de niños, que es conocido como 'velorio del angelito'. A finales del siglo XIX, Granada hace mención sobre cómo se llevaba a cabo la ceremonia en esta área geográfica: '*no toda clase de velorios son velorio: pues los hay harto animados y estrepitosos, que el ínfimo vulgo suele dedicar á la muerte de los párvulos. Reunidos en la casa mortuoria hombres y mujeres (...) se entretienen durante la noche en cantar y bailar y en diversos juegos de prendas, como las aves nocturnas, el pulpero, la cortina de amor*'.[12] Es costumbre también que el velatorio se prolongue más de un día para que la fiesta continúe: '*El velorio de un ángel solía durar dos, cuatro, seis ó más días; pues los vecinos y amigos solicitaban de los padres ó deudos el cuerpo de la criatura para celebrar en su casa la bienhadada fiesta (...) dando motivo á que la juventud se divirtiese, jugando, bailando, chacoteando, comiendo y bebiendo*'.[13] Incluso resulta habitual que los padres presten el niño muerto a los propietarios de las tascas a cambio de dinero para hacer frente a los gastos del entierro.[14] Otro testimonio de la presencia del canto y del baile durante el velatorio nos lo aporta el folklorista Coluccio, quien explica que:

> En el norte argentino no se llora la muerte de los niños chicos. Una boca menos en la tierra, en el cielo un ángel más: la muerte se bebe y se baila, desde el primer canto del gallo, con largos tragos de aloja y chicha y al son del bombo y la guitarra. Mientras los bailantes giran y zapatean, se van pasando al niño de brazo en brazo. Cuando el niño ha sido bien mecido y festejado, rompen todos a cantar para que empiece su vuelo al Paraíso. Allá va el viajerito, vestido con sus mejores galas, mientras crece la canción. Y le dicen adiós encendiendo cohetes, con mucho cuidado de no quemarle las alas.[15]

El lanzamiento de cohetes se realiza con la intención de asustar a los malos espíritus, mientras que con la incorporación de las alas al cuerpo del párvulo difunto se pretende facilitar su ascensión al cielo, por eso debe evitarse que las alas se puedan quemar o bien quedar mojadas de tanto llorar. Para facilitar este tránsito hacia el cielo también es práctica habitual recurrir a la utilización de un cordón con nudos, tal y como nos explica un testimonio entrevistado por Pelegrín en Santiago del Estero:

> [...] Cuando muere un chiquitito se lo prepara con papel crep, se les hace una flor y se le pone en la boquita, la madrina, por ejemplo. La mamá le tiene que echar la leche en la boquita. La madrina le tiene que poner la flor. Después se hacen en forma de alas que se le cose en la ropita aquí, por sobre los bracitos, éste para que vuelen (...)para que algún día, cuando nosotros nos morimos, ese bebé, ese ángel, venga y nos encuentre, entonces que nosotros nos agarramos detrás de ese nudo y llegamos al cielo.[16]

Llega el turno de interesarnos en saber cómo se desarrolla el ritual funerario del velatorio del albaet entre los afroamericanos. En este sentido, en Colombia, en la zona rural de Buenaventura, el promotor de salud Óscar Gómez constata cómo los padres, cuando el médico les explica la imposibilidad de salvar la vida de su hijo, toman la decisión de no desplazarse a otro lugar para recibir una mejor atención médica y optan, pese a que el niño todavía no haya muerto, por destinar el dinero a la realización del velatorio y el entierro:

> cuando notaron que en las iglesias no hay santos, ni ángeles negros, y que el mismo Jesús es mono ojiazul se preocuparon por la falta de representantes de su etnia en el reino de los

cielos… de allí que celebren con 'biche', música y baile la muerte de un recién nacido, pues al no haber alcanzado a cometer ningún pecado, muy seguramente ese será un angelito más de raza negra! Motivo este por el cuál hay que celebrar[17]

En esta región colombiana denominan al ritual 'chigüalo'. Ante la muerte existe el sentimiento de tristeza, pero al mismo tiempo es motivo de alegría, siendo vivida la muerte de manera festiva: '*al niño lo sentaban, lo acunaban y parecía que estuviera vivo; le tocaban la guitarra y comenzaban a bailarle porque el niño es bailado. Un angelito es bailando porque así lo reciben los ángeles en el cielo, con guitarras. Uno lo veía ahí sentadito y así mismo se meneaba él. Cualquiera decía que estaba vivo y no, porque así lo chigüaliamos*'.[18] En estos 'chigüalos' no sólo se despide al niño muerto con cantos, sino que también es frecuente jugar y cantar juegos que reflejan la situación de su pérdida, entre los cuales se encuentran, por ejemplo, los juegos de 'A pilar el arroz', 'Azúcar' o 'El loro y la lora'.

En el Palenque de San Basilio, a setenta kilómetros de Cartagena de Indias, principal puerto de la trata de esclavos del Caribe, hay una notoria comunidad negra descendientes de los cimarrones que se instalaron en el siglo XVII. Uno de los rituales principales que celebran con ocasión de la muerte es el *lumbalú* y los juegos de velatorio. Etimológicamente el término 'lumbalú' es una voz africana compuesta de dos elementos: *lu* es un prefijo colectivo y *mbalu* significa melancolía, recuerdo o reflexión que expresa el sentido de los cantos de muerte.[19] Cuando el difunto es un niño, en el ataúd se le ponen sus juguetes, sus enseres para comer, ropa nueva y sus zapatos para que comparta con otros angelitos sus posesiones. Friedemann establece que en el velatorio de un niño, los niños juegan a canicas y dominó en la calle, mientras que las niñas permanecen sentadas con las mujeres adultas dentro de la casa. En estos juegos es costumbre personificar a varios animales e incitar a la sensualidad y el erotismo.[20] Tanto es así que, según Martínez Miranda, '*un componente a destacar en los juegos de velorio, también presente en otros rituales funerarios afrodescendientes, y tema poco profundizado, es la carga lúdico-erótica (…) los juegos y cantos de velorio son el pretexto dentro del velorio para el enamoramiento*'.[21]

También para Schwegler, estos juegos tienen la intención de distraer a los asistentes al velatorio. Los participantes se agrupan por edades y forman un círculo en el centro del cual se coloca uno de los jugadores, que es reemplazado por otro, hasta que se inicia otro juego.[22] Un aspecto interesante a destacar es que en los juegos de velatorio del Palenque de San Basilio se evidencia la importancia que atribuyen las etnias africanas, especialmente las bantúes, al culto de los muertos. En los cantos y juegos de velatorio se produce una adaptación de sus ritos funerarios y, a su vez, la adopción forzada de los ritos procedentes de la religión católica. Este hecho se puede corroborar en uno de los juegos de velatorio, que recibe el nombre de San 'Benito', en el cual los palenqueros invocan a Lembà, diosa de la procreación. En este juego los participantes forman un coro en el centro del cual se coloca alguien simulando pedir limosna.

En otros lugares del pacífico sur del país colombiano al 'chigüalo' también se le llama 'bunde', 'gualí', 'velatorio', 'mampulorio', 'angelito', 'angelito bailao', 'velorio del angelito' o 'muerto alegre'. Este canto está muy extendido entre las comunidades afrocolombianas del litoral pacífico. De hecho, etimológicamente se deriva de la voz 'wunde', que designa un tono, canto y danza propios de Sierra Leona. El bunde a menudo queda enmarcado en el ámbito de las rondas y juegos infantiles que ejecutan los niños en el patio de casa mientras los adultos se ocupan del ritual mortuorio. Así, encontramos abundantes rondas de juegos que toman el nombre de bundes como son 'El chocolate', 'El punto', 'El trapicherito', 'El florón', 'El pelusa', 'Jugar con mi tía', 'Adiós tía Coti' y 'El laurel'.[23] El 'gualí' es uno de los ceremoniales rituales más representativos de la tradición oral de la costa pacífica colombiana, en los cuales mientras se lleva a cabo la vela del niño muerto se recitan cantos y juegos. En las letras permanecen arcaísmos hispanos ('vide', 'agora', 'enantes'), otros autóctonos ('ñangamente', 'aliprú', 'arrecha'), y de naturaleza aforamericana ('malanga', 'bemba', 'catanga').

En la costa del Pacífico, en Ecuador, la celebración del chigualo también se encuentra muy arraigada, como sucede en Esmeraldas, donde es considerado una fiesta en la cual el canto, la danza y el juego son fundamentales. Esta práctica persigue glorificar a los niños que se van directos al cielo para convertirse en angeles. El chigualo no estuvo nunca bien visto por las instituciones eclesiásticas durante el periodo colonial, porque atentaba contra sus principios religiosos y morales.

En el Caribe, en concreto en la República Dominicana, Jamaica, Haití y Cuba, al 'velorio del angelito' se le denomina 'baquiní', mientras que en Puerto Rico se le conoce por 'baquiné'. En Jamaica, el 'bakinny' responde a un culto fúnebre celebrado entre los campesinos negros para honrar el regreso del espíritu del muerto cuando visita a sus parientes tras nueve noches. Para la ocasión encienden una hoguera y a su alrededor los hombres y los niños practican juegos, mientras las mujeres y las niñas observan las manifestaciones lúdicas.[24] Respecto a Puerto Rico, la celebración del baquiné, como en otros lugares mencionados, consiste en la celebración de cantos, alternados con bailes y canciones-juegos, entre las que podemos citar 'El Quinimán', 'El Alfiler' y 'El Papelón'. También es frecuente que durante el transcurso de la ceremonia, se lleven a cabo juegos de prendas, se formulen adivinanzas, se expliquen cuentos de la tradición oral, así como anécdotas y leyendas. Esta presencia del juego de velatorio se hace patente en un breve fragmento de la novela 'El litoral', donde el poeta Palés, refiriéndose al ritual funerario del baquiné de Puerto Rico, nos explica que *'la sesión se prolonga a lo largo de la noche, con breves intermedios en los que se reparten golosinas y corre libremente el ron de caña para los hombres y el anisado para las mujeres. Organízanse juegos sociales con la participación de toda la concurrencia, la prenda, el castigo, la gallina ciega...'*.[25] La fuente documental conocida más antigua sobre este ritual procede de Fray Iñigo Abbad, que en el año 1788, al referirse a la afición por el baile de los habitantes de Puerto Rico, señala que *'el nacimiento o muerte de algún niño también se celebra con bailes que duran hasta que ya no se puede sufrir el fetor del difunto'*.[26]

No obstante, en el momento de buscar una posible herencia africana dentro de la religiosidad popular de Puerto Rico no hay documentación que permita afirmar que el baquiné sea introducido por los esclavos negros, sino más bien debería destacarse el origen español, lo cual se pone de manifiesto a la hora de revisar varios cantos de baquiné de ritmo trocaico, característicos de la poesía popular y tradicional hispánica medieval: '*puede observarse en las estrofas el típico movimiento de retroceso y avance tan caractarístico del zéjel (estrofa) árabigo andaluz, así como de algunos villancicos gallego-portugueses. Entre los cánticos de baquiné, además de las coplas de arte menor, pueden encontrarse décimas y hasta seguidillas*'.[27] Quizás cabría pensar que la celebración del 'velorio del angelito' no era contraria a las costumbres de los afroamericanos, al menos se evidencia que la adaptaron e incorporaron a sus propias tradiciones. Así, además de las canciones y los juegos, se incorporan con frecuencia cuentos cantados: '*cuentos, con frecuencia de origen africano, que tenían un estribillo que cantaban, repetidamente, los asistentes. Los estribillos cantados, por lo general, tenían frases en lenguas africanas, cuyo significado ya desconocían los participantes, pero junto a los cuentos habían quedado en la tradición oral*'.[28]

Después de este repaso a las aportaciones sobre el velatorio de niños entre la población afroamericana, pasamos a intentar averiguar cómo se materializa el velatorio en las zonas más proclives a conservar una densidad de población indígena más acusada. Así en Ecuador, en lugares como Otavalo, Cotacachi, Ilumán, Peguche y otras poblaciones, los funerales de los niños indígenas se conocen como 'Huahua velorio'. Es frecuente que durante la noche se baile el fandango presidido por los 'achitaita' o padrinos del párvulo, que son los encargados de llevar los músicos al velatorio. Uno de los rituales funerarios que tienen más estrecha relación con el juego es el 'Wantiay'. Los juegos fúnebres comienzan con el juego del 'chunkana',[29] un juego de azar previo con granos de trigo. Entre los juegos más frecuentes se encuentran el 'Tanta Ukucha', 'Gallo', 'Kurikinki', 'Paya' o 'Micha Sinti'.

Otros informantes consultados en los años 1970 y 1973 en la sierra ecuatoriana,[30] relatan otros juegos de prendas, con los cuales se castiga o penaliza a los perdedores del juego de *chunkana* anteriormente mencionado. Entre otros encontramos: traer una mosca por participante, representar varios animales, cruzar un río, o bien intentar coger una moneda del suelo teniendo las manos atadas a la espalda. Debe mencionarse también que el juego de chunkana parece ser una adaptación del juego de la 'pichca', un juego de la época prehispánica que se empleaba para dialogar con los huacas en el Imperio Inca. Con un pequeño objeto con forma de pirámide que tenía grabadas diferentes marcas en sus caras y bases, se consultaba la voluntad divina según caía y si se dejaba o no ver cierta marca. El juego de la pichca, también conocido como 'huairo o pisca', derivaría durante el siglo XX en un juego de velatorio y un juego de fortuna.[31]

CONCLUSIONES

El velatorio, con todos sus componentes, representa, de un lado, una ocasión de agradar al *albaet* o angelito, alegrarlo con música, festejarlo con bailes, danzas y juegos, para preparar su tránsito de la vida hacia la muerte y nuevamente a la vida para que, una vez convertido en angel sea benevolente con sus deudores y protector de sus familiares.

De otro lado, el ritual es una forma de agradar a Dios o los dioses para que le acepten. La muerte del niño es un hecho triste y penoso. La fiesta no es más que la pretensión de separar el difunto de la comunidad, facilitándole su viaje al más allá y a la vez reintegrarlo a los orígenes del individuo, de la comunidad y del mundo. El ritual es necesario para que se produzca la transformación. La madre ha de estar alegre, si llora puede romper el conjuro (mojar las alas). Así pues, debido a la alegría que se experimenta al saber que el niño ha encontrado un lugar mejor más allá del mundo terrenal, el Velatorio de l'albaet o Velorio de Angelito adquiere un tono festivo. En palabras de Zalba, '*esta práctica-creencia manifiesta una profunda valoración de la vida humana. En ella, se dice fuerte y claro que la muerte no puede tener la última palabra. Se intuye un después o, mejor, una suerte de continuidad vital, que se expresa simbólicamente con la imagen del angelito*'.[32]

Los cantos contribuirán a que el alma no se sienta sola en el tránsito de la vida a la muerte y a la vez distraerán al muerto para que no encuentre el camino de vuelta y pueda venir a atemorizar a sus parientes. Con los cantos también se trasladan peticiones a otros mundos en los que residen las almas de los muertos, así como las de aquellos que todavía no han nacido. Los instrumentos de percusión se emplearán para golpear las puertas de estos mundos para que se abran las vías de comunicación y se pueda establecer un diálogo. Y es que, sea como sea, en el trasfondo de los rituales de la muerte '*hay símbolos de una cosmovisión donde vivos y muertos habitan un mundo conformado por varios planos relacionados y compartidos. Y el culto a los muertos es un acto para que los habitantes de los dos mundos dialoguen*'.[33]

Si el ritual requiere de un estado alegre, qué mejor que contar con la presencia de las manifestaciones lúdicas. A nuestro entender no se juega para entretener o distender el ambiente, ni de los asistentes, ni tampoco del difunto. Tampoco es que el muerto se juegue su destino o su eternidad. Las manifestaciones lúdicas, acompañadas de gritos, carreras, saltos, cantos, aplausos, voces, risas y sonrisas etc., se practican durante el velatorio porque si el juego está implícito a lo largo del ciclo vital, como renegar de él durante el ritual de paso a otra vida, con más razón si cabe cuando el difunto es un niño.

De otro lado, señalar que no decimos nada nuevo si recordamos que el hombre ha jugado desde siempre, desde la noche de los tiempos, en una especie de danza celestial que a menudo ha fusionado al hombre con Dios, un Dios que también ha hecho el mundo como un juego, es decir, gracias a una decisión libre que escapa de cualquier tipo de necesidad y determinismo. Como diría Hugo Rahner en *El hombre lúdico* (1952), es la presencia de un Dios ludens la que nos permite hablar de un homo ludens. Así, en el tlachtli, el juego de pelota practicado por los mayas y aztecas desde el 1.400 a. C, los vencedores tenían el gozo y el honor de ser sacrificados para servir de alimento a los dioses con el fin de mantener el orden cósmico del universo y la regeneración ritual de la vida.

En el velatorio del albaet, el corpus lúdico es utilizado también como religión, en el sentido de que nos une y da cohesión, consolidando la comunidad de los vivos, una comunidad que sabe que la muerte es uno de los aspectos fundamentales de la vida.

Porque al fin y al cabo, '*la muerte no era vista como final de la existencia, sino como una parte de ésta; por eso era más bien, una fiesta de la vida*' Guerrero (1998, 13). En definitiva, se trata del triunfo de la incerteza de la vida – y en eso de la incerteza, el juego es una excelsa fuente de aprendizaje – por encima de la certeca de la muerte, de la victoria de la eternidad sobre el tiempo.

## Notes

1   Blázquez y García-Gelabert 1992, 28–39
2   Concepción 2007, 64–65
3   Hernández 2004, 65
4   Hernández 2004, 65
5   Duque 2004, 224
6   Pelegrín 2005, 4
7   Audiencia de Valencia 1788, IV–V
8   Davillier 1874, 409
9   Buil 1927, 26
10  Coluccio 1992, 227
11  Pelegrín 2005, 2
12  Granada 1896, 70
13  Granada 1896, 70
14  Dragoski 1972, 33
15  Coluccio 1988, 673
16  Pelegrín 2005, 11
17  Sevilla *et al.* 2009, 37–38
18  González 2003, 36
19  Escalante 1989, 6
20  Friedemann 1991, 84–85
21  Martínez 2012, 73–74
22  Schwegler 1991, 189–21
23  Cárdenas 1998
24  Álvarez 1961, 276–77
25  Arce 1984
26  Abbad y Lasierra 1788, 281
27  Canino 2010
28  Cruz 2012
29  Cachiguango 2001, 179–186
30  Hartmann 1980, 225–274
31  Gentile 1988, 75–131
32  Zalba 2010, 289
33  Friedemann 1992, 551

## References

Abbad y Lasierra, I. 1788. *Historia geográfica, civil y natural de la Isla de San Juan Bautista de Puerto Rico*. Madrid: Imprenta de Antonio Espinosa.
Álvarez, M. 1961. *El español en Puerto Rico*. San Juan de Puerto Rico: ICP.
Arce, M. 1984. *Luís Palés Matos: obras 1914–1959*. Puerto Rico: Ed. Universidad de Puerto Rico.
Audiencia de V. 1788. *Auto del Real Acuerdo de la Audiencia de Valencia, de seis de noviembre de este ano, en el que a representacion: del Reverendo en Christo D. Joseph Tormo, Obispo de*

*Orihuela, se prohiben las funciones de Bacas, Novillos, Comedias, Mascaras, &c. con motivo de Fiestas de Santos, Imagenes, y demas que aqui se expresan*. Murcia: Viuda de Felipe Teruel

Blázquez, J. M. y García-Gelabert, M. P. 1992. El origen funerario de los juegos olímpicos. *Revista de Arqueología* (Valencia), nº 140: 28–39.

Buil, E. 1927. *El gancho: choget lirica en mig acte y en prosa*. Valencia: Arte y Letras

Cachiguango, L. E. 2001. ¡Wantiay...! El ritual funerario andino de adultos en Otavalo, Ecuador. *Chungara. Revista de Antropología Chilena* (Arica), nº 33: 179–86.

Canino, M. 2010. La religiosidad popular en Puerto Rico y la herencia africana. *Enciclopedia Puertorriqueña de las Humanidades* htpp://www.enciclopediapr.org.

Cárdenas, R. 1998. *Nortecaucanos y su folclor. Negro es mi vivir...* Santa Fe de Bogotá: CINEP.

Coluccio, F. 1988. *Diccionario folkórico argentino,* Buenos Aires, Corregidor.

Coluccio, F. 1992. *Fiestas y celebraciones en la República Argentina*. Buenos Aires: Plus ultra

Concepción, J. L. 1984. *Costrumbres y tradiciones canarias con anexo de santiguados*. La Laguna: Asociación Cultural de las Islas Canarias.

Cruz, Z. 2012. Adaptación del angelito o baquiné: ejemplo del sincretismo mágico-religioso en torno al ritual de la muerte en el Caribe y Puerto Rico" en *Enciclopedia Puertorriqueña de las Humanidades* htpp://www.enciclopediapr.org.

Davillier, C. 1874. *L'Espagne*. París: Hachette.

Dragosky, Graciela y Páez, Jorge 1972 *Fiestas y ceremonias tradicionales,* Buenos Aires, CEAL.

Duque, María del Mar 2004 *El ciclo de la vida: Ritos y costumbres de los alicantinos de antaño*. Alicante: Club Universitario.

Escalante, A. 1989. Significado de Lumbalú, ritual funerario del Palenque de San Basilio. *Revista Huellas* (Barranquilla), nº 26: 6–24.

Friedemann, N. 1991. Lumbalú: ritos de la muerte en Palenque de San Basilio, Colombia. *Revista América Negra* (Bogotá), nº 1: 65–86.

Friedemann, N. 1992. Huellas de africanía en Colombia. *Centro virtual Cervantes. Thesaurus*. Tomo XLVII, 3: 551.

Gentile, Margarite E. 1998. La Pichca: oráculo y juego de fortuna (su persitencia en el espacio y tiempo andinos). *Bulletin de l'Institut Français d'Études Andines* (Lima), nº 27: 75–131.

González, C. 2003. Música, identidad y muerte entre los grupos negros del Pacífico sur colombiano, *Revista Universidad de Guadalajara* (Guadalajara), nº 27: 1–48.

Granada, D. 1896. *Reseña histórico-descriptiva de antiguas y modernas supersticiones*. Montevideo: Barreiro y Ramos.

Hartmann, R. 1980. Juegos de velorio en la sierra ecuatoriana. *Indiana* (Berlin) 6: 225–274.

Hernández, M. 2004. *Enfermedad y muerte en Canarias en el siglo XVIII. Tomo II: La muerte*. Santa Cruz de Tenerife: Ediciones Idea.

Martínez, L. G. 2010. *Del canto del kajambá al lamento del leko: El velorio en el palenque de San Basilio, una encrucijada entre su valor cultural, su costo económico y los procesos de aculturación*. Cartagena: Observatorio del Caribe Colombiano y Ministerio de Cultura.

Pelegrín, M. 2005. Desde el Mediterráneo a tierras de quebrachos. El Vetlatori del Albaet en Valencia y su correlato en el Velorio del Angelito en Santiago del Estero, Argentina. *Espéculo, Revista de estudios literarios* (Madrid), nº 30.

Schewegler, A. 1991. África en América: Los Juegos de velorio y otros cantos funerarios afrohispanos remanentes en la costa atlántica de Colombia, pp. 189–221 en Norbert Boretzky (Coord.) *Akten des 7. Essener Kolloquiums ubre Minoritätensprachen/Sprachminoritäten*. Bochum: Univesitätsverlag Dr. N. Brockmeuer.

Sevilla, E., Sevilla, M. y Valencia, V. H. 2009. *Tejiendo sonidos y sentidos*. Cali: Pontificia Universidad Javeriana Cali y Ministerio de Cultura.

Zalba, S. 2010. Los huahuitas del señor. Angelitos y velorios. *Vida pastoral* (Buenos Aires), nº 289.

# 25

## COMPARTIENDO LA EXPERIENCIA DE LA MUERTE. EL NIÑO MUERTO Y EL NIÑO FRENTE A LA MUERTE

### Virginia de la Cruz Lichet

*Tradition demonstrates that the representation of death is constant in History: the Fayum portraits, the use of mortuary masks or the representation of the deceased in his mortuary bed. The occidental tradition of Ars Moriendi, the art of good death is proof of our concern about afterlife.*

*However, in the case of children, death is more dramatic and surrounded by a complex weave of emotions, feelings and attitudes established around the loss. Premature departure becomes a tragedy in a family. Different categories of representation demonstrate three points of view to represent the experience of child death. The first tentative is to take a picture of the child like an angel. Simbolic and metaforical images are constructed to certify the salvation and destiny of this little soul in Afterlife. The second form is the sanctification of the wake, and specially the place where it takes place. Space like a delimited territory where the dead child is located and surrounded by a metaphorical terrenal paradise. This new place, constructed to share and ritualise the veneration of this representation. Finally, the third possibility revolves around the transformation of this angel-child and the altar-child to the card-child where the representation of the child becomes a new religious picture like a fetish visual objet for the family.*

*Nevertheless, we can see also another form of sharing the space of death. Live children participate in funeral rites: from the wake until the burial. Because death is lived like a natural act and a rite of passage for humans. Pictures demonstrated this active participation where children are protagonist. For that reason, the cementery, the space shared with life and death, becomes a territory for contact between them. The grave is the new place for the deceased, the cementery is the new city of death and photography, used in this place, is a sustitute for the absent body. Often post-mortem photography of a child represents the only picture and evidence of his existence, and is also the replacement of the loss in the family album, like a new virtual space to share with the family, living and dead.*

La tradición ha demostrado que la representación de la muerte ha sido una constante en la Historia de la Humanidad. Desde los retratos de Al Fayum hasta el uso de las máscaras funerarias, pasando por la representación del difunto en el lecho de muerte, o del *Ars Moriendi* como arte del buen morir, han sido la manera de plasmar las creencias que existen en torno a la Muerte y al Más Allá. Por ello, cada imagen, cada representación va unida a nuestras creencias, nuestro imaginario colectivo y nuestra tradición. En este sentido hay que incluir la tradición del retrato *post-mortem* como una forma más de plasmar la muerte, pero también de certificar la existencia de un ser en un lugar y momento determinado.[1]

## EL NIÑO DIFUNTO

La representación del niño difunto ha sido una constante en el mundo del Arte. La pintura primero, pero la fotografía después, han sido medios para representar una muerte, sentida por todos como prematura, para mostrarse como imagen del hecho dramático. Si bien el fallecimiento de un adulto es siempre algo desafortunado, en el caso del niño se hace inesperado y, en consecuencia, todo se acentúa. El dramatismo de la escena se hace mayor, la solemnidad del acto y su representación se acrecientan porque el acontecimiento así lo exige. La muerte de un niño es, en definitiva, una muerte dramática. Su vida no ha llegado a ser y, por lo tanto, su muerte será su mayor acontecimiento y recuerdo. Así pues, el velatorio será más sentido y vivido.

Si observamos algunos retratos de niños, nos percatamos de la dificultad que existía a la hora de realizar la toma. En ejemplos de finales del siglo XIX en España, las representaciones eran más distantes. El pequeño dormido sobre grandes almohadones o apoyado sobre el diván de la casa, se muestran en la imagen bajo una apariencia de vida, negando en cierto modo la realidad de lo que allí sucede. Sin embargo, poco a poco, con la incorporación del ataúd y con el cambio en las tomas fotográficas, el significado de la imagen va a ir evolucionando. Si en un primer momento se busca la negación de la muerte mediante dos estrategias que eran, tal y como las define Jay Ruby en su estudio *Secure the Shadow*,[2] por un lado la representación del niño *as alive*, es decir sentado sobre un sofá en actitud, por ejemplo, de lectura; o por otro mostrándose *as asleep*, como si estuvieran dormidos; ambas pretenden negar la evidencia y mostrar en la representación esa actitud vital que, en realidad, no existe. El simulacro se establece aquí como medida estratégica para lograr el deseado resultado de la imagen: un recuerdo del pequeño, pero no de su muerte.

Sin embargo, poco a poco, estos simulacros irán desapareciendo a medida que los propios fotógrafos van desarrollando y buscando nuevas posibilidades en este tipo de representación. Artículos que salieron en prensa explicando estas nuevas fórmulas, son buena prueba de ello.[3] La mayoría eran de tipo técnico, pero en realidad la gran dificultad se encontrará en los modos de representación y en las necesidades de las familias que solicitaban estos encargos. En cierto modo, la mayor dificultad en cualquier fotografía *post-mortem* reside en la imposición horizontal del propio modelo que obligó a los fotógrafos a buscar nuevas soluciones y sobre todo a no olvidar de ocultar, sobre todo al principio, la evidencia del hecho. Quiere decir esto que se realizarán desde tomas de perfil con formatos apaisados hasta tomas cenitales enfrentándonos a la imagen del difunto, sublimando así la propia imagen.[4]

Pero más allá de estos recursos técnicos y formales, lo importante aquí no deja de ser el resultado de la imagen y la necesaria satisfacción por parte de la familia. Los propios familiares que eran los que en un principio preparaban al difunto y la escenografía para el velatorio, mostraron una gran creatividad a la hora de recrear estos espacios no sólo para la contemplación (como puede ser la etapa del velatorio, es decir contemplar y velar el cuerpo para ir aceptando su marcha), como para su representación. En el caso gallego, podemos distinguir tres modalidades diferentes a las ya descritas por Jay Ruby con ejemplos norteamericanos: desde la representación del pequeño a la manera de ángel, hasta aquella en la que se muestra como *niño-altar*, pasando por una tercera iconografía que denominaremos *niños-estampa*.

## El niño-ángel

La primera en cuestión define la idea más obvia y fácil de asociar el niño difunto con la imagen de *angelismo*. Sin embargo, tenemos que tener en cuenta un subgénero que se define a partir de la última década del siglo XIX y que podemos observar a través de los ejemplos aportados por el fotógrafo Maximino Reboredo: la representación de los niños *carrollianos.*

Reboredo nos presenta a sus pequeños difuntos colocados sobre una mesa, con sus pequeños trajes de comunión o bautizo, en un decorado lo suficientemente minimalista para intensificar el contraste entre el color negro del fondo y el blanco de las vestimentas. Esta intensidad de colores atrae de inmediato nuestra mirada sobre el pequeño. No obstante, en algunos ejemplos podemos observar a su vez la incorporación de una gran variedad de tejidos estampados, utilizados como fondos, buscando una cierta distracción estética, una variedad, incluso un cierto toque de decorativismo en la escena. Así pues el color negro que envuelve todo el conjunto y el blanco inmaculado que funciona como un proyector-reflector de luz, no sólo centran ineludiblemente nuestra mirada en el difunto, sino que nos introduce el concepto de iluminación metafórica de su ser (Figs 25.1 and 25.2).

En este sentido, y en busca de una representación casi paradisíaca, el niño representado como una Ofelia prerrafaelita, se muestra rodeado de flores; de tal manera que en algunos casos tenemos la sensación claustrofóbica de que los pequeños se ahogan entre tanta vegetación, hundiéndose poco a poco entre la suavidad de los pétalos. Esta representación arcaica de una imagen tan romántica, introduce y amplifica el drama mediante este tipo de construcción visual. Sin embargo, hay que puntualizar que esta interpretación que responde a la de un espectador actual y descontextualizado, no se corresponde con la realidad de la época en la que la familia veía en ellas una representación real de la visión del niño en un espacio paradisíaco.

En esa búsqueda irreal, paradisíaca, complaciente, llegamos a la representación, definida por el simulacro de la ascensión. La incertidumbre a la hora de asegurar el

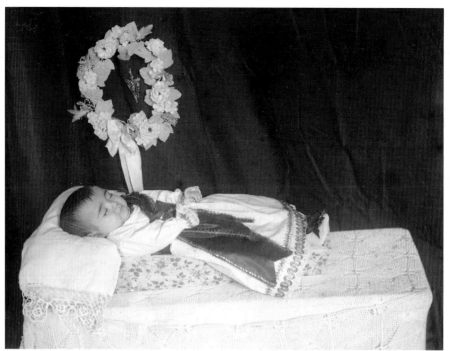

*Figure 25.1. Maximino Reboredo. [Bebé Muerto]. [c. 1892–1899]. © Archivo Histórico Provincial de Lugo.*

*Figure 25.2. Maximino Reboredo. [Bebé Muerto]. [c. 1892–1899]. © Archivo Histórico Provincial de Lugo.*

destino de estas *animitas*, se consolida con esta imagen de *niño-ángel* ascendiendo a los Cielos. Así, imágenes tales como las de Ramón Caamaño, realizadas hacia la década de los treinta o cuarenta, representan el éxito absoluto en la búsqueda del simulacro visual del *niño-ángel*.

De esta manera, este tipo de representación asegura no sólo el destino de estas *animitas,* sino también la materialización visual de la imagen *aparentemente* real de su ascensión. La elevación del torso del pequeño (o de su ataúd en la parte superior) y la colocación de flores o elementos vegetales a su alrededor, unificando fondo y suelo, fue uno de los recursos utilizados por fotógrafos y familiares más eficaces. Tan sencilla estrategia se convirtió con el tiempo en una modalidad más de representación, aunque siempre con el sello y estilo propio de cada fotógrafo.

Tal y como afirma Durand, la idea del angelismo, así como el esquema de la ascensión se opone, en sus desarrollos simbólicos, al de la caída:[5] 'Esta extrapolación natural de la verticalización postural es la razón profunda que motiva la facilidad con que la ensoñación volante, técnicamente absurda, es aceptada y privilegiada por el deseo de angelismo'.[6]

Esta oposición física, la de la colocación de los cuerpos, se desplaza hacia una oposición metafórica en la que la horizontalidad y la verticalidad son claramente definitorios de la idea de vida y de muerte.

De la misma manera, encontramos esta idea en los retratos grupales en los que, de nuevo, vida y muerte se ven enfrentados y donde el fotógrafo debe ingeniárselas para encontrar el mejor punto de vista y mejor encuadre. En consecuencia, el *niño-ángel* aparece representado rodeado de sus seres queridos, como un miembro más del núcleo familiar del que forma parte ocultando, en la medida de lo posible, la evidencia de dicha diferencia (Fig. 25.3).

Así pues, el *niño-ángel* se muestra como tal, buscando la representación de su inocencia, de su pureza y, por consiguiente, la certeza de la salvación de su alma. Las construcciones visuales que se establecen para crear este trampantojo son de una gran ingeniosidad, sobre todo teniendo en cuenta los pocos recursos económicos de las familias, pero también la de los propios fotógrafos.

*Figure 25.3. Ramón Godás. Difunto en Dacón. 1924. © Colección privada.*

## *El niño-altar*

La segunda opción, la del *niño-altar*, se determina como continuación de la primera en la que, tras desarrollar y hacer más compleja la escenografía de estos espacios, observamos la manera en que ésta acaba absorbiendo todo el protagonismo a favor de la imagen de conjunto. Ya no importa la representación del niño, sino la escenografía que lo rodea. Ahora ya empezamos a abandonar los fondos neutros y oscuros a favor de una puesta en escena mucho más compleja. De nuevo, aquí, el espectador es alejado de este territorio sagrado y delimitado por su sacralidad. Tanto el visitante que acude al velatorio como el observador de la imagen, entienden de forma inmediata esta delimitación invisible pero palpable y observan el conjunto desde la distancia.

Para alcanzar estos resultados, la familia construía unos altares artesanales pero de gran belleza. De manera casi intuitiva, las familias buscaban los contrastes de color a través de los fondos, de la vestimenta y de las flores. El conjunto se constituía como un espacio sagrado en el que el pequeño era divinizado e idolatrado. Ejemplos de grandes fotógrafos tales como Pacheco, Ramón Caamaño, Pedro Brey, Moreira, Jose Luis Vega o Virxilio Vieitez demuestran que el difunto seguía siendo el actor principal, pero ya no aislado sino rodeado de diversos objetos, en su mayoría religiosos,

y composiciones florales que permitían constituir no solo unos conjuntos de lo más escultóricos, sino también sus correspondientes construcciones visuales.

En este sentido, estas escenografías, por su complejidad, llegaron incluso a convertirse en verdaderos conjuntos escultóricos similares a aquellos Barrocos o a los utilizados para los pasos de Semana Santa. Un ejemplo a destacar es el retrato de un *difuntiño*, realizado en Dacón por el fotógrafo Ramón Godás en el año de 1924. Esta fotografía representa a la perfección la idea de pequeña capilla creada por la escenografía que nos traslada a ese mundo de lo sagrado y que nos muestra el pequeño deificado para guardar su imagen en nuestra memoria. En consecuencia, la imagen no solo se convierte en el recuerdo de ese día, sino también y sobre todo en la posibilidad de su contemplación a través de la imagen, creando una suerte de *revival* o, como diría el propio Roland Barthes, una prueba irrefutable de lo que ha sido (Fig. 25.4).

*Figure 25.4. Ramón Caamaño. [Bebé difunto]. c. 30s. © Archivo Caamaño.*

## El niño-estampa

Por último, estaría la imagen del *niño-estampa*. Manteniendo esa idea de *niños-altar*, de repente se prioriza otro tipo de representación. El recién nombrado angelito, ya sacralizado, se bidimensionaliza a su vez a través de la *imagen-estampa*. Las tomas cenitales, más características en estos casos, acaban produciendo una suerte de estampas en las que la escenografía pierde interés. Tras la necesaria lejanía que se establece en la tipología anterior, ahora el fotógrafo se acerca buscando nuevos puntos de vista y nuevos encuadres, cercando el rostro del pequeño, su esencia y también, como un acto a la desesperada, el fijar su imagen para siempre. En consecuencia es palpable la celeridad de sus actos. Casi sin miramientos, el fotógrafo se sitúa literalmente sobre el pequeño, encuadra y dispara. En estas tomas cenitales, el pequeño pierde volumen y termina por aplanarse. Este carácter bidimensional lo constituye como imagen en sí misma y lo vemos de forma metafórica cayendo en el abismo, tal y como Lewis Carroll hizo sufrir a su propia *Alicia*.

De esta manera, el objetivo nos acerca de nuevo al cadáver, enfrentándonos a él, anulando la distancia propia de las típicas escenografías. Ahora ya no existe imagen onírica, ni altares sacros, ni ascensiones posibles, ni pequeñas *Ofelias* emergiendo de un mar de flores embalsadas, tan sólo la representación deshumanizada del pequeño en su caja, caja de muñecas, casi abstracta y descontextualizada. Esta imagen se muestra casi como fetiche, como estampa religiosa. Mediante el acto fotográfico se ha recreado un artefacto visual lleno de poder y de magia. De alguna forma, la idea del *niño-estampa* acaba adquiriendo una función protectora y de veneración, conteniendo de forma inevitable una carga aurática añadida a la que ya tiene de por sí.

## EL NIÑO ENFRENTADO A LA MUERTE

Bien es cierto que, en la actualidad, la muerte es ocultada a los niños. Esto es lo que Görer cuenta en 1955 en su artículo *"The Pornography of death"* en el que señala el cambio de actitud del hombre frente a la muerte, en la que ésta había sido desplazada poco a poco hacia los márgenes de lo visible y que se acentúa con respecto a los niños.[7] Ante las preguntas inadecuadas de los niños sobre la muerte, los adultos han configurado todo un elenco de interpretaciones fantasiosas que desvelan la impostura.

Sin embargo, si atendemos a la tradición y costumbres, la muerte no era algo que se ocultaba a los niños, sino todo lo contrario.[8] De hecho, podemos observar la manera en que los niños participaban activamente en el rito funerario sobre todo en los casos de defunción infantil. Cosa que no sorprende porque, en definitiva, la comunidad en la que vivía el pequeño era la de los niños y es lógico entonces que esté rodeado por dicha comunidad. En numerosas fotografías se puede apreciar la presencia de los niños a lo largo del rito funerario e, incluso, su participación activa en determinadas etapas como podría ser el transporte del ataúd. Esta naturalidad con la que la muerte es tratada, facilita y normaliza el cambio acontecido por el fallecimiento dentro de la comunidad. Dicho esto, la participación de todos los niños (en los casos de muerte infantil) ayuda a los padres a suavizar y embellecer el propio rito funerario. El color blanco, símbolo de pureza e inocencia, se impone. Pero sobre todo, la vitalidad natural que acompaña siempre a los niños, se establece como nueva fórmula para luchar contra la muerte y el silencio que nos impone.

A su vez, existen algunos retratos en los que más allá de narrar un momento concreto del rito funerario, pretenden sencillamente hacer un retrato de la familia en el que el difunto aparece rodeado por sus hermanos. Estos retratos que no representan ninguna etapa concreta (salvo que consideremos el acto fotográfico como una etapa más que se añade a las ya conocidas del rito funerario) sino que son un retrato familiar, el último posible, uniendo de cuerpo presente, y antes de la inevitable y definitiva separación, los distintos miembros de la familia.

## El cementerio, espacio de encuentro

Con la inevitable desaparición del cuerpo y de su visión, tan solo nos queda su presencia simbólica mediante su sepultura o su imagen fotográfica. Si consideramos tanto la imagen como la sepultura como dos formas diferentes, e igual de válidas, para albergar el cuerpo difunto, entonces podremos entender la manera en que la fotografía funciona como sustituto de ese cuerpo, pero también como continente de su imagen. Ambos espacios (fotografía y escultura) se configuran como territorios para el encuentro entre vivos y muertos. El recuerdo se establece como un mecanismo que se activa con el fin de mantener viva la memoria y el recuerdo del difunto, hacerlo presente y partícipe tras su muerte de los cambios en el seno de la familia, pero sobre todo de mantener ese encuentro necesario para seguir alimentando la historia y raíces familiares.

De alguna manera, la imagen funciona como una aparición. Apariencia, del latín *apparentĭa*, es el término definido como aquella cosa que parece y no es.

> Poco a poco se dibujaba en una luz vaporosa, la sombra encantadora de una joven. La imagen era primero tan transparente que los objetos situados tras ella se dibujaban a través de los contornos, tal y como vemos el fondo de un lago a través del agua límpida. Sin llegar a materializarse del todo, su figura se condensó lo suficiente como para adquirir la apariencia de una figura viva, pero de una viveza tan ligera, tan impalpable, tan aérea, que se parecía más al reflejo de un cuerpo en el espejo que al propio cuerpo en sí.[9]

Verosimilitud, ocultamiento, ilusión visual, imagen especular, etérea, Gauthier, en su *Spirite,* nos lo describe de esta forma tan particular. En todo caso, la imagen como espacio simbólico de una presencia ausente, funciona como ese espejo que nos devuelve la imagen reflejada del pasado. En cierto modo, el vivo sigue viviendo a través del recuerdo y, lo que es más importante, sigue sintiendo su presencia. En opinión de Erek Parfit, 'la identidad personal radica en la perduración en el tiempo de determinados hechos. Consiste en varios tipos de continuidad psicológica como la memoria que, a su vez, descansan en la continuidad corporal'.[10] El cuerpo, por lo tanto, forma parte de ese conjunto identificatorio y la lápida, con el nombre del difunto, como sustituto de ese cuerpo, al que se sigue adornando *post-mortem* con flores y con el que se sigue comunicando.

Según Bachelard, "el espacio lo es todo, porque el tiempo no anima ya a la memoria. Es en el espacio donde encontramos esos bellos fósiles de duración, concretados por largas estancias".[11] Se recuerdan lugares, aunque parecen tiempos. Estos lugares son los que permanecen como imágenes de otros espacios, envejecidos y amarilleados que permanecen en el soporte de papel como duplicados bidimensionales de recuerdos tridimensionales. Los territorios del recuerdo son lugares con olores, con sonidos, con sensaciones táctiles que, entre todos, constituyen nuestra memoria. Como indica Bachelard, "toda gran imagen simple es reveladora de un estado de alma".[12]

Existen, por lo tanto, estos espacios construidos con el único fin de *recordar*. Los cementerios son buen ejemplo de ello, convirtiéndose en lugares, consensuado por todos, para el recuerdo. No es de extrañar que en las sepulturas aparezcan fotografías de los difuntos, tanto *pre-mortem* como *post-mortem*, imágenes para no olvidar, para ayudar a la memoria a conservarlas latentes, y como dice Philip Rahtz, fosilizando su apariencia *pre-mortem*.[13] En esta misma línea habría que considerar los mensajes y anuncios *In Memoriam*. En las tumbas más actuales, todavía se pueden encontrar estos mensajes, aunque en muchos casos ya están normalizados, repitiéndose las mismas fórmulas.[14]

El uso de las fotografías encastradas en las lápidas o en los monumentos escultóricos era una práctica, según afirma Hallett, rara en Inglaterra, frente a los numerosos ejemplos norteamericanos.[15] Sin embargo existe un caso muy temprano que es el realizado en memoria de John Garmston Hopkins en la parroquia de San John en Bedwardine en Worcester. El monumento mide 1,73 m de alto, y su base es de 0,93 m de ancho por 0,46 m de profundidad. La fotografía del difunto está colocada en la parte alta del monumento en uno de los lados y mide 0,15 × 0,33 m. Dos ángeles de piedra flanquean la imagen y parecen mirar hacia la fotografía del niño.

La fotografía retrataba a John Garmston Hopkins que murió, según fue publicada la noticia en el *Berrows Journal* del 22 de enero de 1871, a la edad de catorce años. Era el hijo mayor de T. M. Hopkins. No hay información sobre la naturaleza de la muerte del niño, pero lo elaborado de la lápida hace pensar en el dolor y la decepción de los padres ante la pérdida de su hijo mayor. La lápida también registra el fallecimiento del hijo más pequeño, Jonathan Edward en 1870, cuando tenía dos años. La figura y reputación del padre explican la razón de ser de este monumento. La fotografía que es un positivo de colodión sobre vidrio, muestra la imagen de un chico, cubierto por un sudario de raso y recostado sobre un sofá. La imagen lo muestra de perfil acentuando la horizontalidad que tanto se identifica con la idea del yacente. Parece que el nombre del fotógrafo es un misterio aunque varios artículos apuntan a un hombre, F. C. Earl, que trabajó en Worcester entre los años de 1860 y de 1872 y que fue uno de los primeros fotógrafos de la zona. Hay que destacar que Hopkins, como importador de vinos, viajó a Italia y Portugal por negocios y vio monumentos conmemorativos con fotografías. Esto fue seguramente lo que le dio la idea a la hora de optar por este tipo de representación escultórica.[16]

De esta forma, entendemos la manera en que el monumento y la imagen se convierten en un espacio en el que colocar y encontrarse con el cuerpo ausente. A menudo, la fotografía *post-mortem* de niños representa la única imagen y evidencia su breve existencia y, sobre todo, la posibilidad *in extremis* de emplazarlo en el álbum familiar, a la manera de un nuevo espacio virtual para compartir con la familia, tanto vivos como muertos.

NOTES

1   Bolloch 2002, 112–38
2   Ruby 1995, 27–75
3   Bool 1878, 84–5; Burguess 1855, 80; Orr 1877, 200–01; Sachse 1891, 350
4   Faeta 1993, 69–81
5   Durand 1981, 122–4, 137–40
6   *Ibid.* p. 122
7   Görer 1955, 49–52
8   Cruz Lichet 2005, 151–175
9   Gauthier 1992, 146
10   Parfit 1986, 6
11   Bachelard 1993, 39
12   *Ibid.* 104
13   Rahtz 1981, 127
14   Batchen 2004, 77–80
15   Hallet 1987, 119
16   *Ibid.* 121

REFERENCIAS

Bachelard, G. 1993. *La poética del espacio. Madrid: Fondo de Cultura Económica.*
Batchen, G. 2004. *Forget me not. Photography & Remembrance.* New York: Princeton Architectural Press.
Bolloch, J. 2002. Photographie après décès: pratique, usages et functions, pp. 112–38 en Héran, E. (ed.), *Le dernier portrait.* Paris: Reunión des Muses Nationaux.
Bool, A. H. 1878. Post-mortem photography. *The British Journal Photographic Almanac and Photographer's Daily Companion,* 84–5.
Burguess, N. G. 1855. Taking portraits after death. *The Photographic and Fine Art Journal,* 8, 3, 80.
Cruz Lichet, V. (de la) 2005. Más allá de la propia muerte. En torno al retrato fotográfico fúnebre, pp. 151–75 in Bozal, V. (ed.), *Imágenes de la violencia en el arte contemporáneo.* Madrid: A. Machado Libros.
Durand, G. 1981. *Las estructuras antropológicas de lo imaginario.* Madrid: Taurus. (traducido de la edición francesa de 1979 por Bordas).
Faeta, F. 1993. La mort en images. *Terrain,* 20, 69–81.
Gauthier, T. 1992. *Spirite.* Toulouse: Editions Ombres.
Görer, G. 1955. The pornography of death. *Encounter. Literature, Arts, Current Affairs.* V, 4, 49–52.
Hallet, M. 1987. The Hopkins Memorial Stone. *History of Photography,* 11, 2, 119.
Orr, C. E. 1877. Post-mortem photography. *Philadelphia Photographer,* 10, 200–01.
Parfit, D. 1986 Identidad personal y racionalidad. *Revista de Occidente.* 56, 5–25.
Rahtz, P. 1981. Artefacts of Christian death, pp. 117–36 en Humphreys, S. C. y King H. (eds), *Mortality and Immortality. The anthropology and archaeology of death.* London: Academic Press.
Ruby, J. 1995. *Secure the shadow. Death and photography in America.* London: The MIT Press. Cambridge.
Sachse, J. F. 1891. Post-mortem photography. *American Journal of Photography,* XII, 350.